HUGO WOLF

A Biography

by

FRANK WALKER

Ja! Ich weiss woher ich stamme!
Ungesättigt gleich der Flamme
Glühe und verzehr' ich mich.
Licht wird alles, was ich fasse,
Kohle alles, was ich lasse,
Flamme bin ich sicherlich.
FRIEDRICH NIETZSCHE

With 8 pages of plates
and music examples
in the text

LONDON: J. M. DENT & SONS LTD

Made in Great Britain
by
The Temple Press · Letchworth · Herts
First published 1951

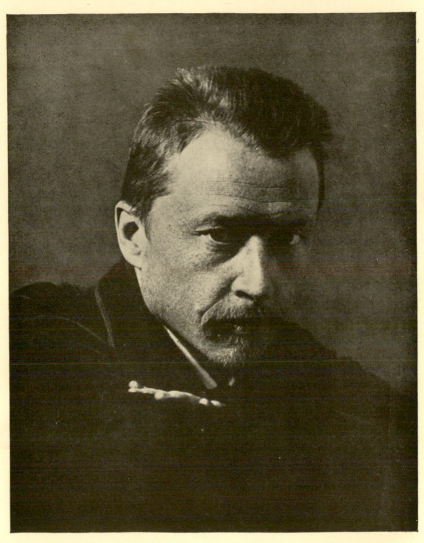

HUGO WOLF, 1895

ACKNOWLEDGMENTS

THIS book has a long history. It was, I think, in September 1936 that Walter Legge, the founder of the Gramophone Company's Hugo Wolf Society, first suggested to me that we should collaborate in a book on Wolf. My private circumstances made me very willing, at first, to leave to him the gathering of first-hand information. In the summer of 1937 he interviewed Emil Heckel and Joachim Kromer, at Mannheim, and Frau Käthe Salomon-Wolf, the composer's sister, Frau Ilse Kautsky (*née* Köchert), Friedrich Eckstein, Ferdinand Jäger, junior, and Johann Scheibner in Vienna. In December 1937 Mr. Legge saw Karl Hallwachs at Kassel and Frau Hilde Wittgenstein (*née* Köchert), Miss Agnes Park, and Friedrich Eckstein again in Vienna. In the summer of 1938 he interviewed Herr Eckstein for the third time and saw Gilbert Wolf, the composer's brother, at Slovenjgradec (Windischgraz), and a lady who does not wish to be named here, Wolf's niece, at Ljubljana (Laibach), Yugoslavia. On each of these occasions I provided my collaborator with a series of questionnaires, to be presented to those he succeeded in interviewing, and many difficult points were elucidated in this way, but the greater part of the information collected on these journeys was obtained through Mr. Legge's independent efforts.

Unhappily the proposed collaboration was not a success. As time went on my colleague's numerous other activities seemed to leave him less and less time for his work with me, which never, at any time, got beyond the stage of collecting material. The whole scheme gradually moved away from the practical sphere into the idealistic, and its execution was postponed until some time in the very hazy future. Meanwhile, a European war was obviously rapidly approaching, and at length in sheer desperation I began to write this book myself. My debt to my former collaborator remains, and I am also indebted, through him, to those named above, although some of them have since given me copies of very numerous and important documents to which Mr. Legge was denied access. Mr. Legge has since laid me under further obligation by criticizing the first version of my manuscript (1942).

When I began, by correspondence, to collect original material on my own account I found almost everywhere sympathetic, even eager response to my inquiries, and much information and unpublished material was given me. I should like to express my gratitude, especially, to Frau Helene Bettelheim-Gabillon, to Herr W. Kleinschmidt, and to Landesgerichtspräsident Edmund Hellmer, for all they did at this stage to make the present biography possible in the course of a voluminous and long-drawn-out correspondence.

I was also indebted, before the war, in greater or lesser degree, to all the following, who provided me with information, copies of unpublished letters and other documents, books, and articles: Ludwig Bösendorfer, Messrs. Breitkopf & Härtel, Frl. Dora Breuer, Max Brockhaus, Carl Blaas, Adolf Fürstner, Frau Rosa Frauscher, Helmut Grohe, Dr. Karl Grunsky, Frau Bertha Hammerschlag, Frl. Elisabet Hefele, Frau Jenny Hoernes-Reuss, Wolfram Humperdinck, Frau Gertrud Lambert, Frau Clara Mayser-Nestle, Hofrat Max Millenkovich-Morold, Musikwissenschaftlicher Verlag and Oscar Brandstetter, Bernhard Paumgartner, C. F. Peters, Prof. Heinrich Rauchberg and his family, Dr. Wilhelm Schmid, Frau Käthe Salomon-Wolf, B. Schott's Söhne, Dr. Max Vancsa, Dr. Otto Werner, Hermann Wette, Frau Josepha Wüllner, the Gesellschaft der Musikfreunde in Vienna and the Directors of the Preussische Staatsbibliothek in Berlin, the Städtisches Schlossbücherei and Theatermuseum in Mannheim and, through Walter Legge, the Nationalbibliothek in Vienna. Through Herr Kleinschmidt I was indebted to Oberstleutnant von Selzam and Dr. Leydheker, and through Walter Legge to the Marchesa Sophie della Valle di Casanova.

The collection of material was interrupted in September 1939 by the outbreak of war. I set to work on what I had and the first version of this book was finished in April 1942. In the following year I was sent abroad on war service and after two years in Italy the opportunity presented itself of getting to Vienna. The nine months I spent in Austria, from August 1945 to the end of April 1946, are counted among the happiest of my life, in spite of the misery in which I too often found old correspondents and new friends. How shall I express my gratitude for all the kindness that was shown me in that time? It extended from the sympathy and encouragement of those who became my dearest friends to the disinterested enthusiasm of the library officials who, with open sores on their hands from the cold, searched for and found for me the Wolf manuscripts in the cellars where they had been deposited for safety.

I shall never forget those evenings with Wolf's nieces, in Vienna, at Graz, and later in Yugoslavia, when we sat and talked, and laughed, about 'Onkel Hugo,' and read his unpublished family letters, and, on one occasion, made coffee in his famous 'Non plus ultra' coffee machine. The grand climax of all my Wolfian adventures was the week I spent at Traunkirchen as the guest of Frau Hilde Wittgenstein, when I first read through Wolf's correspondence with Melanie Köchert, and cycled in his tracks over half the Salzkammergut. In connection with this, I owe a special debt to Frau Ilse Kautsky, whom I first encountered by chance in the Wolf house at Perchtoldsdorf, and without whose kind offices I should probably never have gone to Traunkirchen at all.

Here, in the form of a dry list, are the names of others who helped me personally in Austria: Frau Marianne Boller, Frau Helene Dlauhy, Frau Fritzi Diemer, Dr. Gladt of the Stadtbibliothek, Prof. Robert Haas, Prof. Herbert Haberlandt, Landesgerichtspräsident Edmund Hellmer, Frl. Stefanie Herzeg-Wolf, Heinrich Hinterberger, Frau Gerda Hofmann, Dr. Hans Jancik, Prof. Robert and Dely Kautsky, Hofrat Viktor Keldorfer, Karl Klier, Direktor Koch and the Konzerthausgesellschaft, Frl. Irmina Köchert, Gerhard Köchert, Frau Prof. Hedwig Krauss and the Gesellschaft der Musikfreunde, Walter Krieg, Fritz Kuba, Prof. Erwin Lang, Frl. Edith Obermayer-Paget, Frau Marie Öhn, Prof. Alfred Orel, Dr. Oswald Ortner, René Pasteur and the Vienna Philharmonic Orchestra, Ministerialrat Karl Pichler, Dr. Racek of the Stadtbibliothek, Frl. Cornelia and Frl. Modesta Strasser, Frau Ilse Strzelba, Dr. Umlauf, Dr. Hans Wamlek, Dr. Otto and Frau Emmi Werner, Herbert and Frau Traute Wolf. Since returning to this country I have been further assisted by Kurt Böhmer, Mrs. Käthe Braun-Prager, Frl. Margarete Klinckerfuss, Frau Sophie and Dr. Julius Lichtenberger, Miss Virginian Hendrickson, Dr. Nowak of the Nationalbibliothek, Vienna, Eugen Ochs, Dr. Hans Redlich, Dr. Willi Reich, Frau Lili Schalk, Walter Woschnagg, and, in particular, Musikdirektor Karl Hallwachs.

I have also to thank the editor of *Music & Letters* for permission to make use of material which originally appeared in that periodical, Dr. Mosco Carner for assistance in clearing up certain difficulties, Eric Blom for invaluable encouragement and advice at various stages

of the book's development, and finally Ernest Newman, Arthur
Hedley, and Prof. Gerald Abraham for various corrections and
suggestions, after reading my manuscript.

This book presents the story of Wolf's life, in so far as it is decipherable from the surviving documents. 'A Biography' I have called it
in the sub-title, although it includes fairly extensive discussions of
the music as well. These discussions are there because I regard some
account of the nature of a composer's work as an essential ingredient
in his biography. For the rest, this attempt at a source-book in
English on an Austrian composer is founded on an exhaustive examination of the literature of the subject and on the many hundreds of
unpublished documents made available to me by those named above.
I can only hope that those to whom I am most indebted will not too
strongly disapprove.

One important chapter and a few shorter passages have had to be
omitted from this edition, out of regard for the feelings of living
people.

F. W.

Orpington,
June 1951.

CONTENTS

ILLUSTRATIONS

I

CHILDHOOD AND SCHOOLDAYS

IN the former Austrian Empire Windischgraz was a small town of about two thousand inhabitants in lower Styria: after the Great War of 1914–18 it became part of Yugoslavia and has since been known as Slovenjgradec. It lies in the Miesling valley among gently rolling, wooded hills at the foot of the Ursulaberg, in surroundings of quiet beauty, but the straggling town is not in itself attractive in any way. Its distinction is that, on 13th March 1860, Hugo Wolf was born there, in a building of two storeys towards the end of the principal street. A few minutes' walk beyond the house were the workshops where the family leather business used to be carried on, and over the doorway of the dwelling-house the sign of the trade was hung—an enigmatic-looking sheet of metal in the shape of a pigskin.

Windischgraz was regarded as an outpost of Germanic culture in a countryside inhabited largely by Slovenes. The bilingual character of the district is illustrated by the fact that the teaching in the local elementary school included instruction in both German and Slav languages. The Wolf family was of predominantly German origin, but with a definite strain of foreign blood in its composition. There appears to have been a family tradition that Wolf's mother was of Italian descent. The composer himself is said to have sometimes played with this idea and F. G. Antal, in an article [1] based upon information given him by Wolf's cousin, Anna Klenz, née Vinzenzberg, boldly declared, before any other writer had discussed the point, that 'his mother was an Italian—from her the composer inherited his fiery temperament.' This was of course an overstatement. But she came from Wolfsbach, near Malborghet, in Carinthia,[2] a district where Italian influence was strong, and she retained all her life a strange and passionate desire to read Italian books and to travel south of the Alps. Dr. Rauschenberger's researches into the ancestry of the composer do not completely exclude the possibility of an admixture of Italian blood on the maternal side, as the records, owing to the loss in a flood of the church books of

---

[1] 'Hugo Wolfs erstes Jahr in Wien' (*Neue Freie Presse*, Vienna, 13th March 1910).
[2] Since 1919 Valbruna, near Malborghetto, Italy.

1

Wolfsbach, are imperfect. But it cannot have been very pronounced. Much more important is the indisputable Slovene element in her make-up. Her maiden name was Nussbaumer, which seems solidly German, but we find that her paternal grandfather was born an Orchovnik, at Moistrana, and changed his name to Nussbaumer (the German equivalent of Orchovnik), probably when he transferred himself from Moistrana to Malborghet. The surname of Wolf's mother's maternal grandfather, Stanko, or Stank, also suggests Slovene origins. The Orchovniks were peasants at Moistrana; the Stankos also of peasant stock. Jakob Nussbaumer, the father of the composer's mother, was the owner of a forge at Malborghet. On the paternal side Wolf's ancestors were overwhelmingly German. His great-grandfather, Maximilian Wolff (Wolf), is known to have settled at Windischgraz in the eighteenth century and to have established himself there in the leather trade. Maximilian's son Franz was likewise a leather manufacturer. Franz had two sons, of whom the younger, Philipp, unwillingly took over his father's business.

X This Philipp Wolf, father of the composer, is the first of the family about whom we know much more than the name. He was born on 1st May 1828, and it was regarded as a matter of course that he would in due time succeed his father in the leather trade. This was not, however, young Philipp's idea of a suitable occupation and he pleaded for opportunities to study for a more learned profession. He is said to have wished to become an architect. Franz Wolf, whose industry and energy had brought the family business to a flourishing condition, was unsympathetic to this proposal and Philipp was obliged, much against his will, to become apprentice in his father's workshops, but by private study in leisure hours he strove continuously to better himself, and it was above all in the world of music that he found consolation. Unaided, he taught himself to play with fair proficiency on the piano, violin, flute, harp, and guitar. In the tannery, the fiddle or flute would often be concealed under a pile of hides, ready for an opportune moment for a little extra practice, in Franz Wolf's absence.

On his father's death Philipp inherited the house and business, but he never concealed his dislike for the trade he had been forced to adopt. It was still a recurrent theme in his conversation with his married sister, Katharina Vinzenzberg, when she used to revisit Windischgraz in later years. But the stains and the smells of the tannery brought a material reward, even to an indifferent business man like Philipp Wolf, who would sooner spend money on a new violin than on the requirements of his workshops. At that time the peasants used to repair their own shoes at home and there was consequently a considerable local sale of leather; the business was extended by visits to the neighbouring market towns, and in the course of time Philipp was enabled to marry and bring a large family into the world in fairly comfortable circumstances. Katharina Nussbaumer, who became his wife in 1851, was four years older than Philipp. She was a shrewd, energetic, and practical woman, with a good share of mother wit: she was not much in sympathy with her husband's artistic inclinations, although he is said to have first attracted her favourable attention, among several rival suitors, by his skill as a performer on the guitar. Although by no means intellectual, or even particularly well educated—the spelling and syntax of her letters are very faulty—there is no doubt that she was the dominant partner in this marriage. Katharina's portrait suggests a kindly, homely nature, but she also possessed the vitality and will-power that were conspicuously lacking in Philipp, and in addition a notably sharp temper, displayed not least where her own husband was concerned. This was perhaps a manifestation of that streak of southern blood in her composition. In the genius of Hugo Wolf we see the development and flowering of the crude, unrealized musical talents of his father; from his mother he inherited the temperament that so often multiplied the practical difficulties of his life and the iron will-power which alone enabled him to bring his genius to full fruition.

Within a year of their marriage, on 8th June 1852, the Wolfs' first child, Modesta, was born, and during the succeeding years there were fairly regular additions to the family: Adrienne (1854), who died at four or five years of age, Max (25th April 1858), Hugo (13th March 1860), Gilbert (14th April 1862), Cornelia (7th August 1863), Katharina (26th April 1865), and a second Adrienne (24th February 1867).[1]

Hugo was thus the fourth-born in a family of eight children. His full name appears on his baptismal certificate as Hugo Filipp Jakob Wolf; the father himself preferred to spell his name as *Fi*lipp, instead of the more customary *Phi*lipp.

---

[1] Dates of birth of the Wolf children provided by Frau Käthe Salomon-Wolf and Frl. Cornelia Strasser.

Hugo received his first music lessons from his father, who began to teach him the piano keyboard and the first position on a tiny violin when he was four or five years old.   This instruction was compulsory for the whole family.   The girls were able occasionally to evade the drudgery of daily practice by pleading household duties, but in the case of his sons Philipp Wolf was inflexible.   He used to lock Max and Gilbert in a room on the first floor, until he found that they had devised a system of escape through the window, after which they did their practising in the cellar.   Philipp was not a patient music-master and often struck his pupils over the head with a violin bow.   Little Hugo, however, took easily to this discipline and made rapid progress.   He was no precociously gifted *Wunderkind*, but it became clear that he possessed a remarkable musical memory and a phenomenally acute ear.   He was soon able to recognize intervals and chords when they were struck on the piano behind his back.

Meanwhile his education had commenced at the town school (*Volksschule*), which he attended from 1865 to 1869, passing without difficulty through all four classes.   His intelligence, good conduct, and industry earned him excellent reports during the whole time of his attendance at the town school of Windischgraz.   It was recognized that here was a pupil of exceptional promise, and the parents, and especially the father, followed his progress at school and in the home musical circle with joy and pride.   Philipp became devoted to the gifted boy, who, out of all the children, was easily his favourite. Hugo's musical education subsequently passed out of his father's hands into those of Sebastian Weixler, a local school teacher and member of Philipp's circle of musical friends.   Under Weixler he made good progress in the study of the piano, laying the foundations of his later remarkable command of the instrument.   At the same time, after preliminary instruction in the tuning of the guitar, Philipp taught him the difficult process of tuning the piano, an art which afterwards became a passion with him, and in which his sense of absolute pitch enabled him to excel.

Philipp's friends were largely drawn from official circles.   Windischgraz was the seat of the district court and administrative offices, and many of the provincial officials were keen amateur musicians. Whenever a newcomer came to the town Philipp always asked two questions: 'Is he German?' and 'Is he musical?'   A group of friends used to assemble regularly at the Wolfs' house in the evenings and in this way a small household orchestra came into existence, of which the first and second violins were respectively Philipp and Hugo. Brother Max played the cello, Weixler the viola, and an Uncle Ruess the horn, while additional players and instruments were added from time to time from among Philipp's acquaintances. Hugo at an early age began to tyrannize over his brothers and sisters and would tolerate no conversation, nor was any member of the family permitted to enter or leave the room in the course of a performance. In 1866 this little orchestra made a public appearance at a fancy-dress ball. A 'Mozart costume' was specially ordered from Graz for the six-year-old Hugo. Dressed in this outfit of pale blue silk breeches, buckled shoes, frilled waistcoat, and black velvet jacket, the diminutive violinist delighted every one, playing valiantly all the evening until midnight, when he fell asleep and was carried home by his father with his pockets stuffed with sweets and other dainties.

Some indication of the nature of the musical entertainment provided by the home orchestra is to be found among miscellaneous papers and manuscripts in the possession of the children of Wolf's youngest sister. The collection includes loose manuscript orchestral parts of various dance pieces—polkas and a mazurka—a *cavatina* from Donizetti's *Ugo Conte di Parigi*, and a duet and aria from Bellini's *Norma*. The most curious of all these pieces, however, are two little dances named after two of the Wolf children—the *Katharinen Quadrilles* and the *Hugerl Polka*, by 'S. W.' They are doubtless compositions of the school teacher Sebastian Weixler.

Another extension of young Hugo's musical experience occurred in November 1868, when he was taken, as a special treat, to hear Donizetti's *Belisario* in the opera-house at Klagenfurt. The occasion was one of Philipp's visits to his eldest daughter Modesta, who was taking a domestic science course in that town. This first glimpse, through the agency of a third-rate provincial opera-house, of the alluring world of the theatre made a profound impression on the young Hugo Wolf, who, preoccupied with the music and the fictions of the stage, sat as if spellbound throughout the performance, making no reply when spoken to and retaining such a vivid impression of the work in his mind that he was afterwards able to play long passages of *Belisario* from memory.

At this period of his childhood his attention was much taken up by books and pictures, over which he used to pore for hours, and by the imaginary adventures of 'Hazapitel' and 'Reckobekka'—two strangely named and curiously clothed dolls whose company he seemed to prefer to that of his fellow children.

Shortly before this a catastrophic deterioration had taken place in the circumstances of the family. One day in 1867 an appalling fire, in which the hand of a rival leather manufacturer was suspected, broke out in an attic, soon enveloped the house, and spread to the neighbouring buildings, including the warehouse. The conflagration was not put out before most of the household possessions, many sacks of corn, which had just been harvested, and Philipp Wolf's whole stock-in-trade had been destroyed, and Katharina stood among her children, with only the barest necessities, in the street. All Philipp's reserves of capital were swallowed up in the re-establishment of their home, and from this grievous blow the family fortunes never recovered. Henceforth Philipp's life became 'an unbroken chain of cares and hardships,' as his son recorded twenty years later in a letter announcing his father's death. Some members of the family, in later years, have striven to show that Philipp was not so poor as he has been made out to be, that he was a person of some standing at Windischgraz and could have been Bürgermeister if he had wished. It may be so—his property after his death in 1887 was valued at 19,794 gulden (about £1,650)[1]—but that he was very often desperately short of ready money is conclusively shown, over and over again, by his letters to Hugo. In order to raise a little more money the Wolfs had to let out to strangers some of the best rooms in their house, and once they even had the bailiffs in residence. Philipp added to his cares by the resolution he had taken that all three of his sons should be given the secondary educational opportunities that had been denied to himself, for he did not abandon this honourable ambition in the violently strained financial circumstances in which he found himself after the fire.

In spite of his father's great misfortune, Hugo's childhood at Windischgraz may be considered to have been, in the main, a happy one. His father, not foreseeing the question of a musical career which was to arise later, encouraged the boy to develop the musical talents which he so clearly possessed, and the passion for the art which burned in them both forged an indestructible bond between father and son. Little has been recorded of Hugo's early relations with his mother. She was no great letter-writer, and in later years

---

[1] From documents concerning Philipp Wolf's estate in the possession of Dr. Otto Werner. About 8,000 gulden had been inherited in 1885.

left most of the family correspondence in the hands of her daughters. Katharina Wolf's personally written communications to Hugo were generally sent on special occasions such as birthdays, name-days, or at Christmas, and the warmth and tenderness with which Hugo recalls his childhood in the replies to his mother's occasional letters leave no doubt that it was not only in his father that he found as a boy an unfailing source of deep affection and sympathy.   Preserved in these letters, a few memories from the earliest period of his home life may be added to the scanty material elsewhere available.   The mother's own birthday was celebrated by the children with gifts of flowers and congratulatory poems of their own composition.[1]   On their own name-days and birthdays it was her custom to present them with a silver piece and a sausage, of which the coin was destined for the money-box, to the children's secret disgust, but the sausage consumed on the spot.[2]   Hugo was all his life a passionate lover of home-made sausages, and to him these highly seasoned[3] delicacies were the principal joy of the name-day celebrations.

He also took part in the door-to-door pilgrimage of the children of the town, on the evening of Epiphany.   In costumes representing the kings from the East, they sang for coppers outside each house. The melody traditionally associated with this custom was afterwards employed by Wolf in his *Christnacht*.   His eldest sister, Modesta, in some unpublished reminiscences of her childhood, recalls that the three brothers often played among themselves this game of the Three Kings, wearing their cloaks turned inside out to show the red linings.

There was another gifted musician in the Wolf family.   In addition to Hugo's more orthodox musical accomplishments, he possessed as a boy an absolute mastery of the Jew's harp.   But his younger brother Gilbert excelled even Hugo in this field.   According to information supplied to Hellmer by Katharina Wolf, Gilbert lived as a child in a wholly unreal world, composed entirely of musical instruments.   He seemed to be able to extract music from everything he laid his hands upon; the technique of these improvised instruments he seemed to have at once at his finger-ends.   He played the guitar, too, copying his father and reproducing the same pieces, and in one of Philipp's letters to Hugo he remarks on the progress Gilbert

[1] Letter of 27th January 1891.
[2] Letter of 25th December 1880.
[3] The composer of the *Italian Song Book* had a great liking for garlic.

has made with both piano and violin—with the proviso, however, that 'among the blind, the one-eyed man is King.'

One further youthful acquirement of Hugo's is known to us from his own account in later years. In the eighteen-nineties he was once leaving the house of a friend with Edmund Hellmer: Wolf had been moody and ill at ease all the evening, but while they were waiting for the housekeeper to let them out of the building he suddenly brightened up and to Hellmer's surprise began spitting at the high ceiling of the entrance hall. The force and accuracy with which he was able to direct his expectorations were remarkable, and after scoring several direct hits he desisted, visibly gratified. 'I can still do it,' he remarked; 'as a boy I was a real master at it. Nobody could spit higher than I.'

Hugo left the Windischgraz Volksschule in 1869, having completed the whole course of instruction available there. He seems to have remained at home until the next school year began, in September 1870, when, after passing the preliminary examination, he entered the lowest class of the Gymnasium in the Lichtenfelsgasse at Graz, the Styrian capital. The ten-year-old boy was remembered by one of his teachers, Georg Kaas, as somewhat short and thickset, with full cheeks and fair hair, strikingly earnest in demeanour, and with the soft drawling speech common among German children who have been brought up in Slovene spheres of influence. He lodged, together with his elder brother Max, with a family named Caulerio in the Wielandgasse. Outside the Gymnasium, both Max and Hugo attended the school of the Styrian Musical Association in the Burggasse for violin lessons under Ferdinand Casper, and Hugo also studied the piano with Johann Buwa. Buwa's records show that Hugo's lessons commenced on 30th September and that he left soon after, on 12th November, the reason being unknown. The solitary entry against his name is to the effect that his scale-playing was excellent.

At Graz Hugo's educational troubles began. His stay in the Gymnasium there lasted only one term. At the end of the scholastic half-year he was withdrawn, his work being officially classified as 'wholly inadequate.' Such a complete failure on the part of a reputedly clever pupil of the Windischgraz school is surprising. The course of instruction there may not have been an ideal preparation for the secondary education of a Gymnasium, but it is reasonable to suppose that he was given some coaching for the entrance examination during the year between his completion, in 1869, of the four-year course available at Windischgraz and his commencement at Graz in September 1870. It is most likely that his uprooting from the comfortable home circle where he was petted and favoured, and transference to the less agreeable environment of a lodging-house and a crowded schoolroom, were at bottom responsible, and that, feeling himself in unsympathetic surroundings, his failure was a wilful one. He was back home early in 1871 and spent the whole summer at Windischgraz.

Another attempt to complete his education began in September 1871, when he was sent to the Konvikt attached to the Benedictine monastery of St. Paul, in the Lavant valley in Carinthia. It was a well-chosen school for a sensitive, impressionable boy. Here was comparative solitude and quiet, life among ancient traditions and beautiful surroundings, and treatment, at the hands of the Benedictine monks, more sympathetic than was to be found in the secular educational establishments of the larger towns.

There were only a dozen pupils in Hugo's class, among whom he was well liked. He is recorded on one occasion to have taken punishment for a fellow pupil's offence, his schoolboy code of honour preventing him from clearing himself. He was esteemed especially by his schoolfellows for his masterly performance of *O du lieber Augustin*, enlivened by a simulated impediment in his speech. They used to urge him to repeat it again and again, and he was delighted to do so, as the tune is one of those maddening ones which can be repeated endlessly without a break, and Hugo Wolf had a predilection for such tunes all his life.

Father Sales Pirc, his teacher, retained memories from that time of the boy's love for his parents and his passion for music, and in particular for the piano, on which instrument he was already a remarkable player, although his inability to span the octave was the cause of grief to him. Pot-pourris of operas by Bellini, Rossini, Donizetti, and Gounod were ordered from Graz by Father Sales, and these were Hugo's staple musical diet at St. Paul. He was also chosen to play the organ on weekdays at the students' masses. A trio was formed in which Herr Denk, the secretary of the institution, performed, with Hugo at the piano and another pupil, Ernst Gassmeyer, as violinist. Not infrequently Philipp Wolf himself with his violin would take a place in this group, on the occasions when the marketing of his hides had brought him to the neighbourhood of the monastery. It seems that he drove over from Windischgraz by his own horse and wagon—a distance of about eighteen miles.

During the time of Hugo's schooling at the monastery occurred an accident which illustrates the all importance to him of his music, even at this early age. The accident was followed by a fresh family disaster. In September 1872, during the school holidays, Katharina Wolf arrived back home from a visit to Bleiburg in Carinthia with her three youngest daughters, Cornelia, then aged nine, Katharina (Kathi, or Käthe), aged seven, and little Adrienne (Jenny), aged five. Cornelia had been taken ill on the homeward journey, and when the party reached the house they found Dr. Unger, the family physician, engaged in bandaging Hugo's hand. He had broken a bone in a fall while practising gymnastics on his mother's flour bin, and the remains of Katharina's best damask table-napkins were strewn around, which the helpless Philipp Wolf had, in desperation, torn to pieces for use as bandages. Hugo himself cried out despairingly, not on account of the considerable pain he must have been suffering, but because he feared a permanent injury to his hand that would have put an end to his musical activities.

Cornelia's illness was diagnosed as typhoid fever and soon after, on 19th September, she died.

Hugo's aunt, Katharina Vinzenzberg, was present when he injured his hand, and according to the account given by her daughter to F. G. Antal, it occurred when he was eleven years old, i.e. in 1871.[1] The above version is taken from Hugo's sister Käthe's reminiscences. Although Käthe was herself only seven years old at the time, she is able to connect the incident with Cornelia's death, and the fact that in the term beginning in September 1872 there is a blank space against 'Gymnastics' in Hugo's school reports indicates pretty clearly that this was, indeed, the time of the injury to his hand.

Meanwhile, except for music and history, a subject which also aroused his interest, Father Sales Pirc found no great aptitude or desire for study in Hugo. His school reports, however, which have been printed by Decsey, are reasonably satisfactory. In both terms of his first year at St. Paul he was placed sixth out of twelve pupils. After his promotion to the second class he was placed fifth out of eleven in the first term; in the second term, at the end of which he left

---

[1] In some brief autobiographical notes, 'Daten aus meinem Leben,' which, however, can be shown to be often inaccurate, Wolf himself dates this accident from 1871.

the school, his position is not given. The reports further indicate that his conduct was 'praiseworthy' throughout the whole two years of his stay there. The remark 'excellent' is comparatively rare. He seems to have attained excellence only in gymnastics in the second term of his first year, in geography and history in the second term of his second year, and in singing in both terms of his second year. Languages were his stumbling-block. In his last term he received the lowest classification of all for both Slovene and Latin languages. The Latin reports progressively deteriorate, and although he managed to pass the end of term examination, his difficulties with this subject were the cause of his leaving the monastery school. Professor Hermann, who taught Latin, was exceedingly strict and unbending and demanded much of his pupils. Of the eleven children in Hugo's class, he considered that only four deserved promotion in this school year. From him the young Wolf, who was careless and apathetic towards his Latin studies, could expect little sympathy, and Father Sales in the end advised Philipp to withdraw the boy from the school. The earliest letter of Hugo's that has been preserved, written apparently on 5th June 1873, gives us some idea of the difficulties both of Hugo and of his teachers. He writes to correct the false impression he considers likely to have been made by a recent letter from his teacher to his father, which he has been shown:

Some of it is true, but much shamefully trumped up. He wrote, for instance, that my work is less satisfactory in all subjects. Only this is true —that I did bad Latin compositions but on my honour I will improve. The school Inspector was here on the fourth. I did well in history, knew it so well that the Inspector praised me. You will find a note about it in my history report, as I told you at Easter. Don't forget that! About my conduct he writes that I am proud, rebellious, stubborn, etc. I can't understand at all how he has thought that out. Similarly he lied *most infamously* when he told me, as he wrote to you, that he threatened to get me expelled from the institution and that I replied: 'Anyway, I'm going to Marburg.' He also wrote that I had never begged his pardon. I went once in the first year to him and apologized about something else. But he repelled me and said: 'That's all *hypocrisy*.'

The letter runs straight on without a break to request the dispatch of a new summer coat, bathing-drawers, and photographs of his parents. There follows a postscript:

Secretly written. Don't answer him as to why you didn't come on Tuesday. Please tell him that the horse was lame, not that I wrote to you not to come on account of the prefects being so angry with me.

It happens that three letters of this period, from Father Sales Pirc to Philipp Wolf, have survived. They include the latter part of the letter referred to by Hugo in the quotation above, and allow the affair to be seen in a rather different light. Father Sales deserves to be remembered for his kindness and desire to help the young Wolf. The matter of the first letter is reflected in Hugo's own. It ends:

I have read this letter to Hugo, just as it is, and I hoped thereby to bring him to repentance and reason, in which case I should have set aside the letter and perhaps not troubled you with it. Unhappily I was mistaken. I saw in Hugo no change at all—he did not beg my pardon but, after I had finished reading, turned right about and went away, completely indifferent.

The second letter, dated 19th July 1873, six weeks later, tells how Hugo may perhaps scrape through the mathematics examination, but in the path of further advancement at St. Paul stands the terrible Prof. Hermann, who will not hear of promotion for Hugo. Father Sales suggests already that it might be better, to avoid humiliation, for the boy to leave before the end of term, thus escaping classification. Then if he would study hard in the holidays he would be able to get into a higher class elsewhere—at Marburg, for instance. Or perhaps the humiliation of a second year in the same class would be good for Hugo? But he warns: 'Come yourself to fetch Hugo, if possible, I am afraid the boy could do himself an injury, if he doesn't get through. He is very violent.' A week later, on 25th July, the prospects seemed more hopeful.

I cannot tell you how much I have the fate of your Hugo at heart, for in spite of his occasional thoughtlessness I love the boy very much. . . . To-day they are writing the last so-called Term-Composition. Perhaps Hugo will yet extricate himself, as he was successful in doing yesterday in mathematics and geometry. He is getting on very well in all subjects.

Father Sales promised to use all his influence with the Prelate to secure for his 'dear Hugo' at least a two-thirds reduction of the fees, if not complete exemption from payment. 'But on no account must he cease studying. It would be an eternal shame. "All in good time." He will grow wiser with the years.'

But finally Prof. Hermann prevailed and Hugo was withdrawn from the school.

It is clear that his transference to Marburg was in the air before he left the Konvikt of St. Paul. His brother Gilbert was now old enough for a beginning to be made with his secondary education, so that the new crisis in Hugo's affairs made it convenient to send both boys, together with their sister Modesta, to Marburg on the Drave, where one of their uncles had his home, in the autumn of 1873. From a letter of Hugo's it appears that Max was also living in the vicinity, perhaps even attending the Marburg Gymnasium with his two younger brothers. Philipp Wolf was thus enabled to keep together all the children who had so far left home under the watchful eye of Uncle Liebezeit.

But Hugo was not a success at Marburg.

Conditions in the Gymnasium at that time were far from ideal. The director, Johann Gutscher, was an able and industrious pedant, who carried out his duties with great earnestness, but antagonized the whole school by too great a fondness for the sound of his own voice. In the Tertia, the class to which Hugo was assigned after the entrance examination, the teaching of German, Greek, and Latin was entirely in the hands of a student teacher without any qualifications, either of scholarship or temperament. He was accustomed to pass his evenings drinking in the taverns, and took little interest in maintaining discipline. The short-sighted old professor of religion, Dr. Žager, or Schager,[1] was also incapable of keeping order. He was cruelly treated by the boys, but only roused himself to severity when they played tricks upon him during his Sunday religious services.

Marburg was far less congenial to Hugo than St. Paul had been. In the busier world of the Gymnasium he became more retiring and, as at Graz, outside school hours he did not care to associate much with the other boys. He seems, nevertheless, to have first acquired the nickname 'Wölferl' in Marburg, which suggests the existence of reasonably good relations between him and his fellows. But it was not easy to get really to know him. Only one subject brought him out of his shell. His musical interests were no longer confined to operatic pot-pourris: he talked now of Haydn, Mozart, Beethoven and other composers, but principally, with fanatical zeal, of Beethoven, whose symphonies he played in piano arrangements. His colleagues loved to make game of him on account of these Beethoven transports, but when they exasperated him beyond bearing he used to fly at them with raised fists and pummel them into displaying more reverence before his idols.

In his first half-year at Marburg, Hugo was placed twenty-second out of the twenty-nine pupils in the Tertia, but improved in the second term as far as twelfth place out of twenty-six, which assured

[1] The Dr. S. of the *Familienbriefe*, letter of 29th June 1875.

him of promotion to the next grade. But in the Quarta his decline from grace was devastatingly complete. The reports show him to have been placed last but one in the first term, and last of all his class in the second term. It seems that Hugo's failures were deliberately contrived and were intended to blackmail his father into sending him to the Vienna Conservatoire, for he was now possessed by the fixed idea of a musical career. He told his sister Modesta that if he did well at school he would never succeed in getting into the Conservatoire and there he *must* go—no other course was possible. When one of his teachers, becoming aware of the extent to which his normal studies were being interfered with, restricted his musical activities in the Gymnasium, Hugo told his father that it would have been impossible for him to remain there, had not the more kindly Prof. Nawratil given him permission to use his own piano whenever he wished.

Although he had not received any lessons in composition, he was already covering much manuscript paper with his childish, as yet unformed, musical handwriting. In the autobiographical 'Daten aus meinem Leben'[1] Wolf writes: '1873–74. Attended the Gymnasium at Marburg. Got to know the Haydn symphonies in piano-duet arrangements. . . . Enormously enthusiastic and composed straight away a piano sonata. Shortly afterwards variations. Later songs.' This is a clue with the aid of which we may perhaps succeed in establishing the chronology of Wolf's earliest compositions. The entry for 1875 begins: 'In September travelled to Vienna. Attended the Conservatoire. . . .' Thus all Wolf's comments on his Marburg experiences are compressed into the entry for '1873–74,' although he was at school at Marburg until at least the end of June or beginning of July 1875. Now the early manuscripts in the Music Section of the Vienna City Library[2] bear opus numbers, and the first three of these opus numbers correspond exactly to the sequence of compositions mentioned in Wolf's autobiographical notes—they are given to a piano sonata, a set of variations, and a group of songs. It

---

[1] Already referred to in the footnote on p. 10. I am told that this interesting little document, covering Wolf's life up to 1891, has been lost, but a copy of it still exists, made many years ago by Frau Hilde Wittgenstein, *née* Köchert, who kindly allowed me to re-copy it.

[2] These manuscripts came into the possession of the Vienna Hugo Wolf Verein on the composer's death. When the Wolf Verein was disbanded they were handed over to the Vienna Akademischer Wagner Verein, and when this society, in its turn, ceased to exist, in July 1939, they were presented to the City Library, in the Rathaus.

seems certain that these are the works referred to by Wolf as compositions of his Marburg schooldays. The manuscripts are not
dated, but other evidence suggests that they were written during the
first half of 1875, rather than in 1873 or 1874. In the National
Library in Vienna is a little pocket-book [1] containing, among other
things, carefully written notes in connection with Hugo's German
lessons at Marburg. This was later used as a Viennese address-book
and finally, on the pages that were still blank, developed into a little
musical note-book and diary. On the last pages are some smudgy
pencil scribblings:

> On Sunday, 11th April, at 8.30 p.m. the Sonata begun; written on
> Monday 12th at 11.45 in the Town Park, from 5 till 7.45 in the wood over
> the three ponds. Continuation on Tuesday 13th April, from 3 o'clock till
> 4.45. On Friday from 11.30 to 4.30, with interruption. Continuation
> in the evening about 8.30–9.30. On 29th April at 4.50 in the afternoon.

Now although almost the whole of the contents of this little note-
book, except what is obviously a school exercise, concerns Wolf's
stay in Vienna, the dates and days of the week of *this* entry (at the
very end of the book) are correct only for early 1875, when he was
still at Marburg. Further, a scrap of manuscript paper, also in the
National Library, among the sketches and fragments acquired in
March 1940 from the Köchert family, begins in the same way as
these diary scribblings, this time with the addition of the year:
'Begun Sunday, 11th April 1875, continuation Monday 12th at
11.45. . . .' The rest, and the music itself to which these dates refer,
is torn away, the blank portion of this scrap of paper having been
used later for a sketch for the slow movement of the Violin Concerto,
Op. 6. But, considered in conjunction with the dates at the end of
the little diary, where a sonata is actually mentioned, there can be
little doubt that these dates refer to the Piano Sonata, Op. 1, the
other sonatas in manuscript being all demonstrably later works.
So the catalogue of Hugo Wolf's compositions begins thus:

Op. 1. *Piano Sonata.*
> 'Dedicated to Herr Philipp Wolf.' The MS. is incomplete. All
> that has survived is an Adagio leading to an Allegro, and a Minuet
> and Trio.
> Composed at Marburg in April 1875.

Op. 2. *Variations* for the piano.

[1] See 'Hugo Wolf's Vienna Diary, 1875–76,' in *Music & Letters*, January 1947.

Op. 3. *Lieder.*[1]

 Nacht und Grab (Zschokke).
 Sehnsucht (Goethe).
 Der Fischer (Goethe).
 Wanderlied (Goethe).
 Auf dem See (Goethe).

Op. 4. has not survived, but against the last two of the above songs is written in pencil 'Op. 4 No. 1. (quartet),' and 'Op. 4 No. 2. (chorus),' indicating Wolf's intention to arrange these two Goethe songs for chorus. The alto part of a setting for mixed chorus of *Auf dem See*, by Goethe, was in the possession of Gilbert Wolf at Windischgraz in 1938.

The title-pages of these early manuscripts are often very carefully executed, in imitation of a printed page. Musically all these compositions, and those that were to follow them for some time to come, are completely negligible. The young Wolf's manuscripts reflect, as in a mirror, his early enthusiasms—Haydn, Mozart, Beethoven, Schubert. In these works there is nothing yet to be found that is characteristic of Wolf.

A few further scraps of manuscript, perhaps the earliest of all, were lent to Hans Wamlek's Hugo Wolf Museum [2] at Windischgraz by Wolf's niece, Frl. Cornelia Strasser, of Graz. They consisted of sketches or fragments of unfinished songs—*Das taube Mütterlein*, *Soldatenlied*, and *Der Morgen*. A *Frühlingslied* by Hugo Wolf is remembered only by a title-page, without the music, in Philipp Wolf's hand. This was also in Wamlek's Museum. Two additional songs from a very early period, *Die Sterne* and *Gebet*, are preserved in the family of Wolf's sister Adrienne. They are simple tunes, without accompaniment. *Gebet* is a setting of 'Leise, leise, fromme Weise,' from *Der Freischütz*.

At Marburg Hugo had contrived to obtain for himself a position among the first violins of the orchestra which took part in the performance of religious works at the town church. He began to play

---

[1] The song *Frühlingsgrüsse*, Op. 9, No. 1, dated 3rd January 1875, which has been considered to be the earliest surviving song by Wolf, is undoubtedly from 1876, as will be shown later.

[2] The opening ceremony took place on 25th September 1943. I am not optimistic about the survival of that part of the contents which was left behind when German resistance collapsed in 1945 and the founder of the museum had to flee. The commemorative tablet on Wolf's birthplace has been removed, as I have ascertained for myself, and I have been told that everything written in the German language found in the houses was burnt, and all German books collected for pulping. It is to be feared that many precious Wolf relics, some manuscripts and letters, have been lost to the world through the ill-advised foundation of a Wolf Museum in disputed territory in war-time.

truant for this purpose, especially from the Sunday morning school masses. On 27th June this happened on the occasion of a performance in the town of a Mass in D minor by Hummel. Dr. Žager discovered that Hugo had not been present at the school mass, and encountering the boy the next morning, demanded the reason. Hugo explained that he had been himself performing in the mass at the town church and, as Žager persisted in entering his name in the register as an absentee, remarked that *surely one church service was enough for one Sunday morning*! Richard Kukula, who overheard the conversation, declares that as the professor began to expostulate, Hugo at first let the flow of words pass unheeded over his head, waiting resignedly for the storm to abate, until Žager made an unhappy reference to this 'damned music,' whereupon the boy flared up in defence of his art, verbally assaulting Žager in a fit of uncontrollable fury, and scattering around him the darkly gleaming, piercing, almost maniacal glances peculiar to him in his anger. Žager, who, in spite of his myopia, had further detected Hugo in the act of consuming his breakfast during the hours set apart for religious instruction, reported his unruly pupil to the director of the Gymnasium, who took a serious view of his conduct and called a conference to decide what should be done with him. While the result of the conference was still in doubt, Hugo wrote to his father an account of the position. In this letter he declares that in order to avoid shameful humiliation and the director's 'revenge,' he wishes to leave Marburg. Decent treatment is not to be expected. His father will see for himself that it is better for him to leave the school. At Marburg he will find plenty to occupy himself with, and if his father doesn't write soon, he will leave the place of his own accord.

Whether he walked out at once, as he threatened, or waited until the nearing end of the school year, when he would certainly have been asked to leave, his days at Marburg were numbered and the problem of his future was agitating both Hugo and his father. The letter which relates of the Hummel Mass and its consequences goes on to deal with the greater question of his career. Although music was a necessary relaxation in his own life, Philipp was unwilling that his son should be entirely dependent upon it for his livelihood. He retained his love for the art, for music as the pleasure and consolation of a drab and laborious existence, but the bright flame of his youthful idealism shone only dimly in the middle-aged leather manufacturer. His own ill fortune, the disaster of the fire and the subsequent incessant labour at his uncongenial occupation, in the end brought him near to despondency. He was pessimistic about Hugo's chances of supporting himself in the career he wished to adopt.

We may be sure the matter was frequently and exhaustively discussed between them. The surviving letter on the subject represents the phase which the struggle had reached by 29th June 1875. At that time it seemed that a victory for cold reason and common sense was assured. The son, 'deceived in his fairest hopes,' alternately pleading and despairing, sorrowfully recognizes, in this letter from Marburg, that his father has set his face against the fulfilment of his fondest wishes, and declares that he is now prepared to accept this and to dedicate himself to another profession. 'God grant only that your eyes be not opened,' he writes, 'when it is already too late for me to turn again to a musical career.' He throws the whole responsibility for the unhappiness that he feels is inevitable on to the poor, perplexed Philipp, who perhaps realized that it was with himself that he was struggling, in a reconstruction, a generation later, of his own old contest with paternal authority and prudence.

It was not, after all, the end of the struggle, for assistance came from an unexpected quarter. Aunt Katharina Vinzenzberg paid another visit to Windischgraz that summer, from her home in Vienna, and in the family discussions which arose she gave her support to Hugo. Why not give the boy a chance to show his mettle, by allowing him to return with her to Vienna, to attend the Conservatoire, where her own two daughters, Hugo's cousins Anna and Ida, were already studying? She undertook to give him a place in her own family and to supply his needs for the bare cost of 16 gulden monthly.[1]

Philipp was not entirely convinced: but Aunt Katharina's scheme provided at least an escape from the deadlock in which Hugo's affairs had culminated. The two of them talked Philipp round and at length he consented. Hugo went to Vienna with his aunt, was entered for the Conservatoire there, and in September 1875 eagerly began a new life in the city of his dreams and aspirations.

---

[1] The gulden, or Austrian florin, was worth about one shilling and eightpence.

II

VIENNA: THE CONSERVATOIRE

THE Vienna Conservatoire had been since 1851 under the direction of Josef Hellmesberger, additionally celebrated both as a witty man about town and as the leader of an admirable string quartet. Under his administration the young Wolf studied harmony with Robert Fuchs [1] and the piano with Wilhelm Schenner. He was by no means unfortunate in his masters, for Fuchs seems to have taken a warm interest in him and his early attempts at composition and Schenner was an able musician and teacher. Wolf's playing was sufficiently advanced for him to commence at once with the curriculum of second-year pupils. Among his fellow students in Professor Fuchs's harmony class was Gustav Mahler, who had joined the Conservatoire at the same time.

We have seen that, early in 1875, the young Wolf was already launched upon his career as a composer, with his imitative piano pieces and songs. When he got to the Conservatoire he had to begin all over again with the study of elementary harmony, without regard for what he had been able to pick up for himself out of his father's old text-books of composition. He felt this set-back keenly and was impatient to get on to more advanced work; he is said to have dismissed his teacher's explanations with the airy comment: 'That's all self-evident!' Naturally, his musical studies were not confined to the hours of his attendance at the Conservatoire. The intense musical life of the capital was something new and tremendously exciting to the little provincial, who for the first time found himself in an environment where it was possible to absorb music almost with the air he breathed. The whole of his waking life was devoted to it, and he grudged even the time he had to spend in sleeping as time lost to the study of his art.

There was much music-making in the Vinzenzbergs' house in those days. They lived in the second Bezirk, Leopoldstadt, at Mayergasse 14, a turning off the Praterstrasse. There are various indications, in

---

[1] Not Franz Krenn, as stated by Decsey, who was badly served by the 'higher official' who searched for him for details about Wolf in the annual reports of the Conservatoire.

19

Wolf's diary and elsewhere, to show that he lodged partly in the Mayergasse and partly in the Arsenal. This is very curious. His uncle is thought to have been a master tailor. Perhaps he had business connections with the Arsenal. Wolf's cousins were about his own age and attended the Conservatoire with him—Anna for piano and Ida for singing lessons. They were talented children. Anna once had the honour of playing the Weber-Liszt *Polacca* at a students' concert in the presence of Liszt himself, who was moved, as usual on such occasions, to embrace and kiss the performer.

Unable to progress in the harmony class as fast as he wished, Wolf used to sit at the Vinzenzbergs' piano for hours on end, striking successions of chords, and when he discovered a novel way of resolving a discord, used to call out into the living-room: 'Anna, Anna, another resolution!' and play it over to her a dozen times in succession.

The Vienna opera-house was a powerful attraction. He was frequently to be found among the students who waited for hours in the gallery queue, score under arm, until the doors were opened, when the jostling crowd of long-haired enthusiasts would rush up the staircase to secure their favourite seats.

The dominant influence of the opera-house is evident in what we know of Wolf's musical tastes at this period. The Vinzenzberg sisters, of course, were his chief confidantes, and in his explorations of the repertoire he sometimes tried their patience beyond bearing. He forced his own enthusiasms upon them—Mozart, Weber's *Freischütz*, Kreutzer's *Nachtlager von Granada*, and the *Poet and Peasant* overture of Suppé, which he often played to them from memory. But the work which made the most powerful impression of all upon him was Meyerbeer's *The Huguenots*. He procured a score [1] and was tireless in his study of the instrumentation. It was a characteristic of Wolf's to form attachments of a most intimate and possessive nature for whatever made a special appeal to him, and at this period, we are told, he was never tired of stressing that *The Huguenots* was 'his' music, in the way that Mörike and Kleist afterwards became 'his' poets. Ida Vinzenzberg's voice was frequently pressed into service, but Wolf was always intolerant of imperfect intonation or faulty rhythm in her singing. A slip of this

---

[1] It must have been from this score that he first learned to know and admire the opera, and not from an actual performance. His Vienna diary shows that he only saw *The Huguenots* on the stage *after* he had capitulated to Wagner, and Meyerbeer's work seems then to have made no particular impression upon him.

PHILIPP AND KATHARINA WOLF, 1882

Photos: Historisches Museum der Stadt Wien

kind would be most severely censured, and this generally resulted in a breakdown of the performance. The young lady would retire in a huff, inviting him in doing so to sing the opera himself, which he would, in fact, then proceed to do, representing the whole cast himself, and persisting until the Vinzenzbergs began to wonder whether the maintenance of this musical genius in embryo was altogether worth while.

His behaviour was often freakish and unpredictable. Accompanying his cousins to the Conservatoire, they once passed a hurdy-gurdy in the street which happened to be playing a melody from an opera he had recently heard. That was sufficient to start Hugo singing the music in a loud voice, in the open street, with the appropriate stage gestures. But when an audience began to assemble from the passers-by he became furious.

A good idea of his life at this time is given by entries from the amusing little diary in which he kept notes of the opera performances and concerts he attended.

On October 11th, 1875, at the Court Opera for the first time. Opera: *The Marriage of Figaro*, by Mozart. Countess: Frau Wilt. Pöch [1] was with me. Very rainy weather. The performance very good. Was in the gallery. To-day, October 12th, *Oberon* by C. M. von Weber. Rezia: Frau Dustmann. The scenery was extraordinarily fine. The music wonderful and enchanting. At the close very rainy weather. Almost forgot the biography of Beethoven.

October 16th, *Robert the Devil*. Princess of Sicily: Frau Wilt. Robert: Herr Labatt. Gallery. Anna, Ida, and another young lady. Frightful scrimmage. Ballet: Fräulein Linda. End 10.30.

October 17th, *The Magic Flute*, by Mozart. Pamina: Frau Dustmann. Queen of the Night: Frau Wilt. Was in the pit. Received from Uncle a gulden for the theatre. Magnificent scenery. Then went with Maier [2] to the Napagedl beer-saloon. At 12 o'clock went home. The music was charming.

Wednesday, October 27th, went without head-covering from the Mayergasse to the Arsenal at 7.30 in the evening.

Thursday, October 28th, 1875, played the second Study in the first volume of Cramer and the E minor scale before Professor Dachs at the test. The examination itself went off very well.

Sunday, 31st, the great Gran Mass of Liszt performed in the Hofburg Chapel. The Mass made a powerful impression on me.

Sunday, October 31st, *Don Giovanni*. Couldn't go to the Court Opera owing to very violent headache.

[1] A visiting-card of this friend, Alexander Pöch, is enclosed in the diary (National Library, Vienna).
[2] Hans Maier was another cousin of Wolf's.

On November 1st C major Mass of Mozart in the Hofburg Chapel. Comic Opera, great performance by the conjurer Professor C. Hermann. Herr Gaisser took me in. Second row of the stalls. On this day met Herr Gaisser for the first time in the Black Eagle Hotel. On November 1st as I left the theatre (by the Belvedere line[1]) it snowed for the first time, at about 9.45.

Thursday, November 4th, 1875, *Fidelio* by L. v. Beethoven. Fidelio: Frau Dustmann. Florestan: Herr Walter. Pizarro: Herr Beck. The effect of this opera was tremendous. I was quite beside myself. Aunt, Anna, and Ida were with me in the gallery. Frau Dustmann received a bouquet at the end and was called back four times.

Sunday, November 7th, we all—Anna, Ida, and I—fell into fits of laughter over the word 'Deibl,'[2] after *Manfred* had been performed.

Monday, November 8th, frightful wind and rain on going home from the Mayergasse to the Arsenal.

In November 1875 Philipp Wolf was still mentally uneasy about Hugo's future. He wrote to his sister in Vienna, urging her to do her utmost to persuade Hugo to take up his Latin studies again, and look to his general education. He wished him to become qualified to take 'a decent situation' instead of concentrating the whole of his attention on music. Philipp was also thinking of the question of military service. Without educational qualifications, Hugo would be conscripted, later on, for a period of three years' training, whereas with a high-school Diploma of Maturity he could become an 'Einjährig-Freiwilliger'—a volunteer, liable for only one year's service. Hugo did, in fact, write home, not for his Latin grammar, but for the mineralogy and physics text-books which he had used at Marburg. However, in his next letter he lays stress on his own view that culture can be attained even without the high-school diploma, and he gives his father little reason to believe that he could succeed in Vienna where he had failed at Marburg.

Any hopes Philipp may still have been entertaining that his son would change his mind before embarking upon a musical career were finally dissipated by one of the most overwhelming experiences of Hugo's lifetime—his introduction to the music and personality of Richard Wagner.

The year in which the young Wolf made his appearance upon the

---

[1] The Belvederelinie, part of the old boundary of the city of Vienna, which approximately followed the line of the present Gürtel. Wolf was clearly on his way to the Arsenal again.

[2] 'Deibl' is 'Teufel' ('Devil') in Viennese dialect. Wolf does not let us into the joke.

Viennese scene was one of importance in the long conflict which raged in that city around Wagner, his theories, and his works. The musical programmes of 1875 provided a public avid of sensation with full measure of controversial matter. Wagner himself, after an absence of three years, came twice to Vienna for long periods, and, as always, his presence stirred the musical life of the city to its depths. The Wagner question was one to which no one could remain indifferent, and it seemed that, in considering it, scarcely any one was even able to preserve an open mind and a sense of humour and proportion. It resolved itself into a warfare of the generations, in which even family loyalties were frequently sacrificed to musical party politics. In the eyes of the young men of that day Wagner represented modernity, freedom, and progress; to conservative parents and pedants he was the great iconoclast and seducer of youth. Not only the man's music, but every shade of opinion that could be associated with his name, from anti-Semitism to pan-Germanism and, later on, even vegetarianism, was embraced wholeheartedly by the young Wagnerian party. The Vienna Wagner Verein had been founded in November 1872 and was wholly the product of this youthful enthusiasm. Felix Mottl, the leading spirit in its foundation, who had sought and obtained the master's blessing upon the enterprise, was himself barely sixteen years of age at the time, and almost all the members, in the early years of the society's existence, were drawn from the ranks of the Conservatoire and university students. They were wholly under the spell of that mighty magician and demonstrated their allegiance with all the emphasis of which youth is capable. Max Burckhard once waited for three days at a railway station, having heard that Wagner was expected to arrive there, simply for the honour of setting eyes upon the great man himself. To be young at that time was to be a Wagnerian, with all the earnestness and intolerance, the follies and the exaltations that the term implied.

Against these fanatical crusaders were arrayed all the reactionary forces in Viennese musical life, headed by the most influential critics —Eduard Hanslick, of the *Neue Freie Presse*, and Ludwig Speidel, of the *Fremdenblatt*. These two men, by the bitterness of their attacks on Wagner's music, earned for themselves, in Wagnerian biography, a dubious sort of immortality. For more than a quarter of a century Hanslick's word was law in Vienna. Those who stood up against him, or incurred his animosity in any way, were marked men for the rest of their lives. According to Ludwig Karpath, Felix Mottl paid

B

the penalty for his early misdeeds in 1897, when his chances of becoming director of the Vienna Opera were destroyed by the unrelenting opposition of Hanslick, who had still to be consulted on all important musical matters, although he was himself in partial retirement.

Hanslick's critiques in the *Neue Freie Presse* were exactly suited to the taste of the majority of his readers—witty, stylishly written, at their best as light and easily digestible as the finest Viennese confectionery. But something more than brilliant journalistic talent should go to the making of a responsible music critic, and Hanslick's knowledge was superficial and his tastes were limited. His authority in Vienna rested upon his claim to leadership of the party which venerated Brahms as the saviour of German music from the pernicious influence of the New German school of Wagner and Liszt. He made a great parade in his writings of his admiration for Brahms, but the object of these attentions seems to have been himself under no illusions as to the quality of the understanding that his friend Hanslick brought to his music. The beatification of Brahms was an elaborate sham, necessitated by the musical party politics in which Hanslick indulged. His real tastes were for the light operas and operettas of Auber, Adam, Boieldieu, Rossini, and Johann Strauss. Richard Specht, in his Brahms biography,[1] records that he once saw a a postcard from Hanslick to Richard Heuberger: 'I have just come from the Rosé Quartet's concert, where Brahms's new Quintet was played. I could scarcely endure to remain to the end, so much did this music bore me. . . . The trouble is that Brahms no longer has any ideas and that he is becoming more and more leathern. After this piece, the Suite by Brüll that followed was a veritable feast with its Bachish euphony.' For public consumption, however, Hanslick produced an essay in which Brüll's work was barely mentioned while Brahms's Quintet was eulogized.

January 24th, 1875, had brought the first appearance of Hans Richter in Vienna as a conductor, in a concert organized by the Wagner Verein for the benefit of the Bayreuth fund. The programme consisted of Wagner's *Huldigungsmarsch*, the Prelude and *Liebestod* from *Tristan*, Wotan's Farewell and the *Feuerzauber* from *Die Walküre*, and the first performance in Vienna of Liszt's *Faust* Symphony. The occasion was obviously a field-day for the New German party, and Richter's appearance aroused general attention

[1] *Johannes Brahms* (Dresden, 1928). English translation by Eric Blom, 1930.

among the public, on account of his personal associations with
Wagner, dating from the time of his appointment as copyist of the
score of *Die Meistersinger* at Triebschen as a young man of twenty-
three.   The anti-Wagnerians did their best to minimize the effect of
the concert.   Hanslick declared that the first movement of Liszt's
symphony must have been intended to represent Faust with the belly-
ache,[1] and concluded his concert notice with these words: 'As, half
dead, we escaped into the open air, scarcely knowing what music
was, by good luck a well-tuned barrel-organ struck up the *Blue
Danube*.'

The next big event of the year was the arrival of Wagner himself to
conduct three orchestral concerts of his own music in the city.   The
first was announced to take place on 1st March, the programme
consisting of the *Kaisermarsch* and extracts from *Götterdämmerung*,
the latter comprising the first performance anywhere of any of the
music of the concluding drama of the *Ring des Nibelungen*, which
had been completed towards the end of the previous year.   The
public interest in these concerts was unprecedented.   The commencement of the first concert was delayed half an hour owing to the
crowds who wished to get in.   Wagner was given a tremendous
ovation, which he acknowledged in a speech, after which, according
to Glasenapp, the applause continued for at least a quarter of an
hour, until Wagner again addressed the audience.   The same
programme was repeated at the two other concerts, on 14th March
and 6th May, amid similar scenes of enthusiasm.

Before the last of these *Götterdämmerung* concerts, however, there
had occurred a crisis in the affairs of the Vienna Opera, which had for
long been in a desperate condition from both the artistic and the
financial points of view.   The director was Johann Herbeck, whom
Wagner considered incompetent for the position he held.   He was
an earnest musician and a conductor of compelling power, but it
was evident that he was out of place in the opera-house and in the
middle of April he received his dismissal.   The ex-actor Franz
Jauner, his successor, was very well aware of the state of excitement
prevailing in Vienna after the three *Götterdämmerung* concerts, and
as a born showman knew how to utilize this for his own purposes.
The heightened feelings which the great Wagnerian controversy had
brought about would provide him with the forces he required for
the staging of a major sensation.   With this object in view he had

---

[1] This remark was omitted when Hanslick reprinted his articles in book form.

made his own acceptance of the position of director dependent upon the engagement of Richter as Kapellmeister, and he further determined to bring Wagner himself again to Vienna.

There were difficulties at first. The Vienna Opera had long ago acquired, at a low figure, performing rights in perpetuity of *The Flying Dutchman*, *Tannhäuser*, and *Lohengrin*, and the Intendant had hitherto refused to consider any further payments to Wagner on this account. Jauner managed to secure for Wagner a revision of the agreement concerning the performing rights of these operas, and also gave permission for the artists of the Vienna Opera to take part in the proposed Bayreuth Festival of 1876. By these concessions he succeeded in inducing Wagner to come to Vienna to superintend in person productions, without cuts, of *Tannhäuser*, with the Paris *Venusberg* music, and *Lohengrin*.

Wagner, with his family, arrived on 1st November for a stay of about six weeks. Rehearsals for *Tannhäuser* began on 3rd November and their progress was reported almost daily in the newspapers. Something more than merely local interest was aroused by these performances. Celebrities, such as Joseph Tichatschek, the creator of the role of *Tannhäuser*, came to Vienna for the occasion. The artistic life of the city itself was in a ferment, and in the cafés there was but a single topic of conversation.

Counter-demonstrations were arranged by those hostile to the composer and his followers. On 7th November Richter conducted his first Philharmonic concert, in a programme including the *Faust* overture. The subscribers to the Philharmonic concerts were notoriously conservative in their tastes, the *Faust* overture was received with the utmost coolness, and although Wagner was known to be present, no attempt was made by the audience to call him, while the succeeding item, a familiar Bach Concerto, was received with demonstrative fervour.

The final rehearsal of *Tannhäuser* took place on 20th November and the work was finally produced on the 22nd. It was repeated on 25th November and followed by *Lohengrin* on 15th December.

We shall now see what impression those events made upon the fifteen-year-old Wolf. The young enthusiast for *The Huguenots* was about ready to be overwhelmed by the early Wagner operas, and *Tannhäuser* and *Lohengrin* did not fail to set fire to his imagination. His reactions cannot be better related than in the words he himself wrote in his family letters. We are made to realize, through this vivid personal account of the events of the last two months of 1875, what a young musician of that time really thought and felt about Wagner.

The first letter is dated 23rd November.

Richard Wagner has been since 5th November in Vienna. He occupies, with his wife, seven rooms in the Imperial Hotel. Although he has already been so long in Vienna, I did not have the good fortune and joy to see him until 17th November, at a quarter to eleven, outside the stage-door of the opera-house, from where I went up on the stage and heard the rehearsal, at which Wagner was present.

With a truly religious awe I gazed upon this great Master of Tone, for he is, according to present opinion, the greatest opera composer of all. I went several paces towards him and greeted him very respectfully, whereupon he thanked me in a friendly manner. From that moment forward I conceived an irresistible inclination towards Richard Wagner, without having yet formed any conception of his music. At length, on Monday, 22nd November, I was initiated into his wonderful music. It was *Tannhäuser*, performed in the presence of the great Richard Wagner himself. I took up my place at a quarter past two, although the opera, exceptionally, only began at half-past six (usually at seven o'clock). There was such a frightful scrimmage that I was worried about myself. I wanted to back out, but it was already impossible, for no one near me would make way. So nothing remained for me to do except to stay in my place. At last the door was opened, the whole crowd pushed their way inside, and it was fortunate that I was drawn into the middle, for if I had got to the side I should have been crushed against the wall. But I was richly compensated for my mortal anxiety. I got my good old place in the gallery. The overture was wonderful, and then the opera!—I can find no words to describe it. I can only tell you that I am a madman. After each act Wagner was tempestuously called for and I applauded until my hands were sore. I cried continually 'Bravo Wagner!' 'Bravissimo Wagner!' and so on, so that I became nearly hoarse and people looked at me more than at Richard Wagner. After each act he was continually called for, when he made his acknowledgment from the box. After the third and last act he appeared on the stage and as the jubilation was endless, after being called forth three times he made a short speech to the audience. In my next letter I will let you have the Master's exact words. I have written them out in my note-book. More about Wagner in my next letter. I am quite beside myself about the music of this great Master and have become a Wagnerian.

After *Tannhäuser* young Wolf spent much time hanging about the Imperial Hotel in the hope of again catching a glimpse of Wagner. With his old-fashioned plaid cloak, such as used to be worn in the country districts of his Styrian homeland, he presented a strange appearance in fashionable Vienna, and aroused the interest of the hotel manager, with whom he discussed the possibility of arranging an interview with Wagner himself. It was perhaps in connection with this proposal that, in another part of the letter quoted above, he asks his parents for money to buy material for a new pair of trousers and a waistcoat, which he will have made up in Vienna. New shoes will be required too, he writes—his old ones are quite worn out.

A short but significant entry in the diary reads:

Yesterday, at x o'clock in the night (9th–10th December), Richard Wagner appeared to me in a dream. Thereby I came into close contact with him. I sang him the well-known part of *Tannhäuser* (*Venusberg*).

In further letters to his parents he continues his Wagnerian rhapsodies:

I have been—can you guess with whom??? with—*Meister* Richard Wagner. I shall now relate to you everything, just as it happened. I am writing to you in the very same words that I have used in my diary.

On Saturday, 11th December, at half-past ten I saw Richard Wagner for the second time, in the Imperial Hotel, where I stood half an hour on the staircase and waited for his arrival. (I knew that on this day he would direct the final rehearsal of his *Lohengrin*.) At last *Meister* Richard came down from the second floor, and I greeted him very respectfully while he was yet some distance away from me. He thanked me in a very friendly manner. Then, as he reached the door, I sprang quickly to it and opened it for him, whereupon he stared hard at me for a few seconds and then departed for the rehearsal at the opera-house. I ran as fast as I could in front of the Master and arrived at the opera-house before Richard Wagner in his cab. I saluted him again there and wanted to open the door for him, but as I couldn't get it open, the driver jumped down quickly and opened it for him. Thereupon he said something to the driver, I think it was about me. I followed him then again towards the stage but this time was not allowed in. (I had already been on the stage at the *Tannhäuser* rehearsal, in Wagner's presence.) As I had often waited for the Master at the Imperial Hotel, I had made, by this opportunity, the acquaintance of the hotel manager, who promised to befriend me with Wagner. Who was happier than I when he told me to come to him the next day, the afternoon of Saturday, 11th December,[1] so that he could introduce me to the chambermaid of Frau Cosima (Richard Wagner's wife, daughter of the great Liszt) and Richard Wagner's valet. I came there at the appointed time; my attendance on the lady's-maid was very short. I received the instruction to come there the next day, Sunday, 12th December, at two o'clock. I went there at the time indicated, but found the lady's-maid, the valet, and the hotel manager still at dinner, and I took a *Capuziner* with them. Then I went with the maid to the Master's rooms, where I waited

---

[1] Wolf has clearly reverted here, in his narrative, to an earlier episode than that with which the letter began.

about a quarter of an hour until the Master arrived. At length Wagner appeared, accompanied by Cosima and Goldmark, etc. (He had just come from the Philharmonic concert.) I saluted Cosima very respectfully, but she did not consider it worth the trouble to bestow on me a single glance; indeed, she is known to the whole world as an exceedingly haughty and conceited lady. Wagner went without heeding me into his room, when the chambermaid said to him in a pleading tone: 'Ach, Herr Wagner, a young artist, who has already so often waited upon you, in order to meet you, wishes to speak with you.' He came out, glanced at me and said: 'I have already seen you once, I believe, you are . . .' (apparently he was going to say 'You are a fool.') At this moment he went in and opened the door of the reception room for me, where a truly royal splendour was in evidence. In the centre stood a couch, all velvet and silk. Wagner himself was enveloped in a long velvet cloak with fur trimmings. As I went in he asked me what I wanted. When I was alone with Wagner I said: 'Honoured Master! I have for a long time cherished the wish to hear an opinion upon my compositions and it would be to me——' Here the Master interrupted me and said: 'My dear child, I can pass no judgment upon your compositions: I am very short of time at the moment and cannot even get my letters written. *I understand nothing at all about music.*' When I asked the Master to tell me whether I had musical talent, and whether I should ever get anywhere with it, he said: 'When I was as young as you are now, no one could say from my compositions whether I should ever get anywhere in the musical world. You must at any rate play over your compositions to me at the piano, but just now I have no time. When you are more mature and have written greater works and I come again to Vienna, you can show me your compositions. It's no good, I can give you no opinion.' When I told the Master that I take the classics as my models, he said: 'Well yes, that's right, one cannot be original all at once.' (With that he laughed.) Finally he said: 'I wish you, dear friend, much fortune in your career. Go on working hard and when I come back to Vienna again show me your compositions.' Thereupon I left the Master, deeply moved and impressed.

The precise meaning of Wagner's curious remark, 'I understand nothing at all about music,' has been questioned. Friedrich Hofmann, who heard a version of the story in 1890, understood that it was in particular *piano* music upon which Wagner deemed himself incapable of giving an opinion. According to Anna Klenz,[1] however, the composition which Wolf wished Wagner to examine was *Auf dem See*, one of the Goethe songs of Opus 3. Wolf himself afterwards referred to this incident in an article published in the *Wiener Salonblatt* for 20th February 1887, which seems to have escaped notice in this connection:

When I, as a very young man, was ingenuous enough to lay before the

[1] Antal.

great Richard Wagner some piano pieces of my composition, in order to learn from his mouth whether I had musical talent or not, I could not repress the remark, as the Master obligingly looked through the manuscript, that they were still very much in the style of Mozart. The Master, greatly to my reassurance, replied in tones half earnest and half joking, 'Yes, yes. . . . One cannot be original all at once; I myself was not either.'

From this it would seem that Hofmann's memory was more reliable than Anna Klenz's, upon this small point. There can be little doubt that it was the Piano Sonata, Opus 1, and the Variations, Opus 2, which Wolf showed to Wagner. He had written no other piano compositions at this time.

Clearly Wagner was amused, but could not be bothered with the boy's demands upon his time and attention, made a few conventional remarks, and dismissed him as soon as possible. Wolf, however cast down he may have been about his precious compositions, left Wagner's presence enriched with an experience to which he afterwards loved to return in memory. According to Edmund Hellmer, Wolf used often to tell the story of his interview with Wagner, with the delightful addition of his own reply to the disputed remark of Wagner's—'O Master, you are too modest.'

The performance of *Lohengrin* on 15th December found Wolf, of course, again in his 'good old place' in the gallery of the opera-house, and once again the little diary gives the best record of his thoughts and feelings about this opera, and all the others that followed:

On Wednesday, 15th December, *Lohengrin*. Beginning at half-past six. This is the first work to make an overpowering impression on me. This music is so splendid that one believes oneself transported to quite another world. One finds no words to describe such a masterpiece. At the end of the third act, where Lohengrin takes leave of his Elsa and sings the swan song for the second time, I was so moved by the power of the music that I—wept!

Wagner was repeatedly called out. Before the beginning of the opera four of the violins fell over and broke a lamp. Further I had a squabble with a young man (in the pit) who took my place. To-day (16th December) Richard Wagner leaves at seven o'clock for Bayreuth. Wagner's family were also present—the young Siegfried, with long blond hair, and the little Kriemhilde.[1] The latter I did not see.

Sunday, 19th December 1875, *Der Freischütz*, for the first time since my arrival in Vienna. Although I had looked forward immensely to hearing this opera, I was disappointed. After the performance I went away completely dissatisfied. The reason was, however, only that my

---

[1] Wolf was misinformed. Wagner had no child of this name. Perhaps Eva or Isolde is meant.

head was still full of *Lohengrin*. In the Wolf's Glen much that concerns the stage setting was left out.[1] Frau Dustmann played Agathe in masterly fashion, as usual, and received after the aria 'Leise, leise, fromme Weise' a garland from the performers' box in the fourth tier, and after the second act was called for three times. . . . Only on the following day did I begin to see this wonderful music in its true light. From day to day I like this music more and more. Thereby I came to see that one must hear this opera often, in order to understand it.

Saturday, 25th December, *Don Giovanni*. Last appearance of Frau Dustmann in this opera and her third from last stage appearance in anything. I liked the opera very much indeed, especially Leporello and Don Giovanni. Frau Dustmann sang very beautifully but it provoked me that she composed for herself in almost every bar. Likewise Donna Elvira. . . . Frau Dustmann received a bouquet in the duet between Donna Anna and Don Octavio in the first act, after the murder of the Commendatore. The house was packed. For the benefit of the Pension Fund. I had my old seat. To my joy (ironic) there were some *anti-Wagnerians*, whose necks I should have liked to wring.

On Tuesday, 4th January 1876, taken for the first time to the Court Library by Herr Waldmann. Waldmann wrote repeatedly on a form that the person who had charge of the books should give me Brendel's *History of Music*. Yet I got neither this, nor *Opera and Drama* by Wagner. I took a *Manual of Composition* by Marx and studied it intently, which interested me very much. After we had studied from one o'clock till three, I went home with Herr Waldmann. The latter had the misfortune to lose his umbrella.

On Thursday, 6th January 1876, I heard the magnificent oratorio of Liszt *The Legend of St. Elizabeth*. Bertha Ehnn sang Elizabeth, Herr von Bignio Landgrave Ludwig and Hermann. Beginning 12.30. I was there already at 11.30 and betook myself to the pit, where I had to pay a gulden for the ticket. The oratorio was performed under the direction of Johann Herbeck. I was quite surprised by this music and for the first time admired Liszt as a great artist. The drum and horn duet was very peculiar, but beautiful. I left the large hall of the Musikverein very well satisfied. The storm was especially characteristic.

Sunday, 9th January, Philharmonic Concert. Programme: Mendelssohn, overture *Calm Sea and Prosperous Voyage*; Violin Concerto by Viotti; Weber's *Invitation to the Waltz*, orchestrated by Berlioz; Beethoven, sixth symphony (Pastoral). Professor Fuchs, to whom I had just shown my D major Sonata, gave me a ticket for a reserved seat in the circle. I was for the first time at a Philharmonic concert. I was quite enraptured over the wonderful expression which this orchestra brings out. Naturally the Beethoven symphony pleased me the most. Strangely enough I find no words to describe it. It is the first time that I have heard an orchestral

---

[1] The Vienna City Library possesses a part of Wolf's books and music. Among these volumes is a full score of *Der Freischütz* from this very early period. The stage directions for the scene in the Wolf's Glen are incomplete in this score and Wolf has carefully copied out everything lacking.

*B

work by Beethoven. There was only one round of applause. The violinist, Dragomir Krancsevics, too, was three times called back. The overture *Calm Sea and Prosperous Voyage* was delightful.

Monday, 10th January, *Tannhäuser* by Richard Wagner, for the second time. I was with Pöch in my old position. *Tannhäuser* delighted me even more than the first time, as I now understand the music better. I was at the end quite beside myself. No opera can affect me like *Tannhäuser* or *Lohengrin*. I had then Wallner's overcoat on for the first time.

Wednesday, 12th January, dress rehearsal of the opera *Lucia*, by Donizetti. I went with Fischoff in the circle, where we were then locked in and luckily for us an attendant let us out, who had necessarily to unlock the door. I heard there an Italian opera for the second time and I must say that, although I am a great opponent of Italian music, yet the opera rather pleased me. Herr Nawiasky acted and sang splendidly. Fräulein Riegel as Lucia sang very well, as usual. The second time Wallner's overcoat.

On 14th January 1876, *Lohengrin* by *Meister* Richard Wagner. The impression was like the first time, or even greater in comparison, as I was in the gallery. Anna was moved to tears.

Thursday, 20th January 1876, *The Flying Dutchman* by *Meister* Richard Wagner. At half-past four I took up my position, where I found already three people waiting. I was then the first at the door and the first upstairs, where I took the corner seat in the second row of the gallery. I made the acquaintance of a University student in the next seat, who deemed me too a son of the Muses. The opera was very fine and Beck acted really wonderfully. Characters: Daland (Mayerhofer), Senta (Kupfer), Dutchman (Beck), Eric (Walter), Steersman (Lay), Mary (Worani, mezzosoprano). Walter was quite hoarse, otherwise they all sang well, especially Herr Mayerhofer as Daland. Not for nothing is the Flying Dutchman known as one of Beck's most brilliant roles, for such acting and such singing will not easily be replaced, if he should some day leave the Opera. . . .

Thursday, 27th January 1876, *The Huguenots*. I went there at 4.30, where a whole throng of people were gathered at the outer doors. I went with Walenta to Schiel's,[1] purchased a libretto and arrived back just as the doors were opened. It stands to reason that I pushed my way so far to the front that I got into the fifth row from the barrier. Suddenly I heard my name called out and I caught sight of my new friend Pinkas, with whom I became acquainted on the Ferdinand Bridge,[2] when I was singing the Pilgrims' Chorus from *Tannhäuser*. I lent him my libretto which I afterwards lent to a corporal who was employed with the military band of the *Deutschmeister*.[3] During the race up the stairs I fell down and before I could pick up my ticket, which fell out of my hand, there were quite three score in front of me. Nevertheless I had a good position,

[1] Presumably a bookshop or music dealer.
[2] Now the Schwedenbrücke.
[3] The *Deutschmeister* were soldiers of an infantry regiment recruited from Vienna. The brass band of the *Deutschmeister* was celebrated.

the corner seat in the third row.　That in the second row Pinkas, who got there before me, took, and next to him sat a friend.　The first act of the opera went by without effect upon me.　The scenery was exceedingly fine. There was only one round of applause.

On Tuesday, 8th February 1876, I dreamed for the second time of Richard Wagner—that I came to see him just as he took out a pile of songs, which he had apparently received from somebody for his opinion.　I told him that I had read his biography and learned from it how badly things had gone with him at one time.　If I should fare so badly, I said, I would rather be a tailor.　At that he began to laugh heartily.　Then he went to wash himself, wearing all the while a black soft felt hat.　Finally I asked him to look at my compositions but he wouldn't hear of it.　Incidentally, the action took place in a room in the Imperial Hotel, although the scene was changed (the room different from that in which he received me).

Wednesday, 9th February 1876, Concert by Marie Baumayer, with the assistance of Herren Hellmesberger and Wallnöfer.　Hellmesberger and Baumayer played the A major Sonata of Bach.　Wallnöfer sang Bach, Brahms, and finally a song from *Die Walküre*, which was magnificent.　In conclusion Baumayer and Epstein played the *Hungarian Fantasy* with great success.

It was Wolf's desire to become independent and self-supporting, and as early as November 1875 he had found his first pupil in an engineer, who took violin lessons from him for three hours weekly, at a gulden an hour.　Wolf was hoping also to secure two further engagements as teacher of the piano early in December.　He was optimistic regarding his ability to earn a living in this way.　He asked his father for assistance: 'Sacrifice yourself just once more, and never again shall a request for money be sent to you.'　Actually, he had little enough money to spare.　At Christmas he wrote: 'I would gladly have sent something for the Christmas tree, but the carriage costs too much.'　He was, of course, provided with food and shelter at his aunt's; he needed pocket-money for books, scores, music-paper, and tickets for concerts and opera-house.

He complained to his father that he had already experienced a foretaste of the musician's difficulties in securing performance of his compositions.　In spite of all he could do, the Conservatoire authorities would not allow his works to be performed there, as he was not yet a member of the composition class.

From 18th February 1876 another letter of Philipp Wolf's to Katharina Vinzenzberg has been preserved.[1]　It is not a cheerful letter.　Hugo has not written home for a considerable time, he has

---

[1] Antal.　Original in the archives of the Gesellschaft der Musikfreunde.

not even acknowledged the receipt of 20 gulden sent in the previous
month.   In his last letter he had said that he had mislaid the receipt
for his Conservatoire fees and that he had to wait until a new one had
been made out.   Yet Philipp has received no news for a whole month.

I pity Hugo, that he is dedicating himself to music; I have Lortzing's
biography before me—Lortzing, the great composer of *Czar and Car-
penter*, fared miserably and was driven to attempt to support his wife and
six children by acting with itinerant comedians—in 1850!   *Thus does the
Germany of our time honour and reward her artists!*
Poor Hugo!   If only he would change his mind in time, and continue
his studies, so that such bitter disillusionments may not prostrate him,
when it is too late.   In any case Hugo should read the biography of Lortzing; it is probably obtainable in Vienna.
Very probably I shall myself be coming to Vienna in May with a consignment of leather, and then we will discuss Hugo's future, which troubles
me very much.   And the enclosed sheet from the *Neue Freie Presse* of
recent date is calculated to do anything but remove my gloomy forebodings.   [The cutting was Hanslick's article of 13th February 1876, on
the subject of youthful prodigies, and in particular of the young Busoni.]
I will dispatch the recently completed winter clothes to Hugo at once.   I
thank you for your timely assistance, and I must tell you quite frankly that
you sorely misunderstand my position when you reproach me for doing so
little for Hugo; a month's stay in my house would thoroughly convince
you of the reverse, for it is not possible to relate everything [by letter].
Hugo already knows how things are going, hence his resignation.
While once again requesting you, if occasion arises, to make inquiries of
Hugo's professors about his prospects, I send my most cordial regards to
you and to your dear husband and the children,
                    Your deeply distressed brother,
                                        PHILIPP WOLF.

Hugo was not much concerned about the misfortunes of Lortzing.
He had made contact with a greater musician, and one moreover
who had triumphed over adversity and who lived in princely
magnificence.   Within ten days of the dispatch of Philipp's letter
Hugo was once again planning to interview Wagner.   The latter
had told him to come to see him when he came again to Vienna, and
his return was imminent.   He was to conduct *Lohengrin* on 2nd
March, for the benefit of the singers of the opera-house chorus, and
the young Wolf was going to take him at his word and present himself before the Master with his latest works.
On 28th February, the day before Wagner's arrival in Vienna,
Wolf set out to call upon Richter, with a view to preparing the
ground for his reception by Wagner.   We possess a detailed account

of the events of these days in Wolf's own words, in a family letter of 15th March:

I am now busily composing. When you indicated to me the so-called *Ritterbund* I straight away composed a chorus, *Die Stimme des Kindes*, words by Lenau, for four male voices with piano accompaniment. On 28th February, just as Richard Wagner's opera *Rienzi* was being given, I went with the finished work to Hans Richter, the Kapellmeister of the Opera. I found him at table, had him called out and explained to him the reason for my appearance. Thereupon he led me inside, where incidentally I had to wait a good half-hour until he had finished eating. After that we played the chorus on a Bösendorfer grand piano, he the voice parts, I the piano part, as well as I was able, for Richter played the score much better than I the piano part. The chorus pleased him very much, but as I always have bad luck with part-writing, the basses went, in relation to the tenor, much higher than the tenor itself. Of course, by that the melody was drowned. He indicated to me then the various registers, wrote it all out for me, and gave me permission to bring him some more choruses, but written in the tenor clef. On arriving home I went straight to work upon a new chorus *Im Sommer*, by Goethe, upon which followed three other choruses. These four choruses are without piano accompaniment and written in the tenor clef, which was rather difficult for me at first. They are very finely worked out, and I hope that Richter will be pleased with them. I went principally to Richter to obtain tickets for the Opera and to request the use of his influence with Richard Wagner. The second project did not come off, as Richter said that I ought not to appear before the Master with my first chorus *Die Stimme des Kindes*, as the basses must first be revised. Nevertheless I quickly wrote the second chorus *Im Sommer*, and marched off to the Master. As, however, the members of the chorus were just going to thank the Master, I decided to go to him a few days later, as I had heard that Richard Wagner would stay some time in Vienna. The next day I wrote a letter to him at his hotel, but as the Master departed on that day for Bayreuth and my letter only arrived at the hotel on the following day, it was sent on to the Master. However, since I gave no address, I could not expect an answer. Wagner is coming again in the summer, when I shall ask him for a ticket for the Bayreuth *Nibelungen* festival. This consists of the Prelude *Rheingold*, *Götterdämmerung*, *Walküre* and *Siegfrieds Tod*.[1] The ticket for these performances costs 300 thaler. Then the journey is extra. More about it by word of mouth in the holidays.

My Sonata in G major met with lively appreciation from Professor Fuchs since in it sonata form is better commanded. Stimulated by this praise I wrote on the same day my fourth Sonata, in G minor. In this work sonata form is for the first time really clear to me and here *I break away from all my models and follow a path of my own*. One perceives this

---

[1] It is clear that Wolf had not yet fully digested what he had heard of *Der Ring des Nibelungen*, since he confuses *Siegfried* with *Siegfrieds Tod*, the original title of *Götterdämmerung*.

especially at the beginning. I have only got the first part of the first movement ready, but this is already four pages long. The first movement alone will be fourteen pages long. I shall dedicate it to the Ritter Fischer. At present I am occupied exclusively with choruses and with this Sonata.[1]

Wolf is generally stated to have destroyed, in these early years, a vast amount of music with which he was not satisfied, but this seems extremely unlikely. There are very few compositions mentioned in the early correspondence, or known from other sources to have been written, which cannot be traced to-day among the unpublished manuscripts in the Vienna libraries or in private hands. A few manuscripts have been lost or destroyed, certainly, in the course of time, by Wolf and others, but that there was at any time a wholesale, systematic destruction of works which he considered unrepresentative is incredible. How explain, in that case, the continued existence in the composer's possession of manuscripts with 'Rubbish!', 'Bad!', 'Worse!', etc., scrawled by himself across them? How explain the almost complete survival of his Opp. 1–17, from the very beginnings of his creative life? The last-quoted letter mentions various works, and of these the Piano Sonatas in G major and G minor, *Die Stimme des Kindes*, and three out of the four Goethe choruses have all come down to us in manuscript.

The catalogue [2] of Wolf's early compositions with opus numbers —after about May 1876 he ceased to employ this system—continues as follows:

Op. 5. *Der Raubschütz*, a long, unfinished Loewe-like ballad, a setting of a comically bad poem [3] by Lenau about the ghost of a murdered gamekeeper. The diary has a reference to this work. 'Monday, 13th February 1876. Saw the main stream of the Danube and the Imperial Bridge for the first time, on the occasion of wishing to compose the *Raubschütz*. As however I could not go into the little wood, owing to the snow being too deep, nothing occurred to me and I went home.' From the early opus number, the origins

[1] I have rescued the concluding five short sentences, which do not appear in the printed version of the letter (*Familienbriefe* VII), from the original in the Prussian State Library, Berlin.

[2] Here presented in its clearest form. Sometimes a work received two different opus numbers at different times. Full details of all such variations will be found in Appendix II.

[3] Here is the penultimate stanza:

> Doch an des Walds geheimstem Ort,
> Auf seinem liebsten Stand,
> Wo jüngst die Kugel ihn durchbohrt
> Aus meuchlerischer Hand,
> Da bleibt er stehn und donnert: 'Schau!
> Hier schoss er mich wie eine Sau!'

of this ballad must date back even before this diary entry. As late as 24th June 1876 Wolf was still endeavouring to make something of it, but it was never completed.

Op. 6. *Violin Concerto*, in a reduction for violin and piano. Two movements are complete in the manuscript. The Adagio fades out after twenty-five bars. Wolf mentions in a letter from December 1875 that *three* movements were then completed—only the *finale* was lacking. 'But as I don't care for the moment to carry it further I begin other works. I am now writing three compositions and haven't yet completed any of them.'

Op. 7. *Piano Sonata in D major.*
This also consists of two completed movements and an unfinished Adagio. Undated.

Op. 8. *Piano Sonata in G major.*
'Begun on 9th January 1876, Sunday, at 11 o'clock at night. First part finished after two hours.' This Sonata has three completed movements. The last pages of the final Rondo, begun on 6th February, seem to have been lost.

Op. 9. *Lieder:*
Meeresstille (Lenau). Undated.
Liebesfrühling (Lenau). 29th January 1876.
Erster Verlust (Goethe). 30th January 1876.
Abendglöcklein (Vincenz Zusner). 18th March–24th April 1876.
Mai (Goethe). 25th April, revised 1st May 1876.
Der goldene Morgen. 1st May 1876.
Of *Mai* there are two versions in manuscript, neither quite complete. *Der goldene Morgen* is mentioned on the cover of Wolf's Op. 9, in the Vienna City Library, but the song itself is missing. It is to be found, however, in a sketch-book in the National Library. Another Op. 9, No. 1, exists. The song *Frühlingsgrüsse* (Lenau), dated 3rd January 1875, has been considered Wolf's earliest surviving song. But the date 1875 is certainly an error on Wolf's part—a likely slip, in the first few days of January, for any one to make, and one, moreover, which Wolf made several times over in his diary entries for this month. *Frühlingsgrüsse* evidently never satisfied its composer, as he withdrew it from his Op. 9. It seems to have given him considerable trouble. Two versions exist in manuscript. The first, in G, is unfinished; the second, transposed down a third, with a different ending, is finished, but several bars are crossed out and a third variant written out below.

Op. 10. *Die Stimme des Kindes* (Lenau) for male voice chorus and piano. Mentioned by Wolf in his letter of 15th March 1876, from which it is clear that the chorus was finished by 28th February. There is a note on the manuscript in accordance with what he told his father about Richter's strictures on the composition: 'The two tenor parts must be replaced by soprano and alto. In place of the first bass comes the tenor. As the basses often go too high I am compelled to arrange this chorus for mixed voices, as is also indicated above.'

Op. 11. *Fantasie* for piano.

Begun on 15th February 1876 but abandoned after thirty-two bars.

Op. 12. *March* for piano duet.

Mentioned in the diary: 'On 16th February saw the Danube for the second time, when I composed the beginning of the *March*, near the Rotunda, under a solitary tree.' The right-hand side of the paper is headed 'Trio,' but is otherwise blank.

Op. 13. *Three male-voice choruses*, words by Goethe.

> *Im Sommer.*
> *Mailied*, begun 11th March, finished 3rd April 1876.
> *Geistesgruss.*

Mentioned in the letter above, which shows that *Im Sommer* was begun on 28th February. Several copies exist. On the cover of one of them two other Goethe choruses are mentioned, *Wanderers Nachtlied* (erased) and *Die schöne Nacht*, which have not survived. Op. 13 is dedicated in stiff, boyish script on the title-page to 'Herr Philipp Wolf.'

Op. 14. *Fourth Piano Sonata, in G minor.*

See the letter of 15th March. A first movement, opening in *bravura* fashion, begun in the Conservatoire on 13th March and finished on 31st March, is complete. Only the theme of the Adagio, eight bars in all, was added on 1st April, and the work then apparently abandoned.

Op. 15. *Rondo Capriccioso*, in B flat, for piano.

Begun on 4th April, and finished on 4th June 1876. One of the few completed works, apart from songs and short choruses.

Op. 16. Missing.

Op. 17. *Choruses:*

> *Fröhliche Fahrt* (Edmund Höfer), 6th–7th May 1876. S.A.T.B., unaccompanied.
> *Im stillen Friedhof* (Ludwig Pfau), 10th–28th May 1876. S.A.T.B., with piano.
> *Grablied* (Lenz Lorenzi). S.A.T.B., unaccompanied.

Only the first chorus actually bears an opus number. The date of composition is omitted in the case of the *Grablied*, but it was written in the 'Lechner Wald,' which is a wood near Windischgraz. It is therefore of rather later date than its companions. Lenz Lorenzi, author of the poem, was an acquaintance of the Wolf family.

Not much need be said of these immature compositions. The songs are utterly insignificant, though the choice of poems—Goethe and Lenau predominate throughout the early opus numbers—is interesting. The piano sonatas and the Violin Concerto show Wolf still modelling his work on the Viennese classics, but the form is still helpless, and there is a great deal of empty passage-work. Most of these works in the larger forms were left incomplete. The choruses, designed in the first place for the Ritterbund at Windischgraz—a group of Philipp Wolf's friends who, after the household orchestra had broken up, came together weekly for music and good company —are perhaps the most successful of these student works. The *Mailied* ('Zwischen Weizen und Korn'), although still technically immature, captures something of the freshness and the springing rhythms of Goethe's lovely poem.

Wolf's early manuscripts are dated with extraordinary care and precision. He was accustomed at this period to take his work into the parks and public gardens. At the head of the manuscript of the song *Mai*, from Op. 9, is the inscription: 'Begun on Tuesday, the 25th April 1876, at seven o'clock, in the meadow to the left of the Prater; finished at half-past eight in the morning on Tuesday the 25th April.' On that morning an hour and a half sufficed for the composition of the whole song. The chorus *Fröhliche Fahrt* was 'begun at a quarter past four on Saturday afternoon, the 6th of May' and 'finished on Sunday, the 7th of May, at a quarter past ten in the morning, in the Prater.' Wolf adds the remark, in the German language, but spelt out in Greek characters, 'Very cold.'

The *Rondo Capriccioso* for piano, Op. 15, bears a secret inscription in Greek characters: 'Dedicated to Ritter Fischer von Ankern.' Fritz Fischer, Ritter von Ankern, figures upon the list of extraordinary (subsidizing) members of the Vienna Wagner Verein, but no details of his personal relationship with Wolf have survived. The letter quoted above declares Wolf's intention of dedicating the Piano Sonata in G minor to this patron, whose name also occurs in one of Philipp's letters.

In May the Vinzenzbergs moved out to the suburb of Hetzendorf for the summer, and Wolf, of course, went with them. Among the choruses of Op. 17 is the beginning of a *Mailied* (not identical with the Goethe chorus of the same title in Op. 13), sketched out first for chorus, and then recommenced as a song. This manuscript bears the inscription: 'Begun on Tuesday, the 13th of June 1876, at a quarter to five in the afternoon, near the Gloriette,' indicating that the Schönbrunn Palace Gardens had taken the place of the Prater as his outdoor workshop. The *Rondo Capriccioso* was completed at Hetzendorf, and there too Wolf made a transcription for orchestra of Beethoven's 'Moonlight' Sonata. He seems to have studied orchestration on his own account, for it must be remembered that he was not yet in the composition class at the Conservatoire. A letter to his cousin Anna, written in August of this year, refers familiarly to Berlioz's *Treatise on Orchestration*. In his transcription of the Beethoven Sonata he boldly adds new counterpoints where he feels Beethoven's own material to be inadequate to fill out the new medium.

In May, while living at Hetzendorf, Wolf used to earn himself a little pocket-money by playing dance music in an inn at Meidling. He received only a gulden and a half for playing from eight o'clock until past midnight. Night after night he trudged home on foot, tired, and bitter about the scanty remuneration, but with *some* money in his pocket, at least, for the books and scores he needed.

The books he purchased he read with eyes solely for their musico-dramatic effectiveness, for he was already searching for a subject for an opera. His first choice—the first of the long series which engaged his attention for a time, without finally satisfying his requirements—was Theodor Körner's libretto on the subject of Alfred the Great. He had Körner's complete works, in an edition which also contained the poet's letters, in which he was shortly afterwards to find another suggestion for his projected opera.

But before this happened the Conservatoire year came to an end and Wolf returned to Windischgraz for the holidays, with a certificate of the 'first grade' in his possession for both his subjects. He made the journey to Windischgraz towards the end of July; a letter to his cousin Anna on the 25th of that month is clearly written within a few days of his arrival.

On the very first day of his stay at Windischgraz, Wolf played over to his parents the *Tannhäuser* overture, on the old family piano that had done service in so many musical evenings during the years of his boyhood. But this 'wretched rattle-trap,' as he now called it, was utterly unable to stand up to the assault made upon it by the young Wagnerian—four hammers fell off in the course of the performance.

The idea of a grand opera on Körner's *Alfred der Grosse* was soon abandoned, and a new subject taken in hand. He told his cousin Anna:

I am quite happy in my little room, where I can now create greater works without being disturbed. . . . I shall not utilize 'Alfred the Great,'

but probably 'Alboin and Rosamond,' as to the handling of which
Körner gives some hints in his letters.   Now I am going to compose an
overture, for which, however, I haven't any material yet.

He did, in fact, for a long time play with the idea of *König Alboin*,
a romantic opera in four acts, and began to sketch out the music.
The text was written for him by a friend, an obscure Viennese writer
named Paul Peitl, whose work was published under the pseudonyms
of Paul Günther and Paul Mannsberg.   The subject is the historical
one of Alboin, King of the Lombards, who was assassinated at the
instigation of Rosamond, his wife, whom he had compelled to drink
from her father's skull.   One fragment of this opera has survived,
with twenty-one bars of music representing a duel between King
Alboin and his enemy Lintram, with the stage directions: 'Lintram
redoubles his blows.   Alboin, his weapon hacked to pieces, falls to
the ground, mortally wounded by Lintram.'   The sketches for
König Alboin gave their composer no little amusement when he
looked through them in later life.   'One already discovers in them
the little Wolf,' he told his sister Käthe in December 1892.   'He
howls not with the others, but somewhat apart, and that's something, even if his individual howl is not yet by a long way fully
developed.'

The young composer also occupied himself at Windischgraz with
the instrumentation of the *Rondo Capriccioso*, employing a large
modern orchestra, and with the beginning of a piano quintet, never
to be taken very far.

In the early autumn Wolf went back to Vienna to enter the composition class at the Conservatoire and continue his piano studies
under Schenner.   His professor of composition was the dry-as-dust,
monosyllabic pedant Franz Krenn.   'Old Krenn,' every one called
him, for he gave the impression of never having been young at all.
For Wolf, who needed above all sympathetic guidance at this stage,
the change of teachers was not a happy one.

Very little information has survived about the next few months of
his life.   There are no more letters in existence covering the remaining period of his Conservatoire training.   A record in the composer's own hand of the houses and hotels in which he lived during
his early years in Vienna,[1] with in most cases the precise dates of his
arrival and departure, contributes notably to our knowledge of

---

[1] Made use of by Heinrich Werner for his 'Hugo Wolfs Wohnstätten in Wien'
(*Wiener Neueste Nachrichten*, 16th May 1926).

these few months. It shows that he returned on 15th September to the Arsenal. But in October he left the care of his Aunt and Uncle Vinzenzberg, and transferred himself and his belongings to the Mayerhofgasse in the fourth Bezirk, 'Auf der Wieden,' a district in which he afterwards always preferred to live. The number of the house is not known. 'Family affairs'—perhaps a euphemism for a quarrel between Hugo and his relations—made it impossible for him to continue living with his aunt and uncle. He preferred, too, independence in a cheap lodging-house to the comfortable middle-class family life at his aunt's, and although the Vinzenzbergs were reticent about any break between Wolf and their family, it is certain that he had very little to do with them after this time.

It was the beginning of an endless succession of removals from one lodging to another, in search of cheap, yet decent and quiet 'diggings,' where he could work at his music in peace. Between Wolf's return to Vienna in September 1876 and May 1879, when he found a house in the Rennweg that accorded better with his requirements, there are recorded no fewer than twenty-one addresses where he occupied rooms.

After only a month in the Mayerhofgasse he moved on 1st November into the inner city, and took up his lodging in the Michaelerhaus. He endured this place for a fortnight, and then crossed the Danube canal into Leopoldstadt, where he spent a fortnight in 'a building in the Augarten.' On 1st December he returned to the Wieden district, this time staying at Margaretenstrasse 7. Here he seems to have found something more to his liking, for he settled down for the whole of the remaining period of his attendance at the Conservatoire—about three and a half months.

During this time the sixteen-year-old student composer was turning away from his part-songs and piano music to grapple with the most extended and exacting musical forms. He still had his opera *König Alboin* in hand, and now he conceived the idea of writing a Symphony in B flat. On 26th October he began to compose the first movement, which, although only a fragment has survived, was probably completed at this time. The second movement, a scherzo in G minor, was sketched out in November. The *Rondo Capriccioso*, orchestrated at Windischgraz in the previous August, was taken over and employed as finale of this B flat Symphony. Wolf's struggle with the symphonic form was spread over a long period. His present endeavours seem to have come to an end as the problems arising out of the slow movement became apparent—problems in the solution of which he had never been very happy. Of all his attempts at the larger forms the Piano Sonata in G, Op. 8, is the only one which has a complete slow movement. The Violin Concerto and the Piano Sonatas in D and G minor all break down at this same point. The symphony was laid aside for the time.

A new lyrical impulse made itself felt in the month of December. We possess a little group of songs composed at this time, the earliest examples of his work in this field that have been printed—though not by their composer. *Ein Grab*, begun on 8th December, and finished on the 10th, is a not very distinguished addition to the already overcrowded field of German churchyard songs. The author of the poem was Wolf's friend Paul Peitl, of *König Alboin* fame. Wolf then turned his attention for the first time to the poetry of Heine and produced three songs in five days—on 17th December *Mädchen mit dem roten Mündchen*, on the 18th *Du bist wie eine Blume*, and on the 21st *Wenn ich in deine Augen seh'*, all taken from the *Buch der Lieder*.

Mädchen mit dem roten Mündchen is at once the least ambitious and the most individual of these Heine songs. The manner of Wolf's approach to the poem is his own, and there are prophetically felicitous touches in his handling of the words. *Du bist wie eine Blume* looks like a deliberate imitation of Schumann's setting of the same words.

Wolf returned to Lenau for the words of his *Abendbilder*, which he began on 4th January 1877 and finished on 24th February. It is a curiously designed song in which three odes by Lenau are joined together to form a single text. The *Abendbilder* are rather reminiscent of early Schubert in their undisciplined rambling, with all manner of engaging pictorial detail by the wayside in the accompaniment—an impressive moonrise, tinkling sheep bells, the nightingale's song, and woodland murmurs.

We now come to the farcical final scenes of Wolf's life in the Conservatoire. The pedantry of Professor Krenn was becoming irksome to him, and he was no more ready to submit to a systematic course of instruction now than he had been in the earlier stages of his schooling. He came to imagine that his progress was being retarded in the routine of the Conservatoire, and one day he announced to the director that he was leaving the establishment, where he was forgetting more than he was learning. For this piece of impertinence he was officially expelled 'for offences against discipline,' but he himself always stoutly maintained that he had not been expelled at all but had left the Conservatoire of his own accord before they took the decision to eject him. Wolf was much incensed at what he considered an insupportable insult, and talked wildly of taking legal action against the Conservatoire authorities who had turned him out as if he had not paid his fees.

One day Hellmesberger, the director, received a threatening letter to the effect that his days were numbered. The letter bore the signature 'Hugo Wolf,' but it was really the work of one of his Conservatoire acquaintances who saw in Wolf's circumstances the opportunity for a practical joke. Wolf himself, hearing of what had been done in his name, marched off to see Hellmesberger to explain the deception. By chance, just as Wolf went up to the doorway, Hellmesberger came out, saw the wild-looking ex-student whom he believed to have threatened his life, and cried out: 'I have no business with you. You are no longer at the Conservatoire.' Wolf attempted to explain the situation and wanted to demonstrate his innocence by a comparison of his handwriting with that of the threatening letter. Hellmesberger refused to listen to him. It is said that he was so thoroughly scared that he had Wolf shadowed by the police for a time.[1]

The break with the Conservatoire determined the end of Wolf's first Vienna period; he was naturally recalled by his father after that exploit. There was, however, a short interim period, between his departure from the Conservatoire and the return to Windischgraz, when he remained at liberty in Vienna. The dates of these events cannot be exactly determined; it is not even known precisely when he left the Conservatoire. On 5th March he wrote a short letter to his parents, in which he announced his intention of moving on the 15th. In this letter occur, for the first time in his correspondence, the names of Mottl and Goldschmidt—two friends who were to play a most important part in his cultural development during the succeeding years. Goldschmidt had provided him with an opportunity to earn a little money as an accompanist, while with Mottl he was perhaps going, on the day on which he wrote, to the first performance in Vienna of *Die Walküre*—not in the gallery, this time,

[1] A letter from Wolf to his father, dated 19th December 1882, has this passage: 'To-day I encountered Hellmesberger; he was very friendly, inquired how I was, what I am composing, etc. etc. *He is no longer afraid of me.*'

but in a box. On the previous day he had also been to the Philharmonic concert, and it was perhaps the acquaintances he was
making in these privileged musical circles who were determining
his whole attitude towards the uninspiring instruction at the Conservatoire. But Wolf did not for long enjoy his freedom, for on
18th March, three days after the date announced for his removal from
his Margaretenstrasse lodgings, he went back again to his home at
Windischgraz.

Philipp's despair can be imagined. In his eyes Hugo had now
failed in his chosen profession, as well as in his whole school career.
That was not Hugo's own idea of the situation. Nevertheless, it
may be supposed that his heart was heavy when he set foot on the
train that was taking him, for an indefinite period, away from
Vienna, the concerts, the opera, and the circle of Goldschmidt's
friends, where he was beginning to find appreciation, back to remote,
provincial Styria.

III

VIENNA: GOLDSCHMIDT AND HIS CIRCLE

FOR nearly eight months of the year 1877 Wolf remained cooling his heels at Windischgraz. The sequence of his family letters is necessarily broken during this time, and almost the only information we have as to the manner of his life is to be found in the reminiscences of his sister Käthe,[1] who was a girl of nearly twelve when Hugo returned home in disgrace from Vienna. The younger members of the family got on well with him, and found him always ready to join in their escapades like one of themselves; they used to fool about together in company with 'Schips,' the great, friendly, shaggy house-dog. Hugo was a lively addition to the household. He possessed astonishing powers of mimicry, and would willingly reproduce the rich flow of profanity that he used to hear from quarrelling cab-drivers outside the windows of his Vienna lodgings. Sometimes he persuaded his younger sisters to go with him for walks in the evenings, when he would discourse upon Wagner's operas and cross-examine the children upon the extent of their musical knowledge. They would be required to answer conundrums such as: 'What is the note called that is under the stave, with one stroke through its head and one through its neck?' From these problems they strove to direct the conversation back to Wagner's operas. This subject Hugo was well prepared to expound. There still exist fragmentary librettos of *Lohengrin* and *The Flying Dutchman*, written out in Wolf's boyish hand, and provided with musical examples. Another of his favourite themes was Weber's *Freischütz*. He used to lead his younger sisters, after dark, to a nearby hollow of decidedly uninviting appearance; this was the 'Wolf's Glen.' Hugo would then relate the horrid story in detail, and flinging his overcoat over his head, call upon Samiel in a terrible voice, while his sisters trembled in the bushes at what might follow. This was for them anything but a joke, but Hugo rejoiced greatly when he had succeeded in thoroughly frightening the children.

Wolf spent much time in composition, and would wander away

[1] I have used a copy of these reminiscences as originally set down by Frau Salomon-Wolf. The published versions have been revised and shortened by other hands.

to the quiet of the woody hillsides with his manuscripts. He completed a number of songs—*Ständchen* (Körner), *Andenken* (Matthisson), *An* * (Lenau), *Wanderlied*, and *Morgentau*; the words of the last two songs were taken from 'an old song-book'—likely enough a volume of poems copied out by hand by his father.[1] He was perhaps short of literary stimuli to composition at Windischgraz. He seems to have attached considerable importance to these songs at the time, since he transcribed them, with the earlier *Ein Grab*, into a thin book of manuscript paper bearing the inscription, in elaborate imitation of a printed title-page, 'Lieder und Gesänge. Erstes Heft. In Musik gesetzt von Hugo Wolf.' The composer seems, by this inscription on the 'first volume' of his songs, to exclude his earlier works from the canon. The *Ständchen* and *Andenken* are sprawling, rather uncouthly sentimental compositions. *An* * is an expressive song, very much in Schumann's manner; the *Wanderlied* is rather commonplace. The endearing little *Morgentau*, the earliest of his compositions that Wolf, at the time of his maturity, still thought good enough for publication, is not at all ambitious, but it far surpasses all the other songs in this group in its sureness of touch. Its gentle melodic flow is wholly captivating. The muse of Schumann seems to have assisted in its creation, but the seventeen-year-old Wolf in his tiny song struck a genuine lyrical note that Schumann only rarely attained when he attempted this innocent vein; all too many of his intended simplicities sound forced and unnatural. The Wolfian will prefer to regard *Morgentau* not as a reminiscence of Schumann, but rather as the earliest example of the mood of dewy morning freshness that recurs again and again in Wolf's output, right up to the beautiful Spring Chorus, which opens the tragic fragment of *Manuel Venegas*, at the very end of his creative life.

There is also, among the unpublished manuscripts, a charming *Humoreske* for piano, written in September of this year. Here again the influence of Schumann makes itself felt.

---

[1] Among Wolf's books was one such collection of poems, copied out by Philipp Wolf for Katharina Nussbaumer in 1849, two years before their marriage. This volume does not contain the texts of *Morgentau* or the *Wanderlied*, but is interesting in other ways. All the poems are signed 'Philipp' or 'Wolff,' although many of them are by well-known authors. Was Philipp trying to pass himself off as a poet to his betrothed? However that may have been, a later hand, not unlike that of the young Hugo at about fourteen or fifteen, has gone through the book correcting many of the attributions. The signature to 'Neue Liebe, neues Leben,' for instance, is altered from 'Philipp' to 'Goethe.'

But these shorter works were after all only the by-products of Wolf's sojourn at Windischgraz. His chief preoccupation was with the symphony which he had begun in the previous year. The work was apparently fully completed and scored during 1877, but the original manuscript was shortly afterwards lost, and only scattered fragments and copies of isolated movements remain. The chequered history of this symphony may be conveniently summarized here.

It will be recalled that Wolf had begun, at least, and perhaps completed, a first movement for his projected B flat Symphony in Vienna in October 1876, and during November fully sketched out a scherzo in G minor. He had also the *Rondo Capriccioso*, scored at Windischgraz in the previous August, and intended for use as the finale of the symphony. A sketch-book in the National Library in Vienna throws considerable light on the subsequent history of this work. On 26th April 1877 we find Wolf making sketches for a slow movement in D major, which was to be the third movement of his B flat Symphony. In May, as another manuscript shows, the scherzo was completed and elaborated. Not much more than a fortnight after the completion of the scherzo, however, we find in the sketch-book, dated 17th June, themes for both a new finale and a new first movement—this time not in B flat but in G minor. It would seem that the old orchestrated *Rondo Capriccioso* and the first movement in B flat no longer satisfied their composer. The old scherzo, however, in its elaborated form, he took over for inclusion in the new project—one manuscript, with the title 'Scherzo, from the Symphony in G minor,' shows the erasure of the original main key 'B flat' of the work as first conceived.

The new first movement in G minor was finished in June. Possibly the two remaining movements—the slow movement and the new finale—were also completed during the summer. Wolf in later letters refers to 'the Symphony,' which he played to his friends, as though it were an accomplished whole. After the loss of the manuscript he bravely sat down and began to write it out afresh, but it seems doubtful whether he ever completed this second score. Only the scherzo and a number of fragments have come down to us.

The scherzo and the orchestrated *Rondo Capriccioso* from the earlier planned Symphony in B flat have recently been published. It is interesting to observe Wolf's Berliozian experiments in orchestration, but the rather wooden and jejune *Rondo Capriccioso* need not detain us. The scherzo is another matter. It reveals a prodigious advance upon anything which the young composer had up to this time produced.

In the first place Wolf's command of the orchestra is really surprising. His use of the four drums is particularly interesting and effective—reminding us that as a boy at Windischgraz he was esteemed for his mastery of these instruments. Then the form of this scherzo—the symphonic movement where unconventionality might least have been expected—is novel and arresting.

Over an ostinato figure on the drums the tiny germ motive

enters canonically nine times, or, if we include three further shortened entries, twelve times, on flutes, oboes, bassoons, and strings—all within the first four bars. The rest of the material consists of a rising *pizzicato* passage on the strings, combined with a downward-leaping *staccato* figure in the wood-wind, a rising chromatic scale on the strings, and a few plaintive phrases for the oboe. With this slight material Wolf makes play for eighty-six bars, in the course of which the germ motive recurs almost as many times. It is all extremely light and delicate, and at the same time soundly constructed and satisfying. The trio opens with a sturdy rustic theme on horns and bassoons, which is at once subjected to development, including a polyphonic passage with many and widely ranging key-changes, ending with a flourish of trumpets. A brief connecting passage, in which the ubiquitous germ theme reappears from top to bottom of the score, leads to the return of the scherzo. We expect a conventional repeat, but after only eleven bars it goes its own way. New features are introduced, the most important being a syncopated unison figure on the strings,

answered by fanfares on the brass and wood-wind. The plaintive oboe phrases recur, and seem to have a chastening effect on the furious upward surge of the strings. The animation dies away to a murmur, kept alive by delicate rhythmic touches on the drums; then a sudden rapid downward rush of the violins brings the coda, with a *triple canon.* The ostinato drum figure is answered at a bar's interval by the basses, the germ motive is treated, *fortissimo*, in canon at the octave by wood-wind and strings, while trumpets and horns unexpectedly reintroduce the trio theme in canon. The four drums have the last word.

The insistent use of canon in this movement is interesting and shows an aspect of Wolf otherwise unknown. The fragments of the symphony are valuable in that they make clear that quite early in life their composer possessed a natural feeling for the orchestra—a gift which allowed him, without ever having heard a note of his own scoring, to produce, later on, a work like *Penthesilea*.

To return to Windischgraz—an interesting hand-written concert announcement [1] from this summer of 1877 provides fresh evidence of Wolf's maturing musical tastes. The days were gone by when he used to reward his sisters for little services by playing them *salon* pieces like Kafka's *March Violet* or *The Carnival of Venice*. On 22nd August he gave the first of a projected series of twelve matinée recitals to the family and a few friends, with the following programme: Wagner's *Tannhäuser* overture and *Venusberg* music, the Landgrave's address and the following march and chorus from the same opera, Mozart's Fantasia in C minor, Schubert's songs *Der Wanderer* and *Du bist die Ruh*, the first part of Schumann's *Faschingsschwank aus Wien*, Chopin's D flat Prelude, two songs by Schumann, *Dein Angesicht* and *Kommen und Scheiden*, and Beethoven's 'Moonlight' Sonata. The guests were warned on this programme to arrive punctually, to avoid interrupting the performances. At Windischgraz Wolf seems to have become friendly with a few of the residents with musical interests—the names of Josef Walter and Franz Pecharz, the latter afterwards a district magistrate, recur in the family correspondence—but in general he was very reserved, apart from the company of his little sisters. He spent many hours in long solitary walks, scheming always how to get back to Vienna. An undated letter to Felix Mottl, probably written at this time, declares that, owing to bad business in the leather trade, his father is in no position to assist him financially; his return is dependent upon the efforts made on his behalf by his friends in the capital.

Philipp simply did not know what to do with him. He had three

[1] It is dated simply 'Wednesday, 22nd August.' Of the three possible years 1877, 1879, and 1881, 22nd August fell upon a Wednesday only in 1877.

nearly grown-up sons upon his hands, who should by this time have been helping, at least, to earn their own livings, but the eldest boy Max was only half-way through his long term of three years' military service, Hugo had adopted, against his father's wishes, the perilous calling of a musician, while Gilbert, the youngest, who was intended to follow his father in the leather business, showed remarkably little ability or enthusiasm for the work.   Although Hugo, in spite of his undoubted gifts, did not look like making a great success of his chosen career, he was so ill equipped for anything else that when he was able to procure through his friends in Vienna sufficient employment as music teacher and accompanist to give him the hope of supporting himself there, Philipp's objections were finally withdrawn, and on Saturday, 10th November 1877, Hugo set out joyfully on the first stage of his return journey, to begin a fresh phase of his life as a free artist in Vienna.

Windischgraz was connected by a post-wagon with the railway at Unter-Drauburg and, with his face turned once more towards the capital, even this short drive of about seven miles, which cannot have lasted much more than half an hour, had to be put to good use by the eager young musician.   He set about the composition of a violin sonata, and while waiting at Drauburg he sketched out this work as he had conceived it in the post-wagon.   In the train that took him as far as Graz he found some friends and abandoned composition for conversation, with Wagner as the principal theme.   He had to change at Graz, and there he found time to pay a visit to Dr. Friedrich von Hausegger, the writer on music and aesthetics and professor at Graz University.   Hausegger was a leading spirit in Wagnerian circles of this rather conservative-minded town, and worked hard to expound the new music to his countrymen.   He had instituted a series of semi-public concerts, at which the later operas of Wagner were sung with piano accompaniment and works by promising local composers performed.   Philipp Wolf had great hopes that his son's genius would receive recognition at these concerts and in the columns of the local newspaper, the *Grazer Tagespost*, of which Hausegger was music critic.

After presenting himself at Dr. Hausegger's Hugo seems to have visited a theatre before continuing his journey by the night train. Not until Graz had been left far behind did he discover that he had left the precious manuscript of his symphony in the waiting-room there.   He telegraphed back from the next station at which the train stopped, but the score was already gone, and he never recovered it.

At half-past six in the morning of Sunday, 11th November, he set foot again in the streets of Vienna. Apart from his elder friends and musical well-wishers, his intimates of his own generation were his cousin Hans Maier, Ludwig Schneider, and a certain Basler,[1] the two last probably fellow students from the Conservatoire. Wolf's first action on disembarking from the night train from Graz was to get Maier out of bed. Ten minutes later Basler turned up: he had gone to the station to meet Wolf, but had not arrived there quite in time. The joyful reunion was continued when they picked up Schneider in a coffee-house, and then went on to the Sunday morning Philharmonic concert. Paul Peitl was present and offered another of his poetical dramas as the subject of an opera. After this Wolf encountered almost all his musical friends, and rejoiced in the warmth with which they welcomed him back to Vienna.

Fortunately for his own welfare, the adolescent Wolf possessed, in addition to his manifest musical endowments, very great charm of manner and appearance. In spite of his poverty he always contrived to be neatly dressed, and was really finical about such things as his linen and his shoes. He was slightly built and very short—at this time probably considerably less than the five feet one and a half inches which he attained when fully grown. He had a sensitive boyish face, with a long 'artistic' crop of ash-blond hair, of which a lock or two would keep falling forward over his brow, and wonderfully gleaming, deep-brown eyes. About the mouth in repose there was a touch of precocious wisdom, which when he smiled gave way to a winning, childlike candour. He laughed readily, with a characteristic dark undertone in the voice. Silent and mistrustful among strangers, he expanded in the company of his intimates, where he knew himself loved and his gifts respected. The other side of his character, which he exhibited when he was annoyed, was no less endearing, and very amusing, to those who had no desire to see all humanity cut to the same pattern, and could appreciate his fantastic originality. One who knew him at this time, Helene Bettelheim-Gabillon, has drawn a vivid portrait of him from this viewpoint:

But when our circle was enlarged by company that was disagreeable to him he became at once peevish and silent, or peevish and rude. He sat

---

[1] Perhaps the amateur singer, Ludwig Basler, with whom Mahler was also friendly in his student days.

there with crossed arms, bent forward with sullen face like a little goblin; his yet boyishly youthful features, usually good-natured and winning, took on a completely changed expression through a piercing glance that made his eyes flash in a manner quite diabolical.

The same witness, in a different context, says that in his early youth he struck people often as being one of the most unconsciously humorous figures they had ever encountered.

Wolf's return to Vienna had been made possible by the interest and affection he had won, while still a student at the Conservatoire, in the house of the wealthy Goldschmidt family. They lived on the Opernring, No. 6. The elderly Moritz von Goldschmidt, who had been Prokurist to the house of Rothschild and still carried about with him something of the atmosphere of the Metternich period, occupied with his family the first two floors of this building. He had six sons, of whom the youngest, Adalbert, became the particular friend and benefactor of Hugo Wolf.

Adalbert von Goldschmidt, born in 1848, and thus twelve years older than his protégé, was at first intended for a banking career, but preferred instead to cultivate his remarkable gifts as poet and musician. No difficulties were laid in his way, and the handsome 'Berti' settled down to a congenial Bohemian existence. He surrounded himself with like-minded friends, whose carefree and unconventional manner of life became known to all Vienna. Goldschmidt married a young singer, Paula Kunz, a pupil of Marchesi, who retired from the stage on her marriage, and devoted herself to her husband's compositions, which she sang in private at their Sunday afternoon musical *salon*, where all the greatest artists of the day used to appear. Goldschmidt came under the spell of Liszt and in his best-known work, the secular oratorio *Die sieben Todsünden*, he gave expression to his profound faith and admiration by representing Liszt as the 'Singer' who liberates mankind from the Powers of Darkness. *Die sieben Todsünden* was successfully performed in Berlin in 1876, in Vienna, in spite of Hanslick's opposition, in 1877, at Hanover in 1879, and was published in 1880. It was followed in 1884 by an opera, *Helianthus*. His most ambitious work, the operatic trilogy *Gaea*, remains unpublished and unknown, although the poem, which, like that of *Helianthus*, he wrote himself, has been printed and also translated by Catulle Mendès into French. Goldschmidt's artistic development suffered to some extent from his dangerous double gifts, but much more from his incurable weakness for the pleasures of fashion and society. Everything came far too easily to him. He was very popular, he had money, he excelled at riding, fencing, swimming, and athletics; he became the darling of society. He remained a most charming, generous-hearted, witty man, but he never attained the laurels he sought for as a musician. As he grew older he found his money disappearing; his social pleasures had to be curtailed, and artistic success still evaded him. The extent of Goldschmidt's disillusionment may be judged from the character of his last work for the stage: the erstwhile designer of large-scale idealistic music-dramas turned to Wilhelm Busch for the libretto of his operetta *Die fromme Helene*. An attempt to perform it, at Hamburg, ended in fiasco. In his later years, when his artistic star had long since set, the genial but now somewhat corpulent 'Berti' was a familiar figure in Vienna, driving through the town in his one-horse cab, with long beard and hair, top hat and fat cigar, accompanied by his old black poodle, which he loved more than anything else in the world. He died on 21st December 1906.

In 1877, however, Goldschmidt's sunny nature was not over-clouded by any forebodings of failure to come. In his apartments in the house on the Opernring a group of remarkable men used to forgather regularly. They included the painter, Julius von Blaas, the well-known sculptor Viktor Tilgner, music critics such as Hans Paumgartner and Gustav Schönaich, and the twenty-one-year-old Felix Mottl, at that time only an assistant at the rehearsals at the Opera, but already making a name for himself through his activities in connection with the Vienna Wagner Verein. It was this group of friends who were mainly responsible for bringing the young Wolf back to Vienna.

The contacts he made through Goldschmidt were extremely valuable to him at this early stage of his evolution as an artist. Although in the course of the next few years he was to cut himself off again, in the passionate pursuit of his own austere ideals, from all contact with this easy-living, jovial artistic circle, in these earliest years of independence in Vienna he found in Goldschmidt's house cultural guidance and human sympathy. There he amused them all by the free exposition of his precocious enthusiasms and prejudices, and especially by his uncompromising and forthright nature. As he wrote to his father:[1] 'All, especially Goldschmidt, Dr.

---

[1] Letter of 15th November 1877 (*Familienbriefe* with a few additional words from the original in the Prussian State Library).

Schönaich, Dr. Paumgartner, and the painter Julius von Blaas, are very fond of me, particularly when I begin often to abuse them thoroughly for their frivolous behaviour, whereupon Goldschmidt says: "Now listen to Wolf with his diverting rudeness."' These men went to some trouble to procure him teaching appointments in Vienna. Viktor Tilgner's brother, a youth of nineteen, was persuaded that he needed some lessons in the elements of music, somebody else procured Wolf the position of music master to two little girls, while Goldschmidt himself engaged him to correct the orchestral parts of *Die sieben Todsünden* from the original score, in preparation for the forthcoming first Vienna performance in December. Upon this task Wolf spent some hours daily in the archives of the opera-house.[1] There were prospects of further teaching appointments for him in December. He had bright hopes, when all these arrangements would be concluded, of earning more than a hundred gulden monthly, which would easily suffice for his needs.

He had at first taken a room at Schleifmühlgasse 22, but after about a fortnight he moved to Mozartgasse 7, also in his favourite Wieden district. The Goldschmidts' generosity knew no bounds. Wolf could turn almost at any time from his shabby lodgings to the house on the Opernring and find there unfailing kindness and precious understanding of his ambitions as a creative artist. He could borrow books and scores, which he carried off to study in his rooms; he could also confidently apply to Goldschmidt for money whenever his own earnings had failed to come up to his expectations. It was further suggested that Wolf should be the Goldschmidts' guest at Ischl during the summer months, when all those on whom he depended for a living would have left Vienna for the country. 'He does all this,' he told his father, 'because he is so very interested in me on account of my Symphony, that I played to him, and my Humoresque for the piano, that he found charming. He observes in me an enormous step forward, as much intellectual as musical, and believes firmly that I shall achieve my great object.' Both Mottl and Goldschmidt were delighted with the symphony because of 'the energy and strength that they found in it, in complete

---

[1] Many years later Wolf permitted himself a sly jest at Goldschmidt's expense, when he composed his setting of Goethe's humorous ballad *Ritter Kurts Brautfahrt*. At the mention of Jews he introduced two non-Aryan thematic fragments. Shaking helplessly with mirth Wolf used to explain: 'I got one theme from Goldmark, it 's from *The Queen of Sheba*: the other is from *Die sieben Todsünden*, that in its day I got to know only too well'—a reference to the hours he had once spent collating the parts with the score in the opera-house archives.

C

contrast to the sloppy feelings and phrases of the composers of to-day.'

Wolf wrote home frequently, sharing with his dearly loved father all the exciting experiences of his wonderful new life. His letters, which often recall those of the young Mozart, are of delightful quality—boundlessly optimistic for the future, full of the exuberance and arrogance of youth. These letters become even more revealing when certain passages are restored to them which editorial discretion suppressed when they were first printed.[1]

At midday to-day I went to the Mozart *Requiem*; Mottl, Goldschmidt, Schönaich and I had to smuggle ourselves in, as there were no more tickets to be had. At the first attempt we were all thrown out, but the second succeeded, *chiefly because the rich Goldschmidt let slip a few banknotes.* . . . Yesterday evening I was at the Hellmesberger Quartet's concert, and what is more I went with Goldschmidt in his carriage *with two liveried servants.* By good luck a rowdy group of Conservatoire boys came along just then, who stared their eyes out at me, but I didn't deem them worth a glance. We went proudly up the staircase and took two stalls in the foremost rows, where Anna and Ida Vinzenzberg observed me continually from the gallery with opera-glasses. I could have burst with joy, for the one-time poor devil Wolf sat by the side of the distinguished composer *and rich nobleman (he is Ritter von Goldschmidt) in a stall* in the front row, immediately behind the executants. . . . More good news! Dr. Schönaich, one of the most intimate of Richard Wagner's friends, will take me with him to Bayreuth next year, introduce me to Wagner, and recommend me to him as copyist for his forthcoming *Parsifal* drama. In this way I shall come in immediate contact with the Master himself and the advantage that arises from that one sees clearly in Hans Richter, *who would to-day still be a horn-blower in some theatre if Wagner had not employed him as copyist of his scores.*

Gustav Schönaich (1841–1906) was the stepson of Dr. Joseph Standhartner, with whom Wagner generally stayed when he came to Vienna, and thus, as a member of the inner Wagnerian circle,[2] he

---

[1] Indicated in italics in the succeeding quotations.

[2] Wolf, however, in calling Schönaich 'one of the most intimate of Richard Wagner's friends,' seems to have decidedly overstated the case. It is more than doubtful whether Wagner would have taken any notice of any one recommended to him from this quarter. The following story, told to Albert Gutmann by Mottl, undoubtedly refers to Schönaich.

Mottl visited Wagner at Bayreuth shortly after 'a witty Viennese critic' had been there. Wagner himself referred to this visitor in these terms: 'Recently this dreadful man, Sch . . ., arrived here. By chance I myself opened the door to him, and was horrified. I said to him at once: "Good God, have I got to look at this face?" He came to me in bright yellow boots, this tasteless fellow! But naturally my wife had to invite him to lunch, on account of his stepfather. There he showed himself still more disagreeable. It was my birthday. My

exerted great influence upon Wolf, and became for a time his trusted adviser and friend. Wolf compared him to Faust and himself to his *Famulus* Wagner.

Mit Euch, Herr Doktor, zu spazieren,
Ist ehrenvoll und ist Gewinn.

Schönaich was keenly intelligent and a remarkable talker, although unfortunately he never succeeded in writing himself down. He left behind only a number of articles, forgotten in the dusty files of musical periodicals, and the legend of his own richly eccentric personality. Gustav Schönaich's exceptionally keen appreciation of the good things of this world had made itself apparent in an almost Falstaffian corpulence, and his devotion to the flesh-pots of Vienna led him all too often to disregard the limitations of his income as a music critic, so that he earned the reputation of a persistent borrower from his friends. But when he had any money he disposed of it royally. Wolf himself was undoubtedly often obliged to him for 'loans,' when there seemed little enough likelihood that he would ever be able to repay them; but it is said of Schönaich that if he lent Wolf money then he must have first borrowed it from someone else. Schönaich played a not unimportant part in the development of his young admirer, by encouraging his early work as a composer, by introducing friends who were able to find him employment in their households, and by sharpening his wits and broadening his mind in conversation upon all manner of literary, musical and philosophical themes.

At Goldschmidt's house, in the company of these men, the young Wolf, who still bore about him many traces of the deficiencies of his early education, began to acquire a little worldly polish. At his age it was natural that he should adopt and repeat as his own many of the opinions which he heard from the lips of his elders. Thus in his letters he reflects their attitude towards Richter, who, as we have seen, had been of some assistance to him earlier.

With Richter I have nothing to do, *because he is too lazy to bother himself with me* :[1] I do without him perfectly easily, as I have found a greater

---

good Siegfried made a speech about me; it was really moving. But Sch . . . did not let it interrupt his eating, and said to my wife: "I like this asparagus; give me some more of this asparagus." What a glutton! I won't have anything to do with such gluttons.' (From *Aus dem Wiener Musikleben*, by Albert Gutmann, Vienna, 1914.)

[1] Further restorations in italics (*Familienbriefe*, letter of 18th–19th December 1877).

substitute in Dr. Schönaich. . . . I have just come from the second orchestral rehearsal of the 'Sieben Todsünden,' which however went off no better than the first, for which Richter is chiefly to blame, *who, too lazy to study the score thoroughly, doesn't know how quickly or slowly he ought to set the tempo, when this or that instrument comes in, or whether they play rightly or wrongly.* In a word, it was terrible to listen to and Goldschmidt himself says that if people abuse this music they are quite right to do so. . . .

With Hellmesberger Wolf hoped for a reconciliation, through Schönaich.

It was clearly a very agreeable existence that he was leading at this time. After the *Sieben Todsünden* rehearsal, for instance, there followed supper at Goldschmidt's and talk until half-past one in the morning. During the Christmas holidays he was a guest at the house on the Opernring every evening, and his name was not forgotten when the presents were distributed. On 28th December he accompanied Goldschmidt to a banquet given by the tenor Schott, who had been appearing as guest artist at the court opera. The banquet lasted until 3 a.m. At eight Wolf was up again, giving someone a music lesson. On New Year's Eve he was again at Goldschmidt's, and on this occasion, also, the party did not break up until three o'clock in the morning, after which Wolf, with Goldschmidt's brother Theodor and another friend, went on to a coffee-house for further conversation until half-past four. Wolf then returned to his lodgings, but not at once to sleep. He had begun on 27th December to sketch out a new large-scale composition, an overture, based on Byron's *The Corsair*, which was intended to be the first work of his 'maturity' but which, like so much else, was never completed. After he left the coffee-house in the early hours of the year 1878 Wolf put in another hour and a half's work upon this overture, before finally taking to his bed at six o'clock.

Besides the sketches for the *Corsair* overture he composed only a few songs in this winter. On 29th December he finished *Der Schwalben Heimkehr*, which he had begun at Windischgraz—an unimportant setting of the first verse only of the words of Abt's well-known song *Agathe* (' When the swallows homeward fly '). Among the manuscripts in the Vienna City Library a little strophic song, *So wahr die Sonne scheint* (Rückert) and the first of a projected cycle, *Auf der Wanderschaft* (Chamisso), escaped exhumation even by the editors of the song-volumes of the Posthumous Works. It was across the bottom of the manuscript of *Auf der Wanderschaft* that

Wolf himself scrawled 'Bad!' A few days later he took up the song again, gave it a new rhythmic twist, and then added the further comment: 'Worse still!' We need not appeal against the composer's verdict. Then there are two ambitious settings of poems by Lenau, *Traurige Wege* and *Nächtliche Wanderung*. Both songs show Wolf sunk deep in the luxurious melancholy of his poet's sick imagination. In *Traurige Wege* Lenau's tragic lovers find no response in themselves to the happiness of the woods and streams around them, or even to the peace of the graveyard, while in *Nächtliche Wanderung* a bereaved bridegroom, restrained from suicide only by a deathbed vow to the loved one, calls upon the lightning to relieve him of the burden of existence. They are best regarded, like the earlier song among the tombstones, *Ein Grab*, as symptoms of a prevalent sickness of romantic musical adolescence.

On the chronology of Wolf's changes of residence during these months his own account is misleading, and Werner's article ' Hugo Wolfs Wohnstätten in Wien ' even more so. The letters are the safest guide. On 23rd December he was still in the Mozartgasse, but planning to move on 5th January to a quiet room in the Hotel Goldenes Lamm, in the Wiedner Hauptstrasse. This would cost, with service, 25 gulden—fairly expensive, according to Wolf's standards, though ridiculously cheap according to ours. 'I gladly pay 10 gulden for the service,' he told his friend Pecharz, 'for I only need to press a button on the wall and ministering spirits appear—on pressing once, the chambermaid; twice, the waiter; thrice, the boots. What do you think of that? Could anything be more agreeable? And then I am quite alone, don't bother my head about Death or Devil—I should like to meet any one who still has doubts about being happy in such lodgings.' In spite of those advantages he was in the Hotel Goldenes Lamm for only a few days, then—he must have been desperate—slept for a time in the Archives of the Court Opera, then stayed a few days in the Hotel Erzherzog Karl in the inner city, Kärntnerstrasse 31, until he found, in the same street, house number 39, a more permanent address. This must have been some time in January 1878. His father's letters show that he was there until the end of March.

In February a project was afoot to get some of Wolf's compositions printed. One of Schönaich's friends, Emerich Kastner, was bringing out a *Wagner-Katalog* through the publishing house of Joh. André at Offenbach-am-Main. It was thought that André might undertake

the publication of a group of Wolf's songs. So the young
composer selected four songs that he considered the best he had
so far written, and sent them off to André with Kastner's recommendation. He chose the recent *Traurige Wege* and three songs
from the previous summer—*An* *, *Morgentau*, and the *Wanderlied*—
and looked forward to their appearance in print 'in four or eight
weeks' with complete confidence. Philipp Wolf was urging Hugo to
send his songs to Dr. Hausegger at Graz. On 31st March he wrote
to his son:[1] 'I turn the pages of the *Tagespost* industriously, in the
hope of seeing that your songs have been performed. In it Kienzl,
who played the piano part of the Wagnerian tetralogy, is praised
to the skies: however, it 'll be your turn one day.' So a copy of the
songs was dispatched to Graz. But Hausegger was not so impressed
as had been expected: 'In general the songs, of a Mendelssohnian
character,' he wrote, 'made a not unfavourable impression upon me,
but I won't withdraw my opinion of their superficiality.' Hugo was
quite disgusted.

A greater insult could never be thrown in my face, than to charge me
with the imitation of Mendelssohn, and in the *Lied* moreover! Probably
he looked through them just before going to bed, while not only his
physical, but also his mental, powers were relaxed, for otherwise he could
never have arrived at this conclusion. A strong Schumannian trait runs
through the songs, especially in the *Traurige Wege*, but Mendelssohn?
Never again!

André seems also to have rejected the songs, but Wolf was not at
all deterred by these set-backs. He added the *Nächtliche Wanderung*
to the others, and sent them off again, this time to Breitkopf &
Härtel at Leipzig, 'as this firm,' he wrote, 'is much better known
than André and enjoys a world-wide reputation. . . . In two months
at the most they will appear in the musical trade, and then every one
will have the right to express his opinion—*pro* or *contra*.' Breitkopf & Härtel also decided not to publish these works, and with
that Wolf seems to have given up for the time his efforts to get into
print.

He was finding it more difficult than he had at first expected to
earn a living by giving music lessons. He was ill equipped with the
patience necessary for the teaching of young children, although he

---

[1] This and all succeeding passages from Philipp Wolf's letters to his son are
here published for the first time, with the exception of a short extract from a
letter of 19th November 1878 (p. 79), which was included in Edmund Hellmer's *Hugo Wolf: Erlebtes und Erlauschtes* (Vienna, 1921).

generally managed to get on very good terms with the pupils themselves. By some of the families where he was engaged to give lessons he was treated very much as a servant, and that he would never put up with for long. In such circumstances, he used to say, 'I crouch in a corner and growl.' So it happened that the only situations that he retained for any length of time were those in friendly households where the progress of the pupils was regarded as being less important than the maintenance of the music-master's scanty income. Foremost among these was his engagement to teach the children of Josef Breuer, a well-known Viennese doctor.

Through Schönaich Wolf had become acquainted with Kaiserlicher Rat Leopold Altmann, one of the most warm-hearted and open-handed of all his early sympathizers. The extent to which Wolf would accept help from his friends was a measure of his individual trust and affection for them, and through a period of fully five years he turned repeatedly to Altmann for assistance in his recurrent financial difficulties, and received from him gifts of clothing and very considerable sums of money. He pays tribute to his benefactor in one of his letters:

A man who, judging from his intellect, is a good forty years of age, but whose heart is about twenty years younger ... who has both heart and intellect in the right place. I may pride myself upon possessing his confidence and friendship, so far as the difference of ages allows. ... He is the one righteous man, on whose account, if the fate of mankind lay in my hands, I should like to spare the godless human rabble.[1]

Dr. Breuer was married to Altmann's sister, and it was decided between them that Wolf should be asked to teach the piano to two of the Breuer children—the eight-year-old Robert and his seven-year-old sister Bertha. These children soon grew to love him dearly, in spite of the scenes that often occurred during the lessons, especially those with little Bertha, whose lack of any real musical talent produced outbursts of nervous irritation from the teacher, which in turn reduced his pupil to tears. After a time he added the study of harmony to the curriculum, though here again Wolf did not perceive that the children were capable of understanding very little of what he tried to teach them. Robert, it is true, worked out for himself some little inventions at the keyboard which showed considerable independence of mind, and wrote them out for Wolf who, sadly shaking his head, showed them to the boy's mother: 'Strange!—

[1] Letter to Bertha von Lackhner, 3rd August 1881.

nothing like what I set him to do!' From these lessons there grew up a close friendship between Wolf and the whole family. Dr. Breuer himself, a man of the highest intelligence, remembered for his early psycho-pathological work in collaboration with Freud,[1] delighted in the untamed young musician. The doctor's wife, a lady of very retiring disposition, became as fond of him as the children themselves; there was hardly any one outside the family circle with whom she was so open and friendly as with the young Wolf. He made further allies in the family governess and nurse.

Another branch of Altmann's family, the Kauffmanns, was pressed into service; their children also had to take lessons from Wolf. How much he depended upon these families as a source of income may be seen from a letter of 10th April 1878, in which he reported to his parents that since the Breuer children had been taken away from Vienna for a holiday he had had to reduce his principal meals to one a day. This meal usually consisted of soup, followed by meat and vegetables, and was taken in a restaurant. He believed that he would be able to economize still further by preparing his own coffee, in an apparatus that Goldschmidt had given him, and relying more upon the parcels of food—eggs, home-made sausages, *Reinling* and other Styrian delicacies—which his mother sent him from Windisch-graz. 'I could then easily do without the meal in a restaurant,' he wrote, 'if I made a cup of coffee at midday and ate with it a piece of *Reinling* and a slice of ham or sausage.'

His other problem of finding lodgings that were both inexpensive and quiet had been happily solved at the beginning of April, when he moved once again into a house in the Wieden district, Floragasse 7. There he found a room facing the gardens behind the house, which seemed to be all that he desired. He was wakened in the mornings by the sun streaming into his room and by the multi-tudinous birds in the garden below. Three times a week he worked at his music without interruption from six in the morning until one o'clock in the afternoon, so wonderfully quiet was the Floragasse. He was altogether delighted with the place, and settled down there for the long stay—for him—of about four months.

In these favourable conditions the muse did not desert him. He put in a lot of work upon a large-scale composition for *soli*, chorus,

---

[1] Sigmund Freud and Josef Breuer, *Studien über Hysterie* (Vienna, 1895).

and orchestra, *Die Stunden verrauschen*, on a strongly rhythmic poem by Gottfried Kinkel:

> Ei unter der Linde, wie woget das Fest.
> Es ist Maitag, ist Maitag, sie tanzen aufs Best.

A water nixie dances in the May Day festival, sleeps in the wood with a mortal lover, and at dawn returns to her pool to die. This work was left unfinished like the *Corsair* overture and other works in the larger forms. Besides this there were more songs. On 1st April he began a setting of Chamisso's *Was soll ich sagen?* which he then put aside. On the 5th he began *Die Spinnerin*, to words by Rückert; this seems to have been completed on the 12th. He was reading a lot of Hebbel at this time, as well as E. Kuh's biography of the poet, and produced three Hebbel songs within a few days. *Das Kind am Brunnen*, the manuscript of which bears three dates, 16th, 22nd and 27th April, was nevertheless already all but completed by the 20th of that month, as is clear from a family letter. *Das Vöglein*, after he had for some days striven in vain to hit upon the right musical mood for the poem, was suddenly set down on paper almost in one breath, on 2nd May, while sitting on a bench in the Schwarzenberg Gardens and listening to the song of a finch. The next day he began the third Hebbel song, *Knabentod*, and completed it on 6th May. In the meantime, on the 4th, he had taken up again the unfinished *Was soll ich sagen?* from the previous month, but after adding a few more bars gave up the whole thing, for a reason which he scrawled across the bottom of the manuscript—'Too much like Schumann—on that account not finished.'

In this group of four completed songs, *Knabentod* and *Das Kind am Brunnen* are of minor interest. Hebbel's poems themselves have little that is truly lyrical to invite the song composer, and the subjects of these particular examples do not compel our sympathy. But the remaining two songs, *Die Spinnerin* and *Das Vöglein*, are gems. Both of them were included in the *Sechs Lieder für eine Frauenstimme*, Wolf's first publication, that came out early in 1888, so that the passage of ten years did not affect the composer's estimation of their worth. The playful *Vöglein*, with its chirruping, fluttering accompaniment, so beautifully written for the piano, in contrast with the quasi-orchestral rumblings of such things as the *Nächtliche Wanderung*, strikes a perfectly individual note of fresh, delicate humour that we recognize as peculiarly Wolfian, when we meet it again in

* C

later masterpieces like the *Mausfallensprüchlein, Zitronenfalter im April,* and many another. *Die Spinnerin,* a delightful character-sketch of a young girl conscious of the stirring of the spring, both outside the chamber where she sits and spins, and within her own restless heart, has the same lightness of touch and beauty of work-manship.

The creation of songs such as these, of indisputable technical accomplishment and artistic worth, induced in the young composer a mood of peculiar satisfaction and happiness. Sometimes, it is true, he was driven almost to doubt whether his talents were really com-mensurate with his ambitions. But then suddenly, almost uncon-sciously, a new work would take shape under his hands and restore his faith in the future.

In the fine spring weather the nearby Schwarzenberg Gardens and the Stadtpark attracted him to their fresh green retreats. He lay in the Stadtpark on Easter Sunday, after he had been reading the Easter scene from Goethe's *Faust,* which had thrown him into ecstasies: 'To-day everything seems to me so devoutly in accord,' he wrote. 'I see before me this great park, thick set with the young fresh verdure, hear the birds singing so lovely and clear, and the bells sounding so grave and solemn; only the heavens are covered with clouds, so that the sun is quite invisible.' He never passed the Schubert memorial in the park without falling into reflection; per-haps he already sensed the direction in which his talents were ulti-mately to come to full fruition; perhaps he obscurely felt that in the field of song composition there were to be only two names that could be mentioned in the same breath—Schubert's and his own.

The coming of spring to Vienna, the natural beauties of her parks and gardens, the wonderful new lodgings in the Floragasse, which so delighted him in spite of the inconvenience of the dawn-song of the birds outside his windows, the creation of remarkable and original songs and his friends' joy in these successes—all these contributed to the sum total of his happiness. There was, however, another reason for the strange new emotions that filled his heart. Hugo Wolf had fallen in love.

IV

THE YEAR OF SONG, AND FIRST LOVE

THE full measure of the young Wolf's indebtedness to Adalbert von Goldschmidt can hardly be told. It was not only that the glad companionship, the intellectual stimulation and guidance, the discreet patronage, were so valuable to him in his salad days, but all the most important and most fateful of his friendships seemed to branch out from this original connection with Viennese cultured society.

The third and fourth floors of the Goldschmidts' house, Opernring No. 6, were rented to some of their intimate friends, and under this ideal arrangement the younger members of these families, especially, were continually passing up and down the staircases to and from each other's apartments, so that Wolf, on his visits to Adalbert von Goldschmidt, soon came to know the other occupants of the house as well. These were Anton Lang and his French wife and niece, and the celebrated theatrical family, Ludwig and Zerline Gabillon.

Ludwig Gabillon (1825–96), the great German actor, for more than forty years connected with the Burgtheater in Vienna, was married to the actress Zerline Würzburg, and they had two daughters—Helene, the gifted artist and writer, and Dora, a wonderful red-haired beauty. Wolf was engaged to teach Dora the piano, but as she possessed, like most of his pupils, very little talent, the course of instruction frequently broke down. It was nothing for a lesson to end with the music-master playing Berlioz or Wagner to himself for hours on end, every one else having fled. But in this supremely well-regulated household such incidents were not allowed to disturb the friendly relationship between Wolf and the other members of the family. Dora Gabillon's piano lessons became, like those he gave to the Breuer children, a reliable source of income during the winter months, however little progress his pupil may have seemed to be making.[1] The elder daughter, Helene, who was never his pupil, came to know

---

[1] That Dora Gabillon regarded the eccentricities of her music-master with humorous tolerance may be surmised from an entry in one of Wolf's books in the Vienna City Library. In a copy of Max Haushofer's *Unhold, der Höhlenmensch* ('Monster, the Cave-man') is found the inscription: 'Herrn Hugo Wolf —*ohne jegliche Anspielung*—Dora Gabillon. Weihnacht 1879.'

him very well.   They had common interests in poetry and folk-song, and Wolf spent much time playing and singing Wagner's operas to her.   He declared also that she possessed a voice, which he would undertake to train, and brought her as the first material for study the folk-song arrangements of Brahms—for at that time Wolf was still an admirer of this composer, who later on came to represent all that he most hated in music.   Brahms was himself a personal acquaintance of the Gabillons, but the younger people were not attracted to him.   They knew him among themselves as 'the salted Hamburg herring.'

Anton Lang, the other tenant in Goldschmidt's house, was a good-natured, kindly and charming man, who occupied himself principally with all-too-amateurish painting, and with collecting minerals and plants, somewhat to the detriment of the family business.   He had married the sister-in-law of the learned Adolphe Franck (1809–93), who, after a distinguished career as professor of philosophy at various French universities, occupied a chair, *du droit de la nature et des gens*, founded specially for him at the Collège de France.   Professor Franck's younger daughter Valentine ('Vally'), after the early death of her mother, was practically adopted by her Aunt and Uncle Lang and at this period spent a great part of her life in their household, either in Vienna or at Roskosch, Bohemia, where the Langs owned some property.   Vally Franck and Helene Gabillon were intimate friends; together they founded the Eulonia, a select company who read poetry, sang, and made merry together under the sign of the Owl, their chosen crest.   Hugo Wolf sometimes found himself a guest of the Eulonia.   On such social occasions he spoke very little and never joined in the singing.   His friend Felix Mottl, on the other hand, not only sang, with his rather hoarse voice, in the Eulonia chorus, but used to beat time for them, long before any one realized how preeminent he was to become as a master of the baton.

It may have been at a gathering of the Eulonia that Wolf first encountered Vally Franck, or their meeting may have taken place in Goldschmidt's apartments.   At any rate, he met her in the house on the Opernring, in the spring of 1878, and fell hopelessly in love.

This reaction was quite customary with all those who were brought into contact with this remarkable young lady.   She was an outstandingly attractive, black-haired girl, high-spirited and intelligent, four years older than Wolf.   She delighted such a connoisseur of feminine beauty as Hans Makart, who wished to paint her portrait, as he had painted that of Dora Gabillon. Helene Bettelheim-Gabillon, in a portrait-sketch of Vally Franck written especially for this book, describes her as she knew her in early youth:

The beautifully arched, dark brows, the long lashes, the black hair, and the dull white complexion gave her head, with the profile of some antique gem, an almost tragically earnest expression.

But how deceiving was this impression! She was a calm, joyous artist in life. Quite conscious of her beauty, she liked to be courted and fallen in love with, but love, with her, should not go too deep, never become a source of pain, or too exacting. Existence should remain sunny and unencumbered. She was, too, full of laughter, and had a lively sense of humour. In confidential exchange of thoughts and feelings with her dearest friend she often gave way to unbounded high spirits; she was far more reserved in wider social circles, where her conversation was charmingly enlivened by her own peculiar *esprit*, but where in general it hardly rose above frivolity. Only very seldom did she become more communicative: one had to know her very well before one was able to notice whether anything pained or annoyed her. She hardly ever raised her insinuatingly melodious, soft, rather dark-toned voice, even when she was excited. Wonderful was the uncomplaining, controlled calm with which she bore, at the age of twenty-two, in the full flower of her beauty, the temporary paralysis of the left half of her face—in this matter, as always, full of consideration for her adopted parents, who lovingly cared for and consoled her. Even her confidential friend she advised very calmly of the affliction, allowing herself only a tinge of melancholy irony. Her solitary hours she dedicated to serious reading, as her cultured spirit and true thirst for knowledge demanded. She possessed great talent for languages, and mastered Czech, as well as German, English, and Italian. She not only loved music, but understood a good deal about it; she played the piano very well, and with her friend, or in a chorus of friendly voices, liked to sing folk-songs, or something of Schubert, Schumann, or Mendelssohn—German Romanticism was very dear to the youthful sentimental feelings of those days. Once when the fervent love-song *Aennchen von Tharau* was being sung, with the pledge of troth,

> 'Käm' alles Wetter gleich auf uns zu schlah'n,
> Wir sind gesinnt beieinander zu stahn,
> Krankheit, Verfolgung, Betrübniss und Pein
> Soll uns'rer Liebe Verknotigung sein,'

Vally declared that that was asking too much, and that she would have no use for such constant, self-sacrificing love and truth. But she was never deceitful: if she loved, she loved truly; and when her love cooled she confessed it openly. This was so even when she had managed to present her heart at the same time to three different people, as she wrote to her friend in high spirits from Cannes in February 1881: 'Yes, Lening, shudder—but don't reproach me—I am in love with three young men at once, to the greatest confusion and anxiety of my sister, who has to listen continuously to my dithyrambs, first about this one, then about that one, and does not know to whom she ought to show her sympathy.' This was of course a joke, the expression of her good humour and joy in her social successes, but at the same time an indication that such successive courtships were necessary to her, so that she could rejoice in her youthful existence. In friendship, nevertheless, there was with her no vacillation; she remained true and dependable throughout all the changes of time, never betrayed confidence placed in her, was never capricious, always feeling with understanding for the sorrows and joys of others, always stimulating, enlivening, bringing light and warmth—a gleam of sunshine in the unforgettably lovely gardens of youth.

Hugo Wolf and Vally Franck were thus remarkably dissimilar characters. The impetuous Wolf, often outspoken to the point of rudeness and quick to imagine offence where none was intended, was decidedly a curiosity, with his many strange mannerisms, which some regarded as affectations, in the social sphere of Goldschmidt's residence on the fashionable Opernring. Vally, on the other hand, had grown up amid all the conventions of the best Parisian and Viennese society and knew how to adapt herself to any company and control with serene accomplishment a wide circle of admirers. Nevertheless, the diminutive young musician of genius, with his outrageous behaviour and his extraordinary boyish charm, excited the interest and affection of the twenty-two-year-old Parisian beauty, and there developed between them a strange and unstable relationship which yet endured for fully three years. Wolf loved with all the fervour of romantic adolescence and the peculiar intensity of his own nature. Vally was hardly capable of returning his devotion in like degree. Frau Bettelheim-Gabillon has clearly indicated the limitations of her affection; for all the charm of her person and the fine qualities of her mind and heart, she possessed no great depth of character. Once, as a young girl, she had shocked her friend by declaring that she would never marry, as she could not imagine herself ever remaining faithful to any one man, and by this jocular remark she did herself no great injustice. Nevertheless, although she was incapable of single-minded devotion of the kind that was consuming Hugo, she did come really to care very deeply for him, later on, in her own way. It is fortunately possible to demonstrate this clearly from her own letters.

Since both Hugo and Vally received back and destroyed their letters to each other at the conclusion of their relationship, very little information has been available about the course of their love-affair.

HUGO WOLF, 1877, AND VALLY FRANCK

It first became known through the researches of Heinrich Werner, who collected his information from certain of his relatives, with whom Wolf stayed at Maierling in the summer of 1880. The loss of all direct correspondence between the principals left the episode in considerable obscurity, into which a series of letters written by Vally Franck to her friend Helene Gabillon throw a clear beam of light. These letters prove that the relationship between Wolf and Vally was not a transient affair of a few months, but a vital impulse in the composer's life throughout three whole years.

Wolf had no opportunity of meeting Vally between the time of his return to Vienna in November 1877 and the spring of the following year, as her letters to Helene Gabillon show that she remained in France during that winter, first in Paris with her father and then on the Riviera with her married sister. In February she was still at Cannes, though longing for Vienna. The last letter from Cannes is dated 4th March, and then with the spring Vally came to her uncle and aunt in Vienna. The exact date of her arrival, and thus the date of her meeting with Wolf, cannot be fixed with certainty, but Helene Gabillon's diary shows that on 13th May the Langs left the house on the Opernring and within a few days were at Roskosch. Vally was thus in Vienna for, at the most, two and a half months, during which short period her friendship with Wolf seems to have made rapid progress. The first letter of hers in which his name occurs was written on 2nd July of this year, in the following circumstances. Vally became seriously ill while staying at Roskosch and towards the end of June the Langs brought her back to Vienna. It was thought then that she might derive benefit from the waters at Bad Gastein and they moved on to that resort after only a very few days in Vienna. From Gastein on 2nd July Vally wrote to her friend:

In Vienna I was still rather poorly, and until the departure so weak that I could only by the greatest exertions make the necessary preparations for the journey. . . . That I didn't see you again in Vienna was bitter. . . . It was without that a day of anguish, my little friend departed and the rest you can imagine. The last days in Vienna were unbearable—hot, lonely, sick, and full of longing; it was no life at all. . . . The first letter that I received, on the day after my arrival, was one six pages long from Hugo.

Another passage, in a letter from Roskosch, where the Langs and their niece returned after visiting Gastein, may be quoted, although it contains no reference to Hugo Wolf, for the light it sheds on the character of the girl who wrote it. It is dated 13th–20th July 1878.

My beauty (?) has suffered considerably. Only think! the whole left side of my face is completely immovable, so that in speaking or laughing everything happens on the right side and I look dreadfully crooked. Farewell my so-called 'diabolical' beauty! Now truly any one on whom I smile is to be pitied, but not on account of any danger to his heart! I bear all that with stoical indifference, such as you would not have expected of me, copy extracts from Mignet's *History of the French Revolution*, mend gloves, and from Schubert's Collected Songs play through a few every evening, which always arouses in me a wholly exalted mood, in which I forget all earthly cares and my crooked appearance. . . .

The legacy of her illness, the immobility of one side of her face, remained with Vally for a long time, but gradually yielded to medical treatment. She writes of it again in a letter from Roskosch in the following September: 'I must prepare you for the fact that I am still crooked, and that especially my magical smile has considerably suffered.' She bore traces of this disfigurement for the rest of her life. Vally remained for the whole of the summer and the early autumn in Bohemia. After the above-quoted reference to Wolf in the letter of 2nd July there is no further mention of him in the correspondence for this year, which may be taken to indicate that as yet he played no more important part in her thoughts than did the rest of her admirers.

Meanwhile, important events had occurred in Wolf's lodgings in the Floragasse. We have seen that in January and February he had produced two songs to words by Lenau, in April *Die Spinnerin* to a poem of Rückert's and the first of the Hebbel songs, and at the beginning of May two further settings of this poet, the last being finished on the 6th. In the latter half of May he took up again Heine's *Buch der Lieder*, an obvious choice for a young romantic musician in search of poems to set to music, but one, as it happened, that he had not utilized since December 1876. *Sie haben heut' Abend Gesellschaft* was begun on 18th May. His attention was then temporarily directed elsewhere; on 20th May he composed two little piano pieces, *Schlummerlied* and *Scherz und Spiel*, for a Wolfian equivalent of Schumann's *Kinderszenen*. A few days later he set to music *Über Nacht*, words by Julius Sturm. This was begun on 23rd May and finished the next day. Then he returned to the *Buch der Lieder*. On the 25th he completed *Sie haben heut' Abend Gesellschaft*. On the 26th he began *Ich stand in dunkeln Träumen*, which he finished on the 29th. The 31st saw the production of *Das ist ein Brausen und Heulen*, and there followed in rapid succession

Wo ich bin mich rings umdunkelt (3rd–4th June), *Aus meinen grossen Schmerzen* (5th June), *Mir träumte von einem Königskind* (16th June), and *Es blasen die blauen Husaren* (22nd June), all from the *Buch der Lieder*. *Mein Liebchen, wir sassen beisammen*, the precise date of which cannot be established, was almost certainly composed between 16th and 22nd June. Another Heine song, *Manch Bild vergessener Zeiten*, begun on 24th June, was left unfinished.

The burst of creative energy which resulted in the production of these songs marks the onset of that period of his early life which Wolf used to refer to as his 'days of Lodi.' In the first flush of excitement accompanying the creation of the Mörike songs, in February 1888, the mature Wolf wrote to his friend Edmund Lang: 'The days of Lodi really seem to be renewing themselves. My Lodi in Song is known to have been the year '78; in those days I composed almost every day *one* good song, and sometimes *two*.' The remark refers not to the whole year, but only to certain specially productive periods of it, of which the first was that which, in May and June, saw the composition of the songs from Heine's *Buch der Lieder*.

The manuscripts of these songs are numbered and there exists a fair copy in Wolf's hand in which seven of them are gathered together to form a *Liederstrauss*—'Seven poems from the *Buch der Lieder* of Heinrich Heine, for voice and pianoforte, composed by Hugo Wolf, Volume I. Summer 1878.' This volume was formerly in the Heyer Museum at Cologne. In arranging the songs, Wolf discarded *Wo ich bin mich rings umdunkelt*, the manuscript of which is numbered five, and set the remainder in the following order:

    (i) *Sie haben heut' Abend Gesellschaft*
    (ii) *Ich stand in dunkeln Träumen*
    (iii) *Das ist ein Brausen und Heulen*
    (iv) *Aus meinen grossen Schmerzen*
    (v) *Mir träumte von einem Königskind*
    (vi) *Mein Liebchen, wir sassen beisammen*
    (vii) *Es blasen die blauen Husaren*

The unfinished *Manch Bild vergessener Zeiten*, the text of which is also from Heine's *Buch der Lieder*, was to have been the eleventh song of the *Liederstrauss*, as is shown by the manuscript. It was, however, not until October that Wolf set to work seriously upon the second volume of his cycle, and by that time he had come to envisage a different continuation, in which all the poems should be taken from Heine's *Neue Gedichte*, instead of from the *Buch der Lieder*.

Perusal of Wolf's *Liederstrauss* leads to the conviction that it was composed under the dominating influence of Schumann's *Dichterliebe*. Although there is no indication in the letters or elsewhere that this masterpiece was occupying his thoughts at this time, the internal stylistic evidence of the songs themselves is overwhelming. It is significant, too, that in this year he attempted no setting of any poem of Heine's which had been previously utilized by Schumann, although he had the temerity to tackle *Ich stand in dunkeln Träumen*, in spite of Schubert. Schumann's *Das ist ein Flöten und Geigen* clearly suggested the scheme of Wolf's *Sie haben heut' Abend Gesellschaft*. *Das ist ein Brausen und Heulen* brings a storm of passion and of the elements that foreshadows a later masterpiece of Wolf's own— the Mörike *Begegnung*. *Aus meinen grossen Schmerzen* is pure Schumann, but an exquisite thing, all the same. It happens occasionally that a young artist, working with the technique of one of his great predecessors, and throwing himself passionately and devotedly into the spirit of a past generation, succeeds in producing something that is not unworthy to stand beside some of his master's work. The German romantic movement had lost its innocence by the time Wolf came to write his *Liederstrauss*, but the best of his reflections of Schumann still ring emotionally true, with the freshness of that earlier spring of song, that welled up in the year 1840. The delicately plashing accompaniment of *Mein Liebchen, wir sassen beisammen* seems to echo a prelude of Chopin's. In the last of the cycle we detect a genuine Wolfian note again; it is the first of the brilliantly vivacious little military marches that recur in his work.

The remaining song of this period, *Über Nacht*, the only one for which Heine did not provide the words, is also of interest. Through posthumous publication it has become fairly popular. Its chief significance lies in the first stanza, where the composer for the first time hit upon those uneasy, broken rhythms which he employed afterwards for identical purposes in *Alle gingen, Herz, zur Ruh* and in his setting of Byron's lines to the moon, 'Sun of the sleepless, melancholy star,' to evoke the restless heartbeats, the unquiet throbbing of the pulses of those whom sleep has forsaken.

The summer was now well advanced, and Wolf's pupils were beginning to leave Vienna for the hottest months of the year, establishing themselves in various resorts where the music-master was unable to follow them. The earlier suggestion that Wolf should go with the Goldschmidts to Ischl for the summer seems to have been abandoned. His parents wished him to return home. Philipp Wolf wrote to his son, not always in the best of humours, advocating this course, and stressing his own inability to contribute further to Hugo's support.

That we all wish you the very best for your name-day stands to reason, and that the deed falls short of the intention is the affair of the goddess of fortune, who for a long time has left me in the lurch . . . so accept the enclosed 5 florins as a fresh contribution to the purchase of the over-coat, with the reflection that the present position allows of no more. . . . When you read this letter I shall be on the way to the market at Bleiburg, perhaps your mother with me, to gain—nothing! As it was at Eberndorf and will be in fourteen days at Griffen as well.

You won't wonder about having received no letter from me for such a long time when I tell you that for 350 florins I have let all five rooms to the son-in-law of District Commissioner Arailza, and that we have moved into the back part of the house. You can hardly conceive the disorder. . . . But there was nothing more to be done but to realize on the house, since business is so bad. Modesta remains here until I have 150 florins to spare for her—she 'll have to wait a long time. It reminds me of the bailiff's men in the old days. On 1st May Mother and I travelled home the whole night from Kappel market with 20 florins receipts; on 6th May quite on my own from Schwarzenbach until twelve o'clock at night. I wonder that no accident has ever occurred to me yet. I am heartily sick of this market drudgery, but there 's nothing else for it.

To-day sister Vinzenzberg has written to me and sent me the newspaper cutting about the Conservatoire concert where Anna performed the Weber-Liszt *Polacca* and Liszt kissed Anna, etc. . . . You too don't write very much, and nothing at all about how you 're getting on—it 's to be sup-posed that things are not going well with you. You seem also to have no piano. In this case Maier's lodgings would seem to have been indicated during his absence, but the practical thing never occurs to you. If in my present situation I can't help you, as I gladly would do, yet perhaps the stay here for the summer would be of assistance to you, as you 'll find but little stimulation [in Vienna] and in that case the cares of your existence will interfere with your studies. In the autumn things will turn out differently. Also, although I 've got no piano you could practise at Tomschek's and Arailza has also a very good, new piano. It 's hard for us to see you fighting for existence.

You write nothing about Liszt, but he must be in Vienna, as he kissed Anna. Mottl was at Graz, but his name did not shine among the per-formers; I am on tenterhooks about the reception of your songs at Leipzig. May they be favourably judged, so that the beginning may encourage you to further efforts. Recognition in restricted circles is all very well, but nothing in comparison with the opinion of recognized experts in publishing matters—only they are able to initiate you.

Although your mother would be very much in favour of going to Vienna in the summer I have little hope that it will come about; she won't travel alone, and for both of us the expenses are too heavy, although the question of lodgings would be settled by Maier's house being vacant. What do you say about it?

As we have seen, Philipp's hopes of publication came to nothing. Hugo, as usual, went his own way. He resisted all his parents' entreaties and arguments that he should return to Windischgraz. The situation was saved for him by the thoughtful and generous suggestion of Dr. Breuer that Wolf should accompany his family to Waidhofen on the Ybbs and continue the lessons he was giving to the Breuer children and their relatives the Kauffmanns. Wolf further received loans of 20 florins each from Gustav Schönaich and from one of Adalbert von Goldschmidt's brothers, so that he started out on his holiday well provided for.

It is uncertain when the journey actually took place. We know that on 20th July he was still in Vienna, and that on 9th August he was at Waidhofen. On this holiday he did not stay with the Breuers but rented a little room of his own—according to verbal tradition at Waidhofen he lived at the inn Zum goldenen Pflug. He was with his friends and pupils, however, all day and every day, and was treated almost as a member of the family. They took him with them on various excursions to the beauty spots of the surrounding countryside, and little towns to which the river lends a romantic enchantment. One day Wolf nearly lost his life in the clear, cold, emerald green water of the Ybbs, when he was seized with cramp while bathing.

He had recently purchased the works of Hoffmann von Fallersleben and here at Waidhofen he planned another song-cycle, a *Dichterleben*, with words by this poet. It was to consist of fourteen songs, of which, in a sudden recurrence of creative fever, he completed three in three successive days. *Liebesfrühling* was composed on 9th August, *Auf der Wanderung* on the 10th, and *Ja, die Schönst', ich sagt' es offen* on the 11th. *Nach dem Abschiede* followed on 31st August and 1st September, after which the *Dichterleben* petered out. *Die Nachtigallen schweigen*, begun on 10th September, got no further than the introductory bars. It cannot be said that Hoffmann von Fallersleben's wandering student inspired Wolf very greatly. Indeed, some of these songs approach the commonplace more nearly than anything else in the composer's work in this year of song. *Auf der Wanderung* makes use of the theme of the trio from the scherzo of the lost Symphony in G minor. Echoes of Schumann still abound, as might be expected from the title he chose for the projected song-cycle. *Nach dem Abschiede*, however, the latest in date, seems to reflect another influence—that of Schubert, both in the reminiscence of *Der Doppelgänger* with which it opens and in the fervent, soaring melody of the beautiful continuation. 'Love, give me wings that I can fly to her,' the poet cries, and Wolf in his youthful chastity of heart could respond quite simply to these sentiments, and set them to music that Schubert himself might have written. It is a sincerely felt and finely realized song, quite captivating in its boyish romantic mood.

More important, however, is another composition of these Waidhofen days, a setting of the scene from Goethe's *Faust*, 'Gretchen before the Image of the Mater Dolorosa,' begun on 22nd August and completed on 9th September. 'Ach neige, du Schmerzenreiche' had been, before Wolf's day, finely set by Schumann in his *Faust* music, and by Schubert in a song that unhappily has come down to us only in an incomplete form. When the eighteen-year-old Wolf came to portray Gretchen in her agony, he produced something quite unlike anything he had written before, or was to write again until eleven years later, when in his *Spanish Song Book* he represented Spanish mysticism writhing in agonized consciousness of sin at the foot of the Cross.

Wolf told his father on 27th August that his financial situation was not too bad up to that time. He had his fees coming in for the lessons to the Breuer children, and had made use of the 40 florins he had been lent. He foresaw difficulties in repaying this sum, but for the present had no need of the pocket-money that his father had offered him. 'I am eating at Bronsreiter's,' he wrote, 'very well and fairly cheaply, large portions and, as they say, as good as in the Hotel Erzherzog Karl in Vienna. . . . I eat, besides breakfast, only once a day, because I feel no necessity of doing so again in the evening.' There was perhaps also a motive of economy behind this frugality, so that he need not call upon his father for further sacrifices. At any rate, the reminiscences which Frau Bertha Hammerschlag, *née* Breuer, one of his little pupils, has set down for use in this book tell a different story:

It was an eternal subject of dispute with us that he was not to be induced to eat a single bite in the house. He sat at the piano and played . . . and my parents did not enjoy their meal because they knew how hungry he was. When he was in the garden with us children he ate with eagerness the fruit that had fallen from the trees, and explained to us his invention, the 'Hunger Belt,' that he could fasten more tightly in order to feel his hunger less. But in spite of that he could not be brought to take part in a meal. I remember one scene quite clearly—how my mother sent the governess, of whom he was very fond, over to the piano with a large portion of tart, and requested him to eat it, but in vain.

Others who knew him well at this period had similar experiences. At Gabillon's, when they asked him why he didn't eat at dinner-time like ordinary mortals, he replied with a furious glance that he didn't visit them just to procure his food. They all considered this persistent avoidance of the dinner-table a freakish symptom of his extraordinary pride and determination to be independent of charity. But the possibility must be faced that there may have been another reason for it, which he chose to disguise by the eccentricities of his behaviour. Dr. Breuer himself believed at the time that Wolf's refusal to eat with the family was the outcome of his childish pride; but in later years he formed another opinion. Wolf died in 1903 after years of insanity and general paralysis, and medical teaching is quite explicit that the origin of this condition lies in a venereal infection that may have been contracted many years before its devastations are revealed. Dr. Breuer believed that this infection may have first manifested itself at this early period of Wolf's life, and that, acting on medical advice, he deliberately avoided using common table utensils, for fear of infecting others. Certainly for a period he seems resolutely to have avoided the dinner-table at the houses of his friends, and Breuer's theory is strengthened immensely, if all unwittingly, by the published reminiscences of Helene Bettelheim-Gabillon.[1] With no other intention than that of indicating some of the eccentricities with which Wolf used to amuse them, Frau Bettelheim-Gabillon provides evidence that appears to be almost decisive: 'He was often a guest at our table, but it seldom happened that he touched food other than some *bread, cheese*, and *fruit* from the dessert. . . . On the other hand he plunged quite unconstrainedly into the afternoon tea that was taken after the piano lesson.' It appears, then, that his pride did not hold him back, in this household at least, from certain foods, and it certainly seems significant that these foods should have been precisely those—bread, cheese, and fruit from the dessert and, it may be supposed, bread and butter, sandwiches, or cakes from the tea-table—*which he would be able to consume without conveying them to his mouth with common utensils.*

---

[1] *Im Zeichen des alten Burgtheaters* (Vienna, 1921).

Finally, it may be recalled that one Brunold Springer has stated without qualification in print [1] that Wolf contracted his disease at the age of seventeen years.   Springer does not give us his authority for this statement, which appears nowhere else in the whole Wolf literature, nor does his book inspire much belief in its ultimate dependability. Nevertheless, he must have received a hint from somewhere about the period of Wolf's infection.

That is all that can be said upon this unpleasant subject.   Wolf certainly contracted the disease at some time or other, and it is both more pitiful and more excusable in him that it should have occurred, as seems likely, so early in his lifetime, when he was thrown, without adequate protection, alone into a great city that beneath its romantic exterior concealed much that was vile and dangerous for a naïve youth, such as he really was in worldly matters.   Who played Schober to Wolf's Schubert we shall probably never know.[2]   Philipp Wolf himself was concerned about these unpleasant possibilities. He once wrote unhappily to his son: 'Above all be warned against immoral company, and against women, who are only born to poison the lives of men.'   It can never be sufficiently regretted that Wolf should in his young days, by a pitiless stroke of fortune, have absorbed the slowly operating poison that brought about his ultimate destruction.

From such thoughts we turn gladly to the final scenes of Wolf's visit to Waidhofen, the more so since they are concerned with an example of what human kindness could do to alleviate the difficulties of this poor mortal, who was yet endowed with the divine gift of genius.

About the middle of September, the Breuers and their relations returned to Vienna.   They were considerably surprised when Wolf declared that he would not be coming back with them.   On the day

---

[1] *Die genialen Syphilitiker* (Berlin, 1926).

[2] Alma Mahler, in her *Gustav Mahler: Erinnerungen und Briefe* (Amsterdam, 1940), has this extraordinary passage: 'Hugo Wolf as a very young man was taken by Adalbert von Goldschmidt into the so-called "Lehmgrube" (a brothel), where Goldschmidt played dance music, for which he received each time a young woman without charge.   He presented his honorarium once to his friend Wolf, and Wolf took away with him "the wound that will never heal." '
It *may* be that this is the true story of the origin of Wolf's disease.   I am not prepared, however, to accept it unconditionally.   Not a few of the many entertaining stories in Alma Mahler's book must be regarded as apocryphal, and the account given of the onset of Wolf's madness in 1897, which is very far from according with the recorded facts and reports of eye-witnesses, does not encourage one to place overmuch reliance in this account of the far more obscure events of 1877, or thereabouts.

of their departure he accompanied them to the station, the train arrived, and the fairly numerous passengers began to enter. It was then discovered that Frau Breuer was missing from the party, and indeed she barely reached the station in time. As the train moved out the family learned the reason for her mysterious disappearance. She had guessed that Wolf was unable to travel with them because he could not pay his bill for board and lodging, hesitated to risk his annoyance by openly offering him the money, and had run back, settled the account with the landlord at the risk of missing the train, and just managed to rejoin her family in time, rejoicing like a child in the success of her manœuvre. Wolf was able to return to Vienna a few days later, on 21st September.

It seems that the wonderful lodging in the Floragasse was no longer available. He first took a room in the Hotel Stadt Triest, in the Wiedner Hauptstrasse, just opposite the Hotel Goldenes Lamm where he had stayed in the previous December. But after only two days he moved to the eighth Bezirk, Josefstadt, to a private house in the Tulpengasse. Here too he stayed only two days, and on 26th September he returned again to the Wieden district, to a cheap lodging at Neumanngasse 5, where he was to pay only 14 florins a month. In this place, which did not please him at all, he nevertheless once more began to compose.

We have seen that in the last of his settings of Hoffmann von Fallersleben Wolf seemed to have struck a Schubertian lyrical note; after his return to Vienna he continued to work out this vein in a second series of Heine songs, to poems from the *Neue Gedichte*. *Es war ein alter König* (4th October), the first of these, is of minor interest, but it was followed in the same month by three of the most remarkable of the young Wolf's achievements in song. *Mit schwarzen Segeln*, a tense and violent expression of despair, was composed on 6th October, and on the following day he wrote the wonderfully poignant, Schubertian *Spätherbstnebel*. *Ernst ist der Frühling*, an exquisite song, all melancholy tenderness, followed between 13th and 17th October.

This last was not completed in the Neumanngasse, for on 15th October, following his 'inborn roving impulse,' as he put it to his father, he had returned once again to the Wiedner Hauptstrasse, this time to house number 22—the fourth move since his return from Waidhofen. There he occupied a more elegant apartment, fine and roomy, with outlook into the garden, for which he was to pay his landlord, a house-painter, 20 florins a month.   But on 1st November, after only a fortnight, he moved again.   This time he tried the sixth Bezirk, Mariahilf, Hofmühlgasse 2, only to return on 12th November to the inner city, Himmelpfortgasse 3.   He explained the situation to his parents in a letter on 11th November: [1]

> The one surprising novelty is that I am already moving again, probably into the city.   In bad weather the road is impassable, so that on Sunday of last week I could not step outside the house the whole day.   I am sorry myself to leave these people, but there's no help for it.   If I can only settle down in my future dwelling! . . .   The muses have for three weeks completely neglected me and behave very prudishly, scarcely allowing me a tiny song.

He had now occupied rooms at six different addresses within a period of about seven weeks.   For one reason or another each of these places was found to be impossible.   When he devoted himself to composition the twittering of birds outside his window, or even the tick of a clock in a neighbouring room, was enough to drive him into a state of nervous frenzy.   He spoke often to his friends of the miseries of these lodgings.   Sometimes, pale from lack of sleep, he would come to beg a night's rest in the house of a friend and relate his latest misfortune—once he was put out into the street by an irate landlady who had caught him in the act of removing the pendulum from her kitchen clock.   This unending search for quiet was anything but a joke to Wolf, sensitive to sound, as he was, to a most acute and even phenomenal degree.   'The question of lodgings so greatly occupies me,' he wrote, 'that all the poetry of music has departed. If I could only find a decent lodging, like that in the Floragasse, to be able once again to work undisturbed!'

Philipp Wolf also had something to say about these continual removals.   On 19th November he replied to his son's letter of the 11th.

> Moving again then!   Why don't you reflect beforehand, so as not to offend such rare people?   After all, the bad road won't matter much, and we would gladly hear that you are stopping where you are.   Maier too often has a muddy road, but has been a long time now in this lodging and the people are fond of him.   With this eternal wandering you can

---

[1] *Familienbriefe XXII.* The letter is erroneously dated 11th October, and Wolf makes the same mistake in the text, where he reports that *Siegfried* was performed in Vienna on 9th October. The *first performance* of Wagner's *Siegfried* in Vienna did not take place until 9th November. This mistake caused Werner to apply Wolf's remarks about the bad state of the road to the Neumanngasse, when they really concern the Hofmühlgasse.

have no piano to hold the muses fast. . . . That the muses desert you is the fault of this continual wandering. Settle down comfortably and they will favour you.

Philipp also returned often to his favourite advice that Hugo should send his compositions again to Dr. Hausegger at Graz, who, it seems, had promised to see what could be done for him at a forthcoming concert.

> The *Tagespost* brings a lot of news about concerts and criticisms by Hausegger, but never anything about you. The boy Busoni was dressed up and favourably criticized. I hope that Hausegger will now keep his word if he arranges a concert, which so far has not been the case. You say very little about your musical circumstances, and I have been waiting now a long time for the promised good news. It seems as if a deadlock has been reached. That would be all the more regrettable as the time of *military service* draws ever nearer, and you should be equipped for all eventualities before that time. Enlightenment about your means of existence would also be welcome. The thought that you may be lacking necessities makes me very uneasy. Altmann and Schönaich are to be sure a great consolation, but one doesn't come across such good people very often. Here I recall the Ritter von Ankern, to whom you ought to show your gratitude in some way or other. (5th December 1878.)

In a letter of Dr. Hausegger's, which Hugo enclosed in his own reply to this letter of his father's, there is no mention of any prospective performance of his songs at Graz. Instead we learn that he was again thinking of attempting an opera, if he could only find a suitable libretto. Hausegger's letter is full of advice about the kind of book to avoid. At the end of his own reply, Wolf tells his father: 'I am sorry you worry yourself so much about the performance of my songs at Graz; probably it'll come to nothing.'

About this time Philipp Wolf was involved in various lawsuits and utilized Hugo as his agent in Vienna. Much of the father's correspondence is concerned with these matters, which were drawn out through many months. Hugo was frequently urged to set about arranging powers of attorney, interviewing solicitors, etc., with more energy, so that this or that 'mangy Jew' might have 'life made sour for him.'

Philipp's advice about too frequent removals had its effect upon Hugo only until the beginning of January, when he took himself and his belongings out to the Beethoven House in the Schwarzspanier-strasse, in the Alsergrund district. There he remained only a fortnight, after which he stayed at Berggasse 4, in the same neighbourhood, until 14th February. He then returned to the city and took a room on the Opernring itself, house number 23.

Except for his misfortunes in the matter of lodgings Wolf does not seem to have been much concerned about the future. He reports in his letters that he was present at the first performance in Vienna of Wagner's *Siegfried*; also that he is looking forward eagerly to Brahms's C minor Symphony, so that it seems that he had not yet finally taken sides in the musical party warfare of the times. For some months now he had not complained of financial difficulties, but in a letter of January 1879 he confesses that he has often to apply to Altmann or Schönaich for assistance, as his own earnings amount only to 56 florins a month. He never mentions Vally Franck by name in his letters to his parents of this time.

Vally had returned from Roskosch to Vienna at the end of October and renewed her acquaintance with Wolf. A very interesting question invites consideration: Was it merely coincidence that 1878, the year in which he first fell in love, was also the year of his 'Lodi in song'? Helene Bettelheim-Gabillon, the confidante of both principals in the affair, was definitely of the opinion that Vally inspired this first sustained burst of song composition in Wolf. It must be remembered that he was not yet by a long way the objective artist he became in his maturity. In her printed reminiscences Frau Bettelheim-Gabillon recalls how, when he was especially put out by the unsympathetic conduct of the young lady with whom he was in love —obviously Vally is meant—he used to sing Schumann's *Ein Jüngling liebt ein Mädchen* with peculiar intensity and bitterness, hammering out the accompaniment until it sounded like a street song, while with his peculiarly unmusical voice he gave unforgettable expression to the pain in his heart. She also heard him sing his own setting of

> Aus meinen grossen Schmerzen
> Mach' ich die kleinen Lieder,

with very decided emphasis on its personal application to himself:

About the worth of the composition I could at that time form no opinion, and I cannot recollect whether the song as such pleased me or not—but I knew whom his 'grossen Schmerzen' concerned, and the expression of his passion and of his deeply wounded feelings, that reflected itself in his features and quivered in his toneless, veiled voice, had something about it so affecting that the impression on me has remained unforgotten.

That certainly suggests that the numerous love-songs of this year were inspired by his passion for Vally Franck, and an examination of the songs themselves goes some way to support this suggestion. In *Mit schwarzen Segeln*, for example, we must surely recognize the subjective note. 'Your heart is inconstant, like the wind'—Wolf seems to throw the words in the girl's face. Then with *Spätherbstnebel*, written on the following day, in a mood of complete submission, there cannot be much doubt as to the identity of the 'vielgeliebte, schöne Frau' to whom it is addressed. It is indeed very probable that in such songs as these we possess a record of his feelings that goes far to compensate for the loss of his love-letters. It may have been precisely their subjective nature that caused Wolf to pass over these settings of Heine, with the Lenau songs of the following year, when he came to publish his first volumes of early songs in 1888. The best of them are certainly not at all inferior to some of those which at that time he chose to print. But the songs which then met with his approval, of course, were those that conformed to his by that time firmly established conception of himself as an objective lyrical artist, with a pronounced distaste for the *Ich-poeten* who had claimed so much of his attention in earlier, more sentimental times. Finally, it should be noticed that the flow of Wolf's songs, which had begun almost immediately after Vally's departure in May and continued intermittently throughout their separation, ceased precisely when they were once again together in Vienna.

In December and January he was working on the astonishing String Quartet, on the title-page of which he inscribed the quotation from *Faust*: 'Entbehren sollst Du, sollst entbehren.' It is interesting to note that this Quartet, which so unmistakably exhibits the influence of Beethoven, was in part written while Wolf was himself living in the Beethoven Schwarzspanierhaus.

Only a few details are available of his relationship with Vally in this winter. They were both present at a new year's party at Gabillon's, at which members of the Burgtheater company performed a parody on Shakespeare's *Antony and Cleopatra*, to which Wolf provided burlesque incidental music. Then he is known to have given piano lessons to Vally for a time, and it is probable that she is the 'very beautiful young lady' mentioned as his latest pupil in the letter to his father of 8th January 1879.

This seems to have been the period of his closest association with the young Mahler. They had known each other since 1875, when they had joined the Conservatoire together, and in the years that followed they were friendly with the easy intimacy of old school

colleagues whenever their individual paths brought them into contact.   Mahler's early letters reflect like Wolf's own the ecstasies and
the sufferings of youthful genius.   He shared with Wolf the miseries
of unquiet Viennese lodging-houses.   Heinrich Werner records a
story [1] that Mahler lived with Wolf, and even shared a bed with him,
on the fourth floor of Opernring 23.   Alma Mahler, too, has in her
reminiscences [2] stories of Wolf and Mahler's early life together.
With a young musician named Rudolf Krzyzanowski, one of the most
intimate of Mahler's friends, they rented a single room and lived there
together for a few months.   They were all very sensitive to noise
and whenever any one of the three of them wished to compose, the
other two had to spend the night walking the streets.   Thus Mahler
once wrote a quartet movement for a musical competition in a single
night, while Wolf and Krzyzanowski slept on benches in the Ringstrasse.   The chronology of Mahler's early life is even more confused
than Wolf's has hitherto appeared, and it is not always possible to
assign precise dates to such stories as Alma Mahler records of her
husband's life in the years before she knew him, but it certainly seems
likely that this story may date from the first half of 1879, when,
according to tradition, Mahler lived in the same room as Wolf on the
Opernring.   Wolf's own String Quartet was being written at about
the same time.   Was it, perhaps, originally intended for the same
competition as Mahler's?

Another of Alma Mahler's stories is that the three friends got to
know *Götterdämmerung* at the same time and in their passion for the
work they made such a frightful row in their lodgings, singing the trio
between Gunther, Brünnhilde, and Hagen, that the landlady appeared, trembling with rage, and turned them all out into the street.
Now it is interesting to recall that the first performance of *Götterdämmerung* in Vienna took place on 14th February 1879, the very day
on which Wolf first moved into the lodgings on the Opernring, so that
there is altogether a very strong probability that these stories are
authentic and date from this time.

Early in the year 1879 there occurred an event of considerable
biographical and controversial interest—Hugo Wolf's interview with
Johannes Brahms. We have seen that Wolf's surrender to Wagner had
so far not affected his early admiration for what he knew of the music
of Brahms.   He had brought the latter's folk-song arrangements

---

[1] *Hugo Wolfs Wohnstätten in Wien.*
[2] *Gustav Mahler: Erinnerungen und Briefe* (Amsterdam, 1940).

to Helene Gabillon and spoken of his music with enthusiasm. In December 1878 he had told his parents that he was looking forward eagerly to the C minor Symphony. In later life he often admitted that he had in his early days greatly admired much of Brahms's chamber music, and also the *Magelone-Lieder*. Considering that Wolf moved principally in Wagnerian circles, he showed considerable independence of mind in successfully combining a passion for Wagner with a strong liking for Brahms. So it came about that he set out one day for the Karlsgasse, where Brahms lived, with a bundle of his manuscripts, upon which he intended to invite the master's opinion. For details of the interview we are dependent upon Brahms's biographer, Max Kalbeck.[1] According to this authority:

> Brahms had just sat down at the piano, when he heard a suspicious noise at his glass door. At the same time he saw on the blind the shadow of a man, who seemed to be occupied with the lock of the door. Brahms rose at length and opened it. He had some trouble to get his strange visitor to come into the room, as the latter could not be got away from the door-latch, which he kept on kissing. 'The compositions which he brought to me,' related Brahms, 'did not amount to much. I went through everything thoroughly with him and drew his attention to many things. Some talent was certainly forthcoming, but he didn't take the matter seriously enough. I then told him quite earnestly what it was he lacked, recommended contrapuntal studies, and referred him to Nottebohm. That was enough for him and he did not return. Now he spits poison and gall.'

Kalbeck also records that the composer Richard Mandl saw Wolf in a café directly after his visit to Brahms. With flushed face, and quite beside himself with indignation, he told those who were waiting for him there that Brahms had in fact said: 'You must first learn something, and then we shall see whether you have talent.'

The interview must have taken place before 13th March, as Brahms left Vienna for Frankfurt on that day, with the intention of staying in Germany for about a month at least,[2] while at the end of March and the beginning of April there is some discussion of Brahms's proposal in Wolf's family correspondence. In an undated letter congratulating Hugo on his nineteenth birthday (13th March), Philipp inquires whether Nottebohm, or 'Notebone,' as he calls him, will give lessons free of charge. In another letter, posted on 28th March,

---

[1] *Johannes Brahms. III, zweiter Halbband* (Berlin, 1912). Kalbeck places the incident in 1881 or 1882, but there is not the slightest doubt that he is referring to the interview which took place early in 1879.
[2] Letter to Fritz Simrock of 13th March 1879.

he writes: 'About Notebone I hear nothing from you, although I
would gladly see you studying with him.   There must still be much
that you need, as Brahms advises the lessons.'   Hugo replied to this
on 7th April.   'There is nothing to be done with Nottebohm.   He
wants 3 florins a lesson and won't do it otherwise.   I shall get on now
without him and it's only Brahms's North-German pedantry that
makes him thrust Nottebohm upon me.'   It seems, then, that
Brahms's advice had not been ignored entirely, in spite of Wolf's
indignation.   He did get as far as inquiring Nottebohm's fees, and
gave up the idea of these lessons because he could not afford them.
If they *had* been commenced, they would certainly not have lasted
long.   Richard Specht[1] recalls Nottebohm's

pedantic reliability and love of order, his uprightness that verged on dis-
putatiousness, his morbidly exaggerated Teutomania and self-esteem, his
miserly economy, but above all his fanatical thirst for justice.   Nottebohm
was capable of depriving a postman of his wretched living for having left a
letter with the porter instead of taking it up four flights of stairs, and he
curtly and irrevocably dismissed a pupil who had come a great distance
to study under him because, all too eager to learn, he had impetuously
inquired after the task to be set him at the next lesson.

Certainly Wolf would not have endured such discipline for long.   It
is interesting to find, within two months of Wolf's visit, Brahms
discussing the Vienna Conservatoire and its products with Elizabeth
Herzogenberg, who had asked what the place was like: 'Could one
advise a young student, who is taking up composition, to go there?'
On 29th April Brahms wrote:

Our Conservatoire is in a terrible state as regards the teaching of composition.   You only need to see the teachers, and not—as I often do—the
pupils and their work. . . .   Nottebohm charges 3 gulden a lesson, so far as
I know . . . I can strongly recommend him as a teacher.   I send him
every one who comes my way, and have often had reason to be delighted
with his results.

Kalbeck's account of Wolf's interview with Brahms, as related to
him by Brahms himself, has given great offence in Wolfian circles and
been seized upon and reprinted with glee by the jackals of Brahmsian
biography.   It is perhaps worth while investigating the history of the
passage in question.   In 1904 there appeared the first number of a
sort of Austrian musicians' directory, *Ein Musikbuch aus Österreich*,
edited by Richard Heuberger.   Decsey contributed to this year-book

---

[1] *Johannes Brahms* (Dresden, 1928).   Quotation from the English translation
by Eric Blom (1930).

a 'Hugo Wolf Miscellany' which included an inscription from the back of a photograph of Eduard Hanslick, sent, it was alleged, to Wolf as a birthday greeting.   This, however, seems really to have been the souvenir of a practical joke played upon Wolf by some of his friends, and did not come from Hanslick at all.   Kalbeck, on reading Decsey's 'Miscellany,' having ascertained from Hanslick that the latter had, in fact, never sent birthday greetings to Wolf, denounced the published inscription as a forgery in a review of the *Musikbuch aus Österreich* in the *Neues Wiener Tagblatt* for 9th March 1904.   The *Wiener Salonblatt* was at the same time reprinting some of the musical criticism, with its attacks on the whole Brahmsian circle, including Kalbeck himself, which Wolf had written in the years 1884–7.   Infuriated at this reappearance of his old enemy, Kalbeck, in his review of the *Musikbuch aus Österreich*, wrote so offensively that Wolf's family, backed up by the Hugo Wolf Verein, threatened legal proceedings and Kalbeck was forced to withdraw.   His apology was published in the *Neues Wiener Tagblatt* of 2nd July and there he withdrew 'all passages offensive to the memory of Hugo Wolf' in his article.   The story of Wolf's interview with Brahms appeared for the first time in Kalbeck's review of the *Musikbuch aus Österreich* and it was from this source that he reprinted it, eight years later, in his Brahms biography.   In the original version Brahms is made to say of Wolf: '*Ach Gott!* that's a wretched, needy fellow, a Musikant come to grief, who won't learn anything.   He came once to see me, when he was not to be got away from the door; he kept on kissing the latch "out of respect."   Disgusting!'   By avoiding direct quotation from these preliminary sentences, Brahms's statement was given a less objectionable tone in the biography.   Nevertheless even the later version bears signs of animosity and of something less than perfect objectivity on the part of the biographer, and it would not be at all surprising if the whole improbable episode of Wolf's kissing Brahms's door-latch were originally an invention of the irate Kalbeck, which he retained even in the milder version of 1912.   Kalbeck sought to show that Wolf's later antagonism to Brahms was the direct outcome of Brahms's unfavourable verdict upon his compositions.   It was necessary to show that Wolf's original admiration for Brahms was at least on a par with his known admiration for Wagner—hence the necessity for the kissing of the door-latch.   Probably the broad outline of the Brahms-Kalbeck account is truly drawn, but some of the details sadly out of perspective.   Not long before his death, Heinrich Werner records, Kalbeck paid a visit to the house at Perchtoldsdorf where Wolf created so many of his wonderful songs and said: 'I did him wrong.'[1]

That this unfortunate episode did do something to impel Wolf more forcibly towards the anti-Brahmsian camp is probably true. It must have predisposed him to acceptance of the talk he heard all around him in Wagnerian circles. Do we not seem, in his remark to his father that it was only Brahms's North-German pedantry that made him thrust Nottebohm upon him, to catch the echo of some comforting assurance of Goldschmidt or Schönaich?

With the passage of the early months of 1879 Hugo's financial situation had not improved as he had hoped. Dora Gabillon and the Breuer children were still his only permanent pupils; others, such as Vally Franck herself, were gained and lost from time to time. He was badly in need of new clothes. His younger brother Gilbert had come to Vienna as apprentice in the leather trade, and Hugo had passed on to him most of his clothing, which was becoming too small for him. The renewal of Hugo's wardrobe was no easy matter. His monthly income had fallen from 56 florins in January to about 38 florins in April—'a handsome sum for pocket-money,' he wrote, 'but too little to meet the expenses of lodgings, food, laundry, clothing, etc.' Poor Philipp was called on for no less than 80 florins in April, chiefly on account of tailors' bills. In a letter delivered on the 29th of this month he wrote to Hugo:

I know nothing of Gilbert, whether he arrived in Vienna and, if so, whether he is still there. You too have scarcely enough time to tell me how much money you require. It is, however, very praiseworthy that you have at length conceived the idea of looking for cheaper lodgings, but after all that only shows that things must really be going badly with you. ... As it is I have to send you money at the time when business is slackest, when I receive dunning letters from all sides and collect nothing. I have to-day no money. I will send you 30 florins to-morrow—God knows where it's coming from. Moreover, you must be very ignorant of my circumstances, that you ask for such sums such a short time after each other, and in purchasing the clothes go to work in such an unpractical manner, for in these days only those people who have money to throw away allow themselves to be measured by the tailor. A thrifty man buys ready-made goods.

Eleven days later Hugo was forced again to ask for money.

Couldn't you send me 10 florins by the 15th of the month? Then in

---

[1] 'Hugo Wolf. Zur zwanzigsten Wiederkehr des Todestags' (*Neues Wiener Tagblatt*, 20th February 1923).

D

the middle of June another 10 florins and 10 florins for the journey? Altogether that would be another 30 florins, but it'll be easier in instalments. . . . I have been living now for some time on bread and butter again, but that itself is not so bad as the consciousness of having no money in my pocket.

It will be seen that life was not easy, either for Hugo or for his father. Hugo only applied for help, of course, when it was absolutely unavoidable, and Philipp made every possible sacrifice for his son. But a bitter note recurs continually in the father's letters. Prolonged poverty and bad luck had reduced his vitality to a low ebb. More and more space in his letters is devoted to the recital of his own miseries; he sank ever deeper into prolonged and luxurious fits of melancholy. He seems to have received little sympathy at home, for a quite disproportionate amount of space in his correspondence with his son is taken up with increasingly bitter complaints on this score. Hugo was not his only, or even his greatest, source of anxiety among his children. The youngest son Gilbert caused his father many headaches. Not caring for his life in Vienna, he had made use, after a few weeks, of money given him by Hugo to return home without his father's permission. There had been scenes and Philipp had driven him out of the house.

Hugo in his replies makes hardly any comment at all upon his father's lamentations. He takes no sides in the frequent family disagreements. Although he often has temporary disappointments to relate, he is still, at any rate in the letters he writes to his family, unshakable in his conviction of his ultimate success. It is truly remarkable with what tenacity he clings to the idea that he is a born composer, in spite of everything the practical world can do to convince him to the contrary. He has no sooner conceived the idea of sending his songs to a publisher than he writes confidently that they will be in print in a couple of months. Their ultimate rejection seems not at all to depress him—there are better publishers elsewhere. This sort of thing reduced the pessimistic Philipp to despair; Hugo was always serenely confident that an improvement, success, fortune itself, was just round the corner.

Wolf seems to have made good use of the opportunities afforded by the music lessons he was giving to Vally Franck. In April they were hoping to be able to spend their summer holidays together. Wolf wrote to his father: 'Frau Lang has definitely invited me to Bohemia for the summer months.' Within a few weeks, however, he was thinking of accompanying the Breuer family to Gmunden, 'because the Langs have suddenly decided to go to Paris.' But the Langs did not visit Paris after all; they went, with their niece, to Roskosch as usual, and Wolf was not asked to accompany them. It seems that Frau Lang was beginning to think the affair had already gone far enough. On 25th July Vally wrote to Helene Gabillon:

How can you believe that I would keep secret from you anything so important as Hugo's presence here? By doing so you arouse within me grief's most sorrowful longing—the wish that your supposition were true. . . . I should be only too glad to have him here, but that is also my aunt's opinion (that I should be *too glad!*), and she applies her prudent veto.

On 25th August she wrote again:

The dear creature has remained true to me and to himself. I receive many loving letters and now and then compositions. I cannot withhold from you that I answer the letters, play the compositions, and read the books sent to me. How that will end only the gods can tell; meanwhile the independence and originality of my style are lost, for I write now exactly like Hugo.

The compositions referred to probably included the three Lenau songs which have survived from July of this year. *Herbstentschluss* was composed on 8th July, *Frage nicht* on the 21st, and *Herbst* on the 24th. They were written in his home at Windischgraz, for all his arrangements for spending the summer with his friends had come to nothing, owing to continually increasing financial difficulties. At Windischgraz he also occupied himself again with the String Quartet, begun in the previous winter and then laid aside. The first movement was completed on 8th July.

The grandly sombre *Herbstentschluss* is the most ambitious of these Lenau songs of 1879, and *Herbst* the most beautiful and accomplished; but *Frage nicht* is much more like an intimate personal confession than a composition intended for public performance. The recurring introductory passage for the piano, with its spasmodic eruptions and subsidences, bears the direction 'Convulsive, like a passionate outburst,' and in Wolf's setting Lenau's poem has a feverish intensity that may well have caused Vally to draw back in alarm. The boyish romanticism of the previous year had developed into something more earnest and realistic.

On 4th September Vally wrote from Roskosch:

We should like to remain here until the first of November. Isn't it atrocious that we should *like* to do that? I must, however, for the sake of appearances, also plead for it, so that the erroneous idea be not aroused

that Another besides yourself draws me to Vienna. This Other writes to
me so industriously and so tenderly that it might be supposed that I could
not withstand so much amiability, and so I must be on my guard and
tremendously unconcerned.

There followed on 4th October a cry of distress:

I am wretched! I have quarrelled with my only, best, dearest friend
Hugo. And why? Owing to cursed, stupid virtue and reason on my part.
He wrote me increasingly passionate letters; the flames flickered continually higher and at length I became scared. I thought: 'What will be the
outcome, in this passionate nature, of *such* a love?' and since, with my
heartfelt affection for the little one, I had without that let the affair go too
far, I wrote in an access of virtue an innocently cheerful letter, rather cooler
in tone, *not wishing to understand.* I only wanted to bring him gradually
back into the realm of reason. But this sensitive plant understood at once,
and how alarmed I was when I received a letter in which he told me that as
the result of my writing he had at first desired never to see me again, but
that then he had discovered the golden mean and he would be my friend
in the way I wished. In the coming winter he would move out to Nussdorf
or Währing (as far as possible from us!) and come to us once a week to play
something for me. And how much pain and bitterness was to be read
between the lines! I was too unhappy and wept the most bitter tears
throughout a whole afternoon, and cannot yet accustom myself to the
thought of having lost Hugo, my only joy. Nor do I yet believe that we
can be parted so easily. Now I have received another card with the
remark that he is now travelling back to Vienna, that I may spend October
pleasantly at Roskosch. He did not give his address in Vienna. Does
that mean that for the whole of this month I shall not hear from him
any more? Perhaps *you* can find out something. Should you know his
address don't withhold it from me.

The dispute did not last long. On 18th October Vally wrote again:

As you probably foresaw, my quarrel with Hugo is already long since
fought to a standstill. 'They say Jove laughs at lovers' quarrels.' How
long the peace will endure I do not know, but if it only lasts until our
reunion I will look out for the future.

Wolf returned to Vienna early in October—an existing account
from a Viennese solicitor, Dr. Josef Frühwald, mentions an interview
with 'Wolf junior' on 3rd October. The Langs returned on 2nd
November. Once again there is practically no information about the
course of their friendship during the winter months. One of Vally's
later letters suggests that there were difficulties. It is certain that
Hugo lost all his pupils, with the sole exception of Dora Gabillon,
and was forced to rely more and more upon his poor father for
monetary assistance. Philipp Wolf was growing desperate. He still
had on his hands three grown-up sons without permanent employ-

ment.   His leather business was going from bad to worse and cattle diseases were preventing the marketing of his hides.   His lawsuits had only involved him in further expenses.   He told Hugo that he would have to return home unless he could contrive to earn more money for his own support.

Only one letter of Wolf's from this winter has survived, but Philipp Wolf's correspondence helps to fill out the scanty material. On 3rd November he wrote to his son the following cheerless letter:

Your jeremiad was all that was wanting.   It's not enough that Modesta requires 100 florins for the removal to Graz, Max came home without a job, Dr. Frühwald wants 50 florins in advance, Mother goes to no markets, the cattle plague broken out here, in consequence of which no business, bills to pay at Trieste, Vienna, etc.—on top of all that you come with your immense tailor's bill.   Lack of pupils, therefore no income—what's going to happen???   If now in the winter you have no pupils then you must say farewell to Vienna.

But are your many friends doing nothing for you in this direction, hasn't one, out of them all, enough influence to procure you a few pupils?   Or is it the belief that I am rolling in money?   You can relate some fine things out of my correspondence. . . .   I enclose the power of attorney for Dr. Frühwald.   In the fold [of this letter] you will find 25 florins, out of which, if the worst comes to the worst, you can pay Dr. Frühwald the first expenses, in that case the tailor, who charged so much, would have to wait.

It is time that your friends should not just admire and adulate your mental products, but also procure recognition for them and material profit for you.

In such remarks Philipp was manifestly unjust to Hugo's friends in Vienna.   He seems not always to have realized how very difficult it was to help his son.   Hugo's desperate plight is still the principal theme of his own letter of 17th December, printed in the *Familien-briefe*.   The first page of this letter has *not* been published and is printed here for the first time from the original in the Prussian State Library:

If you knew what has occurred since I received your last letter, perhaps you would forgive my dreadful reticence. . . .   I received the 20 florins and unfortunately also—kept them!   I was in a most critical position, lost all lessons except for Gabillon's.   Altmann was, and still is, at Trieste; Schönaich, Mottl, and all my acquaintances were already completely cleaned out.   I still didn't want to touch the money and hoped, hoped and waited—but all in vain.   There remained nothing further but either to starve or to keep the 20 florins, and if the former would have been preferable to you, then I have failed you, to be sure.   Are you still angry with me?   Should I have rather employed the money according to your opinion and—starved?   No, dearest, beloved Father, I know it—you *don't* think that, and you yourself will say in your heart: 'It's not so completely wasted, after all, and certainly it has been of more use to him than it would have been to me.' Isn't that so? And truly it is so.

The rest of the letter is printed in the *Familienbriefe*:

For never have I so experienced the truth of the proverb 'A friend in need is a friend indeed' as now. . . . The only one who would have been able to help me, and also really *would* have helped me, was Altmann, and he was away. But as if that were not enough, I must make still further demands for your assistance if I am not to go under completely. If you could help me out only until the middle of January, from then on I have good prospects. I require, of necessity, 40 florins, and it is accursed luck that I cannot procure them for myself here. I move to-morrow to Cottage, near Vienna, in order to live more cheaply. Also in order to concentrate more upon my studies and my works. Write therefore to Währing Cottage-Verein, Karl-Ludwigstrasse 24.[1] I don't need the money at once but in any case 20 florins on 5th January. If you could send me just 10 florins for the time, my situation would be considerably eased. . . . If you intend coming to Vienna, you could put up at my place finely. I have a dwelling—living-room, closet, lobby, kitchen, loft, and cellar—at the cheap price of 45 florins quarterly, that is 15 florins monthly, furnished of course. I have also a fine piano, for which I shall not need to pay any rent yet, because my friend Mahler, who leaves my future dwelling to-morrow, has paid up to the 1st. The instrument is excellent.

Here we have further evidence of the close friendship of Wolf and Mahler at this time. A letter of Mahler's,[2] written on 22nd September of this year, gives his address as Rennweg 3—the very house in which Wolf had been living before his return to Windischgraz for the summer, and to which he seems to have returned from October until he followed Mahler out to the Cottage-Verein at Währing, a settlement of detached villas in the English style, at that time still outside the city boundaries and probably used chiefly as a summer resort. In the winter months some of these villas, owing to their isolation, would be to let at very low rentals.

Wolf's extreme penury at this time was not unconnected with his friendship with Mahler and Krzyzanowski. The latter had been engaged as accompanist to Marie Wilt, who was touring the provinces with the pianist Annette Essipoff.[3] It was arranged that during his absence from Vienna Krzyzanowski's pupils should be taught by Wolf. This would have kept him fully occupied for two whole months but unluckily Frau Wilt fell ill and abandoned the concert

---

[1] Now Weimarerstrasse (Vienna XIX).

[2] Hans Holländer, 'Unbekannte Jugendbriefe Gustav Mahlers' (*Die Musik*, August 1928).

[3] 'Christoff' in the *Familienbriefe* is a misreading of Wolf's handwriting.

tour, so that Krzyzanowski returned to Vienna and took over the lessons from Wolf, who was thus left stranded with only the single engagement at Gabillon's with which to support himself.

A letter of Philipp Wolf's, delivered in Währing on 24th December, brought his reply to Hugo's call for help of 17th December. In this letter Philipp surpassed himself in querulous lamentation.

What with my many worries and great shortage of money, your miseries were the only thing lacking. But in heaven's name what's going to happen? No lessons so far, and in March people get ready to go into the country! As I cannot possibly give you the 40 florins there will probably be nothing for you to do except come home, and I should moreover have already made the suggestion, if the military service, that will take effect this year, were not at hand. Nothing remains for you to do, but to take up your quarters with Maier for the present, and instead of rump steak to eat something cheaper. What's the use of all your music writing (three years now) and not a single page published—what a waste of costly time!! Practically nothing is done for you, and you yourself also do nothing. Instead of sending your things to Hausegger, who this year brought to performance all Styrian compositions and especially likes to glorify Styrian composers, your works lie in the cupboard of a Jewess, who one day in a bad humour will throw them into the fire or the waste-paper basket. In this way you will never make your name; you cannot even get pupils; what use to you is your stay in Vienna? In influential circles you are not liked, and with your temperament you never *will* make yourself liked; even your friends do nothing for you, have at the most fair words or charity, that is all. I am sorry for you and your inability to accommodate yourself to circumstances. You are over-particular, spoilt, and pampered, and if you lack the necessary means, you are unable to help yourself—your father must pay the piper, whether it's easy or hard for him. . . . Yesterday I travelled at three o'clock in the night to Schwarzenbach, in 20 degrees of frost and an icy north wind, so that I could send you 10 florins to-day. I cleared about 6 florins and suffered 1,000 florins from the cold. Whether I can send you 10 florins on 5th January I don't know; I have enormous bills to pay. . . . When I hold review of my children it appears that Modesta is badly married, Gilbert just as poor a leather-worker as Max is a witless tradesman, and finally you, withdrawn from the fourth class in order to seek out the most uncertain of all means of existence. That's a nice Christmas present for me! One could joyfully sink living into the grave, in order to hear nothing more about you all.

For six months after this we have no letters of Hugo's, but his father's correspondence indicates that there occurred—not before it was due—a decided improvement in the young Wolf's situation. Firstly, from a letter of 6th January 1880, we learn that his immediate financial embarrassment was eliminated at a wave of the generous hand of Leopold Altmann, who sent a present of 40 florins from Trieste. Secondly, in the surviving letters of Philipp's from the first half of 1880 his previous harsh, complaining tone is nowhere resumed—at least, Hugo is not himself the object of his father's complaints. There is no further mention of any financial difficulties of Hugo's, nor does Philipp seem to have had to contribute anything more towards his son's support. We may surmise, then, that besides being able to settle the more pressing of his debts through Altmann's generosity, Hugo managed to procure and retain further teaching appointments that provided him with a fairly stable income.

He was no sooner in possession of money again than he moved back to his former quarters at Rennweg 3. There in this winter he produced a few more songs, including his earliest surviving settings of Eichendorff—*Erwartung* (26th January) and *Die Nacht* (3rd February). These were included in the volume of *Eichendorff-Lieder* published in 1889, but were withdrawn later, as not being truly representative, when the opportunity arose for a new edition. *Erwartung* is unique in Wolf's work in seeming to reveal the influence of Brahms. On 13th February he reverted to Heine for the words of an extremely delicate and moving song, *Wie des Mondes Abbild zittert*, an addition to his settings of poems from the *Neue Gedichte*.

There exists a sheet of paper, once used as a cover for a group of manuscripts, with the following inscription:

Lieder und Gesänge
von
N. Lenau und J. Eichendorff.
Fräulein V . . . . F . . . . . geweiht,
von Hugo Wolf.

I. Heft.	II. Heft.
1. *Frage nicht* (Lenau)	5. *Traurige Wege* (Lenau)
2. *Erwartung* (Eichendorff)	6. *Der schwere Abend* (Lenau)
3. *Die Nacht* (Eichendorff)	7. *Verschwiegene Liebe* (Eichendorff)
4. *Herbstentschluss* (Lenau)	8. *Nachruf* (Eichendorff)

Besides providing further evidence of the intimate connection in Wolf's mind of these early songs with Vally Franck—the full name on the dedication has obviously been erased and dots substituted—this document records some lost songs. Here are the two *Eichendorff-Lieder* of January–February 1880, together with three of the Lenau songs from 1878–9. *Nachruf* is another setting of Eichendorff, composed on 7th June of this year, but what of *Der schwere Abend* and *Verschwiegene Liebe*? The former is otherwise quite unknown, while the *Verschwiegene Liebe* that we know so well dates from 1888. This title-page must refer to an earlier version. A sketch of the vocal line of a setting of this poem, quite different from the song of 1888, is in fact to be found on a loose sheet of manuscript paper in the Vienna City Library.[1] Other title-pages to songs that have completely disappeared include a ballad by Hebbel, *Schön Hedwig*, from 1878, a 'first volume' of *Romanzen von J. v. Eichendorff*, containing *Der Kehraus*, *Das zerbrochene Ringlein* and *Der traurige Jäger*, and eight songs from *Des Knaben Wunderhorn*. Lost piano compositions are recorded on title-pages to a *Phantasie* in C, from 1878, and a series of *Reiseblätter nach Gedichten von Lenau*. It is possible, of course, that these things never existed, except in name on these title-pages and as projects in Wolf's mind. Except for *Schön Hedwig* and the *Phantasie*, no dates are given.

On 13th March 1880, his twentieth birthday, Wolf was due to be called up for military service, but for this year he was rejected, probably on account of his retarded physical development, or perhaps owing to steps taken behind the scenes by influential friends. In the following years, too, he was able to obtain deferment or exemption —though not, as we shall see, without at one time actually experiencing life in a barracks. Each year, as the time for his calling up approaches, Philipp Wolf betrays intense anxiety in his letters, and sometimes speculates whether Hugo's friends will show themselves helpful in this matter.

As for his further relationship with Vally Franck, he recalls in one of his letters an excursion to the Kahlenberg with her, which seems to have taken place on 12th May, and shortly after this, on 26th May, the Langs left for Roskosch again. Wolf accompanied them only as far as the station restaurant, where farewells were said. Through Vally he had made the acquaintance of another branch of the Lang family, the children of a brother of Anton Lang's. These were Melanie, who was married to Heinrich Köchert, the Viennese court jeweller, Henriette, Fritz, Karl and Edmund. Wolf's first introduction to the Köcherts had taken place as early as April 1879, but for some time to come he had more to do with the younger members

---

[1] No. 29 in a *Konvolut von Skizzen*. One side of this sheet has the heading *Aus dem Liederstrauss von H. Heine. XIII*, and nothing else. On the reverse are these pencil sketches for *Verschwiegene Liebe*.

* D

of the Lang family. He made a confidante of Henriette ('Hansi') Lang, and with her brother Edmund, a law student at the Vienna University, he struck up what was to become the most intimate and enduring of all his friendships.

Vally wrote to Helene Gabillon from Roskosch of a mood of depression that had descended on her since she had left Vienna. Then on 8th June she wrote again of a 'momentary hardening of the heart' on her side. 'Whether that will continue? Surely not, for I am subject to as many changes of mood as the day has hours.' A month later, on 5th July, she told her friend: '"Ulf" writes often, sometimes very crossly, sometimes very amiably, just as his changeful humour decides.' Meanwhile Wolf himself, after a short visit to his parents at Windischgraz,[1] had returned to Vienna and then moved out for the summer to the tiny village of Maierling in the Wiener Wald.

[1] A letter of Philipp's, posted at Marburg on 8th June, requests definite news as to whether Hugo will be returning to Windischgraz. The reply to this letter has not been preserved. On 27th June, however, Wolf was in his home at Windischgraz, and from there wrote to Edmund Lang: 'We shall see each other at Maierling? I go there to-morrow week.'

V

THE MAIERLING IDYLL, AND AFTER

MAIERLING is situated not far from Baden, about twenty miles to the south of Vienna. On a wintry night of January 1889 the suicide of the Crown Prince Rudolf was to bring this insignificant village a tragic fame, but in 1880 it lay almost forgotten in the shelter of the Wiener Wald, remote and very peaceful. On either side of the principal road were the simple peasants' cottages, and then, on higher ground, surrounded by a wall, the church with its attendant buildings and the village inn. After the tragedy of 1889 the whole of this upper part of the village of Maierling, including the church with its old linden-trees, was razed to the ground by order of the emperor.

Some distance beyond the village on the Heiligenkreuz road, among the orchards and meadows at the edge of the encircling woods, was the Marienhof, a somewhat dilapidated but delightful dwelling-house. In 1880 it was the property of a Viennese advocate, Dr. Joseph Reitzes, who had let it for the summer to the architect Viktor Preyss. Wolf had been introduced by Schönaich to Dr. Reitzes and had become very friendly with his family. He often visited them in Vienna and it is very likely that Dr. Reitzes's influence was behind the improvement that had taken place in Wolf's circumstances in the first half of this year.

Viktor Preyss was occupied with his work in the city during the week, so that Frau Preyss, her sister Bertha von Lackhner, and little Lottchen often found life in the Marienhof somewhat lonely. So when Dr. Reitzes asked if they would object to a young musician, who needed solitude and quiet to continue his studies, occupying a room on the ground floor, it did not take the Preyss family long to decide that he would be welcome.

So Wolf came out to the Marienhof, where he spent some of the happiest months of his life. It seems that he felt at home there from the first, so that they saw all the more delightful side of his character. He was soon on the best of terms with the Preyss family, who treated him as one of themselves. They soon recognized that the actions of this gifted youth were not to be judged by conventional standards,

97

while Wolf, for his own part, seems to have made special efforts to avoid displeasing his hosts.

At first he went down to the village inn for his meals, but later on took them with his new friends. These months in the Marienhof were in complete and happy contrast with his mode of life in the lodging-houses of Vienna. For the first time since he had left his Aunt Vinzenzberg's he enjoyed life as a member of a family: he settled down to their daily routine, helped now and then with the household tasks, read or played the piano to his hosts, and behaved generally just as if he were at home. Most precious of all to him was the quiet; a noisy cockerel, which he used to chase with a large kitchen knife in his hand, and Bauxerl the house-dog, whom he used to tie up to a fence and threaten with a stick, were the only disturbers of the peace.

Frau Preyss and her sister, in whose company he was thrown during most of the week, lacked, perhaps, the brilliant wit and intellect of those Wolf had been accustomed to meet in Goldschmidt's *salon*, but they had a profound love for all that is noble and beautiful in life, and saw clearly that their young friend was greatly gifted. Wolf kept up his friendship with Goldschmidt and his circle for a number of years, but in reading his letters one gains the impression that already the day of their greatest influence on him was past. He was ultimately indebted to Goldschmidt for almost all his other acquaintances, including the Langs, Vally, and the Köcherts, who played so immensely important a part in his later life, and the value of the intellectual initiation which the half-baked young provincial underwent in the company of Goldschmidt and his friends cannot be doubted. But it does seem as if he had come to realize, as the novelty wore off the attractions of opera-house, concert-hall, and musical *salon*, that there was a good deal of pose and insincerity about their easy-going artistic existence, and that to follow them up the primrose path of musical dilettantism was for him to court disaster. In the Lang family he had found friends of his own age, and here at Maierling he found warm-hearted, motherly attention to his needs. Frau Preyss's sister, Bertha von Lackhner, adored by every one for her unfailing kindness, received Hugo into her adopted family; she became his 'Aunt Bertha' and he continued to address her as such for the remainder of his life. The latest in date of the many letters which Frau von Lackhner preserved from her adopted nephew 'Wölferl' is one in which he thanks her for a present she sent on his thirty-seventh birthday—seventeen years after his arrival in the Preyss household at Maierling. Aunt Bertha's was a blithe, sunny, Viennese nature, bubbling over with simple humour and yet sometimes touched with melancholy; out of her goodness of heart she undoubtedly did her best to spoil the little Wölferl, who knew well how to wind her round his finger. His love was never entirely free from tyranny; Aunt Bertha's affection was put to many severe trials, but never found wanting.

In addition to this happy family life in the Marienhof, it was the beauty of the surrounding countryside that made Wolf's stay at Maierling so delightful. There was something elemental about Wolf in his relation to nature, something that made him quiveringly sensitive and responsive to her moods. One of his friends has written: [1] 'I seek him instinctively in the open country, as though he were more easily to be found there than anywhere else.' Like a spirit of the earth or the woods, he would be found lost in thought by the streams, on a narrow pathway through the cornfields, or lying dreaming in the long grass, shading his eyes with his hand and gazing into the sky. The same friend retains the memory of Wolf bending forward at the edge of a lonely pond, his hand to his ear, while he sought to estimate the pitch of the croaking frogs in the reeds among which he stood: 'I see him there in the twilight still, standing and listening: stocky, broad-shouldered, thick-necked like a young faun and yet so light and delicate, as graceful in posture and bearing as Puck, the elf.' In his passionate delight in the beauty of the world there was nothing superficial or conventional; in the face of nature an expression of great solemnity came over his own features. Always he was absorbing impressions that were later to be reflected in his music. All the wonderful evocations of the open air in the *Mörike-Lieder*—the floating clouds, the glowing evening sunlight, the streams murmuring in the night, the music of the birds and bees, the delicate fluttering of a butterfly's wings—are drawn from nature herself and in hearing or singing that last ecstatic cry in *Auf einer Wanderung*, one of the composer's truest masterpieces, we experience again what Wolf himself must once so intensely have felt, on some blissful evening in his own dear Austrian countryside.

In those early years he wandered far over the Wiener Wald, knew its hillsides and grassy hollows, its peaceful villages, oak and beech woods and dark pine forests, its running streams and dreaming ponds.

[1] Edmund Hellmer, *Hugo Wolf : Erlebtes und Erlauschtes* (Vienna, 1921).

Here too were romantic ruined castles from the Middle Ages. The monastery of Heiligenkreuz lies very near to Maierling, half an hour's walk over the hill and down into the Sattelbach valley, and this became a favourite excursion of Wolf's. In a letter to his parents on 17th July he describes the powerful impression made upon him by this building and compares it with St. Paul where he had formerly been at school.

There the monastery lies on an eminence, one must gaze upwards; here the road is higher than the towers of the abbey and one must look downwards. That gives one no special opinion of Heiligenkreuz. But one must have been inside it to see all the wonder and dreams of romanticism resurrected. Yes! I was so delighted and so moved that I had no other wish than this—to be a monk! But how mean and dreary St. Paul's is! I can no longer remember quite clearly, but St. Paul has not a cloister in the purest Gothic style, and above all no stained glass, a principal feature of the Middle Ages, and it is essentially the lack of the latter that makes St. Paul look so uninteresting and exert so little influence upon the visitor. Nothing puts me in such a poetical mood as a while (especially in the twilight) spent dreaming in the cloisters, in order to escape for a time from the less poetical present.

Sometimes the great organ of Heiligenkreuz would be heard far and wide over the hills and in the woods. Small wonder that the impressionable young Wolf numbered his Maierling days among the happiest of his life, there where nature and the romantic past seemed to have survived inviolate together.

At first the financial problems which arose especially in the summer months threatened to become troublesome again. The letter which pictures Hugo dreaming blissfully in the cloisters of Heiligenkreuz ends with an appeal for money. 'I've got 2 kreuzers left, must borrow stamps so that I can write to you, and I can assure you, lest you put the blame on Vally, that I have only written to her once. Please, please, send me 3 florins at once and don't blame me for it.' Hugo's request, considering that he was reduced to 2 kreuzers, was modest enough, but poor Philipp's reply is astonishing: 'In the fold [of the letter] you'll find only 2 florins, as I have got no more.' Affairs at Windischgraz must indeed have been in a bad way when Hugo asked for the equivalent of five shillings and his father could only send him three and sixpence! Philipp suggested that Hugo should return home, rather than starve at Maierling, and looked round for possible pupils among his own acquaintances. His next letter, however, reveals that the threatened crisis was evaded by Hugo

borrowing 30 florins.   The kindly Dr. Reitzes was the benefactor in
this case and he also hired a piano for use in the Marienhof from a
dealer at Baden.   It was at this time, too, that Wolf began to take
his meals with the Preyss family.   His father was much relieved at
this turn of events, but was still lavish with warnings, phrased with
his customary felicity: 'Be careful with the money, for it is painful to
have to sponge on such people—I'd rather eat grass!'

Among the visitors who came out to Maierling as guests of the
Preyss family were their relatives the Werners.   Wolf made their
acquaintance in the first weeks of his stay there and this family, too,
became and remained his lifelong friends.   For their little son, the
seven-year-old Heinrich, the meeting with Wolf, about whom he had
already heard various strange stories, was of far-reaching significance.
Heinrich Werner has himself described the occasion.[1]

It was in the dining-room on the ground floor of the Marienhof; all was
prepared for the midday meal, when finally Wolf came in the door.   With
enchanting amiability he greeted every one, those he knew already and also
the strangers, including myself, who stood shyly in a corner.   There fell
forward at each bow his long, dark-blonde hair, which he tossed back again
with a quick movement.   I was decidedly disillusioned.   For I had pictured the 'wild Wolf' to myself as very much wilder!

Young Werner's disappointment was soon dispelled; shyness and
reserve on both sides gave way to trusting friendship.   Nothing is
more likable in Wolf than his captivating way with children.   He
won them at once with his impish sense of humour, his powers of
mimicry, and the extraordinary grimaces into which he loved to twist
his features.   This was a new kind of grown-up, with unusual ideas
about the relative importance of things.   The village schoolmaster
from Alland used to come to Maierling to teach Lottchen in the upper
storey of the Marienhof, and the lessons were sometimes interrupted
by a mocking voice at the window, which Wolf had reached by
clambering up the wooden balcony, or from the top of an apple-tree
outside the house.   In such incidents the children recognized an ally.
They found his conversation fascinating; he would hold solemn discussions on the most unusual subjects, frequently invoking the
Devil.   Wolf was also fond of using curious words and phrases, from
dialects and foreign languages, such as 'ruppig,' 'schnuppe,'
'schnitzu,' and 'meschugge.'   'Ruppig' was the word he always used
to describe his own ill humour.

[1] 'Erinnerungen an Hugo Wolf' (*Die Einkehr*. *Beilage der Münchner
Neuesten Nachrichten*, 26th August 1922).

The young Werner became a great favourite. After only a very short acquaintance he was allowed to address Wolf as 'Du,' while he himself was known as 'Signor Heinrich' or 'Enrico.' He used to climb on Wolf's shoulders and ride him about the garden, roll with him down grassy 'precipices,' and engage him in butting matches. The boy became devoted to Wolf, and as the succeeding years brought no serious interruption of their friendship, he grew up completely under the domination of Wolf's tyrannical affection. An irresistible magnetic force held Heinrich Werner fast till the end of his days. He treasured the memory of this lifelong intimacy and, after Wolf's death had brought it to an end, continued to devote his energies to the Wolfian cause. Besides setting down his own memories in writing in a number of short volumes of great charm, editing many of the composer's letters for publication, reprinting, in collaboration with Richard Batka, the musical criticisms from the *Salonblatt*, and working as secretary to the Hugo Wolf Verein, he was constantly engaged in finding out new material and persuading others to allow their correspondence to be printed. When in 1913 he published his delightful *Hugo Wolf in Maierling*, a book solely concerned with the composer's connections with this little village in the Wiener Wald, which is barely mentioned by Decsey, his account was so rich in happy memories, so full of Wolf's fantastically humorous letters and poems from this period, that there was no little difficulty in reconciling this smiling portrait with the subject of the earlier biographies.

Heinrich Werner's sister Mizzi often sang for Wolf, sometimes his own early compositions. When he was particularly well satisfied he would reward her with a cup of the strong black coffee that he prepared himself. He kept a watchful eye on the development of her musical tastes. One day he found a book of songs by Carl Hofmann in her possession and ruthlessly tore the brand-new score in half. He also thundered against Riedel's settings of poems from Scheffel's *Trompeter von Säckingen*, which were then very popular.

Frau Marie Werner also got on well with Wolf, but with Heinrich's father there were difficulties at first. Like many of the older genera- tion of his time, without possessing any particular interest in music he yet regarded Wagner and the Wagnerians with great suspicion. He therefore looked askance at Wolf's increasing influence over his children, who were being demoralized with Wagner's music and with Wolf's own strong black coffee. But in the end he too was converted and in later years made the pilgrimage to Bayreuth as a confessed Wagnerian. The Werners' own summer residence was at Perchtoldsdorf, or 'Petersdorf,' as the country people call it, half an hour's journey by rail from Vienna and about four hours' walk from Maierling. Wolf often undertook this long excursion on foot. There he lay for hours in the grass with the children, helped to gather the grapes from the vines, and played skittles with great enthusiasm. For a number of years Wolf was to continue to enter this house at Perchtoldsdorf as a summer visitor, and in the winter and early spring of 1888 it was here that the majority of his *Mörike-Lieder* were composed. In those later years he still retained his passion for the game of skittles which he had first acquired in his Maierling days.

So the summer of 1880 went by in the peaceful seclusion of the Marienhof. Each morning the Preyss family gathered for breakfast under the apple-trees; then Wolf would put in an appearance, clad in his brown velvet jacket, with artist's cravat, looking, as every one agreed, exactly like the young Mozart. Often he had something important to communicate—a chapter from Schopenhauer or Jean Paul—before settling down to the meal. Father Preyss would go off to his work in the city, while Wolf would retire to his den to study music or to compose. For he had taken up his unfinished String Quartet in D minor again. The history of this work is very involved and confused, and it is not easy to decide how much of it was written at Maierling in this summer, but, at any rate, at the head of the slow movement stands the inscription in the score: 'Maierling bei Baden, July 9th, 1880.' After the midday meal the two ladies would retire for an hour's rest, and Wolf used to show his disapproval by choosing just this time to make the Marienhof resound with his piano playing. Then towards the evening he would set out on a walk through the woods, or perhaps accompany Aunt Bertha on a shopping expedition to Alland. During rainy weather he used to play to his house companions for hours on end. We hear no more about Brahms, but a good deal about Wagner; the *Ring*, *Die Meistersinger*, and *Tristan*, of which the last had not yet been produced in Vienna, were performed by Wolf from the piano scores. Some curious 'Paraphrases' of Wagnerian operas—*Die Meistersinger* and *Die Walküre*—are probably relics of Maierling days; they were given to Dr. Reitzes, the owner of the Marienhof. It is strange to find Wolf, of all people, producing pieces of this kind. Another favourite work, which, in those days, he used to play to all his acquaintances, was Marschner's *Hans Heiling*. Almost every one who knew him speaks too of the compelling intensity with which he used to sing Loewe's ballads.

At Maierling he had also plenty of opportunity to indulge his passion for reading: Viktor Preyss kept him supplied with books from the city. Wolf is said to have busied himself with Wagner's prose writings and the philosophy of Schopenhauer, although in the latter subject there is no evidence that he had got beyond the lighter reading of the *Parerga und Paralipomena*. Goethe's *Faust*, Gottfried Keller, especially *Der grüne Heinrich*, Heine's poems and *Reisebilder*, Lenau, Kleist, Immermann's *Münchhausen* and *Tulifäntchen*, E. T. A. Hoffmann, and Jean Paul—these names and titles give some idea of his tastes in German literature. Among foreign writers he discovered and liked Turgenev, Lermontov, Leopardi, Scott, Byron, Mark Twain, Dickens, Sterne, Molière, Rabelais, Mérimée, and Claude Tillier's *Mon Oncle Benjamin*. We notice here, besides romantic tendencies, a pronounced taste for the masterpieces of humour.

Hugo passed on some of these books to his father. On 5th September he sent him the Heine *Reisebilder* and Kleist's *Prinz von Homburg* and *Der zerbrochene Krug*. 'The volume of Heine belongs to Frl. Franck, so please take care of the book, so that it doesn't in the end plop into a bowl of porridge. Read the *Harzreise* straight away. The "Ideas" are delightful beyond measure.' Philipp replied on 25th September: 'Kleist gives me much pleasure: Heine also entertains me. I should like, when the opportunity arises, to read more of both of them.'

Only once was there a serious disagreement between Wolf and his hosts in the Marienhof. It arose out of a discussion in which he insisted that only black-haired women were beautiful. This was of course a Wolfian compliment to Vally Franck. Frau Preyss told him plainly not to be so stupid, whereupon he retired to his room in displeasure and remained there until Frau Preyss was persuaded to beg his pardon.

Maierling was the scene of what must be regarded as the climax of the long-drawn-out love-affair between Hugo Wolf and Vally Franck. It seems that Vally herself came alone to Alland, a few miles from Maierling, and took lodgings there for a few days. This is a very mysterious episode, upon which Vally's letters to Helene Gabillon throw no illumination. Vally never mentioned her secret excursion to Alland to her friend, either by letter or word of mouth, for she knew that she would find no support or sympathy for this audacious move, in defiance of prudence and the strict convention of the time. Her silence may also in part have been imposed by Hugo, for earlier in the year he had thrown off in a spleenful moment his teaching appointment to Dora Gabillon by means of an outrageous letter to his pupil's mother.   He could no longer, he had declared, continue to teach such an unmusical goose; it would kill him to have anything more to do with such an untalented person.

The episode at Alland is known only through the researches of Heinrich Werner.   Vally's aunt can obviously never have known anything of her niece's intention of going there.   The previously quoted letter of 5th July mentions a forthcoming visit to Reichenau in August.   There she was the guest of a married friend and it seems likely that she went in secret from Reichenau to Vienna and Alland for a few days.

We can only imagine what burning words of Hugo's could have impelled her to take this step.   His inquisitive friends at Maierling are said to have observed the lovers through a telescope as they embraced and kissed on one of the surrounding woody heights.[1] A wandering tinker carried love-letters between the Marienhof and Alland.

Vally returned to Paris in the autumn; her letters to Helene Gabillon became much more infrequent after this summer, so that her movements cannot be determined with any precision, but she seems to have spent the whole of the following winter in France after her long stay of two and a half years with the Lang family.

Philipp Wolf, in his letter of 25th September, inquired about the artistic results of Hugo's stay at Maierling.

In all your letters you are silent about the products of your summer holiday. Was the Quartet finished? Will it be heard at Graz in the winter? That would truly be a great surprise for us, however much certain people might be annoyed at your better success than their own. You may yourself be annoyed at my insistence, but I am not to be dissuaded that *Graz* is the only right place for the attainment of your aims. . . . You have had enough leisure in the Marienhof to create something decent.

'Was the Quartet finished?' asked Philipp, and the answer to this question still evades us.   It can only be said with certainty that Wolf did some work upon it during this summer at Maierling.   The

---

[1] It should be recorded that Vally Franck is known to have objected to certain aspects of the account of her relationship with Wolf in Werner's *Hugo Wolf in Maierling*.

existing last movement was only added in 1884, but perhaps replaced an earlier one.[1]

Wolf's Quartet shows many signs of a close study of the quartets and sonatas of Beethoven's last period. Although its composer was already acquainted with most of the later works of Wagner, there is little trace of their influence. Apart from the obvious reflection of the *Lohengrin* Prelude at the beginning of the slow movement, it is Beethoven's shadow that is felt to lie heavily over the whole composition, but in place of the unearthly wisdom, joy, and sadness of

---

[1] The following is a summary of what we know of the history of this work.

Wolf told his parents in a letter that the 'third movement' of the Quartet was completed in the night of 30th–31st December 1878. On 8th January 1879 he wrote: 'I am working fairly fast on the String Quartet.' The end of the third movement (scherzo) is dated in the score 16th January 1879. It would seem that between 31st December and 16th January some revision of the scherzo took place, and perhaps also work on another movement.

The beginning of the first movement is dated in the score 20th January 1879. On 7th April Wolf told his father he had given up the Quartet, 'because it did not seem to me good enough to complete.' This decision was later abandoned. The rough drafts of a great part of the first, second, and last movements are among the manuscripts purchased by the National Library in Vienna from the Köchert family in 1940. They show that work on the first movement was resumed (at the point corresponding to p. 18, beginning of line 3, of the published miniature score) at Windischgraz on 25th June, and that this movement was completed there on 8th July.

In the score the opening of the slow movement has the inscription: 'Maierling bei Baden, 9th July 1880,' but there is evidence to show that that date probably only applies to the introductory passage (bars 1–52). The rough draft of the greater part of this slow movement, beginning with the principal melody 'breit, innig' (p. 29, line 2 of the published score), is also in the National Library and the heading 'Second movement' shows that this was originally the opening of this movement. This manuscript is undated but another fragment, this time in the Vienna City Library (*Konvolut von Skizzen*, No. 27), has the principal theme with the date 15th April. This may have been either 1879 or 1880. In either case the movement originally began with this theme, and the greater part of it existed in manuscript before the introductory bars were added at Maierling on 9th July 1880.

No date of composition is given in either the score or the rough draft of the last movement. A letter to Franz Russ says little work was done at Maierling in 1880, and the use of the term 'study' for Wolf's room there was only ironic. A letter to Henriette Lang on 26th January 1881 shows that the Quartet had then recently been performed, from which it would seem that it *must* have been completed either at Maierling or in Vienna in the next few months. But if the Quartet as performed in 1881 had a fourth movement, it was not identical with that of the work as we know it to-day. The theme in B flat (p. 54 of the miniature score) occurs, in B, in a sketch-book preserved in the National Library, Vienna, with the surprising date '11th July 1884.' Further, for the rough draft of this movement a sheet of manuscript paper was utilized which had previously served for the *Prinz von Homburg* monologue—composed definitely in 1884. The whole last movement of the Quartet must date from 1884. But did it replace an earlier *finale*?

Wolf in his 'Daten aus meinem Leben,' under 1879, says 'First Quartet written.' In a letter to Gustav Schur on 18th December 1891 he writes of 'a Quartet from the year 1880.'

Beethoven's third period there is in Wolf's Quartet a turbulent strength and cataclysmic intensity of suffering, such as only youth is able to conceive or support. If the work is seldom performed, this is as much due to just this quality of youthful extravagance of feeling as to the admitted awkwardness of much of the actual writing. The texture of the work is often so close that it is doubtful whether all the details can ever be made to sound clear in performance. We are reminded of how, when he was orchestrating *Der Corregidor* at Schloss Matzen in 1895, Wolf was tempted continually to weave new counterpoints into his score—beautiful but entangling growths which have to be pruned away again before the work can be heard.

A tense, dramatic introduction leads to an *allegro appassionato* of enormous length and tremendous emotional stress. In this movement sonata form is expanded almost out of recognition. The short, pregnant themes are barely presented before they are combined together, transformed, and developed, together with a short figure taken from the introduction, in a complex web of impassioned musical argument. 'Entbehren sollst Du, sollst entbehren,' the quotation from Goethe's *Faust* which Wagner applied as a motto to the first movement of Beethoven's ninth Symphony, stands also at the head of Wolf's score. Some intense Faustian struggle in the young man's soul—the inner conflict, which he confided to no one, either by word of mouth or in his letters—is here worked out in purely musical terms. The introduction to the slow movement breathes something of the peace of the woodland solitudes among which it was written, but hammering, threatening rhythms break in upon the noble cantilena that follows; this movement too is not after all to be free from struggle. Out of the opening high, sustained chords for the three upper instruments, the succeeding recitative-like passage for the cello, which returns later with rich contrapuntal embroidery, the hammering figures, and the sublime, Beethovenian song, like an eloquent prayer of thanksgiving, Wolf constructs an extended movement of really wonderful beauty and nobility. The music is of great strength and, what is especially remarkable in a young man of nineteen or twenty, of great *austerity*. It is utterly free from any suggestion of self-pitying or erotic sentimentality. The forceful, resolute, scherzo-like movement which follows again recalls Beethoven quite unmistakably, both in the thematic material and in its treatment. The last movement, combining elements of both sonata and rondo forms, is by no means free from the sense of conflict that pervades the whole work, though the delicious lyrical second subject brings unalloyed content for a space, with hints of the later humorous manner of the *Italian Serenade*. This finale has inexhaustible vitality and driving energy, and brings this truly astonishing work to a convincing conclusion.

There had been nothing in the young Wolf's output up to this time to suggest that he was capable of such sustained creative achievements. The epic breadth of the design of this Quartet, the daring freedom of its forms, the sheer mastery over stubborn musical material, impel one to wonder what Brahms would have said if, instead of a few songs, he had been shown this work. Could he have been in any doubt about the nature of the 'talent' possessed by the young composer? Would he not have been compelled to recognize an affinity between this Quartet and the heaven-storming works of his own youth?

Wolf returned from Maierling to his old quarters in Vienna, Rennweg 3, at the end of September or the beginning of October. In the succeeding winter he often visited the friends he had made at Maierling—the Preyss family, Aunt Bertha, and the Werners. He became increasingly friendly with Vally's cousins, the Langs. Another friend of his own age whose name begins to appear in Wolf's letters of this time was Heinrich Rauchberg, a brilliant law student at the Vienna University. This was another friendship that was to endure for many years. In the house of Rauchberg's parents Wolf was a frequent and welcome guest. Rauchberg himself was a great admirer of Wolf's music and afterwards wrote the first considerable essay upon his work to appear in print.[1]

There were the usual difficulties about procuring teaching appointments. Wolf had by the end of September spent the 30 florins he had obtained from Dr. Reitzes and had to ask his father for 12 florins to keep him going until he had re-established himself in Vienna. Then a fortnight later came a further request for assistance, which brought forth the following reply from Philipp Wolf on 9th October:

Your last letter has very much grieved and depressed me, and you may now say what you like, you have failed. . . . You read Schopenhauer and the like, instead of music you cultivate thoughts of suicide, you drink the strongest coffee, which undermines your whole nervous system, you worship Wagner as something quite unattainable. Why cleave to an idea

---

[1] 'Neue Lieder und Gesänge' (*Österreichisch-Ungarische Revue*, November–December 1889). It was preceded only by Theodor Helm's concert notices and reviews in the *Deutsche Zeitung*.

that you never venture to realize, of which you yourself despair? What did you do at Maierling? You have used up the 30 florins that Dr. Reitzes lent you; wouldn't it have been more sensible to have remained at home and to have lived in the family circle somewhat more comfortably than is your wont? What will you do in Vienna without lessons? Who gave you so many *vain* hopes?—for you told me that this winter you would get many good lessons and now suddenly *none at all*!!! If it were not for the military service I would say go home and begin to do something else, since music gets you nowhere.

Altmann probably made his escape so that he should not be sponged on by you. It is humiliating to sponge on people for money, it's like beggary. If you can't keep yourself with lessons in Vienna then say farewell and go home—as long as I live we shall still have something to eat, but to send you ready money to Vienna so that you can live is bitter and makes *great* difficulties, for money is hard to earn. There are many markets where I earn nothing, even pay out, and the best market often brings in scarcely 10 florins net gain. How one must plague oneself about a few paltry florins!

I consider as your true friends only those who procure you work, so that you never need blush. Presents are still presents, however delicately they may be given. I can only send you 15 florins to-day, and if you see that you cannot manage to live on your lessons, utilize this money for the journey home, even at the risk of becoming a soldier. There are plenty of people doing that who are as good as you—at least you would not need to be under an obligation to anybody.... Farewell, and take my words to heart, you have no more candid friend than your sorely troubled father.

Philipp always expected the worst, and it seems that Hugo had better prospects than his father thought. He seems somehow to have procured, or to have had the hope of procuring very shortly, no less than 90 florins and to have written to his father in optimistic terms. But Philipp was hard to convince that any great improvement was at hand:

Your professed hope has not raised my spirits. You are a luckless fellow like myself, the sun will never shine clearly for us. In the Book of Fate it is written that my children shall bring me only trouble and no joy, but if it makes an exception of you, that will be gratefully accepted and will reconcile me to my fate, that oppresses me so bitterly. Save your money for bad times. You know that I cannot always keep pace with my good intentions, for trouble often hangs on to me to the point of suffocation. Farewell, and bring soon light into my dark existence.

Philipp's chief cause for anxiety was not so much Hugo, but the youngest son Gilbert, who had returned to Vienna, where he had found employment, but after only one month had thrown over his job and was now, according to his father, 'lounging about in Vienna,' without money and without the intention of finding work. A number of Philipp's letters to Hugo are entirely devoted to the problem of Gilbert.   In the circumstances it is not surprising that Philipp's reactions to Hugo's occasional requests for assistance should have been so violent.   Philipp Wolf was almost broken by his misfortunes; he was certainly a psycho-pathological border-line case. Some of his letters touch measureless depths of despondency.

Modesta will endeavour to get me a position as administrator, or, if nothing else, as housekeeper.   Here I am only a harassed journeyman leather-worker, household menial, and martyr, who has coffee in the morning (so-so!), a scanty midday meal, and supper every Sunday.   For special amusement there are the markets near and far.

On 5th December another letter of Hugo's led to this appalling outburst:

So you have no longer enough money for a stamp, out of the 90 florins! Either you lied to me about that or you are a spendthrift, who retains no money. . . .   You live continually at other people's expense and cannot even support yourself.   This *dolce far niente* you have in common with Gilbert.   Both want to live comfortably and well, do nothing, sponge on the whole world. . . .   You have already contracted all the caprices and bad habits of Beethoven, also his brutal, repulsive behaviour, but of his industry and his economy and creative work there is no trace.   You do just what pleases you.

Yesterday there came into my hands one of the prefect's letters[1] in which he reproaches me that I give you your own way in everything and all too seldom energetically admonish you, and prophesies that nothing will come of you unless I go hand in hand with him.   Unfortunately he was right and I was blind.   Your mother too was right, I was too indulgent, and to your misfortune you are spoiled.   Your parents have borne the pain and the cares of so many sacrifices and privations in order to make something worth while out of you—in vain! . . .   If you have a spark of feeling for your parents pull yourself together, *work and renounce*, else you are lost!!! Enclosed are the last 6 florins of your unhappy father. . . .   Like a tortured man the thumbscrews are put on me by my own children.   My working strength is unscrupulously exploited by so many children in irresponsible ways, in my old age I must *work like a slave*. . . .   Oh, would the last day were already come!   Hope supported me earlier, now that too is gone, life is to me only torment, and God only knows what trials yet stand before me.   All Meizer's children together did not make so much trouble as *one* of mine, and yet he hanged himself!   Have I not a thousand reasons for such a dishonourable action?

Such despairing reflections from Philipp, and the misadventures of Gilbert, are probably the cause of the noticeable diminution at this period in the number of Hugo's family letters which have been made

---

[1] Clearly from the Marburg Gymnasium.

public. It cannot be doubted that Hugo, devoted as he was to both parents, suffered endless pain and distress from the frequent disharmonies in the family life at Windischgraz and from his father's incurable despondency. It at first seems that the young Wolf reveals himself with remarkable clarity in his correspondence with his parents. Yet the doubt persists, in the face of these letters of Philipp's: how much of Hugo's expression of indomitable courage and serene confidence in his success in the near future, sustained as it was through year after year of extreme penury and failure, was a defensive measure against his father's reproaches and despair? Was Hugo consistently *making allowances* for Philipp's pessimism?

Besides the letters of Philipp Wolf there is very little information available about Hugo's life during this winter of 1880–1. A much more pleasant impression, however, is given by two deeply affectionate letters written to his mother at the end of December wherein he recalls with emotion the Christmas festivities of his early childhood. On Christmas Eve Wolf had returned to his room in the Rennweg and had been astonished to find there a gaily decorated Christmas-tree—secretly provided, as he subsequently learned, by his adopted aunt Bertha. This charming and wholly unexpected attention called up innumerable memories of his home and parents, in those earlier years before the fire of 1867 had destroyed his father's property and happiness. He lit the candles and in their friendly light, shining among the tinsel decorations of the tree, he sank deep in meditation, recalling past Christmases and birthdays of his childhood, with all the dear family rites and customs associated with them. Then he went out into the dark streets, where he wandered aimlessly until far into Christmas morning.

Unless we decide to include the problematical last movement of the String Quartet among the compositions of this winter, not very much was achieved in the creative sphere. On 26th November he set to music *Sterne mit den goldnen Füsschen*, another poem from Heine's *Neue Gedichte*. This is a most delicately beautiful song, the glassy transparency of the accompaniment hinting at the later masterpiece *O wär' dein Haus durchsichtig wie ein Glas* in the *Italian Song Book* of 1896. Then on 24th December Wolf composed his first song to words by Eduard Mörike. *Suschens Vogel* is by no means highly characteristic either of Wolf or of Mörike, but the composer's earliest connection with this poet, whose name was afterwards to become indelibly associated with his own, deserves attention. It is possible that he may have been drawn to Mörike by Schumann's song settings, of which there are five, or he may have been first introduced to the somewhat neglected poet by Goldschmidt, who turned to Mörike for the words of a number of his own compositions.[1]

Apart from these two completed songs there are only a few fragments and a variant to the 1878 setting of Heine's *Mir träumte von einem Königskind*, written on 20th January 1881. A letter to Henriette Lang of 26th January is interesting in this connection. Wolf was once again endeavouring to secure publication for his compositions and had sent a group of seven Heine songs to Kistner at Leipzig. It may be surmised that this was the *Liederstrauss* from the *Buch der Lieder* and that the revision of *Mir träumte von einem Königskind* was undertaken while preparing the manuscript for submission to the publisher. Kistner rejected Wolf's songs, like André and Breitkopf & Härtel before him.

The above-mentioned letter to Henriette Lang also reveals that at this time he began to give piano lessons to Frau Melanie Köchert, Henriette's sister, and that his String Quartet was performed for him in private at the house of Natalie Bauer-Lechner, who played second violin in the Soldat-Röger Quartet, and whose reminiscences of Gustav Mahler are fairly well known. The performance of the Quartet did not at all satisfy the young composer, who, as he wrote, 'had to watch with secret shuddering how the four assassins, who at a sign from himself swung their murderous instruments, horribly mutilated his child.'

The winter of 1880–1 seems to have been the period of his greatest intimacy with a group of friends, moving chiefly in artistic circles, which centred round the personality of Dr. Friedrich Umlauft. Umlauft was connected with the Austrian Geographic Society and edited a long series of volumes devoted to the beauties of the Austro-Hungarian provinces. Wolf often visited his household, where he associated also with Franz Russ, the painter, brother of the better-known landscape painter Robert Russ, with a Dr. Crone, and with Dr. Josef Jüttner, a professor at the Mariahilfer Gymnasium. Jüttner, as a young man, had been engaged as tutor to the two Gabillon daughters, and, in consequence, had the honour of becoming one of the earliest of Vally Franck's victims.

[1] *Das verlassene Mägdlein, Erinnerungen, Verborgenheit, Denk' es o Seele, Schlafendes Jesuskind, Zum neuen Jahr*, and *Nachtgesang*, all but two of which were afterwards set by Wolf, who had, however, himself been in possession of Mörike's poems since 1878, as a volume in the Vienna City Library shows.

That young lady herself, as we have seen, had been throughout this winter in the south of France, and from Cannes, on 12th February 1881, she wrote again to Helene Gabillon describing in the highest spirits the joys of the carnival.   This is the letter quoted by Frau Bettelheim-Gabillon in her portrait-sketch of Vally in the previous chapter.   In spite of having fallen in love with three young men at once, however, the dearest of all those who pleased her, she confessed, was still 'the little brown-eyed "Ulf," when he doesn't grumble and when everything doesn't go wrong between us, as in the previous winter.'   That is the last reference to Wolf in Vally's correspondence with her friend.   Within two months of this letter she wrote to Hugo himself conclusively breaking off their relationship.   Nothing is known of her reasons for this step.   Perhaps she had come to realize the lack of any prospect of a happy ending to this strange courtship, in view of Hugo's continued inability to support even himself and the long periods of separation imposed by circumstances, or she may have found the admiration of one of her new friends of the Riviera Carnival more precious even than that of the 'little brown-eyed "Ulf." '

Poor Hugo suffered intensely.   Although he had not seen Vally for the past six months he was so far from forgetting her that the shock of his dismissal almost drove him out of his mind.   Heart-broken, he packed up with tears her letters and a few pitiful souvenirs —a cape, a ring, some coloured ribbons, and fragments of a torn veil —and posted them back to Vally, receiving in return his own letters to her, which he burnt.

The break seems to have occurred in April, or possibly at the end of March.   The earliest evidence of the change in their relationship is the confession and expression of Wolf's tortured feelings in a long and confused letter to Henriette Lang on 26th April,[1] in which involved and remarkably mixed metaphors are carried on through pages. The grievous wound was then obviously almost unbearably painful.

This month of April also saw the composition of the six *Geistliche Lieder* for mixed chorus, to poems by Eichendorff.   *Resignation* was written on the 1st, *Einklang* on the 14th, *Letzte Bitte* on the 22nd, *Ergebung* on the 28th, and *Erhebung* on the 30th; the date of composition of the remaining chorus, *Aufblick*, is not known.   Ignorance

---

[1] No. 2 of the *Briefe an Henriette Lang*, edited by Werner (Regensburg, 1923), where it appears without the date.   This correspondence was previously printed in the *Deutsche Rundschau* for November 1921, and there this letter is dated from Vienna, 26th April 1881.

of the precise time of Wolf's rejection by Vally Franck makes it impossible to decide definitely whether the creation of these remarkable works had any close connection with the emotional upheaval which the composer endured at about the same time. It seems at least possible, however, that they may have been the artistic product and sublimation of his sufferings in this crisis.

The six choruses form a cycle, in the form of a nocturnal meditation in four parts, within the framework of a declaration, *Aufblick*, and a reaffirmation, *Erhebung*, of religious faith. The arrangement of the poems is Wolf's own and he also gave them titles differing from those of the poet, in accordance with the design of his own work. After the introductory *Aufblick*, the heart of the cycle commences with the mystical *Einklang*. Eichendorff's emotional simplicity—in spite of his poetical obscurities—is reflected in Wolf's severe, chorale-like music, after which the opening of the following chorus, *Resignation*, with its rather self-consciously artistic part-writing, is not easy to assimilate. *Resignation*, however, has many beauties:

Come, silent Night, solace of the world! The years like clouds have flown: I am alone, forgotten, except for thy consoling presence. Come, Night, I am so weary of the day: let me rest from cares and pleasures until the eternal sunrise.[1]

The music of the rustling forests among which the poet sits pervades the piece from beginning to end. The same plea is developed with greater intensity in *Letzte Bitte*:

Like a lost warrior, wounded to death, I totter and can go no further. Quiet night covers the earth. Lord, give me peace at last, I no longer wish or hope for anything more.

The music modulates wearily until it finds rest in its closing bars. Then with *Ergebung* comes the ultimate submission:

Thy will be done, Lord! Have mercy upon us sinners; in deepest woe my face is bowed to the dust. Thy will be done.

In this chorus Wolf touches sublimity. The sadness of the music is heart-rending, and in the passionately pleading section in E major:

> O mit uns Sündern gehe
> Erbarmend ins Gericht.
> Ich beug' im tiefsten Wehe
> Zum Staub mein Angesicht,

[1] Freely paraphrased.

the twenty-one-year-old composer, prostrate in the dust, seems to voice the plea of the whole of suffering humanity.   This was the piece which was sung behind the altar of the Votivkirche, with shattering effect, as Wolf's own mortal remains were consigned to the earth after intolerable sufferings.   It has been suggested that these works owe their inception to an emotional crisis in his own life. That may well have been the case, but the products of that upheaval were in no way weakly subjective in character.   Wolf had already attained the artistic detachment from purely personal events and emotions which represented his aesthetic ideal, and to which he remained true for the whole of the rest of his life.   After the nobility and overwhelming sadness of *Ergebung* the final chorus, *Erhebung*, an optimistic affirmation of belief in the power of prayer, is unconvincing.   The music is less interesting in itself, but the real flaw, if the cycle be viewed as a whole, is the lack of any adequate transition from the mood of the penultimate chorus to that of the last.

The composer retained a good opinion of these choruses in later years and his letters show that he thought of publishing them in 1892 and again in 1894.   On one of these occasions he seems to have revised them.

On 12th May 1881 Wolf wrote again to Henriette Lang: since 26th April, he told her, he had written three letters which he had afterwards thought it better to destroy, owing to their confusion of style and extravagance of expression.   Helene Gabillon's recent engagement to Hans Bettelheim had made the thought of the unhappy outcome of his own love-affair unbearable and induced many bitter reflections.   In the destroyed letters, he wrote, he had held Vally to be more to blame than perhaps she really was.

His despair found expression too in letters to his parents and aroused their concern.   Both his father and his mother did their best to provide consolation and advice.   Katharina suggested travel for the sake of distracting his mind, while Philipp found occasion for some characteristic utterances upon the fate of mankind in this vale of woe:

How few mortals are content with their lot; each one has something to wish for; no one is entirely happy, and if any one *were* so, he could not, in the face of so many unhappy people, himself feel content.

So it came about that, after two months of bitterness and black despair in Vienna, Wolf returned to seek his lost peace of mind in his home at Windischgraz.   From there he continued to unburden his heart to Henriette Lang in a series of intimate letters. At first his life there was not so tedious as he had expected. 'When one thinks about something dreadful,' he wrote, 'one is much more despairing than when one actually experiences it; the imagination is everything. So it was with me about Windischgraz. The thought of having to stay at Windischgraz for the summer could thoroughly deject me. But the nearer I drew to the dreaded place the more it lost all dreadfulness for me.' He even seems to have sought consolation in friendship with another woman.

My parents don't let me feel that I am at Windischgraz; also a new acquaintance, the wife of one of the district court officials here, a pretty, young, clever, exceedingly charming, sensitive woman, gifted with an excellent voice and outstanding musical sensibility, makes my stay here more than just bearable. She knows Brahms personally and enthuses dreadfully over his compositions. I was downright envious to have to listen to his praise from such lovely lips. That seemed to me doubly unjust and I suddenly began to prepare a dreadful bath of blood among his musical offspring, like a second Herod.

Wolf then played for her two acts of *Tristan* and was able to look forward with confidence to her conversion. Finally, 'she wishes to hear my songs and to sing them. They first really come to life when *she* sings them.'

But the consolation he found there was only illusory: by 26th June he had come to recognize that he had been deceiving himself. 'The woman,' he then wrote, 'is as ugly as an owl and croaks like a screechowl.' In the same letter he describes his nights of anguish and the recurring dreams of Vally on account of which he was afraid to sleep.

There she appears to me, so fair and gentle, as I have else only seen her with the eyes of the soul. Happy pictures of blissful companionship then flow past, just as it once really was—she loves me—O God! why, *why* must it no longer be true, what I dreamed and what once made us both so happy? This brooding and puzzling, the lack of all hope, her cruelty, which yet stands in such remarkable contrast to her goodness, which then brings me again to the thought that she was not conscious at all of the step she took and is still not yet returned to awareness, to measure the monstrous consequences—in thinking over all that the night passes, broken into by the most violent outbursts of anguish, and only with the grey of morning a good fairy grants me an hour of rest and no longer conjures up dream-spirits in the shape of the loved one. Far more dreadful are the dreams in which she turns away from me, does not know me, in which I hear clearly the words, 'I do not love you.' To wake from that, a thousand times to call her name, often to lie there as if in catalepsy, while the brain glows in fever-heat. Oh, to bear these torments requires much courage!

A letter to Bertha von Lackhner a little later, on 22nd July, also refers to his loss and his intense sufferings, and may stand here, to close this account of Hugo Wolf's first love-affair, as a fine example of the elaborate metaphorical style of many of his letters of this period. The worst was then over. At length he felt solid ground again under his feet after the tragic shipwreck of all his hopes.

Many a storm has passed over my heart since I heard from you for the first and last time. The wind blew from a well-known region, and so violently that the rudder of my will-power broke and 'the waves of the sea and of love'[1] flooded over the wreck of my memories with such violence that only a little more and I should have been destroyed with the wretched vessel in the storm. However, luckily it has fallen out otherwise. 'Weeds don't spoil' and as soon as the storm had somewhat abated I abandoned the wrecked boat of my hopes, sprang into the sea of cold reason, fought my way boldly through it, not without throwing painful side-glances at the ship that once steered so hopefully towards the harbour of bliss, but which had in the course of time changed into a haunted phantom vessel and now into a miserable wreck, and landed luckily on the sandy shore of reality. So there I am, poor as a church mouse; in the far, far distance I see a torn sail on the broken mast—this signal is probably the last farewell of the broken vessel, that conceals in its deepest hold all my memories of wondrously lovely times, which shall drag it down under to the ocean bed, and there below may they quietly sleep and—no, not dream! sleep, sleep the eternal sleep of death!

[1] Grillparzer, *Des Meeres und der Liebe Wellen.*

VI

YEARS OF INDECISION

WOLF spent an unhappy and almost entirely unproductive summer in his home at Windischgraz. He had no love for his birthplace. The narrow, provincial mentality of those with whom he came in contact and the lack of any artistic activities such as could interest one accustomed to Viennese standards combined with his thwarted ambitions and the intolerable pain of his rejected love to embitter his whole existence for a long period. In letters to his Viennese friends he recalled regretfully the happy Maierling days of the previous summer. 'I become altogether too melancholy when I think of Maierling,' he wrote to Frau Preyss on the anniversary of his arrival in her household. He reminded her of how at half-past ten in the evening, one year ago to a day, the 'wolf' had come and broken like a robber into the peaceful dovecot of the Marienhof. 'O God, how much has changed since then! Things will never be the same again. Pitilessly the wheels of time roll onward: only a withered leaf of remembrance, preserved by a pious hand, bears witness to the splendour of long-departed times.'

During his stay at Windischgraz he produced only one musical composition—the song *Da fahr ich still im Wagen*, the first of a projected cycle *In der Fremde*, to words by Eichendorff. It is not specially remarkable, although by no means unattractive—a good beginning to a song-cycle in Schumann's manner, one would say. But for the present the continuation of *In der Fremde* hung fire.

Certainly for a period Fortune seemed to have averted her face. Misunderstandings arose in his correspondence with Henriette Lang and even with his beloved 'Aunt Bertha.' He sought to while away the time by reading Keller's *Der grüne Heinrich* to his assembled family. 'They are all very interested,' he told Henriette Lang, but his sister Käthe has revealed that far from being enthusiastic about Hugo's favourite *Der grüne Heinrich*, she herself was so abysmally bored that for many years she could never bring herself to open any book of Keller's again. She recalls also how he would suffer from lack of sleep. Often at two or three in the morning he would come

to his sisters' room and awaken them: 'Don't you hear that cursed
cockerel? I can't sleep. I shall go back to Vienna to-day if you
don't see to it that the brute is choked off.' In August a planned and
eagerly awaited holiday at Gröbming with his married sister Modesta
Strasser came to nothing.

Family quarrels did nothing to make life at Windischgraz any more
pleasant. There was no love lost between Hugo and his elder
brother Max. The latter, with hardly a trace of artistic feeling in
him, looked upon Hugo as a wastrel, destined surely to end in the
gutter, while to Hugo Max's purely mercenary ambitions were
abhorrent. Some of Hugo's spleen found expression in poetical
forms and a surviving exercise book dated 'Summer and Autumn
1881' shows clearly enough the uncongeniality of his existence during
that time. Wolf had no poetical pretensions; his taste in literature
was sufficiently acute for him to recognize his own limitations in this
sphere. But as a young man he did produce a considerable amount
of occasional poetry, most of it humorous or satirical in intention,
in which the very badness of the verses was part of the joke. The
book of poems from 1881 contains, or contained,[1] the following
items:

I. A short general introduction of eight lines in which the author
begs the pardon of the muse for his poetical trifles, the work, as he
says, 'of a musician who in idle hours has nothing better to do than to
play with verses.'

II. 'In Remembrance of the Werner Family's Skittle-party in
Petersdorf on Sunday, 29th May 1881.' A high-spirited outburst of
nonsense verse in dialect. The poem is printed in full in Heinrich
Werner's *Hugo Wolf in Maierling*, where it occurs in a letter to Bertha
von Lackhner.

III. 'On the Name of my Sister "Katharina," when she changed
the same to "Charita."' Nine lines dated 18th June.

IV. 'A Joke,' in six verses, dated 3rd August, concerning a certain
'Mizerl,' the Belle of Windischgraz, who is free with her kisses to all
and sundry—including the author, he hopes.

V. 'On an effeminate Clown' (*Auf einen weibischen Hanswurst*),
dated 'mid July 1881.' Thirteen derisory 'epigrams' and a

---

[1] It was rather unwillingly lent to Wamlek's Wolf Museum by Käthe Salomon-
Wolf, who tore out and destroyed part of it before doing so. A loose page from
this or a similar booklet survives elsewhere, with two poems, dated from Windischgraz, 17th June 1881, about Wolf's youngest sister: 'To my dearly loved,
loquacious sister Adrienne, for her urgent consideration.'

E

'conclusion' of three verses, about a local pianist of whom Wolf
seems to have made an enemy.

VI. 'Windischgraz Types.' Some pages are torn out: a 'Prologue'
and numbers 2 and 4 are all that remain. Hugo's sister Käthe has
recorded that it was Philipp Wolf who destroyed the others, which
described in scathing terms the Bürgermeister and other local
worthies. No. 2 concerns the garrulity of a certain 'sheep's head'
named Schweiger. 'Schweiger zwar heisst er und doch schwätzt
er immer.' No. 4 is apparently a substitute for one of the poems
torn out by Philipp. The poet compares the study of the Windischgrazers to the dissection of a stinking donkey.

VII. 'A moving Apostrophe, delivered on 4th September as a
Morning Sermon, for it was a Sunday, the Day of the Lord, which
should accord with Devotion and the Love of Mankind. Reproduced faithfully in verses with a note in conclusion by the author,
which witnesses to his Christian disposition, for the moral pointed
thereby is given in the words of Christ, "Father, forgive them, for they
know not what they do."' There follows a poem in thirty lines dated
from Windischgraz, 4th September 1881. It is concerned with a
quarrel between Hugo and his brother Max and makes much of the
latter's infrequent use of his handkerchief.

VIII. 'Something further to the Characterization of my Worthy
Brother Max—Good Advice.' Four lines, composed in the evening
of 6th September.

IX. 'Brother Max's Journey to Hell: a dramatic joke.' A lengthy
fragment, the strangest mixture of truth and fantasy, according to
Wolf's sister. The action takes place in that part of the Wolfs'
house which was used for business purposes and the only characters
are brother Max and the Devil. Max wishes to become a grocer and
offers his soul to the Devil for success in this venture. Mephisto-
pheles rejects this proposition since he is sure of Max's soul in any
case, whereupon Max proposes to include the souls of the rest of his
family in the bargain.

X. 'Interesting Psychological Observations on Max's Skull.'
Five verses.

Certain aspects of the letters of this year lead to the conclusion
that this was the time of Wolf's ultimate conversion to Wagnerianism.
That implied, to the young hotheads of the day, not merely admiration verging on idolatry for Wagner's *music*—Wolf was already a

fully fledged Wagnerian in that sense of the word—but also the openly declared detestation of Jews, the flesh of animals, and the music of Brahms. The first anti-Brahmsian comment in Wolf's correspondence occurs on 11th June in a letter to Henriette Lang, there are two—albeit jocular—references to anti-Semitism in letters to Franz Russ and Bertha von Lackhner on 10th and 15th June respectively, and another letter to Bertha von Lackhner on 3rd August establishes the fact that he had very recently become a vegetarian.

It was in October 1880 that the *Bayreuther Blätter* had published Wagner's essay 'Religion und Kunst,' in which he had expounded for the first time his astonishing and newly acquired beliefs that in meat-eating lay the cause of the decline of the Christian religion and its influence, and in vegetarianism the only hope for the regeneration of mankind. The effect of this article on the faithful had been wide-spread and immediate. We find Gustav Mahler, for example, writing to his friend Emil Freund on 1st November 1880:[1]

I have become, since a month ago, a complete vegetarian. The moral effect of this way of life, in consequence of this voluntary subjugation of the body ... is immense. You can imagine how convinced I am by it when I expect thereby a *regeneration of mankind.*

Wolf was thus some months behind the main body of Wagnerians in adopting this mode of life;[2] he seems to have remained a strict vegetarian for about eighteen months. It is doubtful whether he ever took anti-Semitism very seriously, although there were occasions when he could be outspoken enough upon the subject of certain individual members of the race. But he had too many good friends of his own of Jewish extraction for any rigid upholding of this par-ticular article of faith of the ultra-Wagnerian party. To the third part of their doctrine, however, uncompromising scorn and antago-nism towards the music of Johannes Brahms, Wolf remained faithful to the end of his days.

The people of Windischgraz were by this time aware that Philipp Wolf's second son possessed musical talents of a high order; they knew also that his temperament was not such as would make smooth for him the difficult pathway to fortune. Although the quarrelsome

---

[1] Gustav Mahler. *Briefe*, edited by Alma Mahler (Berlin, 1925).
[2] An unpublished family letter shows that in October 1879, a year *before* Wagner's article appeared, Wolf was taking meals in a Viennese vegetarians' club. But this was, as he himself explains, because they were cheap—20 kreuzers for a large portion of vegetables and pudding.

Wolf family can hardly have been exceptionally popular with their
fellow townsmen, there was considerable interest in the progress of
the local prodigy, and something like a sensation in the town was
caused in October by the news that he had been appointed chorus
master at the Stadttheater at Salzburg.

It was the faithful Adalbert von Goldschmidt who was responsible
for this, his first real opportunity and the long-awaited release from
his confinement in his home town.   The Kapellmeister at Salzburg
was Karl Muck, then in the early stages of his long and distinguished
career; he was finding the work rather more than he could manage
single-handed and had applied to the director, Leopold Müller, for
some assistance.   Goldschmidt had given Wolf a very strong recommendation that resulted in his appointment as Muck's amanuensis.

So Hugo, after months of idleness and boredom at Windischgraz,
was given his freedom again, and on 1st November, in bitter weather,
set out once more with joy in his heart for Vienna.   It must have been
on the evening of the same day that he called at Opernring No. 6 to
express his thanks and say good-bye to the Goldschmidts before
continuing his journey to Salzburg.   In one hand he carried a small
bundle and under the other arm a large and weighty object wrapped
in paper, which he deposited with great care in the hall.   This
mysterious parcel aroused Goldschmidt's curiosity and he asked his
visitor what it contained.   Wolf undid the wrappings and revealed
a large plaster bust of Wagner. 'So equipped,' says Decsey, 'the
Kapellmeister set out for his first engagement.'   It is perhaps a pity
to spoil this story by pointing out that a clean shirt and a bust of
Wagner did not constitute his *entire* worldly possessions when he left
to take up his duties at Salzburg.   The fact is, as his father's letters
show, that he had as yet no idea of where he was going to live and had
just taken with him enough clothing for his immediate needs and left
his trunks to be sent on when he had discovered suitable lodgings.
A letter to Franz Russ shows that he had left the Wagner bust in
Vienna in the previous May.

Wolf arrived at Salzburg on 2nd November and soon settled down
in rooms at Bergstrasse No. 8, on the second floor.   A number of
letters from his father indicate clearly the mingled joy and appre-
hension with which Philipp viewed this new and unexpectedly favourable turn in his son's fortunes.   Was it indeed possible that Hugo
was going to make good?   Voices were not wanting at Windischgraz
to suggest that it was somewhat unlikely.

The first letter from his father which Hugo received at Salzburg was already waiting for him there on the day of his arrival. It is addressed to 'Chorus-Director Hugo Wolf at the Imperial Theatre at Salzburg.'

I greet you as director in your new place of refuge. From my heart I hope that your appearance there may create a favourable impression and that you may fill your post obediently, in accordance with Director Müller's ideas. . . . I look forward with anxiety to your first reports, for fate always strikes an ugly, discordant note whenever I most rejoice. But may *this* joy be an untroubled one! . . . Good luck a thousand times in your new and first situation—it is the sole joyous consolation in my life of misery that all goes well with you and that you are achieving your aims. So—*Industry, Patience,* and *Endurance* !

The next letter was written on 10th November and delivered at Salzburg on the following day:

It affords us all a measure of relief that you were so well received both in Vienna and at Salzburg. May things always continue in the same way. I should like to experience *one* untroubled joy! I am awaiting yet another letter from you—about your début and also the various details of your life. You must have a lot of subject-matter and your letters could serve at the same time as a diary. You can increase more particularly the length of them, even at the risk of your hieroglyphics being only partially decipherable. You know that I follow your fortunes with great anxiety and interest myself greatly in each one of your steps and experiences.

A few days later Windischgraz received the surprising news that Hugo had been promoted. Philipp wrote on 16th November to his son 'Kapellmeister Hugo Wolf':

Your appointment as Kapellmeister has greatly rejoiced us all. . . . I was congratulated on all sides. I cherish only the one wish that in this position you will control yourself—of that many are doubtful on account of your fiery temperament. Show that you can also command *yourself.* . . . Congratulations on the Salzburg newspaper.[1] Whenever a criticism of you appears in it send me the page. Such printed evidence would make the Windischgrazers sit up, who are already quite agape about your appointment and the high salary. For here you are a Kapellmeister with 80 florins a month and at Ischl an additional 200 florins.[2] There is no need for the Windischgrazers to know that there exists besides yourself a *first* Kapellmeister!

Wolf's duties at Salzburg were mostly confined to rehearsing the soloists and chorus in popular operettas, such as those of Millöcker and Johann Strauss. In this he must at first have given satisfaction since he so soon won promotion to the post of second Kapellmeister.

[1] Presumably the public announcement of Wolf's appointment.
[2] For the summer season.

It is recorded that in this capacity he conducted Lortzing's *Waffen-schmied* on 21st December. The critic of the *Salzburger Volksblatt* did not think much of the performance, but did not actually single out the conductor for particular praise or blame. As might have been expected, however, Wolf made no very good impression upon the musicians of the orchestra, who on one occasion actually refused to play under him. He had had no experience of the work and lacked the technique of the baton—he admitted himself that in the perform-ance of some incidental music to a play of Anzengruber's he had broken down completely. Above all, he was disqualified, as his father had feared, by the excesses of his temperament. Little of the music performed at Salzburg was of much interest to him and the long hours he had to spend on the preparation of trivial operettas were a severe trial of his patience. Karl Muck recalled one occasion when Wolf abandoned altogether the rehearsal of a Strauss operetta with the words: 'Oh, leave the stuff! I'll play you something from *Tristan* instead.'

Leopold Müller, the Salzburg director, afterwards discussed his young assistant Kapellmeister with Decsey. He commented on Wolf's undoubted gifts and his punctual attention to his duties and criticized only his lack of experience and temperamental unsuitability for the post. He does not seem to have revealed how the Salzburg interlude came to an end. For that we must return to the family correspondence.

On 1st January 1882 Philipp Wolf wrote his son a long, despairing letter. He had already read between the lines of recent letters of Hugo's and divined that things were not going smoothly at Salzburg. The poor man sought confirmation for his own fears that the cup of happiness was again to be dashed from his lips:

It stands in the Book of Fate in flaming letters that I may never give utterance to a joy—that none is ordained for me. Hope, like a Northern Light, flares up often but disappears the next moment—the dream is over. With your star falls my own—hold this constantly before your eyes, for severe trials await you and many disappointments. . . . But you were at first so happy at Salzburg—what happened? Where's the trouble? Is your salary withheld? The director hostile? Have you quarrelled with Muck? Why is it that you want to leave?

Hugo replied on 4th January: [1]

DEAREST FATHER! Your melancholy letter has really alarmed me. Who is going to despair like that straight away? Courage! Courage! We

---

[1] *Familienbriefe XXXVI*, with a number of suppressed passages (indicated by italics) from the original in the Prussian State Library.

will present a brow of iron to all affliction. Now, when everything con-
spires against me . . . now for the first time I am come to consciousness of
my strength. Muck, the director, the orchestra—they are all furious.
But I remained indifferent to their ravings and quietly looked about for
something else. *The radial lines of the spider's web in which the whole gang
shall stick fast are already drawn.* Frankfurt is the solution. Mottl, who
passed through Salzburg ten days ago and to whom I related my position,
undertakes my release from it. *Then the gang shall repent of what they
have perpetrated against me.* Intrigues on intrigues! The theatre here is
more an intriguer's school than a school of art. *I will publicly brand it as
such when the chosen moment arrives.* A violent verbal exchange between
me and the director led to the mutual giving of notice. *From the 16th
onwards I belong no more to this pigsty.* Only now am I glad; I am in my
element; I will extinguish my unlucky star and replace it with a star of
fortune. But woe to the Salzburg theatre when I have got my breath.

With such dauntless courage, breathing defiance at the entire hostile
world, Wolf faced up to yet another failure in his tenaciously pursued
musical career.

He had made only one friend at Salzburg, the Mozarteum Director
Hummel, who had himself been Kapellmeister at the Stadttheater
until his resignation in the previous year. They put their heads
together and compared notes upon their experiences under Müller's
directorship. '*The two are sworn enemies,*' Wolf told his father,
'*and at Hummel's I can allow my gall to flow to my heart's content.*'
Hummel would gladly have found his young friend a position at
the Mozarteum but there was no vacancy there. Wolf's hopes
of Mottl being able to find him employment at Frankfurt were also
to be disappointed. His career as Kapellmeister was at an end.
He was none too well off financially—a dentist's bill had swallowed
up most of his savings and he was again forced to ask his father for
15 florins. '*I should have written to Altmann before now,*' he confessed, '*but I am ashamed to sponge on him now that I have taken
on a job.*'

He got the 15 florins, and, as was to be expected, a long lecture from
Philipp Wolf, who described himself as being

more out of tune than our piano. . . . Why did you have to let the
sparrow *out of your hand*, because Mottl showed you the *dove on the roof*?
. . . You don't consider the degree of mortification that you have inflicted
on me by your dismissal. It was the first joy, the first fruit of this costly
upbringing. Oh, the consciousness that I have reared with great sacrifices
only good-for-nothing scamps is galling. Even more so is the derision and
mockery of the people among whom I have to live, and whose scornful
remarks I must accept with a 'mea culpa.' You, to be sure, shake yourself

free like a wet poodle, but I can't do that.   Your education was a Sisyphean labour.   Graz, St. Paul, Marburg, the Conservatoire—the stone came always rolling back.   At last at Salzburg it seemed to find support. It begins to roll again, and I am not strong enough to check it.   I am too tired now, have exhausted all my strength and hope.   It will roll over me, over my useless life.

Neither Philipp Wolf nor Hugo himself looked forward to his encountering the Windischgrazers again after so short an interval and so apparently inglorious an end to his Kapellmeistership. Philipp suggested desperate measures—that Hugo should go to stay with his brother-in-law Strasser at Gröbming, and announce from there that he was ill, to give his father a chance to explain away the conclusion of his Salzburg appointment.   This of course Hugo did not do, and in the end there seemed to be nothing for it but to return to the old drifting existence as a music-teacher and accompanist in Vienna.

A member of the Wolf family once told Edmund Hellmer that there was for a time a breach between Hugo and his father.   There is no direct evidence of this in the family letters, but the tone of some of them, and the fact that there is a gap of some months in Philipp's correspondence after the return to Vienna, suggest that such a severance of relations was not impossible, and that if it did occur it may well have been at this time.   Twice in letters to Gilbert, who had also gone back to Vienna, Philipp relieves his feelings about Hugo, and seeks for news of him.   In both he remarks that things must be going badly with him, but that that will do him no harm—in the end he will perhaps come to recognize his own limitations.   He complains that no acknowledgment has been received of money that had been sent him—Hugo not seeming to think it worth while to say 'Thank you' for 'a lousy 5 florins.'   There is nothing quite so bitter as this in all Philipp's correspondence.

In the 'Daten aus meinem Leben' Wolf writes:

1881. Breach. Misery. Despair. Only one song composed. Summer at Windischgraz. Winter at Salzburg, Kapellmeister at the theatre. An awful time.

1882. Frightful moral hangover. Winter Rennweg. Summer Maierling. Nothing composed but *Mausfallensprüchlein* and some cradle songs. Bayreuth for the first time.

Our information as to Wolf's way of life at this time is very scanty. After the return to Vienna there is only one dated letter—an unimportant one—until the middle of May, when the documents again become plentiful. The Library of Congress, Washington, however, possesses an undated visiting-card, which must almost certainly be assigned to the early months of 1882, and which conveys some exceedingly curious information. Both sides of the card are closely written over. Here is the text:

CARISSIMA!

Fleas, bugs, and other afflictions overcome. I am, from to-day on, wholeheartedly in favour of universal military service. Truly a fine thing, death for the Fatherland, but properly to enjoy this elevated sentiment one must experience it in the case of other people. I must confess that after to-day even the fair Gregurich is no more agreeable sight to me than—a barracks. That is not to say, however, that I wouldn't like to see the Gregurich more often than the barracks that I have daily before my eyes. But I should like also to see you once again. Saturday evening? Perhaps you will invite Frau Karabatschek for that evening—perhaps, too, by then my sore throat will be better and I shall be able to sing *Siegfried*—and perhaps you will be disposed to hear it and (which requires more disposition) —me—but perhaps not? Don't increase endlessly my painful suppositions. A few lines from your hand will set me at rest. I etc. etc. etc. remain in etc. etc. etc. and sign etc. etc. etc. as etc. your etc. and so on.

The only possible conclusion, after reading this card, is that Wolf wrote it while serving as conscript in the Austrian army. It is presumable that on the day in question he had been drilling or route-marching, since he was so glad to get back to barracks. His father's letters show that in 1880 and 1881 he had been exempted or deferred. It seems that in 1882, the last year during which he would normally have been liable for military service,[1] he had, in returning to Vienna from Salzburg, not complied with all the regulations. A card from Philipp Wolf, delivered on 14th February, says: 'Why no letter? To-day your call-up card [*Stellungskarte*] received, because you have not applied to present yourself in Vienna but simply sent in your name—so apply at once, or you will be treated as a deserter.' How obscure these early months of 1882 are is shown by the fact that not only is nothing known from other sources of Wolf's conscription for military service, but the person to whom this card is addressed ('Carissima') is unidentifiable, as is 'the fair Gregurich' mentioned in it. Frau (Karoline) Karabatschek was Edmund Lang's eldest sister. The period of military service cannot have lasted very long. It was not uncommon for young men to be called up and then

---

[1] It seems, however, that the period of military service for Wolf's age group was extended to include 1883.

*E

released again after a few weeks if they were found physically unfitted for the life of a soldier.

The significance of Wolf's remark, in his autobiographical notes, about his 'frightful moral hangover' ('Greulicher moralischer Katzenjammer') must not be underestimated. Without it, however, one would have said that the farcical interlude of his sojourn as Kapellmeister at Salzburg had had a most beneficial effect upon his spirits, making a clean break with the melancholy introspection and ill temper of the greater part of the previous year. We know that he returned to his old lodgings in the Rennweg, and it is clear from the scraps of information that we have that old friends made him welcome—above all, the Preyss family, with 'Aunt Bertha,' and their relatives the Werners. They took him into their homes and lovingly saw to his needs. He spent long hours music-making with Mizzi Werner, keeping a close watch upon the development of her tastes, studying *Figaro* and teaching her some of his own songs. Other intimate friends of the period were the Lang children, in particular his confidante Henriette or 'Hansi' and her brother Edmund. In time all those painful memories receded farther and farther into oblivion behind him. All the later letters of the year, to say nothing of numerous high-spirited poems, suggest that he was wonderfully happy again. How different was the nonsense poetry that he now wrote from the cruel, jangling rhymes of 1881! In place of 'Brother Max's Journey to Hell' he now celebrated 'Aunt Bertha's Resurrection' and expressed his deep thankfulness and love in verses for all the members of the Werner family.

We have no knowledge at all of how he earned his living, but must presume that there were still mothers to be found in Vienna who would entrust the musical talents of their daughters to his uncertain direction.

As an out-and-out Wagnerian he now took his meals in a little vegetarian restaurant on the corner of the Wallnerstrasse and the narrow alleyway of the Fahnengasse. A little glass door showed the way from the street downwards over stone steps into a dark cellar, with tiny latticed windows high up in the wall, where naked gas flames burned the whole day long. In this restaurant was always to be found a rich collection of cranks of all denominations, as well as many really notable personalities who, for one reason or another, had forsworn the flesh of animals. A Socialist vegetarian group included Dr. Viktor Adler and Heinrich and Adolf Braun. The

Wagnerians had recently greatly increased the custom of the establishment, and among them came Mahler, with his friend Krzyzanowski, and August Göllerich, Liszt's amanuensis, with a mane like a lion. Then there were various other groups faithful to the teaching of Pythagoras or Empedocles, clad in summer and winter alike in natural-coloured haircloth or entirely in linen garments, mostly with full beards and hair falling down over their shoulders. Among this strange company Wolf now appeared regularly at meal-times—'a slender youth with blond hair, fluffy chin, and a light down on his upper lip, with pale face and somewhat piercing glance. He spoke hardly a syllable and his utterances were mostly a shyly hostile growling.'[1]

Very much the same company, including Wolf, was often to be seen at the nearby Café Griensteidl in the Schauflergasse. This was the recognized meeting-place of artists and originals of all kinds and was known to the populace as 'Café Grössenwahn' ('Megalomania'). It was a typical Viennese café of the older sort where an exclusively masculine clientele—it was not thought fitting, at that time, for women to be seen in the coffee-houses—was dimly discerned through intense blue clouds of tobacco smoke. No word was ever spoken aloud here—the patrons were entirely engrossed in reading the newspapers.

It may have been at this time that Wolf undertook to accompany Mizzi Werner in some of his own compositions at a musical evening held by the Austrian Alpine Society. He stipulated, however, that the songs were to be announced as Schumann's and not as his own. So it was agreed. The master of ceremonies rose to announce that Frl. Mizzi Werner would sing a group of songs 'by Schumann—er—I believe'—with a meaning glance at Wolf, who had already seated himself at the piano. But the form of this announcement was itself enough to infuriate Wolf, who seems to have been intent on passing off some of his imitations of Schumann as the real thing, and this particular item of the Alpine Society's programme had to be abandoned forthwith, for the pianist and composer leaped up in a fury, rushed off the platform, and was seen no more that evening.

In the spring, on 16th May, Wolf abandoned his town lodging for the peace of Maierling again. The Preyss family had again taken the Marienhof for the season but they themselves were not making use of it until June, so that Wolf was alone there for a time, quite content with his hand-made cigarettes, his coffee-machine, and some

[1] Friedrich Eckstein, *Alte unnennbare Tage* (Vienna 1936).

milk-groats for his dinner. 'Here it is warm, flowery, pleasant, sunny,' he told Henriette Lang,

and I feel so much at my ease, am so divinely lazy, as if I were in the Land of Nod. I have not for a long time found myself so well as in these few days at Maierling. That was a melancholy time two years ago in comparison with now. . . . Future and past are far from me; I live only in the present and that makes me so glad and happy. That once upon a time I could be so foolish as to allow my head to hang like a hypocrite's would vex me now, if I were not so very much inclined to laughter.

On Sundays he generally walked over to see the Werner family at Perchtoldsdorf, where the day passed swiftly with skittles and music-making. Then he would set off back on his lonely walk of three or four hours, by the forest road to Maierling, accompanied for the first part of the way by all his friends.

While he was leading this carefree existence in the sun of Maierling, Wolf's head was full of new plans for the composition of an opera, for which he thought he would be able to write his own libretto, if he could only find a suitable subject. He had been reading Heine's *Harzreise* and certain stanzas in it had set his imagination working.

Ich bin die Prinzessin Ilse,
Und wohne im Ilsenstein,
Kommt mit nach meinem Schlosse,
Wir wollen selig sein.

. . . . .

Ich will Dich küssen und herzen,
Wie ich geherzt und geküsst
Den lieben Kaiser Heinrich,
Der nun gestorben ist.

This legend of the fairy princess Ilse, Wolf thought, might be the subject for which he had been searching. From Heine he turned to Grimm, and in Grimm's notes was referred back to the collections of folk-tales made by Otmar and Quedlinburger. He found, however, that neither of these authorities was available in the Vienna Court Library and was temporarily at a loss. He told his friend Dr. Crone of his difficulties and was advised to write to a Dr. Gustav Winter, who, if anybody could, would be able to give him the information he wanted about the various forms of the legend. Wolf first wrote on 23rd May,[1] calling attention to Heine's connection of the Princess Ilse

---

[1] Wolf's three letters to Dr. Winter were published in *Der Merker* (Vienna) for 1st March 1913 ('Ein Opernplan Hugo Wolfs, mit ungedruckten Briefen'), but without the name of the recipient. The originals are in the possession of the Gesellschaft der Musikfreunde.

with King Henry the Fowler, and to his reference to a story of Ilse
and a certain Knight of Westenberg—a story which seemed to have
been very finely treated 'by one of our best-known poets,' as Heine
put it.   It was important to discover the identity of this poet; possibly
his version of the legend would prove to be adaptable as an operatic
text.   Dr. Winter supposed that the reference was to Wilhelm
Blumenhagen, who in his *Rostrapp und Wanderungen durch den Harz*
touches on the Ilse saga.   But it seems that in the end no copy of the
once popular works of Blumenhagen could be unearthed, even in the
second-hand bookshops, and very soon Wolf's interest in the subject
diminished and died away.

With the arrival of the Preyss family at Maierling, the old happy
family life of two years before was renewed, although the cares of
'Aunt Bertha,' who prepared Wolf's meals, were now greatly
increased by his insistence on a severely vegetarian regimen.   His
father once sent him a parcel with some sausages and bacon, and
received it back, to his extreme annoyance, by return of post.

With Mizzi Werner's youthfully fresh light soprano voice in mind
he composed on 18th June his *Mausfallensprüchlein*, a little song, with
words by Mörike, to be sung while walking three times round a
mouse-trap.   Its practical value as an aid to trap, cat, and poison
has yet to be proved, but regarded from a purely artistic standpoint
the *Mausfallensprüchlein* is simply enchanting.   So sprightly and
delicate a sense of humour had hardly before found expression in
music.   The tiny piece scurries by with inimitable youthful grace—
an authentic Wolfian masterpiece in miniature.   It seems only fitting
that such a happy flight of fancy should have originated at Maierling.
One other composition came into existence there on 6th July—a little
canon for the piano, a by-product of the music lessons he was now
giving to Lotte Preyss.

Wolf was now relieved for some months of all anxiety about food
and lodging and declared his intention of idling away no more of the
precious years of his apprenticeship.   He rose at six and went to bed
at midnight and was fully occupied during the whole of the day—no
doubt at first with his opera libretto and then, when that had been
abandoned, with the study of *Parsifal*.   Aunt Bertha had procured
at Baden a copy of the recently published vocal score and brought it
out to Maierling.   For weeks he was deeply engrossed in this work,
which aroused his most passionate admiration.

A great and exciting project was afoot.   *Parsifal* was to be produced for the first time at Bayreuth this year, and Wolf had been successful in procuring one of the free tickets available to impecunious students. Various friends contributed towards the expenses of the journey and lodgings at Bayreuth—from Dr. Breuer alone he received about 70 florins. In preparation for this, his first visit to Germany and the Mecca of all Wagnerians, his wardrobe had first to be overhauled. A new summer suit was made for him at Windischgraz. But when it arrived Wolf was far from satisfied. 'The tailor at Windischgraz,' he wrote, 'must have a decidedly hazy conception of the normal build of mankind, for when one considers the twill suit, one is very much inclined to believe that it was measured for the body of a gorilla.' 'Try it yourself,' he invited his father, 'you will be able to play hide and seek in it quite comfortably.' In this predicament Leopold Altmann came once more to the rescue with a coat, waistcoat, and two pairs of trousers which could be altered to fit Wolf's tiny frame.

On 12th August Wolf left Maierling at six in the morning, arriving at Bayreuth shortly before midnight. On the next day he attended the ninth performance of the *Parsifal* festival, although he had to pay 30 florins out of his pocket-money for the experience, as his free ticket was not yet available. Two days later he heard the work for the second time. It was everything he had hoped—'colossal,' 'Wagner's most inspired, sublimest creation.' Wolf tried hard to see the master himself, to renew the acquaintance he had made as a boy in 1875, and visited Amalie Materna to ask for a personal introduction. He was kindly received by the great singer but learned that Wagner was quite unapproachable, being surrounded by innumerable courtiers and satellites. All Wolf could do was to stare at the windows of 'Wahnfried,' which, as far as he could see by peering in from the outside, was 'fabulously luxuriously furnished.' On this first visit to Bayreuth everything found favour with him—*Parsifal*, the performance, the singers, the town itself, and the surrounding countryside. He wandered out to Eremitage and Fantaisie and visited the grave of Jean Paul, where he plucked leaves of ivy and lilac for remembrance.

It was all over too soon. He had to leave Bayreuth early on the 16th and intended visiting Nuremberg and, if his money lasted out, Munich as well on the return journey. Whether he carried out these projects we do not know, but on 18th August he was at Gmunden, in the Salzkammergut. There he visited Dr. Breuer, who had done so much to make his Bayreuth journey possible, and spent the day, despite rainy weather, in sailing on the lake with his ex-pupil Dora Breuer and her father. That was an incomparable joy to him. 'If I were at Gmunden for a longer period,' he wrote, 'I should, like a water rat, seldom come on land, but allow myself, like the Flying Dutchman, to be driven aimlessly astray by the wind and waves.' Afterwards he played for his hosts as much as he could remember of *Parsifal* and discussed with Dr. Breuer all aspects of Wagner's music and Wagnerian doctrine before catching the night train back to Vienna.

Wolf returned to Maierling tired, hoarse, and nearly penniless, with a heavy cold brought about by his one day's sailing on the Traunsee in the rain, but enriched with the unforgettable experiences of Bayreuth, which continued for long to occupy all his mind. On 30th August, the date of the last *Parsifal* performance of the Bayreuth Festival for 1882, his thoughts ran continually on the distant gathering of the faithful around the ageing master, as they paid homage to the last fruits of his genius, and he seemed cast down by his own inability to be present. He determined to live over again his experiences at Bayreuth, to realize at Maierling a Wagner festival of his own. He shut himself in his little room, which he darkened, and punctually at four o'clock, when the Bayreuth performance was due to commence, began the Prelude to *Parsifal*. Between that time and about half-past nine he played and sang, with 'Aunt Bertha' for audience, the whole music drama.[1]

The middle of September saw Wolf back in Vienna in his winter quarters in the Rennweg. Pupils were no easier to find than before. A suggestion that he should take up again the piano lessons in the household of Dr. Breuer came to nothing, but the situation was eased for him once again by his old friend 'Berti' Goldschmidt, who with characteristic kindness and discretion arranged for his wife to take some singing lessons from Wolf. This led to a renewal, in some degree, of the happy relationship of earlier years, and Wolf now came again frequently to the Goldschmidts' house, where he became friendly with, among others, the comedian Alexander Girardi from the Wiednertheater. He taught Paula Goldschmidt his new *Mausfallensprüchlein*, which she sang with success in numerous *salons*.

[1] See the letter to Henriette Lang of 31st August. Heinrich Werner (*Hugo Wolf in Maierling*, pp. 56–7) describes this scene as taking place on 26th July, on the occasion of the *first* (private) performance of *Parsifal* at Bayreuth. There was probably some little confusion here in the memory of Werner's informant.

In October he learned from the Goldschmidts of the death of
Anton Lang, Vally Franck's uncle and guardian, on his estate at
Roskosch, and also that Vally and her aunt were to reside permanently in France for the future—a matter of indifference to him
now, he declared.

An important new friendship had its origin at about this time in
the vegetarian restaurant. There often sat next to Wolf a young,
bearded Pythagorean, wearing linen garments and possessing a
remarkable shock of hair, of whom many strange stories were current
in Vienna. This was Friedrich Eckstein, a man of more or less
independent means, who studied music as a private pupil of Anton
Bruckner's. Wolf at first showed marked animosity towards his
neighbour at table, but he afterwards became more agreeable, and in
the course of time the two young men discovered that they had many
interests in common and struck up a close friendship. Eckstein, like
Wolf, had been at Bayreuth for the production of *Parsifal*. He had
chosen to make the journey, however, not in a prosaic railway carriage but entirely on foot—although the particular version of the
legend of this pilgrimage which represents him as travelling, like
Tannhäuser, in *sandals* is not confirmed by Eckstein himself, who
refers plainly to the mountaineering boots which he wore on that
occasion.

In Wagnerian circles at that time *Parsifal* was an inexhaustible
source of wonder and argument, and Wolf and Eckstein often saw the
day break before they had finished discussing it. Eckstein's knowledge was encyclopaedic: his rooms were lined from floor to ceiling
with books and scores. They discussed *Parsifal* together in relation
to German and Spanish mysticism, Palestrina's masses, free-
masonry, vegetarianism, and various oriental religions; it is to be
suspected that Eckstein did most of the talking on these subjects.
Upon literary matters, as of course upon strictly musical ones, Wolf
could more than hold his own. He could recite by heart whole scenes
from the plays of Kleist and Christian Grabbe, men of unbalanced
genius for whom he had a special predilection. With Eckstein's
library to draw on he could now embark on a wider course of reading.
One task he set himself was to read through all the novels of Jean
Paul. One of these, *Der Titan*, he found desperately hard to digest.
Repeatedly the book was flung to the ground in rage and despair,
only to be ruefully retrieved and continued later, for Wolf made a
point of always finishing any book he had once begun. In the end

Der Titan became one of his favourites. He was fascinated by the Hellish language in Berlioz's *Damnation de Faust* and on meeting Eckstein would sometimes exchange greetings with him in that tongue: 'Marexil burrudixe formy Dinkorlitz, Tradium, Merondor, Irkymur, Irimirikarabrao!' Wolf had heard somewhere that Berlioz had taken this mysterious language of Hell from the works of Emanuel Swedenborg, and Eckstein was invited to make a search for its origin and meaning. They looked through many books of Swedenborg's, including the sixteen volumes of the *Arcana Coelestia*, but found nothing. Wolf had a great liking for this sort of elaborate verbal buffoonery and delighted also in the scene from Immermann's *Münchhausen*, satirizing the Schwabian cult of mysticism of its author's day, in which occurs a passage in diabolical language: 'Fressaunidum schlinglausibeest, pimple timple simple feriauke, meriaukemau,' for which, it seems, the German equivalent is simply 'Ja!'

During these years Wolf was also becoming increasingly friendly with the Köchert family, and their house in the former Mehlmarkt,[1] in the heart of the city, was henceforward the asylum to which he generally turned from the stress of circumstance. There occurred in this house during this winter a strange episode, the last scene of Wolf's youthful love-affair. Heinrich and Melanie Köchert, with their three young children, occupied the fourth floor, and below them lived Heinrich's brother Theodor and his family. The lady who afterwards became Marie Lang was at that time married to Theodor Köchert and has related the story in a forgotten article.[2] It was her first meeting with Wolf, who was wearing a most elegant velvet jacket, probably Altmann's gift. The introduction had barely taken place when she was called away to attend to her child [3] on the floor below. A quarter of an hour later she was able to return.

But as I set foot on the narrow, winding staircase, Wolf rushed headlong past me with noisy clatter, fierce as a wounded boar, fell, picked himself up again in a flash, and dashed downstairs. The host and others followed him, calling and shouting 'Stop there! Come back, Wolf!' It was no good, he was gone—gone in wild haste without his jacket, which the owner of the house held in the hands with which he had attempted to arrest him.

It was Vally's presence in the room above that had led to Wolf's panic-stricken retreat. Without warning she had by arrangement

---

[1] Now Neuer Markt 15.
[2] 'Hugo Wolfs Entwicklungszeit' (*Die Zeit*, Vienna, 3rd January 1904).
[3] Erich Köchert, born 27th September 1882.

with the hostess suddenly confronted him and held out a friendly hand. But Wolf in great distress warded her off brusquely and turned his back. When others tried to induce him to show a more friendly spirit he became unruly, lost all control of himself, and took refuge in flight. That ghost had been laid once, with manifold prayers and sighs and bitter mental conflict, and yet it had returned to disturb once more his hardly won peace of mind. How could he have faced it again? It was better to flee.

Thus ended in painful confusion a first love-affair which had brought much happiness throughout a critical period into an existence that without its transforming, warming radiance might have become insupportable to a hypersensitive nature such as Wolf's in conflict with an often sordid environment. Once in later life Vally Franck again crossed his path and by that time he was completely indifferent towards her, but to his friend Eckstein he often spoke, never with bitterness, of lovely, fickle Vally, who had captured his heart in the first penurious, storm-shaken years of his youth in Vienna.

During all this time Wolf seems to have been happy enough on the whole, although apparently as far as ever from any conclusive justification of his adoption of a musical career. For the time being he drifted and waited, building up friendships and absorbing experience and knowledge of books and music, making whatever use he could of these not very profitable years. In this winter he attempted to put together an operatic libretto of his own invention, the sketches for which are still in existence.[1] The action was to take place at Seville in carnival time. The title-page gives the names of the principal characters—Don Antonio, a rich nobleman; Don Alphonso, his brother, disguised as a Chaldean; Gregorio, a music-teacher; Donna Angela, Antonio's daughter; and Donna Clarissa, her cousin. There are half a dozen different drafts of the first two acts, with many variations of the plot. The whole thing was left by Wolf in a fragmentary condition after a few months' desultory labour. Its chief interest, in view of the composer's later operatic achievements, is the southern *milieu*.

It must have been with a certain relief that in December he experienced a reawakening of his creative abilities. In the past twenty months he had only produced two songs to maintain his claim to be considered seriously as a creative artist. Now at last the lyrical

[1] Vienna City Library.

impulse was upon him again and, inspired by the poems of Eichendorff and, in particular, of the painter-poet Robert Reinick, happy songs flowed from his pen with comparative freedom.   In the latter half of December he wrote three Reinick songs—*Wiegenlied im Sommer* on 17th December, its companion, the *Wiegenlied im Winter*, on the 20th, and *Wohin mit der Freud?* on the 31st.   On 12th January there followed the Eichendorff *Rückkehr*, and two further settings of Reinick, *Ständchen* and *Nachtgruss*, on the 19th and 24th respectively. Another Eichendorff poem, *Wolken wälderwärts gegangen*, intended for the projected cycle *In der Fremde*, was composed on 30th January. After that new songs became less frequent, but each of the next three months saw an addition to the little group of settings of Reinick's poems—*Frühlingsglocken* on 19th February, *Liebesbotschaft* on 18th March and *Liebchen, wo bist du?* on 12th April.   Another Eichendorff song for *In der Fremde, Ich geh' durch die dunklen Gassen*, followed on 3rd May.

The best of the Reinick songs are among the happiest of Wolf's early inspirations; the two endearing cradle songs, tender yet completely unsentimental and even lightly humorous variants of this old theme, and the enchantingly fresh and melodious *Wohin mit der Freud?*—these reveal all the charm and sweetness of the gentler side of Wolf's personality.   *Liebesbotschaft* is attractive mock-Schumann and *Frühlingsglocken* a brilliant imitation of Loewe's *Kleiner Haushalt* manner.

The two songs for the Eichendorff cycle *In der Fremde* seem to show Wolf endeavouring to revive, without much conviction, the subjective romantic manner of four or five years earlier.   But the impulse which had then driven him on to exalted and passionate lyrical expression was no longer within him; the new songs cannot compare with the best of the Heine and Lenau settings of the earlier period.   Their sentiments are unconvincing, their melodies halting and forced, never really taking wing.   *Rückkehr*, the isolated Eichendorff song, not connected with the projected *In der Fremde* cycle, is quite distinctive and original, with noteworthy resemblances to the peerless *Das Ständchen* of 1888.   It exhales the typical atmosphere of Wolf's mature *Eichendorff-Lieder*, that of a happy students' world of carefree song to the plangent music of the lute, but like *Das Ständchen* itself, *Rückkehr* is tinged with sadness and regret by the singer's detachment from the happy scene he describes.   This gives Wolf the opportunity for the employment of what afterwards became one of his favourite devices—the depiction, in voice and accompaniment, of two conflicting emotions.

In January Wolf had begun to renew his efforts to achieve the publication of some of his compositions, and had gone as far as to approach Hanslick with a request for his opinion upon some songs and for advice as to the possibilities of getting them into print. Goldschmidt's friend Viktor Tilgner, who lived in the same block of flats as Hanslick, seems to have acted as intermediary. There exists a letter from Hanslick to Wolf which, although it does not say very much, is perhaps worth reproducing here as a curiosity, in view of the subsequent hostility between critic and composer. It is dated 1st February 1883.

DEAR SIR,

Although it was not easy for my eyes to master the miniature writing of your manuscripts, yet I owe to them the acquaintance of a new, very promising talent and have the honour to return your sensitive, interesting songs with best thanks,

Yours sincerely

DR. EDUARD HANSLICK.

Some time after this the two met personally, but no details of their encounter have survived, except that Hanslick recommended Wolf to try his luck with the publishing house of Simrock.

By 17th February, however, Wolf had decided to offer his work to Schott, and on the next day he sent off some of his songs to this firm. His sudden decision to offer the songs to Schott rather than to Simrock can be clearly understood when we consider the catastrophe that had shaken the whole musical world only a few days before. On 13th February Wagner had died at Venice. On the next morning, when the news reached Vienna, Wolf had called at the Werners' house, taking no notice at all of young Heinrich, who was the only person about, had gone to the piano, played the Funeral March from *Götterdämmerung*, and departed again without saying a word. He had spent the day in the branches of a tree, and in the evening he had reappeared in a subdued and sorrowful mood. 'I have wept like a child,' he told them.

The death of Wagner seems only to have exacerbated the feelings of the two hostile parties in Vienna. On 26th February Wolf wrote to Mottl an account of a recent concert at which the *Faust* overture had been 'shamefully bungled' and extremely coolly received by the audience, while the succeeding item, an arrangement for full strings of a movement from a Mozart Quartet, was received with acclamation.

It sounded like a demonstration against the departed master, of whom, moreover, I dreamed to-day that he was only apparently dead. . . . We spoke together about this for a long time, he complained besides of constant indisposition. It was in the same room in Wahnfried in which I visited him once before in a dream, when he showed me with visible pleasure his Chinese vases and figures. How strange! Even to-day I can hardly believe that the man is dead *who first made men of us wretched clay figures.*

In the emotional reaction of those first days of shocked mourning, the thought of offering his work to Simrock, the publisher of Brahms, on the recommendation of Hanslick, Wagner's bitterest opponent, was not to be endured. So his manuscripts went off to Schott, the publisher of Wagner's *Ring*, *Parsifal*, and *Meistersinger*.

Ill luck, however, continued to dog his efforts to get into print. In the above-quoted letter to Mottl he had to report that

Schott refuses in the politest manner the publication of my songs and regrets the rejection of the same all the more since you pressed my affairs so warmly upon him. I will now try my luck with Breitkopf & Härtel, since I cannot make up my mind, in spite of Hanslick's recommendation, to offer my compositions to Simrock.

Wolf's fineness of feeling in this matter has been much commended, but a later family letter, which continues the melancholy story of his repeated rejections, shows that in the end he did not have the strength of mind to forgo entirely his chances of acceptance by Brahms's publishers. He sent his father the printed reply of another publisher and explained:

From this printed rejection slip you should be able to gather how difficult it is to find a publisher, for most of them do not look at the manuscript at all, but straight away add the printed rejection to the unseen manuscript and send it back. I could show you letters from *Simrock*, Breitkopf & Härtel,[1] etc. etc., they all decline the manuscripts and, I am convinced, without previously having examined them. So you can't lay the blame on me, for I have as little command over the heart of a publisher as I have over his understanding. They're all alike—stingy, heartless rogues.

Philipp had been continually urging his son to renewed efforts. He caustically remarked that he hoped Hugo would soon gain public

---

[1] In the case of Breitkopf & Härtel, at least, Wolf actually made use of Hanslick's letter to him. See Wolfgang Schmieder, *Musikerhandschriften in drei Jahrhunderten* (Leipzig, 1939).

notice, as it was improbable, with his way of life, that he would live very long. He railed against vegetarianism:

Your whole behaviour displeases me. Strong coffee (poison) and then peas—in that way you'll certainly perish. A donkey has put some idea into your head which you have not understood. The food to which one is accustomed from youth is the right food—everything else is folly and swindle.

His anxiety on this point was relieved before long. In February he was able to send home-made sausages again, 'for an hour can still come when the goose-liver pie is not just at hand.' After the death of Wagner Philipp redoubled his admonitions. 'Now I suppose it's the turn of Wagner's disciples,' he wrote on 19th February,

Press into the foreground! Only fools are modest. Boldly ventured is half won. Be your own supporter! If you wait patiently until others raise you up, you'll grow old meanwhile. Strain every nerve—if your strong coffee hasn't already paralysed them—and show that Wagner has not lived and written in vain, that he has worthy disciples! ... Seize fortune by the ears and don't let go! Make every effort! Act as many others before you have done! Nothing venture, nothing win—see Wagner's example!

Wolf's disappointing experiences with so many music publishers were offset in April by the stimulation of the personal encouragement of one of his idols. Liszt came to Vienna in that month for a few days and on the 6th, through Goldschmidt's good offices, Wolf obtained audience with him. He played through some of his songs and Liszt confessed himself delighted and embraced the young composer and kissed him on the brow. He expressed, however, the hope of hearing from Wolf soon a work on a larger scale. This remark of Liszt's, in all probability, may be regarded as the germ-cell from which there developed, in the succeeding months, Wolf's great experiment on a symphonic scale—the orchestral tone-poem based on Heinrich von Kleist's poetic drama of *Penthesilea*. The first recorded mention of this work, written in a form so peculiarly associated with Liszt's name, and employing the Lisztian process of theme transformation, occurs in a letter to Philipp Wolf on 31st July, less than four months after the interview. Furthermore, a sketch-book in the National Library, Vienna, acquired by Wolf on 2nd May 1883, *within a month of the meeting with Liszt*, contains, first, a sketch for an orchestral work, not used in *Penthesilea* (5th May), and then, on the next and succeeding pages, sketches for *Penthesilea* itself. The Penthesilea theme, in its normal form, as used in the third section of the work (bar 520 and on), is dated 19th July in the sketch-book, and is followed by the greater part of the slow second section in short score.

A by-product of this period, composed in Vienna on 16th June, was the famous setting of Justinus Kerner's *Zur Ruh, zur Ruh!* in which Wolf speaks his individual language—a language largely derived from late-Wagnerian sources—with confident mastery. It is surprising indeed to note the small extent to which his earlier music had been affected by his cult of Wagner. In song, Schubert, Schumann, and to some extent Loewe, had represented his ideals and remained his models. In his String Quartet and occasionally elsewhere he had, it is true, seemed to echo effects from *Lohengrin*, but before this date the influence of Wagner's later works was most surprisingly absent from Wolf's own compositions. In this respect, as first pointing the direction in which he was to find his most fruitful field for development, the application of Wagnerian technique and principles to the older forms of the German *Lied, Zur Ruh!* is a milestone in Wolf's own progress towards mastery and in the history of song.

Wolf left Vienna on 6th July for his second visit to Bayreuth, travelling this time with Mottl, Schönaich, and other members of the Wagner Verein. He attended performances of *Parsifal* on the 8th and 10th and then left for Gmunden, where he intended to spend a fortnight with some friends.[1] It seems that there was some misunderstanding about the arrangements for this visit, however, for when Wolf arrived he found there was no room for him in the house where he believed himself to have been invited to stay, and had to depart at once to look for a room. This in itself was sufficiently annoying, and his opinion of Gmunden sank lower and lower when for day after day it rained continuously. As soon as the weather cleared a little he set out for Rinnbach at the other end of the lake, where the Köchert family had taken a house for the summer. This was on 19th July; he returned on the same evening. There followed three more days of rain at Gmunden and then for four days he was the Köcherts' guest again and made use of this opportunity to find a cheap room for himself at Rinnbach, which seemed to have many advantages over rain-soaked Gmunden. He moved into his new quarters on 1st August, but within a few days was already regretting the move. 'What does Rinnbach offer me?' he inquired of Henriette Lang,

---

[1] Probably the Breuers.

'Food fit only for dogs, *no* coffee, a dwelling that is pretty, to be sure, but highly disturbing on account of the enormous number of children in and about the house. If I want to work I must go out into the open air. If I do go out, it begins to rain!'

Nevertheless, he spent seven weeks at Rinnbach, often visiting the Köcherts' house, and it was there that Hermann Bahr became acquainted with him. Bahr had been until recently a student at the University of Vienna, but had been expelled after a revolutionary speech he had made at a meeting of the three thousand young Wagnerians who attended the university. The gathering had begun as a ceremony of mourning for Wagner but had ended in uproar as a pan-Germanic demonstration, when the hall had been cleared by the police. Bahr had afterwards been sent to Graz University, but very soon it had been indicated to his father that there too he was not looked upon as a desirable character, with the result that he had been sent into exile at the lonely Steinkogl Inn in the woods between Ischl and Ebensee. Bahr's father, however, did not know that at Rinnbach, only an hour's walk from the Steinkogl, Edmund Lang, another student of the Vienna University and a close friend of Bahr's, was staying with his brother-in-law Heinrich Köchert. Bahr's banishment did not therefore turn out to be so very unpleasant, as he was able to spend almost every day from morning to night with his friend: sailing, swimming, drinking, and talking endlessly. His first impression of Wolf, the other visitor in the house, was of a taciturn, rather insignificant-looking young man, entirely lost in his own thoughts. Only by degrees did it come out that he too could do his share of the talking, but then he did so to such effect that Herr Köchert had to separate them before anybody could get any sleep. As they lay in the long grass of a meadow bordering the lake, Bahr encouraged Wolf to relieve his feelings about the popular composers and writers of the day, and Wolf, his face distorted with rage, used to rave and curse with such effect that boatmen far out on the lake were disquieted and gazed apprehensively towards the shore. A certain poet was the particular object of his abhorrence at this time; the friends would become aware of a shrill giggling and screeching; they knew the signs—Wolf had found another bad poem. Red in the face, his hair dishevelled, he would rush up to them: 'You rogue! You confounded rogue! Why didn't you become a porter? Or a waiter? Or a court councillor? No, the rascal must write poetry. Well then, please listen. Wait a bit, rascal. Oh, you accursed

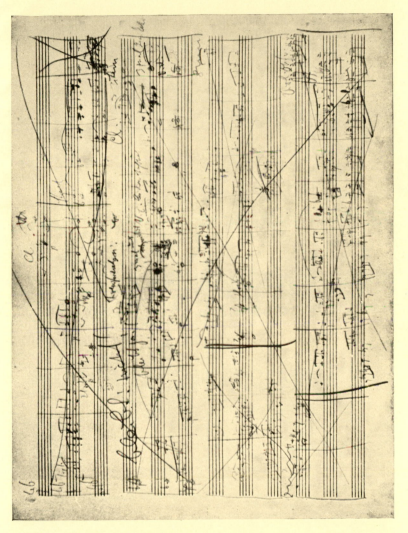

SKETCHES FOR 'PENTHESILEA,' 1883

National Library, Vienna

gallows bird!'[1] Then he began to read, with voice full of scorn and malice, his latest discovery.

During this time he was wrestling with his ideas for the tone-poem on the subject of Kleist's *Penthesilea*, and his serious reading was almost entirely confined to this play. He carried it about with him everywhere, like a breviary, he read and quoted it constantly to his friends. 'He doted on it,' wrote Bahr. 'His hands trembled when he read only a few lines from it, his eyes shone and, as if in sight of a higher and brighter realm, whose doors had suddenly sprung open before him, he appeared as if transfigured.'

How far *Penthesilea* was carried at Rinnbach cannot be precisely determined: it was certainly very far from being completed. We have seen how his work was interrupted by noisy children in the house and how the weather seemed to conspire to prevent him continuing it in the open air. There also seems to have been no piano available, which was a great handicap, as he always liked to work out his ideas at the keyboard when composing. On 13th September he wrote in no very agreeable mood to Henriette Lang, telling of his various disappointments. He had been hoping to obtain employment in Germany, his 'promised land,' but had not succeeded in procuring even a position in an opera-house chorus. 'Oh, I shall learn yet to despise mankind, and with good reason,' he cried. 'Lies and deceit, dirty work, falsehood, self-interest, malice, narrow-mindedness, professional jealousy, against which the devil himself cannot make his way, turn out to be my dear, kindly disposed, helpful, self-sacrificing friends.'

In an evil moment he brought his valuable friendship with the

---

[1] Hermann Bahr, *Buch der Jugend*. It is very likely that the poet who so aroused Wolf's anger was Richard Kralik von Meyrswalden. Kralik's first book of verse came out in this year, and Wolf's contempt for his work is expressed repeatedly in the *Salonblatt* criticisms. Here are two examples of Kralik's 'poems' (from *Büchlein der Unwesenheit*):

> O Tag! O Sonne! O Morgenrot!
> O Wald! O Quell! O Hain!
> O Gott!—Wem klag ich meine Not?
> Zu lang bin ich allein.

> Spielet mir, o spielt mir vor
> Jene Tänze, die im Chor
> Ich tanzte mit der Trauten!
> Spielt den Ring des Nibelung,
> Jene Götterdämmerung,
> Die wir zusammen schauten!
> Ach, jene Tänze tanzt ich nicht,
> Und jenes Schauspiel schau ich nicht,
> Weil ihre Augen mir blauten.

Breuer family to a sudden end. He appeared at their house at Gmunden one evening while they were having supper and sat down with them. He came from Rinnbach and had obviously been drinking, so that the children found him quite changed from the friend they knew and loved. It happened that an infant prodigy, the later celebrated pianist Ilona Eibenschütz, was giving concerts at that time at Gmunden, and Wolf, regardless of the presence of the children, began to speak in outrageous terms of the mother of the prodigy. Frau Breuer endeavoured to silence him, and when his remarks grew worse and worse had to tell him outright: 'Herr Wolf, I cannot permit that another lady should be spoken of in such terms at my table.' Wolf stopped talking suddenly, got up, and left the house. Next morning a card arrived whereon he thanked the Breuers for all their past kindness to him; it was his leave-taking, and with it he passed entirely out of their lives.

Rinnbach became finally unendurable to him when one of the Köchert children developed measles, which meant the end of his visits to their household for a time. He was hard put to it to know what to do, but accepted, after some hesitation, a kindly offer by Fritz Flesch, a wealthy leather manufacturer who had been a member of the Wagner Verein party at Bayreuth, to make his home for the time at his house at Unter St. Veit, a suburb of Vienna, and continue work upon *Penthesilea*. So that he could work undisturbed, Flesch put the whole first storey of a house in the St. Veiter Hauptstrasse at Wolf's disposal.

Wolf left Rinnbach on 17th September and remained at Unter St. Veit until about the end of the year. The manuscript full score of *Penthesilea*, in the National Library in Vienna, is clearly dated 'Summer and Autumn 1883' at the foot of the last page. But it is certain, in spite of this inscription, that the tone-poem was *not* actually finished in this year.[1] The date is undoubtedly that of the

---

[1] In his 'Daten aus meinem Leben' Wolf says, under 1883: '*Penthesilea* sketched (*entworfen*), and under 1884, '*Penthesilea* scored.'   In my opinion, even this does not give the true facts of the case.   The work seems to have occupied Wolf up to 1885.

That the inscription on the score gives a wrong impression can be easily shown. According to information supplied to Decsey by Wolf's brother-in-law Josef Strasser, *Penthesilea* was still occupying his attention in the summer of 1884, while he was Strasser's guest at Öblarn.   Then again in 'Ein Monolog,' an article about the programmes of the Philharmonic concerts for the season then commencing, written by Wolf for the *Wiener Salonblatt* on 1st November 1884, there occurs this significant passage: 'Goldmark's *Penthesilea*—a noble subject for musical treatment, but the composer's talent is not equal to the grandeur of the

earliest draft, which with Wolf usually took the form of a piano score, the details and orchestration of which were worked out later. In later copies and completions of his works he always retained the dates of the original inception of his musical ideas—for him the most important thing in composition.

At Flesch's he was made extremely comfortable. It seems that his host kept a very well supplied table and cellar—Wolf refers several times in his letters to the liqueurs and champagne that were consumed there. He seems, however, to have been unhappy about this life of comparative ease and luxury and to have longed for the freedom of an independent existence again, even if it were only in an attic. Thus it came about that, with characteristic abruptness and seeming ingratitude, he broke away from the golden cage in which he felt himself confined and sought his liberty once more. The critical moment occurred during a meal. Flesch made use of a toothpick to pass a pear across to Wolf, and for no other discernible reason than this Wolf rose from the table and left the house—for ever. He made his way to the old Trattnerhof, Graben 29, where Edmund Lang had his quarters in the attic, and took up residence there with him. Then one day he announced that he was going to America, since he could not earn a living in his own country or in Germany. A friend of Eckstein's, Artur Gebhardt, whom Wolf had met through Amalie Materna, made the arrangements. Gebhardt was half American and the son of a silk merchant who had a New York branch, and he had suggested that Wolf should go with him

---

theme. Only a Makart could have represented Penthesilea in colour, only a Liszt or a Berlioz in music. No other could do it.' That certainly suggests that Wolf himself had not at that time succeeded in completing his own *Penthesilea* in a manner satisfying to his artistic conscience. Further, after the earliest of all references to the work in his letters, when its composition was barely begun, on 31st July 1883, where Wolf optimistically spoke of a performance in the succeeding winter under Mottl at Karlsruhe, there is no other suggestion of even the possibility of a performance until 1885. Then in September of that year he set to work vigorously to secure its performance in Vienna. What more likely than that *Penthesilea* and the music to Kleist's *Prinz von Homburg* were the unidentified 'greater works' which, as he told Strasser in a letter of 9th June 1885, he wished to finish before the autumn? What other works *could* have been meant?

Dates given in the *Penthesilea* sketch-book (National Library, Vienna,) are: 19th July 1883, Penthesilea theme, as at bars 520 and on; followed, without further dates, by the greater part of the second section of the work, 'Penthesilea's Dream,' in short score; 20th August 1883, opening of the first section, 'March of the Amazons'; this section is also almost completely sketched out on the succeeding pages; only a comparatively small part of the long third section of the work exists in sketch form, without further dates.

A letter to Gustav Schur of 18th December 1891 declares that *Penthesilea* was written in 1884–5.

there to try his fortune in the United States. It is said that they got as far as buying the ticket, but at the very last moment Wolf decided, after all, that he would not go. At about the same time he brought another old friendship to an end. During a conversation with Gustav Schönaich, Wolf was holding forth in a very extravagant manner, so that Schönaich was impelled to say: 'I can't take you seriously.' That was enough for Wolf, in the mood in which he was then; all past benefits forgotten, all affection and respect apparently wiped out in a moment by a careless remark, he went away and never spoke to Schönaich again.

Disagreeable incidents such as these were probably only the unfortunate outward signs of a conflict then going on deep within Wolf's nature. This inner struggle had nothing whatever to do with the consistent material difficulties of his life, but was concerned solely with his artistic and creative existence. We have seen how Wolf had been drawn more and more under the all-powerful influence of Wagner, so that his waking thoughts were never far removed from this theme, while the form of the master even appeared repeatedly in his dreams. The genius of Wagner had brought to the young Wolf supreme happiness and an artistic faith that, while it caused him to be unjust to other schools of music not professing allegiance to Bayreuth, yet ennobled all his being and steeled his resolve to be content with nothing that was second-rate in his own creative efforts. But Wagner's monopoly over his thoughts and feelings brought with it terrible waves of dejection. The more prodigious, the more unapproachably sublime the creations of Wagner appeared to his eyes, the more circumscribed and overshadowed he felt his own talents to be. 'What remains for me to do?' he lamented. 'He has left me no room, like a mighty tree that chokes with its shade the sprouting young growths under its widely spreading branches.' As one who knew him at this time has written: [1] 'Deepest despondency seized him. The discernment of Wagner's immeasurable greatness, of his monstrous wealth, of the universality of his genius, exerted a crushing effect upon Wolf.' To procure relief for his anguish of heart he used to discuss at great length with Edmund Lang the unhappy fate of the artist born too late in time. Though sometimes he wondered whether in song or in light opera there might not still remain a field worth his cultivating, he seemed for the present to have lost all joy in creation. 'Wagner, who had overshadowed completely his whole

[1] Marie Lang, 'Hugo Wolfs Entwicklungszeit.'

being, all his thoughts and feelings, Wagner the superhuman, the Titan, grew for him until he darkened the sun.'

On that account he felt himself so immeasurably drawn to Kleist, to whom Goethe had barred the way, whose impotence to achieve his highest aims and whose sorrow and despair had compelled his deepest sympathy. On that account he could not satiate himself with *Penthesilea*, 'the truest but at the same time the cruellest tragedy that ever sprang from a poet's brain.' With sighs and tears he read it many thousand times. It was the tragedy of his own soul.

It was in this mood of despair for his own creative abilities that, at the beginning of 1884, he turned aside from his attempt to translate Kleist's *Penthesilea* into musical terms, to try his hand at musical journalism for the fashionable weekly, the *Wiener Salonblatt*. The Köchert family, who as court jewellers were important advertisers in the *Salonblatt*, exercised their influence to secure the post for Wolf and thus brought a period of painful indecision to an end. Henceforth he would at least be provided with fixed employment and a regular, if modest, source of income. Not before it was time! Many of his older friendships lay in ruins behind him; he had to get along now without the help of Altmann or Dr. Breuer, the Gabillons, Schönaich, or Flesch.

Poor Hugo! He was going to make a name for himself at last, but in somewhat different circumstances from any he had imagined in the days of his youthful self-confidence and pride.

VII

THE CRITIC

THE *Wiener Salonblatt* was the creation of Moritz Engel, an ex-officer, well known in Austrian aristocratic circles in the days of his gallant youth, who in later years had made good use of these connections to build up the circulation of his magazine, the mirror of Viennese society. With its portraits of the nobility, its accounts of the season's balls, reviews of sport, and guidance to the vagaries of feminine taste, it was digested every Sunday by all fashionables and would-be fashionables in the city. Wolf's uncompromisingly severe and outspoken voice of criticism thus began to make itself heard among this ballroom chatter with effects that have been aptly compared by Ernest Newman to the entry of a howling dervish into a lady's boudoir. It was not in Wolf's nature to do anything by half-measures and soon the fanatical intensity of his attacks upon everything in the musical life of the capital which did not meet with his approval—the adulation of Brahms, the neglect of Liszt and Berlioz, the hide-bound conservatism of the Philharmonic programmes, the depravity of taste of the opera-going public and the vanity and indolence of some of its favourite singers—brought the *Salonblatt* to the attention of a far wider public than ever before. It was passed from hand to hand in the cafés and discussed and devoured with relish by the Wagnerians and with anger and distaste by their opponents. The 'wild Wolf' of the *Salonblatt* became a Viennese institution.

Wolf's critical reviews of the musical life of the city were a feature of the *Salonblatt* for more than three years; the first, signed 'x.y.,' appeared on 20th January 1884, and after that articles under his own name followed on almost every Sunday during the concert and opera seasons, up to 24th April 1887. Considered in isolation, the almost incredibly foolish-seeming attacks upon the staid and eminently respectable muse of Brahms would convey, and often *have* conveyed, the impression that the so-called 'critic' was nothing better than an ignorant *farceur* with a taste for self-advertisement, but any reader of the *Salonblatt* criticisms as a whole, who keeps in mind the polemical intentions of their author, must repeatedly recognize the keenness of Wolf's perception and not seldom the brilliance of its expression in words. His humour is sometimes a little heavy-handed, his writing, like his thoughts, somewhat undisciplined, but the general impression is certainly that of a most acute and discerning mind. Unlike Schumann, who, in his critical writings for the *Neue Zeitschrift für Musik*, gave generous praise not only to Chopin and Brahms, but to dozens of mediocrities who have never been heard of since, Wolf was never taken in by the third- and fourth-rate composers who had access to the public ear in his day. Undoubtedly he overrated Liszt and Berlioz, as was inevitable in a critic who deliberately set himself to oppose the reactionary tendencies of his time, but, apart from the undisguised antagonism to Brahms and composers such as Dvořák who were associated with the Brahmsian party, there is surprisingly little in the whole of Wolf's critical writings that is unacceptable to-day, after more than half a century, as a just, if severe, comment upon the works in question.

He took his stand upon Wagner, Beethoven, and the classical masters of the eighteenth century. Opportunities of hearing the music of Bach and Handel were limited in the Vienna of Wolf's day, and it is doubtful if he ever became acquainted with more than a small fraction of their total output. We know that he used to play the forty-eight Preludes and Fugues, but his own musical library contained only Bach's *Inventions*, *Chromatic Fantasy* and *Italian Concerto*—the last a great favourite—and nothing at all by Handel. The programmes of the concerts of the Gesellschaft der Musikfreunde during the years of Wolf's work for the *Salonblatt* included Bach's cantata *Es ist dir gesagt, Mensch, was gut ist*, *Magnificat*, *St. Matthew Passion* and the first complete performance in Vienna of the B minor Mass. Of these Wolf reviewed only the cantata. During the same period the only Handel work he wrote about was the oratorio *Saul*, in which he found much that was faded and out of date, especially in the recitatives and arias, but in the choruses 'an impetus, a dramatically impelled life, a titanic strength, a transporting power of expression, that still fill us to-day with wonder and admiration, and will surely do so as long as music is made at all.' There is, however, a remark of Wolf's on record that he was once bored stiff by a performance of *Messiah*.

His real interests began with the operas of Gluck and Mozart, and the symphonies, chamber music, and sonatas of Beethoven. 'Let

Gluck, Mozart, and Wagner,' he wrote, 'be for us the holy trinity, a holy trinity that only in Beethoven becomes one.   We owe them the greatest pleasures of life, deepest woe, and the most joyous exaltation, the torments of Prometheus and the bliss of Nirvana, every mortal emotion is opened up for us through the tones of these masters.' A boundless veneration for Mozart and Beethoven was presupposed in his readers from the start, so that no important discussions of the music of these composers are found in Wolf's writings.   For the most part comment is directed on the defects or qualities of the performance; devotion to the music itself and the recognition of its unquestioned eminence was taken for granted by Wolf.   The one exception was the *Grosse Fuge*, which the critic declared was a piece of music he simply did not understand.

Schubert he loved, but criticized with detachment and justice. Of the lightweight sixth Symphony he wrote:

> The real Franz Schubert whom we love and revere is far from being revealed in the recently heard Symphony.   On the contrary, the great composer appears here as a weak imitator of his afterwards so antipathetic rival Weber, there even as a copier of Rossini.   Pure Schubertian blood pulses only in the freshly springing scherzo with its striking reminiscence of the well-known *Reitermarsch* orchestrated by Liszt.

The Octet called forth the following little prose poem:

> The smiling earth in its spring finery, joyful mankind in the simplicity of its heart, with its passionate longing for pleasure and contentment—that is the world of which these harmonies relate.   Only in the introduction to the last movement does it seem as if a distant storm approached.   One hears the roll of the thunder, lightnings cleave the night; it is as if the composer raised the curtain over the window of his magic chamber to observe the rebellious elements.   But no shadow shall fall to-day over his serenity of mind.   He shuts out this gloomy scene and, turning his inspired glance inwards, heavenly bliss flows through his heart and a world full of love and goodness is transfigured in the melodies springing forth in the depths of his breast.

A passage from the notice of a performance of the Unfinished Symphony gives also a clear statement of Wolf's attitude towards the whole Schubertian heritage.

> The B minor Symphony, a true reflection of the artistic individuality of its creator, was unfortunately left a fragment.   So it compares in its form with the external existence of the master, who in the flower of his life, at the height of his creative powers, was snatched away by Death.   Schubert lived only half a lifetime, as a man and also as an artist.   His life barely sufficed for him to write two symphonic movements consummate in content

and form. We possess to be sure a precious legacy from him in the C major Symphony, but all the flowering riches of his ideas, the voluptuous spell of his melodies, cannot hide from us the loose construction of its symphonic architecture. The B minor Symphony is not only more compact, more formally unified than the C major, in its themes the pathetic Schubert speaks as convincingly as the dreamily elegiac. He reveals himself as completely as in his songs, in which he attained the highest.

Wolf retained his early admiration for Weber, and particularly for *Der Freischütz*. He recognized the failure of *Oberon* as an opera, in spite of the beauty of the music. There is not a great deal about Schumann in the *Salonblatt* articles, but Wolf's devotion is evident. His chief admiration was of course for Schumann as song-writer; other works which appealed strongly to him were the *Manfred* overture and the String Quartet in F major. He drew the line, however, at performances of later compositions such as the *Neujahrslied* and *Des Sängers Fluch*, which reveal all too clearly the clouding over of the mind that conceived them, with the gradual onset of mental disease. The *Provenzalisches Lied*, like a spring of sweet water in the midst of a desert, was too dearly bought at the cost of a performance of the whole of *Des Sängers Fluch*.

We know that Wolf profoundly admired Chopin, and was violently opposed to certain members of the Wagnerian party who criticized the Polish master as 'a *salon* musician' and 'un-German.' His pre-eminence among composers for the piano is emphasized in a review of a Chopin concert by Anton Rubinstein. There is not, however, anything outstanding about Chopin's music in the *Salonblatt*, apart from a rather flowery passage on the B flat minor Sonata.

Upon all aspects of Wagnerian interpretation, problems of production and of performance by both singers and orchestra, stage business, costume, and gesture, Wolf was always ready to discourse with authority and eloquence. The Isolde of Lilli Lehmann he found too much the virago.

The Isolde drawn by the poet is wholly woman, inflamed with love for Tristan but rebuffed by him, a rejected, outraged, derided woman. But never is a woman more feminine than when she is in love, and Isolde is in love from the first scene to her love-death. Isolde raves, fumes, rages, curses—whom? Her lover. Why? Because she loves him. Further, Isolde is far too much a woman, that is, loves Tristan far too much, to be able to dissemble, to appear as if she were wholly indifferent about him. Her cold, scornful speeches accord badly with the passionate beating of her heart, with her impetuous urging to the draught of expiation, with the subterfuges and diplomatic intrigues that she employs to shatter Tristan's

F

imperturbable composure.   Ah!   She loves him only too much, she is all too womanly.

Similarly he expounded to another singer the psychology of Lohengrin:

> The narration at the end of the opera could have been delivered by Herr Vogl in a more tranquil, serene, mysterious manner.   He put too much passion into it, he showed himself too human.   Lohengrin's eyes during the narration pass absently over the circle of his surroundings.   His spirit dreams of the wonders of Monsalvat, while his earthly part still dwells among common mortals, to speak to them for the last time.   So should his voice be nothing but the means of expressing his spirit's fair dream in transfigured melody.

There were certainly curious things to be seen and heard on the Wagnerian stage in Wolf's day—a Kurwenal who, so that the public should be under no misapprehension, used to tap his forehead significantly during Tristan's vision; a Venus in pink ballroom gown and corsets; singers who altered the text of their parts to suit their voices. With all this sort of thing Wolf dealt faithfully and severely, and hence made many enemies among singers and conductors.   'Herr Fuchs may be an excellent time-beater,' he wrote, 'but to conduct *Tristan*!! Herr Fuchs is a metronome.'   The customary cuts in the performance of *Tristan* infuriated Wolf:

> Among the Red Indians the most respected person is he who can show the greatest number of hacked-off scalps.   Quite certainly, too, that Kapellmeister enjoys the greatest regard among his colleagues who flays the scores the most, who can boast of having trimmed off with his red pencil (red pencil! how significant! the pencil reddens itself in the heart's-blood of the scores, as it burrows in their vital parts) not only the scalp but the whole head, together with the feet of the plot.   The Indians content themselves with the scalp and are savages.   The Kapellmeister mangle their victims and are for the most part civilized, yes, and wish also to be artists.   Artists!

His preoccupation with Wagnerian stage ideals led Wolf to detest Italian operatic mannerisms and the public which delighted in them. 'An Italian singer,' he declared,

> will relate with unexampled calm the news of an affecting event, so long as no B flat or C appears there for him, whereas the most indifferent circumstance can put him in a state of excitement and commotion, if only his larynx is sufficiently considered by the composer. . . .   The Italian *rabbia* overcomes the most abandoned villain in the most horrible aria of revenge just the same as the sentimental lover in the tenderest lyrical outpourings. The high notes are decisive.
>
> They are to repeat *Trovatore* in order, as in the last performance, to hear

a succession of the high notes which Signor Mierzwinski so generously
supplies to the frequenters of the Italian season. 'Good appetite!' one
would like to call out to the stalls, to whom each B flat or C of Mierzwinski's is at least as precious as a fresh, fat oyster. Observe them in that
exalted moment when the tenor from the beatific heights of his C or C
sharp smirks down transfigured on the stalls; they contentedly smack their
chops, stroke their stomachs in ease. . . . The ambitious among them
attempt to imitate him by singing with him at the same pitch; the more
modest choose the safe course of the lower octave; but the real enthusiast
joins only in the pantomime of the singer (a sign of great emotion) while
separating his upper and lower jaws as widely and for as long as the height
and duration of the notes attacked.

Wolf made no comment at all upon the music of any of the Verdi
operas which he attended as critic; he seems hardly to have been
aware of the significance of this composer. The weaker products of
the Italian operatic school, however, were torn to shreds in the
Salonblatt; operas accorded this treatment included Ponchielli's
Gioconda and Boito's *Mefistofele*:

> Indicative of the corruption of our theatre-going public are the continued
> performances of *Mefistofele*, this infamous work, to characterize which no
> expression can be strong enough. That Vienna is no German city, or
> draws upon no German theatre-going public, is becoming a melancholy
> certainty through the applause that the public gives to this wretched
> caricature of Goethe's *Faust*. The German, long-suffering as he is, how-
> ever much he might let pass, would never allow the pride of his country,
> Goethe's *Faust*, to be ravished before his eyes.

Other operas which were condemned included Rubinstein's *Nero*
and Goetz's *Taming of the Shrew*. On the other hand, Wolf appreciated Marschner and Lortzing, and showed a pronounced liking for
the light music of Auber and Suppé. Another of his early idols
had come down in his estimation, as the following comment makes
clear: 'What is one to say when for a whole month no Wagnerian
opera has been performed, but Meyerbeer three times a week? Are
we in Palestine, or in a German city?'

No consideration of Wolf's writings about the music of Brahms
can ignore the provocation to which as an ardent Wagnerian he was
subjected by the incessant pro-Brahmsian and anti-Wagnerian propaganda of Hanslick and his colleagues. For more than twenty-five
years Hanslick and his friends in Vienna had been slinging mud at
Wagner with impunity. They occupied the most influential critical
situations and set the tone for countless minor hacks who, in the name
of musical morality, gave vent to their spite and envy at the very real

success of Wagner's music with a great part of the public. For, as has been shown in an earlier account of the Viennese scene, the Wagnerian cause excited enormous enthusiasm in a large section of the populace; the hostility of Hanslick and Speidel in no way represented the real feelings of musical Vienna, but the Wagnerians lacked an outspoken advocate in the city press. Honest, responsible voices, such as that of Theodor Helm, Wolf's immediate predecessor in the pages of the *Salonblatt*, were to be heard here and there, giving out their impartial judgments upon the music of both Wagnerian and Brahmsian schools alike, but in the nature of things their sober thoughts found rather colourless verbal expression and their writings lacked entirely the flashy brilliance of the more spectacular mountebanks of the anti-Wagnerian school.

When Wilhelm Tappert, in 1877, first compiled his so-called *Schimpflexikon*, an anthology of abuse from the writings of Wagner's opponents, he culled twenty-four of his examples from the work of Hanslick and twelve from that of Speidel. What these gentlemen wrote about Wagner was quite as silly as anything that Wolf was to say later about the works of Brahms. One does not expect Hanslick to have shared the excitement with which Vienna witnessed the production of *Lohengrin* under Wagner's own direction, but his remarks on that occasion were astonishing enough: 'On 15th December 1875, the centenary of Boieldieu's birth should have been celebrated by the Opera and that this was not done was simply unpardonable.' The *Lohengrin* prelude sounded to Speidel like 'a boxful of cockchafers,' while Hanslick found the *Meistersinger* overture 'a musical product of painful artificiality and positively brutal in its effect.' Sachs's Cobbling Song was 'alleged to be comic, but suggests an infuriated hyena rather than a merry cobbler. . . .' 'A cannibal who had burnt his mouth with too hot a piece of human flesh would compose music like this.' *Das Rheingold* was 'a musical goose-march three hours long,' while as for *Tristan*, Hanslick felt impelled to 'protest most emphatically against the idea of accepting this assassination of sense and language, this stuttering and stammering, these bombastic, artificial monologues and dialogues, void of all natural sentiment, as a poetic work of art.'

It was inevitable, in these circumstances, that Wolf, when the opportunity came his way, should do everything in his power to redress the balance by counter-attacking along the entire Brahmsian front. It would be extremely instructive if we were able to set the contemporary comments of Hanslick and Wolf side by side, but this is not practicable, as Hanslick was at this time resting somewhat on his laurels and not writing at all regularly for the *Neue Freie Presse*. Neither Wolf nor Hanslick made any attempt to cover the entire field of Viennese musical activity; concerts reviewed at length by Hanslick are ignored by Wolf, and vice versa.

Here is the *Salonblatt* commentary upon Brahms's third Symphony:

As a symphony of Herr Dr. Johannes Brahms it is to some extent a capable, meritorious work; as a symphony of a second Beethoven it is a complete failure, since one must ask of a second Beethoven all that which is lacking in a Dr. Johannes Brahms—originality. Brahms is the epigone of Schumann and Mendelssohn and as such exercises about as much influence on the course of the history of art as the late Robert Volkmann, that is, he has for the history of art just as *little* importance as Volkmann, which is to say *no* influence at all. He (Brahms) is a proficient musician who knows his counterpoint, to whom occur ideas now and then good, occasionally excellent, now and then bad, here and there familiar, and frequently no ideas at all. . . .

Schumann, Chopin, Berlioz, Liszt, the leaders of the revolutionary movement in music since Beethoven (in which period Schumann himself hoped for a Messiah and in the person of—Brahms!) have passed by our symphonist without trace; he was, or pretended to be, blind as the eyes of astonished mankind opened and overflowed before the radiant genius of Wagner, as Wagner, like Napoleon, borne on the waves of the Revolution, led them into new channels by his despotic power, created order, and performed deeds that will live on eternally in the memory of mankind. But the man who has written three symphonies and apparently intends to allow a further six to follow these three cannot be affected by such a phenomenon, for he is only a relic from primeval ages and no vital part of the great stream of time.

As in those days people danced minuets, i.e. wrote symphonies, so Herr Brahms also writes symphonies, whatever may have happened meanwhile. He comes like a departed spirit back to his home, staggers up the rickety staircase, turns with much difficulty the rusty key which creakingly opens the cracked door of his deserted dwelling, and sees with absent-minded gaze the cobwebs pursuing their airy constructions and the ivy staring in at the gloomy windows. A bundle of faded manuscript paper, a dusty inkpot, a rusty pen arouse his attention. As though in a dream he totters to an antediluvian arm-chair and broods and broods and can't rightly recollect anything at all. At length his mind begins to clear: he thinks of good old Father Time, whose teeth have all fallen out, who has become shaky and wrinkled and who cackles and chatters like an old woman. He listens long to this voice, to these sounds—so long that at length it seems to him as if they had shaped themselves into musical motives. With an effort he reaches out for the pen and what he writes down are notes, to be sure, a

whole host of notes.   These notes are now stuffed into the good old form
according to the rules and the result is—a symphony!

Upon a performance of the B flat Concerto Wolf wrote:

Whoever can swallow this Piano Concerto with relish may look forward
with equanimity to a famine; it is to be supposed that he rejoices in an
enviable digestion and in time of famine will be able to help himself out
excellently with food substitutes such as window-panes, cork stoppers,
oven-screws and the like.

Of the D minor Piano Concerto he said: 'Through this composition blows an air so icy, so dank and misty, that one's heart freezes,
one's breath is taken away.   One could catch a cold from it.   Un-
healthy stuff!'   The Violin Concerto was 'a most disagreeable piece,
full of platitudes and meaningless "profundity."   The virtuoso
executed this thankless task with great bravura and did his utmost to
breathe life and warmth into the frozen composition.'

The whole mass of Wolf's critical writings is permeated through
and through with such sneers and gibes.   No matter what subject is
under discussion, sooner or later Brahms's name, or that of one of his
champions, Hanslick, Kalbeck, Dömpke, or Bülow, occurs with acid
comment.   'I once knew a celebrated music aestheticist,' remarks
the *Salonblatt* critic, 'who professed a dislike of cheese and yet
enjoyed Brahms's music.'

Brahms's Variations for orchestra on a theme of Haydn bear eloquent
witness to his peculiar gift of artistic manufacture.   Herr Brahms under-
stands the variation of given themes better than any one else.   His whole
works are nothing but a great variation upon the works of Beethoven,
Mendelssohn, and Schumann.

Striking is the crab-like retrogression of Brahms's productions.   He has
to be sure never been able to raise himself above the level of mediocrity,
but such nullity, emptiness, and hypocrisy as prevail in the E minor Symphony have come to light in no other of his works.   The art of composing
without ideas has decidedly found its most worthy representative in
Brahms.

Brahms himself seems to have taken these attacks in good part;
indeed, his whole personal attitude towards the controversies of his
time compels admiration.   He did not entirely relish his own
election as anti-pope.   He had, of course, publicly demonstrated his
hostility to the music of Liszt by the abortive manifesto of 1860 and
he also developed, later, a fathomless contempt for poor Bruckner,
when the latter was taken up by the Wagnerian party in their need of
a symphonist.   But towards Wagner, as distinct from the Wagnerian

party, Brahms's standpoint was one of great admiration for the man's purely musical gifts, tempered by dislike of his aesthetic theories. He always regretted that he had never been to Bayreuth and confessed that it was his fear of the Wagnerians that had prevented him from doing so. Perhaps the most illuminating of Brahms's recorded remarks concerning Wagner's music is that which he made to Carl Friedberg after a walk following a performance of the *Siegfried Idyll*, which they had attended together. Brahms did not utter a single word until they parted, when he blurted out: 'But one can't listen to such music *all* the time!' There was also the odious position taken up by Wagner himself in relation to his rival. It must have been extremely difficult for Brahms to think without prejudice of the man who publicly referred to him as a 'Jewish czardas player' and 'the Eunuch of Music.' Wolf's 'criticism' at least did not descend to that level.

We have seen, in discussing the interview of 1879, that Brahms attributed Wolf's animosity to the unfavourable verdict that had been passed upon the latter's early compositions when he had brought them to the Karlsgasse. Wolf's criticism seems to have interested Brahms more than his compositions had done. During a luncheon at the house of Rosa Papier, Brahms once humorously excused himself by saying: 'It's Sunday and I must buy the *Salonblatt* to see what Hugo Wolf has written further about me.' At a later date Richard Specht was invited to look up Wolf's criticisms in the *Salonblatt*.

There you will find that an original melody has never occurred to me and that I only produce mathematics in sound. At that time we used to laugh a great deal at the crazy modern Davidsbündler, when I recited his ferocious criticisms, which I carried about with me day and night.

Strangely enough, there were occasions when something of Wolf's early admiration for Brahms again overcame his later animosity. The String Sextet in G and the Alto Rhapsody he thought two of the best of their composer's works, while the String Quintet in F, Op. 88, even gave rise to one of his prose poems.

The imagination of the composer revels in picturesque images; we find no trace of the frosty November mists that elsewhere brood over his compositions and stifle each warm tone from the heart before it can sound out —all is sunny, now brighter, now more dim; a magical emerald green is diffused over this fairy-like picture of spring; everything grows green and buds, one really hears the grass growing—nature is so mysterious, so solemnly still, so blissfully transfigured—the composer could only by a sudden effort of will withdraw himself from this magic, so closely did the muse hold him under her spell.   In the second movement the shadows sink lower.   Evening, and then night, shroud the fantastic creations that moved so wonderfully in the first movement.   Deep meditation and silence.   An animated form moves through the deep solitude.   It is as if glow-worms danced their rounds, it flashes and sparkles so in the rushing figures of the instruments.   But the form disappears.   The former silence returns, to be once again broken by a similar motive.   In strange harmonies, that modulate between dream and waking, this mysterious tone-picture dies away.

After these two movements, however, the composer, according to Wolf, felt himself ill at ease in the magic gardens of romanticism,

for with a jerk he is sitting on the school-bench at Altona and recalls in the finale with much gladness his contrapuntal studies under Marxsen—whither however we have no desire to follow him.

In Wolf's references to the works of Liszt there is always an element of fanaticism.   A performance of the symphonic poem *Tasso* drew from him the following outburst:

If you want symphonies to-day as Beethoven wrote them, then turn back our century, waken the master from the dead, but don't set up in his place our epigones, these impotent symphony writers of the present day. . . . Beethoven, as absolute musician, has in the symphony spoken the last word.   Liszt, as poetic musician, the first (and perhaps at the same time the last) word in the symphonic poem. . . .   Such bold, original creations of genius as those of Liszt are nevertheless disposed of by our critics with sovereign contempt, or with a pityingly sarcastic remark, while the glue-factories, these disgustingly insipid, from the bottom of his soul mendacious and crazy symphonies of Brahms are praised by them as a wonder of the world.   Who could keep silent in those circumstances?   In a single cymbal clash from a work of Liszt's is expressed more spirit and feeling than in all Brahms's symphonies and his serenades besides.   To compare Liszt with Brahms at all!   Genius with the Epigone of Epigones!   The eagle with the hedge-sparrow!'

A performance of the orchestral *Mephisto Waltz* ('The Dance at the Village Inn') caused a riot at a Philharmonic concert on 18th April 1886.   The young enthusiasts in the cheaper seats and standing-room at the back of the hall applauded violently, while the reactionaries in the stalls hissed.   Wolf's voice was heard above the din: 'Outside with the hissers!' and this cry was taken up all around him.   The demonstrators were only silenced when the police were sent for. This episode was celebrated in the *Salonblatt* a week later:

Utterly determined, the standing-room and part of the galleries opposed the stalls, the mountain against the swamp.   On the one side youth, intelligence, idealism, discernment, enthusiasm, conviction; on the other side stupidity, frivolity, lack of principle, ignorance, conceit, and Abderitism.[1]

Of Berlioz Wolf seems to have most admired the *Symphonie fantastique* and *La Damnation de Faust*. He admitted the defects and limitations of lesser works, such as the *King Lear* and *Corsair* overtures. Opportunities of hearing the less well-known compositions did not come often in Wolf's day; surprisingly, he had practically nothing to say of the *Grande Messe des Morts* when it was performed in April 1884, and the first performance in Vienna of the *Te Deum* on 14th December of the same year is not even mentioned in the *Salonblatt* criticisms. Of *La Damnation de Faust* he said truly:

Berlioz was incapable of creating an organic work of art, congruent in form and content, like the two compositions of Wagner and Liszt [the *Faust* overture and *Faust* symphony]. His *Faust* is a fragmentary mosaic, a building without plan, full of the most beautiful detail but without a conscious aim. The Faust theme, in its purely human features an inexhaustible spring of artistic ideals, disintegrates with Berlioz into the idle play of arbitrary fancies, which, though admirable in themselves and full of genius, shatter the poetic intention to pieces and do not allow complete enjoyment of the whole work. This reproach applies also to Schumann's *Faust*. An inner instability is common to both, and if Schumann's *Faust* follows with finer feeling Goethe's original, Berlioz's work surpasses it in musical content. But whatever one may think of Berlioz's conception of the Faust idea, one thing is certain—that almost every number in this work invites our most ardent admiration.

After the *Symphonie fantastique* had been more coolly received than Wolf considered fitting, he grew almost incoherent in the expression of his indignation. He enjoined the Philharmonic orchestra, which had at length summoned up enough courage to perform the work, not to despise the enthusiasm of youth, which alone, from the galleries and standing-room, had shown appreciation of it.

Let us not be disconcerted by the spleen and the dishonourable conduct of our critical opponents. We have the shield of truth to guard us, we carry the sword of inspiration to overcome our adversaries; let 'War against the Philistines, War against the Critics' be henceforth our battle-cry.

At first Wolf did not accept without reservations the symphonies of Anton Bruckner, 'this Titan in conflict with the gods,' as he called him.

It is their intellectual deficiency, notwithstanding all their originality,

---

[1] 'The air of Abdera was proverbial as causing stupidity.' *Encyclopaedia Britannica*.

* F

greatness, force, imagination, and invention, that makes the Bruckner symphonies so difficult to understand. Everywhere a will, colossal preparations, but no satisfaction, no artistic solution.

Nevertheless, he yet considered these works the most important creations in symphonic form that had been written since Beethoven.

They are works of an unfortunate genius, comparable to the colossal poems of Grabbe. Bold, magnificent conceptions are as common to them both as are confusion and formlessness in their execution.

From this attitude to Bruckner's work Wolf's friend Eckstein and others long strove to move him. At length Wolf confessed he had seen the light. Eckstein arranged a meeting between the two composers, which took place on Corpus Christi day, 1885, at Klosterneuburg, and after that Wolf was an active adherent of the Brucknerian faith. In March 1886 he greeted the belated Vienna performance of the E flat Symphony, which had already achieved success at Munich, Leipzig, Hamburg, and Hanover, but reminded the Philharmonic Committee that in the composer's desk lay half a dozen other symphonies which had never been performed at all, the least of them, to his mind, a Chimborazo compared with the Brahmsian molehills! When, in the same year, Bülow hoaxed the simple-minded Bruckner by sending three telegrams announcing that he had been elected to the Bulgarian throne, that ten thousand photographs of him were required at once, as the populace were crying out for portraits of their sovereign, and that the critics who had broken lances for him were to receive places in the Cabinet, Wolf, along with Theodor Helm and Gustav Schönaich, was named for ministerial appointment.

Bizet's *L'Arlésienne* delighted Wolf; in the *Vysehrad* and *Vltava* of Smetana he recognized two masterpieces. Of the Russians he liked what he heard of Tchaikovsky and Glinka, but a whole programme of Russian music was more than he could stand. 'We certainly do not belong to the apostles of moderation,' he wrote.

Abstemiousness, self-laceration, and mortification of the flesh we have never preached. We are no musical Trappists. But to listen for a whole evening to Russia's hopeful music of the future would put out of humour even the most nihilistic patriot of the czar's realm. I would just as soon be transformed into an old bassoon as live through another such evening.

There were various general reforms that Wolf was constantly urging upon the Viennese musical world. In a strange article entitled 'From the Diary of a Chinaman' he imagined himself

intendant of the Court Opera.   Under his regime the whole decoration of the theatre was to be altered, the claque done away with, all
pretentious 'star' singers ejected, the ballet halved in numbers, the
theatre closed twice a week to allow of adequate rehearsals, the entry
of the audience during the playing of an overture forbidden, disturbers of the peace quietly but firmly removed, and only good works
performed in the most perfect way possible.   On other occasions he
protested against the use of the larger concert-halls for the performance of chamber music and the production of the more intimate
operas on the vast stage of the Court Opera.   Works such as Lortzing's *Waffenschmied*, he thought, had been infinitely more effectively
given at Salzburg, during his period as Kapellmeister there, with
inferior resources but a smaller stage.   He wished in certain circumstances to forbid applause.   If the Viennese public were to witness an
eclipse of the moon, a thunderstorm, a prairie fire, a rainbow, an
earthquake or volcano, it would seem that their first reaction would
be to applaud the good Lord for his excellent performance.

In the name of Heaven and all angels and archangels, must the kindling
lightning of enthusiasm always travel to the hands and feet?   Must there
be clapping and stamping? . . .   I ask whether in all circumstances
applause is called for?   Whether applause is a law of nature or only a
silly, bad habit?

There were occasions when it was by no means out of place.
'Continue to applaud, but only where the work of art itself invites
applause—at resounding conclusions, in pieces of cheerful, festal,
warlike, heroic character.'   At other times it was offensive and
stupid.   He instanced Beethoven's *Coriolan* overture:

The eye still stares drunkenly forward, as if into a magic mirror, wherein
the gigantic shadow of Coriolanus slowly floats away, the tears still run,
the heart throbs, the breath is caught, the limbs are incapable of movement
—and the last note has scarcely died away, when you are again cheerful
and contented, making a noise and criticizing and clapping.   Oh, you have
looked into no magic mirror, you have seen nothing, felt nothing, heard
nothing, understood nothing; nothing, nothing, nothing at all!   But you
applauded well.

Such were the chief musical tastes, the opinions and prejudices, of
Hugo Wolf the *Salonblatt* critic.   In later years Friedrich Eckstein
once suggested that these writings should be collected and republished
in book form.   Wolf's reaction was surprising.   He jumped up from
his chair in a rage and rushed at Eckstein with raised fists, as though
he would strike him.   'No, no, no!' he cried.   'Never!   Don't talk

about it. May God grant that these articles be soon entirely forgotten, as they richly deserve! There is nothing that could harm me
more than that somebody should unearth them and print them
again.' He was, it appeared, *ashamed* of his *Salonblatt* articles—not,
however, on account of their content; it was only because of their
literary imperfections that he would have resigned them to limbo.
On several later occasions he laid stress on the fact that he retracted
nothing of what he had written as a critic, that his actual opinions had
not become modified, or moderated, with the years, and, indeed, the
fanatical elements in Wolf's make-up became more, and not less,
pronounced as he grew older.

The period of musical journalism forms a characteristic episode in
the story of Wolf's uneven progress through life; it was not, however,
of any significance in his development as an artist. Nor did he
succeed in leaving any enduring influence behind him. But if none
of the reforms that he advocated was ever carried out, if Brahms
continued to be performed and Berlioz comparatively neglected, if
his writings in themselves had little real importance, they nevertheless
added a good deal to the interest and gaiety of musical Vienna in his
time, and for us to-day they throw a valuable sidelight upon his
character. It was only in its consequences upon his own life and
struggle to attain artistic recognition that the critical interlude was
wholly deplorable. It was of course highly imprudent in a young
musician to risk making so many enemies in high places. What
Wolf had to say he said vigorously and distinctly, regardless of
whether his remarks, and the highly characteristic voice in which they
were uttered, were pleasing to all those within earshot or not. There
were many that heard with violent distaste and they did not forgive,
and the misdeeds of Wolf the *Salonblatt* critic were long remembered
against Wolf the composer of genius.

VIII

THE ARTIST AND THE WORLD

THE years during which Wolf was working as music critic to the *Wiener Salonblatt* are the least well documented of the whole of his career. His collected criticism forms a substantial volume of 368 pages, but in addition to this the most painstaking research has produced only a handful of letters, spread over more than three years. His letters to his parents seem to have disappeared almost entirely, and his father's surviving correspondence is also scanty and comparatively uninteresting. Fortunately for the biographer, Wolf's life during this period was necessarily a good deal less erratic than it had been in earlier years, since his movements were restricted by his work for the *Salonblatt*. He was busy in the Vienna concert-halls and opera-house until about June of each year and resumed these duties in September or October. Some of the few letters that we do possess are of extreme interest and importance, and personal reminiscences do something to fill in the outline of Wolf's activities during these years devoted to musical journalism.

Shortly after the new critic commenced his work for the *Salonblatt* there appeared in its pages the following small advertisement:

A musician wishes to give tuition in the pianoforte, harmony, and counterpoint, etc. etc. Strongly recommended by the editors of this journal, who will also give fuller particulars.

It is very probable that this referred to Wolf himself, who hoped to be able to supplement the 60 gulden a month which he was drawing as music critic of the *Salonblatt* with some teaching appointments among the high society whose affairs it chronicled. In this he was helped by Engel, who was not unappreciative of the original qualities of his new assistant and who was secretly amused at the indignant letters which began to arrive from readers whose taste and intelligence had been insulted in Wolf's articles. There were, nevertheless, sometimes scenes in the offices of the *Salonblatt*, when the critic discovered that his more extravagant outbursts had been toned down by the editor.

Very amusing are the reflections of Hugo's critical writings in Philipp Wolf's letters. It had been, of course, a source of endless satisfaction to Philipp that his son had at length found work that gave him a settled, if modest, income.   Copies of the *Salonblatt* were sent home regularly, passed from hand to hand at Windischgraz, and everywhere commented upon.   Philipp shared Hugo's antipathy towards Brahms, Brüll, and others of that circle, but feared greatly that his attacks upon them would lead to trouble.   In March 1884 he noted the increasingly passionate character of Hugo's diatribes and uttered a word of warning.   'Anxiety haunts me that that could cause you harm.   Poor Grün!   For Brahms I am less sorry—he was never sympathetic to me.   I have always held him to be a musical swindler, who was raised up by patronage.'   A little later, after the article in which it was stated that there was more spirit and feeling in a single cymbal clash from a work of Liszt's than in all Brahms's symphonies and serenades, Philipp wrote again:

I am always worried that your criticism could involve you in a duel, and set your Jewish friends against you.   You have squashed the wretched Brahms like a flea between your fingers.   The fellow quite deserves it, to be sure, but won't they all pounce on you one day, when you appear before the public with the offspring of your imagination?

This is a recurring theme:

May fortune for once thoroughly empty her horn of plenty before you, so that you may look forward to the future without cares, so that you need not write your fingers sore with criticism and thereby lay yourself open to the danger of having to fight a duel with a singer (Rokitansky) or with Brahms, as I have several times feared—these people must be very tame natures.

The idea of Brahms and Wolf squaring accounts with rapiers or pistols is inexpressibly comic.   Philipp often praised Hugo's writings and was undoubtedly very proud of him, but at the same time urged him repeatedly not to neglect composition.   The position as music critic to the *Salonblatt* represented for Philipp a reasonably satisfactory solution to his son's problems, and a happier outcome of his adoption of a musical career than had seemed possible in earlier years.

The old Trattnerhof, in the attic of which Wolf, early in 1884, occupied a room rented by his friend Edmund Lang, had associations with Mozart, who is thought to have been at one time in love with Frau von Trattner, the wife of the publisher who gave his name to the building.   Mozart lived in the Trattnerhof in 1784 and in it his son Karl Thomas was born.   Wolf's own stay there was limited to a few months.   In March Lang and Wolf were joined by Hermann Bahr, who, since they had left him in the Steinkogl Inn near Rinnbach, had succeeded in getting himself expelled from the University of Czernowitz; Bahr's scholastic record is worthy of comparison with that of Wolf himself. There were three rooms in Lang's apartments, of which the farthest, reached only by passage through the other two, belonged to Wolf. He had installed a piano there and friends had provided various household utensils and a few pieces of furniture. Bahr occupied the middle room and the unselfish host the narrow outer chamber. Bahr and Lang celebrated their reunion by many a nightly carousal, returning in the small hours of the morning heavy-eyed with lack of sleep and too much liquor. As they threw off their shoes and clothing and prepared to retire from the world for a space the door of the farthest room would open and Wolf appear in his long night-shirt, a flickering candle and some book or other in his hand, very pale and strange in appearance in the uncertain light. He would chuckle and mock the revellers and then sit down on Bahr's bed and begin to read aloud, generally out of *Penthesilea* but often also from Grabbe's *Scherz, Satire, Ironie und tiefere Bedeutung*. Bahr compared Wolf's absolute understanding of his favourite poets to that of certain fanatical followers of Verlaine or Baudelaire he had met in Paris, who knew every line of their master's work. To hear Wolf read *Penthesilea* in the grey dawn in a Trattnerhof attic was to forget weariness and fuddled heads; Bahr and Lang only knew that they were in the presence of genius. Wolf's astounding ability to bring a poem or a dramatic scene to life, to master the words and meaning until they seemed almost to belong to him alone, to be the creations of his own brain, was to be a decisive factor, fully equal in importance to his purely musical gifts, in the make-up of the greatest song-writer of modern times. It was owing to this that he was able, in his most inspired moments, to fuse fine poetry and his own music into one whole, the incomparably beautiful and enduring alloy that is Wolfian song.

It is uncertain how long Wolf remained in the Trattnerhof. Letters of his father's were addressed there up to 12th March, but towards the end of May and in June we find him living at Karlsgasse 4, on the third floor. It does not seem to have been noticed that this was the house in which Brahms had been living since 1871, and the scene of that unfortunate interview in 1879. It is surely an extraordinary thing that Wolf should have returned to live there, and on the very floor on which Brahms himself had his flat. Wolf did not like the place, however, and thought his landlady dirty and negligent. He had ideas of spending a third summer at Maierling and made inquiries of the Preyss family, stressing the fact that he had grown up a bit and lost some of his unruliness. He believed that the servants would have an easier time with him than had been the case in former years. But the peasants of Maierling had long memories and nothing would induce them to undertake again the tasks of blacking Wolf's shoes and washing his clothes, making his bed, and cleaning his coffee-machine.

The last critique for the season appeared in the *Salonblatt* on 15th June and a few days later Wolf went to Rinnbach as the Köcherts' guest. The name of this family has recurred, and will continue to recur, with increasing frequency in the story of Wolf's life. The brothers Heinrich (1854–1908) and Theodor Köchert (1859–1936) were active supporters and members of the Vienna Wagner Verein and proprietors of the firm of A. E. Köchert, goldsmiths and court jewellers, established in Vienna since 1814 in a wonderful old house in the inner city, at Mehlmarkt (Neuer Markt) 15. Photographs show these lifelong friends and benefactors of Wolf as tall, heavily bearded figures—Heinrich dark and Theodor fair. But the portraits do not reveal very much, and both men have remained rather shadowy personalities in Wolf literature, whose names crop up from time to time in the letters and biographies, who were obviously on extremely intimate terms with the composer, but about whom practically nothing is known. While others, including some who were only remotely connected with Wolf, have published their reminiscences and almost invariably exaggerated the degree of their intimacy with him, the members of this family have been so reticent that there has been serious danger until recently that the decisive and fateful roles which they played in the drama of the composer's life would never be clearly understood owing to sheer lack of documentation. Only three letters to Theodor Köchert have survived. They are very important in the history of *Penthesilea*, and their high-spirited tone of banter suggests a carefree companionship based on understanding and a common sense of humour. But Theodor's part was a minor one, compared with those of his brother Heinrich and Melanie, the latter's wife. Wolf's letters to Heinrich Köchert have been lost, which is nothing short of a calamity, from the biographer's point of view. He seems to have been more retiring, more serious-minded, than his brother. A very sympathetic character emerges when we piece together the scraps of information available—one would like, very much, to know more. Wonderful tact and kindness characterize Heinrich Köchert's aid to Wolf, which never failed through half a lifetime. Although Wolf himself never knew it, his retention of the position as music critic to the *Wiener Salonblatt* was solely due to the generosity of this friend, who arranged to pay in with the bill for his advertisements a sum which was then paid out to Wolf as his salary. Then he would go off to the races, promising to 'put something on' for the composer. Wolf's horse always won, and on his return Heinrich would hand over his winnings, which actually came out of his own pocket. In a thousand other ways Heinrich Köchert covertly or openly smoothed Wolf's rock-strewn path. A considerable part of the composer's life was spent as guest of the Köcherts, either in their town house in the Mehlmarkt, at Döbling, where they owned a suburban villa, or in the Salzkammergut, at Rinnbach or Traunkirchen. Posterity owes an enormous debt to Heinrich Köchert. He had much to put up with as a result of this relationship, and it is to his eternal credit that, whatever the difficulties and however great the provocation to act otherwise, he recognized always that genius is not to be judged by the standards of normality.

How far Wolf himself appreciated what was done for him by this man, and through what vicissitudes their friendship endured, cannot be shown owing to the loss of their correspondence. Something of what Wolf owed to Melanie Köchert, however, is now on record in the wonderful series of letters that have come down to us— incomparably the most beautiful, interesting, and revealing that he ever wrote, some of them in their way as consummate as his finest songs. They provide an annihilating answer to the whispering campaign of denigration that was afoot in some circles in Vienna. It has been said: 'She was not capable of understanding him or his music.' A hundred passages in the letters give the lie to this statement, and if that is not enough there is this dedication in a volume of his songs:

> An Frau Melanie.
> Von Allen, die der Tonkunst Zauber tief empfunden
> Hat Niemand mich so ganz wie Du verstanden.

It is not too much to say that without Melanie Wolf's life-work, the songs on which his reputation rests, would probably never have been written. This he himself recognized when he laid the manuscripts of them all—a kingly present—at her feet. Two years older than Wolf, she was an extremely handsome woman, with a high clear brow and the most wonderful liquid brown eyes. Even in a portrait from childhood these eyes seem already to prefigure, with sadness and compassion, all that was to come. Wolf used to call this the 'Mignon portrait.' It was Melanie Köchert's destiny to stand beside Wolf for twenty years, to encourage and console him in his struggle for self-expression and for recognition, to rejoice with him in his creative ecstasies, and then to watch him, for five long years, die by inches in a mental home. Throughout his creative life she watched over his material and spiritual welfare with unending benevolence and devotion, and, when the dark hours came, she never left him. Unfalteringly she drank the bitter cup to the dregs and, some time after his death, brought to an end her own life, which had lost all its meaning.

The house at Rinnbach, named 'Krähbauer,' where, in the second half of June and the whole of July 1884, Wolf was a guest of the Köcherts, stands at the top of a rather steep grassy slope, facing the Traunsee, among the last little group of buildings before the lake's eastern margin is hemmed in by the mountains. It was here that he had visited them in the previous year and begun work upon *Penthesilea*, and here he was often to return. The immediate surroundings are unchanged to-day, but industrial Ebensee has spread its tentacles and almost engulfed once secluded Rinnbach. For the lover of Wolf a poetic aura must ever surround this spot, in spite of the encroachment of all too prosaic Ebensee.

From Rinnbach Wolf moved on 1st August to Schloss Gstatt, near Öblarn, in the valley of the Enns, in Styria. In this beautiful country district his brother-in-law Josef Strasser held office as inspector of taxes and in his household Wolf spent the rest of the summer. He was thoroughly happy there with his sister Modesta and her children, and for his brother-in-law he conceived a profound affection. There were few people indeed of whom Wolf was as fond as he was of Josef Strasser, as many passages from his correspondence testify:

Friend of my heart! How did Nature contrive to fabricate such a fine fellow as you are? No, you cannot in the least divine how your dear lines delighted me. You are the only man to whom I am devoted with my whole heart, whom I love, esteem, and admire. You are the only person who makes me still believe that man is not entirely beast, and in this 'entirely' is great praise for you, for generally speaking I have found mankind far worse than beasts. In short, and without beating about the bush, I love you. . . . My dear, dear friend! I *must* see you again this year. By God!

I am a hard-boiled fellow but when I think of you I become as soft as butter.   It is not exactly my way to be tearful, but you, with your boundless simplicity and goodness of heart, could make me sob like two dozen mill-wheels.

He compared Strasser to the hero of Claude Tillier's *Mon Oncle Benjamin*, a book he passionately admired.   In his correspondence, however, Wolf often signed himself as 'Benjamin' and addressed Strasser as 'Beisskurz,' the German equivalent for 'Machecourt,' the brother-in-law of Uncle Benjamin in Tillier's novel.

The mornings Wolf generally spent composing.   While staying at Rinnbach, on 11th July, he had produced a new Mörike song, *Die Tochter der Heide*, and begun work on the new last movement of his String Quartet; now in Schloss Gstatt he completed this and returned to wrestle again with the scoring of his *Penthesilea*.   During this summer he was also working at music to another of Kleist's plays, *Prinz Friedrich von Homburg*.   No one was allowed to disturb him in his room; when his sister called him for his meals he used to spread his arms out quickly over his papers and ask irritably: 'Must the body be fed again already?'   When he could make no progress with his score he was continually out of humour, until the moment came when he saw a way out of his difficulties.   This happened during a visit to Schladming on 30th August, when he conceived the Funeral March for his *Prinz von Homburg* music and in his excitement jumped for joy like a child.

Of the incidental music to Kleist's *Prinz von Homburg* very little has survived.   The National Library in Vienna has the sketches for the brief monologue in the fourth act: 'Das Leben nennt der Derwisch eine Reise'; the Vienna City Library has the full score of the same piece and a short fragment, also in full score, of the Funeral March (*Trauermusik*) for the end of the second act.   This Funeral March was completed in Wolf's head, at any rate, and probably in sketch form on paper.[1]   He played it sometimes to Eckstein, who had a high opinion of it.   All that remains is a powerful introduction of sixteen bars, scored for a much larger orchestra than Wolf could have hoped to find in any theatre where this music might have been employed, and the first four bars of the main march theme.   For the Prince of Homburg's Hamlet-like meditation in the fourth act Wolf provides thirty-five bars of dark-toned accompaniment to the spoken

[1] In 1890 Wolf wrote to Grohe: 'Music to the *Prinz von Homburg* lies before me in sketch form, but a very expressive Funeral March, which is also partly scored, could be extracted from it.'

text. These fragments are impressive, but too short to allow an opinion to be formed on the importance of the work as a whole.[1]

When not preoccupied with musical problems Wolf spent much time during his summer holidays at Öblarn in walking among the surrounding mountains, and he also made various excursions of several days' duration into more distant parts. Strasser had to travel a good deal, in his official capacity, and Wolf used to accompany him. Thus they visited the Aussee district, a favourite resort of Viennese artistic society, and it was there, no doubt, that he introduced his brother-in-law to the Goldschmidts. There too he met the folk poet and composer Johann Kain, known as the 'Bachwirth,' and after his return to Schloss Gstatt Wolf used to plague his sister with endless repetitions of some of Kain's songs which he had learned by heart. He taught them to the children, who remember them to this day. He later rehearsed the three Köchert girls in one of these songs, an endless enumeration of all the different kinds of dumplings favoured by the composer, took the children to Aussee, and made them sing it to Kain, who listened with tears running down his cheeks and declared it was the happiest day of his life.

In the evenings Wolf read Kleist's comedy *Der zerbrochene Krug* to Modesta and Strasser, and one day he showed them with pride a letter from Liszt. He had sent a copy of *Die Spinnerin*, the song he had played on the occasion of his interview with the master, and had received it back with a gracious letter and a necessary correction in Liszt's hand on the margin of the manuscript.

With the end of the summer Wolf went back to Vienna to resume his duties for the *Salonblatt*. The exact date of his return is uncertain, but his first critique of the new season appeared on 19th October, a review of a performance of Marschner's *Vampyr* on the 15th. On 22nd October he was able to inform Strasser that he had on the previous day, after a short stay in a too expensive hotel, found a new lodging in the inner city at Kumpfgasse 9. Here he lived on the fourth floor of an old house called the Becherlhof, from a relief over the entrance with the figures of children bearing goblets. 'I am happy about my new home,' he wrote. 'Just what I have sought for so

---

[1] An article by Fritz Kuba, 'Hugo Wolfs Musik zu Kleists Schauspiel "Prinz Friedrich von Homburg,"' in the *Jahrbuch der Kleist-Gesellschaft*, vol. xvii (1937), describes not only the Funeral March and the monologue but various other disconnected sketches which are found together with this music among the manuscripts formerly in possession of the Vienna Wagner Verein. Kuba failed to notice that these are sketches, not for the *Prinz von Homburg* music, but for *Christnacht*.

hard and so long—a room entirely separated from the staircase. At last I have found it, and with a pleasant ante-room besides, that gives the living-room an appearance worthy of a critic.' This dwelling, so conveniently situated high up over the centre of the city, roomy and well lighted, seemed to him a bargain at 24 florins a month, including service, and he settled down thankfully for a long stay. The furnishings could not be said to be luxurious—a rickety bed, a hired piano under the window, a small table with two chairs, and, right in the middle of the room, an enormous indiarubber bath-tub, this last now and henceforward his indispensable companion wherever he went to live. Except during the summer months, he made his home in these rooms in the Kumpfgasse for the best part of the succeeding three years.

A letter to Ludwig Koch, the chairman of the Wagner Verein, shows Wolf in November endeavouring to secure the performance of his String Quartet and his Eichendorff choruses. Arnold Rosé, at that time only twenty-one years of age, but already Konzertmeister of the Vienna Philharmonic orchestra and the leader of the string quartet bearing his name, had given Wolf reason to hope that his D minor Quartet would be played at one of their chamber concerts. For some reason Rosé then changed his mind and Wolf turned to the Wagner Verein and offered both the Quartet and the Eichendorff choruses for performance at their private concerts—concerts intended, as he reminded Herr Koch, for the production of just such good and little-known works as he believed his own compositions to be. The Wagner Verein seems not to have shared this opinion, for nothing came of the proposal.

On 21st January 1885 Wolf had further bad news about the fate of his own works to report to Strasser. The Viennese publisher Gutmann had at length been persuaded to undertake the publication of some songs but had in the end broken his word and returned the manuscripts. 'I console myself with the words of Berlioz,'[1] Wolf wrote to his brother-in-law. "Let us raise ourselves above the miseries of life, let us banish all black thoughts and sing with cheerful voice the well-known lively refrain:

Ex 3

di – es i - rae, di – es il - la cru - cis

---

[1] Quoted from Berlioz's *Grotesques de la musique*.

In spite of these further disappointments, Wolf had evidently regained a measure of self-confidence, and in the summer of 1885 he resolved upon a great new effort to lift himself out of the dreary round of musical journalism and win recognition as a composer. He told Strasser that he had regretfully decided that he could not this year visit him at Gröbming.   He would have to do without a holiday, as it was essential that he should complete some large-scale compositions before the autumn.   For this purpose he needed a piano and as his financial means would not permit the hiring of an instrument for the summer months he preferred to remain in Vienna and to take advantage of the hospitality of the Köchert family, who had placed a room at his disposal in their house in the Mehlmarkt.   He moved from the Kumpfgasse lodgings to the Mehlmarkt on 13th June and there he worked in ideal conditions at the unparticularized 'greater works' mentioned in a letter to Strasser on 9th June.   There can be little doubt that Wolf was here referring to the *Prinz von Homburg* music and to *Penthesilea*.   The reason why he was anxious to complete these works by the autumn is that he would then be able to submit them to the Philharmonic orchestra for consideration among the season's novelties.

In a series of letters to Strasser, Wolf refers from time to time to his labours.   He sorely missed his holiday and often thought of the happy summer of the previous year.   On 23rd July he wrote:

I have been rummaging about in my manuscripts to-day and found among them many things that were scribbled by me in Schloss Gstatt. Schladming too, with the date of 30th August, is immortalized (?) on a sheet that is scrawled over with a sketch for the Funeral Music from the *Prinz von Homburg*.   What wonderful memories awake for me in gazing at these pages!   It was the happiest time of my life.

On 1st August he was still 'head over heels' in his tasks, but in the course of the next few weeks *Penthesilea*, at least, was completed to his satisfaction and in time for inclusion, with luck, in the Philharmonic programmes for the new season.   The members of the Philharmonic orchestra had the final word as to whether a new work should be included in their programmes or not, and their judgment was given by vote after a trial performance, which usually took place before the beginning of the concert season.

The normal course for any composer who aspired to the performance of his music by the Philharmonic orchestra was to submit his work officially to the committee.   Wolf, however, preferred to tackle Hans Richter personally and enlist his support beforehand. Years before, as a boy of sixteen, he had already benefited by Richter's advice, and later received through his recommendation free tickets for the Bayreuth festivals. He therefore repeatedly sought for Richter at the opera-house, where he knew him to be engaged on rehearsals, but did not succeed in obtaining an interview.

The fellow is as inaccessible as the Czar of Russia, I thought—and a thing or two else besides. The affair is too silly. The devil take Richter and my *Penthesilea*. I will bother myself further neither with the one nor the other. *Penthesilea* I'll hand in. If it's accepted, good; if not, good as well.

So he wrote to Theodor Köchert on 18th September. But three days later he made a last attempt to interest Richter in his work and this time he succeeded.

He had moved at this time to the Köcherts' suburban villa at Döbling and from there, with his score under his arm, he walked to the Cottage district of Währing, where Richter lived, and pulled on the conductor's door-bell. 'To my fright,' he told Köchert in a letter of 21st September,

Richter himself rolled forth out of the background and let me in. He was somewhat astonished over my visit and looked at me in great distress when he became aware of the score. I assured him in the cheerfullest manner that with my score I in no way intended a treacherous assault upon his, to me, sacred repose, and asked only the tiny favour that he should look over the notes for their appearance and not for their content. My modest request visibly relieved him. He praised my musical handwriting and found it very legible, but couldn't wonder enough at the resemblance between my handwriting and Richard Wagner's. . . . Finally he asked for my score for more detailed examination and promised me a performance, in spite of Bachrich and his associates, if he should find the work a good one. He expressed quite warmly his joy over my musical activity and regretted that I had become a writer. He declared to me that, to be sure, he had never read a line of mine—fortunately!—but that the worst *Musikant* is dearer to him than the best critic, in which matter I was quite of his opinion. The arrival of his wife brought our agreeable discourse to a rapid end. I commended myself to Richter and the good Lord, since everything had gone off so well, and, arriving home breathless, sat down at once at the writing-desk to acquaint you with this happy turn of events. God only grant that *Penthesilea* may please Richter, for it would be devilish if nothing were to come of it.

Besides the exciting prospect of *Penthesilea* being included in the Philharmonic programmes, Wolf had further renewed hopes of a performance of his String Quartet. Among the editorial staff of the

Salonblatt was Richard Kukula, who had known Wolf during his schooldays at Marburg, and it was he who pressed and finally persuaded Wolf to send the Quartet again to Rosé, in spite of the latter's refusal of it in the previous year. Kukula was friendly with Anton Loh, the second violinist of the Rosé Quartet, who had promised to do his best to secure the acceptance of the work by his colleagues. Wolf received no acknowledgment of his Quartet for a long time. A letter to Theodor Köchert relates how, on 4th October, before a performance of Gluck's *Alceste*, he went for a stroll under the arcade of the opera-house, 'with the intention of abusing Rosé, and if need be of thrashing him as well.' He missed his intended victim but encountered instead a violinist named Siebert, a member of the Kretschmann Quartet, whom he also invited to try over the work which Rosé had 'high-handedly ignored.' Siebert agreed at once and was only amused when Wolf thought it necessary to warn him of the hair-raising difficulties for the players. A date and time were soon arranged and Wolf was already preparing to turn a complete somersault for joy when he felt himself seized from behind by the collar. It was Hans Paumgartner, the music critic, at that time still very friendly with Wolf. 'At once he greeted me as the composer of *Penthesilea*,' Wolf told Theodor Köchert,

and as I amazedly questioned him about the import of this strange harangue, I learned that Richter is very much interested in my work, that he considers it—I scarcely dare to repeat it—an *important* one, and that he will use all his influence to see it through the trial. You can imagine in what spirits I was, with what attention I listened to *Alceste*. I could have shouted, grunted, giggled, howled, squeaked, wept, and laughed all at once. O holy Radagunda! If I survive the performance of *Penthesilea* I shall become as old as Methuselah.

Wonderful vistas now spread themselves out in Wolf's imagination; dreams of success attained at length and of the triumphant justification of the long years of apprenticeship and the sacrifices that he had been compelled, from time to time, to exact from his parents. These new hopes, too, were certainly built upon more secure foundations than some which had led to earlier disappointments. Now that he had learned on good authority that Richter regarded *Penthesilea* as an important work, and would do his utmost to bring it to performance, and had Siebert's promise to compensate for the now dwindling hopes of a performance of the Quartet under Rosé's leadership, surely the future was bright with promise, the turn of the tide near at hand?

Alas! Wolf had still to learn the full penalties which the world imposes on those who refuse to conform to its mediocre standards, and to compromise in life and in art.   Of Siebert and the Kretschmann Quartet nothing more is known, but certainly they gave no public performance of Wolf's work, and Richter's reported great interest in *Penthesilea* was only to lead, after many months of disappointments and hopes deferred, to an experience of overwhelming bitterness and pain.

In the meantime, possibly after a reminder from Wolf, the Rosé Quartet did at length make known their decision upon the work submitted to them.   One day in October he received this letter:

Honoured Herr Wolf!

We have attentively played through your D minor Quartet and unanimously resolved to leave the work for you with the door-keeper of the Court Opera-house (Operngasse).   Will you have the kindness to send for it as soon as possible? He could easily mislay it. With heartiest greetings,

The Quartet,

Rosé, Loh, Bachrich, Hummer.

The players of the Rosé Quartet were all members of the Philharmonic orchestra and it may be that by this rebuff they thought to avenge Wolf's outspoken criticism of the Philharmonic's policy and programmes.   The Quartet was also closely connected with Brahms, who often entrusted it with the first performances of his chamber works and appeared on occasion as pianist at its concerts.   It is likely, however, that the wounded vanity of the viola player, Sigismund Bachrich, was the principal cause of their hostility towards Wolf, who, both before and after this incident, had himself nothing but praise for the artistry and musicianship of the Rosé Quartet. Bachrich, who was twenty-two years older than the young Rosé, and must thus accept a good deal of responsibility for their common action,[1] was the composer of two operettas, *Muzzedin* (1883) and *Heini von Steier* (1884), which had aroused Wolf's contemptuous derision.   Bachrich had become one of the figures of fun—like the shockingly bad poet Richard Kralik—who reappeared from time to time, in and out of season, in Wolf's contributions to the *Salonblatt*.

---

[1] In a book of reminiscences, *Aus verklungener Zeiten* (Vienna, 1914), Bachrich wrote: 'Rosé had in me, the older and more experienced man, unconditional trust. He appointed me also his Minister for—Disagreeable Affairs, and Heaven knows they were not wanting.'

The Rosé Quartet's communication to Wolf (facsimile in Werner's *Hugo Wolf und der Wiener Akademische Wagner Verein*) is actually in Bachrich's handwriting, including all the signatures.

In this year of 1885 there were jeering references to Bachrich's
prowess as composer on 11th January, 8th February, and 8th March,
the last being a suggestion that he should be engaged to orchestrate
Czerny's *School of Velocity*, to enliven the Philharmonic programmes.
It was thus hardly to be expected that Bachrich and his friends should
have welcomed an opportunity of performing Wolf's own compositions, and rather surprising that Wolf should have laid himself
open to their retaliatory action: he was, in fact, clearly asking for
trouble in doing so. Bachrich would have had to be more than human
to resist the temptation of administering in his turn a sharp snub.

Wolf's reply took the form of an article in the *Salonblatt*, written
on 23rd October. This was not one of his happiest ideas, and the
article itself is surely one of the dampest of all the squibs in Wolf's
collected criticism. It was written not so much in anger as in rather
plaintive protest against the manner of the rejection of his work, with
a good deal of schoolboyish buffoonery.

Kukula records that Wolf himself had had no very high hopes of
acceptance, and had only with difficulty allowed himself to be persuaded to submit the work. After its rejection he raged for a few
days and then there came over him a notable change. He became
quite calm again, the manuscript of the Quartet was no longer to be
seen and he seemed to have lost all interest in it. When pressed by
Kukula to say what had become of the work, Wolf told him that he
had left it behind in a tramcar. Kukula's impression was that this
had not been entirely an accident and that Wolf had decided to settle
in this way the fate of his unfortunate Quartet. If this was so, however, he certainly retained the separate parts, from which the score
could have been reconstructed at any time, for he was able to send
them to Grohe in 1890, when there was a possibility of the work being
performed at Mannheim, and as he put his friends to considerable
trouble to try to discover the score itself among his belongings, he
clearly had at that time no recollection of having lost it; the tale of
his leaving it, by accident or deliberately, in a tramcar was thus
probably only an invention to escape from the importunate Kukula.

Wolf's reaction to the condemnation of his Quartet would certainly
have been far more violent if the performance of *Penthesilea* by the
Philharmonic orchestra had not still been an inspiring possibility. It
was upon this that his chief hopes were centred and his heart set, and
there was no room in his head for serious thought upon any other
matter.

All seemed prepared for the trial of the work, and with Richter's influence behind him Wolf certainly stood a good chance of getting his symphonic poem accepted for public performance, in spite of the hostility of Bachrich, Rosé and their friends within the orchestra. Yet it was not until *more than a year* after he first heard of the interest *Penthesilea* had aroused that the work was actually played through by the Philharmonic orchestra under Richter's direction. What happened to prevent the performance in 1885? We do not know; the source of all our information about this period dries up; after the previously quoted letter to Theodor Köchert of 5th October we have nothing until a letter to Strasser on 23rd December:

How comes it that we have heard nothing from each other for so long? Do you know? I don't. But wait! I for my part *do* know now. I wanted to surprise you with some news that, with your sympathy in the fate of my artistic activities, would have given you, too, great pleasure. But I waited, waited, and waited—until the present day. I was fed only with prospects, hopes, assurances, and the like beautiful things, that to be sure whet the appetite pleasantly but allow the stomach to go empty. I have good prospects of bringing my *Penthesilea* to performance in Munich and Vienna. It must be decided before the end of January. Pray for me.

It is evident that Richter must have deferred the trial of *Penthesilea* until a later date and that Wolf must have recovered the score and sent it off for consideration at Munich. The next letter to Strasser, written on 25th January 1886, shows that Munich rejected the work and that there was still nothing definite to be learned in Vienna. 'Whether it will achieve performance in Vienna,' Wolf then wrote, 'Heaven alone knows.'

This letter of 25th January 1886 also reported that the String Quartet was to be performed privately at Goldschmidt's house before an audience of sixty to eighty guests—additional evidence that the score had not really been lost. Whether the performance really came to pass is problematical; at any rate Goldschmidt himself, when Decsey sought information from him, could remember no such occurrence. This was a period of renewed intimacy with Goldschmidt. 'We are together almost every day,' Wolf told Strasser, 'and chaff each other to our hearts' content. In the coming summer I shall have many droll stories to tell you about him.' According to Friedrich Klose, the Swiss composer, who arrived in Vienna in 1886 to study under Bruckner, one of the critiques which appeared in the *Salonblatt* under Wolf's name was actually written by Goldschmidt. Wolf complained, as they sat in a café, that he had still a

Philharmonic concert and a performance of *Lohengrin* to write up that night and Goldschmidt volunteered to do it for him. From the details given this would seem to have been the critique of 14th February 1886.

Klose, in his reminiscences of his student days,[1] recalls various meetings with Wolf. They were both present at Goldschmidt's house on 13th March, when Liszt, on his last visit to Vienna, was the guest of honour. This day was also memorable for the creation of a new song by Wolf, *Der König bei der Krönung*, the first for very many months.

The 1885–6 concert season came to an end with Richter's promise of a trial performance of *Penthesilea* still unfulfilled. Nothing could then be done about it until the early autumn and Wolf decided to spend the summer months again with Strasser, who had in the meantime been transferred to Murau, a little old-world town in the Mur valley. No doubt he received from Richter further polite assurances before he left Vienna.

He arrived at Murau on 12th June, loaded with toys for the children, and anticipating a long and happy holiday. The visit began inauspiciously, for it was raining when he arrived, and the mountains invisible. Then when he reached Strasser's house he found Modesta confined to her bed, having three days before Wolf's arrival presented him with an additional niece. He was so little prepared for this event that he was only with difficulty persuaded not to leave again at once. 'A baby in the house?' he asked. 'I'm off!' In the end he stayed, but his misfortunes proved to be by no means yet over. He was showing the presents he had brought for the children when he was accidentally struck in the eye by one of the toys. He only escaped losing his sight by a hair's breadth and as it was he was compelled to remain in a darkened room for more than a week with a cold compress over the injured eye, and it was fully another week before he was able to leave the house.

Further unpleasantness arose when he was asked to act as god-father at the christening of the new baby. He seems to have been still incensed with the child for having chosen such an inopportune moment for its entry into the world, for he refused outright to have anything to do with the ceremony. At midday he disappeared, hiding himself somewhere in the woods until the christening was safely over. They saw no more of him that day, but next morning

---

[1] *Meine Lehrjahre bei Bruckner* (Regensburg, 1927).

Strasser found a sheet of paper on the breakfast-table, with the confession of Wolf's remorse for his churlish action.

'My dear Beisskurz,' he had written,

> I would like best to fall weeping on your neck, and on yours, too, Modesta. I am wretched and at the same time furious with myself. Pity me, for now I know with certainty that it is my fate to wound all those who love me and whom I love. It is unfortunately not the first time that I have found myself in such a wretched state of mind. I have gained thereby the conviction that my mental constitution is a thoroughly morbid one and will remain so. What would I not give to have done for you that little service, to have acted as godparent to your child! And believe me at heart I was wholly agreeable, but there whispered in my ear a devil (and I harbour legions in me) that I should not do it, because that would hurt you. I assented at once and as I perceived that it mattered a lot to you I refused outright. And yet by midday to-day I wanted to open my mouth and tell you that I was ready to do everything, and that with pleasure. Then I remarked your ill-humoured faces, which took away my power o speech.
>
> Now laugh at me, I pray you, for you will have to seek in the world a long time before you find such a magnificent example of a fool as your worthy brother-in-law, who dearly loves you and your wife. Only think! I had already resolved once more to leave you because I think myself so disagreeable. I shall not see you any more to-day, because I cannot bring myself to look you in the face. Burn this sheet of paper and never talk to me about this business again.

After reading this Strasser went at once to the church, found, as he had hoped, that the christening had not yet been entered in the books, and readjusted matters. The records in the church at Murau show that Alphonsa Maria Strasser, born at 12.30 a.m. on 9th June 1886, at Rindermarkt 24, had as her godfather, after all, 'Hugo Wolf, musician in Vienna, represented by the midwife.'

It is of interest to recall that the hero of Tillier's *Mon Oncle Benjamin* also once refused to be godfather at the christening of a nephew. It looks as though Wolf may have been posing a little to himself as his favourite character in fiction.

After their reconciliation, and for the whole of the rest of the four months spent by Wolf with his brother-in-law, there was no more ill humour between them. The sun shone again in the Mur valley, causing him to revise his hasty judgments upon both Murau itself and upon his latest niece. The longer he stayed the better he liked them, and the new baby became his favourite, over which he would willingly keep watch when Modesta had to go out.

Strasser's house stood next to an old church, at that time disused and neglected, so that it was much overgrown and romantic in appearance. The garden led down to the river and Wolf lay there on the banks of the Mur for many hours, gazing at the stream or reading for the thousandth time the poems of Mörike. For weeks this book accompanied him everywhere. A young Viennese lady [1] who was staying at the time at Murau heard a lot about Mörike from Wolf, who would have liked, he said, to lend her his own copy of the poems, but could not bear to be parted from it for a single moment.

During this summer an *Intermezzo* for string quartet, begun in Vienna in the previous April, was brought to completion. The manuscript is dated at the end: 'Murau, 1st October 1886.' An isolated scrap of paper in the National Library in Vienna with this theme in pencil:

Ex. 4

bears the early date of 3rd June 1882. This old idea became the germ of the principal theme of the *Intermezzo*:

Ex. 5

The work is practically monothematic. Out of the material of this opening the whole composition grows. The main theme itself recurs in its entirety, in the main key, thrice, each time in a different setting —first as a dialogue between the violins, then in a similar colloquy between viola and second violin, and later on the viola alone. Between these statements of the main subject are highly elaborate developments of its elements, contrasted with each other or combined together with infinite resource. The second of these development sections starts up a 6–8 movement, wherein all the material is still clearly derived from the original theme, however widely it may range from its starting point, and into this 6–8 pattern phrases from the

[1] H. von S., the unidentified author (*not* Henriette von Schey) of 'Von Hugo Wolf. Erinnerungen einer Wiener Dame,' published in the Viennese newspaper *Die Zeit* for 18th July 1903.

main theme in 2–4 gradually reassert themselves in a passage of considerable rhythmic complexity.   When the viola brings the third presentation of the principal subject the 6–8 rhythm still lingers in the two upper instruments.   A brief coda rounds off the work with a final reminiscence of the opening idea.   The *Intermezzo*, or *Humoristisches Intermezzo*, as Wolf calls it in a later letter, is an arresting little work.   The development process which forms so large a part of it is perhaps overdone, making a rather laboured effect at times, but the whole thing is most cleverly contrived and full of life and vigour.   It has been strangely neglected.

On 7th October Wolf said good-bye to his sister and brother-in-law and set out upon his return journey to Vienna.   He had learned at length that his *Penthesilea* was to be played through at a Philharmonic trial on the 15th, and although it was the rule that a composer was not allowed to be present at the trial performance of his work, Wolf knew well enough that there were ways and means of evading this.   He was not going to miss the first opportunity of hearing his symphonic poem if he could possibly help it.

Accordingly on 15th October he presented himself at the concert-hall, in company with Edmund and Marie Lang, and by giving a tip to the attendant secured a position in the gallery, where his presence would not be noticed.   What he experienced there was told in a letter to Strasser three days later:

You could not dream what I have gone through in recent days.   I am charged like a dynamite bomb, and woe to those upon whom my wrath falls.   What does it matter to me now if I myself fly in the air with it?   I know at any rate that my missile dispatches to the devil all the —— who so much enraged me; they shall be roasted in hell's brimstone and immersed in dragon's poison—I have sworn it.   I will publish an article against [Richter] [1] that shall make the devil himself grow pale.   Oh, there will pass a cry of rage through [Vienna] [1] such as no Indian brave has ever yet experienced.   But listen!

Last Friday my *Penthesilea* was performed in the trial of the novelties.   *My Penthesilea?*   No, the *Penthesilea* of a madman, an idiot, a jester, and anything else you please, but *my Penthesilea* it was not.   I can't describe to you how this piece was played.

[1] Proper names omitted in Decsey and the *Familienbriefe*.   The full text of this letter would be of extraordinary interest.   Decsey had to suppress all references to Richter and the Vienna Philharmonic orchestra; the editor of the *Familienbriefe* never had access to the original, but merely reprinted the extracts quoted by Decsey.   This important letter was in the possession of Frl. Cornelia Strasser, at Graz, but, with others, was *stolen* from her about 1930.   Its present location is not known.   The proper names here inserted are suppositious only, but almost certainly correct.

The letter went on to tell how a shameful travesty of his work distressed his ears and how Richter continued calmly beating time, apparently indifferent to the unholy discord with which the orchestra responded. 'It was Babel itself.' Afterwards there was 'resounding laughter on the part of the orchestra' and then Richter turned to the players and said: 'Gentlemen! I should not have let the piece be played to the end, but I wanted to see for myself the man who dares to write in such a way about *Meister* Brahms.' 'Now how does the moral of this story please you?' Wolf asked his brother-in-law.

Very amusing, isn't it? Damned amusing! My first reaction to these words was to send [Richter][1] a challenge. The efforts of my friends who were present succeeded in convincing me of the uselessness of such a step and in turning me from this purpose. Now I am collecting data for a pamphlet that shall throw light upon the behaviour of [the Philharmonic],[1] so that they shall curse the light of day, envying the owls and bats their photophobic existence.

This appalling anticlimax to what had seemed likely to bring the realization of his long-drawn-out hopes of success, the total destruction of the whole fabric of his dreams, made the Philharmonic trial of *Penthesilea* the most bitter experience of Wolf's life of travail as an artist. He suffered terribly over those fair promises and their cruel disappointment, and his letter to Strasser leaves us in no doubt at all that he himself believed that his work had been deliberately and maliciously sacrificed to make a Brahmsian holiday.

What were Richter's real intentions? In the programme book of the Stuttgart Wolf Festival of 1906 Karl Grunsky recapitulated the generally accepted Wolfian version of these events and drew from Richter a defence of his own actions of twenty years earlier.[2] In this he characterized the current account of his own and the Vienna Philharmonic orchestra's relations with Wolf as a legend and a lie:

Hugo Wolf did not 'trustingly submit' the Overture [*sic*] but played it over to me in private. I told him at once quite frankly that the work, in the form it was *then*, had no prospects of being performed in the Philharmonic concerts. On his remarking that he would dearly like to hear the piece I promised him that it should be played through at a trial, but he would have to keep out of sight because nobody had entry to the Philharmonic trials. I did not allow a vote to be taken on it because I only let the piece be played through as a favour to Hugo Wolf, who—as he told me—had never yet

---

[1] See footnote, p. 181.
[2] Open letter to the editor of *Die Musik*, published in the first November number 1906, with further correspondence from both Grunsky and Richter in the second December number of the same periodical.

heard a work of his own scoring. . . . I should like to know how, at the first reading-through, one can play a work in a distorted form from beginning to end. How is that done? The musicians, who are completely occupied in reading a new work, really have no time for private jokes, which in any case would not be tolerated either by the conductor or by the great majority of the players. 'Resounding laughter' is a strong exaggeration. In a company of over a hundred people there are always a few thoughtless ones who do not reflect that their unmannerly behaviour will bring discredit upon the whole body. . . . After the playing-through of the Overture I said audibly to those about me: 'The composer of this Overture has not the right to write so disrespectfully about a master like Brahms.' I should, however, have suppressed this remark if I had known that the composer was within hearing distance, for it could not have been my intention to offend the gifted man personally.[1]

It is exceedingly difficult to pass judgment upon the conflicting stories of Richter and of Wolf's friends and biographers. Both sides tend to simplify their own cases. Richter's version of the interview with Wolf leading up to the agreement to play through the score at one of the Philharmonic trials cannot be reconciled with Wolf's own letter to Theodor Köchert of 21st September 1885 (p. 173). Richter found it convenient to forget that he had ever thought more favourably of the work and encouraged Wolf's hopes of performance. But the Wolfians themselves have preferred to ignore the fact that a whole year passed between the time when Richter's interest was first aroused in the work and the date of the actual trial. Although Wolf's letter undoubtedly presents a reliable report on the interview of 1885, the possibility cannot be excluded that another interview, in accordance with *Richter's* account, may have taken place in 1886. Since Wolf presumably sent the score away to Munich in December 1885, the trial performance in Vienna in 1886 can hardly have come about without further negotiations, either with Richter himself or directly with the Philharmonic committee.

Was 'Penthesilea' officially submitted by Wolf and accepted by the Philharmonic committee, or was it played through as a favour by private arrangement with Richter? We know from Wolf's own letters that in 1885, at any rate, he did not submit *Penthesilea* to the Philharmonic committee, but aroused Richter's interest by a personal visit. But the letters also show that he was bent on a public performance, to which his interview with Richter was only

[1] Ludwig Karpath, in his *Begegnung mit dem Genius*, gives another version of this defence, as related in a private conversation, according to which Richter knew quite well that Wolf would overhear what he said to the musicians after the performance. The little speech itself appears in a third version.

G

a helpful preliminary. He then heard indirectly that Richter intended
to do his best 'to see it through the trial.'

The trial, however, did not take place until a whole year later.
There is no evidence at all in Wolf's letters as to whether he submitted
the work officially in 1886 or again interviewed Richter, or as to
whether he had accepted the fact that a playing-through at the trial
was the most for which he could then hope. Richter, however,
remarks in his final words to the editor of *Die Musik* that if the work
was officially submitted there should be a covering letter and an entry
in the books of the Philharmonic orchestra to that effect, and that 'in
the exemplarily carefully kept books of the Philharmonic there is
nothing about it to be found.'

Through the kindness of the archivist of the Vienna Philharmonic
orchestra I have been able to investigate this matter for myself, and
have reached a conclusion somewhat at variance with that of Richter.
It is true that there is no letter of Wolf's regarding *Penthesilea* in the
Philharmonic archives, but neither are there letters from some other
composers, like Glazounov, whose works *were* officially submitted.
It is true that in the minutes of the committee meeting on 1st October
1886, where there was discussion of the novelties to be played through
at the trials, there is no mention of *Penthesilea*. But a separate later report of the season's trials includes not only *Penthesilea* but no less than
five other compositions which were not discussed at that committee
meeting, two of which received after the trial a few votes in favour of
their acceptance. So it is clear that either the Philharmonic records of
these events—and especially the minutes of the committee meetings—
are misleadingly incomplete, or that the personal line of approach was
a common one and in no way precluded consideration for public
performance. In any case, *Penthesilea*, in spite of Richter's denials,
does figure on the official report of the trial of 15th October 1886.

Here is the astonishing programme, which must have required
three hours or more to perform:

> Glazounov: Overture on three Greek themes
> [1] Prince Reuss: Symphony
> [1] H. Finck: Serenade
> [1] Degner: Symphony
> [1] H. Hofmann: Suite: *Im Schlosshof*
> [1] Herzfeld: Overture: *Im Frühling*
> Krinninger: Serenade
> [1] H. Wolf: Symphonic poem: *Penthesilea*

[1] Not mentioned in the minutes of the committee meeting of 1st October.

A majority vote was required for acceptance. Out of a possible 83 votes, Glazounov received 9, Finck 9, Hofmann 5, Krinninger 2, and the rest none at all, so the whole eight works were rejected.

Was the performance of 'Penthesilea' in 1886 deliberately contrived to wound and ridicule Wolf?   It is necessary to remember that the conditions of a Philharmonic trial allowed of no rehearsal or polishing; the normal purpose of these trials was to provide a rough practical test, from which the players would form their opinions before casting their votes, for or against the work's inclusion in the season's programmes.   On this occasion they had played through at sight two symphonies, two serenades, two overtures, and a suite before they came to *Penthesilea*, which is an extremely complex and difficult score—in the pre-Straussian era in which it was written something of a phenomenon.   In these circumstances the performance was bound to be rough and ready in the extreme.   But Wolf, in a condition of high nervous tension, looked for the miraculous realization of his ideal, and in place of the beautiful and terrible vision of Kleist's heroine which he had conceived in his imagination he saw only a hideous caricature.   The sensitivity of his ear made a torment of every lapse on the part of the players and every miscalculation of his own in the scoring.   There were similar occurrences at other early rehearsals of his works in the larger forms; the String Quartet was 'murdered,' according to Wolf, when it was first played in 1881 at the house of Frau Bauer-Lechner; in Berlin in 1894 Siegfried Ochs at one time really thought Wolf was going mad; similar scenes are recorded of the *Corregidor* rehearsals at Mannheim in 1896.   To go through most of the symptoms of an epileptic fit was, in fact, Wolf's normal reaction to the first imperfect performance of any one of his works. But if the quality of the performance at the trial of *Penthesilea* is excusable, what occurred *afterwards* can be less easily forgiven.

Between his first introduction to the work in 1885 and the trial in 1886 Richter's attitude towards *Penthesilea* clearly underwent an important change, that cannot entirely be explained away by the fact that a more detailed examination had revealed defects in the scoring. It is certain that in the meantime his attention had been drawn to Wolf's anti-Brahmsian writings in the *Salonblatt*, which, as he told Wolf himself in 1885, he had not then read, but about which he made his speech to the orchestra after the trial of 1886.   Richter was certainly incensed at what he had read, or been told, of Wolf's criticism of Brahms, and may well have regarded the trial as a form of punishment for those misdeeds. Yet still in his ponderous way he may have meant no more than to *teach this young man a lesson*, after performance had demonstrated certain deficiencies in the latter's musical equipment. If this was so he unfortunately failed to take account of the temperament of the young man with whom he had to deal, and failed also to realize that among the players were some who nursed a burning hatred for Wolf and would make use of any such opportunity to vent their spite against him. Richter sought to minimize the laughter amongst the orchestra after they had scrambled through the score, but he did not deny that something of the sort had taken place. There is no doubt at all that Wolf had enemies within the orchestra—Bachrich and colleagues—who were chiefly responsible for his bitter experiences at the trial of his *Penthesilea*, but that Richter himself, who had shown kindness to Wolf on various occasions in the past, was acting with malicious intent seems improbable—however unpleasant the self-righteous tone of his apologia of 1906 and however many half-truths, or worse, it may be shown to contain. It would be fully in accordance with some estimates of the man's character[1] if his little speech were made not for Wolf's benefit at all, but rather for *his own*, with the object of rehabilitating himself with the players, when he realized the full extent of their hostility towards Wolf's symphonic poem. This seems, indeed, more than a possibility when we consider that he can hardly have known exactly where Wolf was concealed in the hall, and thus whether his words to the orchestra would be audible to the composer or not.

The unfortunate thing was that Wolf *did* overhear Richter's remarks and put the worst construction on all the conductor's actions preparatory to, during, and after the trial performance of *Penthesilea*. He never forgave, or forgot. His later comments on Richter in the *Salonblatt* are all hostile. Some of his most violent diatribes were suppressed by his editor, as may be seen from the original manuscripts of his *Salonblatt* criticisms in the Vienna City Library. A long passage abusive of Richter was cut from the article which appeared on 9th January 1887, and from that of 16th January a similar passage commenting on the censorship of his previous critique. The editor did well, and the world lost very little. The following remarks

---

[1] e.g. Dame Ethel Smyth's in *As time went on*, p. 47: 'I, however, had heard a good deal in Germany about the great man's "peasant astuteness," and knew that once in England he would realize that I was not in the swim, and then good-bye to his enthusiasm.'

may be quoted from one of these generally unhappily expressed and, in the circumstances, rather pitiful outbursts:

Although secretly he has only a shrug of the shoulders for Brahms, he turns somersaults for enthusiasm before his critical patron [Hanslick] and declares that without Brahms Beethoven could never have composed the ninth Symphony. (Whoever heard the like?) Although he has publicly sworn, body and soul, in pompous phrases brimming over with cordiality to encourage our inspired Anton Bruckner and to perform his works, on the quiet he does everything he can to bar his way to the concert-hall.

Penthesilea was first published posthumously in 1903, after revision by Josef Hellmesberger the younger, assisted with advice by Ferdinand Löwe and Willibald Kähler, and at the time of Richter's letters to the editor of *Die Musik* this version of the work had already been successfully performed on various occasions. It was not until 1937, however, that the real nature of the 'revision' to which Wolf's score had been subjected became known. In that year a full score was issued [1] which reproduced the work exactly as it stands in the manuscript and revealed the remarkable extent to which the editors of the earlier version had departed from the composer's intentions. In addition to a thorough overhaul of the orchestration, an enormous and unacknowledged cut was made, one hundred and sixty-eight bars in length.[2] The new edition of the score represents the work as Richter knew it in 1886, except that it includes the additional percussion (triangle, gong, side and bass drums) and the substitution of cor anglais for one oboe, which were the results of the composer's own revision in 1897.[3] The original version has been performed with success in various German cities and study of the score encourages the belief that in this work, which has been all too often dismissed, even by Wolf's own biographers, as a misapplication of his energies and a secondary offshoot of his genius, we possess one of the grandest romantic conceptions of the nineteenth century.

In Kleist's poetic drama, Penthesilea, Queen of the Amazons, leads her followers into battle during the Trojan wars, with the object of capturing heroes with whom the Amazons may mate at their Festival of the Roses. Penthesilea herself dreams of conquering Achilles and leading him back to be her prisoner and temporary spouse. In the battle, however, she is herself defeated. Achilles, enamoured of her,

---

[1] Musikwissenschaftlicher Verlag.
[2] The idea seems to have been Kähler's.
[3] See Hugo Wolf, *Briefe an Heinrich Potpeschnigg* (Stuttgart, 1923), letter of 15th December 1897, and compare with the critical apparatus accompanying the new edition of the full score.

and aware of the sole condition under which an Amazon may mate—
when she has conquered a man in battle—leads her to believe, as she
awakes from a deep swoon, that she has been victorious and he himself defeated.   Penthesilea, however, learns the truth.   Achilles then
challenges her to a new struggle, with the intention of allowing himself to be defeated, but the Amazon's wounded pride turns her love to
madness and hate; she falls upon the prostrate Achilles and assists
her hounds to tear him to pieces.   On returning to her senses she kills
herself.

Wolf's symphonic poem is divided into three sections, headed
respectively 'Departure of the Amazons for Troy,' 'Penthesilea's
Dream of the Feast of Roses,' and 'Strife, Passions, Madness and
Destruction.'   They are not to be regarded as three separate movements; the material of the first two short sections, lasting about five
and three minutes respectively, is made use of and developed in the
long third section.   The entire work plays for about thirty-five
minutes.   The apparent disparity in length and weight between the
three 'movements' may have been responsible for the drastic cut,
from bar 556 to bar 723, which the first editors of the work made in
its longest section.   By this mutilation they made it clear that they
had no conception of the design of the work, which is subtly and
beautifully organized.

'The Departure of the Amazons for Troy' begins with a syncopated
theme of wild power and majesty, thrown out over furious rumblings

Ex. 6   **Lebhaft, wuchtig**

in the basses.   Much of the subsequent material of the tone-poem is
related to this theme, in particular by its characteristic interval of
the falling minor second.   After the complete presentation of the
first subject there follows a fanfare on trumpets, posted on either side
of the main orchestra, and horns, leading up to a climax and the
commencement of the Amazons' March.   This illustrates a passage

Ex. 7

in Kleist's play describing the stealthy advance by night of the
women warriors—a Berliozian scene, full of the muffled beat of
horses' hoofs and the clash of arms.   After a subsidiary motive,
beginning *dolce* in the strings, has been developed to another climax,
the nocturnal march is resumed and dies away in the distance in a
coda.   A pause, and the beautiful theme of Penthesilea's love-dream,

an obvious relative of the initial theme of the whole work, is given out
on woodwind and muted strings, while divided violas and harp
create a spell in the background.   For all too short a space the
marvellous haunted dream continues, woven of extraordinary
arabesques and floating melodies, until it is broken into by fragments
of a new theme, the principal subject of the final section of the work;
the love theme endeavours to retain its hold but is rapidly disinte-
grated until we are thrust without a break into the waking world of
'Strife, Passions, Madness and Destruction.'   The most important
subject of this section, almost certainly symbolizing Penthesilea's fury
and madness, appears in various shapes and fragments in the course
of what is still in the nature of a symphonic exposition, but its
ultimate shape and full force are withheld until a later stage of the
tragedy.   In one of its earlier forms, presented on the trombones,

it is opposed by wild figures on woodwind and strings, formed from
the initial phrase of Penthesilea's love-dream.   Shortly afterwards
the tumult dies away, the love theme itself returns, and is then
developed at length in passionate conflict with the ideas of hatred and
destruction.   Almost the whole of this crucial section of the work
was cut in Hellmesberger's edition of the score.   The excitement
intensifies and leads through a big climax to the recapitulation of the
opening of the whole work, the initial theme—Penthesilea the
warrior queen—and the succeeding fanfares.   This bold stroke has
all the effect of the return of the first subject in the recapitulation of a
symphonic movement and at the same time falls into place to portray

the Amazons' preparations for the renewal of the conflict. The subsequent tumult, through which is heard the loud baying of Penthesilea's hounds, at length brings in the thunderous presentation of the main theme of this part of the work in its complete form, and then, after a final climax and a shuddering *diminuendo*, leads to the inversion of the first phrase of this theme, undoubtedly illustrating Penthesilea's awakening from her insane fury to realization of her appalling deed. From this point begins Penthesilea's *Liebestod*; the love theme and weary reminiscences of madness and fury portray the death of the Amazon queen. In the last bars, over a death roll on the drums, the love theme reappears tenderly on the strings and is given a turn into the major—a last gleam of beauty passes over the anguished face of the dying Penthesilea—before soft minor chords bring the work to a close.

Most authorities are agreed that the orchestration of Wolf's great experimental tone-poem stands in need of some revision, and it is comforting to know that the composer himself, on mature consideration, came to the same conclusion. When his *Christnacht* was performed at Mannheim under Weingartner in 1891, Wolf admitted that he was dissatisfied with the effect of his own scoring. He showed his *Penthesilea* to Weingartner on that occasion and is said to have listened carefully and quite humbly to the conductor's strictures and suggestions. From that time onwards he recognized that a complete overhaul of the scoring of the work was necessary and in 1894 nearly quarrelled with his friend Grohe when the latter took steps to arrange for a performance. Unhappily the long-intended revision of *Penthesilea* was not undertaken until 1897, when Wolf was no longer capable of reasonable judgment upon this or any other matter. He was then confined in Dr. Svetlin's asylum, and made alterations to the orchestration which actually *added*, by the use of additional percussion, to the generally thick and noisy effect of the original scoring. It was nothing less than a tragedy that Wolf, in 1885 or 1886, did not receive, in a form acceptable to his proud and stubborn nature, such advice from a more experienced friend as would have led to a clarification of the texture of *Penthesilea*, and made its instrumentation worthy of its magnificent conception and design.

It was perhaps as well that Wolf, in 1886, did not allow himself to be cast down over his own share of responsibility in the failure of *Penthesilea*, or we might have been deprived of a series of striking songs and other works which he produced in the months that followed. For the first time since he had taken up his critical work for the *Salonblatt* he devoted a considerable measure of his energies to composition during the winter. December 14th saw the creation of a new song, *Der Soldat* (subsequently *Der Soldat II*), to words by Eichendorff. Then on Christmas Eve, after a suggestion by Eckstein that Wolf should write something seasonal on the lines of Bach's *Christmas Oratorio*, he began the composition of *Christnacht*, a work for *soli*, chorus, and orchestra on a considerable scale, based on a poem of Platen's. This, however, was laid aside in an unfinished state, and was not to be taken up again and completed until May 1889. On 26th December he composed another song, *Biterolf*, with words by Scheffel, and on 24th January 1887 a further setting of the same poet, *Wächterlied auf der Wartburg*. Two Goethe songs, *Wanderers Nachtlied* and *Beherzigung*, followed on 30th January and 1st March respectively. Then came more settings of Eichendorff's poems. *Der Soldat I* on 7th March, *Die Kleine* on the next day, and *Die Zigeunerin* on 19th March, to which were added at intervals of about a month *Waldmädchen* (20th April) and *Nachtzauber* (24th May). Between 2nd May and 4th May the well-known *Italian Serenade* for string quartet came into existence.[1]

Although none of the ten songs in this group would inevitably suggest itself for inclusion in a representative selection of their composer's best work, they are nevertheless in many ways characteristic of the real Wolf, and, with the exception of such isolated earlier masterpieces as *Mausfallensprüchlein* and *Zur Ruh*, really comprise the first fruits of his most individual manner. The songs indicate, in particular, his command of half a dozen varied moods and styles, and his remarkable powers of dramatic characterization in little.

Soldat I and *II*, *Die Zigeunerin*, *Waldmädchen* and *Die Kleine* are all character pieces, chosen for musical illustration with a particular object in view. Wolf wished to produce a volume of Eichendorff settings that should supplement those of Schumann, notably the *Liederkreis*, Op. 39. With all his admiration for the many beautiful songs to which Eichendorff's poems had inspired his predecessor,

---

[1] Earlier writers have thoroughly misunderstood and confused the chronology of the different versions of this work. The dated manuscripts of the first pencil sketches on two staves and the first draft for string quartet (National Library, Vienna) show that the string quartet version published in 1903 was the original form of the work and that it was composed in 1887. See 'The History of Wolf's *Italian Serenade*' (*The Music Review*, August 1947).

* G

Wolf recognized that there were aspects of the poet's nature to which musical justice had never yet been done. Schumann had pictured the mysterious world of Eichendorff's twilit woods and meadows, ruined castles in the moonlight, and faery spells; Wolf deliberately concentrated more upon poems of a realistic or humorous character. *Nachtzauber* alone, among this group of the Eichendorff songs, breathes the atmosphere of romantic enchantment that had appealed so strongly to Schumann, and in this song Wolf looked forward beyond his master's range of vision towards an almost Debussyan impressionism.

Wanderers Nachtlied is the more likable of the two Goethe songs. *Beherzigung*, though of interest as the earliest example of Wolf in didactic mood, is not so convincing as a song. In *Biterolf*, the weary crusader stands among the burning sands of Acre and thinks of his green Thuringian homeland. The music characterizes with superb simplicity his faith and courage and the longing in his heart. The new year's song of the watchman on the Wartburg strives hard to live up to its splendid opening. The poem contains a good deal of pedestrian stuff that was no help at all to the composer in shaping his song, but the best parts of the *Wächterlied* have a brazen magnificence all their own. It was, however, clearly conceived with something more than a piano accompaniment in mind, and there does in fact exist an unfinished later arrangement of this piece for male voice chorus and orchestra.

The *Italian Serenade* is a very curious and original conception, for which it is difficult to find a musical parallel before modern times. It treats an old and commonplace subject with ironic detachment. A modified rondo form is employed. After preliminary strummings, the instrumental serenade commences with its sinuous, jocular theme, succeeded by a whole string of variants or related melodies. It is all enchantingly light-footed and delicate, until a change of rhythm brings an expressive passage in which we seem to hear the voice of the lover himself. His plea appears to be favourably received, for the entertainment is resumed and a crescendo leads to the passionate outburst of a fiery melody of southern cast. A bridge passage or short development of the initial theme then brings the return of the whole first section of the work, with fascinating elaborations of the themes by the second violin. The musicians then pause, while, in a passage of recitative on the cello, a manly voice makes a declaration of love. Three times he presents the lady with his heart, each time in more hyperbolic language, that is not allowed to pass without mocking comment by the other instrumentalists.[1]   A pause, and over an accompaniment of deliberate monotony a comical new theme makes its appearance; it is succeeded by another lilting, dancing melody which is developed up to a crescendo and climax, after which the musicians decide in another bridge passage to satisfy the demands of musical form by repeating their principal material for the third time and completing the rondo.   This they do, and the delicious little composition ends as it began with the twang and the drone of guitars.

Before the last of this group of compositions from the early months of 1887, Wolf had already written his last concert notice for the *Salonblatt*.   The issue of 24th April contained his final contribution.[2] Nothing is recorded of any quarrel with the proprietor or editor of the paper, or other external incident, to account for his retirement and forfeiture of his principal source of income.[3]   We have no evidence at all about the direction in which his thoughts were turning, but it is likely enough that the recent revival of his creative powers, with the production of a whole series of works of decided worth and originality, went far to convince him that it was time to make an end of unprofitable hack-work such as the *Salonblatt* demanded of him. The interlude as a critic, begun in a mood of despondency over ambitions that had seemed beyond his power to realize, came to an end with these unmistakable signs that fulfilment was, after all, still possible.   Nevertheless, it must have needed not a little courage to abandon the comparative security of the *Salonblatt* offices and plunge once more into the uncertainties of the old vagrant hand-to-mouth existence.   No doubt he could depend upon his friends to provide a roof above his head at night and see that he did not actually starve; but it was no longer the ingenuous youth of earlier years, sanguine in

---

[1] The element of caricature in this passage is almost invariably missed in performance of the work.   In Wolf's opera *Der Corregidor* (1895) there occurs a reminiscence of this part of the *Italian Serenade*, at the point where the senile magistrate is about to begin his wooing of the fair Frasquita (vocal score, p. 25). This sufficiently indicates, I think, the character of the passage in question.

[2] Overlooked when the criticism was reprinted in book form.

[3] The widely held belief that the death of Wolf's father was responsible for his abandonment of his critical work will not survive the elementary test of a comparison of the dates.   He was kept in ignorance of his father's illness until the very last moment, and by that time two numbers of the *Salonblatt* had appeared without contributions from his pen.

A supplementary source of income was an engagement to give music lessons to the Countess Harrach, mentioned in an unpublished family letter of 10th March 1887. and continued for several years.

expectation that the world would recognize, welcome and reward his genius, that now resought the artist's independence. The hardening and ripening process that had been necessary before the inner nature of the man could develop and express itself in song had left a core of bitterness within him. Wolf was a grown man of twenty-seven, very well aware of the immense obstacles that stood in his path, a composer, not one of whose compositions had yet been published or even performed in public, and who had made for himself numerous and powerful enemies.

Fortune, he was now to learn, had still one more blow in store for him before fulfilment came—a blow more severe than any that he had yet been called upon to suffer.

Philipp Wolf, the composer's father, has not figured prominently in the narrative of the past few years. In February 1885 an inheritance had relieved him from the most pressing of his money difficulties and this, with Hugo continuing to hold his *Salonblatt* appointment, meant that his last years were calmer. His melancholia continued, but Hugo's stability was a source of endless consolation. One of the last of Philipp's letters congratulates his beloved son on his name-day:

> My wishes are the same as your own—they culminate in your success. It is a task of Sisyphus in which you wear yourself out. Your striving is mirrored in your critical essays—but don't despair, the sun of recognition will shine upon you yet. That I may witness it is my only wish, it would be the greatest joy in my wretched existence—but hush! nothing shall disturb your name-day. Think only that you have a father who loves you and whose only joy and hope you are.

As for Hugo, half the incentive behind his long struggle had been the overwhelming desire to justify himself in his father's eyes, to prove that he was, after all, not the failure that he seemed as a composer. In following his star so tenaciously, and so often to the bewilderment and sorrow of his parents, he had done nothing that was not a necessity of his nature, and to bring Philipp to recognize this fact, to give him the happiness of witnessing the end of the struggle and the presentation to the victor of his laurels—this was Hugo's most heartfelt longing, and it was precisely this of which at the last moment a malignant fate was to deprive him.

In the first months of 1887 Philipp Wolf's health had begun to fail. It was decided at home that Hugo was not to be told. For the joint festival of his mother's name-day on 30th April and his father's fifty-ninth birthday on 1st May he sent from Vienna congratulations

and a gift of wine. Only a week later the family learned that the
father was sinking and on the doctor's advice Hugo was sent for by
telegram. On the morning of 9th May Katharina was able to tell
poor Philipp that his favourite son was expected by the midday train.
At first the sick man was angry that the news of his illness had been
conveyed to his son, for he did not realize how desperate his condition was. Then his glance began to stray ever more frequently
towards the clock; repeatedly he asked whether the post-wagon was
not yet in sight. At one o'clock the coach at last came rattling down
the principal street and even before it had drawn up at the Windischgraz halting place Hugo leaped from it and ran to his home and up
the stairs. 'Is Father still alive?' he cried, and burst into the sick-
room and threw himself into the dying man's arms. Philipp's face
was transfigured with happiness, while Hugo sank down sobbing at
the bedside. His father tried to console him, but a few words only
were allowed him; with his dying breath they heard him sigh: 'Hugo,
my Hugo!' Then poor Philipp Wolf's earthly troubles were over
and his son with his handkerchief wiped the perspiration from the
dead forehead and gently closed the glazing eyes.

Wolf was inconsolable for the loss of his father—so close a bond
had joined them. His grief was measureless and he mourned for
years. How great an impetus the desire to gladden his father's heart
and justify himself in his eyes had been is shown by his exclamation to
Marie Lang: 'What does it matter to me if my songs are published
now? No success can any longer give me pleasure,' and by a letter
written five and a half years later to his sister Käthe, when she had
sent him a parcel of his own early manuscripts, one of them with a
comment by his father:

And the inscription by so dear, so unforgettable a hand!! You cannot
measure how indescribably the sight of it touched and moved me to the
depths. 'In the quiet churchyard'—it was the only song that Father's
dear hand provided with an inscription. And now he lies in the quiet
churchyard and none of my songs can reach him. Ah, why do I go on
composing when he can no longer hear?—he, who only in music lived and
breathed, and for whom *my* music never sounded, to whom my song never
spoke!!!

Youth came to an end for Hugo with the death of his father. We
are accustomed to think of him as a hopeless bungler in the ordinary
affairs of life, as a fine-nerved artist quite incapable of adapting himself to the requirements of the everyday world, and up to a point, of

course, this was undoubtedly the case. Nevertheless, compared with his two brothers, Hugo was a monument of dependability and resource in mundane affairs, and although not the eldest son he felt, far more than the others, the responsibility for the welfare of his sisters and his ageing mother. Any improvement in the none too happy conditions of their lives, he knew, was entirely dependent upon his own success or failure. Luckily for themselves, since Hugo could only rarely contribute anything to the family finances, the girls seem to have inherited their mother's practical sense and shrewdness, and to have been able to keep their little business at Windischgraz going. A part of the house was converted into a grocer's shop. It is touching to read in the family correspondence how Hugo kept his eye upon them, now inveighing against this or that scheme of the eldest son Max, which would, according to Hugo, have driven the mother from home, now urging his own advice upon them, returning to the attack in letter after letter. He only rarely visited Windischgraz after the death of his father, and felt no affection at all for the place, but his family ties were still enormously strong and to the end of his days he honoured these obligations to the full, working always for the betterment of those he loved.

IX

FULFILMENT

HARDLY more than the bare outline of Wolf's movements is known of his life in the summer of 1887.   After his father's funeral he returned to Vienna, where he stayed for a short time before going with the Köcherts to Rinnbach.   There, on 17th June, while playing with the children on the grassy slope before the house named 'Krähbauer,' he had the misfortune to break the fibula of his right leg, with the result that he had to spend five or six weeks in bed.   When sufficiently recovered he paid a visit to Strasser at Leibnitz, in Styria, and in the autumn he was back again in Vienna.   From that time onwards there is more abundant information about his activities.

As his leg still needed a certain amount of attention, he did not return to his Kumpfgasse lodgings but took up residence with Edmund and Marie Lang in their home at Belvederegasse 9, in the Wieden district, sleeping in his friend's study on a divan.   One day he returned from a walk and told of a meeting in the Kärntnerstrasse with Friedrich Eckstein.   Wolf had not seen Eckstein for some time and in response to the latter's inquiries had begun to complain of his continued inability to get any of his work published.   Eckstein had looked thoughtful for a moment and then said that if that was all that was amiss he would soon remedy it.   He had assured Wolf that he could find a publisher for some of his songs.

Wolf was tremendously excited and wished to bring Eckstein at once to the Belvederegasse; the Langs were eager to meet him, and on 21st November a special vegetarian dinner was prepared in his honour.   On his appearance he was rapturously greeted by them all. The lady of the house, who was obviously much attached to Wolf, told how a joyful feeling of liberation had taken possession of him now that at last, for the first time in his life, some of his compositions were to be printed.   It was quite simple, Eckstein explained.   He would approach the small Viennese firm of Emil Wetzler, whom he had already induced to publish some of Bruckner's shorter choral works, and himself guarantee the costs of the publication of twelve

197

of Wolf's songs, afterwards calling upon all his own and Wolf's friends to take as many copies as they could conveniently afford.

In this way, by Eckstein's generosity and common sense, the apparent miracle was achieved.[1] Wolf chose from among his manuscripts of many years the songs *Morgentau* (1877), *Die Spinnerin* (1878), *Das Vöglein* (1878), *Mausfallensprüchlein* (1882), *Wiegenlied im Sommer* (1882), and *Wiegenlied im Winter* (1882): these were to be published in one volume, dedicated to his mother, as *Sechs Lieder für eine Frauenstimme*. Another volume, *Sechs Gedichte von Scheffel, Mörike, Goethe und Kerner*, dedicated to the memory of his father, was to contain *Zur Ruh* (1883), *Der König bei der Krönung* (1886), *Biterolf* (1886), *Wächterlied auf der Wartburg* (1887), *Wanderers Nachtlied* (1887), and *Beherzigung* (1887).

The jubilation in the Belvederegasse was endless. Eckstein was greeted with a song of welcome whenever he visited the Langs' house. Once the fragments of Wolf's earliest attempt at an opera, *König Alboin*, were unearthed and a chorus from it performed in honour of the 'mighty Eck': 'Hail, King Alboin! The battle is won through thee, all-conquering hero!' On another occasion he was welcomed with the carol *Ihr lieben Hirten*, sung by the Windischgraz children on the eve of Epiphany, and made use of in *Christnacht*.

All this excitement and happiness aroused in Wolf only one desire —to compose more songs. Relieved from the bonds of doubt and indifference, he felt there was nothing he could not do. All that was lacking was a place where he could live in solitude and quiet, to reduce his teeming ideas to order and set them down on paper. He then remembered the Werner family's house at Perchtoldsdorf, where he had so often played skittles in the sunny Maierling days of 1880 and 1882. In the depths of winter it would be cold and deserted, but certainly peaceful, and there he decided to go, with a mass of manuscript paper, a few volumes of poems, his coffee - machine and portable bath, to try the affections of his muse in conditions of almost arctic severity. After he had been warned of the many hardships he would encounter, permission to use the house was gladly given, and

---

[1] Eckstein's services to Wolf are indisputable, but there is evidence to show that on this occasion he was probably not called upon to defray the costs of publication. The legal correspondence of Dr. Reitzes, who acted for Wolf after the death of his father, shows that the composer inherited just over 1,700 gulden. Letters of Dr. Reitzes to a colleague at Windischgraz, in December 1887 and January 1888, request the advance payment of 200–300 gulden, required by Wolf for his 'artistic purposes.'

in the middle of January 1888 he said good-bye to the Langs and set out for his new asylum.

The market town of Perchtoldsdorf, half an hour's journey by rail from Vienna, was at that time quite isolated from the city suburbs and surrounded by vineyards, on the outskirts of the Wiener Wald. With its many old houses, Gothic church, and massive stone watch-tower, it was a place of singularly harmonious character and quiet charm, and had become a favourite summer resort of artists and scholars from the capital.

The Werners' house was at Brunnergasse 26. The building had belonged in 1775, and perhaps also before that date, to the monastery of Monte Serrato and had probably been used to house the keeper of the vineyards. In 1888 a round door in the thick outside wall gave entry to the courtyard, where the watch-dog Diana lived. A wooden fence divided the courtyard from an extensive garden, with a huge mulberry-tree, probably nearly as old as the building itself. A low doorway led into the house; on the right was the dairy, on the left the dining-room, and a narrow winding stone staircase led the way to Wolf's combined bed-sitting-room and study. This was a fine, large, tower-like chamber with windows on all four sides. In the middle of the room an old leather settee stood near a great round table, upon which were spread Wolf's books, writing materials, and tobacco. Under the pier-glass on one of the walls was a bed. A Promberger grand piano stood in one corner, and near it a writing-table, a cupboard and a commode. The *non plus ultra* coffee-machine was erected on a little cane table of its own and in another corner hung the portable indiarubber bath.

The house had no water laid on and was poorly lit by oil lamps, but the chief drawback, as Wolf had been warned, was the very indifferent performance of the old tiled stove, and in the first weeks of his stay at Perchtoldsdorf he suffered severely from the cold and was glad to avail himself of an occasional invitation to visit the Werners or Frau Preyss. Perhaps on 24th January the weather was a little warmer, for on that day he unfroze sufficiently to produce two new songs, *Wo wird einst*, the latest in date of his settings of Heine, and *Gesellenlied*, to a poem of Reinick's. *Wo wird einst* represents neither Wolf nor Heine at his best but the *Gesellenlied*, in which the David of Wagner's *Meistersinger* reappears, is a jolly thing. But far more important events were to follow.

On 16th February Wolf set to music *Der Tambour*, a poem of

Mörike's, and six days later his creative imagination took flight on the wings of this poet's genius. There began to pour from his pen a veritable flood of impassioned song, such as had hitherto been known only to Schubert at his most inspired and to the Schumann of 1840. Wolf himself watched with incredulous amazement and joy while strange new songs, all settings of Mörike's poems, formed themselves under his hands almost without conscious volition on his part. The composer seemed to have become the helpless instrument of a higher power. In letters to Edmund Lang he tried to give expression to the tumultuous emotions that filled and overflowed his heart. On 22nd February he told his friend:

> I have just written down a new song. A divine song, I tell you! Quite divinely marvellous! By God! it will soon be all over with me, for my cleverness increases from day to day. How far shall I get? I shudder to think about it. I have not the courage to write an opera, as I am still afraid of the many ideas that would be necessary. Ideas, dear friend, are dreadful. I feel my cheeks glow like molten iron with excitement, and this condition of inspiration is to me exquisite torment, not pure happiness.
>
> To-day I have sketched out at the piano practically a whole comic opera. I believe I could write something really good of this kind. But I am afraid of the exertion. I am too cowardly for a proper composer. What will the future yet unfold for me? This question torments and distresses me and preoccupies me waking and dreaming. Have I a vocation? Am I really one of the elect? God forbid the latter. That would be a pretty kettle of fish.
>
> I believe I am mad; I rattle off such silly stuff to you.

A copy of the poem just set to music, *Der Knabe und das Immlein*, was enclosed with this letter. Later in the same day Wolf wrote to Lang again, conveying the news that two further songs had come into existence since his first letter.

> The days of Lodi really seem to be renewing themselves. My Lodi in song is known to have been the year '78; in those days I composed almost every day one good song and sometimes two. Now prick up your ears!
>
> Scarcely was my letter dispatched than, taking the Mörike in hand, I wrote a second song, in 5–4 time, and perhaps I may say that seldom has 5–4 time been so fittingly employed as in this composition. You too, a layman, will at once discover the 5–4 measure in the rhythm of the poem and understand the necessity for it.

Jägerlied

Zierlich ist des Vogels Tritt im Schnee,
Wenn er wandelt auf des Berges Höh':
Zierlicher schreibt Liebchens liebe Hand,
Schreibt ein Brieflein mir in's ferne Land!

In die Lüfte hoch ein Reiher steigt,
Dahin weder Pfeil noch Kugel fleugt:
Tausendmal so hoch und so geschwind
Die Gedanken treuer Liebe sind.

Ex. 10

Zier - lich ist des Vo - gels Tritt im Schnee, wenn er *etc.*

Now congratulate me, or curse me, just as you please.

Should Polyhymnia be sufficiently attentive to threaten me with a third song, I will personally convey to you the dreadful news very early in the morning.

At the moment nothing musical is happening around me, except for the regular evening prayer in long-drawn howls on the part of a respectable maiden—our Diana.

Despise me! The hat-trick is complete. The *third* song, *Ein Stündlein wohl vor Tag*, is also achieved, and *how*! That is an eventful day.

After these three songs on 22nd February there followed *Der Jäger* on the 23rd and *Auftrag* and *Nimmersatte Liebe* on the 24th. After composing the latter song Wolf sat down again to acquaint his friend Lang with his latest achievements.

It is now just seven o'clock in the evening and I am as happy as a king. Another new song is successfully completed. Dear fellow, when you hear it the Devil will take you with pleasure.

The end breaks out into a regular student's song. It goes deuced merrily. Here are the words:

Nimmersatte Liebe

So ist die Lieb'! So ist die Lieb'!
Mit Küssen nicht zu stillen:
Wer ist der Tor und will ein Sieb
Mit eitel Wasser füllen?
Und schöpfst du an die tausend Jahr'
Und küssest ewig, ewig gar,
Du tust ihr nie zu Willen.

Die Lieb', die Lieb' hat alle Stund'
Neu wunderlich Gelüsten;
Wir bissen uns die Lippen wund,
Da wir uns heute küssten.
Das Mädchen hielt in guter Ruh',
Wie's Lämmlein unterm Messer;
Ihr Auge bat: nur immer zu,
Je weher, desto besser!

So ist die Lieb' und war auch so,
Wie lang es Liebe gibt,
Und anders war Herr Salomo,
Der Weise, nicht verliebt.

(EDUARD MÖRIKE.)

It just occurs to me that you may as well save yourself the purchase of Mörike's poems, as in my wonderful creative zeal I should be in the happy position of making you acquainted, sooner or later, with the entire poetical works of my favourite.

On the following day he told Marie Lang: 'To-day two new songs (by Eduard Mörike) have occurred to me, of which one sounds so weird and strange that I am quite afraid of it. There has never been anything like it. God help the unfortunate people who will one day hear it!' *Zur Warnung* was written on the 25th, but the second song mentioned does not seem to have been set down on paper on that day. After an interval of three days came the *Lied vom Winde* (29th February) and *Bei einer Trauung* (1st March).

All through the month of March this feverish creative activity continued with hardly a break. Twenty new songs were written in this month alone.

Wolf would rise very early and permit himself a short walk over the heath, or more usually only as far as the top of the 'Hochberg,' a little grassy hillock behind the house, rising to a height of 306 metres above sea level, or just 46 metres above the level of Perchtoldsdorf market-place. There he breathed the morning air, while his gaze strayed far over the vineyards to the forest-clothed hills of the Wiener Wald. He loved this view. 'What more do I need?' he used to ask visiting friends, who were always taken to the Hochberg. After a breathing space on the summit he would return to the Brunnergasse and begin the day's work. He would read through aloud several times a poem that attracted him and afterwards work out at the piano his musical ideas. Almost all his later work was done at the keyboard. Hasty sketches on odd scraps of paper would be amplified, developed, and varied many times before they took their final shape. The whole composition was built up in his head and sketched out on loose manuscript sheets. The later process of writing it out was a purely mechanical operation and this is the reason why all Wolf's manuscripts, in their definitive form, are so beautifully clean and clear, with only a very occasional erasure or correction here and there.

But these manuscripts are not, as was for so long believed, the first drafts at all.[1]

At lunch-time he would go out to the Black Eagle Inn for some boiled beef and vegetables—the cheapest dish—and then, after a cigarette and a cup of coffee of his own preparation, at once recommence his labours. In the evenings, unless Polyhymnia was being exceptionally attentive, he would generally read or write his letters.

In this routine the weeks passed and the pile of 'Mörikeana,' as it was at first called, grew ever larger. Each new success was at once communicated to his friends, in letters that reflected the composer's pride and joy. On 20th March he wrote to Edmund Lang:

> To-day, immediately after my arrival, I created my masterpiece. *Erstes Liebeslied eines Mädchens* (Eduard Mörike) is by far the best thing that I have done up to now. Compared with this song everything earlier was child's play. The music is of so striking a character, and of such intensity, that it would lacerate the nervous system of a block of marble. The poem is mad, the music not less so, and so is your Fluchu.[2]

But on the very next day he told his friend:

> I retract the opinion that the *Erstes Liebeslied eines Mädchens* is my best thing, for what I wrote this morning, *Fussreise* (Eduard Mörike), is a million times better. When you have heard this song you can have only one wish—to die.

Strasser was told the good news on 23rd March:

> I am working incessantly with a thousand horse-power from dawn till late at night. What I now write, dear friend, I write for posterity too. They are masterpieces. At present only songs, to be sure, but when I tell you that in spite of many interruptions due to my absence in Vienna, that is absolutely necessary twice a week on the Countess Harrach's account, I have nevertheless since 22nd February composed twenty-five songs, of which each one surpasses the others, and about which there is only one opinion among men of musical discernment—that there has been nothing like them since Schubert and Schumann, etc. etc. etc. etc.—you may imagine what sort of songs they are.

On 27th March he told Eckstein:

> This afternoon I wrote a quite exceptionally successful song, *Storchenbotschaft* (Mörike, naturally), and so I have hopes that the mill will continue to clatter. On Saturday I composed, without having intended to do so, *Das verlassene Mägdlein*, already set to music by Schumann in a

---

[1] The early sketches for many of Wolf's compositions are now in the National Library in Vienna, and put an end to many romantic legends about his methods of composition spread by Decsey and his followers.

[2] One of Wolf's many nicknames. This one arose out of his liking for violent oaths and curses.

heavenly way.　If in spite of that I set to music the same poem, it happened almost against my will; but perhaps just because I allowed myself to be captured suddenly by the magic of this poem, something outstanding arose, and I believe that my composition may show itself beside Schumann's.

On 2nd March the famous contralto Rosa Papier, the wife of Wolf's friend Hans Paumgartner, had given a recital at the Bösendorfersaal at which she had sung, for the first time in public, two of Wolf's earlier songs.　These were *Morgentau* and *Zur Ruh*, and the composer had his first taste of public recognition in the applause that followed their performance.　A sad little incident occurred at this concert.　One of Wolf's earliest friends in Vienna, Frau Breuer, with whose family he had had no further relationship since the summer of 1883, saw him among the crowd in the foyer when leaving the concert-hall, and went up to him impetuously to express her happiness at the success of his songs.　She had the unpleasant experience of seeing him flinch from renewed contact and almost crouch down in a corner to avoid her.　Shortly after Rosa Papier's recital Wetzler brought out the two volumes of songs.　No great sensation was of course to be expected, Wetzler being a very minor publishing house, but the volumes were favourably reviewed by Theodor Helm, the critic of the *Deutsche Zeitung*, who was always one of Wolf's supporters, and who, as a distant relative of Frau Preyss, had had the opportunity to learn something of the agreeable sides of Wolf's nature.　It is amusing to observe Wolf, in a letter written just after Rosa Papier's recital, informing Dr. Helm of the way in which he would like his work to be reviewed.　The results did not satisfy him.　He told his sister Modesta: 'Unfortunately the critic of the *Deutsche Zeitung* is a monstrously stupid beast, a straw-head, the like of which doesn't exist on this planet.　He is the cross I have to bear.'

While he was working feverishly at the *Mörike-Lieder* at Perchtoldsdorf, Wolf's friends were not encouraged to visit him without invitation.　Everything that interfered with the solitude and quiet so necessary to his work was a torment to him.　When the schoolboys played with their whips and tops in the Brunnergasse he used to rush out and confiscate their toys.　'On his creative days,' writes Hellmer, 'it was somewhat difficult to get on with him.　Everything about him was excited and exaggerated, he himself as though harassed and hunted by invisible spirits—in his own words, a man possessed.'　It was otherwise on the days he himself set apart for the revelation of his new songs to his friends.　While actually at work solitude was indispensable; but afterwards the necessity to communicate the gifts of his muse to others was equally urgent, and once a week, on Sundays, he would invite his intimate friends to Perchtoldsdorf and play and sing to them his latest compositions. Besides Eckstein and the Langs and Werners, there came to these gatherings Rudolf von Larisch, a government official who lived at Perchtoldsdorf and became Wolf's close friend, and an important group of professional and amateur musicians from the Vienna Wagner Verein. They included the chairman, Dr. Viktor Boller, the artistic director, Joseph Schalk, and Ferdinand Löwe, Richard Hirsch and Karl Bernhard Öhn. These men, drawn from various stations in life, were united in their love and admiration for Wolf and his work. Öhn was a bank clerk and amateur composer, who bought up, out of his none too abundant means, many copies of Wolf's songs for distribution among his friends. Richard Hirsch was an official in a government finance department; his modest, gentle, and sunny disposition won Wolf's deepest affection, as is apparent from even the slightest of Wolf's letters to him. Ferdinand Löwe was then a teacher of the piano at the Vienna Conservatoire, Boller the Austrian equivalent of a king's counsel; Joseph Schalk, the outstanding figure of all this group, was, like Löwe, a professor at the Conservatoire. He was three years older than Wolf, bearded and short-sighted, frail in body but extremely vigorous and courageous in mind. An idealist, he had from the first devoted himself with great earnestness to the furtherance of the cause of Wagner and Liszt. At the Conservatoire he had been one of Bruckner's pupils and, with Löwe, he had afterwards worked unceasingly to spread the knowledge of this composer's music. He made piano reductions of Bruckner's symphonies, which were performed by him and Löwe at public concerts long before they were able to get a hearing in their orchestral form. The necessity for the many and far-reaching alterations which these two men induced the simple-minded Bruckner to make in his original scores has been called in question of late, but none would deny the self-sacrificing devotion with which they worked for his recognition. When Schalk, in October 1887, became artistic director of the Wagner Verein, he was in a position to do a great deal for the furtherance of the music that gained his admiration, and for this reason, and the fact that with his idealism he coupled great practical ability and drive, his friendship was of the greatest importance to Wolf. They had met in early years at Goldschmidt's, but the acquaintance did not develop into anything more until 1887, when Schalk's brother Franz—who later became a celebrated conductor and ultimately director of the Vienna Opera—together with Löwe and Richard Hirsch, who had had the opportunity of getting to know some of Wolf's later songs, such as the *Wächterlied auf der Wartburg*, *Biterolf* and *Der König bei der Krönung*, insisted on his visiting Joseph Schalk's flat at Jordangasse 7, in the inner city, and playing and singing his own compositions. After that this group used to meet fairly frequently, either in Schalk's flat or in Wolf's own rooms. By his Mörike songs in 1888 Wolf won Joseph Schalk's unconditional allegiance and support.

After one of the Sunday gatherings at Perchtoldsdorf, Wolf was invited to visit the Wagner Verein and play his new songs to the wider circle of the members. His work, introduced by Boller and Schalk, aroused so much interest there that impromptu recitals by Wolf of his own compositions became a frequent feature of the Thursday evening meetings. In the letter to Strasser of 23rd March, Wolf told his brother-in-law: 'The Wagner Verein, on an evening when I performed my latest songs, I made downright mad. The fellows will go through hell for me, if necessary. I was celebrated there like a king.' With his poor, almost toneless voice, he was able to hold his hearers spellbound. None that heard him ever forgot the experience, or ever heard any performance comparable in intensity from any trained singer.

Throughout April and the first half of May new songs continued to be produced at Perchtoldsdorf with only slightly less frequency than at the beginning of the Mörike period. The total had reached forty-three by 18th May, when *Die Geister am Mummelsee* was composed. This song brought to an end the first great creative eruption of this miraculous year.[1]

At the end of May it became necessary for Wolf to vacate his in that month idyllic refuge at Perchtoldsdorf, as the Werner family wished to use it themselves. He set out on 27th May for a well-earned holiday at Bruck on the Mur. In company with Strasser he made a walking tour of Upper Styria and Carinthia, in the course of

---

[1] In the earlier chapters of this book some consideration of Wolf's compositions has generally followed the account of their origin. In the period now being described the compositions are so numerous and so important that their discussion is more conveniently reserved for an entirely separate chapter.

Full details of the Mörike and other songs, with precise dates of composition, are given in Appendix II.

which they visited the castle of Hoch-Osterwitz, near Glandorf.
As they walked through the deserted halls, Wolf suddenly stopped
short and listened intently. Strange sounds came to his ear, as if
somebody were playing a piano in the distance. He walked towards
the sound and discovered its source in an Aeolian harp, set in the
window of the last chamber of the castle. For a time he listened
enchanted, then ran back to Strasser and said: 'That is really wonderful. Look, I have *never* heard an Aeolian harp in my life until
this moment, and yet I divined it just so, exactly as the Aeolian harp
there sounds; so it is in my song. That is most remarkable.' Then
he sat down and wrote out for Strasser a few bars from his lovely
song *An eine Äolsharfe*, composed just seven weeks earlier. A letter
readdressed from Bruck to Windischgraz shows that Wolf visited his
mother during this summer, probably in the course of his walking
tour.

In July and August he was back again in Vienna. The friendship he had brought about between Edmund and Marie Lang and
Friedrich Eckstein had led to a decision to pool their resources and
take a house for the summer months away from the centre of the city.
In this way there was founded a communal summer colony of friends
in Schloss Bellevue near Grinzing, on the 'Himmel,' a spur of the
Kahlenberg. Other friends of Eckstein's, including the architect
Julius Mayreder, joined them and helped to bear the expenses, each
giving what he could afford. They all went about their own work in
perfect independence and gathered together in the evenings for a vegetarian dinner prepared by Marie Lang and served on the terrace or
under one of the great lime-trees in the garden. Wolf lived there with
them for a period. He spent a long time pulling to pieces, repairing and rebuilding an old piano that had been left in Schloss
Bellevue; such was his skill and knowledge of such matters that in the
end he had it in excellent condition and often played his own and
other music to his friends upon it.

On 21st August Wolf, Eckstein and various other friends left for
Bayreuth on the Vienna Wagner Verein's special train. On the 22nd
he heard *Parsifal* again, after an interval of five years, and once again
he was moved to the depths by the experience. An acquaintance
afterwards saw him sitting on a bench in the grounds of the theatre,
quite lost to the world, supporting his head in his hands and sobbing
as though he were heart-broken. It seems to have been during this
visit to Bayreuth that Wolf was introduced by Eckstein to a Mrs.

Elizabeth Fairchild, an American lady, a relative of Emerson, very cultured and charming, who afterwards purchased many copies of the Mörike volume and paid part of the costs of publication of the Goethe songs. Wolf was soon on good terms with this lady and agreed to perform his latest works for her. An excellent piano was available, which Mrs. Fairchild had had specially tuned for the occasion. Eckstein, who knew Wolf's idiosyncrasies, insisted that the composer should be allowed to try the instrument first, and it was as well that he did so, for Wolf, pulling from his hip-pocket the tuning-key without which he never ventured out, spent half an hour before he had sufficiently improved upon the professional tuner's work for his own satisfaction. He was in the best of humours, and although he at first threw mistrustful glances towards Mrs. Fairchild's English and American guests, their friendliness and the youthful alertness with which they awaited his songs reassured him. He asked Eckstein to read the poems first, very clearly and distinctly, so that they all understood them before they heard his musical settings. Then, in his own incomparable manner, he sang and played his Mörike songs, holding the listeners in a sort of spell.

At the end of August Wolf returned through Munich to Vienna, and from Eckstein's account it seems that he rejoined the summer colony in Schloss Bellevue. But on 31st August, at least, he was at Eckstein's Vienna residence, Siebenbrunnergasse 15, in the Margarethen district, for it was there, and on that day, that the Eichendorff song *Verschwiegene Liebe* was written. Perhaps he had accompanied Eckstein to town on some business trip to his factory, which was near the house in the Siebenbrunnergasse. Wolf was walking to and fro in the garden behind the house, a book of Eichendorff's poems in his hand, reading *Verschwiegene Liebe* again and again, sinking himself into the mood of the poem. The nearby factory disturbed him, someone was idly whistling in the courtyard, and from another house came the persistent sound of the beating of carpets. Suddenly he turned about, entered the house, and went up to Eckstein's room. There he sat down and wrote out the complete song, finished in every detail, with hardly a pause for breath.

This experience seems to have decided him that it was time to disappear into solitude again, for in September he sought and obtained permission to make use of the Eckstein family's country house[1] at Unterach am Attersee in the Salzkammergut. It lies on the

[1] Now Villa Jeritza.

shores of the lake, just outside the little secluded town, and looks across to the Höllengebirge, the mountain mass dividing the Attersee from the Traunsee.　Once again Wolf had cause to be thankful to his friends for idyllic surroundings in which to work at his songs. There he intended to set further poems of Eichendorff's to music, for publication with the best of his earlier settings of this poet.　Even before he settled down at Unterach he had added two more Eichendorff songs to his collection, *Der Schreckenberger* being written out, not, as usual, at the piano, but in the open air at Rettenbach, near Ischl, on 14th September, and a related song, *Der Glücksritter*, being composed, after the example of Schubert with *An Schwager Kronos*, in the post-wagon on the journey from Ischl to Weissenbach on 16th September.　Arrived at Unterach, Wolf completed his projected Eichendorff volume before the end of the month by the composition of ten songs in nine days.

With a break of only four days, three of which were spent in a visit to his old friend Henriette Lang, now Baroness Schey, at Rinnbach, Wolf turned once more to the poems of his darling Mörike. The following letter,[1] scrawled at breakneck speed to Eckstein in Vienna, reveals not only the beginning of the wonderful achievements that followed this return to his favourite poet, and the exultant, almost arrogant mood which these further successes induced in the composer, but much that is interesting besides.　Eckstein, it is apparent, was becoming a sort of honorary private secretary to Wolf, as he was to Bruckner, and was engaged upon various negotiations connected with the publication of the Mörike songs, to which Wolf looked forward with great impatience.　Wetzler was to bring them out, and it seems that Wolf had decided upon a volume of fifty songs. The idea of including a portrait of the poet at the head of the book of songs was already agreed upon, and was eventually carried out, although Wolf did not succeed in obtaining the portrait of Mörike in his youth that he would have preferred.　The beginning of the letter is evidence both of Wolf's reliance upon Eckstein's generosity and of his own sense of responsibility for his family's welfare.

DEAR FRIEND!

In the greatest haste.　Send me *at once* 20 florins.　The enclosed letter from my sister justifies, I hope, my impetuous demand.　I shall, as I run the risk of presenting myself to my dear friends with frostbitten nose and ears, hasten my departure from here.　I only want to set the *Feuerreiter*

---

[1] Facsimile in Decsey, facing p. 128 in vol. ii.

to music here, so that the fifty is complete. Yes, dear Ecksteinderl, I have
in recent days once again industriously 'Möriked' ['*gemörikelt*'], and what
is more, nothing but poems that you especially adore: *An den Schlaf, Neue
Liebe* (both on 4th October), *Zum neuen Jahre* (5th October), *Schlafendes
Jesuskind, Wo find ich Trost?* (both on 6th October). Just now I am
working on *Karwoche*, which will be magnificent beyond all bounds. All
the songs are truly shatteringly composed. Often enough the tears rolled
down my cheeks as I wrote. They surpass in depth of conception all the
other settings of Mörike. God only grant that I succeed with the *Feuerreiter*, for only then will the fifty be complete.

Have you taken any steps in the matter of the separate printing of the
poems? Do have them copied out so that the matter may get under
way. I am working *day and night*. I no longer know what rest is.

I want to publish the songs with an *introduction*. What do you say to
that? One thing more. Ask the publisher of Mörike's poems whether he
can procure for you a portrait of the poet *in his youth*, for the purpose you
know of. But be quick, be quick, be quick! Mörike must appear before
Christmas, or I'll kill both you and myself.

One thing further: Wetzler must renounce the copyright of my published
volumes. Tell him that. This business has already tormented me long
enough. He gets his percentage and—*basta!*

Something further yet: I shall naturally spend the first few nights at your
place. Get yourself ready then to receive me on this day *in a worthy
manner*.

Servus,
Your
FLUCHU.

Unterach, 8th October 1888.

Karwoche was successfully brought to an end on the same day, but
instead of completing the fifty songs with *Feuerreiter* alone, he wrote
Gesang Weylas on the 9th, *Feuerreiter* on the 10th, and *An die Geliebte*
on the 11th,[1] bringing the total up to fifty-two. A dated railway
ticket is preserved, showing that he set out on the first part of his
return journey, from Kammer to Linz, on the following day, 12th
October.

Hardly had he got back to Vienna, where he stayed, presumably,
with Eckstein at Siebenbrunnergasse, than he started off on a great
new cycle of songs, this time to poems of Goethe. The first twelve of

---

[1] Decsey in his original biography, and all subsequent writers, give 10th
October for the date of composition of *An die Geliebte*. The second December
number of *Die Musik* for the year 1904, however, gave a list of misprints in
Decsey's second volume; they included this one of 10th October instead of 11th
for *An die Geliebte*. Decsey himself never made the correction, either in later
editions of his original four volumes, or in the shorter biography which he wrote
many years later. That *An die Geliebte* was composed on 11th October I have
confirmed from the manuscript.

these, all the manuscripts of which give simply 'Vienna' as their place of origin, were composed in the twenty days between 27th October and 15th November.   Then, after a short pause, there followed an odd Mörike song, the second *Auf eine Christblume*, written on a visit to Perchtoldsdorf on 26th November.   Two days later *Gutmann und Gutweib*, Goethe's version of an old Scotch ballad, was set to music in Vienna and then on 7th December Wolf moved out to new winter quarters at Döbling, a suburb of Vienna, where the Köchert family had a residence at Hirschengasse 68, now Billrothstrasse, in the XIX Bezirk.

At Döbling no less than thirty-seven new Goethe songs were written in the succeeding ten weeks, making fifty in all since he had returned from Unterach.

On many occasions during this year Wolf had accompanied Schalk to the Wagner Verein's Thursday evening gatherings and sung and played his own songs to the members.   In addition to these impromptu recitals, the Wagner Verein used to arrange periodically more formal musical entertainments, for which well-known artists, outside the ranks of the society itself, were often engaged.   On 8th November one of these private concerts included the performance of three of Wolf's Mörike songs by Ellen Forster, a soprano of the Vienna Opera, accompanied by Joseph Schalk.   Among the audience at this recital was Ferdinand Jäger, who had sung Parsifal at Bayreuth, a Wagner interpreter of unsurpassed nobility.   He had recently retired from the stage and come to Vienna as a singing-teacher.   He was then nearly fifty years of age, very tall and commanding in presence, with a noble head, and in his manner an assurance that bespoke no little self-esteem.   Frl. Forster's performances did not please him, but Wolf's music made a great impression.   On the next day he visited the Köchert family and spoke with enthusiasm about it.   He then learned that Wolf himself was an intimate friend of the family and a meeting between him and Jäger could easily be arranged.   Soon afterwards Wolf played and sang his own songs to Jäger and Schalk in the music-room of the Köcherts' house in the Mehlmarkt and the experiences of that evening won for Wolf the lifelong allegiance of the great singer, who henceforth played a part in his life comparable with that played by Vogl in Schubert's.

Only a month later, on 15th December, Wolf appeared for the first time at a public concert as accompanist in his own songs, when

Jäger sang in the Bösendorfersaal four settings of Mörike, *Fussreise*, *Der Jäger*, *Peregrina I* and *Der Tambour*; two of Goethe, *Anakreons Grab* and *Der Rattenfänger*; two of Eichendorff, *Der Soldat I* and *Seemanns Abschied*; and the Reinick *Gesellenlied*. The rest of the programme consisted of Beethoven's Piano Sonatas, Opp. 53 and 106, and the Variations, Op. 35, played by Joseph Schalk. The success of Wolf's songs with the audience was immediate and remarkable; what had begun as a Beethoven concert became a Wolf festival before the evening was over. Schalk's challenging juxtaposition of the names of Wolf and Beethoven, however, was too much for the critics, and even the well-disposed Theodor Helm, of the *Deutsche Zeitung*, felt called upon to administer a rebuke. Wolf himself wrote to Strasser: 'That on the programme stand only the names of Beethoven and my unworthy self has already given much offence among those inimically disposed towards me. On the other hand you will understand from it how highly my things are valued.'

In the Wagner Verein itself opposition to Schalk's unceasing propaganda on Wolf's behalf was beginning to arise and the Beethoven-Wolf concert brought forth a leader of the opposition in the person of Wolf's former friend Dr. Hans Paumgartner. In the *Wiener Abendpost* of 18th December he attacked the policy of the society under Schalk's leadership and severely criticized Wolf's music.

Many of the Wagner Verein members did not want their Thursday evening meetings monopolized by Wolf and his songs. They thought that too much was being made of this new star appearing over the horizon. Furthermore, the business of the Wagner Verein was the furtherance of the understanding of Wagner's music and not that of anybody else. It seems that Wolf had a poor opinion of the general level of intelligence of the members which he did not much trouble to hide. He loved and respected some of them as individuals but, in spite of everything that he owed to the existence of the Wagner Verein and its hospitality towards himself, he disliked the stuffy intellectual atmosphere in which the Wagnerian old guard lived, and he despised most of the composers in the Wagnerian manner of whom they approved. He was anxious himself for recognition as an original artist in his own right and not as an epigone of Wagner's, delving in a corner of the territory which the master himself had not found time to cultivate. With Jäger's support, a successful public concert behind him, the Mörike songs in an advanced stage of preparation for publication and whole stacks of Eichendorff and Goethe songs ready to follow them, perhaps he considered that he was already past the stage at which the Wagner Verein could play any part in his progress towards recognition.   In a letter at the end of this year he told his mother:

> If my successes can only give your life some sort of bright coloration, from now on you shall see everything in the rosiest gleams, for my youthful renown is now mightily in the ascendant and in very little time I shall perhaps act the principal part in the world of music.   The imbecile critics, to be sure, have not yet by a long way fathomed my form and ideas, as my art is too new for them and all critics are as dry as dust.   But already I have won the unbiased public and among the people the desire is continually increasing to get to know my things.

He spoke happily of the 'unheard-of wonder' of the past year:

> It was the most fruitful and on that account also the happiest year of my life.   In this year I have composed up to to-day no less than ninety-two songs and ballads, and of all these ninety-two songs not one is a failure.   I think I may be content with the year 1888.   What will the year 1889 bring forth?   In this year must be finished the opera, the execution of which I intend to set about in the next few days.

That the idea of writing an opera was occupying him a good deal at this time, and being discussed with his friends, is seen from a letter of Franz Schalk's, who had secured an engagement as conductor at Richenberg, in Bohemia, and thus learned of Wolf's recent extraordinary activities only at second hand, to his brother Joseph. 'Wolf's successes,' he wrote on 16th November, 'find in me the warmest sympathizer and I rejoice for him and also for all those for whom in him a new light of pure creation shines.   He doesn't need to be in a hurry with the opera, and it remains doubtful whether his peculiar gifts will sufficiently support such an undertaking.'   The subject of Wolf's projected opera was Alarcon's *El Sombrero de tres Picos* ('The Three-cornered Hat'), of which a German translation had been published in 1886 in Reclam's handy and inexpensive Universal Library.   An unpublished letter to Strasser, dated 10th September 1888, already mentions his intention of treating this subject in operatic form and of writing his own libretto.   But many years were to pass, and many other operatic projects to occupy temporarily his mind, before he returned to Alarcon's story and produced *Der Corregidor*.

The song *Epiphanias*, as a note by Wolf in the Goethe volume indicates, was an occasional composition, written for Melanie Köchert as a special tribute of his thankfulness and devotion.   It was composed on 27th December, and sung on 6th January, the lady's birthday, by the three Köchert children dressed in fancy costumes, Wolf himself playing the accompaniment behind a screen.

Meanwhile at Döbling the Goethe songs had been continuing to accumulate, in spite of certain minor annoyances such as the doves, which at Wolf's request were killed, as the noise of their cooing was unbearable to him, and a neighbour's three geese, which Dr. Dlauhy, Heinrich Köchert's brother-in-law, had to buy up and make use of for the family's Sunday dinner. Relief from the noise of the latter birds was only temporary, however, as the neighbour straight away bought some more. Nevertheless, the mighty *Prometheus* came into existence on 2nd January, *Königlich Gebet* on the 7th, and *Grenzen der Menschheit* on the 9th. On 10th January Wolf made his second public appearance as accompanist in his own songs. The brothers Willy and Louis Thern, well known in their day for their recitals on two pianos, gave a concert in the Bösendorfersaal at which Jäger had been invited to sing two groups of songs by way of relief. Unfortunately for the brothers Thern, the success of Wolf's songs with the public was far greater than that of the main part of the programme; eight of his songs were sung by Jäger, instead of three, and the annoyance of the duettists was such that they neither thanked Jäger for his co-operation nor ever again asked for it.

The rest of January was spent by Wolf at Döbling in the furious composition of his Goethe songs. The creative impulse was, if possible, more imperious in its demands than ever before. After *Ganymed* on 11th January there was an interval of four days and then an outburst which resulted in the composition of fifteen songs in ten days, all taken from the *West-östlicher Divan*. A few more isolated songs brought the total of the Goethe settings up to fifty by 12th February. As in the case of the Mörike songs there was a straggler added some time afterwards, *Die Spröde* not being written until 21st October.

A group of three portraits of Wolf by the Viennese photographer Heid, taken in February 1889, show us the composer as he was at the peak of his artistic career. The Mörike songs were then expected from the publishers at any moment, the Eichendorff volume was in preparation, and fifty new Goethe songs had recently been completed. In all one hundred and sixteen songs, or more than half of the work upon which his fame now chiefly depends, had been composed within a year. He had tasted public success, and controversy

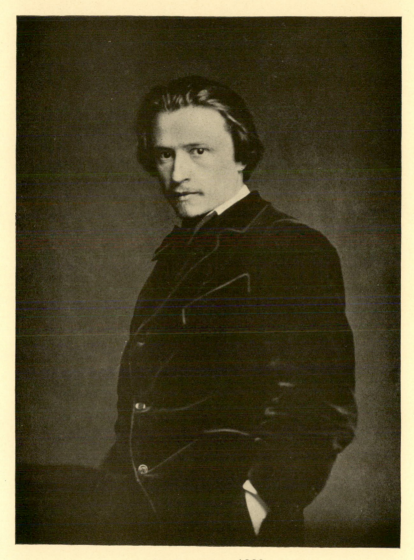

HUGO WOLF, 1889

raged round his name. In these portraits he still wears the worn
brown velvet jacket, with the artist's cravat and long mane of hair.
In two of them he stands, hands nonchalantly thrust into his trouser
pockets, with a challenging, almost disdainful look in his gleaming
eyes. In the third his expression is altogether milder and more
melancholy. To all the portraits the large mouth and heavy lower
lip give a tinge of sadness. The moustache and short goatee beard
are in course of development, but are still very thin; Eckstein has
explained that Wolf had a nervous habit of plucking the hairs out
from his chin, and never shaved. In the photographer's studio he
generally appeared more relaxed, less tensely strained in muscle and
nerve, than his friends knew him in everyday life, and to complete the
portrait we must visualize him in movement. He attracted attention
by his quick, jerky walk, and as he hurried on his way would often be
heard talking to himself. He was a man who always ran upstairs.

The split in the ranks of the Wagner Verein members over Schalk's
pro-Wolfian policy grew ever wider. Rumours were spread by
fanatical anti-Semites that both Schalk and Wolf were of Jewish
extraction. This was true in neither case. The frequency of the
occasions when Wolf performed his songs during the meetings of the
society led to disgruntled remarks about 'howling dervishes' and
the 'wolf's glen' and the suggestion that the name should be changed
to Wolf Verein. On 7th February a violent scene occurred between
Wolf and various disturbing elements in the society. He arrived in a
bad temper owing to a quarrel with his publisher Wetzler, and
although he agreed to accompany Jäger in a group of songs he
ignored the applause and just glared at the audience from the piano.
The Eichendorff *Heimweh*, with the concluding line 'Grüss' dich,
Deutschland, aus Herzensgrund,' was made the occasion for a pan-
Germanic demonstration by some of the company, violent applause
breaking out before the conclusion of the grandiose piano postlude.
Wolf stopped playing and gazed angrily at the interrupters, who were
calling for the song's repetition. Dr. Boller rose and reminded the
audience that an important part of the song followed after the singer's
last line. *Heimweh* was begun again, and again, in spite of Boller's
warning, the postlude was broken into by applause. Wolf was
furious. He slammed his music together, turned to the audience and
ejaculated with unmistakable contempt: 'In the *Wagner* Society!'
Pandemonium was let loose by this remark, Wolf's supporters
quarrelled loudly with his enemies, and order was only restored when

H

Schalk sat down at the piano and played the *Siegfried Idyll*. The opposition left in a body, and later on those who had stayed asked for more songs; but Jäger now was out of humour and excused himself on account of the tobacco smoke in the hall. Wolf played some of his songs, and then suddenly went up to Jäger and asked his forgiveness. The great singer returned to the piano and gave magnificent performances of many of Wolf's latest compositions, to which he had been devoting all his time and attention, and the evening ended in yet another Wolf festival in the Wagner Verein.

On the day after these events Wolf, to whom the whole affair had been intolerable, and who had no desire to attain notoriety at the expense of his self-respect, sent to Joseph Schalk one of the most revealing of all his letters, declaring his intention never to visit the Wagner Verein again. 'Dearest Josephus!' he wrote,

Don't expect me to-morrow. Since yesterday evening a quite dreadful shyness has come over me, so that it seems to me wholly impossible to look anybody in the face. I want from now on more than ever to belong to *myself*. I am not fit for society. I am a man who in everything acts only on impulse, and when a sufficient quantity of electricity has accumulated in me something happens, in thought, words, or deeds that may be good or bad. Wise people, however, act always according to the laws of logic and reason, etc., etc., and on that account there are frequent differences between them and me. I shall certainly not wound my friends any more by my impulsive actions, for I am firmly resolved, once and for all, to shun the Wagner Verein. Dearest friend! Will you not be forced to declare me an arch-scoundrel if I continue to court the favour of the Wagner Verein? In truth my behaviour to date accords badly with my declaration that I am wholly content if my things please just *you three*,[1] and that I am quite indifferent to the public, whether it decides for or against me. What do I want with the Wagner Verein? What do I want with singers? Do I wish to become a famous man? Yes, I was in a fair way of striving with full power towards that goal. Folly! Madness! Idiocy! As if the satisfaction of common vanity could offer compensation for the manifold sacrifices, worries, infamies, insults, and outrages that are bound up with the attainment of such an aim! Ten thousand devils may fetch me on the spot if I ever encumber my brain with such anxieties again. Let's hear no more of it! I will have nothing more to do with publicity; publicity is an infamous *canaille*. I wish to be just a private individual. Oh, if I were only a cobbler, like the incomparable Sachs! How merrily, how happily could I shape my life! Mending shoes on weekdays and composing in my best clothes on Sundays, and that only as a pastime, quite privately, only for myself and a few friends—for example, you, Löwe, and Hirsch. Yes, that would be a fine existence! You see, dear friend, that I am becoming a

[1] Schalk, Löwe, and Hirsch.

philosopher. I am not sufficiently the philosopher to disregard the envy
and the machinations of my enemies, but just sufficiently the philosopher
to live for myself alone and to ignore publicity entirely. If I did not wish
to demonstrate in public—in the way that you have stood up for me—my
thankfulness to you and Franziskus,[1] no power on earth could bring me to
publish the Eichendorff songs.[2] But with them, once and for all, the
business comes to an end.

I don't see why I should bother myself with the Wagner Verein, or why I
should publish my things, when the only reason for putting up with trouble
and persecution proves to be insufficient—I mean the material gain. Am I
a fool, to sacrifice time and money for the fine pleasure of being made the
object of the silliest judgments from sundry unwashed mouths? Is it not
much better, and finer, to be loved and understood by a few men than to be
hated and reviled by thousands?

The devil of vanity and inordinate ambition will not catch me by the
forelock again, you can depend on that. I am no senseless Mohammed, to
propagate my things with fire and sword, and none of my friends shall lose
a single hair on my account. Let each seek to win through on his own
account; each one has enough to do to look after himself. So let's have
no apostles!

This letter is in striking contrast with that Wolf had sent to his
mother little more than a month before. He had then betrayed
ambitions to 'act the principal part in the world of music' and had
spoken of his 'youthful renown' being 'mightily in the ascendant.'
The two letters illustrate phases of Wolf's relationship to his work
that were probably constantly recurring, as the impulse to secure
recognition of his genius alternated with revulsion from the public
contacts and annoyances that the attainment of such recognition
involved. It was the task of Wolf's friends to dissuade him from
such sensitive shrinking within his shell, and, while protecting him as
far as possible from friction with his environment, to persuade him
that he owed it to his *work* to endure the world's importunities.
The outcome of the devoted efforts of Schalk, Jäger, and Löwe, and
their refusal to accept Wolf's renunciation of their discipleship,
is seen in the calendar of events in the succeeding weeks and
months.

The *Mörike-Lieder* were at length published by Wetzler, on commission for the composer, at about the beginning of March. On
5th March Wolf accompanied a group of his songs at another public
recital by Jäger, and on 9th March the latter sang eight Wolf songs at
a further concert, this time with Ferdinand Löwe at the piano. On

[1] Franz Schalk.
[2] The Eichendorff volume was dedicated to Franz and Joseph Schalk.

19th March we find Wolf inviting Theodor Helm to be present at the performance of some of his songs in—the Wagner Verein! Finally, on Good Friday, 18th April, the Wagner Verein itself organized a programme of religious music at the Minoritenkirche and included Wolf's *Seufzer*, *Schlafendes Jesuskind*, and *Gebet*. The singer was Louise Kaulich, accompanied at the organ by Joseph Schalk.

At the end of April Wolf arranged to return for a time to the Werners' house at Perchtoldsdorf. He was there in May, as is shown by inscriptions on some of his scores. Although the first great lyrical impulse of his maturity had almost spent itself with the completion of the Goethe songs in February, various minor musical activities continued to occupy him in the months that followed. *Christnacht*, for chorus and orchestra, which had been begun at the end of 1886, was completed at Perchtoldsdorf in May 1889. The *Elfenlied* for soprano solo, women's chorus and orchestra, 'You spotted snakes with double tongue,' from *A Midsummer Night's Dream*,[1] and the *Lied des transferierten Zettel*—Bottom's 'The ousel-cock so black of hue'—were both composed on 11th May. They are in all probability fragments of the music intended for an opera based on *A Midsummer Night's Dream*. Decsey records that Wolf one Sunday rushed into Löwe's room, where Richard Hirsch was also having lunch, and spoke for about half an hour about this play, saying that it would be impossible to find a better text for an opera. There would seem to be little reason for a musical setting of Bottom's song, apart from the proposed opera, while there is some evidence, even in the printed version of the *Elfenlied*, of its conception in other terms than those of the concert-hall. Although only a single soloist is called for, the two verses of the poem are divided between the 'first fairy' and 'second fairy,' and shortly before the end the stage directions, 'Fairies vanish' and 'Titania sleeps,' remain in the score.[2]

The *Elfenlied* is an exquisite thing, comparable with the fairy music in Berlioz's *Damnation de Faust*; the orchestral texture is like gossamer, and glistens and sparkles with all the mysterious activities of

---

[1] Only the piano score was prepared in this year. Decsey attributes the *Elfenlied* to 1888, but Wolf's dates on four different manuscripts show his first biographer to have been mistaken. The work was scored in October 1891. It is not true, as is often stated, that the *Elfenlied* was originally conceived as a solo song. Even the first manuscript sketches already bear the indication 'chorus' above the section: 'Philomel, with melody . . .' although the parts are not written out.

[2] Some sketches and notes for Wolf's *Midsummer Night's Dream* libretto are in the Vienna City Library.

an enchanted wood at night.　The leaves rustle with invisible movements, the nightingale sings, and in the background is heard the magic horn of jealous Oberon.

Next came a group of Wolf's arrangements of his own songs for voice and orchestra—perhaps as the result of hearing some of them played on the organ at the Good Friday concert.　The orchestral version of *Seufzer* is dated 28th May and that of *Karwoche* 29th May. *Auf ein altes Bild* was also scored in this year, but the precise date is not known.

In June Wolf lived with Eckstein and the Langs in the summer colony in Schloss Bellevue.　The first part of July he spent with the Köchert family at Rinnbach.　Later in this month he visited the Bayreuth Festival again, for performances of *Parsifal*, *Tristan*, and *Die Meistersinger*.　He was there introduced to Blauwaert, the great Belgian bass, and at an improvised concert the latter sang various Mörike and Goethe songs at sight, to the composer's accompaniment. On 26th July Wolf left Bayreuth for Munich, where he stayed until the 29th, when he left again for Rinnbach.　The drinking-song *Skolie*, to words by Reinick, was composed there on 1st August. The whole of September and part of October he spent in his home at Windischgraz.

During these summer months he was corresponding with the music-printing house of Brandstetter at Leipzig.　The Eichendorff songs were being published, not by Wetzler, but by another small Viennese firm, C. Lacom, in the Tuchlauben.　Wolf himself watched over the preparation of the volume with the greatest care and entered upon a lively, and frequently agitated, correspondence direct with the printers.　Just as he could not bear to see a speck of dust anywhere on his clothes, and kept his lady friends busy repairing any minute hole or fray that appeared, so every detail of the format of his published works had to be precisely to his specification.　All his publishers found him exceedingly difficult to please in this respect, and it is no reflection on the world-famous music-printing house of Brandstetter that in the many letters and cards which reached them this summer from Rinnbach and Windischgraz Wolf frequently overstepped the bounds of politeness.　That was a characteristic of all the hypersensitive composer's dealings with the business world. After the *Eichendorff-Lieder* came out in September the correspondence continued over the preparation of the Goethe volume, publication of which Lacom had also undertaken.　The composer declared that he was not seeking a popular edition of his works and insisted on a really handsome volume, with nothing skimped about it.   He specified the dimensions, the quality of the paper, the number of lines of music to the page—many of the Goethe songs had to be reprinted because he objected to the use of five staves to a page—the number of bars to a line, the colour of the covers and the lettering, ink and ornamental border used on the title-pages.

For assistance in financing the publication of these volumes Wolf was again indebted to Eckstein, who in 1937 still possessed a receipted bill from Lacom for 163 florins, 26 kreutzer, dated 22nd August 1889.   In his reminiscences Eckstein says that Mrs. Fairchild, the American lady whom Wolf had met at Bayreuth, paid part of the costs of the Goethe volume.   It seems certain, however, that Wolf himself invested part, at least, of the money inherited from his father in the publication of these early volumes.   Decsey, in his shorter biography of 1919, records that Gustav Schur remembered how the composer spoke to him of the money he had spent in this manner and so sharply stressed the words 'mein Geld' that Schur forbore to inquire about its source.   The letter to Joseph Schalk quoted above also refers to the sacrifices of time and *money* involved in the publication of the songs.   The difficulty was to understand how he could afford to do this.   Everything becomes clear when we know that he had inherited 1,700 gulden on his father's death.

In October Wolf returned to Vienna and without delay re-established himself in his Perchtoldsdorf retreat—a certain indication to all who knew him that the fever of creation had seized him again.   At first he rented a house at Mühlgasse 6, recommended him by Joseph Schalk, but after only a fortnight he moved again to the Werner family's house in the Brunnergasse.   There on the 21st of this month he composed *Die Spröde*, the last of the Goethe songs, which was then sent off to join the others in the volume in course of preparation. Then with *Wer sein holdes Lieb verloren*, on 28th October, he began his *Spanish Song Book*, settings of ten religious and thirty-four secular Spanish poems, in the German translations of Paul Heyse and Emanuel Geibel.   Twenty-six of these songs were written in the next two months, in a state of burning inspiration similar to that in which the Mörike and Goethe volumes had been produced.   On no less than five different occasions a single day saw the completion of two songs.

It is interesting to find that Wolf, writing to his sister Käthe on

12th November,[1] when only nine of the songs had been written, told her that he intended the *Spanish Song Book* to consist of forty-four songs in all—the precise number which it did in fact eventually contain. It would seem that, in spite of the volcanic and apparently unpredictable nature of Wolf's inspiration, he knew beforehand precisely which poems he was going to set to music when his inconstant muse allowed. Similarly, his letters reveal that he had a fixed idea of the desirable numerical content of the Mörike, Goethe, Keller and Italian volumes also.

The progress of the *Spanish Song Book* was halted by an attack of the influenza which, at the end of this year, ravaged half Europe. The intense cold of this winter may also have affected the flow of the Spanish songs, which was interrupted for two whole months. Whenever Perchtoldsdorf became unbearable Wolf returned to Vienna, where he stayed with the Köcherts.

The two months during which the *Spanish Song Book* hung fire were not entirely barren. Wolf turned from original work to the task of orchestrating some more of his Mörike and Goethe songs. The score of *Der Rattenfänger* is dated 5th February 1890, and those of *Er ist's* and *Gesang Weylas* 20th and 21st February respectively of the same year. Other scores almost certainly produced at the same time were the orchestral versions of *Schlafendes Jesuskind, Anakreons Grab, Kennst du das Land?* and *Ganymed*. Their existence, along with that of the others, was mentioned in a letter to Grohe on 16th April. This letter shows that the orchestration of *Prometheus*, although the score is dated 12th March 1890, was still uncompleted. A few days would suffice for the task, however, if a singer could be interested in it.

While Wolf had been busy at Perchtoldsdorf with his Spanish songs his friends had not been idle. In the November–December number of the *Österreichisch-Ungarische Revue* had appeared a notable article, 'Neue Lieder und Gesänge,' by Heinrich Rauchberg, dealing with the Mörike and Eichendorff volumes. In 1890 it was reprinted separately by the author to assist in spreading the knowledge of Wolf's work. On 17th December Jäger had included three Wolf songs in the programme of a concert at the Vienna Singakademie. At the instigation of Gustav Schur, a banking official and the treasurer of the Wagner Verein, a group of Wolf's friends and

---

[1] 'Briefe Hugo Wolfs an seine Schwester Käthe' (*Neue Freie Presse*, 25th July 1926).

supporters was next formed, with the object of relieving the composer from all financial embarrassments. Their first intention was to present him with an annual honorarium to cover his personal expenses, but they found that he would not accept the money in this form. For himself he wanted nothing, but he allowed that the fund should be administered for the benefit of his work. Thus in the years that followed difficulties with publishers and printers were smoothed over by Schur and his associates, and Wolf's travelling expenses paid for him.

When Wolf's propagandists sought to interest further singers of repute in his work they encountered strong opposition from certain sections of the press. Marianne Brandt, who had sung *Der Genesene an die Hoffnung* at a private concert in the Wagner Verein at the end of November, included three Wolf songs in the programme of a public concert on 4th January. Before that date, however, she received a visit from Wilhelm Frey, the critic of the *Neues Wiener Tagblatt*, who intimated that unless Wolf's songs were removed from the programme not a single representative of the press would attend her concert. The songs were replaced by three of Grieg's.[1] Amalie Materna, who had created the parts of Brünnhilde and Kundry at Bayreuth, a great singer whose support would have been of considerable importance to Wolf, also withdrew from an engagement to sing some of his songs in the Wagner Verein on receiving a threat of a critical boycott.[2] The composer Richard Heuberger, Hanslick's underling on the *Neue Freie Presse*, refused to allow his own songs to be performed in the same programme as Wolf's. For the rest, apart from Helm and August Göllerich, the professional critics either ignored the concerts at which Jäger worked so nobly to pass on his own enthusiasm for Wolf's music, or wrote vicious and evil-intentioned nonsense about them. A leader of the latter school was Max Kalbeck, later the author of a monumental biography of Brahms, who, presumably in attempted revenge for what Wolf had written in the *Salonblatt* about his hero, made an incomparable ass of himself

---

[1] See the instalment of Theodor Helm's 'Fünfzig Jahre Wiener Musikleben' in *Der Merker* (Vienna) for 1st April 1917, and pp. 13–14 of Heinrich Werner's *Der Hugo Wolf Verein in Wien* (Regensburg, 1921).

[2] Wolf was on friendly terms with Materna. In a letter to Melanie Köchert of 30th August 1890 he remarks, with a neat reference in conclusion to one of his own Spanish songs: 'Yesterday I visited Materna. She was, as always, amiable and garrulous. Rational conversation was not possible—every third word is Paris, Paris, Paris. There she promises to sing everything for me. When I sighed and spoke of Vienna, "Paris," she softly replied. There's no help for it.'

in the pages of the *Alte Presse* by characterizing such masterpieces as *Anakreons Grab*, *Der Rattenfänger*, and *Frühling übers Jahr* as 'childish, tinkling, barren stuff' with 'oddly banal melodies and ludicrous harmonic convulsions.'

Herr Hugo Wolf, who accompanied in a very individual manner at the piano, and spared neither the instrument nor the singer, has earlier as a reporter, by some singular proofs of his style and taste, aroused involuntary merriment in musical circles. The advice was given to him, rather to apply himself to composition. The latest productions of his muse have shown that this well-meant advice was harmful. He should go back to writing criticism.

It was perhaps the greatest of all Joseph Schalk's services to Wolf that by the publication of his long and splendid article 'Neue Lieder, neues Leben,' in the *Münchener Allgemeine Zeitung* for 22nd January 1890, he broke through the barriers of enmity and prejudice that surrounded Wolf in Vienna and kindled a flame of enthusiasm throughout south Germany. It was a most important step forward —the beginning of something more than local fame. The sensation produced by Schalk's essay was so great that Wolf even wrote to his rather unsympathetic brother Max about it. 'The *Münchener Allgemeine* has struck home like a bomb,' he told him, 'my enemies are disconcerted, my friends rejoice.' One direct result of Schalk's propaganda was that on his thirtieth birthday, 13th March, Wolf received an enthusiastic letter from a perfect stranger, one Emil Kauffmann, music director at the University of Tübingen, in which was enclosed as a gift the original manuscript of Mörike's poem *An Longus*. Kauffmann's father had been a personal friend of Mörike's from his schooldays, had married the sister of the poet's intimate friend Rudolf Lohbauer, and, as an amateur composer, had in his time set most of the poems to music. Two of his compositions were published in the original edition of Mörike's novel *Maler Nolten*. When Kauffmann had read in the *Münchener Allgemeine Zeitung* about the fifty-three new Mörike songs by Hugo Wolf he had naturally been extremely interested, had sent away for copies of the music, and on studying it had recognized at once its originality and importance and the composer's profound understanding of the poet. Wolf for his part was delighted to receive recognition from one so intimately associated with Mörike's family and friends.

Not long after this he received a letter from a second stranger, whose attention had likewise been attracted by Schalk's great article.

* H

This was Oskar Grohe, a judge of the lower court at Mannheim, who
had at once begun to introduce Wolf's music to his own friends,
including Karl Heckel, the music publisher, and Felix Weingartner,
then Kapellmeister at the Mannheim Court Theatre.   Under Weingartner, the Mannheim Wagner Verein was arranging an orchestral
concert in commemoration of the master's birthday (22nd May),
and Grohe wrote to ask whether Wolf had any works which might be
performed at this concert.   Wolf replied enthusiastically, offering
the choice of eight orchestrated songs, *Penthesilea*, *Christnacht*,
the Funeral Music from Kleist's *Prinz von Homburg*, the String
Quartet, the *Humoristisches Intermezzo* and the *Italian Serenade*.

The Goethe songs were published early in 1890 and on 21st March
Jäger sang six of them at a meeting of the Vienna Goethe Verein.
Wolf himself played the accompaniments.   Of equal importance with
the efforts of Jäger and Schalk on Wolf's behalf were the negotiations undertaken by Gustav Schur to procure him a first-rate
publisher to replace the small Viennese firms whose names were
practically unknown outside the borders of Austria.   Wetzler, the
first of Wolf's Viennese publishers, went bankrupt at about this time,
and on 28th March we find Wolf writing to Schott's at Mainz.
Seven years before they had rejected some of his early songs, but with
the recommendations that Schur had been able to procure, and the
great interest shown by their reader, Engelbert Humperdinck, in the
bulky parcels of manuscripts and printed songs which were submitted
for his opinion, the house of Schott declared itself willing to undertake the publication of Wolf's compositions.   The negotiations,
chiefly carried out by Schur, had still a long way to go before complete agreement was reached and all the difficulties caused by
Wetzler's bankruptcy removed, but in principle, at least, Wolf was
accepted as a composer of sufficient importance to merit the attention
of one of the foremost music publishers of Germany.

On the same day that Wolf wrote from Perchtoldsdorf to Dr.
Ludwig Strecker, the head of Schott's, declaring how much of an
honour he considered it to be allowed to present his works to a larger
public under their world-famous name, he returned again to the
Spanish Song Book, of which the remaining sixteen songs were
completed within a month.   During this time there were further
encouragements and successes.   On Good Friday, 8th April, Jäger
sang some of Wolf's religious songs in the Minoritenkirche.   On the
12th he gave a quite phenomenally successful concert at Graz.   The

deputy chairman of the Graz Wagner Verein, the architect Friedrich Hofmann, had in the course of a visit to Vienna been introduced by Jäger to Wolf's songs. He had returned to Graz with copies of everything that had then been published. His friend Dr. Heinrich Potpeschnigg, a dentist who was also a fine pianist, shared his admiration, and it was decided that Graz, the capital of the composer's Styrian homeland, should have its Wolf concert. Dr. Potpeschnigg accompanied Jäger in a programme that had originally included twelve of the Mörike, Goethe and Eichendorff songs. In point of fact, including the encores, no less than twenty-six were sung.

After the concert at Graz Dr. Potpeschnigg wrote to Wolf inviting him to stay at his country house at Krumpendorf on the Wörthersee some time during the summer. Jäger had brought back to Vienna glowing accounts of Potpeschnigg's enthusiasm and musical gifts, and Wolf was eager to make his acquaintance. Circumstances prevented the proposed visit, and the two men did not actually meet until later, but correspondence between them followed, and the foundations were laid of yet another enduring friendship.

Wolf's fame did now really seem to be 'mightily in the ascendant,' as he had earlier expressed it to his mother. At the close of this period of almost exclusively lyrical expressio , the most prolific of his whole life, we see him happy and confident, upheld in Vienna by staunch supporters, with new friendships multiplying farther afield, and his work finding increasing recognition and a publisher in Germany.

X

THE ACHIEVEMENT: FOUR SONG-BOOKS

EDUARD MÖRIKE, the Swabian poet (1804–75), had not lacked admirers among composers of an earlier generation. According to Challier's *Liederlexikon*, there existed no less than fifty musical settings of *Das verlassene Mägdlein* in 1885, three years before Wolf's own was written, and also, among others, sixteen settings of *Er ist's*, twenty-one of *Agnes*, thirteen of *Verborgenheit*, nine of the *Jägerlied* and eight of *Lebe wohl*. There are nine settings of Mörike by Schumann, of which five are solo songs, and several by Brahms and Franz. The Schumann songs include some attractive things, but it cannot be said that any of these composers succeeded in clothing much of Mörike's poetry in music of comparable quality. It was left to Wolf, with his great volume of fifty-three songs, to illustrate in music the range and the intensity of the poet's inspiration. By his peculiarly sensitive and ympathetic response to this poetry his name has become associated with that of Mörike, in the way that Schubert's name is for ever associated with that of Wilhelm Müller, the author of *Die schöne Müllerin* and the *Winterreise*. The parallel, however, is not an exact one, for while Müller's verses are only kept alive by the music to which they inspired Schubert, Mörike was a great poet in his own right, whose work would never have fallen wholly into oblivion. But although in Mörike's own south-German homeland his work was much beloved, the outside world had not paid a great deal of attention to it. Only four editions of the poems, of one thousand copies each, were called for in the thirty-seven years between their first publication and the author's death, and Joseph Schalk, writing for a Munich paper in 1890, could refer to 'the half-forgotten Schwabian poet' in the course of an article on Wolf's songs.

Mörike was a Protestant pastor with leanings towards Catholicism, a man who had known both the happiness and the bitterness of love, and, in his youth, in the encounter with the mysterious 'Peregrina,' plumbed the depths of erotic emotion, a man profoundly responsive to the moods of nature, a lover of his kind blessed with an observant eye and a sense of humour. His poetry reflects all this, sometimes

226

with overpowering emotional intensity, sometimes with classical measure, very often with inimitable sensual grace. Every characteristic of the poet is faithfully mirrored in Wolf's music. In this volume alone are depicted a wider range of subjects, human and elemental, realistic and visionary, and a greater diversity of moods and emotions, than had ever before found expression in song. It was this infinite variety, of Mörike's subject-matter and Wolf's methods of handling his poetic material, that gave rise to Ernest Newman's challenging passage, in his English biography of 1907, in which the *Mörike-Lieder* are compared favourably with a selection of the best of Schubert's songs from all periods.

Der Genesene an die Hoffnung, which stands at the head of the Mörike volume, is said to have been regarded by the composer as an expression of his own thanksgiving for the renewal of hope and creative strength that he owed to the poet. If this was so it perhaps accounts for its most unsatisfactory feature. In the mounting climax and triumphant fanfares which greet the mention of the convalescent's victory over his illness the *present* mood of the poem, which is nearer dejection than triumph, is forgotten. This is a flaw in a song that otherwise has great beauty and a Beethovenian nobility.

We turn the page and with *Der Knabe und das Immlein* we are wholly under the spell of Mörike's enchanted world. The song begins as a charming fable and ends as a fervent hymn to love. Wolf slyly followed it, in the published volume as in the order of composition, with the thematically related *Ein Stündlein wohl vor Tag*, in which an unhappy girl learns in the comfortless dawn how little reliance may be placed on the fine sentiments expressed at the close of *Der Knabe und das Immlein*. The little *Jägerlied* is the perfect musical expression of the rhythm and the sentiment of the verses. The ballad of the homesick and sleepy drummer-boy, *Der Tambour*, is a companion piece to Schumann's most successful Mörike song, *Die Soldatenbraut*.

Das verlassene Mägdlein, that had attracted fifty earlier composers, was in Wolf's Mörike volume, it is generally agreed, set to music once and for all, and even Schumann's song, that Wolf so much admired, is in consequence to-day almost forgotten. In masterly fashion the scene is re-created—the chill of the dawn, the stillness of the hour before the world is out of bed, the little comfort of the warming flames as the jilted maid-of-all-work kindles the household fire—these things are almost physically sensible. And with what economy of means Wolf produces his inevitable-seeming effects! The falling figure of which the listless rhythm pervades the whole song, a few bare and cold harmonies, the sense of strain given by the use of the augmented triad—out of these the whole scene is composed.

There is a setting of *Er ist's* by Schumann, too, and in this case there is less to choose between the two composers. Wolf's song, with its brilliant piano part, makes an effective concert piece and is known to many who have little interest in the rest of his work, but it hardly ranks among the rarer gifts of his muse.

No one but Mörike could have handled the theme of *Nimmersatte Liebe* with such delicacy and charm. 'Love is not to be stilled with kisses,' the poet declares. 'Who but a fool would try to fill a sieve with water?' No one but Wolf could have set the poem to music without offence. Half the attraction of this adorable song lies in the caressing touch of the musician's hand, as he translates into the terms of his own art Mörike's smiling comprehension of the troubles of youth. In *Begegnung* a girl encounters her first admirer in the rain-swept street after a night of storm. The meeting is not without embarrassment—a 'storm' within her own little room had last night disarrayed her tresses. Wolf does not omit to give the singer an opportunity of underlining the point. The attraction of the endearing *Fussreise* lies less in the obvious rhythmic tramp of Mörike's heavy walking boots than in the fact that he meditates as he goes, praising God for the morning, and, in the exhilaration brought about by the exercise, finding the heart of mankind less black than it has been sometimes painted. The song is often taken at a ludicrously fast tempo. *Verborgenheit* to-day enjoys a popularity out of all proportion to its worth. It did so even in the composer's own lifetime and he was once irritated into saying: 'It's not by me at all,' which is true in the sense that the song is uncharacteristic of Wolf at his best. *Rat einer Alten* is another popular song of which the composer himself afterwards tired. In 1923 Dr. Alfred Heuss, editor of the *Zeitschrift für Musik*, criticized both *Rat einer Alten* and *Nimmersatte Liebe* on the grounds that Wolf in his musical settings had not fully realized everything that is in the poems.[1] It must be admitted that in the case of *Rat einer Alten*, at least, there was considerable point in his remarks. There is an interesting background to the

---

[1] See 'Einiges über Hugo Wolfs geistige Potenz' in the second January number for 1923, and 'Weiteres zur Kritik Hugo Wolfs' in the first February number.

poem, implied in the sequence of the verses. It is clear that Mörike imagined the old peasant woman as intervening in a wrangle between her neighbour and his daughter, who has been discovered to have a sweetheart. In the introductory stanza the old woman stresses her age and experience: 'I too have been young, and am now grown old, so my words have authority.' In the next stanza she addresses particularly the father: 'Fine ripe berries hang on the trees. Neighbour, no fence is any use to keep the birds away from the fruit.' She implies, of course, that no pretty daughter can be expected to remain for long unmolested either. After this she turns to the girl, with advice about the handling of her love-affair and marriage. Wolf's setting of the poem lacks subtlety in suggesting the little drama behind the words. For instance, although the chirruping accompaniment of the second stanza may aptly convey the suggestion of the thieving birds, the dancing folk-style melody to which the words themselves are set is less well fitted to reflect the tone in which the old woman would pass on her word of warning. The verbal accentuation is not of the finest. '*Drum* gilt mein Wort,' says Wolf, instead of 'Drum *gilt* mein Wort,' and '*Mit* den zwei Fädlein' ('with the two threads') instead of 'Mit *den* zwei Fädlein'—'with *those* two threads' (the 'love' and 'respect' previously mentioned in the text) 'twisted into one, you will be able to draw him along by your little finger.' Brahms might have set this poem to music on such broad lines, but we are accustomed to seek something more subtle from Wolf.

An eine Äolsharfe, Im Frühling and *Auf einer Wanderung* are songs on a more extended scale. There are melodic phrases in many of the songs mentioned above that might have been taken directly out of folk music, and although Wolf uses the strophic and other simple song-forms with a great deal of licence, they are nevertheless still felt to underlie much of his work in a more popular vein. In these more personal and extended songs all such simple melodic and formal scaffolding is abandoned. The voice is left utterly free to reflect the emotions and point the verbal nuances of each line of the poem in a kind of 'endless melody' of marvellous beauty and flexibility, while the piano develops its independent themes in the symphonic manner. It is a type of song peculiarly associated with Wolf's name and used by him with increasing frequency and unsurpassable mastery in his later volumes. It enabled him to declaim the poem with all the freedom and subtlety that his fine literary sense demanded, while at the same time it gave abundant opportunities for the employment of his outstanding musical gifts—the invention and development of short, pregnant ideas and the shaping of the resultant 'symphonic' material into forms that satisfy both musical requirements and the poetic, or programmatic, requirements of the text. This type of Wolf song is, in fact, nothing less than a miniature symphonic poem for voice and piano. *An eine Äolsharfe* is elegiac in mood—the text refers to a brother of Mörike's who died in early boyhood. *Im Frühling* paints the uneasy longings and presentiments that spring brings to the heart of youth. In *Auf einer Wanderung* the poet is almost intoxicated by the loveliness of the world in the sunset hour, and at the climax of the poem ecstatically sweeps the strings of his lyre and addresses his muse in a phrase of immortal beauty. Illustrative of the possibilities of Wolf's 'symphonic' method of song construction is the postlude, in which the piano's initial theme, a strongly rhythmic 'wander-motiv,' is resumed. Before it dies away in the distance there recurs a reminiscence of the second principal theme of the song, associated with the poet's rapturous tribute to the beauty of the scene and his moment of inspiration. It is as if he turned for a last fond glance, before disappearing into the dusk.

Elfenlied, *Der Gärtner*, and *Zitronenfalter im April* are among the slighter of the Mörike songs, though the second conceals great depth of feeling in its graceful rhythms, and the last has pathos as well as gentle humour. *Um Mitternacht*, again, is quite simply constructed, but is nevertheless among the most profound things in the volume. Night broods over the woodlands and the streams sing to her, and in the beautiful monotony of his song Wolf seems to suggest the passage of endless time in remote fastnesses, accessible only to the poet's imagination. The first *Auf eine Christblume* is one of the more arcane delights of the Mörike volume. It contains almost a superfluity of musical invention. The free poetic reverie of the voice part is less securely held together by the instrumental part than in other songs of this type, and the effect is somewhat diffuse. Perhaps that is inevitable in any setting that attempts to follow the twisting thread of the poet's thought. The song is an elegy, a nature picture, a religious meditation, a vision of elfland, and a hymn to beauty all in one. The second *Christblume* song, though it has the same chaste and delicate air, is queerly indeterminate and far less attractive.

We come now to the very heart of the Mörike volume, a group of songs on religious and related subjects which includes some of Wolf's most highly individual creations.   The setting of *Seufzer*, Mörike's translation of a passage from the Passion Hymn of Fortunatus, shows us a monkish soul in torment from consciousness of sin.   The piece has a medieval atmosphere.   There is a suggestion of tolling bells in the accompaniment.   *Auf ein altes Bild*, the modal, chorale-like melody of which seems to have developed out of the cadence of *Seufzer*, which was written two days before it, is a tender meditation over an old picture of the Christ-child playing happily on his mother's knee.   It is a summer landscape and, as Wolf told Edmund Lang on the day on which he wrote the song, everything shimmers in green before the eyes.   Only at the thought that somewhere in the pleasant wood there is perhaps growing the stem of the cross there comes a momentary stab of pain.   *In der Frühe*, from its position in the volume, is probably to be regarded as a religious song, although there is nothing in the poem itself to indicate the nature of the doubts and spectres of the night that are vanquished by the bells of morning. The first half of the song is concerned with mental anguish and dejection following a night without rest or sleep.   Morning breaks on the chamber window.   A tolling figure that had, in minor keys, pervaded the first half of the song, modulates suddenly to a clear E major; the dull tolling becomes a sweet chiming of distant morning bells; doubts and torment depart with the dawn of day.   Wolf employs his favourite chain of mediant modulations, that he seems to have always associated with effects of changing light, and particularly of morning light;[1] the heart-easing chimes pass from E major to G major, to B flat major, and finally to D major, in which key they gradually die away.   The beauty of the song is itself almost sufficient to restore faith to a mind darkened and despairing.   *Schlafendes Jesuskind* is another religious meditation on an old picture; Mörike's poem arose from the contemplation of a painting by Francesco Albani (1578–1660).   Particularly beautiful is the effect of the postlude, in which Wolf, instead of leaving the summing-up wholly to the piano, instructs the singer to repeat the first line of the poem, to the original melodic phrase, very softly, 'as though lost in deep thought.'   *Karwoche* has atmosphere but no outstanding musical invention.   The popular *Gebet* begins rather feebly but improves towards the end, with a soaring cantilena like an angelic violin solo. *An den Schlaf* employs the resources of late romantic harmony to

---

[1] See, for other examples, *Und steht Ihr früh am Morgen auf*, *Ganymed* and *Morgenstimmung*.

suggest the shadowy boundaries of sleep and death. *Neue Liebe* is one of the least sympathetic of the Mörike songs. Its subject—the acceptance of the perfect love of God as compensation for the imperfection of all human relationships—seems hopelessly unfitted for the melodramatic treatment it receives at Wolf's hands. Instead of a solemn private meditation we are given an almost operatic exhibition of religious emotion. The song seems to be related with *Wo find' ich Trost?* which follows it in the volume and depicts the spiritual agony consequent upon neglect of that divine love which is all too easily accepted in *Neue Liebe*. There is no doubt that here the sinner inspired Wolf far more than the righteous Christian. It is strange indeed how the materialistically minded Wolf reverts again and again to this theme of the remorseful sinner, fearful of damnation. We find these anguished appeals for divine grace and mercy in the choral *Ergebung* of 1881, in *Seufzer* and *Wo find' ich Trost?* among the Mörike songs, and later, repeatedly, with overpowering intensity of expression, in the religious section of the *Spanish Song Book*. *Wo find' ich Trost?* derives spiritually and musically from *Parsifal*, but Wolf has fused his material in the fires of his own creative imagination. Extraordinary is the effect of the widely spaced *fortissimo* chords that accompany the great cry: 'Watchman, Watchman, is the night nearly over? What shall save me from death and sin?' In the orchestral version of the song this passage is given to the brass instruments. Possibly the mind of the composer reverted to the song of the watchman on the Wartburg, with its brazen chorus, or a suggestion of the Day of Judgment may even have been intended. The effect is sufficiently awe-inspiring.

There are numerous love-songs in the Mörike volume, but most of them represent the happiness or sorrow in love of this or that character depicted by the poet. A smaller group have a personal application. They include the two *Peregrina* songs, *Frage und Antwort*, *An die Geliebte* and *Lebe wohl*. There are five *Peregrina* poems by Mörike, commemorating the extraordinary episode of his youthful passion for, and renunciation of, Maria Meyer, a beautiful but half crazy girl, who was found unconscious by the roadside near Ludwigsburg one day, without any indication of how she had got there or where she had come from. She was given shelter and employment by an innkeeper and attracted to the inn many admirers, including Mörike and his student friends. The whole affair is shrouded in mystery, but it appears that a passionate love-affair was in course of

development between Mörike and 'Peregrina' when he either discovered that she was morally irresponsible, or, according to a theory
once put forward by Harry Maync,[1] learned that she had formerly
been in a convent, and drew back in horror from what threatened to
become a physical relationship with one who, as he believed, was
already the dedicated bride of Christ. The poem set to music by
Wolf as *Peregrina I* represents an early stage of Mörike's love, when
he had first become conscious of the stirrings of physical desire.
Wolf's *Peregrina II* is the fourth Peregrina poem in Mörike's
Gedichte. It expresses in poetical terms how the image of the loved
one, after Mörike had cast her aside, continued to haunt his imagination. The two difficult, little-known songs will not yield their secrets
at a casual inspection. They are studies in erotic psychology comparable with the pathological studies of figures from *Wilhelm Meister*
that appear in the Goethe volume. They contribute something
unique towards the complete picture of the poet that Wolf strove to
present in his Mörike songs. The remaining love-songs are nearer
normality. The devoted adoration of *An die Geliebte* is worlds
removed from the sensual yearning expressed in the chromatic
motive common to both *Peregrina* songs. Like many other things in
the volume, *An die Geliebte* suffers from the quasi-orchestral effects in
its piano part—we are reminded of the innumerable hours spent by
Wolf in playing from the vocal scores of Wagner's operas—but it has
nevertheless great beauty of its own. It commemorates the happier
side of the poet's love for Luise Rau, of the heart-broken ending of
which *Lebe wohl* is a memorial.

The nostalgia of the home-sick wanderer is a theme that recurs
frequently in the German *Lied*; it has seldom been more convincingly
expressed than in the dispirited, plodding tread of *Heimweh*. The
rushing, breathless *Lied vom Winde*, almost a piano solo with a
declamatory vocal commentary, looks at first as if its pages had been
extracted from the third act of Wagner's *Flying Dutchman*, but Wolf
keeps the whole on the miniature scale suited to Mörike's fairy-tale
world in which the passing winds converse with children. There
are many happy touches in the declamation of this song. *Denk' es,
o Seele!* brings intimations of mortality, but no earth-shaking,

---

[1] In *Das Urbild von Eduard Mörikes 'Peregrina,'* published in *Westermanns
illustrierte deutsche Monatshefte* (Brunswick) in October 1901. Maync did not revive,
or further discuss, this theory in his later biography of the poet. Nevertheless,
there is much in the poems and letters of Mörike and his friends that is not easily
explicable without it.

Berliozian revelations. There is one moment, before the end, as the passing horse-shoes flash in the sunlight, of shuddering realization of the proximity of death—a moment marvellously caught up into music by Wolf. For the rest, poet and composer clothe even these solemn thoughts in grace and delicate beauty. Wolf himself thought highly of *Der Jäger*, as the following passage from an unpublished letter [1] to his mother will show: 'For the rest, the criticism of the concert is beastly enough. This ass of a critic calls *Der Jäger* a freshly felt "Liedchen"! . . . a "Liedchen"!! On those lines one would have to call *Tristan und Isolde* a droll little "Operettchen." Oh, these sheep's heads of critics!' The scene where the huntsman fires off his gun and listens to the echoes is not without its ludicrous side, but as the incident is described in the poem the composer could hardly pass it over without some attempt at illustration. This song, and a group including *Der Feuerreiter, Nixe Binsefuss, Die Geister am Mummelsee*, and *Storchenbotschaft*, are probably rightly regarded as a tribute to Carl Loewe, whose ballads and songs aroused Wolf's most passionate enthusiasm. That enthusiasm seems to us to-day to have been somewhat excessive. Loewe had his moments of inspiration, notably in his *Erlkönig*, and also wrote a number of charming songs in a lighter vein, but his musical talents are spread out pretty thinly through the seventeen volumes of his collected *Balladen und Gesänge*. Wolf's ballads are enormously more interesting musically, but sometimes, as in *Die Geister am Mummelsee* and some of the ballads in the later Goethe volume, on that very account less effective, because over-elaborate. He could rarely resist the temptation to provide clever musical illustrations to the narrative, almost line by line, and the story's progress is impeded by excessive detail. The great *Feuerreiter* suffers a little from the obscurity of its subject. Most people have at one time or another been swept off their feet by the furious rhythmic drive and demonic power of this ballad, but few would be able to give any lucid account of what it is all about. That a mill is on fire, and that somebody called the 'Fire-rider' dashes to the scene on a horse and meets his death in the flames, is obvious, and it is all very exciting, but exactly why he behaves as he does is far from clear. We are told that Wolf himself, before he set the poem to music, insisted on getting a clear explanation of its contents. In the *Magikon*, a periodical of

---

[1] Written on 19th April 1890, after Jäger's first Wolf concert at Graz. (Original in the Prussian State Library.)

Mörike's day devoted to psychic research, he learned of the Fire-seers, Fire-feelers, and Fire-riders, gifted with the power of detecting distant fires, to which they were irresistibly drawn. They were forbidden by magic to extinguish these fires, and Mörike's *Feuerreiter* had disobeyed this injunction by making use of a chip of the true Cross to quell the flames. In punishment for this, the mill collapses round him and he is burned alive.

The favourite *Storchenbotschaft* is perhaps the finest piece of broad comedy in all music. It is a set of droll variations upon a ridiculous theme. The birds' ungainly antics as they strive to make their meaning understood, their gathering excitement as the shepherd begins to comprehend, and their frantic, gleeful chattering and flapping when he finally realizes the full extent of nature's generosity —twins!—these are portrayed in the music with such vivid effect that the postlude of the song is never heard in the concert-hall—no doubt to Wolf's posthumous displeasure—as it is invariably drowned in happy applause. *Nixe Binsefuss* is equally enchanting—an exquisite thing of brittle, fine-spun glass. It is clearly enough a product of the refinement of musical ore taken from one of the richest veins tapped by Loewe. At the end of the song, as the cock crows, the voice of the singer dies away in a long *diminuendo* from *pianissimo*—the nixy Bulrush-foot disappears into thin air. This device is also taken from Loewe; the seductive voice of his Erlking dies away in just this fashion after each speech.

Often sung though it may be, *Gesang Weylas* does not seek popular acclamation. It is a noble, mystic hymn, sung by a goddess. Weyla is the protecting deity of the imaginary island of Orplid, invented by Mörike and his student friend Ludwig Bauer, who also wrote poems about it. They spent summer nights in the woods, peopling the island with gods, fairies, and heroes out of their imaginations. In Mörike's novel *Maler Nolten* is included a shadow play, *Der letzte König von Orplid*, where the curious will meet various inhabitants of this fairy world, including the Silpelit mentioned in the *Elfenlied*. Wolf told Kauffmann that he imagined Weyla sitting on a reef in the moonlight, accompanying herself on the harp. The island rises out of the waters, shining from afar; the sea-mist ascends from its shores to lave the cheeks of the gods, where high in their temples they are attended by kings. Wolf's arrangement of the accompaniment of this song for harp, with additional counterpoints for clarinet and horn, added notably to its magical, legendary atmosphere.

The last five songs of the Mörike volume ask not to be taken too seriously. Some of them do not amount to much more than the musical equivalent of a practical joke. We can well believe that among his intimates Wolf was able to extract an enormous amount of enjoyment from such a thing as *Abschied*, and we can imagine with what malicious pleasure he set at the end of his song-book this account of how an opinionated critic was kicked downstairs, but the song hardly merits serious discussion as an example of the composer's art. *Zur Warnung* likewise gives the impression of being an occasional piece, written for Wolf's own amusement and that of his friends, and somewhat out of place in cold print. The humour of *Bei einer Trauung* is somewhat laboured, and neither *Selbstgeständnis* nor *Auftrag* is musically inspired, although the latter has enormous vitality and gusto. It appears, in more than one respect, to show the influence of the music-hall.

Such were the extremely varied contents of the Mörike volume, by the composition of which, within a few months, Wolf won for himself a place among the greatest song-writers that the world has ever seen. Much has been written in explanation of the importance of these songs, and it is with perfect justice that critics have stressed that it is in the relationship of the composer to his poet that the unique quality of Wolf's work lies. When the volume was published, the title-page did not read 'Fifty-three Songs by Hugo Wolf, words by Mörike,' but 'Poems by Eduard Mörike, for voice and piano, set to music by Hugo Wolf.' The musician stood at the service of the poet, offering the resources of his art to illuminate the words and recapture the emotions that had inspired them. The peculiar resources which Wolf brought to this task included all he had learned from a close study of his predecessors, Schubert, Loewe, and Schumann, together with an exhaustive knowledge of everything that, since their day, Wagner had taught about the possibilities of verbal and emotional expression in music. The free declamatory methods of Wagner's operas, applied to the miniature form of the song, opened up new fields for cultivation by a composer of genius, and his enormous enrichment of harmonic resources, in particular, made possible the full expression of complex sensations that had been beyond the reach of earlier masters of the *Lied*. Many lesser men, the epigones of the Wagnerian school, worked on similar lines without achieving anything of permanent value at all. Wolf took over these things from Wagner but employed them, happily, in a manner that was his own, and not just an imitation in the song of Wagner's methods in the opera. In the extraordinary beauty and flexibility of his declamation, in particular, he went far beyond anything Wagner had achieved, either in the epic style of his music dramas, where stage requirements demanded comparatively broad effects, or in the few songs of his maturity. The Wesendonck songs, indeed, demonstrate very clearly how thoroughly Wolf must have thought out for himself the problems of the post-Wagnerian song and how fundamentally individual was his solution.

Although Wolf's approach to song-writing was primarily a literary one, it is necessary to insist, at the risk of seeming to emphasize the obvious, that his importance ultimately depends on purely *musical* factors—his rare gifts of melodic, rhythmic, and harmonic invention, his quite exceptional power of design, and his almost Beethovenian command of musical 'development.' Beyond these fundamentals lay his incomparable powers of characterization and atmospheric suggestion, and the limitless scope of his imagination. Any attempt to systematize his methods of song-writing must fail. He is so many-sided, so protean, that he refuses to be pigeon-holed and labelled. Each poem presented him with new problems, and in the vast majority of cases he was able to find solutions that satisfy at once both musical and poetical requirements. Some of these solutions, such as the setting of *Auf einer Wanderung*, a peerless example of the 'symphonic' style in song-writing, are of great subtlety and complexity. On the other hand, a song may be quite simple, like *Gesang Weylas*, with its few arpeggio'd chords supporting a freely declamatory vocal line, and yet still be essentially Wolfian and original. Each new poem was a fresh challenge to his powers of invention and design and each volume of songs contains within itself an astonishing variety of manner and matter. Yet with each new poet he seemed to take on a new musical personality, giving each of the song-books its own individual style and atmosphere, as distinct from that of the others as is the style and emotional atmosphere of Wagner's *Tristan* from that of *Die Meistersinger*.

Something has already been said, in considering the Eichendorff songs of 1886 and 1887, of Wolf's attitude towards this poet. The thirteen new songs of 1888 continued to stress the realistically humorous aspect of Eichendorff's poetry at the expense of his more familiar romantic vein. The most convincing justifications of this attitude are to be found in the figures of the swashbuckling braggart, *Der*

Schreckenberger, with his irresistible swaggering gait, and the devil-may-care sailor who looks forward, in *Seemanns Abschied*, to floating on the high tide into the harbour of paradise, while landsmen are drowning in a second Flood. In *Der Glücksritter*, the *Schreckenberger's* less arresting companion, Wolf seems for once to have tried to repeat himself. *Der Scholar*, in its quieter way, is an exquisitely drawn, gentle and affectionate caricature. The precise *staccato* counterpoint of the accompaniment serves the double purpose of suggesting the patter of raindrops and underlining the pedantic element in the amiable scholar's make-up. Wolf's *Musikant*, too, is a likable fellow, though hardly an inspired melodist.

That the composer was in holiday mood is often apparent in these songs. The temperature at which his inspiration burned was markedly lower than in the case of the Mörike volume; the songs are altogether more detached and less personal. Here and there we have the impression that Wolf has read rather more into a poem than is actually there, that Eichendorff has been overcharged with the composer's own intenser emotions. Thus it is hard to see in the poet's innocuous *Liebesglück* the origin and justification of the rhythmic and harmonic excitement of Wolf's setting.

Verschwiegene Liebe is more in the Schumann tradition, but so delicately beautiful that few would wish to barter it away for another *Glücksritter, Lieber alles, Der verzweifelte Liebhaber* or any other of the lesser anti-romantic conceptions. The self-consciously noble and heroic *Der Freund* represents Wolf at about his worst, as Mr. Newman has been for years at pains to point out. The song follows directly after the dedication in the Eichendorff volume, and perhaps the words were set to music less on account of any direct poetical appeal to the composer's imagination than because they seemed to him to form a fitting tribute to his own friend, Joseph Schalk. *Heimweh* develops curiously in its course. Out of the traveller's sentimental longing arises a mood of intense patriotism, to which Wolf gives fullest expression, after the voice has sung its last phrase, in a magnificently exalted piano postlude.

Incomparably the finest of all the Eichendorff songs is another reversion to the romantic manner—*Das Ständchen*. A student sings to the lute before his sweetheart's door. An older man, from a window near by, gazes over the moonlit roofs and overhears the student's song, which recalls to him his own lost youth and love. Many years ago he himself had sung out his heart in just this fashion.

The left hand of Wolf's piano part sketches in the idealization of a lute accompaniment, while the right hand suggests nothing so obvious as the actual song of the student, but the half-forgotten melody of long ago as it hovers elusively in the consciousness of the onlooker.   The voice part is wholly concerned with the older man's soliloquy.   His present loneliness and his memories are exquisitely blended against the background of another's happiness.   The vocal line is absolutely free, reflecting with the utmost subtlety every turn of the man's thoughts and every inflection of his voice.   All semblance of a formal melody is abandoned; phrase follows phrase of ever-new counterpoints to the instrumental framework of the song; each phrase is moulded to express the sentiment of each line of the poem.   It is one of Wolf's most perfect and original songs.

The Eichendorff volume as a whole is the slightest, in bulk and in significance, of all the composer's greater collections of songs.   Its limitations are those of the poet, who lacked the profound humanity and almost universal appeal of Mörike.   A little known religious or mystical aspect of his personality had been illuminated by Wolf in his early choruses, but in the song volume it does not reappear.   The mature Wolf was chiefly interested in the more objective poems, and Eichendorff's characters, where they are not just picturesque dummies, are mostly uncomplicated, self-explanatory natures, who do not present their musical interpreter with any very deep problems.   Nor do the poet's facile verse-forms and metres call for any great subtlety of treatment.   There are lovely things in the volume, such as *Nachtzauber* and *Verschwiegene Liebe*; there are brilliant character pieces, from the dainty, delicate *Der Scholar* to the bluff and blustering *Seemanns Abschied*; there is the great *Das Ständchen*, in a class by itself; there are other songs, such as *Liebesglück* and *Heimweh*, which miss greatness by a narrow margin, where it seems that the poetry is just not good enough to call forth the musician's finest response. The rest, clever, charming, and amusing as it often is, is secondary Wolf, and the Eichendorff songs alone would not have sufficed to establish their composer as more than a minor master of the *Lied*.

We may say that the Mörike songs were written because Wolf could not help himself—because he was possessed by the poet.   The Eichendorff songs give the impression of having been more of a relaxation.   The Goethe volume, on the other hand, seems almost the product of a conscious stiffening of the musician's will and girding of his loins to meet the challenge of the greatest of German

poets.   To match the splendour of this poetry, in which the heart and
the intellect are so uniquely blended, its depth and range of thought,
its wisdom, and its beauty—here was a test that no singer who aspired
to the highest could decline.   Wolf's response was magnificent.
His Goethe volume is not the most immediately attractive of his
works; there is here no profuse lyrical outpouring as in the Mörike
song-book.   The response is intellectual rather than lyrical.   Mörike
is like a mellow country landscape, full of flowering meadows and
streams and gentle hills.   Goethe resembles more a lofty mountain
range, where exquisite flowers are to be found, to be sure, and homely
merriment in the villages on the lower slopes, but where the main
prospect is one of grandeur and space, and where the solitary peaks
reach upward to the stars.

Wolf's volume opens with the ten songs from *Wilhelm Meister*.
Comparatively few of the poems in his Mörike and Eichendorff collections had been set to music before him by composers of the first
rank, but every song in this group invited comparison with settings
of the same words by Schubert or Schumann, or both, to say nothing
of Beethoven.   Wolf was, of course, perfectly aware of this.   He
never set to music any poem which he considered had been successfully treated before him.   Goethe's *Geheimes* and *An Schwager
Kronos*, for instance, he knew had been given their musical counterpart once and for all by Schubert, and gave this as his reply when a
friend asked him why he had never set them himself.   But he spoke
disparagingly about others of Schubert's Goethe songs, including
some of the most famous.   In the great trilogy, *Prometheus*, *Ganymed*, and *Grenzen der Menschheit*, he held that Schubert simply had
not understood the poet.   Hence his own settings of these poems,
which he placed at the end of his Goethe volume, were, like the
Wilhelm Meister songs at its beginning, a criticism and a challenge.

In conversation with his friends Wolf stressed the fact that in his
Wilhelm Meister songs he had not simply written music for the poems
as they stood, but had tried to realize in his music the characters of
the singers as they appear in Goethe's novel.   It had been his conscious aim to bring out the pathological element in the pathetic waif,
Mignon, and the mysterious, half-crazed Harper, who between them
share the majority of the songs.   This attitude towards the poems is,
of course, a perfectly legitimate one, but Wolf's settings do not, on
that account alone, invalidate those of earlier masters of a less literary
turn of mind, because the poems are really much more Goethe's own

than the Harper's or Mignon's, and were, it is apparent, in most cases only fitted into the framework of the novel with considerable difficulty.   The songs in *Wilhelm Meister* are the conceptions of the poet in Goethe while working as a novelist, and while their existence is bound up with that of the novel, they are not really the spontaneous expression of the characters themselves.

Schubert's principal settings of the Harper's songs were all written in September 1816, when he was nineteen years old.   *Der Sänger* and an unimportant version of *Wer sich der Einsamkeit ergibt* date from the previous year.   Schumann's Mignon and Harper songs, with Philine's *Singet nicht in Trauertönen*, form his Op. 98.

Schubert gives his Harper a tenor voice and quiveringly responds to his pains and sorrows.   The songs are deeply felt, melodious and beautiful, but it is idle to pretend that Schubert at nineteen was temperamentally attuned to this subject.   Even in what is musically the finest of these songs, the version of *Wer nie sein Brot mit Tränen ass* in Op. 12, he shows clearly a failure to grasp the poet's intention. The Harper's theme is that he who has never eaten his bread with tears, or spent sorrow-filled nights weeping upon his pallet, knows not the heavenly powers for what they are.   They lead us into life, they lead the innocent into guilt and then abandon him to his fate. The first stanza closes with the line: 'Der kennt euch nicht, ihr himmlischen Mächte,' and Schubert here introduces a relaxation of tension and a turn from minor to major, as though the singer were finding reconciliation to his fate in the knowledge it has brought him of the nature of the heavenly powers.   The composer then underlines this mistaken point by repeating the whole stanza in the major, with a cadence, this time in F major, which is further than ever removed from the requisite note of bitterness.   The only one of Schubert's three settings of these words which does not show this weakness is that in 2–4 time, 'etwas geschwind'—a remarkable conception, vigorous, almost defiant, but musically too slight to bear the full weight of the poet's thought.   The third setting, in lilting 6–8 time, is almost complacent in tone.

Schumann gives the Harper his passionate melancholy, and presses home the bitter point of *Wer nie sein Brot*, but his *Wilhelm Meister* songs were written when his musical invention had lost its first freshness and the shadow of insanity was already slowly advancing towards him.   Here, if anywhere, is the true 'pathological' treatment of the Harper, reflected, however, in the sometimes laboured workmanship and flagging inspiration of the composer, as well as in his sympathetic personal response to the melancholy poetry. In his setting of *Wer sich der Einsamkeit ergibt* the eternal sentimentalist in Schumann intervenes, at the point where Goethe compares the grief and torment that overcome the Harper in solitude to a lover that creeps in whenever his mistress is alone. At 'Es schleicht ein Liebender lauschend sacht, ob seine Freundin allein' we hear the voice of Eusebius in an exquisite passage that is, however, quite flagrantly out of place in this song.

Wolf's settings are wonderfully taut and sinewy, with none of Schumann's luxuriant word repetition or indulgence in purely musical delights. The composer all the time holds in his mind's eye the figure of the stricken Harper and allows nothing to deflect him from his purpose of tragic portraiture. Wolf's *Wer sich der Einsamkeit* is exceptionally fine and surpasses those of the other composers with comparative ease, but his *Wer nie sein Brot* has been thought to be too violently emotional and declamatory. This is a consequence of his reading into the poem the circumstances of the novel. The tremendous weight and intensity of the latter part of his song, in which the guilt is referred to, into which the heavenly powers lead poor mortals before they abandon them, is explicable when we know the secret of the Harper in *Wilhelm Meister*—the incestuous love which had sent him wandering half crazed over the face of the earth and of which, unknown to him, Mignon is the offspring. *An die Türen*, according to the novel, is only a fragment, the last verse of one of the Harper's monologues: 'It turned on the consolations of a miserable man, conscious of being on the borders of insanity.' All three composers have written plodding melodies that illustrate the dragging footsteps of the wandering Harper, and Schumann here is particularly impressive, but Wolf again cuts deeper than either of his predecessors.

Der Sänger, although it is one of the Harper's songs in *Wilhelm Meister*, is not in the same category as those discussed above. It is one of the old man's public performances, a finished ballad, whereas the others are the expression of his intimate thoughts and feelings, and sung for his own solace. Wolf, like Schubert and Schumann before him, did not find *Der Sänger* a source of much inspiration. In later years he considered withdrawing it from his Goethe volume.

Nur wer die Sehnsucht kennt has been set to music innumerable times, but seldom with outstanding results, and the poem has never really found its inevitable musical reflection.   In the novel it is sung by the Harper and Mignon as 'an irregular duet' and among the six settings by Schubert there is one which conforms to this description. The poem, however, is generally felt to be altogether too personal an utterance for anything but a solo song and is almost invariably associated with Mignon.   In *Wilhelm Meisters theatralische Sendung*, an earlier, unfinished version of Goethe's novel, written at various times between 1772 and 1786, of which a copy was discovered in 1910, *Nur wer die Sehnsucht kennt* is not a duet but is, in fact, assigned to Mignon.   Wolf's setting is astonishingly unlike anybody else's.   We see in it what he meant when he said that he had brought out the pathological element in Mignon, as well as in the Harper.   This Mignon of Wolf's is feverish and agitated, not only in that part of the poem where she cries out, in an untranslatable line, 'Es schwindelt mir, es brennt mein Eingeweide,' but all through her song of loneliness and longing.   It is a wonderful little thing, strange, even rather repellent at first, then increasingly fascinating and convincing.

Heiss mich nicht reden and *So lasst mich scheinen* invite some further interesting comparisons between Wolf, Schubert, and Schumann.   Schubert set each of the poems twice.   If it is desirable that these poems should be sung to music appropriate to the pitiful, *childish* Mignon, then Schubert's first settings, written in April 1821, are without doubt to be preferred to all others.   In just such innocence of heart, with just such naïveté of expression, one feels, would a child sing these verses, the meaning of which is deeper than she can understand.   As Richard Capell has observed,[1] the simple but terrible words of *Heiss mich nicht reden* are 'obscurely indicative of some tragic destiny.'   Is the suggestion of 'Death and the Maiden' in the opening of Schubert's first setting entirely accidental?   The rhythm of the song undoubtedly springs from the opening words of the poem but thereafter is felt to dominate the music at the considerable expense of the verbal accentuation.   The same rhythm, in reduced note values, is utilized in the more celebrated later setting, at first with similar constrictive effect, but after a few lines Schubert throws it off and the conclusion of the poem is declaimed with perfect freedom.   The later setting of *So lasst mich scheinen*, however, is

---

[1] In his affectionate survey of *Schubert's Songs* (1928), by far the best book of its kind.

seriously handicapped by the composer's preoccupation with an inflexible rhythmic scheme, leading to this sort of false emphasis:

In this respect the 1821 version is superior to that of 1826. While both the later songs are admirable pieces of music, each with its incomparable Schubertian touch of genius—in the pathos of 'Dort kann die Brust in Klagen sich ergiessen' in the first, and in the wrenching modulation at 'doch fühlt' ich tiefen Schmerz genung' in the second—one still feels that any other poem of similar rhythmic scheme and similar sequence of emotions would have served the composer's purpose as well, or even better, if the vital words happened in it to coincide more often with the metrical stresses than they do in Goethe's poem.

Wolf's *Heiss mich nicht reden* makes use of the same rhythm as Schubert's but his vocal line is, of course, completely liberated from the rhythmical pattern of the accompaniment. For the passage in the poem describing daybreak, and the rock that cleaves its bosom to reveal the hidden streams, Wolf finds nature music of elemental power, that seems, however, to have little enough to do with Mignon. Fine as his setting is, it has to yield the palm to that of Schumann, who is here intensely inspired. His remarkably original conception involves the repetition at various points of the opening line of the poem, and it may be that this was felt by Wolf to be too great a liberty to be taken with Goethe. Schumann begins startlingly with 'Heiss mich nicht reden' as an anguished cry, which breaks dramatically into the poem again between the first and second stanzas. 'Ein jeder sucht im Arm des Freundes Ruh' is given an extraordinary effect of unbearable inner tension, striving for release—a release that is denied it by an oath that only God can absolve. This reference in the poem to God is treated dramatically—almost melodramatically—by Wolf and also by Schubert in both of his settings. Schumann's treatment of the passage is undoubtedly more fitting:

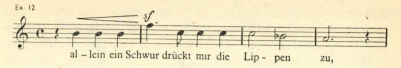

'Nur ein Gott!' is then repeated as an exclamation, after which follows an interlude on the piano, culminating in an astonishing discord. 'Heiss mich nicht reden' is then brought in for the third time, quietly, and the last two lines of the poem repeated with an effect of resignation.

Wolf's *So lasst mich scheinen* is extremely beautiful and surpasses the settings of other composers as does Schumann's of *Heiss mich nicht reden*. The poem, much more than the others, reflects the circumstances in which it appears in the novel. In the eighth book of *Wilhelm Meister*, Mignon has been lodged in Natalia's academy and, on the birthday of two of the other pupils, has been chosen to deliver to them a present. For this occasion she was dressed up as an angel, in a white robe, with a golden girdle and garland. The composer who would set to music the transfigured Mignon's naïve paradisal vision must find accents that express at once her childish innocence and her strange foreshadowing of her own doom. Her early blighted life is about to close and she welcomes death as a release. Schubert's most ambitious attempt, apart from the rhythmic pattern it imposes on the poetry, is, as even Mr. Capell is constrained to admit, altogether too rich and too material. 'It is no less sweet than sorrowful. The renunciation it expresses is felt to have a background of earthly delights. Schubert, in fact, sang as he was, of what he knew.' Schumann's version is care-worn and laboured. Wolf's Mignon, against a background vaguely suggestive of angelic shapes treading solemn measures, bids farewell to the earth in an aura of silvery radiance.

Kennst du das Land? is another celebrated poem that has attracted innumerable composers without inspiring any of them to unsurpassable flights of genius. The settings by Beethoven and Schubert are not important; Liszt's has been accurately characterized by Ernest Walker as 'a moderately inexpensive chromo-lithograph.' That by

Schumann is both his Op. 79, No. 29, and his Op. 91*a*, No. 1. The earlier opus contains his songs for children, and although this *Mignon* has distinguished admirers, it does seem as though the composer was imaginatively constrained by the nature of his intended audience. To indicate that the two last verses of a strophic song are to be sung 'with increased expression' is rather an easy-going solution of the problems which this poem presents to its interpreter, and it is hard on the singer to have to present the third stanza, with its mist-wreathed mountains, dragon-brood, precipices, and torrents, in the identical notes that served for the balmy breezes from blue heaven in the first. Wolf's setting is extremely rich and passionate. Schubertians have sometimes appealed against it on the grounds that it is out of character with the child Mignon, but this criticism is not really valid. Editions of the Goethe songs published in Wolf's lifetime show that he grouped it among the 'Ballads,' with *Der Sänger* and the three following songs, and reference to *Wilhelm Meister* shows that he was perfectly justified in doing this. Goethe set the poem as we know it at the head of the first chapter of the third book of the novel, and did not pretend that it was anything but a free transcription, by Wilhelm, of what Mignon sang to him in Italian. 'The originality of its turn he could imitate only from afar; its childlike innocence of expression vanished from it in the process of reducing its broken phraseology to uniformity, and combining its disjointed parts.' Wolf's song is one of those in which the piano is felt to be quite inadequate to express the composer's intentions. There are two orchestral versions made by Wolf himself, from 1890 and 1893 respectively. The descending counterpoint in small notes on the first page of the piano version is a detail added from the score of 1893.

The two remaining songs from *Wilhelm Meister* are the *Spottlied*, in which a member of the party of actors makes mock of his noble patron, the play-writing baron, and *Singet nicht in Trauertönen*, the ditty of fickle, frivolous, sensual Philine. Neither is important. The *Spottlied* hardly called for musical treatment, and Philine's song is necessarily superficial, for all its sparkle.

The rest of the Goethe volume consists of a selection of twenty-one songs and ballads from various periods, seventeen settings of poems from the *West-östlicher Divan*, and the *Prometheus-Ganymed-Grenzen der Menschheit* group.

Ernest Walker has expressed the opinion, in the course of an

examination of what the great composers have achieved in setting
Goethe's poems to music, that 'all said and done, Wolf, of all song-
writers, comes nearest to Goethe in that, for better or worse, he
adventured everything.'[1] Dr. Walker's verdict is preceded by other
remarks, suggesting that in a good many of his settings Wolf seems to
have acted on Gluck's advice to 'try and forget one is a musician,'
and to have succeeded rather too well. 'In his passionate striving
for characterization he again and again took brave risks; sometimes
he won through triumphantly (as, among these songs, in *Genialisch
Treiben*, *Epiphanias*, the first *Cophtisches Lied*), sometimes not.' It
must be admitted that there are uninviting stretches among the
miscellaneous songs in Wolf's Goethe volume. The composer seems
to have had to search far afield to find unhackneyed poems for
musical treatment, and among the garland with which he returned are
some rather prickly, thistle-like growths. After *Der Rattenfänger*, a
genial masterpiece, unflaggingly brilliant and melodious, come two
long ballads, *Ritter Kurts Brautfahrt* and *Gutmann und Gutweib*,
which must be counted among Wolf's failures. Both poems are
provided with an elaborate musical commentary which gives us
repeated occasion to admire the composer's ingenuity, but which in
the end leaves us not far removed from either tedium, or nervous
exasperation at the lack of a plain statement, sung to a phrase that is
pleasing in itself as well as 'characteristic.' The simpler, direct
method of Loewe and Schubert with such narratives is seen to have
its decided advantages. The two songs entitled *Frech und Froh* are
further examples of Wolf's at times wilful-seeming avoidance of the
agreeable. They are unlikable things, full of harsh and discordant
laughter, reminiscent of the biblical 'crackling of thorns under a pot.'
Beherzigung and the second *Cophtisches Lied* are didactic in tone—
fine things in their way, if somewhat ponderous and dry. The first
Cophtisches Lied is enlivened by a touch of humour, and glows with a
breath of mystic poetry. In *Genialisch Treiben* the not very significant words set the composer off on a wonderful little instrumental
scherzo; the middle section, in particular, is full of boisterous,
Beethovenian musical humour.

In many of these songs, and, indeed, throughout the greater part of
the Goethe volume, the singer has to be content with a declamatory
style that is far removed from the normal conception of a 'song,'
while the composer makes his desired effect chiefly by means of

[1] 'Goethe and some Composers,' *The Musical Times*, June 1932.

I

harmony, rhythm and the change and contrasting of tonalities in the piano part.   The preponderance of songs of this type, as well as the choice of poems, suggests that Wolf considered that the more obvious lyrical aspects of the poet had been almost exhaustively treated by earlier composers.   Was he perhaps impelled so forcibly towards the 'characteristic' song by the riches of the Schubertian heritage? When we consider that the Goethe songs followed close on the heels of the Mörike and Eichendorff settings, we can only feel astonishment at the change that they reveal in Wolf's musical mentality. 'They fairly threaten me with Schubert,' he once cried in some annoyance, 'but I cannot keep my mouth shut because a man of genius lived before me and wrote splendid songs.'   Nevertheless, it is possible that he was driven, in creating his Goethe songs, to repress the purely lyrical side of his own nature, which had ranged at will in Mörike's world only a few months earlier, and to concentrate more on poems that made a call upon the intellect, wherein he knew his own strength lay.

Those few poems of simpler sentiment that he did set to music, in a more normally singable, lyrical manner, are so enchanting that it is only natural that we should sometimes wish there had been more of them.   Is there in all Wolf's work, or in anybody else's, a more exquisite love-song than *Frühling übers Jahr*?   The sense of the title is 'Spring throughout the whole year.'   The loved one vies with the spring and remains in spring-like beauty when the sweet season itself has passed away.   Then there is *Anakreons Grab*, marvellous in its pagan calm and peace.   Exquisitely beautiful is the drooping phrase that sinks caressingly, like a graceful tree over the grave of the poet; except for turtle-dove and cricket, the air is hushed round the mound, which nature has yet adorned with vigorous, springing life.   In the contrast between the two words 'Grab' and 'Leben' lies the whole secret of the successful interpretation of this most wonderful song. Other delights of the volume of which we can never tire are the jewel-like *Gleich und Gleich*, the rococo charms of *Die Spröde* and *Die Bekehrte*, and the endearing *Blumengruss*, which in some ways points prophetically to Wolf's later 'Italian' manner.   Half the fascination of the song lies in the composer's manipulation of his little cadential figure in the accompaniment, which itself seems to wish to pay tribute to Schubert's *Geheimes*.

Epiphanias should always be sung in the spirit of its first performance by the three Köchert children; anything but solemn, there is yet a certain innocence in its humour, that is also tinged with piety. *St. Nepomuks Vorabend* is a setting of a somewhat obscure poem, connected with the festival of John of Nepomuk, patron saint of Bohemia, who, according to the legend, was tortured and flung into the river Moldau for refusing to betray the confession of Sophia, the wife of King Wenceslaus IV. It is difficult to convey the impression made by Wolf's song; there is in it something of mysticism, something, too, of childlike, unquestioning belief, that is deeply affecting; the whole is enveloped in the ethereal, crystalline bell-tones of the accompaniment. The nobility of *Königlich Gebet* is somewhat self-conscious and pompous, and *Dank des Paria* suffers from similar defects. But these two songs are by no means negligible.

Among the *West-östlicher Divan* songs *Phänomen* is beautiful and singable; *Erschaffen und Beleben* belongs to the other class, the 'characteristic' type. The five songs from the *Schenkenbuch* are by no means easy, either to perform or to appreciate. Who but Wolf would have thought of making songs out of these poems, the musings of a philosophic drunkard, or drunken philosopher? [1] *Ob der Koran von Ewigkeit sei?* refers to the Mohammedan controversy as to whether the Koran was created, or existed from eternity. The bacchantic *Trunken müssen wir alle sein* is wild and unconstrained, tremendously forceful and rhythmically exciting, making the utmost demands upon both singer and pianist. *Sie haben wegen der Trunkenheit* treats of that 'drunkenness of love, song and wine' which is the poet's, and which no ordinary 'sober' drunkenness can approach. *Was in der Schenke* is another furious rhythmic outburst, almost barbaric in effect. No one will quarrel with those who do not find expressed here their ideal in the sphere of lyrical song; this is the 'characteristic' *Lied* pushed to something like its extreme limits. But Wolf's music is a fair equivalent of Goethe's extraordinary tough and difficult poetry.

In the *Buch Suleika* of the *West-östlicher Divan* Wolf found a thoughtful lyricism that was ideally suited to his needs, in the love poetry of Goethe's old age, cerebral, riddling, masked in oriental imagery, and yet richly, even turbulently, emotional at heart. Here Schubert, in comparatively simple poems, found material for three long and splendid songs—the two *Suleika-Lieder*, the poems of which are attributed to Marianne von Willemer, and *Versunken*. Some of Wolf's settings burn and flame with a power and vehemence without

---

[1] Schumann has two mild settings from the *Schenkenbuch* in his *Myrten*, Op. 25.

parallel in song.   Such are *Hochbeglückt in deiner Liebe*, the poem of
which is also Marianne's, *Nimmer will ich dich verlieren*, and, above
all, *Locken, haltet mich gefangen*.   This poem contains the passage:

> Du beschämst wie Morgenröte,
> Jener Gipfel ernste Wand,
> Und noch einmal fühlet Hatem
> Frühlingshauch und Sommerbrand,

in which the first and third lines only rhyme when the name 'Goethe'
is substituted for 'Hatem.'   The emotional intensity of songs such as
these strains to the utmost limit the resources of the medium for
which they are written; the passions of Wolf's Hatem and Suleika
are worthy of the Völsungs or the intoxicated lovers of the second
act of *Tristan*.   It is, however, to the more reflective pages of this
section of the Goethe volume that we return most often, to the
barcarolle-like fragment *Als ich auf dem Euphrat schiffte* and Hatem's
two dreamy meditations, *Wie sollt' ich heiter bleiben* and *Wenn ich
dein gedenke*, with their kaleidoscopic effects of harmony and
shifting tonality.

Prometheus, Ganymed and *Grenzen der Menschheit*, the last three
songs in Wolf's Goethe volume, are among the grandest, the most
inspired things that he ever wrote.   The poems illustrate three aspects
of man's relationship to divinity.   In the first, a monologue extracted
by the poet from an unfinished early drama, we have the rebel.
Prometheus is portrayed by Goethe in his workshop, but, curiously
enough, Wolf, who seems not to have investigated the sources of the
poem, depicts him chained to the rock in the mountains of the
Caucasus.   The song, or rather dramatic *scena*, is one of those which
were obviously conceived with the orchestra in mind and we do in
fact possess Wolf's own scoring.   It is true that the composer, as one
of his letters [1] shows, considered in later years that his orchestral
arrangement of *Prometheus* needed revision, to allow the voice part to
be better heard above the instrumental tumult, but, nevertheless, this
imperfect score enables us to realize, far better than we could do if we
had the piano version alone, the magnificence of Wolf's conception.
In the opening bars of the orchestral introduction we feel the hero
draw himself up to hurl his defiance in the face of Zeus, whose
presence is revealed in the lightnings, the thunderbolts, and the
menacing growls that follow.   Then above the raging storm is heard
the voice of Prometheus in proud mockery, as he compares the god's

---

[1] To Grohe, 16th November 1894.

assaults on oak and mountain-top to the idle pastime of a boy beheading thistles. At each fresh climax of audacious defiance the fury of Zeus, the thunders and the lightnings, are renewed, until in the end they are felt only as the expression of the god's impotence in the face of Prometheus's courage and independence. Where the text refers to mankind's childish belief in the existence of a beneficent deity the music has noble sorrow and compassion; where the theme is almighty time and everlasting destiny, to which the gods themselves are subject, it has a cosmic grandeur and amplitude. The voice of the protagonist is heard still, dauntless in strength and defiance, while in the orchestra great swirling string passages threaten to overwhelm him. In the conclusion he remains, magnificent in his human dignity and courage, to found a race in his own image, to suffer and to weep, but also to rejoice in its independence. *Ganymed* is another of Goethe's adaptations from ancient myth. In the beloved of Zeus he saw a figure through which to express his own pantheistic moods, his love and worship of nature. Ganymede lies on the earth, overcome with rapture at the beauty of the spring, and presses to his heart the flowers and grasses. The morning breeze blows only to cool his bosom, the nightingale sings for him alone. He yearns to embrace the whole of nature, and the clouds descend to carry him off, to the arms of the 'All-loving Father.' No greater contrast with the foregoing song can possibly be imagined. Here all is radiance and sweetness; after the heroic poetry of Prometheus's defiance, the composer was able no less wonderfully to find tones to express Ganymede's acceptance and adoration. These profoundly poetic pages are among Wolf's finest. Schubert, too, was inspired by this poem to create music of imperishable beauty. His *Prometheus*, for all its noble qualities, cannot really be compared with Wolf's mighty tone-poem, principally because the requisite notes of burning anger and contempt were not in Schubert's nature. But in the milder air and sentiment of *Ganymed* he was thoroughly at home. His setting most successfully reflects the broad general mood of the poem, though at the expense, here and there, of the natural rhythm and accentuation of the words. The final invocation lingers long in the memory. Schubert's song is expressive of contented love, Wolf's of yearning for ever closer union. Those who place Wolf's setting before Schubert's do so because here, as elsewhere in Goethe's poetry where the two composers enter into rivalry, a controlling intellect, an absolute grasp of the poet's meaning and intention in every phrase, every sentence, and throughout the poem as a whole, as well as an unfailing regard for the niceties of verbal accentuation, are felt to be more essential than any purely musical outpouring, however rich and generous. Wolf was not deficient in musical inspiration. His work may not always glow with the intensity of Schubert at his finest, but he knew better how to harness his music in the service of the poet's ideas, to compel it to fulfil an appointed task, rather than range in freedom through the fields of its own imagination. The loss of Wolf's own orchestral arrangement of his *Ganymed* is much to be regretted.

Grenzen der Menschheit passes far beyond either love or revolt. Man recognizes his own littleness, in space and eternity, and has no more room in his heart for anything except awe and submission. Across infinite distances in space the harmony of the spheres is perceptible; some force, some creative spirit, is there, but it is one that is utterly indifferent to mankind and its transient joys and sorrows. To bow the head is all that is possible. Man strives to raise himself to the stars, but finds nowhere a foothold; in his own station on the earth he lives only as the oak or the vine. The stream of eternity raises him on its waves for a moment and then engulfs him. His life is only one link in the endless chain of existence. The settings of both Schubert and Wolf have nobility and grandeur. Schubert seems to take as his starting-point God's majesty and power, Wolf, as his, man's insignificance. Both songs are splendid and inspired compositions.

The forty-four songs of the *Spanish Song Book* were the first fruits of the passion for Spanish literature, folk-songs and dance that pursued Wolf, not always to his artistic advantage, throughout the whole of his life. The *Spanisches Liederbuch* of Emanuel Geibel and Paul Heyse contains translations of a representative selection from sixteenth- and seventeenth-century Spanish poetry. About half the poems are of unknown origin, but the rest are by celebrated Spanish authors, some of whom are world figures. In all, seventeen of the poems set to music by Wolf are by known authors, and it is not a little curious that it should not be generally known that such writers as Cervantes, Camoens and Lope de Vega are represented in his *Spanish Song Book*. The originals of *Weint nicht, ihr Äuglein* and *Die ihr schwebet* are by Lope de Vega; *Tief im Herzen trag' ich Pein* is by Camoens, author of the *Lusiads*, who was Portuguese. This is one of his occasional Spanish poems. Comendador Escriva's

Komm', o Tod, von Nacht umgeben is quoted in *Don Quixote*, while Cervantes himself is represented by *Köpfchen, Köpfchen* ('Preciosa's Recipe for Headache'). Preciosa is the heroine of the first of Cervantes's *Novelas Ejemplares*, or moral tales. She is also known to music through Weber's *Preciosa* overture and incidental music.

The volume opens with the religious songs. Geibel and Heyse separated the sacred from the secular poems in their anthology, and of the thirteen religious poems which they translated Wolf set ten to music. This section of the *Spanish Song Book* contains some of his greatest masterpieces.

Nun bin ich dein, Die du Gott gebarst and *Mühvoll komm' ich und beladen* portray the sinner, writhing in an agony of fear and repentance, passionately imploring the merciful intervention of Mary or Jesus to save his soul from eternal damnation. *Ach, wie lang die Seele schlummert* has a similar theme, but is more in the nature of a personal meditation than a prayer. The means employed by Wolf to represent in musical terms the masochistic fanaticism of these poems consists generally of a vocal line, somewhat suggestive of ecclesiastical chant, moving in small intervals, mounting painfully or wearily sinking back, over an accompaniment in which a brief rhythmic figure is reiterated again and again, in various guises, like a nagging thought that defies exorcism. Wolf had frequently, in earlier works, made use of discord in the expression of pain and unease, and here, where all is anguish and distress, he employs grinding dissonances that are truly excruciating. Some of these songs are more successful than others—the finest of all is perhaps *Mühvoll komm' ich und beladen*—but all are remarkable and extremely beautiful in their own extraordinarily original way. *Herr, was trägt der Boden hier* and *Wunden trägst du, mein Geliebter* both consist of mystical dialogues between Christ and the Catholic Christian believer. His heart torn with pity and anguish, the latter addresses his crucified Saviour, to an accompaniment of chords each one of which is like a stab of pain. Calm, passionless, infinitely remote, and laden with a more than human burden of sorrow and love, the voice of Christ is heard in reply. *Herr, was trägt der Boden hier* contains within its twenty-seven bars the whole tragedy of Calvary. *Wunden trägst du, mein Geliebter* is less well known, but is fully as poignant and moving.

In striking contrast to these studies of almost morbid religious emotions are three tender visions of members of the Holy Family,

such as might have been painted by Murillo—*Nun wandre, Maria*, in
which Joseph encourages the weary Mary along the road to Bethlehem; *Ach, des Knaben Augen*, Mary's song of devotion to the Christ-
child; and *Die ihr schwebet*, in which she beseeches the angels to
protect the sleeping Jesus from the cold winds that sough in the palm-
trees under which she has taken shelter.   Mary and Joseph are
portrayed as very human figures.   They plod along towards Bethlehem together and he promises rest and sleep only a little farther along
the road, and declares he would give even the little donkey, the
companion of their wanderings, in exchange for tidings of the safe
delivery of her child.   The accompaniment suggests the rhythm of
their footsteps and also, by the imagery of its thirds progressing
together, the close companionship that supports them in all the
difficulties of the journey.   In *Führ' mich, Kind, nach Bethlehem*,
another song of this group, thirds are also employed to suggest two
people journeying together.   *Die ihr schwebet* was set to music by
Brahms, who made of it, in his *Geistliches Wiegenlied*, with viola
obbligato, what is essentially a conventional, if very lovely, German
cradle-song.   But how the imagination of Wolf was able to light up
the scene and bring the poem to life!   In his setting the air is full of
the rustling of branches—or is it the beating of angels' wings?   There
is infinite tenderness in Mary's voice, but she is all the time in a
flutter of anxiety for the welfare of her child.   And how convincingly,
too, amid all the charm and beauty of the song, the deeper note is
sounded, when Mary sings of the weight of earthly sorrow that
already oppresses the Holy Child and from which in sleep He finds
temporary release!   In the end it seems that her appeal is heard, the
branches are stilled, and Jesus sleeps on.

In the secular section of the *Spanish Song Book* Wolf frequently
makes use of local colour.   Guitar- and mandoline-like effects and
pseudo-Spanish dance rhythms are a feature of many of the songs, as
they had been of some of the earlier settings, by Schumann and
Jensen, of poems from the *Spanisches Liederbuch*.   The Spanish
cloak, however, does not sit easily upon German shoulders, and in
spite of all the composer's subtlety and ingenuity in the handling of
his material, even Wolf's song-book is sometimes felt to be rather an
unhappy hybrid.   The Spanish convention is most easily accepted
in the lighter songs, such as the entrancing *Auf dem grünen Balkon*;
elsewhere it is apt to become not a little tiresome.

The first of the secular songs, *Klinge, klinge, mein Pandero*, is

pervaded throughout by dance rhythms and by the pianistic representation of the jingles of the *Pandero,* or tambourine.   The singer
complains that her heart is not in accord with the merry music of her
instrument.   Here the nature of the poem demanded some attempt
at musical illustration of the dance, and Wolf's song, if it is not a
masterpiece, is probably as effective a setting as was possible of the
German translation of the words.   The Spanish element in the
favourite *In dem Schatten meiner Locken* is not obtruded, and the
song ranks among the finest products of Wolf's genius in lighter
vein.   Very effective is the use of key-changes to indicate the
changing thoughts of the singer.   The main key is B flat.   The
graceful rhythmic movement that distinguishes the song dies away at
the end of the singer's first sentence and then recommences in D
major, before the query 'Weck' ich ihn nun auf?'   As Wolf interprets the poem, this suggestion that the girl should waken her sleeping
lover is a sudden idea that strikes her mind, and its onset is depicted
by the abrupt entry of the new key.   For a moment she plays with
the idea, then abandons it—the music slips into another fresh key,
G flat.   This second key-change, before 'Ach, nein!' has a curious
softening effect and indicates a sudden access of pity and affection in
the girl's heart.   Wolf probably read more into these lines than
Heyse himself knew them to contain, but his insight and ingenuity
were wonderfully effective in bringing the little scene to life. *Seltsam
ist Juanas Weise* is attractive enough, but is completely overshadowed
by *Auf dem grünen Balkon,* which treats a similar theme with incomparable grace and humour.   It is the finest of a group of songs in
which a lover complains of the vacillation or coldness of his mistress.
In this case she has the provoking custom of luring him on with her
eyes and then admonishing him by a gesture of her finger, and Wolf,
by the skill with which he places the notes of his vocal line, is able to
suggest all manner of coquetry through the inflections of the singer's
voice.   The accompaniment is strongly rhythmic, in the Spanish
manner, but the declamation in this song is much more flexible than
is the case in some of its companions, where the demands of local
colour may compel even the voice part to mark the rhythm of the
dance.   This is so in *Treibe nur mit Lieben Spott,* which is not one of
the most arresting things in the volume.   Some of the finest of the
songs bear no trace of Spanish coloration.   This is the case of the
lovely *Wenn du zu den Blumen gehst,* which is completely naturalized,
an elaborate compliment in Spanish becoming a tender German

* I

love-song. In setting the recurrent opening line of the poem, the composer deliberately sacrifices the natural accentuation of the words to achieve one of the evocations of movement or gesture which are such a feature of his music. The even quavers with which the voice enters suggest, at each return of the phrase, the rhythm of the beloved's footsteps, as she walks amid the flowers. The accompaniment of this adorable song suggests all the stirring of nature within a beautiful flower garden—not a Wagnerian 'Waldweben,' but a sort of 'Gartenweben.' Another very melodious song, *Wer sein holdes Lieb verloren*, follows *Wenn du zu den Blumen gehst* in the order of the volume, and Wolf probably intended the two to be associated with each other. *Wer sein holdes Lieb verloren* tells how the lover failed through timidity to gain his heart's desire in that garden, how when she spoke of love to him he was lost for an answer, and when she sank down among the flowers failed to take advantage of his opportunity. 'Grösster aller Toren' he must have been, indeed! Wolf scored both these songs for inclusion in his *Manuel Venegas* in 1897.

The blended passion and melancholy of *Ich fuhr über Meer*, a fine dark-toned complaint, are typical of the more earnest of the men's songs in the *Spanish Song Book*. From this point in the volume onwards, although the women are given numerous songs of forthright passion, the men are portrayed almost always tormented by desire, unhappy and embittered. *Blindes Schauen, dunkle Leuchte* is more of a curse than a love-song; it is dominated by a single motive that is repeated again and again in the piano part, in the manner of some of the anguished religious songs, moving inexorably onwards, with gathering intensity, towards its powerful culmination in the last bars. *Eide, so die Liebe schwur* is a disillusioned complaint, *Herz, verzage nicht geschwind* a savage indictment, of woman's frailty. The theme is taken up again in some of the later songs.

Sagt, seid Ihr es, feiner Herr is a woman's song of mockery, but most of the portraits in Wolf's gallery show the Spanish women, no less than the men, in the toils of passion. The love of these hot-blooded, southern creatures is very different from that of the German women of the earlier volumes. It is not for the seventeen-year-old of *Schmerzliche Wonnen* to sing an 'Erstes Liebeslied eines Mädchens!' The girl in *Wehe der*, whose lover has deserted her for another, does not express herself in a broken-hearted lament, as characters similarly placed in the Mörike volume do, but pours out a burning torrent of threats and abuse against her rival. The word 'leidenschaftlich' recurs again and again in the directions for the performance of these songs. *Bitt' ihn, o Mutter, Liebe mir im Busen zündet einen Brand, Schmerzliche Wonnen, Wehe der* and the great *Geh', Geliebter, geh' jetzt* all flame with erotic emotions of the utmost intensity. Among all the characters depicted by Wolf, only the pseudo-oriental Suleika, of the *West-östlicher Divan* songs, had previously been capable of feelings such as these.

Trau' nicht der Liebe and *Wer tat deinem Füsslein weh?* are examples of a type of dance-song, with recurrent refrain, that is found in the *Spanish Song Book*. The melodic interest is about equally divided between voice and accompaniment, with fascinating effect, but these songs are chiefly remarkable for their rhythmic impulse, lilting in *Trau' nicht der Liebe* and impetuously whirling in *Wer tat deinem Füsslein weh?* On similar lines, for a male voice, is *Da nur Leid und Leidenschaft*, which contains in its accompaniment the material for a first-rate instrumental scherzo.

Ach, im Maien war's is attractive, in a way that is not very characteristic of Wolf. The melody, for once, does not seem to belong naturally and inevitably to these words, nor is it obvious why a guitar accompaniment should have been provided for this lament from a lightless dungeon. The prisoner sighs for May-time and love and freedom. He could yet count the days by the singing of a bird outside the walls of his prison, until a fowler destroyed for him this last source of pleasure. He calls down God's curse on the fowler. We seem to lack the clue to Wolf's approach to the poem. He keeps up a conventional guitar figure in his piano part from beginning to end, under a vocal melody that is oddly indifferent to the normal accentuation of the words, and quite inadequate to express the emotions of the unhappy prisoner.

Ex. 13

and   Ach,   im   Mai - en   war's,____ im   Mai - en
Nur   an   ei - nem   Vög - lein merkt' ich's

Is this Wolf? The only possible explanation of the peculiarities of this song seems to be that the composer had noticed that the words were a translation from one of the anonymous romances of Spain, kept alive for centuries in the popular imagination by vagrant singers, and set them to music as a snatch of balladry, and not as a representation of the actual scene in the dungeon. In the last stanza 'im Maien sang' should read 'im *Baume* sang,' as Heyse wrote. The bird's song was not confined to the month of May.

The sombre and profoundly moving *Alle gingen, Herz, zur Ruh* is one of the outstanding masterpieces of the volume. A man lies awake in the night, tormented by thoughts of a hopeless love. The broken rhythms of the accompaniment are a symbol of sleep-for-saken unrest and pulses throbbing against the pillows. The weary chromatic complaint of the opening takes on a more urgent note, swells to a great heart-broken cry, and then dies away again in the mood of its beginning. The last three words of the poem are repeated, not because Wolf found it necessary to expand his musical structure at this point, but because thereby he was enabled to extract the last shade of meaning from the text. The first statement of 'seiner Liebe zu' is dramatic, forming the emotional climax towards which the whole song has been unrestingly moving from its first bar; the second is reflective, like a regretful, longing sigh.

Dereinst, dereinst, Gedanke mein, Tief im Herzen trag' ich Pein and *Komm', o Tod, von Nacht umgeben* form a group of expressive songs of pervadingly melancholic cast, in a mood into which Wolf is some-times felt to have slipped rather too easily and rather too often. The songs are fine ones, but somewhat lacking in musical interest and in the glow that lights up their prototype, the wonderful *Zur Ruh* of 1883. *Ob auch finstre Blicke glitten* and *Weint nicht, ihr Äuglein* are two other songs written to Wolfian formulae but lacking in inspira-tion. *Bedeckt mich mit Blumen* is a beautiful love-song, swooning ecstatically, dying—temporarily, one suspects—of the bliss and torment of love. *Und schläfst du, mein Mädchen* is an unimportant but attractive fragment, the *aubade* of an abductor. In *Sie blasen zum Abmarsch* the singer laments that her soldier lover is called away to battle. The brilliant little military march, however, out of which Wolf fashions his accompaniment, is so irresistibly vivacious that the poor girl has difficulty in securing our interest in the troubles which she simultaneously relates.

Geh', Geliebter, geh' jetzt, which brings the *Spanish Song Book* to an end, is a magnificent song on the grandest scale. The love of which it treats is illicit—the song is a woman's farewell to her lover at dawn—but it is ennobled and given something like grandeur by the splendour of its musical treatment. Tremendously emotional, it yet keeps something in reserve and is not overstrained in its expression, as some of the other passionate women's songs in the *Spanish Song*

Book may be considered to be.   *Geh', Geliebter* has great beauty, as well as great power, and the freshness of the winds of morning blows through its pages.   A verse of the poem is omitted in Wolf's setting —the only case of its kind in the whole of his mature work.

The Spain of Wolf's imagination is peopled by a race ruled by violent emotions, religious and erotic.   Love, sacred or profane, dominates the minds and hearts of all his characters.   In the *Spanish Song Book* there is nothing like the variety of mood and subject-matter of the composer's earlier volumes.   There are here no fairy stories or ballads and no philosophical meditations; there is nothing expressive of love of nature, and little humour, except that of a mocking beauty or her embittered victim.   The result of this, undeniably, is a certain monotony, accentuated, in the secular songs, by the persistent use of guitar effects, and it is probable that this section of the *Spanish Song Book* contains a higher percentage of perishable matter than any other of Wolf's greater volumes.   The lesser songs, though often attractive enough in themselves, are out-weighed by others of similar style and mood but greater individuality and musical worth.   One even feels sometimes that the composer might have done worse than listen to Strecker's advice to publish only a selection of the best of this group of songs.   Nevertheless, as a whole, in its passion, its intensity, its rich colour, and its dancing or driving rhythms, the Spanish volume is unique.   The flame of genius in it may burn less steadily than it does elsewhere in Wolf's creative achievement, but when, as happens at frequent intervals, it does leap up again, warming and illuminating, it is seen to have lost none of its brilliance or power.   Those irritating externalities by means of which Wolf hoped to capture the spirit of the south fade into insignificance when the fire of his inspiration is kindled.   We have to accept the fact that his mind was obsessed by his idea of Spain, and rejoice that this allowed him to reveal another aspect of himself.   It was his first attempt to attain that Nietzschean Mediterranean spirit that was so valuable a counter to the sometimes oppressive influence of Wagner. It may be that it was necessary that he should first work out this vein before he could attain to the limpid beauty and refinement of the later Italian songs.

XI

UNWRITTEN OPERAS, AND FRIENDS IN GERMANY

WE have seen that as early as September 1888 Alarcon's *Three-cornered Hat* had attracted Wolf's attention as a suitable subject for a comic opera. Adalbert von Goldschmidt is said to have first brought it to his notice. According to Marie Lang,[1] Wolf was wholly occupied with the possibilities of making an opera libretto out of this novel at the time when he was introduced to Geibel and Heyse's *Spanish Song Book*. He had been diligently gathering knowledge of the Spanish people and their music but in the end had not been able to reduce the story itself to a form suitable for operatic treatment. All his accumulated enthusiasm for the subject was poured out in the music of the *Spanish Song Book*.

Julius Mayreder, one of the members of the Langs' summer colony at Schloss Bellevue, then suggested that his sister-in-law Rosa Mayreder should try to make something out of *The Three-cornered Hat* for Wolf's purpose. There were lively discussions about it among the composer's friends. Marie Lang herself was decidedly against the idea that a poetic dilettante should write a libretto for one who in his songs had found inspiration only in poetry of the highest quality. Mayreder, however, reconciled everybody to his suggestion in the end, on the understanding that Wolf himself was not yet to be told anything about it. Rosa Mayreder's experimental first act was found to be surprisingly successful and everybody then encouraged her to proceed with the rest of the libretto. The work was completed early in 1890 and sent anonymously to Perchtoldsdorf. Two days later Wolf came rushing into Lang's flat, threw the manuscript libretto on the table, and sat without speaking for a time on the divan. Then he looked earnestly at Lang and asked: 'Did you write that?' 'No.' 'Or your wife?' 'No, neither of us.' 'Thank God! That would have been dreadful.' Then he told them, savagely and pitilessly, everything that was wrong with Rosa Mayreder's script. The banality of the language especially infuriated him. 'Take it away!' he ordered. The manuscript went back to its author.

[1] 'Wie der *Corregidor* entstand' (*Die Zeit*, Vienna, 23rd February 1904).

The ambition of producing a comic opera—with which was bound up his chief hope of achieving financial security—remained with Wolf and, indeed, was seldom absent from his thoughts for long during the rest of his life.   Opera is the one field open to the musician in which he may score a resounding and even sensational success— a success that is measured by box-office receipts as well as by critical notices.   There was in Wolf, as various passages in his correspondence show, a lively desire to attain a real success of this kind.   He once related to Hellmer a dream that kept recurring to him.   He found himself in an opera-house, listening to a new opera, and suddenly realized that the music he was hearing was his own.   He was filled with anxiety that something would go wrong, that the performance would break down.   But nothing of the kind ever did happen. The opera was brought to an end without mishap and Wolf found himself on the stage, before the curtain, with the applause of the audience in his ears.   He dreamed that again and again, and his daydreams, too, were on similar lines.   Various friends, notably Joseph Schalk and Oskar Grohe, also urged him on to the composition of an opera.   The only obstacle seemed to be the lack of a libretto.   The friends made innumerable suggestions of what they thought were suitable subjects, but neither Wolf and his friends nor the friends among themselves were ever entirely in agreement about these things. The restless search for the right opera book was the characteristic feature of the next period of the composer's life.

After the completion of the *Spanish Song Book* Wolf remained at Perchtoldsdorf until nearly the end of May.   On 6th May he scored the Mörike song *In der Frühe*.   On 8th May there was a particularly successful private concert of the Wagner Verein, the programme including the first performance of the *Elfenlied* from *A Midsummer Night's Dream*, for soprano and women's chorus,[1] and eleven of Wolf's songs, more than half of which had to be repeated.   The artists were Ellen Forster and Jäger, with Joseph Schalk at the piano. On 12th May Wolf wrote a patriotic song for Jäger's use, a setting of Reinick's poem *Dem Vaterland*.[2]   While working on this piece,

---

[1] Performed on this occasion with piano accompaniment, the work not being yet scored.

[2] Decsey (vol. ii, p. 33) says this was composed at Perchtoldsdorf at the same time as the Mörike songs.   Heinrich Werner, in his *Hugo Wolf in Perchtoldsdorf* (p. 137), gives the date of its composition as 'probably the end of January 1888.'   A facsimile of the first page of the solo version of *Dem Vaterland*, dated in Wolf's hand 12th May 1890, is reproduced in the German edition of Newman's biography (facing p. 198).

however, he realized that the subject called for something more than a solo voice with piano, and began to rewrite it for male voice chorus and orchestra. He was still occupied with the scoring towards the end of the month.

On Whit Sunday, 25th May, Wolf returned to the Eckstein family's empty house at Unterach, in the Salzkammergut, in the expectation of being able very soon to complete a new cycle of songs that he had in mind. He had hoped in the previous year to celebrate the seventieth birthday of the Swiss poet and novelist Gottfried Keller, the author of his favourite *Der grüne Heinrich*, with a volume of songs, but the intention had remained unfulfilled. Now in the solitude of Unterach he set about this task. He chose a number of poems from the *Alte Weisen*, and the first of them, *Tretet ein, hoher Krieger*, was set to music on the very first day of his stay at Unterach. The other songs followed at rather greater intervals of time than Wolf had expected or been accustomed to in his bouts of composition of late. He humorously lamented this fact in a letter to Gustav Schur on 28th May:

> My hope of being able to astonish you in my usual way has unfortunately come to nothing. If you now learn that I wrote on Whit Sunday one of my finest songs (and, as I hope, most popular in days to come) that will leave you cold, for you will rightly expect that I composed on Whit Monday two, on Tuesday two more, and to-day at least three. Ah, how completely different everything has turned out! I have since the one (*Tretet ein, hoher Krieger*, by Gottfried Keller) written no more at all.

A second Keller song, *Singt mein Schatz wie ein Fink*, was composed on 2nd June, on 4th June the orchestral version of *Dem Vaterland* was completed, and four more of the *Alte Weisen* followed in the course of the same month. According to the manuscripts *Wie glänzt der helle Mond* was written on the 5th, *Das Köhlerweib ist trunken* on the 7th, *Wandl' ich in dem Morgentau* on the 8th and *Du milchjunger Knabe* on the 16th, but letters to Melanie Köchert show that the first three of these were not actually completed on the dates indicated. On the 24th Wolf sent an exultant brief note to Melanie at Rinnbach: 'Hurrah! The spell is broken. Yesterday the blessed apple-blossom wonderfully set to music. St. Peter curses with might and main. The charcoal-burner's drunken wife likewise completed from a sketch of the 7th. Howls atrociously. Have at last, at last, the six all together. Now come what may, my task-work is completed.'

It would seem from this that the third verse of *Wandl' ich in dem Morgentau*, the last two lines of *Wie glänzt der helle Mond* and part of *Das Köhlerweib ist trunken* were all completed on the 23rd. *Frohe Botschaft*, a setting of Reinick that was never published by the composer, was written on 25th June.

This is a rather disappointing group of compositions. Only *Wie glänzt der helle Mond*, an old peasant woman's vision of heaven, is wholly worthy of Wolf's genius. With its luminous and devout atmosphere, its exquisite modulations, and, at the end, its vivid little representation of a disgruntled St. Peter, crouching by the door of heaven and mending his old shoes, to a piano accompaniment that somehow succeeds in suggesting the very rasp of the thread drawn through the leather, this song is one of its composer's supremely lovely things. *Wandl' ich in dem Morgentau* is interesting as seeming to anticipate the style of the *Italian Song Book* in its accompaniment derived wholly from a single figure, of only one bar's duration, and has freshness and charm, particularly in its opening and closing sections. *Das Köhlerweib ist trunken* begins splendidly, with a hiccuping accompaniment that accords well with the voice of the drunken charcoal woman bawling in the woods. But Keller's poem goes on to relate how she was once the belle of the district and to reflect on the transitoriness of mortal beauty, and to all this Wolf seems to give only perfunctory attention. In an amusing letter to Melanie Köchert Wolf wrote:

Larisch visited me to-day, and as my Keller songs were still unknown to him, I played him as a substitute two Keller songs by Brahms which I have just borrowed from Lacom's choice assortment. Oh, you would have enjoyed it. What a master of the bagpipe and concertina Brahms is! . . . I cannot forbear to quote one passage remarkable for its quite outstandingly original declamation:

Ex 14

And so in the well-known, noble folk-song strain it yodels along to the end. Brahms has luckily only conferred immortality on two Keller poems, under the titles *Therese* ('Du milchjunger Knabe') and *Salome* ('Singt mein Schatz'). In the first the last stanza is varied. There it reads:

> eine Meermuschel liegt
> auf dem Schrank meiner Bas':
> da halte dein Ohr dran,
> dann hörst du etwas.

B. seems to have used an older edition of Keller's poems for his criminal purposes.

The Brahms quotation is atrocious, but is Wolf's own setting so very much better?

Ex 15

O ihr Jung-fraun im Land, vom Ge - birg und ü - ber

See, ü - ber - lasst mir den Schön-sten, sonst tut ihr mir weh!

Dem Vaterland was defended by its composer against friends who pointed out its weaknesses. 'When the German Kaiser hears it,' he told Melanie,

he will make me Imperial Chancellor on the spot. It's by Reinick . . . and ends with the words: 'Heil dir, heil dir, du deutsches Land.' Well, one can shout 'Heil dir' for a long time before it gets into one's marrow in the way it does with my music. How I arrived at this death-or-glory patriotic strain is a riddle to myself. I begin by degrees to believe I can do everything. Jäger will turn somersaults. It's written for him.

Wolf seems to have clung to the work, which underwent three further revisions before it was finally completed in full score, in the rather pathetic hope that it would bring him a great popular success. It sings the glories of the Fatherland with much pomp and ceremony but leaves the masses to whom it was intended to appeal without the satisfaction of a great *tune*. The music makes noble gestures, but is not sustainedly eloquent. It contains much that is admirable, but little that can inspire much affection.

Other projects were filling Wolf's head and exciting his imagination while he was working on these compositions. Some of his Viennese friends wanted him to produce a new orchestral work [1] and he had

---

[1] In this connection a sheet of pencil sketches in the Vienna City Library (*Konvolut von Skizzen*, No. 21) is interesting. A theme for 'cellos and basses, jotted down on 22nd December 1889, has the superscription: 'Einleitung zu Hamlet.' Nothing further is known of this project.

decided upon 'a symphonic illustration to Shakespeare's *Tempest*.'
But in thinking it over he found that the idea behind the play stimulated him less than did the fantastic scenes and characters themselves,
which made him think that perhaps *The Tempest* could best be set to
music in another form.   On 28th May he wrote to Schur:

The more I strove to get the piece clear to myself in its simplest outlines,
the more vividly the multicoloured splendour of these uniquely contrasted
pictures crowded before my imagination.   Good God, I thought, if that
isn't the material for an opera, fallen from Heaven into your lap, what else
are you waiting for?   What do you say, friend Schur?   Prospero!   What
a majestic bass!   Ferdinand, Miranda—a pair of lovers like Adam and
Eve.   Ariel!—I hear already the loveliest *colorature*!!?   And then Caliban
and Trinculo and Stephano?   This trio!!   What do you say?   I have
already sketched out a scenario.   The first scene remains, the second ditto,
only considerably shortened (but how Wagnerian—Prospero in the second
scene!)   From page 17 (Universal Library, Schlegel's translation) the
scene with Caliban falls out and Ferdinand comes on straight away (see
page 19).   The act can end as in Shakespeare.   In the second act the first
scene drops out entirely; it begins at once with Caliban's prodigiously
characteristic complete second scene.   Now think of the crazy scene
between Caliban, Trinculo, and Stephano—it'll be side-splitting.   In this
scene the attempt on Prospero's life would have to be prepared.   It can
close with the bestial drinking-song of Caliban.   The beginning of the
third act in Shakespeare gives the second scene of the second act; on the
other hand the second scene in Shakespeare would have to come out and
form the third scene of the second act (see page 57).[1]   The second act
closes with the hunting of the conspirators by Ariel and his sprites.   In the
third act, which in Shakespeare is the fifth, the whole personality of
Prospero unfolds itself.   Antonio, Gonzalo, etc. etc., would, as in general
throughout, in this act move somewhat into the background.   This, in
hasty outline, is my scheme.

Wolf asked Schur to obtain the opinion of Richard Genée, the
operetta composer and librettist, upon this plan.   Soon afterwards
Schur himself was urged to attempt a libretto, 'for necessity has made
many an honest man into a poet.'   'One of us,' Wolf told his friend,
'must become a poet, and I would rather this misfortune happened
to you than to me.'   He admitted that he had himself already tried
his hand at poetry without success, but it is not certain that he meant
by this that he had recently attempted a *Tempest* libretto of his own.

At about the same time Wolf received through the post two
volumes of poems by Detlev von Liliencron, whose attention had

---

[1] Wolf's meaning is not clear here.   Why 'on the other hand,' if the first two
scenes of Shakespeare's third act follow each other as second and third scenes of
Wolf's second act?   Why has Shakespeare's second scene 'to come out,' if it
forms the third scene of his second act?

been drawn to Wolf's songs by articles by Schalk and M. G. Conrad. In consequence, Liliencron too was asked by Wolf to undertake the *Tempest* libretto. The poet, however, would not venture to rewrite Shakespeare, and suggested instead that a drama of his own on the subject of Pocahontas should be used. 'He offers me a tragedy,' Wolf told Schur, 'the action of which takes place in North America. But in spite of my enthusiasm for Buffalo Bill and his unwashed crew, I prefer the soil of the homeland and its offspring, who appreciate the advantages of soap.'

Grohe, too, was not in favour of *The Tempest* as an opera, and recommended a poetic drama on the life of Buddha by his friend Karl Heckel, the Mannheim music publisher. This drew from Wolf a remarkable letter, in which were clearly defined his attitude towards Wagnerian music-drama and his own operatic ideals:

So I must set Buddha to music, a sort of second edition of *Parsifal*, perhaps with variations on Wagner's motives? Really, I don't understand you. How little familiar you are with my artistic nature, that you expect me to solve such sublime problems. The world has as yet scarcely an inkling of the philosophical profundity which is expressed in the most extraordinary manner in the Master's last words, and already something else must come into existence to give people a new headache. . . . Shall we then in our time never again be able to laugh heartily and be merry, must we strew ashes on our heads, wear garments of repentance, cover our foreheads in thoughtful furrows, and preach self-laceration? Let him redeem the world who feels in himself the redeemer's calling; that is little to me. I for my part will be merry, and if a hundred people can laugh with me, I am content. Nor do I strive for any 'world-redeeming' merriment. Anything rather than that. That we gladly leave to the great geniuses. Wagner has in and through his art already achieved such a mighty work of redemption that we can now at last rejoice that it is quite unnecessary for us to storm heaven, since it is already conquered for us, and that it is wisest to seek for ourselves in this fair heaven a really agreeable little nook. And this pleasant little nook I should much like to find, but on no account in the desert with water and locusts and wild honey, but in happy and original company, with strumming of guitars, sighs of love, moonlit nights, champagne carousals, etc.—in short in a comic opera, and a quite ordinary comic opera to boot, without the sombre world-redeeming spectre of a Schopenhauerian philosophy in the background. For that I need only a poet, and truly for that one *must* be a poet and a devil of a poet too. . . . Procure him for me and you shall see that a dozen Buddhas are unable to outweigh one such quite ordinary but original little comic opera.

Another suggestion of Grohe's, Gozzi's *Il pubblico segreto*, was found too antiquated, the characters stereotyped and conventional.

At the end of June Unterach was exchanged for the Köcherts'

house at Rinnbach. There Wolf stayed during the whole of July. With Joseph and Franz Schalk, who were spending their holidays not far away, he went to Ischl to see Nikisch, who gave a never redeemed promise to perform *Penthesilea* at Boston. On 2nd August Wolf returned to Vienna, to the Köcherts' residence at Döbling.

An article by Hermann Bahr, published in the Berlin weekly *Deutschland* on 16th August, led to renewed correspondence with the poet Liliencron. Bahr suggested that the pantomime might be the art form needed to bridge the gap between the older art of the stage and the modern, and actually named Liliencron and Wolf as those who might collaborate with Böcklin in such a pantomime. 'After six weeks,' Bahr was ready to wager, 'the three of them would be quite fantastically rich millionaires.' 'What do you think of me as a fantastically rich millionaire?' Wolf asked Melanie Köchert.

Liliencron takes it up in all seriousness and proposes for this purpose his Red Indian thriller *Pocahontas*. But Böcklin? He will make eyes like one of his own sea monsters. A devil of a fellow, Bahr! Liliencron is, moreover, as you will see from the enclosed card which I have just received, quite enchanted with Bahr's genius. Heaven alone knows how he has become infatuated with this hothead. I could do with the millions, however, even if I had to make 'pantomimic' music with repeaters and rifles.

Wolf never seems to have discovered that the subject proposed by Liliencron had no connection whatever with Buffalo Bill. As a result of this article the story of Cupid and Psyche, from *The Golden Ass* of Apuleius, was considered for a time as the possible subject of a pantomime. Then this followed *Pocahontas* into oblivion, as did another libretto, *Hildebrands Heimkehr*,[1] with an exclusively male cast.

During all this time Schur had been engaged on Wolf's behalf in negotiations with Schott's and other publishers in Germany. Schott's first offered to publish twelve songs selected from the *Spanish Song Book* and offered 600 marks for them. Wolf replied that he would just as soon give the whole lot away as sell twelve of them separately for this beggarly sum. He suggested that Schott's should publish the whole song-book and share the profits with the composer, after deduction of the costs of the production of the volume. This was the arrangement eventually agreed upon, but it was not at once accepted. The publisher declared that the *Spanish Song Book* contained 'a whole series of uncomposable poems.' This was communicated to Wolf by Schur, who received the following reply:

Schott can . . . ! Yes, I would rather continue in the old way than do

---

[1] Presumably based on the epic poem of Wilhelm Jordan.

business with this cheese-monger. I am tired of bargaining. Tell Schott that I *insist* on the division of the net profits, that I am *determined* on a complete edition of the Spanish songs, and that he needs to print, for all I care, only twelve songs separately. But I insist on the edition in volume form; if he doesn't like it, he must immediately return the copies and the three volumes. This is my mature, well-considered decision and my last word. . . . Add to your answer to Schott that it falls to my judgment, and not that of the publisher, to choose poems that are suitable or unsuitable for setting to music. That was all that was lacking, to allow to be dictated by this primeval blockhead what is composable and what isn't. 'A whole series of uncomposable poems'!!! Oh, you Caliban! Since I composed them, they were composable.

Schur passed on Wolf's decisions in more diplomatic language, leaving the way open for a renewal of the negotiations in case no other publisher could be found. It was as well that he did so. The songs were next sent to Breitkopf & Härtel, but Breitkopf's reader reported that 'the songs of Wolf are among the most absurd that the extreme left wing of the New German school has as yet brought forth, and have nothing more in common with my conception of the musical art than the bare elements of sound and rhythm.'[1] On the strength of this report the works were rejected. Wolf next proposed to publish them through Lacom at his own expense, but happily Schur was able to induce Schott's to reconsider the matter. After further correspondence, first through Schur and then directly with the composer, Schott's showed themselves much more amenable, and it only needed a personal visit on Wolf's part for everything to be settled between them satisfactorily.

At Döbling in September four further orchestral arrangements of Mörike songs came into being. *Gebet* and *An den Schlaf* were both scored on the 4th of this month, *Neue Liebe* on the 5th and *Wo find' ich Trost?* on the 6th. On the 10th Wolf left for Kövecles, in Hungary, where he stayed with Baron Schey for about a week, then went to Rinnbach for a few days and towards the end of the month returned once more to Eckstein's house at Unterach. On the 24th he told Schur: 'I feel ominous signs of composition in me, and await an explosion at any moment,' and sure enough, next day he was able to write out *Mir ward gesagt, du reisest in die Ferne*, the first of his

---

[1] See Oskar von Hase, *Breitkopf und Härtel, Gedenkschrift und Arbeitsbericht*, vol. ii, 4th edition (Leipzig, 1919), and a footnote by the translator on p. 24 of the German edition of Newman's *Hugo Wolf*. What the latter footnote does not make clear is that it was not the early songs, which Newman refers to on this page of his biography, but the Mörike, Eichendorff, Goethe, Spanish, and Keller songs, that were rejected by Breitkopf's reader in this way.

songs from Paul Heyse's *Italienisches Liederbuch*. On this day, too, he all but completely scored the first *Auf eine Christblume* song from the Mörike volume. Four new songs in all were thrown up by this 'explosion,' the others being *Ihr seid die Allerschönste* on 2nd October, *Gesegnet sei, durch den die Welt entstund* on the 3rd, and *Selig ihr Blinden* on the morning of the 4th. On the next day Wolf was again at Rinnbach, where he stayed until the 9th, when he set out on an important journey, combining business and pleasure, far into Germany.

The objects of the journey were twofold: to conclude the negotiations with Schott's, and to make the acquaintance of various friendly correspondents and see what could be done for the furtherance of his art in the districts in which these friends lived. There was Liliencron at Munich, with whom some sort of collaboration might still be possible; there was University Music Director Kauffmann at Tübingen, in the heart of the Mörike country; there were Grohe and Weingartner at Mannheim, the latter still considering the possibility of introducing *Christnacht* at one of his concerts.

Munich was Wolf's first stopping place. He got on famously with Liliencron, who as an amateur singer was well acquainted with the work of the great German song-writers, and, unlike most poets, actually wanted his own poems set to music. This had undoubtedly been his object in sending copies of his books to Wolf, but the latter found nothing sufficiently lyrical to inspire him to song. Nor did anything come of the various projects for operas and pantomimes that were discussed between them. Wolf found in Liliencron a friend and supporter, who afterwards worked hard to spread the knowledge of his work, but not a collaborator. No doubt the poet, 'who could cut such a dashing figure and always suggested one who has just dismounted from a good horse and is about to sit down to oysters and champagne,'[1] had much to tell of his adventures, first as a captain in the German Army, until compelled to resign his commission on account of debts, and then in the United States, where he lived for a time in poverty, paying five cents a night for the privilege of leaning on a rope at the Alligator Hotel, New York, and acting in turn as house-painter, school-teacher, horse-dealer, and pianist in a beer-garden.

Another new acquaintance was Liliencron's friend Michael Georg Conrad, editor of the periodical *Die Gesellschaft* and a leader of the

[1] Arthur Eloesser, *Modern German Literature*, trans. Catharine Alison Phillips (London, 1933).

naturalistic movement in German literature. At midday on 11th October Conrad returned from a walk to find his house resounding with music. Someone was violently assaulting his old piano, while singing in a rough but arresting voice words that he recognized as those of Mörike's ballad, *Der Feuerreiter*. An agitated servant-girl explained that this sort of thing had been going on for an hour already. As Conrad entered the room the pianist introduced himself: 'Hugo Wolf from Vienna.' Then he passed his hands through his hair and sat down again at the instrument. 'I wanted to show you these,' he said, and opened the Mörike and Goethe volumes here and there in rapid succession: 'Listen to this . . .' 'Listen to that . . .' 'And what do you say to *that*?' He played and sang untiringly, carrying the music-loving Conrad off his feet. 'You must help me,' he said. 'Munich must get to know me.' It was decided that a group of influential musicians, critics, and writers should be invited to meet Wolf and be introduced to his music on the following morning.

Late that night a full report on the day's activities was sent to Melanie Köchert.

My chances here at Munich are improving. Levi made me welcome in the most friendly fashion and handed me straight away a letter of recommendation to Eugen Gura, to awaken the singer's interest in my things. Gura was amiability itself. He avowed that he had ordered songs by Wolf, but received those of a false Wol*ff*. Gura is an intelligent, modest, and go-ahead singer and above all he really knows a thing or two—he knows a great deal, possesses a *divine* voice, and sings in *heavenly* fashion, of which I had the best opportunity to convince myself. He gave a recital and obliged me by presentation of a ticket to attend the concert. The programme was, as you will see from the enclosure, very rubbishy. Schumann was a complete flop. Altogether the applause, in spite of Gura's great art, was very feeble, for which the second-hand, long, slow, and boring compositions bore the blame. The intervals passed off, God be thanked, without the piano-thumping customary in Vienna. I had the feeling that if Gura had sung a rousing piece, like my *Rattenfänger* or even *Fussreise*, or something like that, all the people would have gone mad with delight and happiness at such a change. Gura is tremendously interested in my things. Now at 10 a.m. to-morrow we meet Levi, Porges, Merz, Liliencron, and Conrad. . . . To-day I played my things to Conrad and Liliencron. Both were literally *overpowered*. One wept and the other shouted. It was enough to send one raving mad. Liliencron wants at any price to write about me. Perhaps I'm the hero of his next novel. The one bawled: 'That's better than Wagner'; the other roared that the Devil himself couldn't put such things together; in short, the fellows have gone raving mad. It's to be hoped that the others will do likewise to-morrow.

The meeting took place at the piano sale rooms of Alfred Schmied, a music-dealer in the Maximilianstrasse. 'On the whole it went well,' Wolf wrote later in the same day to Schur, 'but I was understood only by a few. Gura was delighted with my Harper's songs, all the more as in his song recital the day before he had suffered fiasco with Schumann's settings.' Melanie Köchert was given a more detailed account.

The production has taken place and they all turned up except Merz. I performed almost exclusively Goethe, but much of it was not understood in the least—for instance, *Phänomen* and *Dies zu deuten bin erbötig*. The three Holy Kings, also, did not make their usual effect. In short, it fell rather flat. Gura, who held out longest, sang for me, while Liliencron was still present, my Harper's songs at sight and in downright consummate fashion. He was quite carried away and puts them far above Schumann's and Schubert's settings. He was quite delighted with *Auf einer Wanderung*, which he wants to sing just as it is in the original. Levi liked best the two Coptic songs, *Als ich auf dem Euphrat schiffte* and, strangely enough, *Wenn ich dein gedenke* and *Wie sollt' ich heiter bleiben*. The *Rattenfänger* wouldn't ensnare but on the other hand every one was in ecstasy about *Trunken müssen wir alle sein* and *Komm, Liebchen, komm*. On the whole I got the impression that I was *not* understood, that they occupied themselves too much with musical matters, and thereby forgot what is new and original in my musico-poetical conception. Continual chatter of musicians! Ah, how very differently *you* understand me, and even my Viennese friends!

From Conrad's account, it seems that every one at this meeting was very flattering and agreeable, but that all those best able to serve Wolf hesitated to commit themselves to anything definite. Gura, in carefully chosen words, weighed the chances of the new music's success at Munich. The conservatism of the public made it hazardous to venture upon even the less well-known songs of Schubert and Schumann. Extraordinary caution and wisdom would be necessary in Wolf's case. He pressed the composer's hand warmly, wished him well, and departed. Heinrich Porges, then critic of the *Münchner Neueste Nachrichten*, agreed to give his support 'as soon as his pen was required'—but no call was made upon it for a very long time. The sole positive result of Wolf's visit to Munich was Liliencron's poem *An Hugo Wolf*, which appeared in his next volume. Liliencron proclaimed the arrival of a young King of the new Art:

> Platz da, Platz da, Gesindel,
> Ein junger Germanenkönig kommt,
> Ein König der neuen Kunst,

but the people of Munich were afraid, and turned aside hastily to their sentimental operettas and music-halls.

On 13th October Wolf was at Stuttgart, where he saw the conductor of the 'Liederkranz' Choral Society, Wilhelm Förstler, who agreed to perform *Dem Vaterland*. Next day the traveller arrived at Tübingen. He left his luggage—which included the portable bath—at the station and made his way to Prof. Kauffmann's address, Neckarhalde 60. Although Wolf had not forewarned any one of his intention of visiting Tübingen, he was immediately invited to stay at the house.

Kauffmann, who had held the position of director of music at the University of Tübingen since 1877, and was well known in Württemberg as a choral conductor, was twenty-four years older than Wolf. This difference in their ages was no bar to their mutual understanding and friendship, but seems to have induced in Wolf an attitude of respect, mingled with deep affection, that was unique among his friendships. Small disagreements, that with others of Wolf's friends would have led to a sharp exchange of words, were in Kauffmann's case passed over in silence. Perhaps the latter's intimate relationship with Mörike and his circle also had something to do with this, in Wolf, quite exceptional respect for an elder friend.

Before this meeting, at the very beginning of their correspondence, when Kauffmann had published an article on the Mörike songs, in which he had unfortunately referred to Wolf as 'a son of the time that had brought forth a Wagner and a Brahms,' and discovered in the *Peregrina* songs and others examples of the less happy consequences of Wagner's influence, Wolf had vigorously protested, quoting Nietzsche's verdict upon Brahms: 'He has the melancholy of impotence,' and expressing his own belief that in Brahms was to be found nothing of that 'stern, harsh, inexorable *truth*,' which represented his own undeviating artistic aim and ideal. The question of Brahms came up again in the course of conversation at Tübingen, and Wolf went to the piano and played an extract from *Lohengrin*, an expression of that exultation, the lack of which, in his estimation, was the chief deficiency of the music of Brahms. Kauffmann, on this as on later occasions, forbore to spoil their relationship by expressing his disagreement.

A far more profitable subject of conversation was Mörike, about whom Kauffmann had much to tell, including what he knew of the history of Peregrina. He also read Wolf the letters that his father had received from the poet. 'Dear Heavens, what letters!' exclaimed the composer in a letter to Melanie. 'They are almost to be preferred to his poems, so much that is splendid is revealed in them. We were all moved to tears.' On the afternoon of the day of Wolf's arrival he accompanied Kauffmann and his son-in-law, Wilhelm Schmid, professor of classical philology at Tübingen, through the Schönbuch woods to Bebenhausen, the hunting castle of the kings of Württemberg, and all the way he had a copy of Mörike's poems in his hand. In the evening Kauffmann invited a number of his friends from the university to hear Wolf sing and play a large number of his Mörike, Goethe and Eichendorff songs. On the next morning Kauffmann and Schmid were introduced to the unpublished *Spanish Song Book* and the Keller songs, as well as the scherzo from Bruckner's ' Romantic ' Symphony, which was a revelation to them both. Wolf told them many comical stories about Bruckner, and also something about the sad neglect of his work in Vienna. In the afternoon of this second day the three friends walked to Reutlingen. On the way Wolf spoke much of his operatic ambitions. He said that he envied Mendelssohn his success in writing music to Shakespeare's *A Midsummer Night's Dream* and was looking about for a similar fantastic subject. Kauffmann suggested that he should consider Mörike's story *Der Schatz*; Schmid recommended Aristophanes' *Birds* to his attention. Wolf himself spoke of Alarcon's *Three-cornered Hat*. Arrived at Reutlingen, they spent a pleasant hour in the Black Bear Inn, and at six o'clock Wolf departed by train for Stuttgart again. He was in buoyant spirits and all amiability. Shortly before the train left, he jumped down again on to the platform to shake his new friends repeatedly by the hand.

The visit had been wholly delightful, and undisturbed by the slightest disharmony. Wolf afterwards sent Kauffmann his photograph, inscribed with the opening bars of the Mörike song *Auf einer Wanderung*, and described how he looked back with joy and delight to the happy hours he had spent at Tübingen—the 'freundliches Städtchen.'

At Stuttgart he had arranged another meeting with Förstler, who seems to have undertaken to bring together the town's musical notabilities to hear Wolf's compositions, as had been done by Conrad at Munich, but the proposed gathering had to be postponed and Wolf, finding himself also unable to sing owing to catarrh, did not linger at Stuttgart but proceeded on the 16th to Heidelberg. His stay there—it seems to have been purely a pleasure trip—was spoiled by his cold and by persistent rain, so that he was able to do little more than inspect the castle ruins. On 18th October he arrived at Mann-heim. He met Weingartner by arrangement in the reading-room of the Pfälzer Hof. Grohe arrived there later to find the two deep in animated conversation and already on friendly terms. Weingartner induced Wolf to play through with him Strauss's *Don Juan* as a piano duet; it was his intention to perform the work in the same pro-gramme as *Christnacht*. Wolf showed little interest in *Don Juan*, thought the piano duet a waste of valuable time and played the bass part thoroughly badly.

Grohe insisted that Wolf should leave the hotel and be his guest while staying at Mannheim. In Grohe's residence a little later the composer played his Spanish songs from the manuscripts for his host and Weingartner. They were quite overcome as song followed song with scarcely a pause, in apparently endless succession. Wolf would probably not have stopped until he had sung them all the forty-four songs in the volume, if Weingartner had not begun to run up and down the room, holding his head in his hands, and begging him to cease. It was too much. He could for the time absorb no more new impressions. Grohe too was glad when it was over, and was too deeply moved to speak.

Weingartner found that although Wolf did not take kindly to criticism of his songs, he was ready and willing to listen to advice about his treatment of the orchestra. Weingartner pointed out various instances of thick, overladen scoring in *Penthesilea*, and Wolf listened quite quietly and then shook him warmly by the hand. He seemed almost childishly thankful for the advice. 'You tell me all these things so kindly,' he said. ·'In Vienna they simply run me down, and I can't stand that.' He complained a good deal about the condition of music in Vienna. The subject of Brahms came up again in conversation and, although Weingartner himself at that time was not a particularly warm admirer of this composer, he found Wolf's burning hatred hard to understand.

At Mannheim Wolf attended a performance of *Tannhäuser* under Weingartner and was quite overcome. At the end of the opera he seemed hardly to know where he was. He trod on people's toes, and if it had not been for Grohe would have left his hat and coat behind. He embraced Weingartner with tears. Again and again he repeated that in Vienna, with all their rich resources, they were unable to achieve anything like this *Tannhäuser* performance at Mannheim. He told them that Wagner's music left him quite disheartened. Always the thought recurred that his own work was utterly unimportant compared with that of Wagner and he considered destroying everything he had written.

Weingartner had recently completed his own opera *Genesius* and played the first act to a group of friends, including Wolf. The latter maintained an icy silence, but expressed his belief afterwards to Grohe that Weingartner would suffer bitter disillusionment over the work.

On 21st October Wolf left Mannheim, after making Grohe a present of his copy of Mörike's poems, from which he had often read aloud while breakfasting. In Grohe he left behind him one of the staunchest of all his friends, a man who, although not a professional musician or writer, managed to do more than almost anybody else in the fight for the recognition of his genius. He was not by any means an uncritical admirer and told Wolf what he thought and felt even when he knew this would not be altogether palatable. In consequence Wolf too was frank and outspoken in his relationship with Grohe and the large collection of letters written to this friend are among the most valuable that we possess.

At Mainz, the next stage of his tour, Wolf stayed at the Hotel Stadt Coblenz. He made his way at once to Schott's and there made the acquaintance of the head of the firm, Dr. Ludwig Strecker. He found he had to do business with a younger man than he had expected—Strecker was only seven years older than Wolf himself—and, moreover, with a man of great culture and refinement—not at all the barbarian, the 'Caliban,' that he seems to have been expecting. Strecker led the way to a room where part of the *Spanish Song Book*, beautifully printed, lay awaiting the composer's inspection. Then Wolf sat down at the piano to try to arouse more enthusiasm for the Spanish songs than the publisher had shown in some of his earlier letters. 'On the whole,' Schurs was told next day, 'he still doesn't understand the Spanish things very well, but shows goodwill and zeal.' Strecker's wife was more enthusiastic than her husband, and Wolf prided himself on the diplomacy with which he had secured this important ally. The Keller songs brought difficulties, as neither Strecker nor his wife cared much for the poems of the *Alte Weisen*. At this first meeting no definite conclusion was arrived at regarding the publication of the songs. The house of Schott, however, provided splendid food and wines, and the evening passed rapidly and pleasantly in doing justice to these, discussing and making music. On the 22nd Wolf returned to the attack, this time playing his *Christnacht*, and with this Strecker was delighted, though he prudently decided to await the outcome of Weingartner's performance of the work before discussing terms. Strecker continued to make himself very agreeable. Wolf was taken over the printing works and then shown various interesting manuscripts, including Wagner's 1861 draft of the *Meistersinger* libretto. The next day he dined with Strecker and Humperdinck, who had originally recommended Wolf's songs to Schott's, while acting as their reader. He had no longer any connection with the firm, having in the meantime secured a teaching appointment in the Hoch Conservatoire at Frankfurt; he had come to Mainz specially to meet Wolf. Humperdinck records in his diary that they discussed Wagner together and that Wolf played *Christnacht* again. After Humperdinck left, Wolf also played a large number of his Eichendorff and Goethe songs, including all the settings of poems from the *West-östlicher Divan*. 'You should have seen how Schott [1] opened his eyes!' he wrote to Schur. 'He and his wife were completely lost. I now have them both in my pocket.' When he returned to his hotel, just before one o'clock in the morning, Strecker had agreed finally to publish on commission for the composer the Spanish and Keller songs, and to take over the Mörike, Eichendorff and Goethe volumes besides. The terms were those that Wolf had already suggested months before—the profits to be shared between Schott's and Wolf, after deduction of the costs of production, and Wolf to retain the copyrights—in spite of the fact that this was entirely contrary to Schott's usual policy. It was a triumph for the composer.

Humperdinck had provided Wolf with letters of introduction to Franz Wüllner, conductor of the Gürzenich concerts, and to Hermann Wette, his own brother-in-law, at Cologne. Wolf arrived there on the 24th and quickly made friends with Wette, who already knew his published songs. He was an ardent admirer of Wolf's art and had been the first to call attention to it at Cologne.

Wüllner was interviewed without result, but Otto Neitzel, the critic, pianist and composer, agreed to write an article about Wolf's music for the *Kölnische Zeitung*. On the 25th Wette took Wolf to the house of his great friend Arnold Mendelssohn, the composer, a relative of Felix Mendelssohn's. Arnold Mendelssohn wrote a successful opera,

---

[1] Wolf meant Dr. Strecker, of course.

Elsi, die seltsame Magd, to a libretto by Wette. On the occasion of Wolf's visit, he returned home after a tiring round of music lessons and was not overjoyed at first to learn that Wette had brought an unknown composer from Vienna to perform his own works; but when he heard the Mörike songs, and then the Eichendorff and Goethe settings, his tiredness left him. Wolf's manner, at first somewhat unprepossessing, became confidential and winning when he saw that his music was understood. He gave them a charming account of the first performance of *Epiphanias* at Frau Melanie Köchert's birthday party, and insisted that Mendelssohn's wife, who had been called away to attend to her own children, should return before he sang it. 'That's a song for the *home*,' he said; 'the lady must be present.' He sang and played until one o'clock and it was Mendelssohn's impression that he omitted not one of all the songs in the three volumes he had brought with him.

Next morning Wette accompanied Wolf as far as Rüdesheim, where they exchanged the 'du' and drank to their future friendship before taking leave of each other, Wolf returning by rail to Mainz. On the 27th he was at Frankfurt. He called on Humperdinck, who showed him round the town in the afternoon. In the evening they visited the music-dealer André's, where Wolf found a piano duet arrangement of Bruckner's third Symphony, which he and Humperdinck played through together. In the morning of the following day Wolf accompanied his friend to a rehearsal of Friedrich Lux's operetta *Die Fürstin von Athen*, upon which he made sarcastic comments. Humperdinck then took him out to lunch and afterwards saw him off at the station upon his return journey to Vienna.

Wolf's travels, whether considered from a purely business and propagandist viewpoint, or from one comprehending the artist's desire and need for friendship and understanding, had been eminently successful. Himself in the best of humours, and exercising the unique charm that was his when he cared to use it, his journeyings had developed into a sort of triumphal progress from one new friend to another. Everywhere he went he left behind him men's hearts more closely bound in his service, their minds more determined to struggle for his recognition. Enthusiastic and affectionate letters followed him to Vienna from all the towns he had visited. Wette sang his praises in a manner that was almost embarrassing. On 3rd November Wolf wrote in reply to a letter from this friend: 'Your exuberant hymns in praise of my art have almost frightened me. I am not accustomed to such strong tobacco. I have always been pledged in the potion of rapture only in homoeopathic drops, and now, dear savage, you pour whole barrels full of enthusiasm over me and drown me in it.' Kauffmann was soon able to announce a new article on the Goethe songs, published in the *Münchner Allgemeine Zeitung* for 22nd November, and shortly afterwards the delivery at Tübingen of a lecture on the progress of music during the past century, of which the conclusion was a performance of Wolf's *Kennst du das Land?* to illustrate the culminating point in the development of the art song. Humperdinck, too, had the intention of publishing an article in the *Frankfurter Zeitung*; he was only waiting for the appearance in print of the *Spanish Song Book* before setting to work. In the meantime he believed he had succeeded in interesting Julius Stockhausen in Wolf's songs. Schmid sent a German translation of Aristophanes, as a sequel to his suggestion that the *Birds* might be found a suitable subject for a comic opera. In this idea Wolf was at first much interested, but he found that the innumerable learned footnotes that had to be consulted while reading the book destroyed all his pleasure in it. He decided that the matter was too satirical and could not possibly be used without drastic revision. Liliencron sent a copy of *Der Heidegänger*, a new volume of poems containing *An Hugo Wolf*, but unhappily the composer's earlier favourable opinion of the poet's talents had undergone a change by this time: apart from the poem about himself, he found nothing of any value in the new volume and advised Kauffmann, who had also received a copy of the poems from their author, *not* to read them. He told Liliencron himself, in his candid way, how lacking in musical feeling he found the poems and how he looked for something more song-like, more purely lyrical. After this their correspondence languished, but Liliencron, in his later years at Hamburg, still busied himself with Wolfian propaganda.

In the correspondence with Schott's regarding the publication of the Keller and Spanish songs there arose the same disputes as had occurred with Brandstetter over the printing of the Eichendorff and Goethe songs. Wolf objected to every attempt to economize in plates by compressing his music upon the page and to every variation, however minute, from his stipulations with regard to paper, print, marginal decoration, pagination, and so forth. Printer's errors drove him near to madness. He would not allow the songs to be issued in transposed editions.

Schott's wished of course to advertise the publication of these fifty new songs by an almost unknown composer, and asked Wolf for a few biographical details and a photograph for use in this connection. Wolf refused outright to provide any such material. The music, he thought, was good enough to speak for itself. He wanted the songs announced only in the musical journals and without any information at all about the man who had written them. He considered that 'their quantity alone should suffice to excite in high degree the curiosity and interest of the public.' For the rest, he trusted in 'Gott und Schott.'

Wolf for a time expected the new volume to be in print by Christmas, but, with the repeated discovery of fresh errors in the proofs, its preparation dragged on a long time after this. In spite of a whole series of postcards, with impatient inquiries and reminders from the composer, it was not until the beginning of March 1891 that it actually appeared.

Meanwhile, on his return to Vienna from his German tour, Wolf, after a week or ten days in the Köcherts' house in the Mehlmarkt, had retired on 11th November to their suburban residence at Döbling, where he had earlier written most of the Goethe songs. There, in spite of the handicap of an upright piano—a type of instrument he despised and detested—he added three new settings of poems from Heyse's *Italian Song Book* to the four he had written at Unterach shortly before setting out on his German travels. From these exquisite and original creations he then had to turn to the less agreeable task of writing incidental music to Ibsen's early drama *The Feast at Solhaug*, commissioned from him by Max Burckhard, the new director of the Vienna Burgtheater. Wolf had had to contribute 500 marks in cash towards the cost of the publication of the Spanish songs and had in consequence run into debt. This commission to write music for the Burgtheater, secured for him by Gustav Schur, would bring in, he hoped, an honorarium of 300 or 400 florins to stabilize his finances.

At first Ibsen's drama had impressed him; for a time he even thought of making an opera out of it. Within a very few days, however, he had changed his opinion completely. On 14th November he told Grohe: 'I like the Ibsen play less every day. It is right honestly botched—with damned little poetry. I really don't know where I shall get the plaster from, to clothe in music this home-made carpentry. The whole thing is repugnant to me and yet I must get on

K

with it.' The production of Ibsen's play was expected in the middle of December, and time pressed. Wolf began 'working like a madman' at the task he had undertaken and at first made good progress. By the middle of December most of the music, as originally planned by Wolf,[1] was completed—only Margit's ballad in the first act and the overture, in which the theme of the ballad was to be introduced, still remained to be done. These two pieces, however, caused endless difficulties and delays. The performance had to be put off until January; on 30th December Wolf wrote unhappily to Grohe: 'The accursed ballad just *won't* occur to me and consequently the overture cannot be written. I fear that this work will remain a torso. But I can't get on with the Italian songs either. I can't get on with anything at all. It's a dog's life when one can't work.'

It was not until the end of January that he was able to announce that he had 'sweated out' the ballad, and although it had turned out quite different from what he had originally intended, he was 'happy to be at length free of this plague.' There remained the overture. The production of the play had meanwhile been further deferred until March, but in the middle of that month Wolf, although he had added an orchestral introduction to the third act and one of Gudmund's songs to the original scheme, was still struggling with his overture. He envisaged a full-scale symphonic movement with a slow introduction and an *allegro*. All that actually materialized, after further months of delay, was a short slow prelude, introductory to Margit's ballad, from which its themes are derived. The sketches

---

[1] Gudmund's two songs and the orchestral introduction to the third act were afterthoughts, not included in Wolf's earliest plans. The dated sketches for the *Fest auf Solhaug* music (National Library, Vienna) clarify considerably the history of the work.

20th November 1890, introduction and chorus 'Nun streichet die Fiedel.'
22nd November 1890, final chorus 'Gottes Auge wacht.'
23rd November 1890, march and chorus 'Bei Sang und Spiel.'
23rd November 1890, chorus 'Es locket ins Freie.'
Letters of 27th and 29th November show that Wolf was then hard at work on the scoring of the above.
11th December 1890, chorus 'Wir wünschen Fried und Glück.'
A letter of 18th December says the music is finished except for the ballad and overture.
23rd January 1891, Margit's ballad 'Bergkönig ritt durch die Lande weit' (almost complete).
11th February 1891, introduction to third act.
7th March 1891, Gudmund's second song 'Ich fuhr wohl über Wasser.'
11th March 1891, prelude to first act.
30th October 1891, Gudmund's first song 'Ich wandelte sinnend allein.'
Thirteen bars dated 11th May 1891, with the opening of the never completed *allegro* of the overture, exist elsewhere.

show this to have been composed on 11th March, but an unpublished letter to Wette, written as late as 26th July, has a note on the margin of its first page: 'The overture to *Solhaug* I hope to finish before the winter.' It looks as if what was intended to be the slow introduction to the overture was utilized as the prelude as a last resort, when it became apparent that the *allegro* would never be completed. Another song for Gudmund was added at the end of October 1891, three weeks before the play was at length produced.

The incidental music to *Das Fest auf Solhaug* was the first and only music written to order by Hugo Wolf. The amount of hard labour it cost him was hardly repaid by the few hundred gulden that he received for it, but on the other hand the Burgtheater authorities, for their part, cannot have been particularly pleased with the result of their commission. In addition to the repeated delays in the production of the play that had been caused by Wolf's inability to complete his score, it was found that he had written for a much larger orchestra than was actually available. He wanted the opera-house chorus and members of the opera-house orchestra engaged to reinforce the normal complement of the Burgtheater, but this was out of the question. For this reason when the play *was* finally produced only a part of Wolf's music could be performed with it.

The composer himself, in spite of the trouble it had cost him to produce, and his contempt for the material he had had to work upon, thought highly of his *Fest auf Solhaug* music. He looked forward to a concert performance with a large chorus and orchestra, and to its employment in German theatres with better musical resources than the Burgtheater of that time. It seemed to him 'genuine theatre music, straightforward and full of life' which would 'assuredly not fail in its effect upon the public' and, certainly, by all normal standards, he had done well. If, as is on record, Wolf's music to *Das Fest auf Solhaug* is not very effective in the theatre, that is the fault as much of the dramatist as of the composer. Wolf's desire to achieve bold, simple effects is evident throughout his score, but the brief choruses of Ibsen's play, with their conventional stage sentiments, expressed in what is, in the German translation at least, language of shameless banality, gave him no opportunity of building up any impressive musical scene. To what expedients he was driven in the endeavour to fill out his wretched material may be judged from the amount of verbal repetition in the chorus 'Bei Sang und Spiel' in the first act. Yet the result is by no means unimpressive. The musical material may not be exactly inspired but it is employed with considerable ingenuity and resource, and the same is generally true of most of the rest of the score. The dancing chorus, 'Nun streichet die Fiedel,' in the second act, has life and gusto, and the fresh, open-air quality of the nocturne 'Es locket ins Freie,' in the last scene of the same act, is quite attractive in its rather commonplace way. A long orchestral introduction to the third act utilizes material from other sections of the incidental music. A theme from the short chorus, 'Wir wünschen Fried und Glück,' with which the third act itself opens, is worked up in a sort of 'Wedding anniversary at Solhaug' atmosphere, after the precedent of Grieg, but with some of Wolf's own characteristic modulatory restlessness. In the middle section a somewhat unpromising theme, also used in the accompaniment of Gudmund's second song, is most resourcefully developed. As incidental music to Ibsen's play this is all excellent stuff. It is only when it is considered apart, as a product of the same brain that had given to the Mörike songs their genial warmth, to the Goethe volume its intellectual passion and grandeur, that had conceived, only a few days before, some of the most exquisite miniatures of the *Italian Song Book*, that the *Fest auf Solhaug* music is felt to be unworthy of a great artist. It is safe to say that nobody, hearing this music for the first time, would think of attributing it to Wolf. In one of his letters to Humperdinck, Wolf wrote that he had almost decided to borrow some ideas from Brahms for *Das Fest auf Solhaug*, on Loge's principle: 'Steal from the thief what the thief stole.' Phrases in Gudmund's two agreeable songs arouse the suspicion that in this emergency Wolf may have extracted a leaf or two from the book, not of Brahms, but of Grieg. Margit's ballad is the only music in the whole score with a really individual character. The legendary, northern atmosphere is finely realized, the whole piece coloured with the dark tones of the cor anglais. This ballad alone deserves to be rescued from the limbo to which the rest of the *Fest auf Solhaug* music has already been consigned—a fate that no lover of the essential Wolf need excessively deplore.

Another work that has dropped out of the concert repertory is *Christnacht*, for *soli*, chorus, and orchestra, of which the beginning dates back to December 1886, but which was completed in full score only in May 1889. Occasion would have been found for its discussion before this if its chronology had been less uncertain, but as we do not know how far it was taken in 1886 or 1887 and how much remained to be completed in 1889, or how long the composer was working upon it on either of those occasions, it seemed preferable to withhold consideration of the work until it could be discussed in relation to its first performance.

Ever since Wolf's visit to Mannheim there had been prospects of *Christnacht* coming to performance there under Weingartner, but in the succeeding months there were so many delays that Wolf often doubted whether anything would ever come of the project. But at length the work was put down definitely for the last concert to be conducted by Weingartner at Mannheim before he left to take up an appointment with the Berlin Opera. The rest of the programme consisted of Beethoven's second Symphony and the *Faust* Symphony of Liszt. Wolf was 'formally invited' to attend, and decided to make Mannheim his first stopping place on a second tour of his friends in central Germany.

In an article in the Mannheim *Generalanzeiger* on 9th April, the day of the concert, Grohe prepared the ground for the work's reception by quoting passages from one of Wolf's own letters, outlining the scheme of his *Christnacht*. In the letter he had told Grohe:

The work begins with two motives which in their development—swelling out to the greatest brilliance and then gradually dying away again—dominate the whole introduction. These two motives form the basis of the composition, symbolizing the personality of Christ, the Child, and the World-conqueror. To a simple, child-like melody in the woodwind—a genuine folk-song that, in the naïvely rustic representations of Christmas night customary in Styria, I myself as a child joined in singing—the horn replies—later the trombones—with a pathetic phrase. It is the motive to which in the course of the piece the Chorus of the *Believers* sing the words 'Praise we offer to the new-born Child.' I stress the word 'Believers' because I did not consider a Shepherd's song, as specified by the poet, compatible with the solemn, grandiose character of this passage. The first simple theme in its complete and original form, however, first appears in the Shepherds' song 'The angels hover, singing and playing, on the breezes,' but in the *orchestra*, while the chorus intones in counterpoint a melody wholly in keeping with the character of the scene—by which means, as I flatter myself, a fine effect is achieved. Towards the end of the work, in the prophecy of the Angel of the Annunciation, and the answering double chorus of the Shepherds and Believers, entirely fresh musical ideas appear that only with the final conclusion of the whole piece flow into the previously mentioned pathetic theme, which, borne on and encompassed around by the whole orchestra, unfurls in flaming outlines the dogma of Divinity become Man and of Redemption.

A certain rhythmic monotony, or stiffness of gait, which characterizes much of the music of *Christnacht*, as well as the programme underlying the orchestral introduction, points to *Lohengrin* as one of its forbears and also gives some grounds for supposing that the work belongs essentially to 1886 or 1887, rather than to 1889. The thematic material is fresh and tuneful and it is easy to understand the affection in which Wolf held these reminiscences in music of the faith and innocence of his childhood. However, by taking some of Platen's words out of the mouths of the Shepherds, and giving them to a supplementary chorus of Believers, Wolf did not solve all the *musical* problems involved in the attempt to portray at once a childlike simplicity and a Wagnerian, world-redeeming conquest of evil. The simple carol and the fresh, flowing counter-melody of the Shepherds are not too happily placed among the rich, late-romantic harmonies and modulations of their setting. The later part of the work, from the Chorus of Believers to the end, is somewhat pompous and overbearing, with too liberal an employment of Wolf's favourite modulations—modulations that could at times become almost an obsession with him.

The use of naïve melodies in folk-style in combination with Wagnerian harmonies gives the music an effect akin to that of Humperdinck's, and indeed the whole piece, in theme and in treatment, resembles some colourful dream interlude in a Humperdinckian opera.

Christnacht was fairly well received at Mannheim, both by the public and by the critics. After the performance Wolf was called for, made his bow, and received two tributes in the shape of laurel wreaths. But he was not himself altogether happy about either the performance or the work. Humperdinck, who had come from Frankfurt for the occasion and encountered Wolf at a rehearsal on the morning of 9th April, afterwards noted briefly in his diary that the latter seemed despondent over his *Christnacht*. On the day after the performance Wolf expressed his partial disappointment in a letter to Heinrich Rauchberg. 'It was only a *succès d'estime*,' he told this friend. . . . 'The blame for that may perhaps be assigned to me as well as to the Mannheim orchestra. Anyway, the trouble lay in the orchestra, where from time to time curious things were to be heard.' Many passages, he admitted, had sounded badly because they were too heavily scored, but the orchestra for their part had done nothing to hide these defects by discretion and restraint in their playing.

Afterwards, in Vienna, he told Ferdinand Löwe that he recognized the faults of his scoring in both *Christnacht* and *Penthesilea*. *Christnacht* was offered for performance after this at Cologne, Vienna and Graz, with the proviso, in at least one of these cases, that some alterations in the scoring would first be necessary. Nothing came of any of these projects; the firm of Schott decided not to publish the work, and Wolf himself later on lost interest in it. It was first printed after his death, after revision of the scoring by Ferdinand Foll and Max Reger.

Since Wolf's previous visit to Mannheim his friend Grohe had married and removed to nearby Philippsburg. After the *Christnacht* performance he went there to stay for about a fortnight as the first guest that the Grohes had entertained in their new home. Jeanne Grohe was the daughter of Jean Becker, of Mannheim, the violinist and leader of the Florentine Quartet, and her brother was Hugo Becker, the cellist; she herself was an excellent pianist. She and Wolf quickly became very friendly. During all his visit Wolf was in the best of humours, and at Frau Grohe's request, however late the hour, would willingly undertake to play his own songs, an act of *Die Meistersinger* or a Beethoven sonata. On one occasion he even played Brahms's D major Symphony as a piano duet with his hostess —which speaks volumes for the influence she had so quickly won over him. With Grohe himself he played, in arrangements for four hands, the *Siegfried Idyll*, several of Bruckner's symphonies, and the Symphony in F major by Goetz—another composer of whose work he had no very high opinion.

On 20th April he left Philippsburg for Frankfurt, where Humperdinck met him at the station. In Humperdinck's dwelling Wolf played through his *Spanish Song Book* and after an agreeable evening he passed the night there on a sofa. Perhaps because he could not sleep, he spent the whole night in studying the score of *Parsifal* by moonlight. It seems that Humperdinck's house was to Wolf in some way suggestive of the Alhambra—perhaps furnished in Moorish style, or containing mementoes of Humperdinck's travels in Spain—and that in this atmosphere, bathed in brilliant moonlight, he fell into a mood of romantic ecstasy over the score of *Parsifal*.

A letter from Humperdinck to Wette, written on the 23rd of this month, gives insight into the relationship of these two men to Wolf and the impressions they were forming from their contacts with him.

Wolf on Monday spent the night upon my sofa and waking delighted himself with the splendour of my moonlit 'Alhambra dwelling.' He has almost killed me with his 'Spanish' songs. I hope that he soon finds occasion to proceed with an opera, for in them I find no advance at all upon his Mörike, Goethe, Eichendorff. His style will, I fear, with his uncontrollable creative impulse, become mannered if he continues much longer at this *genre*. He is and remains a capital fellow, intercourse with whom brings one only profit. He sends his best greetings to you. When he has further need of you he will certainly write to you again. In that naïve men of genius are fortunate, as they never need put themselves to inconvenience. What I showed him from *Hänsel und Gretel* pleased him very much.

It is worth remarking in this connection that although Wolf's correspondence with Humperdinck bears witness to the warmth of their friendship, on Wolf's side almost every letter asks Humperdinck to do something for him—to forward some cigars left behind after a visit, to write articles about his compositions for the *Frankfurter Zeitung*, to give him hospitality for a few nights, to intervene with Schott's on his behalf, or to give him information about Strecker's attitude to his works. Humperdinck, for Wolf, was a dear friend, but essentially a musical journalist and publisher's adviser, who could be very useful to him, just as Wette and others were poets who might perhaps supply him with the long-sought libretto. This attitude of Wolf's explains, though it cannot excuse, the unpleasant things he later said and wrote about *Hänsel und Gretel*. In the end it was Humperdinck, and not Wolf, who achieved a brilliant operatic success and became a rich man almost overnight, and it was hard for Wolf, conscious as he was of his own much greater genius, to see the lesser man successful in his place.

As it happened, Wolf himself played a small part in Humperdinck's subsequent triumph, for when, during this visit to Frankfurt in 1891, he was shown some of the music for *Hänsel und Gretel*, a play by Adelheid Wette, he advised Humperdinck to set the whole book to music, instead of isolated passages of it, and was thus responsible for the eventual operatic form of the work.

On 21st April Humperdinck accompanied Wolf on a business trip to Schott's at Mainz, where hopes that the publisher would purchase *Christnacht* were disappointed, after which they parted, Humperdinck returning to Frankfurt and Wolf to Philippsburg. On the 22nd he visited Karlsruhe, where he spent an evening with Mottl, without, however, being able to persuade him to take an active interest in his work. He came away somewhat disillusioned about this friend of his Conservatoire days. Next day he was back at Philippsburg

again. On the 24th he finally left the Grohes' hospitable house
for Tübingen, where for a few days he was to stay with the Kauffmanns.

In the course of this visit he went, with Kauffmann and Schmid, to
Urach, hallowed by its Mörike associations, and in spite of none too
favourable weather received an unforgettable impression. On the
way back by carriage to Metzingen, the railway station for Urach,
fairly late in the evening, the Brahms question cropped up again in
conversation between Schmid and Wolf. Although Schmid was no
out-and-out Brahmsian, he could by no means accept Wolf's violent
opinions and, as neither would give way, a somewhat heated discussion arose. Wolf declared that his attitude was in no way
influenced by personal motives, that it was the 'falsity' of Brahms's
music that was the cause of his aversion, and said finally: 'If you
have left any residue of sympathy for Brahms, then you are not ripe
for my music.' He turned in the dark carriage to appeal to Kauffmann: 'And what do *you* say about these things?' There was no
reply—Kauffmann was asleep, or pretending to be. In the train on
the way back to Tübingen further discussion of the Brahms question
was once and for all abandoned and Wolf recovered his good
humour, but it was notable that in giving proofs of his knowledge of
palmistry, he read in Kauffmann's hand everything that he could wish
for, but could promise little good fortune to Schmid.

The day after this excursion there was a 'musical academy,' as Wolf
described it to Grohe, at Kauffmann's house. 'Programme: Wolf.
Performer: Wolf. Audience: Wolfians.' Yet among Kauffmann's
pedagogic friends there were some with whom he was clearly not in
sympathy, and some persuasion was necessary before he would
consent to perform his songs. It was as if he hesitated to lay bare
his inmost thoughts before strangers, who were perhaps assembled
more out of curiosity than from real sympathy with his work. He
seemed also to have the idea that some of these people, richer and of
better social standing than himself, looked down upon him. Schmid
found him on the morning of the gathering sitting at the piano,
engrossed with a tune from Lortzing's *Waffenschmied*, 'Riches alone
are worth nothing.' Intentionally he included in his programme
for the evening the *Spottlied* from *Wilhelm Meister*, 'Ich armer
Teufel, Herr Baron,' and he read and sang it in markedly ironic
manner. He was extremely rude to a certain Prof. F., whom he
suspected of being unduly proud of his noble descent. The professor

* K

recommended an opera text, *Der Meisterdieb*, and began to relate the plot at some length. Wolf said: 'If the story is as boring as the manner in which you are telling it to me, I don't want to know anything about it.' When the same professor mentioned that the singer Karl Scheidemantel was a friend of his, Wolf cut him short with a remark that all singers were good for nothing. Nevertheless, the evening seems in the end to have passed off successfully. Wolf told Grohe: 'I had a regular triumph with the performance of my songs, that ought to take away the bitterness of the defeat sustained in Karlsruhe. All the people, men and women, were as if mad. I too was in my best mood, and played and sang as if possessed of the devil—at least so they declared.'

On 27th April he began his homeward journey, via Lake Constance, where he hoped to enjoy some magnificent scenery. He stayed one night at Singen. Directly upon his arrival there he climbed up to the ruined castle, and at the sight of the peaks and glaciers, all coloured in the sunset glow, and of the far-away, shining lake, he cried aloud with amazement, delight and wonder. The spectacle overwhelmed him. Then it faded, leaving him to melancholy reflections, among the ruins of past splendour, upon the transitoriness of everything earthly—the expression, this, of a spiritual malaise that increasingly beset him with the passing of the years. In this mood the worldly philosophy of Papageno seemed to him the highest wisdom. What use all the years of privation and struggle, if everything was doomed to ultimate extinction? 'Truly, one should enjoy life, and drain its sweetness to the dregs, even at the risk of remaining a pickpocket all one's days'—so he told Kauffmann in a strange letter.

Next day he paid a visit to the Rhine falls at Schaffhausen, celebrated in one of Mörike's poems, and there for three hours he revelled, in his elemental way, in the thunderous weight of tumbling water. Then he passed on to Constance, but his enjoyment of the scenery there was marred by gathering mists and clouds. While he was traversing the lake by steamer, on what should have been the most interesting part of all his journey, it began to rain and even the shores of the lake were for the most part invisible. Near Friedrichshafen a cold wind arose, with driving rain, and sent Wolf and all the other passengers below decks.

Bregenz was worst of all. The mist was so thick that it was impossible to see more than ten paces ahead and impossible to say, from the balcony of Wolf's lakeside hotel, where the land ended and the lake began. Life in such conditions was insupportable, and on 29th April he was glad to leave by train for Vienna.

Back at Döbling he scored *Denk' es o Seele* on 4th May. On 10th May the deferred performance of *Dem Vaterland* took place at Stuttgart. The composer was afterwards sent an honorarium of *5 marks*!

Depression and weariness are reflected in all Wolf's letters of this summer and autumn. To Grohe he wrote on 8th May: 'I feel myself, bodily as well as mentally, utterly exhausted. Of composing I have no longer the remotest conception. God knows how it will end. Pray for my poor soul.' The *Fest auf Solhaug* music was, even now, still incomplete. 'If only the *allegro* for the overture were written! This thought lies now like a ton weight upon my heart. But to compose without ideas—terrible! And yet this dream-like, indolent lounging about brings me to despair. If only there were a war on, or something else exciting! This idyllic vegetable existence will bring me to the grave. It is not to be borne.' He began increasingly to suffer from those prolonged bouts of catarrh and inflammation of the throat, lasting for weeks on end, that are probably correctly interpreted as the secondary symptoms of his malady. On medical advice he went to Unterach at the end of May for a change of air. Unable to smoke, forbidden to bathe, barely able to talk, he lived alone in the Ecksteins' house where formerly he had conceived many splendid songs, entertaining himself with *Don Quixote*, but otherwise wretched, brooding over the failure of his creative powers and the elusive opera.

To Kauffmann on 1st June he wrote: 'I should almost like to believe that I am come to the end of my life. I cannot possibly continue for thirty years more to write songs or music to Ibsen's dramas. And yet the eagerly desired opera will never come. I am just about at an end. May it soon be a complete one—I desire nothing more.' On 12th June he told Grohe: 'It's all over with me as a composer. I believe that I shall never write another note. So stupid and dried-up I have never found myself before in all my life. I thoroughly despise myself.'

In the middle of June he moved to Roith, near Ebensee, where his health improved a little. He suffered, however, from lack of sleep, as the very cheap lodgings he had taken turned out to be next door to a quarry, where blasting operations began at half-past three in the morning. The whole district, too, according to Wolf, 'swarmed' with cocks and hens, whose cackling and crowing drove him half mad. His thoughts, and those of his friends, still turned continually to the problem of the unwritten opera. In desperation he even discussed the possibility of advertising for a libretto in the newspapers. *Der Meisterdieb*, which had been recommended to him at Tübingen, was actually sent to him at about this time. He found it absurd, inept, hare-brained and insipid, 'the most atrocious piece of bungling since the creation of the world.' He collected, in the course of time, a small library of these impossible librettos, sent him hopefully by his friends. Otto Ludwig's *Hans Frei* was another suggestion that he rejected. He found the book prosy and old-fashioned in manner and the plot too reminiscent of Shakespeare's *Much Ado About Nothing*. A fit subject, he thought, for Lortzing rather than for Wolf.

On 18th July he left Ebensee for Bayreuth, where Humperdinck had found him accommodation for the festival period. Wolf's nerves were still in a pitiable state and he continued to suffer greatly from insomnia, with the result that he fell asleep in the opera-house during the performances. On the 19th he slept through part of the first and third acts of *Parsifal*. He lamented his lot in a series of ruefully humorous letters to Melanie Köchert.

I am eating almost nothing, and even the beer tastes bad. I no longer have a clear conception of what sleep means. One can't go to sleep before two o'clock and at four or half-past five one is roused by noises of all kinds. I am truly already quite knocked up and long for nothing more than that this Bayreuth crusade may for me come to a rapid and peaceful end. I loathe *all* the people here (except perhaps Humperdinck, who while I write this broods over a report for the *Frankfurter Zeitung* and from time to time urges me to hurry up). My circular-tour ticket makes me mad with vexation. What stupidity to set out by way of Nuremberg, when one can get the journey over in *one* day via Weiden! Now I shall have to spend a night at Nuremberg, if they won't permit me to travel by the other route. If I can travel via Weiden I shall be at Ebensee by Thursday evening, otherwise unfortunately only on Friday. Can't tell you much about the performance of *Parsifal*, as I only participated with half ears and ditto eyes. It is asserted that it was very fine and probably it was too. *Tristan* to-day. God keep me awake! Was with Levi, Porges, and Merz—they were very agreeable. Mottl not yet seen, Paumgartner avoids me—suits me well enough. Now thank God that you aren't at Bayreuth. Soon I shall be able to be human again and enjoy eating, drinking, and sleeping—ah, sleeping! To the Devil with all intellectual pleasures, when the body is knocked up. [Next day.] It was the voice of a good angel which most pressingly whispered to me *not* to go to Bayreuth. Had I only listened to this exhortation—how many trials and tribulations would have been spared me! Thus, for example, through the fault of Humperdinck, who procured me accommodation, I got to-day into an almost dangerous situation. It was after *Tristan*; the performance, which I attended in full possession of my mental and physical powers (I had previously had my sleep out in Joseph Schalk's dwelling), was almost throughout first rate. Certainly and above all Plank as Kurwenal unique and unbeatable. We were together after the performance in the Sun Restaurant until half-past one in the night—Viennese to a man and well known to each other. As I took my way back home with Franz Schalk and Löwe there was still light and quite lively activity in the beer-house in the lowest part of the building. I had of course to await the retirement of the nocturnal revellers before I could even think of sleeping. After about thirty minutes of impatient waiting it seemed to be quietening down. But scarcely had I lain down in bed when in the first storey beneath me a small child began to howl atrociously. That finally went on so long that I had to get up, dressed myself, and decided to await the morn promenading. But in order to get out into the open it was necessary to unlock two house doors and I had the key only to one of them. All my knocking, calling, and shouting for the housekeepers was in vain. So I put myself in immediate contact with the family on the first floor, which at first led to a violent dispute, interlarded with insulting language and threats of all kinds. Finally the raving fellow unlocked the door for me and I rushed out. As, however, the weather was cold and I was not exactly ideally equipped for that, I made up my mind to wake Löwe and Schalk, who were living opposite to me, in which after some exertions I succeeded. I related to them the whole story, at which they split their sides with laughing and in the end I had myself to laugh with them. The night, which I passed on a wretched sofa at their place, is reckoned, none the less, among my most evil memories. I hardly slept at all, I need scarcely mention. It is still very early, as I write these lines. Löwe and Schalk slumber peacefully while my pen runs scratching over the paper. God permit the bitter cup of the joys of Bayreuth to pass from me! This is my only wish.

Humperdinck's diary shows that Wolf on the morning of the 21st moved to a new lodging, which he hoped would be quieter, but that at nine o'clock on the following morning, after another disturbed night, he returned to ask Humperdinck to let him sleep on his sofa. On the 23rd, at four o'clock in the morning, he left Bayreuth and returned to Ebensee. On 2nd August he moved to Traunkirchen, where he found an almost ideal retreat, at very little cost, in the house of the pastor. For 12 florins a month he was given a large room with three windows, overlooking the lake, which is at its widest at Traunkirchen, and directly facing the Traunstein, on the opposite shore. The pastor allowed him to use his old Bösendorfer grand piano. But

here too he was pursued by the phantom of that unwritten opera and
the fear of having for ever lost the heavenly talent entrusted to his
keeping.   On 6th August he wrote to Kauffmann: 'You ask me
about the opera!   Dear God, I should be content if I could write the
tiniest song, let alone an opera!   I firmly believe that I am finished—
completely finished.'   In a remarkable letter to Hermann Wette on
the 13th of the same month he wrote:

> Since about a fortnight ago I dwell in the parsonage at Traunkirchen, the
> pearl of the Traunsee and its vicinity.   Everything agreeable that a spoiled
> human child can wish for unites to prepare for me a contented lot.   Deepest
> peace and solitude surrounds me, the most delightful scenery, the most
> refreshing air—in short, everything that a hermit of my kind could ever
> desire.   And yet, and yet, my friend, I am the most unhappy creature on
> this earth.   Everything around me breathes felicity and peace, everything
> lives and moves and does what it has to do; only I—O God! only I live
> through the days stupid and insensible like a brute beast. . . .   It's all over
> with composing.   I cannot any longer conceive what harmony, what
> melody, is and begin already to doubt whether the compositions bearing
> my name are really by me.

He compared his fate with that of his beloved Kleist, who had said:
'Heaven gives either a whole talent or none at all.   Hell has given me
my half-talent.'   He told Kauffmann that even his growing recognition as a song-writer was a cause of distress to him, for it only
indicated that he was thought incapable of producing anything more
important.

On 12th October he returned to Vienna and took up residence
again at Döbling.   The only artistic result of his stay at Traunkirchen had been the orchestration of the *Elfenlied* from *A Midsummer Night's Dream*.   Meanwhile, some of Wolf's friends had
succeeded in interesting the Gesellschaft der Musikfreunde—or, at
any rate, some musicians connected with that body—in *Christnacht*,
but at the time of the negotiations the score of this work was at
Cologne and could not be recovered as Wüllner, who was considering
it for performance at one of the Gürzenich concerts, was away from
home and inaccessible.   Wolf seems to have put forward the
Elfenlied as an alternative to *Christnacht*, and for a time he spoke
confidently of a performance in Vienna, to take place on his birthday,
13th March, in the following year.   In this, however, he was once
again disappointed.   Wüllner, after months of delay, finally rejected
Christnacht, and the Gesellschaft der Musikfreunde decided not to
include the *Elfenlied* in their programmes for this season.   Wolf was

promised that both *Christnacht* and the *Elfenlied* would be performed
in the succeeding year, but by this time he was too thoroughly exasperated to put much reliance in any such assurances.

The Burgtheater produced *Das Fest auf Solhaug* on 21st
November. The blue pencil was freely used in Wolf's score and
what little music remained after this was, according to Wolf himself,
atrociously mangled. 'It was positively scandalous. Happily, my
music was for the most part *inaudibly* played, else the instruments
would have run away from under the hands of the musicians.'
Georg Reimers, who was to have sung Gudmund's two songs, found
them too difficult and recited the poems, instead, to a harp accompaniment. The play was withdrawn after only four performances
and Wolf was glad enough to receive 200 florins—considerably less
than he had originally expected—for his share in the production.

The completion of the *Fest auf Solhaug* score and the orchestration
of *Denk' es o Seele* and the *Elfenlied* constituted the whole of Wolf's
musical activities in the first eleven months of 1891. After the
wonderful achievements of the foregoing years, it is not surprising
that he grew dejected over this state of affairs. Although he had
from the first recognized the spasmodic nature of his inspiration and
had already experienced various periods of apparent sterility which
had in turn given place to renewed creative vigour, no recollection of
past experience was able to comfort him in present trouble. He was
a man who lived to compose; he had renounced almost everything in
life for that single purpose, because he believed in his genius, and
when he was unable to compose he was more than unhappy—he
could see no justification for his existence at all.

In the last month of this year, to his own and his friends' joyful
surprise, he succeeded in completing fifteen songs from Heyse's
Italienisches Liederbuch. The new burst of creation began on 29th
November, with *Dass doch gemalt*, and ended on 23rd December,
with *Man sagt mir, deine Mutter woll' es nicht*. These fifteen songs,
with the seven settings of poems from the same collection that had
been written in the previous year, made up the volume published in
1892. Wolf had earmarked thirty-three poems for eventual musical
setting and at first hoped to complete all these in the month of
December. But after *Man sagt mir* the muse again withdrew her
favour. It was more than four years before she relented and allowed
Wolf to complete the second part of his *Italian Song Book*.

The new songs were considered by their composer to be 'the most original and artistically consummate' of all he had written, and there has been none since to dispute this verdict. These exquisite miniatures have captivated all sensitive minds and hearts. Nothing in the *Spanish Song Book*, Wolf's last important lyrical outburst, had suggested that he would develop in this direction, towards serenity, limpidity, delicacy, and restraint. It was as if in the meantime his art had passed through a refining fire. One or two of the Keller songs had hinted at certain stylistic features of the later volume, but the *Italian Song Book*, when it came, was from first note to last the perfected expression of a wholly original musical mentality. Once again Wolf had demonstrated his extraordinary ability to develop almost a new character in response to a new poetical stimulus.

Paul Heyse's *Italienisches Liederbuch* contains sections devoted to translations of *rispetti* and *velote* (the Venetian equivalent of the *rispetto*), *ritornelle*, popular ballads, songs in folk-style and Corsican songs and death laments. In all the first part of his song-book, and, with one exception, in all the second part which followed in 1896, Wolf took his material from among the *rispetti* and *velote*.

The *rispetto* may be described as a sort of intellectual exercise for lovers in verse that is mocking, gallant or passionate. It employs an end-stopped, ten- or eleven-syllabled line, and is invariably quite short. Most of the examples set to music by Wolf consist of only six or eight lines; a few are somewhat longer. In translation into German some of the poems are given a more serious cast than is warranted by the Italian originals, but on the whole Heyse succeeded admirably in conveying their characteristic flavour. Wolf, however, undoubtedly approached the *Italienisches Liederbuch* as a collection of *German* poems. In contrast with his procedure in the majority of the Spanish songs, he made no attempt to introduce into his music any characteristically national features. An occasional suggestion of a lute accompaniment in the piano part, not essentially very different from those in the Eichendorff volume, is his sole slight concession to local colour. More than this, however; the whole emotional world of Wolf's song-book is, it is not too much to say, utterly foreign to the Italian character. He himself told Kauffmann: 'A warm heart, I can assure you, beats in the little bodies of my youngest children of the south, who, in spite of all, cannot deny their German origin. Yes, their hearts beat in German, even if the sun shines in Italian (as the moon in French in *Der Tambour*).' Heyse translated the words of these poems into the German language;

Wolf translated their *sentiments* into a new language of feeling. It was one of marvellous richness, beauty and expressiveness. Perhaps because of the anonymity of the verses, because there was here no revered shade of a great poet compelling the musician's absorption in his world of thought and feeling, Wolf was able to put much of *himself* into his Italian songs. That is not to say that their nature is subjective, as had been the Heine and Lenau songs of his early manhood. Personal confessions they are not, but, taking these translations as a starting-point, and without greatly concerning himself with their original character, the composer allowed his imagination to play about them freely. Often he imposed his own will upon the words, expressing by the virtuosity of his handling of the vocal line shades of meaning and emotion that certainly never occurred either to the unknown authors of the original Italian poems or to Heyse. Examples of this will be noticed later. Everything that Wolf touched he refined and enriched. Almost all the serious songs became intensified in expression in his hands. The emotion, for instance, of the song *Der Mond hat eine schwere Klag' erhoben* is of a different order—infinitely deeper and more concentrated—than that of the Italian poem from which it arose. Here is the poem:

> La luna s'è venuta a lamentare
> Inde la faccia del divino amore;
> Dice che in cielo non ci vuol più stare,
> Che tolto gliel'avete lo splendore.
> E si lamenta, e si lamenta forte,
> L'ha conto le sue stelle, non son tutte.
> E gliene manca due, e voi l'avete:
> Son que' du' occhi che in fronte tenete.

It is only a fancy, a compliment, a piece of gallantry, in accordance with the rules of the game of love. Heyse, by introducing the speaker's own emotion, in the 'die mich verblendet' of his last line, for which the Italian has no equivalent, prepared the way for Wolf's entirely serious treatment of the whole poem. But the extra intensity of the song is Wolf's own. It is noteworthy that Heyse did not care for these songs, although he admired some of Wolf's other work. He listened with ears attuned to the music of the south, and of this there is only a distant echo in the *Italian Song Book*. After merging his own personality almost wholly in those of Mörike and Goethe, after making a brave but not entirely successful attempt, in the Spanish songs, to get under the skin of an alien race, Wolf here gave free rein to his own imagination and his own feelings. We can only be thankful that he did so, even if it does upset all our notions of his relationship with his poets, even if it means that we must recognize that some of the richest treasures of all music came into existence as the result of a sort of inspired misunderstanding.

Auch kleine Dinge, which opens the *Italian Song Book*, serves as a beautifully appropriate introduction to a collection of tiny jewels of song. The theme is the virtue of little things—the beauty of the pearl, the savour of the olive, the scent of the rose. It is not thought of as a love-song, though in the Italian original the words were almost certainly intended as an indirect compliment to a *petite* mistress. For Wolf, and for us, their face value is sufficient. The song is universally beloved for its almost miraculous daintiness and delicacy of feeling. A chromatically descending bass weaves a thread of melancholy—the melancholy of beauty that fades—through the texture of the lovely composition. At the end we hold our breath to hear that final phrase for the voice, which seems to exhale all the fragrance of the rose of which it speaks.

Mir ward gesagt is a song of parting, to the even rhythm of the footsteps that lead lover from lover. So simple a device as a down-ward-stepping bass, in the pianist's left hand, that strains away from the generally upward-tending phrases of the voice part, while the pianist's right hand maintains an almost unbroken sequence of quaver chords, is sufficient to allow Wolf to express a world of untold tenderness and longing. The poignant dissonances that occur as the result of the movement of the parts, in voice and piano, tear at the heart-strings. *Gesegnet sei, durch den die Welt entstund* is an extreme instance of the clarity and simplicity of means whereby the composer of the Italian songs attains the profoundest expressive ends. A figure of three notes is sufficient to suggest unmistakably the gesture of God's all-powerful hand in the act of creation. The singer passes from the general praise of His handiwork to rapt contemplation of one particular detail of it—the face of the Beloved. The emotional climax of the song is the *pianissimo* passage 'er schuf die Schönheit und dein Angesicht.' The voice is suddenly hushed in adoration, while the piano maintains its gentle throbbing, and the motive of 'creation' rings quietly in bass and treble. *Ihr seid die Allerschönste* is a more outspoken utterance, and is given a broader sweep and richer colouring. It contains one of Wolf's boldest strokes. The line 'der Dom von Siena muss sich vor dir neigen' (in the Italian original 'Lo porti il vanto del duomo di Siena') means in Heyse no more than that the cathedral of Siena is surpassed in beauty by the singer's mistress. But Wolf interprets the metaphorical 'neigen' *literally*, as is evident from the contour of his vocal line (compare 'und neiget Euch' in *Und steht Ihr früh am Morgen auf*), and with proud and rapturous hyperbole calls forth an image of the cathedral itself in the act of bowing low before a greater marvel. This might easily have become ludicrous, but the passion and sincerity of the song carry it off triumphantly.

As has already been suggested, *Der Mond hat eine schwere Klag' erhoben* treats a fanciful poem with deep seriousness. No trace of a smile is discernible on the face of Wolf's sore-smitten lover, who seems to have brooded over these thoughts until he has come to believe that the moon is in fact lamenting the loss from the sky of two of its fairest stars. 'With how sad steps, O moon, thou climb'st the skies!'—that is very near the feeling of this exquisite song. The graceful, lilting measure of *Nun lass uns Frieden schliessen* is enchanting. The vocal line, more than is usual in the *Italian Song Book*, contributes towards the rhythmic flow of the whole, but the view of Eugen Schmitz, who sees this piece as something simple and folk-song-like, is a very superficial one. The voice part is studded with felicities of declamation and those added meanings that Wolf permitted himself in these songs. It is doubtful whether *all* its subtleties have ever been brought out in performance, unless it was by the composer himself. The song is a lovers' reconciliation, a plea for a peace that, to judge by the smiling sweetness of the music, has long since ceased to be seriously endangered. The third and fourth lines of the poem may be quoted in their musical setting to illustrate the extraordinary sensitiveness of the vocal line and its ability to hint at shades of meaning that would never occur to the ordinary reader of the verses:

EX 15

Wenn du——nicht willst, will ich mich dir er - ge - ben;

wie könn - ten wir uns—— auf den Tod be -krie-gen?

The lover lingers affectionately over the 'du,' amid the generally speech-like declamation of the rest of the passage, but the real point of the gentle emphasis given to this word is only felt in conjunction with the later prolongation of the normally unaccented word 'mich.' This prolongation is only for an extra quaver but it covers the second main accent within the bar and this, together with the rise of the voice to E flat, the highest point reached in this phrase, suffices to give 'mich' a certain prominence. A tone of mild reproach is thus imparted to the passage—'If *you* are unwilling, *I myself* will yield'— as though the speaker were hinting that it was really the *other's* part to make the first peace overtures, that there lies some special virtue, of loving forgiveness and swallowed pride, in his, or as is more likely, in *her*, surrender. And then, how eloquent is the line that follows! By slightly underlining 'wir' and 'uns'—pronouns that would be passed over lightly in any straightforward reading of the line—these two little words themselves become a sort of whispered endearment, making it seem indeed unthinkable that two such devoted lovers could disagree for long. 'How *could* we—*you and I!*—continue to quarrel?' is the sense of the line as Wolf declaims it, and although the difference between this and the normal reading may seem slight, it is sufficient to bring the words thrillingly to life, by suggesting the inflections of the voice in the most intimate exchange of thoughts with the loved one. Another subtlety of the same kind, very easily over-looked, is the similar slight emphasis given to the word 'ein' in the last couplet of the whole poem:

> Meinst du, dass, was so grossen Herrn gelingt,
> Ein Paar zufriedner Herzen nicht vollbringt?

The effect here is that the indefinite article is given for a moment the force of the numeral, and the sense of the passage charmingly altered from 'a pair' to '*just one* pair' of contented hearts, who may surely find peace together.

The regularly end-stopped lines of equal length that are character-istic of the *rispetto* undoubtedly influenced considerably Wolf's musical style in the *Italian Song Book*. A song like *Der Mond hat eine schwere Klag' erhoben*, which is built up from beginning to end of balanced two-bar phrases, corresponding to the couplets of the verses, shows this very clearly. After the declamatory freedom of other volumes the effect is not unlike that of a poet expressing himself within the formal limits of a sonnet. Elsewhere Wolf was able to split up the ten- or eleven-syllabled line into shorter phrases; it was only very rarely, when Heyse did not find it possible to retain in his translation the normally end-stopped line of the original, that he had the opportunity of spreading a broader wing.　One such opportunity he seized magnificently in *Dass doch gemalt all' deine Reize wären*, another wonderful, richly coloured love-song.　The fifth and sixth lines of the poem are forged together in Wolf's setting into one mighty sweeping phrase, strikingly different from the general style of the volume.　More remarkable still is the effect in *Selig ihr Blinden*, where each of the musical phrases encompasses *two* lines of the poem. The result is that this song does not seem to belong to the *Italian Song Book* at all.　In other ways, too, in its intensity of feeling, and in the inexorable, ruthless movement of its piano part, *Selig ihr Blinden* claims affinity, rather, with the Spanish songs.

Ernest Newman, in his valuable notes to the Hugo Wolf Society's gramophone records, has called attention to the way in which the Italian songs are divided between the sexes, most of the serious love-songs going to the men, while the women are exhibited in moods of scorn or mockery, resentment, or humorous tolerance of their lovers' defects; or, if the women are deeply in love, they are nearly always unhappy, in contrast with the numerous songs of contented love given to the men.　'Hardly ever,' says Mr. Newman, 'does Wolf allow the women to soar to the heights or compass the depths of forthright passion, as he does the men.'　This is so, although there are exceptions, but it is the result, not of deliberate selection by the composer, but of the nature of the material with which he worked. It is, as an examination of Heyse's *Italienisches Liederbuch* makes clear, a reflection of the prevalent moods of the *rispetto*.

In *Wer rief dich denn?* a woman gives vent to her anger and distress at her lover's evident lack of enthusiasm.　She sends him away, protesting violently that she has never called him, never wanted to see him, never been interested in him.　This song provides a remarkable example of Wolf's psychological insight.　It would have been quite possible to set the poem as a straightforward outburst of scorn. There is nothing in the words themselves indicative of any mental conflict in the speaker.　The character as portrayed by Wolf, however, is made incomparably more interesting and convincing by subtle indications that she is torn by conflicting emotions.　For all her protests, she is at heart desperately unhappy, and she betrays this from time to time.　After the scorn of the opening, we get an unmistakable expression of her real feelings at 'Wer hiess dich kommen, *wenn* es dir zur Last?'　'Who asked you to come, *if* it is a burden to you?'　The emphasis on 'wenn' is inexplicable except on the assumption that she still secretly hopes that it is not, after all, a burden to her lover to attend her. The thought of her rival causes her anger to flare up again, but several times in the course of the song she slips back into sad self-pity and longing. She breaks down in the last phrase of all in the voice part, although the piano postlude seems to indicate that her anger and indignation are renewed.[1]

Du denkst mit einem Fädchen is another of this series of wonderfully vivid little character-sketches, and again Wolf gives an original twist of his own to the poem. A girl taunts a too confident lover. 'You are quite right,' she says, 'I *am* in love—but as it happens, not with *you.*' Wolf repeats this last line of the poem, 'Ich bin verliebt, doch eben nicht in dich,' but gives his second setting of it an entirely different character. 'Ich bin verliebt' dies away this time in a dreamy *pianissimo*, a simulated swoon of delight, before the wicked, laughing malice of 'doch eben nicht in dich' delivers the knock-out blow to the lover's pretensions. The graceful, kittenish *Nein, junger Herr* and *Mein Liebster ist so klein*, the decidedly vexed complaint of one whose lover is undersized, are other examples of this type of woman's song. Very remarkable is the depiction, in the piano postlude of the latter song, of the diminutive lover's eager, tiptoe-straining, upward stretching for a kiss. It is not easy to say whether *Wie lange schon* and *Ihr jungen Leute* are entirely free from malice. Certainly the Italian originals of the poems are mocking in intent, but Wolf seems to smile *at*, rather than *with*, the characters represented in his songs. The over delicate soldier lover of *Ihr jungen Leute* and his violinist counterpart in *Wie lange schon* are presented to us with a certain naïveté.

Geselle, woll'n wir uns in Kutten hüllen stands somewhat apart from the rest of the Italian volume. It has been aptly described as a scene out of Boccaccio's *Decameron*. The appalling cynicism of 'die Welt dem lassen, den sie mag ergötzen,' the caricature of the sanctimonious whine of the begging monk, the unctuousness of the proposal to take the sick girl's 'confession'—these things show Wolf's genius for characterization at its best. The song demands, however, an artist of the calibre of a Chaliapin for its interpretation.

---

[1] Paul Müller is certainly wrong in his view of this song. He objects to the singing of the final 'Wer hat dich herbestellt?' in a tone of melting distress, as if entreating pity. He thinks the *piano* and 'zurückhaltend' of the end indicate repressed menace. (See the introduction to the Peters edition of the *Italian Song Book.*) But the *diminuendo* on the word 'herbestellt' surely makes the 'menacing' interpretation of this phrase utterly impossible. Müller does not consider the earlier phrase 'wenn es dir zur Last' and other indications of Wolf's conception of this character.

Each one of these miniature masterpieces has its own particular virtues; hardly anywhere in all the volume does Wolf's inspiration falter. In mood the songs are extraordinarily diverse, but the composer's imagination was equal to every demand that was made upon it. He hit off the spirited banter of *Ein Ständchen Euch zu bringen* with the same assurance and success as he did the passionate urgency of *Man sagt mir, deine Mutter woll' es nicht* and the languorous, amorous contentment of *Und willst du deinen Liebsten sterben sehen*. This latter song is one of his supreme achievements. The mood is one of trance-like, almost hypnotized rapture. The lover is in thrall to the beauty of his mistress's long golden hair. The piano part of the song is a notable example of the kind of creative development of which Wolf was so great a master. The whole grows out of a little figure of three chords, such as might have arisen from the contemplation of the slow, rhythmical movement of a woman's arm in the act of combing her hair. In the second half of the song this figure, in diminished note values, quickens, expands, floats upward, and is elaborated into a lovely, shimmering, waving background to the voice. The rhythm and general outline of the germ phrase remain the same, while the melodic intervals and the harmonies are constantly changing.

Heb' auf dein blondes Haupt is another exquisite love-song. One curious feature of the Italian *rispetto* is a tendency to say the same thing twice, or three times, in different words, or sometimes, even, in the *same* words in a different order. So, in *Heb' auf dein blondes Haupt*, no one of the four weighty matters that the lover has to communicate to his mistress is of greater import than the others, for they all amount to the same thing—'I love you.' Accordingly, this song has no emotional climax; from beginning to end it is uniformly expressive of an unspeakable tenderness and adoration. The concentrated essence of the song, after the voice has ceased, is conveyed in the surpassingly beautiful piano postlude. *Wir haben beide lange Zeit geschwiegen* provides another example of such almost static emotion. It is perhaps worth while reproducing the Italian original of this poem, which shows clearly this characteristic of the verse-form:

> È tanto tempo ch' eravamo muti!
> Eccoci ritornati alla favella.
> E gli angeli del cielo son venuti,
> L'hanno posta la pace in tanta guerra.

E son venuti gli angioli di Dio,
L'hanno posta la pace nel cor mio.
E son venuti gli angioli d'amore,
L'hanno posta la pace nel mio core.

The fifth and sixth lines, and the seventh and eighth, are only variations on the third and fourth, at the end of which everything that is
essential in the poem has already been said.   Wolf made of Heyse's
translation of this *rispetto* a truly wonderful song.   The two opening
lines of the poem he treated as a slow introduction, with the voice
part almost wholly in monotone, and with sullen octaves in the piano.
Then, when the lovers' quarrel has been made up, all the rest of the
song is given up to the angels of peace.   A tender animation and
warmth comes over the music, and, while the voice sings beatifically
of the heavenly blessing, a melodic figure of four notes, so simple and
lovely that it seems incredible that no one should have discovered it
before Wolf did, is developed in the piano part, rising and soaring
somewhat in the manner of the three-note motive of *Und willst du
deinen Liebsten sterben sehen.*   There are no words to describe music
such as this.   Here, and in *Auch kleine Dinge, Der Mond hat eine
schwere Klag' erhoben, Nun lass uns Frieden schliessen, Mein Liebster
singt* and half a dozen other things in this volume, Wolf as an artist
had attained the rarest of all distinctions—he could point with pride
to these tiny, jewelled blossoms of song and say: 'Here is perfection.'

The Italian songs are as fresh to-day as on the day when they came
into existence and no amount of repetition can impair their charm.
It is impossible to imagine that they can ever fade or lose their
significance while civilized humanity endures.

XII

LEAN YEARS

BOTH Wolf's friends and his publishers were anxious that his music should be made known by a series of concerts in Germany, and, on Strecker's advice, Berlin was chosen for the first of these. The concert agent, Hermann Wolff, was interested in the proposal, and after various changes of plan it was finally agreed that Wolf should make a personal appearance as accompanist at a recital of his songs in the Singakademie on 24th February 1892. The singers were to be Ferdinand Jäger, without whom a Wolf concert appeared to the composer's friends unthinkable, and Friederike Mayer, a young mezzo-soprano, who had been a pupil of Mme Artôt in Berlin. Wolf had met her at Schur's house, had been initially pleased with the way she approached his music and had formed a high opinion of her artistry. He had written his Keller songs in 1890 with her type of voice in mind.

An engagement to sing Wolf's songs with Wolf himself at the piano was not to be lightly undertaken. He paid no regard at all to the presence of an audience, and if his artistic feelings, or his abnormally sensitive ear, were outraged by a slip of memory, an error of taste, or lapse of intonation or rhythm, he would rebuke the singer audibly even during a public performance. If he thought his associate showed a tendency to sentimentalize one of his songs he would begin the accompaniment at twice the normal tempo. Untimely applause he would cut short with cascades of *fortissimo* chord sequences, and he had other methods of showing his displeasure, such as stamping his feet on the platform or slamming down the lid of the piano. One of Wolf's letters shows that he formed the opinion that Frl. Mayer did not work hard enough at his songs and gave too much thought to the technical accomplishment of her singing and too little to questions of interpretation. It should, however, be remembered to her credit that she was the first singer, apart from Jäger himself, to co-operate with Wolf in the public performance of his songs.

The group of friends within the Wagner Verein who, under the leadership of Gustav Schur, had pledged themselves to Wolf's

financial support, provided 500 florins towards the expenses of the
visit to Berlin and prevailed upon Wolf, as the advancement of his
art was concerned rather than his personal fortune, to accept the
money.   So that nothing should be lacking that might contribute to
the good impression he hoped to make on the Berliners, they also
fitted him out with evening clothes and a top hat.   Behind the
ironically humorous attitude towards this outfit expressed in some of
Wolf's letters may be discerned a naïve pride.   'The good Berliners
may perhaps shrug their shoulders about my songs,' he told Jeanne
Grohe, 'they will certainly not do so about my dress suit.   For it
fits.'

He left Vienna for Berlin on 18th February, intending to spend a
few days before the concert in seeing the sights and making new
acquaintances.   He was well provided with letters of introduction.
Fritz Volbach, who had met Wolf at Mainz in the previous year, and
who had published an article on his songs in the *Allgemeine Musikzeitung*, wrote to Lessmann, the editor of this paper, on Wolf's
behalf, and provided also, through Dr. Strecker, information about
influential critics in Berlin.   But it was Jeanne Grohe who did most
for him in this matter.   She supplied a handwritten 'Führer durch
Berlin für Hugo Wolf' with many pages of names and addresses of
acquaintances of hers in the city.   Through the attentions of his
friends Wolf found himself overwhelmed with invitations to teas and
dinners.   He suffered badly from boredom at some of the more
aristocratic gatherings, but found consolation among the Austrian
colony, notably at the house of Richard Genée.   Genée was then
living in Berlin with his daughter Anna, who had been a close friend
of Heinrich Rauchberg's first wife.

The concert itself seemed pursued by persistent ill luck.   First of
all Jäger, who was suffering from gout, sent a telegram to say he could
not take part.   A Berlin tenor named Grahl agreed to take his place
—'not a star of the first magnitude,' as Wolf found, but nevertheless
'a very decent singer.'   Wolf worked hard to teach Grahl eight of his
songs.   Then on the very morning of the concert Friederike Mayer
awoke feverish and completely hoarse.   After three hours' rehearsal
with a Frl. Finkenstein, a last-minute substitute, Wolf believed that
his concert would still be able to take place, but in the end the
substitute also withdrew from the engagement out of sheer nervous-
ness and the concert had to be deferred until 5th March.   Wolf was
200 marks out of pocket over the hire of the hall.

The interval was filled with rehearsals and with a constant round of visits and entertainments. The longer Wolf stayed in Berlin the better he liked it. He formed many valuable new friendships. One of the most important was that with Baron Lipperheide, the wealthy proprietor of the *Modenwelt*, a fashion paper published in many different countries, with an enormous circulation. For the Baroness Frieda von Lipperheide Wolf had the greatest respect and affection; he afterwards dedicated to her his Shakespearian *Elfenlied*. In Siegfried Ochs, the conductor of the Berlin Philharmonic choir, Wolf found a kindred spirit. Ochs, the greatest choral conductor of his time, was also an extremely entertaining and witty companion, and Wolf much enjoyed his gift of musical parody, even when he found himself the victim of it. Ochs readily agreed to perform the *Elfenlied* in Berlin, a promise which he fulfilled two years later. Other valuable friendships were formed with Richard Sternfeld, one of the directors of the Berlin Wagner Verein, and with Heinrich Welti and his wife, the opera singer Emilie Herzog-Welti. Wolf's first visit to the Weltis began under a cloud. He made an unfavourable impression by his taciturnity, by his attitude of suspicion and mistrust, and by his disgruntled remarks about the lack of a grand piano. But when he began to sing his Mörike songs the atmosphere soon cleared. Frau Herzog-Welti was attracted by the *Elfenlied* and repeated it at sight without error. Wolf in his turn was delighted at this and because she and her husband shared his own enthusiasm for the *Erstes Liebeslied eines Mädchens*. After two hours the three were already good friends. Frau Herzog-Welti afterwards did much for Wolf's music in Germany. He spoke of her to his friends as 'a charming person and a great artist.'

Under Weingartner Wolf heard a splendid performance of *Die Meistersinger*. He also attended one of Bülow's concerts where among other things he heard 'a horrible piece of music'—the *Macbeth* of Richard Strauss. He slipped out of the concert-hall before Brahms's second Symphony began.

The Berlin Wagner Verein arranged for Wolf to give a private recital of his songs, before the public concert. It took place in the afternoon of 3rd March in the Duysenscher Saal. About a hundred people were invited, and an afternoon was decided upon so that the critics would be able to attend. Sternfeld, who was primarily responsible for these arrangements, was painfully surprised when he arrived with Wolf at the hall, to find that only a dozen people had put in an appearance, and among these there was not one of the critics. Max Friedländer, the singer and Schubert scholar, was there, but most of the others were musical amateurs. Among them were Fritz Mauthner, the writer, and Paul Müller, a school-teacher who afterwards founded the Berlin Hugo Wolf Verein. The programme began with a group of songs from Grahl, which did not make much impression. Grahl then had to hurry away to another engagement, leaving Wolf in sole command of the field. A small, select gathering like this was really far more to his taste than the hoped for critical assembly would have been, and he gave of his best. He first read the poems aloud, drawing attention to their beauties, and then played and sang his settings in his incomparable manner. After reading through Mörike's *Auf einer Wanderung* he asked: 'Isn't that beautiful enough to make you weep?' and before embarking upon *Der Feuerreiter* he remarked: 'Now I'll sing you something that will make your hair stand on end.' As always, the listeners forgot the unlovely voice and the deficiencies of the singing, as singing, in the passionate intensity of his interpretations.

Two days later the public concert at length took place. It was a decided success. Although the audience was not large, it gave Wolf and his music a cordial reception. Only two of the songs were encored, but the warmth of the applause would have justified the repetition of at least six, if Wolf had been more gracious. Except for a small lapse in *Der Tambour*, Grahl, within his limitations, did well enough, but Wolf was displeased with Friederike Mayer. She was still incompletely recovered from the illness that had caused the postponement of the concert, and perhaps Wolf should have given more consideration to this fact. But the real cause of his displeasure was that on the concert platform she took liberties with his music which he had already forbidden during the rehearsals. During the performance of *In dem Schatten meiner Locken* he spoke angrily to her. The song was admirably suited to Frl. Mayer's dark, velvety, mezzo-soprano voice and the audience tried to obtain its repetition. This Wolf utterly refused to allow. In the artists' room he strode ill-humouredly up and down with his hands in his pockets, while the singer alone acknowledged the applause. He went out separately later to receive an ovation. Frl. Mayer left Berlin immediately afterwards and never saw Wolf again. But the artistic success of the concert was indisputable and afterwards, in the Hotel Monopol, the composer was overwhelmed with congratulations and real or pretended admiration. The Baron and Baroness Lipperheide were there with Weingartner and his wife, the physicist Helmholtz, and other celebrities. Hermann Wolff, the agent, gleamed with satisfaction, in spite of a financial deficit.

The Berlin critics were on the whole favourably impressed, although few of them showed any real understanding of Wolf's importance. They patronizingly spoke of his 'very considerable talent,' recommended that his songs should be given 'attentive consideration,' and discovered that he was a successor to Jensen, rather than a follower of Brahms. Wolf told Kauffmann that in intelligence, knowledge and power of judgment, his critics left almost everything to be desired. Although they had for the most part treated him well, they remained asses.

It goes almost without saying that operatic projects were discussed during Wolf's Berlin visit. He was eager to meet Hermann Sudermann, with whose *Frau Sorge*, *Der Katzensteg*, and *Sodoms Ende* he had been very much impressed. He thought he might find in this writer the collaborator he had been so long seeking. But, in spite of his realistic novels, Sudermann turned out to be altogether too well groomed and worldly a person to concern himself with the troubles of a relatively obscure musician from Vienna. Wolf was twice in the same company as the novelist. On the first occasion, at a dinner, he was scarcely able to exchange a word with him, and by the second occasion, at Fritz Mauthner's house on 7th March, he had himself lost all interest in the meeting, as Sternfeld had told him that Sudermann had no understanding of operatic requirements and would certainly not agree to write a libretto. It is typical of Wolf that after this disappointment he no longer found much to admire in Sudermann's novels and plays. Another important suggestion was put forward during one of Wolf's visits to the house of Richard Genée. It will be remembered that he had, through Rauchberg, got in touch with Genée when he was considering Shakespeare's *The Tempest* as an operatic subject. Now in Berlin he played his Spanish songs and both Genée and his daughter at once came to the same conclusion— that Wolf was the man to make good use of *Manuel Venegas*, the German translation of Alarcon's novel *El Niño de la Bola*. This book had been sent to Genée by F. Zell, his collaborator, and he was himself greatly interested in its operatic possibilities, although he had had to recognize that his own musical talents did not permit him to venture on such a tragic subject. He therefore showed it to Wolf, and the latter, who had already considered another of Alarcon's novels, *El Sombrero de tres Picos*, for use as an opera, fell at once into a fever of enthusiasm for *El Niño de la Bola*. The idea of writing an opera on this subject pursued him during the whole of the rest of his life.

On 9th March Wolf was back in Vienna and, as before, he fell ill as soon as he arrived. He was put to bed at the Köcherts' house in the Mehlmarkt with fever and a badly inflamed throat, and there he remained for about a week. He got up for his birthday on the 13th but was back in bed again on the following day. It was the 19th before he felt well enough to return to his hermitage at Döbling.

He had reason to be well content with the results of his trip to Berlin. He had laid the foundations of a reputation there and on this foundation his new friends were not slow to build. In the *Magazin für Literatur*, a periodical edited by Fritz Mauthner, Richard Sternfeld had published on 12th March an enthusiastic article, 'Ein neuer Liederfrühling,' the first important piece of writing about Wolf's work to be printed in north Germany, and on 8th April Emilie Herzog included five of his songs in the programme of a recital in Berlin and achieved with them a remarkable popular success. In Vienna, in the Bösendorfersaal on 11th April, Jäger made amends for his involuntary defection from the Berlin concert by singing twelve of Wolf's songs to Joseph Schalk's accompaniment. No less than eight of them had to be repeated. It was a real triumph; Wolf himself, who was in the audience, described the success as 'colossal': 'It seems in fact as if I were becoming fashionable. It is high time.' In May the Graz Wagner Verein instituted a 'Hugo Wolf Evening,' at which August Krämer and his wife, Marie Krämer-Widl, sang eighteen songs, the piano parts being played by Potpeschnigg.

At Döbling in April and May Wolf was occupied in scoring his *Italian Serenade*, originally written for string quartet in 1887, for small orchestra. The existing movement, in its new form, was now intended as the first movement of a larger work. On 2nd April Wolf told Kauffmann: 'At present I am working on the instrumentation of the first movement of an *Italian Serenade* for small orchestra, for which two further movements must be composed.' On 19th May he told Potpeschnigg: 'I have recast the *Serenade* for complete orchestra, but am not yet at the end of the task.' Perhaps 'the task' here is the larger scheme, and not merely the orchestration of the first movement. We cannot be sure. There is no evidence to show precisely when this first movement, the *Italian Serenade* as we know it to-day, was completed in its orchestral form.　It is likely enough that the scoring was finished at this time.　The idea of an orchestral *Serenade* in several movements occupied Wolf intermittently for the rest of his working life.　Fragments of a slow movement were composed in 1893, a complete new movement, of which only a sketch of the first forty-five bars has survived, was added in 1894, and about forty bars of a Tarantella finale were written in December 1897, when Wolf was in Dr. Svetlin's asylum.[1]

The *Italian Serenade* for small orchestra as we know it to-day—i.e. the first movement of the projected larger work—was published posthumously in 1903, edited by Max Reger.　Whether Reger did anything more than edit the work is a point on which there has been much confusion.　On the title-page of the score is a note: 'Die Partitur bearbeitete Max Reger,' and there has always been doubt as to the extent of Reger's share in the work.　From the first the erroneous idea got about that he was responsible for the whole orchestral arrangement, and although it is on record in Decsey's biography (vol. iii, p. 157) that Reger himself, when questioned on the point, said merely that he had ' seen the proofs through the press,' the idea persists even to-day.　The *Serenade* often appears on concert programmes with the misleading attribution 'Wolf-Reger' or 'Wolf, arranged Reger.'　Some writers [2] have come to the conclusion that Reger must have transcribed the solo part, which was originally written for cor anglais, for solo viola.　Wolf's manuscript of the orchestral version of the work, in the National Library, Vienna, allows us to dispose of all these mistaken ideas.

The manuscript shows that Wolf first gave the principal theme and a prominent part throughout the first section of the work to the cor anglais.　After the first double bar (published orchestral score p. 8, bar 8, to p. 13, bar 4) he employed the cor anglais as an ordinary orchestral instrument, without any specially prominent part.　The *second* presentation of the main theme (p. 13, from bar 4, to p. 15, bar 15), with flute counterpoint, he gave to a solo viola, the cor anglais playing with the viola for only a few bars (p. 15, bars 6–11) towards the end.　From p. 15, bar 15, the solo viola part was discontinued and the cor anglais continued to be

---

[1] For details of the unpublished fragments see Appendix II and 'The History of Wolf's *Italian Serenade*' (*The Music Review*, August 1947).

[2] A recent instance is Richard Litterscheid (*Hugo Wolf*, Potsdam, 1939).

used as an orchestral instrument without particular distinction.   At
p. 27, bar 8, the oboe began to present the main theme for the
third time, but the cor anglais after a few bars took it over again in
a solo capacity.

So, in the original scoring, the *first* presentation of the main theme
was given to the cor anglais, the *second* to a solo viola, the *third* to the
cor anglais again.

Later Wolf decided to dispense with the cor anglais and allow
the solo viola to present the main theme on all its appearances.   In
order to save himself the trouble of recopying the score he scribbled
a note on the first page: 'Solo viola to play instead of cor anglais
throughout.'

All Reger had to do was to recopy the score in accordance with
this note of Wolf's and make a very few minute editorial amend-
ments.   In relation to the whole, Reger's retouches are *microscopic*.
The scoring is, practically, one hundred per cent Wolf's.   The
expression marks and the phrasing are all his.[1]

The arrangement for small orchestra, with its rich colouring, is
greatly to be preferred to the original version for quartet.   It brings
out all the latent romanticism of the music, concealed beneath its
satirically humorous manner.   In all performances of the work, the
real difficulty is to strike a balance between its wit and its sentiment,
and this is closely bound up with the question of tempo.   The
orchestral version seems to require some modification of the indication 'sehr lebhaft' at the head of the score, if much exquisite detail
and luscious colouring is not to pass unnoticed.

The previously mentioned letter to Potpeschnigg of 19th May, in
which Wolf wrote that the recasting of the *Serenade* was not yet
completed, also reveals that he was at the same time working on an
orchestral version of the Spanish song *Geh', Geliebter, geh' jetzt*.
Original creative work, however, still hung fire.   From day to day
he awaited the time when he would be able to take up again the
Italian songs and complete the volume according to his plan, but the
favourable mood continually eluded him.

On 15th June the Vienna Wagner Verein included the music to
Das Fest auf Solhaug in a concert in connection with an International
Musical and Theatrical Exhibition.   The performance, conducted

---

[1] A complete list of every variation, in addition to the transfer of the solo part
from cor anglais to viola, between the manuscript and the score as edited by Reger,
is given in 'The History of Wolf's *Italian Serenade*' (*The Music Review*,
August 1947).

by Joseph Schalk, was not a good one.   The copyist was so late in
delivering the parts that the orchestra had to play the work almost at
sight, and in letters to Siegfried Ochs and Humperdinck Wolf freely
expressed his dissatisfaction.   According to him, the contralto sang
persistently a semitone sharp, while the other soloist, described as 'a
dreadful amateur baritone,' lagged half a note behind the orchestra
throughout.   'The piece was so badly rehearsed, the vocal forces so
beneath all criticism, that it was no wonder that the work achieved
only a *succès d'estime.*'

It will be remarked that those singers who did take up engagements
to perform Wolf's songs rarely got any thanks for it from him.
There were sometimes good reasons for this, but very often it seems
that he was guilty of both injustice and ingratitude towards those who
worked hard to help him.   There are, for instance, many passages in
his letters where even Jäger is treated with scant courtesy.   Nor was
it only Wolf's singers who were often ill rewarded for their devotion.
During these years when, for prolonged periods, he could do little but
brood over the disparity between his ambitions and his actual achievements, his self-centredness increased until he seemed almost to take it
for granted that not only his own life, but also the lives of his friends,
should be wholly at the service of his genius.   There were many
friends who were well content that this should be so; there were others
who were disconcerted at Wolf's increasing egotism, which took
every advantage of their devotion and gave little or nothing in return.
In this mood of frustration his whole character seemed to be altered
for the worse.   Generally speaking, *success alone*, in endeavours to
help Wolf, could count upon his gratitude; to try to assist him and to
fail was to be sent away, not only without thanks, but with contempt.
Instances of this will be seen in the tortuous negotiations which went
on in this year over the preparation of a scenario for the opera he
hoped to write on the subject of *Manuel Venegas.*

Wolf had returned from Berlin with his head full of ideas about
Manuel Venegas.   Among the friends who were told about his plans
was Gustav Schur.   Schur was ill at the time and Wolf came up to
the sick-room, sat down beside the bed and related the whole plot of
Alarcon's novel.   When he reached the end he rose in feverish
excitement and represented the violent culmination of the tragedy,
panting, sighing and choking as he portrayed Soledad's end.   As a
result Schur was impelled to prepare a *Manuel Venegas* scenario for
Wolf.   The latter's verdict upon this scenario, however, was that

L

while it was quite a creditable performance for an artistically inclined banking official, provided another like-minded banking official could be found to set it to music, it was no use at all to *him*. From the time of his rejection of this scenario Wolf had very little more to do with Schur, hitherto his trusty financial adviser and friend. In his memoirs Schur wrote that Wolf returned from his concert in Berlin with increased self-confidence: 'Of us he seemed to have no further need.' It seems likely, however, that it was actually *Manuel Venegas* that brought an end to any real intimacy between these two men.[1]

From Schur Wolf turned to Genée, who promised excellent results from a dramatization of the novel. Wolf told Grohe, however, that if Genée's scenario should prove disappointing he would entrust Ernst von Wolzogen, the brother of the editor of the *Bayreuther Blätter*, with the task. How the negotiations with Genée came to an end is uncertain, nor do we know if an approach was actually made to Wolzogen, but we do find Wolf in July in possession of a *Manuel Venegas* scenario by a third party, Adalbert von Goldschmidt, his old friend and benefactor. There is not the slightest doubt that he had been treating simultaneously with Goldschmidt and with Genée. Wolf approved of the scenario, but Goldschmidt could not be induced to undertake the versification as well, and Wolf in his need turned to Humperdinck again, to ask him to interest Hermann Wette in the subject. Sad to relate, these negotiations over *Manuel Venegas* next cost Wolf Wette's friendship. The stages by which their relations deteriorated may be followed in Wolf's last four letters to Wette, between 22nd July and 3rd August, and by a commentary on these letters, written out by Wette, apparently for Arnold Mendelssohn's benefit, of which a copy is preserved in the Humperdinck archives at Boppard-am-Rhein.

After the Wagner Verein's performance of the *Fest auf Solhaug* music Wolf had moved from Vienna to Traunkirchen for the summer, to the house of the pastor where he had stayed in the previous year. On 22nd July, having heard from Humperdinck that his brother-in-law was definitely interested in his proposal, he sent Wette a joyful letter, enclosing Goldschmidt's scenario:

Humperdinck has just given me the gratifying information that you would welcome the forwarding of my scenario. I hasten to send it to you immediately, but at the same time would ask you first of all to read Pedro

---

[1] Schur reappears, to play a restricted role in Wolf's life, after a number of years. In 1897 he became treasurer of the Vienna Hugo Wolf Verein.

de Alarcon's novel, which under the title *Manuel Venegas* is to be had for 60 pfennigs in Spemann's edition.   I am unfortunately not at the moment in possession of the book, else I should of course have sent it to you.

The scenario, drawn up by the composer Goldschmidt, has my approval; may it have yours also.   It seems to me to be extremely effective and well adapted for the stage, even if at times violence had to be done to the story—as, after all, was unavoidable.   For the unmusical name Soledad you will probably be able to find a better-sounding one; the other figures retain their names.   Arregui, with whom in the novel there was not much to be done, has in the adaptation, it seems to me, become quite a respectable personality.

Probably I do not need to tell you beforehand what trust I place in your poetical powers and what hopes are bound up with your benevolent co-operation.   Only one thing further.   Do not lay the least restraint upon yourself with regard to metre.   The freer the better.   Let verse and prose alternate and above all let there be no lack of strong accents.   The Devil must be in it if we do not bring to light a noble work.   The action must take place in the seventeenth century, and not in the nineteenth as in the novel.   Thereby the religious element will acquire greater validity and also the jurisdiction at the end of the second act will appear more credible.

And now may God grant that you may share my enthusiasm for this subject, so that from the compact of love may spring a vigorous creature, capable of life.

On receipt of this letter, Wette read through *Manuel Venegas* and Goldschmidt's scenario.   The former excited his profoundest admiration, the latter he thought utterly worthless.   He told Wolf this quite frankly and sent him his own *Elsi, die seltsame Magd*—an opera book written for Arnold Mendelssohn—in order that Wolf might be able to form an opinion of his work and in particular might learn what he understood by 'sound tragic art.'   In his letter Wette also inquired what proportion of the royalties on the opera would fall to his share and stressed the fact that he was already fully engaged in collaboration with Arnold Mendelssohn, had no real need of any other musical associate, and that if he undertook to provide a *Manuel Venegas* libretto it would only be because of his admiration for Wolf's music and the extraordinary appeal that Alarcon's novel had made to him.

Wolf's reaction to *Elsi, die seltsame Magd* may be gathered from his curt reply, written on 27th July:

I have read through *Elsi*, the tragedy sent to me, and in accordance with your wishes send it back in all haste, with sincere regret not to be able to share your conception of a 'sound tragic art.'   Return to me if you please the scenario for *Venegas* and let us remain, in spite of all this, good friends.

Wette's commentary to this says that he returned Goldschmidt's scenario and asked whether an operatic version of *Manuel Venegas* was still contemplated, as he had been quite overwhelmed in reading the novel and would have pleasure in working out an operatic version. He had in the meantime drafted a scenario of his own which gave, he thought, a true reflection of Alarcon's masterpiece.

Wette had followed up his previous letter with another in which, as he feared that Wolf might misinterpret his inquiry about the financial side of the proposed collaboration, he gave some account of his circumstances. Wolf received this letter on the 27th, just after he had posted off *Elsi* with the short note given above, and later in the same day he wrote again to Wette:

A short time after your libretto was consigned to the post there arrived from you a lengthy letter, in which you thought it necessary to vindicate yourself to me on account of the allusion to the matter of royalties. Certainly it did not affect me very pleasantly that such importance was attached to this subject, yet this was not at all the reason which decided me to say nothing more about the case of *Venegas*. I did this out of purely artistic considerations, occasioned by your opera poem, of which I absolutely could not approve. I did not recognize therein the author of the splendid Wind songs,[1] which still retain a good place in my memory. I regard it as useless to go into details about your opera poem, as with your preconceived idea of this work you would be absolutely impervious to a contrary opinion. Let each one be happy in his own way. I must most sincerely regret that your wretched pecuniary circumstances hamper the free exercise of your artistic abilities. May you succeed in alliance with Mendelssohn in defying the dark Demon and charming to your side Fortune in the shape of continually renewing royalties.

Wette says that he next wrote 'in a grimly humorous vein' ('in galgenhumoristischer Weise') that he much regretted having to give up *Manuel Venegas*, that Goldschmidt's scenario was hopelessly inadequate, in that the characterization of the novel was weakened and the plot debased into a piece of common scandal-mongering, 'but certainly no word that would give Wolf the expectation that I was still prepared, by setting aside my own art, or rather, my own and my friend Mendelssohn's art, to be of service to his muse.'

Nevertheless, on 3rd August Wolf wrote as follows:

I see from your last letter, which one could characterize with the saying: 'You don't seem to know, my friend, how rude you are,' how near to your heart *Venegas* lies. So I will take your 'free observations,' as you euphemistically put it, in the way they were meant, 'in the honest desire of being serviceable to my art and my fortune.'

[1] Wette's poems *Was der Wind erzählt* (1884).

So let us leave aside our differences over *Elsi*, of which, as you presume, on account of a 'mistake,' I could not approve, and let us stick to *Venegas*.

If you are still willing, and if your precious time allows, I ask you to prepare for me as soon as possible a scenario according to your conception, with the reservation that I shall be at liberty either to accept or to decline it. You will see the reasonableness of this proposal, as it is obvious enough.

Something in this letter seems to have very much offended Wette. In his commentary he again expresses the greatest surprise that Wolf could conceive that, after what had happened, he (Wette) would still be willing to co-operate over *Manuel Venegas*. 'Is it then possible,' he asks Arnold Mendelssohn, 'that this man can be so blinded by the consciousness of his musical talents as to believe that he need only beckon, and every one will stand ready for the honour of being poet to his music?' There is a good deal more in his commentary in a similar vein of personal bitterness.

Wolf's letter is not too happily phrased, nor remarkable for its tact, but after the 'galgenhumoristische Weise' of Wette's previous communication, Wolf probably believed, reasonably enough, that he could express his mind quite openly. As Wette had already, after he knew of Wolf's disapproval of *Elsi*, himself suggested that they should still collaborate over *Manuel Venegas*, and as in his commentary he says that he was 'somewhat reconciled' by Wolf's second letter of 27th July, it is difficult to see why his reaction to this last letter should have been so violent. If he did not any longer wish to write a libretto for Wolf, a few remarks 'in galgenhumoristischer Weise' would probably have settled the matter quite amicably. As it was, however, he came to the conclusion, as he told Mendelssohn, that there were only two courses open to him—either not to reply at all, or to tell Wolf outright that he no longer considered him worthy of his friendship and, unhappily, he seems to have chosen to do the latter. On 10th August Wolf told Grohe:

About the 'progress' of the projected opera I have little that is favourable to report. Wette sent me as proof of his 'genius' an opera libretto that he wrote for the composer Arnold Mendelssohn in Darmstadt which surpasses in amateurishness, imbecility, crudity, and silliness everything that has hitherto been achieved in this much defiled *genre*. When in the most conciliating way I declined his co-operation, he became swinishly impolite and looks down on me as an ignoramus.

Wolf himself does not come out of this affair with much credit. The latter part of the above quotation gives an account of the end of his association with Wette that is definitely untrue. It was Wette, and not Wolf, who ultimately broke off the negotiations, and Wolf's last action was to ask Wette to provide a scenario of his own. The whole episode is far from pleasant to contemplate. To induce Schur to write for him a scenario, to reject this with scorn and, as it seems, practically to cut Schur out of his life, to undertake simultaneous negotiations with Genée and Goldschmidt—to say nothing of Wolzogen—to accept Goldschmidt's scenario and recommend it to Wette, and then to be prepared to switch from Goldschmidt's conception of the work to Wette's when it appeared that the latter would not otherwise undertake the versification, and afterwards to give his friends a false impression of the course of his association with Wette —these are the proceedings of a man quite blindly obsessed with his own needs. Even Goldschmidt, the one person who did succeed in giving Wolf something of which he approved, did not receive much thanks for it. A letter of 14th September tells Grohe that Goldschmidt 'has not the courage' to proceed with the work.

On or about 20th September Wolf returned to Vienna from Traunkirchen and again took up residence in the Köchert family's unoccupied house at Döbling. In October, in letters to Strecker and Sternfeld, he still spoke of the longed for *Manuel Venegas* libretto, with which, however, only a great and true poet could provide him.

His thoughts during this autumn ran on the possibility of returning to Berlin, where he had been so kindly received in the previous winter. He seriously considered spending the whole of the coming concert season there, and to cover his expenses—Schur's Wagner Verein fund being no longer available—he actually sold outright to Schott's the first part of his *Italian Song Book* for 1,000 marks. For a long time he played with the idea of a great concert of his own works in Berlin, with soloists, chorus and orchestra, but although Siegfried Ochs offered him the use of the Philharmonic orchestra and chorus without fee and Emilie Herzog agreed to sing for him, he still hesitated to commit himself, partly owing to the apparent impossibility of finding a suitable tenor—in Wolf's view the *sine qua non* of any concert of his music—and partly because he feared his financial resources were still inadequate for such a venture. In the end he remained in Vienna, the deciding factor being an engagement to rehearse Wagnerian roles with the Dutch tenor Ernest van Dyck, who was appearing at the Vienna Opera at this time. After paying off debts to the amount of 200 gulden, he found himself in the, for him, extremely unusual position of having about 400 gulden to his credit in a savings bank. It was to his credit in another sense that he offered the use of the whole of this money to his mother, in case difficulties should arise at home.

At Döbling in these months, before he began work with van Dyck, he was not wholly idle. In October and November he completed the massive arrangement of *Der Feuerreiter* for chorus and orchestra, that has done as much as anything to carry his name beyond the borders of his native country. The ballad of *Der Feuerreiter* seems always to have been one of Wolf's own favourites among his compositions. In his own performance of it his avowed endeavour was to make his friends' hair stand on end. Demonic power, excitement, the thrill of the supernatural—these were the elements in it upon which he laid stress. The orchestra allowed him obvious opportunities to intensify these effects, to paint in glowing colours what he could only imperfectly indicate in the black-and-white of the piano. The work gains much from the transference of the vocal part from solo voice to chorus, suggesting crowd scenes wholly in keeping with the subject-matter of the poem. The repetition of phrases, such as the fire-alarm, in the different voices, at different levels of tone, vividly suggests the excited clamour of the populace, gathering from far and near.

The first part of the *Italian Song Book* (numbers 1–22) was published by Schott's in December.

From the connection with van Dyck Wolf foresaw possible great advantages to himself. The best account of his plans is to be found in a letter to Kauffmann of 23rd December, in a passage that was omitted when the correspondence was published in book form:[1]

The porter has just brought me a letter from Tübingen. What a pleasure! I gather from it that you are not yet informed of the latest turn of events. You shall now learn what is necessary about that straight away. First of all, I have to inform you that I have dropped my plans for Berlin, and that I shall remain in Vienna. The occasion for this was offered me by the singer van Dyck, with whom I have been rehearsing for several weeks. You must know that van Dyck to-day counts as a celebrity of the very first rank, and that it cannot be a matter of indifference to me to be associated with this artist. Although strangely enough I have not so far found a suitable opportunity to confer with him about my affairs, I confidently cherish the hope of making capital (naturally in the artistic sense)

[1] Published in 'Hugo Wolf und der Tübinger Kreis,' by W. Schmid (*Neue Musik-Zeitung*, Stuttgart, 1st January 1925).

out of him in the future. If I should be successful in interesting van Dyck seriously in my things I am, so to speak, made for life. But I must go to work in the matter with extreme caution, in order to avoid all suspicion of my egotistic purpose, for these confounded tenor-singing gentlemen are incalculable in their insane vanity and, moreover, revengeful as Corsicans. For the present I am still occupied in laying mines, which, however, must not go off before the right moment. You marvel at my diplomatic abilities? Ah, let us first wait for the result; I fear in spite of everything that I am not born for a diplomat. You will grasp the situation at once when I tell you that van Dyck's best friends are my bitterest enemies. That means one must be constantly on one's guard. Fortunately my personality is sympathetic to him and he knows also how to value me as *Correpetitor*. The chief thing, however, is and remains how he will conduct himself towards the *composer*, but about that there is absolutely nothing to be got out of him. But he shall now learn from me how to speak and, if God wills, how to sing too. But time, foresight, and patience!

It would seem that by 2nd January the 'mines' had been exploded with apparent success, for Wolf, through Potpeschnigg, then inquired of the agent responsible for arranging a concert of van Dyck's at Graz whether there would be any objection to the inclusion of six Wolf songs in the programme. Later in the same month he told his friends that he was very intimate with van Dyck and that the latter possessed copies of his songs and was prepared to sing them. But although the rehearsals of Wagnerian roles, including the study of the part of Siegmund in Wilder's French translation—for Wolf at once a joke and a torment—continued until March, van Dyck's interest in Wolf's own songs was not sustained. Kauffmann was told on 10th March:

With van Dyck, who as the 'créateur' of 'Sigmond' travels on the 20th to Paris for the performance of *Die Walküre*, I shall scarcely do very much. In the first place he has little interest in my things, and then he is in general interested only in opera singing, and in well-paid, highly profitable opera singing at that.

The last is heard of van Dyck in a letter to Potpeschnigg of 28th March: 'Unfortunately he could not find time to give a concert at Graz, although perhaps it was just as well, for as a *Lieder*-singer van Dyck seems absolutely unable to qualify.'

Meanwhile, the quest for the opera text continued. During this winter Wolf told Grohe that he had only escaped the attentions of two 'professional librettists,' 'of unexampled tenacity,' by declaring bluntly that, once and for all, he wished to hear nothing more about operatic composition. Now the question of the identity of these would-be collaborators is a point of considerable interest. The suspicion cannot be withheld that Wolf may have been referring to the end of the complex negotiations over *Manuel Venegas*, and that the two 'professional librettists' were in all probability Richard Genée, whom Wolf had earlier referred to as his 'fatherly friend' and asked to prepare a scenario, and Genée's literary collaborator F. Zell. It is difficult to see what other professional writers could have been so extremely interested in supplying Wolf with an opera text, and such conduct towards them on his part would be entirely in keeping with his treatment of the rest of those who tried, in the matter of *Manuel Venegas*, in all sincerity to satisfy his requirements.

The statement that he wished to hear nothing more of operatic composition was, of course, very far from the truth. In the same letter to Grohe in which Wolf relates of his escape from these two librettists, he sighs: 'And yet, if only the right one, the true one, could be found!' and describes the joyous frenzy with which he would throw himself into the arms of the poet-elect who should provide him with the opera poem of his dreams.

The next operatic hare—or perhaps we ought to say the next operatic red herring—was started by Dr. Strecker. He informed Wolf that the Duke of Coburg-Gotha had offered a prize of 5,000 marks for a new one-act opera and urged him to enter the competition. In this connection he sent for Wolf's consideration Scribe's libretto *Actéon*, that in its day had been used by Auber. The 5,000 marks were an undoubted attraction, but the closing date for entries for the competition left very little time to prepare even a one-act opera and *Actéon*, though the subject was by no means unattractive, was not usable in its original form. A modern opera on the subject would require an entirely new libretto, which brought Wolf up against his old obstacle, the lack of a suitable poet. Almost immediately after he had rejected the idea of setting *Actéon* to music, we find him examining with great interest Grillparzer's comedy *Weh' dem, der lügt*. He got as far as drafting a scenario of his own for this, in which the five acts of the play were reduced to three, and thought of inviting Fritz Mauthner, one of his Berlin acquaintances, to undertake the poetical elaboration. Then this project, too, was dropped. A Herr G. S.[1] next sent a libretto called *Zenobia*, but this, Wolf reported, was distinguished even among *his* collection for its outstanding silliness. He told Grohe that in this matter of opera

[1] Not Gustav Schur this time.

*L

texts he entertained the suspicion that he was the victim of the machinations of evil spirits, who always interfered with his plans at the critical moment.

For example, I have a good subject. You recommend me a clever poet —thus everything seems to be in order. Then comes the devil in the shape of a friend who dissuades me from the subject, casts suspicion on the poet, but suggests to me another subject and a better adapter—agreed! The recommended author, held to be a genius *non plus ultra*, turns out to be an impertinent youngster who, as Shakespeare [1] says, still carries the egg-shells on his head and drips behind the ears. What is there to do? You see, pure devil's work! And so it is repeated *ad infinitum* and in the end muddles one up completely.

Since the last of the Italian songs in December 1891 Wolf had composed no original music except a few bars of an unsuccessful attempt at a slow movement for the *Italian Serenade*. In eighteen months his musical activities comprised only this and the orchestration of *Geh', Geliebter* and the first movement of the *Serenade*, and the arrangement of *Der Feuerreiter* for chorus and orchestra, and over this state of affairs he was rapidly becoming almost desperate. With increasing irritation he replied to the well-meant inquiries of his friends as to whether he was 'industriously composing' and his letters reflect, for long periods, only despondency and bitterness. Thus he told Kauffmann on 26th April 1893:

What I suffer from this continuous idleness I am quite unable to describe. I would like most to hang myself on the nearest branch of the cherry-trees standing now in full bloom. This wonderful spring with its secret life and movement troubles me unspeakably. These eternal blue skies, lasting for weeks, this continuous sprouting and budding in nature, these coaxing breezes impregnated with spring sunlight and fragrance of flowers, this 'ich sehne mich und weiss nicht recht nach was,' [2] make me frantic. Everywhere this bewildering urge for life, fruitfulness, creation— and only I, although like the humblest grass of the fields one of God's creatures, may not take part in this festival of resurrection, at any rate not except as a spectator consumed with grief and envy.

In order to keep his brain active he began to learn French and reported that he had made sufficient progress to be able to read with some trouble a novel of George Sand. He returned also to Schmid's present of the works of Aristophanes, extracting much knowledge from the notes and great pleasure from the works themselves, but

[1] Probably a confused memory of Hamlet's 'This lapwing runs away with the shell on his head' (Act v, Scene ii).
[2] Mörike, *Im Frühling*.

not finding, it is hardly necessary to add, anything suitable for his comic opera.

On 17th May he left Vienna and established himself, for the third summer in succession, in the Pfarrhof at Traunkirchen. In solitude there he was disturbed, so early in the season, only by the finches. His earlier offer to his mother of his surplus 400 gulden had evidently been accepted, for in an unpublished letter to his sister Käthe we find him on 19th May asking whether 50 gulden cannot be spared for him from home, to make his stay at Traunkirchen more agreeable. In his family letters Wolf reveals himself in all his human frailty, but often in such a way that the heart is rent with pity for the petty vexations and deprivations that his circumstances engendered. So in this case. Here he was at Traunkirchen, condemned, by lack of funds, to spend his time walking round the shores of the lake instead of sailing over it. He proposed to buy himself a flat-bottomed boat, a so-called 'Plätte' ('flat iron'), costing 18 to 20 gulden (about thirty shillings), this being the best he could hope to do to satisfy his passion for aquatics. But he had to give up the idea of acquiring even this humble craft, as it would have cost him another 15 gulden, which he could not afford, for the use of a boat-house to keep it in. His money had probably been all swallowed up by the 'Bude,' the little grocer's shop that Katharina Wolf and her younger daughters still ran at Windischgraz, to Hugo's intense annoyance. He never ceased to urge them to abandon it.

He went to Traunkirchen with the intention of getting a lot of work done in this summer, took much music paper with him, and had an old Bösendorfer grand piano, given him by Henriette von Schey some years before, sent there and installed in his lodgings. He had never before been able to use it, as he had never had a room big enough to keep it in, and for years Ludwig Bösendorfer had taken care of it for him. It was delivered at Traunkirchen on 23rd May. 'My delight in it is simply indescribable,' he told Melanie Köchert. 'Like an infatuated ape I stare continually at this piece of yellow, old-fashioned furniture and ask myself incredulously whether this thing really belongs to me or whether I am not perhaps dreaming? Heavens, if this time I compose nothing, then it is definitely all over with me.' The possession of this instrument, however, the peace of Traun-kirchen, his own good resolutions—they availed him nothing. It was as if he were bewitched. He could not write a note of music. 'I could just as soon begin suddenly to speak Chinese,' he told Grohe, 'as compose anything at all.'   He described himself as leading the existence of an oyster.   Once he did get as far as setting down four bars of music on paper, but explained to Melanie:

The instantaneous perception that only a 'wish' and not a 'compulsion' brought me to attempt this made me ashamed and so I gave it up again and was glad to have caught myself out in a falsehood in good time.   All the same, my heart almost breaks when I consider how one day after another goes by in idleness, and this fair solitude, just made for composure and self-communion, means to me nothing more than it does to the most ordinary holiday-maker—a *dolce far niente* with more or less boredom or entertainment, just as may happen.   And yet the others are as a rule harassed people in need of relaxation, who have a right to be lazy and to graze like the cows and take a comfortable siesta—but I, I, for whom the calendar reckons only holidays, who is rightly accounted superfluous among the thousands, who is nothing, who knows nothing, and above all *does* nothing —God in heaven, how will that end?   Siegfried Ochs wrote to me recently and dispelled my fears concerning his long silence with the remark: 'Everything in the best of order,' and held out hopes of a more detailed account to follow.   But, Heaven knows, the propaganda for Berlin no longer gives me any pleasure.   There exists for me very little cause of rejoicing at all on this mad planet; it would be quite agreeable to me if some disorderly comet gave it a hearty bump on the nose so that it smashed into a thousand pieces.

This strain was upsetting to Melanie and she begged him to be more cheerful.   In his next letter he attempted to comply with her wishes, for 'in the end even the grizzly bears have learned to dance; shall that be forbidden only to a little grizzling Wolf?'   But it was no use.

I *can't* dance and *don't want* to dance, any more than I can now compose, and any more than I can do anything at all to which a powerful inner compulsion does not drive me.   Now Satan has got me in his jet-black claws and there's nothing to do but to wait, wait, and once again to wait.   Therefore *no* dancing, gracious lady, not even the tiniest little hop.   What purpose would it serve?   The world without that drives one mad enough. Can and should one make a fool of oneself?'

He read Max Stirner's *Der Einzige und sein Eigenthum*, which anticipated many of Nietzsche's ideas.   There is a reference to this book in one of the letters to Melanie, reflecting one of his happier moods:

To-day the air is thoroughly mild and the sun is more generous with 'heat and lighting' than in all the last few days.   So this morning, although I found myself on an inclined plane (on a slanting plank of the steamer landing-stage facing the church), I could really revel for hours on end in enjoyment of the warm sunshine and wrapped in contemplation of the lake and its romantic shore, and, now and then glancing at Stirner's book, lying by me, reflect on his wonderful world of ideas. At such times I really don't apprehend that I am in no mood for composition. To-day, for example, everything is so quiet, so solemn, round about me, even the chattering finches, that I hate, are become more still; only the flies hum their sleepy melodies—else nothing but deepest peace and solitude. Truly, life is still fair!

The strange little man, who hated finches, sitting lost to the world on a sloping plank all the long summer morning! Stirner led him again to Nietzsche, whose entire works he had borrowed from Eckstein, and he found some consolation in passages from *Die fröhliche Wissenschaft*. The philosopher teaches that there exist among artists and contemplatives certain fastidious souls who would rather perish than work without joy in their work, to whom no reward can be of use, if their work is not itself the reward of rewards.

They fear boredom less than work without pleasure in it: they even have need of much boredom, if they are to achieve *their* work. For the thinker and for all inventive spirits boredom is the disagreeable becalming of the soul which precedes the joyous winds and the prosperous voyage.

This was balsam in Wolf's wounds, but he still feared that he would be one of the unfortunate ones who perish while awaiting the propitious breeze.

The primary cause of his condition, apart from possible pathological factors, lay without doubt in his unsolved operatic problems. There was in him the imperative need to express himself fully in an opera, and between him and the satisfaction of his need there were two apparently insurmountable obstacles—the lack of a poet collaborator and the repressive effect of the enveloping shadow of Wagner. The former, the more obvious hindrance, has already come in for much discussion, both here and elsewhere; the latter, though its importance is beyond all doubt, has always received less than its due attention, and in the principal biographies is barely mentioned at all. It was Marie Lang who first pointed out this omission in Decsey's first volume and other literature of the period, and her account of how Wagner's towering greatness weighed heavily upon the young Wolf, with depressive influence upon his spirit and deterrent effect upon his own creative work, has been utilized in an earlier chapter of the present biography. 'He has left me no room,' he had cried, 'like a mighty tree that chokes with its shade the sprouting young growths under its widely spreading branches.'

That had been ten years before the present crisis in his life, but the period of comparative sterility and spiritual malaise which went before the composition of the Mörike songs corresponds closely to these later barren years preceding *Der Corregidor*, and there is no lack of evidence to show that the effect of the impact of Wagner's music upon him did not change with the passing of time. In 1888, only very shortly after the creation of the Mörike songs had seemed to promise the fulfilment of his artistic aims, he was seen by Dr. Zweybrück sitting alone and apart, in the grounds of the Bayreuth theatre, weeping bitterly after listening to *Parsifal*. Gustav Schur has recorded how he and his wife tried in vain to comfort Wolf when, after a performance of *Götterdämmerung*, he was lamenting, in floods of tears, the cruel fate that had made him a musician after Wagner. On this occasion he suddenly sprang up and cried in tones of defiance: 'Friends! One thing I can do, which Wagner could not. I can go hungry!' Then, as we have seen, at Mannheim in 1890, after *Tannhäuser* under Weingartner, Wolf had declared that whenever he heard one of Wagner's operas he was tempted to destroy his own work, which then seemed to him purposeless. In the year at present under discussion, 1893, he told Kauffmann in a letter from Traunkirchen on 5th August that he had been playing the last piano sonatas of Beethoven and described his reactions:

After the intoxicating narcosis of Wagner's art, Beethoven's music seems like heavenly ether and woodland breezes. The former takes my breath away and dashes me to the ground, but the latter expands the lungs and frees the spirit, and veritably makes one a good man, just as Wagner's art in its excess degrades one into a worm. You must not, however, suppose that I have suddenly joined the anti-Wagnerians, although I have in all seriousness to guard against doing that, if only in order to justify my own artistic existence. But Wagner is and remains the supreme god, even if he arouses in his worshippers perhaps more fear, or, if you like, more veneration, than love.

It is not surprising that Wolf sometimes attempted to revolt against the tyranny of Wagner's hold on his mind and emotions. There is a sense in which Wolf's letters to Grohe in 1890 concerning Karl Heckel's *Buddha* contain a criticism of Wagner—a criticism suggested no doubt by Nietzsche's *Der Fall Wagner*, which we know from Eckstein to have cost Wolf many a night's sleep, horrified and fascinated by it as he was. Karl Heckel himself felt this so strongly— and felt also, it is reasonable to suppose, the desire to explain away Wolf's rejection of his own Wagnerian librettos—that he wrote and published a remarkable essay [1] in which he sought to show 'the fundamental antagonism of Wolf to Wagner's nature.' The faithful Heinrich Werner replied to this essay in an article [2] which, while arguing that the suggestion of a 'fundamental antagonism' was somewhat far-fetched, did not deny that there was something in Heckel's thesis. Werner revealed the significant fact that in the 'transvaluation of all values' that held sway while Wolf was interned in Dr. Svetlin's asylum in 1897 he rejected Wagner entirely. Even after he was released from the asylum he still retained for a time the remnants of ideas that had completely dominated him in his insanity, and in January 1898 he said in conversation with Werner himself, smiling as though he scarcely believed his own words: 'No, my dear fellow, there's nothing in *Parsifal*!'

From time to time Wolf would leave Traunkirchen for a few days to visit friends who were spending the summer in different parts of the Salzkammergut—the Langs and Eckstein at Unterach, the Köcherts at Rinnbach, other friends at Gmunden. In August Wolf himself played host to his Mannheim friend Oskar Grohe. A few months before, Grohe had had the great misfortune to lose his wife Jeanne after the birth of a son, Helmut, and he had been invited by Wolf to seek consolation among the mountains and lakes of Austria. The following passages from letters written by Grohe to his relatives during this visit to Traunkirchen give some impression of Wolf's way of life there:

To Frau Jean Becker, Grohe's mother-in-law, 14th August :

Through a peculiar mishap we missed each other at the station. I overlooked him, which with his diminutive size certainly seems plausible enough. But that he should miss me too! [Grohe was very tall.] So it happened that I sought out the Pfarrhof alone, and sat already deep in the reading of your letter when Wolf rushed into the room and impetuously embraced me. . . . Wolf is a capital, loyal, and upright man, who had great admiration for Jeanne, and also understanding. He keeps her letters, like a treasure. Of Helmut's portrait he said: 'Ah, that's a fine fellow!' Yesterday we conversed until midnight. He said that he only writes what pleases himself, that he hates the public and despises it. Proud words! . . . Wolf takes his very simple meals in the house for economy's sake.

To the same lady, 20th August:

Wolf went to Ebensee to a Tarock-party to which he was invited and

---

[1] *Hugo Wolf in seinem Verhältnis zu Richard Wagner* (Munich, 1905; reprinted from the *Süddeutsche Monatshefte* for June 1905).

[2] 'Hugo Wolf und Richard Wagner' (*Österreichische Rundschau*, Vienna, 10th May 1906).

only returned in the evening. . . . On Thursday I wanted to visit the Atter-see with Wolf, but we had to turn back when we had gone half-way because the Kaiser was hunting there, which Wolf declared was a devil's trick, so that I had difficulty in calming him down. . . . We do not make music far into the night as two elderly ladies dwell on the same floor who need rest, but in the day-time there is much conversation and music. Not long ago he played me a work for chorus and orchestra, which will be performed in Berlin next winter. His imagination and inventive powers are astounding, as is also his art. From time to time he plays Beethoven sonatas also. *Les Adieux*, which Jeanne used to play, powerfully affected me. . . . Wolf often stays in the house for pecuniary reasons. He has to parcel out his money, and does so conscientiously.

To Frl. Vera Becker, Grohe's sister-in-law, 25th August. Grohe describes a violent thunderstorm over the lake:

Wolf shouted for joy over this battle of the elements. He is a splendid fellow and a genius from the top of his head to the soles of his feet. Each morning after breakfast we have a discussion and make music. At present he is working on an *Italian Serenade* for orchestra, the scherzo of which he played for me to-day, a piece full of sparkling life and originality, and moreover full of bold ideas. His songs take on a quite different aspect when he plays them himself at the piano. We also often play duets together. Then when we come to a passage in which a cello solo appears he always says: 'Hugo Becker! [1] . . .' I showed Wolf Jeanne's Waltz. He considered the basses very good and altered very little, and said we ought not to make it too difficult, so that Helmut would soon be able to play it.

The 'scherzo' of the *Italian Serenade*, referred to by Grohe, was presumably really the first movement. A fragmentary slow movement—28 bars, which he could take no further—was the sole artistic product of Wolf's four months' stay at Traunkirchen in this year. Even this seems to have been composed earlier, and only scored at this time.

Towards the end of September he left to pay a visit to Windisch-graz—the first since 1889. For a long time he had had it on his conscience that he had not more often revisited his home, and now his mother was nearly seventy years old. At Windischgraz he spent three unhappy weeks, tormented by the noise made by his mother's neighbours and by his old enemies, the cocks and hens of the district. It was a question, he told Grohe, of whether the noise of hammering or the cries of the poultry would first bring about a nervous break-down. In the middle of October he fled from the Windischgraz 'inferno.' On the 15th and 16th of this month he was at Graz. It may have been remarked how completely Josef Strasser has dropped

---

[1] Jeanne's brother, the celebrated cellist.

out of the story of the composer's life. The reason is that he and Wolf's sister Modesta had separated. It was in reference to this that Wolf, in a letter of 14th February 1891,[1] had written to his sister: 'With great joy I have gathered from your letter that you have recovered your inner peace of mind, and that your external situation seems to content you.' The rights and wrongs of the case are not clear, but it is certain that Modesta was left with a large family to support on very little money. Wolf, however, continued from time to time to hear from Strasser, and repeatedly assured him that the separation would make no difference at all to their friendship. Now at Graz on 15th October 1893, he determined to try to renew their former personal relationship and set out to call on his brother-in-law. But the next day he had to tell his sister Käthe: 'Yesterday I looked up Strasser, but when I arrived before the door of his office I suddenly lost all courage to speak to him and returned to my hotel without having accomplished my purpose.' On a later visit to Graz the two men did meet again, but in the circumstances the old friendship could not be renewed. 'With my brother-in-law I am friendly,' Frau Köchert was told, 'but reserved—very reserved—and I try to avoid him.'

From Graz Wolf returned to Vienna and was soon once again settled, for the fourth successive winter, at Döbling. In everything except original creative work his affairs now began to move forward again. Siegfried Ochs had definitely put down both the choral version of *Der Feuerreiter* and the Shakespearian *Elfenlied* for performance by the Philharmonic chorus in Berlin on 8th January 1894, and it was proposed also to produce at the same concert several of the songs in their orchestral dress. After this there were prospects of a number of concerts in various German cities. At Tübingen, on the initiative of Emil Kauffmann, an all-Wolf concert took place on 31st October, the singers being Emma Dinkelacker, soprano, Karl Diezel, tenor, and an amateur bass-baritone named Hugo Faisst. Schmid and Kauffmann shared the piano parts between them, and Schmid had also prepared the ground for the reception of Wolf's music by an article in the *Tübinger Chronik*. The enthusiasm of the audience was unbounded and more than half the twenty-two songs on the programme had to be repeated. Diezel, it seemed, might well be the tenor Wolf had been seeking so long; negotiations were opened and the singer declared himself ready to appear in any of Wolf's

[1] *Familienbriefe.*

projected concerts in Germany. Faisst, who contributed ten songs to the Tübingen programme, wrote an enthusiastic letter to their composer and enclosed his photograph, from which Wolf received his first impression of this fellow countryman of Mörike's, who later became one of the dearest of his friends.

Ochs soon announced from Berlin that the Philharmonic chorus was 'sweating blood' over *Der Feuerreiter*. Wolf's wishes concerning the section of the programme devoted to solo songs with orchestra were not wholly to be fulfilled. Emilie Herzog, his chosen soprano, was unable to obtain leave to appear at the concert from the intendant of the Berlin Opera, and the five scores intended for Berlin—*Geh'*, *Geliebter*, *Ganymed*, *Er ist's*, *Anakreons Grab* and *Mignon* ('Kennst du das Land?')—were left behind in a tramcar and lost by Wolf himself, when on his way with them to the post.[1] He at once set about the task of re-scoring the songs and completed a second orchestral version of *Mignon* on 31st October and a second *Anakreons Grab* on 13th November. To these he added Margit's ballad from *Das Fest auf Solhaug*, which, with *Anakreons Grab*, was finally included in the Berlin programme, *Mignon* dropping out owing to difficulties about the choice of a singer.

On 27th November Wolf went again to Graz, where he had arranged to appear as pianist in a recital of his songs by August Krämer and his wife, Marie Krämer-Widl, on 1st December. The artists gave their services without fee and Wolf was also provided with free lodgings by Josef Purgleitner, a previously unknown admirer who kept a chemist's shop in the Sporgasse. Musical circles in the Styrian capital were beginning to realize the importance of their countryman's work and to take a real interest in his growing celebrity. Numerous articles appeared in the local papers before his first appearance in public at Graz, and these included one by Friedrich von Hausegger, who recalled his early connection with Wolf, dating from his Conservatoire days. Twenty-seven songs were on the programme. Potpeschnigg had carefully rehearsed the artists in their songs before Wolf's arrival and the whole concert was eminently successful. Wolf was left with 230 gulden towards the expenses of his journey to Berlin. After the concert he visited the Balthahof, the home of the Krämers near Graz, and accepted an invitation to stay

[1] *Ganymed, Geh', Geliebter* and the first version of *Anakreons Grab* were never recovered, but *Er ist's* and the first version of *Mignon* came into the possession of the Hugo Wolf Verein many years later and were posthumously published.

there in the following summer—on condition that all the cocks and hens in the district were 'choked off' beforehand.

Not long after his return to Vienna he made another—unexpected —appearance in public. This was at a concert of the Wiener Sing-Akademie in the Bösendorfersaal, where Lili Leschky was to give a group of his songs in a programme principally of choral works. Ferdinand Löwe was to have played the accompaniments but did not put in an appearance, so that Wolf, who was among the audience, had to be lifted up, 'in his street clothes and with dirty boots,' on to the platform from the body of the hall to take his place. The singer was somewhat unnerved and Wolf himself did not improve matters by a bad lapse of memory in the piano part of *Gesang Weylas*. In consideration of this he did not slate Frl. Leschky with his usual severity, but he told his friends he would not undertake to appear in public with her again.

Siegfried Ochs was meanwhile sending most encouraging reports about the rehearsals of *Der Feuerreiter* and the *Elfenlied* in Berlin. Wolf, for his part, was still uncertain whether he could really afford to make the trip. He would have liked to arrange another song recital there during his visit, but Hermann Wolff, the concert agent, would not risk another concert without a financial guarantee, and Wolf, without Schur's fund behind him, was unable to find one. He still retained, however, somewhat vague plans for concerts in other German cities, if sufficient funds were forthcoming. The Wagner Verein at Darmstadt, through its president, Oberstleutnant von Selzam, was, in particular, pressing him to attend a concert of his music there and willingly agreed to refund all his expenses. The financial difficulties of the journey to Berlin were finally removed at the end of December by Grohe, Ochs and other friends, who subscribed together and put 300 marks at Wolf's disposal. In addition, he received a charming letter from the Baroness von Lipperheide inviting him, although the baron and his family were unable to leave Schloss Matzen, their Tyrolean castle, to make use of their Berlin residence, at Potsdamerstrasse 38, during his stay in the German capital.

On 4th January he left Vienna for Berlin. Travelling by the same train was Anton Bruckner, whose *Te Deum* was to be performed under Ochs's direction in the same Philharmonic programme as Wolf's works.

Bruckner was a strange apparition in the streets of Vienna, dressed in a wide-brimmed, black slouch hat and a suit made of rough black homespun material, with the very short but extraordinarily wide trousers which he favoured because they allowed him the free use of his legs when pedalling at the organ. Above a monstrous collar that might have been worn by a clown in a circus rose the noble, massive head, with the profile of a Roman emperor. Bruckner and Wolf often met on friendly terms at concerts, at rehearsals or in the streets, and Wolf later repeatedly visited Bruckner in his home in the Hessgasse. Bruckner showed some interest in Wolf's music and referred affectionately to him as his 'Wölferl.' Any really close intimacy between them, however, was impossible owing to temperamental, religious and intellectual differences.

The brothers Schalk, Eckstein, Göllerich, Löwe and others formed a band of pupils and disciples of Bruckner's on whom he placed great reliance, and Joseph Schalk and Löwe, in particular, were able, through the Vienna Wagner Verein, to do much to make his music known. When the Wagner Verein, in 1888, under Schalk's leadership, began to devote much of its time to Wolf's music, Bruckner became childishly jealous and pretended to himself that he was being neglected, although he remained on apparently friendly terms with his 'rival.' It was perhaps on account of this attitude that, on the occasion of this journey to Berlin for the performance of his *Te Deum*, Bruckner declined to travel in the same carriage as Wolf, saying that the latter was too lively for him.

At midday on 5th January the Vienna train drew up at the Anhalter station in Berlin. Bruckner's appearance, as, among the last passengers, he stepped down from the carriage, aroused general amusement, for he had clothed himself in so many woollen garments as to be almost unrecognizable. Wolf, for his part, was in trouble. It was his custom to provide himself with some cotton wool, which he used to dip in oil and fit into his ears, to deaden the clatter of the train. On this occasion he had brought none with him and in consequence had tried in vain during the night to get to sleep. In desperation he had stuffed quantities of bread into his ears, which in the morning he had been unable completely to remove, so that in Berlin he had to see a doctor, who relieved him at once of the bread in his ears and 20 marks.[1] He was afterwards directed by friends to

<hr>

[1] This story, very solemnly related, occurs in Natalie Bauer-Lechner's *Fragmente, Gelerntes und Gelebtes* (Vienna 1907), in a section of the book devoted to hygiene. Melanie Köchert was given an account of the incident in a letter of 8th January.

a shop in the Leipzigerstrasse where a kind of ear-plug, the 'Antiphon,' was obtainable. He purchased a pair of these and henceforward was never without them. He habitually slept in them and often used them during the day-time as well. They became for him a necessity of life.

In Baron Lipperheide's Berlin residence Wolf was given every attention he could desire. He lived there 'like a prince in a fairy-tale, who has only to utter a wish, to see it at once fulfilled.' The baron possessed an enormous collection of pictures, engravings, armour and antique bronzes, and a unique library of costume (later presented to the Prussian State). His house was like a museum. Wolf wrote to the baroness that the angels in heaven might almost envy him his feeling of comfort and well-being.

On the day of his arrival he attended a rehearsal of *Der Feuerreiter* and the *Elfenlied*. He was well pleased with the effect of his scoring, which, of course, he had never heard before this. The solo part in the *Elfenlied* was charmingly sung by Jeannette de Jong. On the 7th there followed the rehearsals of the songs with orchestra, but here everything did not go smoothly. The singer, Anna Corver, took Margit's ballad very slowly, but Wolf objected to this and worked himself up into an indescribable state of agitation. When Ochs pointed out that they were only following the directions on the score, Wolf replied: 'You ought to have seen at once that that was a piece of stupidity on my part!' Georg Ritter, the singer of *Anakreons Grab*, wished to end on a high note and Wolf fairly howled with rage.

Wolf sent similar accounts of the concert to most of his friends, of which the best is perhaps that to Kauffmann:

Margit and *Anakreons Grab* were simply not understood, either by the conductor, by the singers, or by the audience. They were, so to speak, rejected. On the other hand the public went after the *Elfenlied* like a bear after honey. They didn't know how to contain themselves in their delight. Naturally it had to be repeated. *Der Feuerreiter* struck home like a bomb. Endless applause, calls, and clamour, '*da capo!*', 'Wolf!'—but I did not appear. Meanwhile I hid myself among the standing room. When, after the uproar had died down, I took my place again in the box assigned to me, the infernal noise broke out again and, willy nilly, I had to make the most artistic bows to right and left from my box. So the public enforced its wishes. The performance of both choral pieces was excellent. Chorus and orchestra achieved everything humanly possible. The *Feuerreiter* made a splendid impression. It was fearfully beautiful. Everything was at high tension. The effect was shattering. What a shame, what a shame, that you were not there! You would have opened your eyes. The

Elfenlied sounded heavenly. It glittered and sparkled in moonbeams, so that in visualizing it one almost forgot to listen. Ochs brought out in the best way all the characteristic instrumental witticisms. Yes, yes, it was indeed lovely.

Now I am only waiting to see if Lilli Lehmann is to be won over for a song recital. I will introduce myself to her to-morrow. If the venture comes off my success will be complete.

The papers are almost wholly appreciative and kindly disposed. Even the wild Tappert approves of me. More one cannot wish for.

Wolf did not succeed in interviewing Lilli Lehmann; through the wife of Fritz Mauthner the singer sent word that her co-operation was not to be depended on owing to other engagements. Through the success of the concert, however, Wolf found himself, for the first time in his life, approached by publishers with offers for his works. Some time before this the *Elfenlied* had been offered to Schott's, but Dr. Strecker had decided that it would be better to await the public performance, as Wolf might find that he wished to make alterations, as had been the case with *Christnacht*. The composer interpreted this—not quite justifiably—as a rejection, and considered himself at liberty to dispose of it elsewhere. Ries & Erler were the first to make an offer for the work, but it was eventually sold outright to Fürstner for 300 marks.

Wolf's stay in Berlin was prolonged into three weeks. During this time he renewed many of the friendships he had formed during his first visit two years previously. His most frequent companions were Ochs, Sternfeld, and Mauthner. With Ochs he visited the museums. During a long walk through the Grunewald there was some discussion between Wolf and Mauthner of the latter's *Vom armen Franischko* as a possible source of a one-act opera.

New acquaintances were the singer, composer and writer Ernst Otto Nodnagel, and Prince Bojidar Karageorgevitch.

Nodnagel was a young man of twenty-four, with all the enthusiasm of his years. Two years earlier Arnold Mendelssohn had introduced him to Wolf's songs and from that time he dated his own artistic maturity, with the attainment of what he considered a new and individual style. In the music-room of the Villa Lipperheide Wolf went through a number of these songs of Nodnagel's with their composer, pointing out unnecessary modulations and other defects. It was a new experience for Wolf to have a disciple and he seems to have treated the young man with kindness and shown considerably

more patience than was usual with him.   He let off steam, however,
afterwards in a letter to Melanie Köchert:

I have just been disturbed by the visit of a man who wants at all costs to
play me his songs.   I must therefore break off. . . .   After an interruption
of three-quarters of an hour I continue this letter in a condition of the
deepest dejection.   The man, Nodnagel by name, an enthusiastic admirer
(as he believes) of my songs, has carried out his cruel design and massacred
me with a dozen of his songs.   You know, dear lady, what I can do in the
matter of listening to and playing the most miserable music, but what I had
to listen to from Nodnagel beats the band, as they say.   Countless love-
songs, like those that adorn the modern schoolgirls' annuals, performed in
a strident baritone voice with the insanely affected fervour and passion
common to all those who fancy themselves men of genius—it reminded me
of Goldschmidt.   In addition, the most pitiless scourging of the poor
instrument, which cracked in all its joints, to say nothing of the actual composition—this paragon of cretinism and bestiality. . . .   Ah, it was
maddening.   And to all that, as he ingenuously asserted, the acquaintance
with my 'famous' songs had inspired him, without, to be sure, as he candidly added, impairing his 'individuality'—in which conclusion I acquiesce
with all my heart. . . .   On one volume of his nefarious compositions
stands the dedication: 'To the great Hugo Wolf, from the would-be great';
on the other: 'To the inspired tone-poet Hugo Wolf, in respectful admiration.'   And an honourable man must swallow insults like these!

Nodnagel had included the Mörike *Elfenlied* in the programme of
his début as a singer on 24th January 1893, and on 5th October of the
same year he had sung *Der Freund* in public as far afield as Kibarty,
in Russia.   After meeting Wolf in Berlin in January 1894 he gave
Wolf concerts in the same month at Darmstadt, on the 10th, and
Worms, on the 13th.   In Berlin a little later he sang in two concerts
over forty of Wolf's songs.   In 1897 he published a long essay,
'Hugo Wolf, der Begründer des neudeutschen Liedes' in the *Magazin
für Literatur*, and in 1904 he introduced Wolf as a character in a
novel, *Käthe Eisinger*.

Prince Bojidar Karageorgevitch, a cousin of the later King of
Serbia, had accompanied Bruckner to Berlin.   During one of the
rehearsals for the Philharmonic concert he had approached Wolf,
who had had tears of rage in his eyes, and asked what was the matter.
He had been told sharply to mind his own business.   On the following day the two men found themselves fellow guests at a supper
party and Wolf shyly asked the prince: 'Are you still angry?'   They
became friends and later, back in Vienna, Wolf often visited Karageorgevitch and was insatiable in his demands for Spanish folk-songs,
which the latter had learned in the course of his travels and could

accompany on the guitar. Karageorgevitch made the first French translations of the words of some of Wolf's songs.

The Weltis were other old friends whom Wolf looked up during his second Berlin visit. At their house, he was just about to show his *Italian Song Book* to Emilie Herzog, when the door opened and another guest appeared. It was Richard Strauss, who had also brought his latest songs with him. Welti introduced the two composers to each other but no conversation took place between them. Strauss's music was antipathetic to Wolf, who blamed Nodnagel for mentioning it in the same breath as his own.

Other people's songs continued to plague him. Sternfeld produced some. 'Insipid stuff,' Wolf reported.

I praised them, naturally. There's nothing to be done about it. *Mundus vult decipi, ergo decipiatur.* An old story! And Sternfeld is a dear, nice fellow, but beyond a certain point one can't talk openly with him. He must compose *too*. But who doesn't compose these days? Upon my soul, I believe I am the only one who doesn't compose to-day.

The letters to Melanie Köchert are full of these amusingly outspoken comments upon his experiences. 'To-day I visited Erich Schmidt and Frau Ida Becker,' he wrote on 17th January.

The latter, a sentimental old frump, but thoroughly good-natured, very rich, and uncommonly fond of music, received me like a prodigal son. Once again she sang me *Auf ein altes Bild*, once again she brought me thereby to the verge of despair, and once again I complimented her in the most courteous fashion. For Saturday she is inviting in my honour—that is to say to my affliction—a large company of people. Among others will appear the celebrated Julius Schulhof. In God's name! This cup of bitterness, too, will pass from me. . . . Lipperheide's cutlets and beefsteaks are mighty tasty. If that goes on much longer I shall be in condition for a fat stock show. . . . As Ochs told me to-day, Bruckner travelled back to Vienna yesterday alone. Not a soul accompanied him in the train. You will shortly hear—but don't give away the secret—wonderful things about Bruckner the future spouse. . . . But silence! That I'll only tell you when we're quite alone. Blab it out to no one—agreed? It is a deep secret, or should be, until it's made public. So keep it dark.

This was a reference to the comical episode of Bruckner's brief engagement to the chambermaid of a Berlin hotel.

Perhaps the most enjoyable function attended by Wolf in the course of his visit to Berlin was the celebration of the tenth anniversary of the foundation of the Zwanglosen, a select company, including Sternfeld, Ochs, Welti, Max Friedländer, Paul Schlenther and Otto Brahm, who met once a week in a beer-garden. For the anniversary celebrations, on 21st January, guests were invited, including Wolf and a number of ladies. It was some time before Wolf came out of his shell. From nine o'clock in the evening until one o'clock in the morning he passed almost unnoticed; from one until five in the morning he was among the merriest of them all and, as he sat at the piano performing innumerable musical japes, the central point of the whole gathering. At 4 a.m. he had a tremendous success with the first *Cophtisches Lied* from the Goethe volume and the Mörike *Abschied*.

On 24th January, the last day of his stay, Sternfeld, at Wolf's request, took him to Potsdam, to the palace of Sans-souci and to the Wannsee, where is the grave of Heinrich von Kleist. For a long time Wolf stared in silence at the resting place of the author of *Penthesilea*.

On the next day he departed for Mannheim, accompanied for part of the way by Fritz Mauthner. During the journey the proposal to make a one-act opera out of Mauthner's *Vom armen Franischko* was revived. A scenario was outlined, but beyond this the matter was never taken.

Mannheim was Wolf's headquarters during the succeeding three weeks. He stayed with relations of Grohe, who had returned to live in the city again. On 29th January the two friends went to Darmstadt for the recital of Wolf's songs arranged by the Wagner Verein there. This was not an engagement that the composer had particularly looked forward to, for he knew that Arnold Mendelssohn was likely to be present and feared that their former amicable relationship would have been affected by his quarrel with Wette, Mendelssohn's best friend and artistic associate. He did in fact encounter Mendelssohn, with some embarrassment and distrust, but to his surprise and pleasure learned that it had been Mendelssohn himself who had been responsible for the organization of the Darmstadt concert. The occasion was the twenty-second meeting of the Wagner Verein, in the hall of the Hotel zur Traube. The programme consisted of eighteen of Wolf's songs, the artists being Richard Senff, who included among other things the great *Prometheus*, and Frieda Zerny, a young soprano attached to the opera-house at Mainz. At the outset the audience received the songs rather coolly, but they gradually warmed up in the course of the evening until in the end the enthusiasm grew to a climax unprecedented in the town. Wolf let the singers appear alone in response to the applause, but after his Berlin acquaintance Nodnagel had several times urged him not to spoil the success of the concert, he made his bow, was repeatedly recalled, and became very heated and excited.

After the concert he learned that a supper party had been arranged in his honour by the Wagner Verein committee. He took one look into the dining-room and then turned about and fled from the hotel. He anticipated speeches and formalities of a kind for which he had little liking and it was in vain that Grohe tried to persuade him to return. 'I must have some fresh air, and will go for a walk,' Wolf said. 'I'm not at all hungry.' He disappeared, leaving Grohe to explain to the committee and their guests that the composer had been suddenly 'taken ill.' An hour later Wolf and Grohe were on their way back to Mannheim.

Grohe found that the Berlin atmosphere had not improved the state of Wolf's nerves, and Arnold Mendelssohn gained a similar impression from his second meeting with him. At Mannheim he suffered much from sleeplessness, in spite of the use of his new ear-plugs. He told Grohe that in the Spanish song,

> Alle gingen, Herz, zur Ruh,
> Alle schlafen, nur nicht du,

he had sung of his own innumerable waking nights. The peculiar arrangement of Mannheim's streets and blocks of buildings, which form squares of uniform size, caused him much annoyance and confusion. It was his custom to walk very rapidly through the streets, with head sunk forward, looking neither to left nor to right, and very often he lost his way in the town, and even in houses that were known to him he found himself sometimes on the wrong floor, or blundered into the wrong doors.

During this stay with Grohe at Mannheim Wolf first made the personal acquaintance of Hugo Faisst, the amateur singer who had appeared at the recital at Tübingen in the previous October. Faisst came to Mannheim specially to meet him, and in a very short time the two had become friends for life. Faisst lived in Stuttgart and was by profession a barrister. He had been introduced to Wolf's songs by Kauffmann and had responded to them with all the enthusiasm of his ardent heart. Although his voice was not a particularly good one by professional standards, he possessed much of Wolf's own power of bringing a song to life by the intensity and warmth of his expression. Burly, pugnacious, superbly generous and loyal, he won a place in the composer's affections that was all his own. There was nothing that he would not do for Wolf. He sang the songs on every possible occasion in public and in private, besides arranging at his own expense concerts at which other artists performed them. To his munificence there was simply no limit. In the course of his visits to the Kauffmann household at Tübingen Wolf had been known to grumble at the rather antiquated piano available there. When Faisst learned of this he gave Kauffmann a magnificent Bechstein as a Christmas present, so that Wolf should have a worthy instrument to play on when he came there again.

An account of the Darmstadt concert in a letter of 2nd February from Wolf to the Baroness von Lipperheide contains this passage:

Frl. Frieda Zimmer, of Mainz, sang the soprano songs with a beautiful warm voice and much understanding. Moreover, she distinguishes herself, too, by a rare physical beauty, and if I don't leave Mannheim very shortly—she is coming to Grohe's to rehearse with me this evening for a concert which is to take place at Mannheim on the 8th of this month—I shall be foolish enough to fall head over heels in love with her. That would be the limit, with all my bad luck! Let us hope for the best!

This Frieda Zimmer, or Frieda Zerny, to give her the stage name she preferred to use, was an extremely handsome and attractive woman of about thirty years of age. Wolf did not escape the predicament foreshadowed above. The following passage occurs in an unpublished letter to his sister Käthe: [1]

You need not be so very much astonished at my being in love. When I love anybody, that always implies that I am loved in return, as for example is now the case. Frl. Zerny is moreover an altogether exceptional phenomenon. Quite apart from her enormous artistic capability—she possesses a splendid mezzo-soprano voice—she also distinguishes herself by quite outstanding culture and an energetic character that is unmatched in the whole world. Besides that she is young and beautiful—not pretty, but *beautiful*—and sings my things with a devotion and an understanding such as one cannot conceive bettered even in a dream.

With his two new-found interpreters, Faisst and Frieda Zerny, and the tenor Konrad Diezel, Wolf gave successful concerts of his own music at Stuttgart on 7th February and at Mannheim on 8th February. On the 18th the same three singers joined Wolf in a matinée recital at Tübingen. This concert was also successful—even financially. After paying Diezel's fee, Wolf and Frl. Zerny had 500 marks to share between them.

After the Tübingen concert Wolf stayed with Faisst at Stuttgart, at Archivstrasse 5. For a week Frl. Zerny, who had obtained leave of

[1] Written 14th March 1894, from Vienna. Original in the Prussian State Library.

absence from the Mainz opera-house, was there too, and every day they dined together with Faisst, their 'guardian angel,' as Wolf called him, 'who by his generosity certainly earned for himself a stall in heaven.'

These were memorable days in Wolf's life, when for a time he was raised above care and depression and nervous irritation into a world of friendship, love and understanding.   His love-affair prospered and through Faisst he greatly extended the range of his acquaintances in Swabia.   He was taken, with Frieda Zerny, to see his friend's mother, Frau Henriette Faisst, at Heilbronn, and there encountered another admirer of his songs in Dr. Edwin Mayser, a high-school teacher and savant, who was also an accomplished amateur musician and became later the pianist of Faisst's Stuttgart Hugo Wolf Verein. Wolf also became friendly with Apollo Klinckerfuss, the representative at Stuttgart of the firms of Bechstein and Blüthner.   His wife Johanna was a pianist, a pupil of Liszt's, and his daughter Margarethe also became a well-known player.   Through the Klinckerfuss family Wolf came to know Silvio della Valle di Casanova, an Italian *marchese*, poet and patron of the arts, the friend of Busoni and of many other musicians, writers and artists.   He possessed a fine villa at Pallanza, on Lake Maggiore, but at this time was living a simple student's life in Germany.   Other new acquaintances were August Halm, the composer and critic, then a divinity student, Emil Engelmann, whose poems Wolf talked of setting to music, the publisher Adolf Nast, of Degerloch, and the Lambert family.

Another encounter of this time was with the poet and novelist Richard Voss, who was at Stuttgart for the production of his play *Malaria*.   Voss was a friend of the Marchese della Valle di Casanova, who introduced him to Wolf.   The circumstances of the meeting were rather unfortunate, for Voss was for three days continuously engaged in cooking risotto in Italian costume at a charity bazaar.   In this he was an enormous success, using up a whole hundredweight of rice and earning a large sum of money for the bazaar funds.   But for Wolf this was all a stupid waste of time that might have been more profitably spent in discussing the possibility of Voss writing for him an opera book.   Voss, in his reminiscences, says that Wolf did suggest a subject to him, but that he knew he had no talent for that sort of thing and the subject was an impossible one.   A few days after the bazaar the two men met again in the company of the *marchese*, but Wolf was in a bearish mood and chaffed the poet by

FRIEDA ZERNY, *c.* 1894

inquiring whether the order which he wore round his neck had been awarded him for his services to cookery. Although he saw little chance of their successfully collaborating, Voss himself was inclined to be friendly and regretted the unmistakably unsympathetic attitude adopted towards him by Wolf.

The Voss episode was the only cloud that formed in the sky during these singularly harmonious days in Stuttgart and its environs. A letter to Melanie Köchert on 20th February had reported:

I am enjoying my stay here quite exceptionally and the intercourse with my friends here (and I have only too many of them) is extremely pleasant and stimulating. Herr and Frau Klinckerfuss outdo each other in attention to me. What a shame that you cannot witness all the love and admiration that is given to me here in fullest measure! My friend Faisst is never failing in kindness. He reads my every wish in my eyes. There is never any disputing or quarrelling, for we are one in body and soul. This wonderful man only lives in my music and he can't do enough to give me continual new proofs of his boundless devotion. Ah, I have learned for the first time in foreign parts what friendship really is. The thought of my so-called Viennese friends fairly makes me shudder. Thus you will understand how this pure atmosphere delights me. I feel too that I am becoming by degrees a better man and I begin to acquire anew faith and trust in mankind.

Wolf arrived back in Vienna on 28th February. It was necessary to work out a practical scheme whereby he and Frieda Zerny could both live. To remain in Vienna seemed impossible and the first plan was one of flight together to the United States. In a letter to Kauffmann on 7th March he wrote:

'We' now busy ourselves with important plans. She wishes to leave the stage, in order to live entirely for the propagation of my songs. We have therefore decided to travel to America, to the Land of Gold, to lay the foundations of a decent existence on a safe basis of dollars. I have already taken the first steps and written to an influential impresario at Boston.[1]

It was probably at this time that Wolf, in company with his friend Öhn, began to take English lessons from Miss Agnes Park, the former governess of the Köchert children.[2]

---

[1] From a passage restored by Wilhelm Schmid in the article already cited.

[2] Wolf made several attempts to learn the English language. The first was at the end of 1883, when he contemplated going to America with Eckstein's friend Gebhardt. His teacher on this occasion was a Miss Bowring. In 1887 Miss Park came out to Vienna as governess to the Köchert children and gave English lessons to Wolf in exchange for German lessons from him. The subject of Miss Park's first German lesson was Kleist's *Penthesilea*! This arrangement was soon given up. At the time of Wolf's third attempt Miss Park was established independently as a teacher of English in Vienna.

While awaiting developments in connection with this proposed American concert tour, he turned his attention to the unfinished *Italian Serenade* for orchestra. On 16th March he told Grohe: 'Since a few days ago I have been working again at the *Italian Serenade*, for which I have composed a new movement.' This new movement has not survived in its complete form, but there is a pencil sketch in the National Library, Vienna, with more than forty bars of music, dated 8th March 1894. A few days later Wolf quoted the opening theme:

in a letter to Frieda Zerny and said that the movement he was developing out of it was 'intended to take the place of a scherzo' in his *Italian Serenade*. The completion of this by the 16th was a step forward towards the planned work in several movements, but later in this same year he had to tell Grohe: 'Unfortunately there are still difficulties with the suite. To be sure, a new movement has come into existence, but the *adagio* languishes still in its fragmentary opening bars, and will embark on absolutely no further discussion, no matter what I do.'

On 24th March Frieda Zerny came to Vienna. During her stay there she was given hospitality by Wolf's friends Edmund and Marie Lang. A week later Faisst arrived, and on 3rd April Frl. Zerny, Faisst, Jäger and Wolf gave a concert in the Bösendorfersaal. This was actually the first concert wholly devoted to Wolf's songs to be given in Vienna. According to the composer himself, its success was a downright sensational one. Jäger was in better voice than he had been for some years and Frl. Zerny's temperament found perfect opportunities for expression in such songs as *Die Zigeunerin*, *Erstes Liebeslied eines Mädchens*, *Geh', Geliebter, geh' jetzt!* and *Das Köhlerweib ist trunken*. Her performance of the last-named song caused the audience itself to be seized by a kind of intoxication. Nearly half the songs on the programme had to be repeated. It is noteworthy that such scenes of enthusiasm were frequent whenever Wolf himself appeared at a concert of his own works. It cannot be said that the audiences of his own day were at all slow to recognize his genius. If his music did not make the headway towards general recognition that might have been expected from the almost invariable

acclamation it met with at his own concerts, that was no doubt partly
due to hostility in high places, particularly among the Viennese
clique, and to professional jealousy; partly to the restrictions Wolf
himself imposed upon his publisher in the matter of advertisement;
and partly, perhaps principally, to the inertia and overweening
vanity of the majority of singers, who would have nothing to do with
a development of the art which made increased demands upon skill
and intelligence without offering compensating advantages in the
matter of limelight for themselves.   But at the hands of devoted
artists such as Ferdinand Jäger, Frieda Zerny or Hugo Faisst,
Wolf's music was at once accepted and understood by the concert-
going public.

On 5th April Wolf introduced Faisst and Frl. Zerny to the Vienna
Wagner Verein.   On 14th April he gave another concert with them,
this time at Graz.   Jäger was to have sung here too, but at the last
moment indisposition caused him to retire from the engagement.
Partly owing to this, which meant that Wolf appeared at Graz with
two unknown singers, and partly owing to the very hasty arrangements for the concert, the Rittersaal was not very well attended on
this occasion.   Only half the seats were occupied and, without Wolf's
knowing it, many of these were only filled because his supporters had
bought tickets and given them away to their friends.   The greater
part of the audience consisted of women, who, in Wolf's opinion, did
not sufficiently show appreciation of Frl. Zerny's performances, and
at the end of the first group he led her back to the artists' room, in
silence laid her cloak about her shoulders, put on his own coat, seized
his hat, and turned to leave the building.   Heinrich Potpeschnigg,
who, with Faisst, had been listening from behind the scenes,
cried in alarm: 'Herr Wolf, you are not going to leave us?'   At this
Wolf stopped and looked more closely at Potpeschnigg, in whose
eyes he saw tears.   'You are weeping?   Why are you weeping then?'
Potpeschnigg confessed that he was overcome by the beauty of the
music, whereupon Wolf, deeply moved, agreed to stay and finish the
concert.   'I will play for *you*,' he said to Potpeschnigg, and after the
concert exchanged with him the brotherly 'du.'

On the next day Frieda Zerny, Wolf and a number of his admirers
at Graz, including Hausegger and August and Marie Krämer-Widl,
were the guests of the architect Friedrich Hofmann, who in 1890 had
been responsible for the arrangement of the first Wolf concert in the
town.   Faisst was unable to be present on this occasion, having left

for Stuttgart immediately after the concert. At Hofmann's Wolf
was in his best mood and accompanied Frieda and the Krämer-
Widls, who vied with one another in the performance of his songs.
Wolf and Frieda returned to Vienna on 16th April.

From Graz, two hours before the concert there began, Wolf
had sent Melanie Köchert a letter with the following surprising
passage:

> About my attitude towards Frl. Zerny I can give you the fullest reassur-
> ance. You are quite right. She is an egotist and to love is the last thing
> she can do. If you only knew how coolly and indifferently I behave
> towards her! I scarcely give her a glance. She's becoming downright
> repugnant to me. Happily, my visible aversion to her seems to make no
> particular impression upon her and so I hope to get well rid of her shortly.
> ... My theory of waiting and seeing has to my greatest contentment
> proved successful. I always said to you: 'Let us wait and see!' Since
> then I have become uncommonly clear-sighted.

This was assuredly not dissimulation, but reflected only the mood
of a moment. He was soon blinded again. Back in Vienna they
spent a few more days together and then on 20th April Frieda went
back to Germany. After her departure Wolf was with the Köcherts
and he did something unheard of with him in these years. He went
to the piano and played one of his own early songs, the first *In der
Fremde*:

> Da fahr ich still im Wagen,
> Du bist so weit von mir,

in a caricature of his youthful romantic manner. Then he began to
laugh, and he laughed until the tears rolled down his cheeks. From
this little episode, and the letter from Graz, it might be supposed
that Frieda's reign was over, or rapidly drawing to its close. But
Wolf's succeeding letters give no support at all to this idea. They
are among the most outspokenly passionate that he ever wrote her.
He proposed a secret meeting. Frieda was to go to stay with a friend
at Ulm, and from there make her way to Munich, where they would
spend a few days together, incogniti, in an hotel. This project forms
the subject of most of Wolf's many letters during the next few weeks.

He occupied himself at this time with a complete revision of the
orchestration of *Dem Vaterland*, which the performance at Stuttgart
in 1891 had shown to be necessary.

In the middle of June Wolf went to Munich. He intended travelling on 13th June, and it seems probable that he did so. A later letter

shows that he called on Frau Else Bernstein[1] at Munich on the 14th
and there is a letter to Schott's from this city on the 15th.[2]   By the
18th he was back in Vienna.   He allowed his house companions to
understand that he was paying a visit to Graz to see his family, and
on his return was able to give them comforting reassurances about
the health of his relatives.

Back at Döbling, he delayed writing to Frieda for a few days and
when he did resume his correspondence with her there was a most
marked change of atmosphere.   At Munich he had suffered complete
disillusionment, and this time there was no turning back.   He seems
to have cut his visit short on the plea of sleeplessness in the noisy
hotel.   In the succeeding correspondence he is comically unable to
conceal the fact that a great change had indeed taken place in his
feelings towards Frl. Zerny; he lets her down, as he probably thought,
in gentle stages, but, in point of fact, in a series of violent *decrescendi*
—if such a thing can be imagined.   The lady, after what she had done
for him, deserves our sympathy.   The very first letter prepares her
for probable delays and gaps in his correspondence, as he is busy
correcting the proofs of the choral arrangement of *Der Feuerreiter*
and also working on a similar new version of the *Wächterlied auf der
Wartburg*.   Then: 'After the exciting Munich days,' Frieda was told,
'a succeeding period of quiet is doubly agreeable'—a statement that
certainly falls within the category of 'things that might have been
more happily expressed.'   Further:

My mood in the present circumstances wavers between the uttermost
unease and the most depressing melancholy.   Even the Munich days were
only a deceiving ray of sunshine, which fled away all too soon.   I fear truly
that I am only fit for solitude—at least I feel happiest far from all the world,
in quiet retirement, attending only to my fancies.   But I begin to remark
that I am becoming positively impolite and that it is high time to leave this
key, even if I cannot yet find the modulation to a more cheering one.

It would seem that, in Wolf's mind, his love for Frieda Zerny was
closely bound up with his hopes of breaking the spell that had now
lain upon him since the completion of the first part of the *Italian*

---

[1] Heinrich Porges's daughter, who under the pseudonym 'Ernst Rosmer'
wrote *Die Königskinder*, afterwards set to music by Humperdinck.   Wolf was
of course, in search of an opera libretto even at this time.
[2] The letters of the 10th and 11th to Faisst are both wrongly dated in the
published volume.   They were not written in Vienna on the 16th and 17th June
1894, but on the 6th and 13th respectively.   It looks almost as though someone
were trying to conceal the fact that Wolf was at Munich at this time.   The
original letters are in the Vienna City Library.

M

Song Book at the end of 1891.   Before the Munich episode he had
written:

   As you know, the spring of my creative work has been practically dried
up for several years.   What this appalling realization means to me is quite
indescribable.   Since then I have led, truly, the existence of a frog and not
even that of a living one, but that of a galvanized frog.   To be sure, I
appear at times merry and in good heart, talk, too, before others quite
reasonably, and it looks as if I felt, too, God knows how well within my
skin; yet the soul maintains its deathly sleep and the heart bleeds from a
thousand wounds.   The one thing that sustains me in this sore affliction is
my love for you.   I seek in it solace and forgetfulness; to it I fly when the
spectre of loneliness reaches out towards me all too greedily its dead arms.
From it I hope for salvation from the unworthy shame to which my un-
blessed condition continually condemns me.   Your love for me shall be
the rainbow that shall drive away the black clouds from the horizon of my
life.   Then, my heart, we will gaze with joyful hope towards the future.
Then alone, and not before, we will conquer together a heavenly kingdom
for ourselves. . . .

And now, when, in spite of everything, the old misery came welling
back into his heart once more, he was forced to recognize that he had
been hoping for too much from this association, and with the fading
of his hopes of renewed creative powers there faded, too, his love for
Frieda Zerny.   The second letter after the Munich meeting, on 26th
June, admits frankly the change that has come over him, but seeks to
explain and excuse it in these terms:

   If our love shows itself insufficiently powerful to soothe this dread, then
in any case I am the suffering party, for with the decline of this sweetest and
strongest consolation I must sink into a condition of the completest hope-
lessness.   You may gauge from that in what spirits I am now.   It is not
the cooling of my love for you that has brought about an apparent estrange-
ment between us, or, more correctly, in me.   You must lay the blame for
all the evil that has overtaken me to the daemon which once possessed me
and inspired me to action, and which now weighs upon me, like a dragon,
sluggish and malignant, depriving my soul of air and light.   Until this
monster is overcome and transformed into a ministering spirit, nothing
on earth can give me again complete contentment, such as makes blessed
the most insignificant of mortals when he fulfils his calling.   To be sure,
it's easy for you women.   For you, love itself is a vocation.   But we must
choose such for ourselves, or let it be chosen for us, and if the choice was a
good one—well for him whose existence is crowned by the happiness of
love.   But love *alone* as a vocation for a man may perhaps be in place in a
novel or on the stage.   There it may suffice to fill out several volumes or
five acts, but in reality it certainly doesn't serve as calling for a man's whole
life.

Within a few days he is regretting that their next meeting will have
to be put off until the winter and then excusing himself for not writing
owing to the heat.   There is no need to follow in detail the steps that
led, two months after the Munich meeting, to Frieda offering to
release him from all obligation to her, an offer which he at once
accepted.   Their correspondence was to continue still for some time.
There occur in his letters conventional phrases, such as have been
employed, more or less sincerely, in innumerable similar cases.   He
wishes to remain on friendly terms with her, will always be glad to
hear from her, etc. etc.   Twice Frieda suggested a renewal of their
earlier relationship and twice Wolf rejected the proposal, the first
time protesting against her irresolution and lapse from the 'friendly'
character of their new connection, the second time in a kindly but
positively avuncular manner: 'You will become a celebrated singer;
will forget a poor devil like me and marry a marquis, if not a baron of
the realm.   That shall be the end of the novel that we began so well,
but unfortunately may not finish.'   He never actually wrote to Frieda
in the offensive terms which later references to her in letters to others
suggest.   'If you meet Frl. Zerny at Bayreuth,' he told Faisst on
17th July, 'do *not* tell her that I am invited to the Köcherts'.   Speak
in general as little as possible about me.   Between ourselves, the
party has already become antipathetic to me.   Her egotism does not
please me.   I'm not going to be her milch-cow.'   Accordingly
Frieda was told he was going to stay with Baron Schey at Traunkirchen.

In July, in letters to Kauffmann and Sternfeld, Wolf reported that
the *Wächterlied auf der Wartburg* of 1887 was 'on the anvil' for
transcription for male voice chorus and orchestra.   Some progress
was made at this time with this work but it was never completed.   A
few fragments are in the National Library in Vienna.   The *Italian
Serenade* continued to defy all Wolf's efforts to complete it.   He
found little distraction from the interminable nagging thought that as
a creative artist his life was over, the heavenly talent entrusted to him
wasted or lost, unless he could find the poet-collaborator who should
release the music imprisoned within him, who should provide the key
to the opera he had sought so long.

Here some necessary remarks upon Wolf's character may find
place.   He was, it must be admitted, a man wholly self-centred.   He
was wrapped up in himself and the ideas that possessed him to the
point almost of mania, and the manifestations of this characteristic

of his were often unpleasant enough.   Instances of what looks like
the basest ingratitude, by ordinary standards, are all too frequent in
the story of his life.   Apart from the case of Frl. Zerny, there is
hardly one of all the wonderful band of his intimate friends—and no
man ever had better friends—whose relationship with Wolf does not,
at some time or other, supply an instance of this.   But at the same
time Wolf was never greedily 'selfish,' in the ordinary sense of the
word.   His demands for himself, as a man, were minimal.   'Entbehren sollst du, sollst entbehren,' the words that he had written at
the head of the score of his youthful String Quartet, might have stood
as the motto of his whole life.   As a mere boy he had endured the
direst poverty and knew what it was to feel real hunger; as a man he
had for years existed on little more than coffee and bread and cheese,
or a slice of sausage or boiled beef, and was quite content to do so.
The key to his whole life is found in the unshakable idea that
possessed him that he had been sent into the world for one purpose
and for one purpose only—to compose music.   His attitude towards
his art was mystical.   In conversation with Müller, who had deplored
the early death of Schubert, he declared that a man was not taken
away before he had finished his life's work.   It was the work that
mattered, not the man.   The composer himself was merely the means
to an end.   He was an instrument, through which music sounded, to
be recorded thankfully as the divine gift of the gods to humanity.
It was this gift, expressed through himself, for which Wolf endured all
things, and for which he was ready at any time to sacrifice love,
friendship, money, comfort—honour even.   Selfish he was indeed,
if by selfishness is meant an unending desire to serve his own genius.
His interest in literature, even, may be considered at bottom a selfish
interest: the poets he loved best were those who possessed the
mysterious power of releasing the music within him.   Contemporary
music, apart from Bruckner, did not exist for him, or only existed
as a series of obstacles to the recognition of his own.   Why should
people bother themselves with Strauss, Humperdinck or Weingartner when they might have been performing Wolf?   He knew the
worth of what he had created, and only asked that he might be
allowed to go on producing other things from the same mysterious
source within him.   When he could do so he was gloriously happy;
when it appeared that the creative spring had run dry he was the most
miserable man alive.

On 25th July, in this year of 1894, Wolf left Vienna once again for the delectable shores of the Traunsee. He did not return, as in previous summers, to the Pfarrhof at Traunkirchen, but stayed with the Köcherts at 'Puchschacher,' their newly acquired property on the lakeside. There his only musical activity was the final correction of the proofs of the choral version of *Der Feuerreiter*, which was to be published by Schott's in September. In August Faisst spent a week as the Köcherts' guest at 'Puchschacher,' where he conquered all hearts.

After just over a month at Traunkirchen Wolf left on 1st September for Schloss Matzen, near Brixlegg, in Tyrol, where, with Grohe, he was the guest of the Lipperheides. After ten days he returned to Traunkirchen, intending to continue his journey back to Vienna in a few days, but on the 17th, at the pressing request of the Lipperheides, he was back again in Schloss Matzen. He was then, except for short periods, the only visitor to the castle and was treated like one of the family. The baroness was like a second mother to him. In the castle itself, according to Wolf's own account of his circumstances, the comfort and luxury defied description. He had a splendid Bechstein piano at his disposal, a large library in which to browse, and more fine food and drink than was really good for him. Outside lay the estate of five hundred acres, with gardens, ornamental waters, woods and parklands, and beyond that again much magnificent mountain scenery. When the weather permitted, various tours of the district were made on foot and by coach. It was all immensely agreeable, but Wolf's happiness in it was spoilt by the lack of one essential thing—'ideas,' or musical inspiration.

He was at this time becoming increasingly bitter about the opposition to his work in Vienna and the impossibility of his earning a decent living there, and talked again of migrating permanently to Berlin, where, on both his visits, he had been so cordially received and formed so many friendships. The Lipperheides did their best to persuade him to this course, and offered him a home in their Berlin residence.

In October there reached Wolf in Schloss Matzen another opera text by Grohe's friend Karl Heckel, the author of the unfortunate *Buddha* of 1890. At the time when he had rejected that libretto, Wolf had been full of ideas for turning Shakespeare's *Tempest* into an opera, and now, four years later, the result of that temporary enthusiasm was put into his hands in the form of a second Wagnerian hodge-podge by Heckel. He complained first to Faisst:

To-day I received from Grohe an opera text that his friend Heckel at

Mannheim has perpetrated. The piece calls itself *Prospero*, and is nothing but an unheard-of, indescribable, positively scandalous travesty of Shakespeare's *Tempest*. I do not understand our friend that he wishes to burden me with such muck. How long-suffering paper is!

Then in a letter to Grohe the full blaze of his anger burst out:

Only read this piece of bungling, and you will with horror become aware of how far amateurishness in poetry can go. And such a scrawl boldly calls itself an 'opera poem' and impudently ranges itself by the side of the poems of Wagner! Oh, you accursed brood of 'poets,' with your insane vanity, your ridiculous pretensions, your absurd complacency and self-infatuation! Into a sack with you and be submerged in the most poisonous of swamps, beneath toads and loathsome creeping things, for there you belong, you who make so free with sun, moon, and stars, which would have to extinguish themselves for shame and grief, if they were not happily deaf to your despicable whining! Dear friend, don't come to me ever again with any so-called poets.

Poor Heckel! No wonder he was anxious to demonstrate Wolf's 'fundamental antagonism' to the spirit of Wagner!

From Schloss Matzen Wolf returned on 18th October to Vienna, where he stayed with Eckstein at Siebenbrunnengasse 15. Already his plans for removal to Berlin had been abandoned. Earlier in this year, before his visits to Traunkirchen and Schloss Matzen, he had spent many a Sunday with the Werner family in their summer retreat at Perchtoldsdorf. Everything there reminded him of the wonderful days when the Mörike songs had been created in a surging, unbroken wave of inspiration. Almost every week he returned—to bathe in that atmosphere, so friendly, so memory-laden, to steal away from his friends and climb the Hochberg alone, there to gaze away over the Wiener Wald as in bygone days, to listen in hushed expectancy for some faint echo within him of the old rapturous singing. Always, then, he returned to the house melancholy and regretful. 'So many cherished memories are bound up with my dear Petersdorf,' he said, 'I wish I could live out here again.' In November he obtained permission to set up his winter quarters again in the Werners' house in the Brunnergasse.

At first he was hopeful of bringing to an end the long barren years. But the old complaints of insomnia, nervous irritation and mental and physical exhaustion recur again in his letters.

Soon he was back in Vienna, staying either with the Köcherts or with Eckstein. The latter recalls in his reminiscences incidents that illustrate all too clearly the perilous state of Wolf's mental and nervous health at this period. He would be woken in the morning by his friend walking rapidly to and fro in the next room, talking to himself as he did so, and as Eckstein listened Wolf's conversation with himself would mount to a confused shouting and cursing that was fearful to listen to. Often he would be surprised and alarmed at the wild grimaces that passed over the composer's face and at his habit of angrily pulling the hairs out of his beard. At such times Wolf would disappear from the Siebenbrunnengasse early in the morning and only return in the evening.

December was spent partly at Perchtoldsdorf and partly in Vienna. Two events of considerable importance brought him back to the city for a time and provided distraction from the burden of his own thoughts—the performance on 2nd December of the choral *Elfenlied* and *Feuerreiter* at one of the concerts of the Gesellschaft der Musikfreunde and, later in the month, the arrival in Vienna of Humperdinck for the production of his *Hänsel und Gretel*.

The concert of 2nd December was conducted by Wilhelm Gericke, the remainder of the rather nondescript programme consisting of Beethoven's E flat Piano Concerto and pieces by Rubinstein and d'Albert, including the latter's cantata *Der Mensch und das Leben*, which had, curiously enough, also been performed in Berlin with Wolf's *Elfenlied* and *Feuerreiter*. The soprano solo in the *Elfenlied* was sung by Sophie Chotek.

The inclusion of anything by Wolf in the programmes of the conservative-minded Gesellschaft der Musikfreunde was in itself a decided step towards recognition. Official notice was being taken of him for the first time in Vienna. In a brief biographical notice included in the printed programmes he was even claimed as a pupil of the Conservatoire. Wolf himself, having had long experience of Viennese ways, looked forward to the concert without excessive optimism, but, in point of fact, it brought him a decided success. The public was enthusiastic. Brahms was present and was seen to be warmly applauding Wolf's pieces. The critical notices were almost wholly favourable and even Hanslick himself, perhaps as a result of the interest shown in the works by Brahms, wrote a gracious, if rather condescending, notice. He praised the declamation, the vocal writing, and, apart from some noisy scoring in *Der Feuerreiter*, the orchestration, and declared, somewhat equivocally, that the works were the best that he knew of Wolf's: 'In the Gesellschaft concert Herr Hugo Wolf has for the first time presented himself with success before a wider, not exclusively Wolfian-minded public. Undoubtedly a man of intellect and talent, he needs only to guard himself from his good friends.' The composer himself had his doubts about the reality of Hanslick's conversion, but nevertheless found he had become a local celebrity overnight and, as he told the Baroness Lipperheide, was congratulated from all sides, 'chiefly because of Hanslick's review, which everybody who is conversant with the conditions found "quite wonderful."'

Humperdinck and his wife arrived in Vienna in the middle of December for the production of *Hänsel und Gretel*, and their presence brought Wolf back from Perchtoldsdorf on the 16th. On that day he called to see them at the Hotel Sacher and during the succeeding week he spent much of his time in their company. He was at the dress rehearsal of *Hänsel und Gretel* at the opera-house on the morning of the 17th and in the evening of the same day he and Eckstein, with whom he was staying, took Humperdinck and his wife to supper at a typical Viennese resort, the favourite Gartenbau restaurant, where so-called 'folk-singers' used to perform, one of them to improvised verses in dialect. In the course of this evening's entertainment the singer made punning reference in one of his impromptus to the presence of both Wolf and Humperdinck, to the astonishment of the two composers, who were not to know that a friend of Eckstein's had primed the artist with the necessary information beforehand. On the following day Wolf and Eckstein witnessed the resounding popular success of *Hänsel und Gretel* from Humperdinck's own box. They thought the performance excellent in every way and were very surprised when Humperdinck declared that that at Dresden earlier in the month had been incomparably better. The opera was having remarkable successes throughout Germany. The Vienna production was the fourth that Humperdinck had attended within a week and everywhere his work had been received with acclamation. Afterwards the much-fêted composer invited his guests to have supper with him and, in company with other friends, the party had made its way into the very doorway of a first-class restaurant near the opera-house when Wolf stopped and declared categorically that he would not enter an establishment where the Wiener Schnitzel cost a gulden. Humperdinck and the whole company was compelled to follow him to the less expensive Spatenbräu, where the remainder of the evening was passed in celebrating the triumph of *Hänsel und Gretel*. There was another performance of the opera, in the presence of the Austrian emperor, on the 21st and Wolf was again present in Humperdinck's box, this time with Jäger and his wife.   In all, *Hänsel und Gretel* was repeated twenty-five times in the 1894–5 season of the Vienna Opera-house and was invariably sold out.   Humperdinck's stay in the Austrian capital only came to an end, on 22nd December, because he had to hurry away to yet another first performance at Stuttgart.

How far were these happenings responsible for the solution of Wolf's own operatic difficulties, that followed with surprising suddenness and baffling illogicality only a very short time afterwards?   The reception given to his *Elfenlied* and *Feuerreiter* in Vienna, by the public and by the critics, including the representatives of those forces which he had always held to be his mortal enemies, intent only on blocking his path, the attainment overnight of the status of a 'local celebrity,' and the further successes which the same two works attained soon afterwards under Franz Wüllner, at Cologne, on 8th January, and under Hermann Zumpe, at Stuttgart, on 29th January—these things undoubtedly acted as a tonic upon him, renewing his confidence in himself and strengthening his will-power.   In addition, the witnessing of the triumphs of his charming and modest friend, Humperdinck, whom he had never taken seriously as a composer, seems to have powerfully affected him, to have spurred him on not so much to solve his own operatic problems as to persuade himself that they did not really exist.   Eckstein has recounted how Wolf returned from the performance of *Hänsel und Gretel* in a very excited state and how the two of them spent the whole night in animated conversation about Humperdinck's success, about the work itself and its performance.   Wolf discussed from all points of view Humperdinck's choice of subject-matter and the way in which he had handled it, he dissected the whole work, pointing out its particular beauties and also what appeared banal and uninteresting to him in it.   He compared with it the operatic experiments of Adalbert von Goldschmidt.   Eckstein also seems to attach particular impor-tance to the experience of Wolf and Humperdinck in the Gartenbau restaurant: 'The totally unexpected homage of the improvising singer, of which he could not suspect the true background, had obviously given great pleasure to him, too; it was assuredly the first time in his life that he had had the feeling of having become "popular." [1]   According to Eckstein's account the episode took place

---

[1] *Alte unnennbare Tage.*

* M

later in the same evening as the first Vienna performance of *Hänsel und Gretel* and it may well be imagined that in those circumstances such an incident, trivial in itself, might have had important consequences in its effect upon Wolf's excited imagination. Humperdinck's diary makes it clear, however, that Eckstein's memory was at fault and that the visit to the Gartenbau restaurant occurred on the day *before* the performance of the opera.

It can at least be said that in the month of December events took place which concentrated Wolf's thoughts anew upon the possibilities of operatic success, at a time when he was made aware that, even in reactionary Vienna, he had won a certain standing, popular and official, by his work in other fields.

Within a few weeks the subject of his first opera had been conclusively decided upon, the complete and, as he thought, perfect libretto was in his hands, and he was only awaiting the end of a period of exceptionally severe winter weather before returning to Perchtoldsdorf to pour out the music that he felt simmering within him.

XIII

'DER CORREGIDOR'

A MIRACLE, a miracle, an unheard-of miracle has taken place. The long desired opera-text is found; it lies before me quite complete, and I am burning with eagerness to get on with the musical treatment. You know the novel *The Three-cornered Hat* by Pedro de Alarcon. It's published by Reclam. Frau Rosa Mayreder, a gifted woman I have known for some years, has achieved the clever feat of turning the story into an extremely effective opera book and yet remaining artistically on the poet's level. Friend Schalk, to whom I read the book, expressed infinite delight in the extraordinary art and skill of the authoress and asserted that it is the comic opera *par excellence*.

So Wolf wrote to Grohe on 18th January 1895.

Strange indeed were the circumstances in which he reached the end of his quest and became possessed of what he had sought so long. After his endless difficulties over *Manuel Venegas* he bethought himself again of that other novel, by the same Spanish author, which had occupied his attention five or six years earlier. He spoke of it to Gustav Schur and mentioned Rosa Mayreder's unfortunate attempt to provide him with an operatic version of the tale. Schur suggested that the then chairman of the Wagner Verein, Franz Schaumann, might be the man to do this for him. Schaumann's *Die Abenteuer einer Neujahrsnacht*, after Zschokke, had been set to music by Richard Heuberger and he was well known in the circle of the Wagner Verein as a writer of witty light verse. He was not a close friend of Wolf's and it was Schur who approached him and suggested he should turn his attention to *The Three-cornered Hat*. Schaumann spent his holidays in preparing a libretto, which reached Wolf's hands at the end of December. Those who had the opportunity of reading Schaumann's version are agreed that it had many excellent qualities, but Wolf himself, while admitting the author's wit and intelligence, found it unsuitable for his purpose and very soon handed it back to Schur, who had the unpleasant task of restoring it to its author. Wolf spoke of Schaumann's libretto to Edmund Lang, cursing his bad luck in such matters, and Lang laughingly remarked that Rosa Mayreder's had been a better one. 'You're right!' was the reply. 'I had completely forgotten it. I would like, decidedly, to look through it again.' He expressed this wish again, more pressingly, and after some hesitation Marie Lang undertook to procure the manuscript for him from the authoress.

Wolf's friends were dumbfounded when he began, for the second time, to read Rosa Mayreder's libretto. Eagerly, greedily, this time, he skimmed through the pages that had earlier aroused only his anger and contempt. 'The text was not so bad,' he cried time and time again. 'I can't understand what I was thinking of.' Half joyfully, half in anxiety, he took the book under his arm and hurried off to read it to Schalk, Löwe and Hirsch. Their enthusiasm fanned his own, until he could no longer doubt that his years long search was at an end. He returned to the Langs in a state resembling drunkenness.

No one was more surprised than Rosa Mayreder herself when she learned that Wolf was going to set her text to music. The complete reversal of his earlier judgment was as much a mystery to her as to every one else. He never spoke of it to her, and she remarked how painfully he was affected by every recollection of his former rejection of her work. His approval now was positively embarrassing. What she had regarded as a preliminary draft, a basis for discussion between them, he looked upon as the finished product and was hard to persuade that any alterations at all were necessary. A copy of the book was made and dispatched on the round of his friends in Germany. Grohe did not withhold the expression of his misgivings, which were also shared by Heckel, but Wolf was impatient of criticism of his libretto and would not listen to their objections. He told Kauffmann that he had unbounded confidence in the poetical powers of his associate and did not in the least doubt the successful conclusion of the undertaking. To his mother he wrote of 'the vast, vast sums of money, and fame and recognition, and the deuce knows what else,' that would be his.

With hardly contained impatience and excitement he awaited the coming of the spring. On 27th January he wrote to the Baroness Lipperheide:

If only the bad winter would come to an end! As soon as it gets a little bit warmer, I want to go back to Perchtoldsdorf and give myself up completely to composing the opera; I cannot read the libretto without being seized with a musical fever. What prospects for the future! Two years of ardent, constant labour, concentrated on a single work nourished with my heart's blood: compare this with those recent barren years with day after day passed in idle dozing. . . .

Those bitter years, spent almost wholly in idleness, had left their mark upon him.   A remarkable photograph taken at this time by Richard Sommer contrasts strongly with the Heid portraits of 1889. The old velvet jacket is the same, the rest—how changed!   The hair is now close-cropped, but tending to become unruly and to stand on end; it is as if he had himself hacked off the 'artistic' mane that suited him so well in earlier years.   The face, which was the colour of old ivory, is leaner, and haggard in expression.   Suffering is written all over it.   The brow is furrowed and the whole face covered with a network of tiny wrinkles.   The marvellous eyes are the same, but the gaze is narrower, fixed, hostile, almost maniacal.   It might almost be the portrait of a man who had been subjected to physical torture.   It is well to remember that there was another aspect of him, which the camera never succeeded in catching, that his friends have recorded that his laughter was Homeric, that those who never saw Wolf rejoice have simply no conception of what joy is.   But the sadness and loneliness of the man that gazes out at us from these later photographs is unmistakable and unforgettable.

'Two years of ardent, constant labour' was Wolf's first estimate of the duration and intensity of the effort that would be required of him in order to bring into being *Der Corregidor*, as he had decided to call his opera.   During that time he needed to live, and, if possible, to be free from monetary cares.   In these circumstances Baron Lipperheide generously consented to make Wolf an annual grant of 1,000 marks, and an additional 500 marks was contributed jointly by Faisst, Grohe and Hermann Hildebrandt, a banker at Mannheim.   The moving spirit behind this plan was Grohe.   It proved to be less difficult than had been anticipated to persuade Wolf to accept the money. According to Marie Lang, he remarked in conversation: 'High time! High time that that occurred to someone!   Really it should be the cursed liability and obligation of the State to support its musicians and poets.' [1]

[1] 'Wie der Corregidor entstand' (*Die Zeit*, Vienna, 23rd February 1904).   In this article Marie Lang described how she herself took her courage in her hands and approached Baron Lipperheide, who was at the time staying in Vienna, with a request that he should liberate Wolf from all anxiety about the future by providing him with an assured income, and how the baron agreed to do this.   Decsey accepted this account of Marie Lang's, but there are in existence some letters from Grohe to Rosa Mayreder, written shortly after the article appeared, in which he protests that this part of it is not in accordance with the facts.   Wolf's

The first notes of *Der Corregidor* were actually written while Wolf was still staying with Eckstein in the Siebenbrunnengasse. On the evening of 12th March, the day before his thirty-fifth birthday, he set to music the Night Watchman's call at the beginning of the fourth act. Ten days later he wrote the first part of Tio Lukas's *Spanish Wine* song in the second act—perhaps out of compliment to the bottles of Marsala, Malaga, Madeira and sherry, which, together with a wonderful birthday cake, bearing an effigy in marzipan of the Corregidor, had been given him by the Köcherts. The weather was now improving, but he was kept in Vienna by rehearsals for a performance of *Dem Vaterland*, under Eduard Kremser, by the Wiener Männergesangverein. An entry in Heinrich Werner's diary for 24th March reads: 'Wolf and I go together to the Männergesangverein concert, where his hymn *Dem Vaterland* is performed. Wolf is called for and appears once—only, as he afterwards said, to annoy Brahms, who sat opposite. He was very pleased with the performance.' *Dem Vaterland* was published soon after this by Schott's, but only in vocal score.

On 1st April Wolf moved out to Perchtoldsdorf again and threw himself 'like a madman,' as he himself said, into the task of composing his opera. He reported the progress made in a wonderful series of letters to Melanie Köchert.

The piano I found hardly out of tune at all; Marie's preserves still in good condition. Kitchen and lobby were scrubbed clean and everything in its place. Altogether this had an extremely soothing influence upon me. But what is all that in comparison with the deep peace that surrounds me here, which leads again to my arms the so bitterly renounced joys of solitude, which restores me to myself? This indescribable feeling of the most complete seclusion almost stupefies me. I begin almost to be afraid of myself, for it seems to me as though in the short period of my being here I am become another man. A better one, let us hope. To-morrow morning work begins. To-day I don't venture to tempt fortune. I am still too confused by the first intoxicating impressions of this sudden change. To-morrow I shall be more collected and, God willing, write something fine and beautiful. [1st April.]

---

letter to Grohe of 18th January 1895 shows conclusively that the protest was justified: 'The magnanimity and truly magnificent generosity of my patron the Baron von Lipperheide, of whose friendly intentions you have informed me, could, as far as I am concerned, manifest themselves at no more convenient time than just now, when all my thoughts and aspirations should be directed only to one thing—the great throw of the dice that shall decide my future fate.' Later in the same letter Wolf names the sum—1,500 marks—that would be sufficient for his needs. Lipperheide's visit to Vienna, during which, according to Marie Lang, she broached the subject to him, did not take place until April, as letters show.

It is eight o'clock in the evening and I employ the gathering twilight for a walk on the nearby Hochberg. . . .   I have just returned from this walk in the moonlight, which, in thought at least, I undertook in company. Heavens, what a night!   Cool and fresh, scarcely a cloud in the sky, and so light that I could have written these lines quite as well by moonlight.   I suppose you are surprised that I write letters at all, but except to my sister I have not yet written to any one from here.   It wouldn't be possible, for I work now without pause from seven in the morning (I get up at six) until darkness sets in and often also far into the night.   Yesterday and to-day I was especially fertile in invention.   I have already reached as far as the concluding verses of the second act,[1] after yesterday also conceiving the festal march music at the end of the first act.   The tipsy song of Don Pedro, 'Wenn dich Einer küssen will,' will amuse you greatly.   I consider the scene with Manuela especially successful.   There's something in that! To-morrow, God willing, it's the turn of the conclusion of the second act. [8th April.]

I shall come after all on Friday.   I *must* play you the new things—else it gives me no rest.   The end of the second act was completed yesterday morning.   The tone of the parodistic heroics of the two drinking companions Tonuelo and Pedro can't be better imagined, let alone composed. But why am I talking?   On Friday you shall judge for yourself.   [10th April.]

Just working on the first scene of the first act, of which I originally despaired and which I had already considered cutting out of the libretto.   But now a most happy idea has occurred to me and I believe the piece will be quite magnificent.   The holidays I shall probably spend here, as the cold weather will hardly lure out any visitors.   The riddle of the missing cuff has now been solved.   It was discovered in the drawer of my laundry cupboard.   In my haste I forgot to put on the second one.   On the other hand I forgot my door-key in my winter coat.   Please bring it with you on your proposed visit.   [13th April.]

To-day there are occurring to me the most sublime ideas.   I don't know how I shall be able to master them.   Come out here soon, for God's sake, to your cordially greeting, beyond human conception blissful, Hugo Wolf. [16th April.]

A thousand thanks for attending quickly to the gold band on the cigarette holder, which is incomplete without it.   The lost little gold ring I found yesterday.   I'll bring it with me some time.   I write just before lunch, so must hurry, else I'll get a poor meal.   Swarms of ideas!   Yesterday evening and early to-day thirty bars of orchestral interlude composed which for passion and sweetness leave behind everything that has flowed from my pen to date.   To-day is a wonderful day—not in other respects, to be sure, for it is cold and dull.   But within me it glows and blazes as in a crater.   [19th April.]

---

[1] Wolf began work at Perchtoldsdorf with the second scene of the second act, from the *Spanish Wine* song, begun in Vienna on 22nd March.

A letter from the Berlin publishers Ries & Erler was enclosed with the above:

Would you be inclined, and for what honorarium, to set to music the *Erl King* of Goethe for mixed chorus, soloists, and orchestra? Father, baritone; Child, soprano; Erl King, tenor. We believe the idea is not a bad one, as it is wholly in the spirit of the poem.

Across the margin of this Wolf scrawled:

Received to-day. What an ass! Wrote back: 'Regret have neither desire nor time to take up your proposal. Full stop.'

He found in practice that further minor alterations were necessary in the text. For the most part these consisted of extensions of lyrical passages. Thus he asked for one or two additional verses for the love duet in the second act and for a new opening to the second part of the same act. He wished also to make more use of the chorus, which was originally to be employed only at the conclusion of the fourth act. Rosa Mayreder satisfied his wishes in these respects and he accepted her emendations with expressions of the warmest gratitude. He found every line 'magnificent,' and so great was his respect for his poet that every trifling verbal alteration that he made on his own account had to be explicitly pointed out and justified by reference to the demands of musical declamation.

On Easter Sunday Heinrich Werner and Edmund Hellmer, another young friend, the son of the sculptor of the same name, called to see Wolf at Perchtoldsdorf. Fearful of disturbing him at his work, they waited about until midday, when he appeared at a window and waved to them to come in. He was radiantly happy and at once played over the scattered scenes from the opera that he had already composed. 'That will become something,' he said. 'They won't throw *that* on one side for ever. That *must* succeed.'

On the following day he conceived the lovely motive associated with Frasquita, and the opera began to forge ahead with irresistible impetus. For day after day he took up his task at six, or half-past six, in the morning and continued with scarcely a break until seven o'clock in the evening. The music took shape in his mind as he worked at the piano and he afterwards set it down on paper with such certitude that the manuscript took the form of a perfect vocal score, ready for the printer. The extent of each day's work was carefully recorded.

Twice he had the joy of communicating to a gathering of his friends the achievements of his solitude. On Sunday, 28th April,

Edmund and Marie Lang, the Mayreders, Rudolf von Larisch and Richard Hirsch paid a visit to the Brunnengasse. As they entered the garden gate he ran down the narrow winding stairway with hands outstretched towards them. His dark eyes gleamed. His countenance and bearing were expressive of a blissful pride—a pride, in Rosa Mayreder's own phrase, 'such as a man feels who has prepared for his guests a kingly gift.' He led them to his room, where Baron Lipperheide, who was on a visit to Vienna, was already present, with his nephew, the painter Karl Rickelt, and played and sang what he had written—about half of the first and second acts. Every one was deeply moved; the friends embraced each other in happiness and tears of joy were shed. In a letter to Melanie Köchert Wolf reported: 'Now you can imagine how the story struck home. Even Lipperheide was beside himself and assured me that he understood everything, for he says that music like that to my opera must be understood by everybody. Frau Mayreder swam in bliss, Marie naturally howled, and Hirschlein looked quite stupified. What a shame that Schalk wasn't there!' In this state of excitement and emotion Wolf spoke of his gratitude to his librettist. She had brought fulfilment of the deepest longing of his life. 'You have given me more than any one,' he told her, 'more than my mother, who gave me life.' The same Viennese friends, with the addition of Heinrich Werner and Ferdinand Löwe, met again at Perchtoldsdorf a week later, and by then the first act was complete and most of the second as well.

So rapid was the progress he was making that he very soon abandoned his earlier estimate of two whole years for the length of time that would be necessary for the opera's completion. After four weeks' work he was already dreaming of performance in Vienna in the succeeding winter. On 29th April he wrote to his mother:

About myself I have to inform you that I spent the whole month of April, from early morning until late in the evening, working like a slave. To be sure, my work is now no hardship, but unalloyed pleasure and most blissful indulgence. I have in the short space from the first of April to to-day composed almost two acts of my opera and expect to complete the whole work by the autumn; it is to be hoped that it will come to performance in this very winter. But then you must come to Vienna for the performance; it will make an immense sensation.[1]

A few days later he told Kauffmann:

The music to *Der Corregidor* puts in the shade everything that so far has come from my pen. It is above all much more plastic and of astounding

[1] From an unpublished letter in the Prussian State Library.

simplicity and clarity. But that cannot be described in writing, that sort of thing must be heard. In two more months I hope to complete the composition. Then for the orchestration, and in the winter the performance must come about; that is my plan.

Owing to the Werner family wishing to occupy their house at Perchtoldsdorf, Wolf was compelled, on 10th May, to give up his retreat there. For a few days he stayed in Vienna with the Mayreders, before leaving, on the 16th, for Tyrol. Baron Lipperheide had invited him to spend the whole summer and autumn as his guest in Schloss Matzen, and so that he could continue to work undisturbed had put at his disposal a charming little dwelling, the so-called 'Jägerhaus,' which stood, completely isolated, on a gently rising hill in the middle of the castle park. Wolf had made it a condition of his acceptance of the baron's hospitality that he should have absolute freedom to live as he pleased, without any sort of social obligation, and at Matzen he buried himself completely in his work and saw his host only once a day, when he visited the castle for the midday meal. His other meals were brought to him in the Jägerhaus, where he lived, worked and slept. From dawn to dusk he thought about nothing but *Der Corregidor*, which continued to make rapid progress. Conditions at Matzen were wellnigh ideal—only his old feathered enemies continued to plague him, as may be seen in some further extracts from letters to Melanie Köchert:

The finches again are often bothersome. I have borrowed a gun from the painter Rickelt, to fire off warning shots. But so far I haven't got as far as shooting, I am so absorbed in my work. [22nd May.]

To-day I have allowed myself a day's rest. To-morrow I begin the third act. The recently composed music for the second act boundlessly pleases me. I consider it the best that I have so far written. There follows blow upon blow in rapidest succession and *every note* has sense and meaning. If only you could hear some of it! How amazed you would be, and how you would rejoice! I myself cannot play this music often enough—candidly, I revel in it. God, how fortunate I am that it lies in my power to give myself such pleasure! If someone else had written this music it would certainly not please me any the less, but as nobody else has rendered me that service, I must do it myself and, God knows, I do it truly only for my own pleasure, for to write for humanity would never occur to me in a dream. *I* like it, and that's sufficient. . . . To-day I have shot dead a finch, which frightfully maltreated me. But when I saw the poor thing lying there dead, great uneasiness came over me and I wished most heartily that it had remained alive. I stole away with the little corpse into the nearby wood and buried it in the earth in a remote spot. What must a murderer feel like, who has the death of a man on his conscience? I had to-day a presentiment of it.   The devil take all murdering.   But *must* one not, when one's own neck's in danger?   [25th May.]

If it rested with me I should write to you ten times a day; I certainly think of you a hundred times daily.   But I was so completely in the spell of the muse in the last few days that with the best will in the world I could not find time for letter writing.   Even now I only steal the time.   I am writing by lamplight in my comfortable little work-room.   For a few days now we have had splendid weather here.   The sun shines warm and bright and not the smallest cloudlet disturbs the blue heavens.   What a joy it is to greet the morning at five o'clock, to breathe in the splendid fresh air, and to eye the noble panorama that presents itself in majestic beauty to the intoxicated gaze—it is indescribable.   Truly, you should take a trip here with friend Faisst—it is really rewarding.   A lovelier view than that from the Rolandsbogen, twenty paces distant from my little house, is probably not to be found in the whole world.   That sort of thing one *must* see.   If paradise is only a fable, here it becomes reality.   And then I enjoy such splendour so entirely undisturbed, as if it were only created for me.   God knows, I have enjoyed much happiness on this earth, but more happy, more blissful have I never been than here in this wonderful solitude.   And how conveniently everything is at hand, how clean and tidy everything is kept! My servant, a married woman, as I subsequently learned, is a real paragon. Above all, she makes herself as scarce as possible, so that I am not disturbed on this account either.   Cleaning up is done while I share lunch with the baron, which occurs in the castle.   Supper is served me in the Jäger-häuschen.   Breakfast and supper I partake of on the balcony which sur-rounds my bedroom on two sides.   Then straight away after breakfast to work.   [30th May.]

In the meantime I was under the painful necessity of settling the hash of a couple of feathered disturbers of the peace.   Ah, one gets accustomed to everything!   [12th June.]

Further alterations in the text were found to be necessary and letters flew between Matzen and Vienna, between composer and librettist.   The latter was bidden to 'saddle her poetical racehorse' and provide two further stanzas for the duet of Frasquita and Repela in the third act.

But quick, quick, quick, for heaven's sake, or, as the Corregidor says,[1] 'for the nails of Christ!'   Quick!!! . . .   It just occurs to me that the damned holidays are nearly on us.   Before it was Easter, now it is Whitsun that threatens.   A curse on this infamous Catholic system!   But you won't, for heaven's sake, allow yourself to be kept from the job by the holidays, and during that time abandon me to despair?   You could not be so cruel. . . .   If you send me the verses this week, I hope you have pleasant holidays.   Otherwise . . . !

Before the verses arrived, he had already sketched out the music to

---

[1] Not in Rosa Mayreder's libretto, as published.

them.   He went to Brixlegg himself to fetch the letters and devoured them on the way back to Matzen.   The new verses did not fit the music he had written in anticipation of them, but that did not matter. The music could be used in the orchestral interlude during the change of scenes, and the new verses would inspire him with new ideas.

And now, most esteemed friend, a thousand, thousand thanks for your so uncommonly rapid and so delightful response.   Your mill clatters away even more merrily than my own.   Well, we suit each other.   What won't we get up to yet *ad majorem artis gloriam*?   *Vivant sequentes!*   Cordial greetings and, *now*, a pleasant holiday!

He was, in fact, already planning possible successors to *Der Corregidor*.   Wilhelm Meinhold's novel *Maria Schweidler, die Bernsteinhexe* aroused in him a wave of enthusiasm, and Rosa Mayreder was urged to get on at once with the task of converting it into an opera text, before someone else snapped it up.   He also inquired about *Die Königskinder* and had not yet given up hopes of a *Manuel Venegas*.   For a time he hoped for the collaboration of J. J. David.

There were times when inspiration failed him and the spring of music within him ceased to flow.   Lukas's monologue in the third act was only written after immense effort, as recounted in a letter to the librettist on 8th June:

Your splendid letter caught me just on the point of completing Tio Lukas's great scene.   Consequently I am writing to you in the most excited state imaginable, which may account to you for these lines and also for the shaky handwriting.   I am overjoyed that I have this fearful piece at length behind me.   You cannot imagine what mental anguish I have suffered on its account.   For some days I went about like a man in despair and cursed myself and composing and the opera and the whole world. For three days I tormented my poor brain in vain to find the right musical expression for the passage: 'Wenn es Gott gefallen hätte, mich durch schlimmen Schein zu prüfen.'   I was baffled.   Every attempt failed and, as everybody knows, nothing can be extorted from art by force.   What was to be done?   I wrote at once to friend Larisch to send me the score of *Die Meistersinger*, in order, by occupying myself with that score, to stimulate myself to orchestrate the first act of *Der Corregidor*.   The score has since then arrived, but the good mood has also again arrived, and so nothing came of the orchestration.   God be thanked!   Superstitious as I now am, I read in the passage in question in Lukas's monologue my own condition, as if all the joy of creation had been only to make me feel its futility by a sudden cessation of it.   For what should I have been able to do with half an opera?   Such infamous thoughts increasingly dragged me down, and only in order to escape such tormenting notions did I wish to seek salvation in the task of the orchestration. Now, as I have already said, that has come to pass without it. To-day I am so joyful, so confident, so intoxicated with the future, that I should like to embrace the whole world. And what has been made of the scene! As I played it to myself to-day I was so affected by it that I had to break off, from horror and emotion.

On 16th June the third act was completed. The work moved on with giant strides towards completion. As the end approached the excited letters that had earlier been dispatched every few days to the friends ceased altogether. For fifteen days there was nothing, except a postcard to his publisher and a brief note to Melanie, and then, on 9th July, came joyful messages to them all; to Rosa Mayreder he sent a telegram: 'Finis coronat opus—vale Lupus.' The composition of the final chorus, 'Guten Morgen, edle Donna,' caused last-minute difficulties:

I had already despaired of the accomplishment of a proper conclusion, and had accustomed myself to the idea of letting the piece come to an end with the last words of Mercedes, even at the cost of renouncing the finest concluding effect. But my artistic conscience rebelled mightily against such faint-heartedness and with the expenditure of my last reserves of strength, truly with the courage of despair, I set about the difficult task and worked uninterruptedly for a week on the composition. And lo!—it was successful, and splendidly successful. The last chorus, with the sunrise, now worthily closes the work. The effect with chorus and orchestra will be overpowering.

The whole opera, with the exception of the Prelude, had been completed in fourteen weeks of intensive effort—a wonderful achievement. Wolf's joy in his work was unbounded, his confidence unshakable: 'The public will howl. My personal enemies can say what they please. People will no longer talk about anything but this opera. All of them, Mascagni, Humperdinck, *e tutti quanti*, will be unable to compete and will fade away.' Sternfeld suggested that the work should be performed in Berlin and Wolf urged his friend to do his utmost to bring this about. 'About the effect of the opera,' he wrote,

you can make yourself easy. The public will, at the first hearing, at once stand on their heads for pleasure. I tell you only one thing: Mascagni, Leoncavallo, and the third, the weakest of the group, the insipid Humperdinck, these three heroes of success, will tremble and grow pale when *Der Corregidor* stages its triumphant procession through the theatres.

On 19th July the orchestration was begun. By the beginning of August the first act was nearly complete. The most enchanting letters continued to arrive from Matzen for Melanie Köchert every few days.   Here is a peerless example:

> I write these lines to-day on an incredibly lovely Sunday morning after a short walk in the vicinity.   I am wholly in holiday mood ánd my thoughts dwell only on lovely things; so it is then quite natural that I should think also of you.   Since four o'clock this morning I have not closed my eyes, for just at that time the morning bells rang in the day.   What a contrast to the actual cause of my awakening!   Late home last night from a visit to the painter Grützner, I was woken up at 3 a.m. by the scratching and gnawing of a mouse.   I thus slept, as I had not put out the light until 1 a.m., only two hours.   Full of rage I got up and searched for the disturber of the peace.   He, however, did not allow anything to divert him from his sinister activity and bit and scratched and scraped continually, in spite of my energetic counter-measures.   What was I to do?   It was impossible to get at the monster, naturally I could not sleep any more, and so I got up and wandered about like a dreamer in the twilight of the dawn.   When after some time I returned again to my room the scoundrel was still working away as though possessed, and as free and easy as if he were quite alone in the world.   Furious again I took a hammer and banged away at the place whence the noise came.   For the moment that was effective, but immediately afterwards the racket recommenced.   Then the morning bells began to sound and—gone, as if by magic power, was my rage and vexation over the little beast.   I was almost thankful to the brute that it had been for me the involuntary cause of such an exalting, harmonious delight.   The philosopher draws therefrom the moral that evil does not always bring more evil in its train, but is even sometimes a source of good. [28th July.]

The activities of this mouse resulted in his procuring two cats, which prevented any further nocturnal disturbances, but tyrannized over him completely by day, following him about wherever he went, setting up a pitiful mewing when he left them, strolling about, quite at their ease, on his work-table, and even sitting on his shoulders, purring blissfully, while watching him scoring *Der Corregidor*.

Baron Lipperheide was away from Schloss Matzen for two months of the summer and during his absence Wolf was given permission to invite his own friends to the castle.   He was allowed to make use of the baron's carriage and a staff of servants was left to look after him and his guests.   In August visits were paid to Matzen by Faisst, Grohe, Potpeschnigg, Larisch, August Halm and the Mayreders. Wolf's attention was divided between his friends and his score.   He still spent many hours a day at the orchestration of his opera, working, now that Baron Lipperheide was away, in the castle itself.

During the visit of the Mayreders an attempt was made to climb one of the surrounding peaks. The excursion began in fine weather and the end of the first day saw Wolf and Karl Mayreder arrive at the hay-hut in which they were to pass the night before setting out again, at two o'clock in the morning, for the summit to watch the dawn break. In the morning, however, thick mist and pouring rain compelled them to turn back before reaching their objective. They descended the mountain in safety but had then still to walk for several hours through the valley, in streaming rain, and for Wolf this was the most fatiguing part of the trip. During the climbing he was always the first, nimbly clambering from rock to rock, but on the level ground his short legs put him at a disadvantage and, in spite of strenuous efforts, he was unable to keep up with his lanky companion. That annoyed him more than anything else on this unfortunate excursion. When the weary travellers arrived back at Schloss Matzen Mayreder fell at once into a profound sleep, but Wolf, exhausted as he was, sat down straight away at his desk and continued his work upon *Der Corregidor*.

The scoring of the opera entailed just as strenuous efforts as its actual composition had done. After his friends left he saw little of the world outside his study windows. For week after week he worked all day long, up to ten o'clock at night. He got little sleep, and was followed in his dreams by thoughts of the many pages that still awaited orchestration. 'How I envy all those men who have no need to write operas,' he wrote to Hirsch. 'Ah, that was a fine time when I still composed songs! Then everything went swimmingly. But now I must sit and sweat.' The work was not made easier by his 'crazy way of continually adding new counterpoints.' A thousand times he swore to himself not to do it, but nevertheless continued.

It is clear that Wolf was firmly convinced that with the composition of his opera he had reached the end of all his misfortunes. Apart from the naïve pride in his own work that can be seen in letters already quoted, a note of increasing arrogance recurs in his correspondence, particularly in references to affairs of publication and performance. 'The publisher Brockhaus at Leipzig has made a proposal to me. The time, however, has not yet arrived when it will be *my* turn to make conditions. But it *will* come, and then—woe to the publishing gentry! Woe! Woe!' For a long time he had been dissatisfied with the efforts made on his behalf by Schott's and he now determined to bring his connection with this firm to an end. On 5th October he told Rosa Mayreder: 'My publisher Schott sent me yesterday the long-delayed account. The result is magnificent. I have, in the five years during which Schott has sold my things, actually earned 86 marks and 35 pfennigs.' Strecker had written that he had not expected that the result would be so favourable. On 19th October Wolf replied that *his* expectations regarding the account had been pitched somewhat higher: 'As I am not, like you, in the happy position of being a capitalist, to be able to look on the further progress of the sale with that enviable indifference which does not need to worry itself over "trifles," I find myself compelled to sever our connection and to seek my salvation elsewhere.' The sum of 86 marks, 35 pfennigs, the composer's net profit on the sales of those of his works published on commission for him by Schott's, was a miserable enough material reward. In fairness to Schott's, however, it should be remembered that the terms of Wolf's connection with the firm were his own, that he had refused to co-operate with his publishers in the matter of advertisement, and that the amount due to him did not represent the total sales of his songs during the period in question, but the balance left in his favour after the subtraction of the costs of production, which, under the terms of the contract, were to be borne by the composer. He had also received 1,000 marks for the first part of the *Italian Song Book* and 300 marks for the choral version of *Der Feuerreiter*, both of which had been sold outright to the publishers. Wolf was afraid that if Strecker got to hear about his opera, for which he foresaw a brilliant and lucrative future, he would make difficulties about the transfer of the songs to another publisher. Strecker's letters give the impression that Wolf went as far as to tell Schott's, at the very time when he was working furiously on its composition, that he had given up the idea of setting *Der Corregidor* to music.[1] He certainly allowed Strecker to suppose that he had abandoned the opera, but did so, without actually telling a lie, by hoisting him very neatly with his own petard. Strecker, on first reading the libretto, had expressed doubts about its effectiveness and urged Wolf not to begin a musical setting before taking the opinion of experts in stage matters upon it. So Wolf on 5th May told his publisher: 'About *Der Corregidor* you are quite right. *Stage experts*

---

[1] Strecker to Wolf : 'What's the position regarding *Corregidor und Müllerin?*' (27th April 1895.)
'Your letter with the news that there is nothing doing with *Der Corregidor* was only a very painful confirmation of my fears. I assure you, I think every day about the piece, of which the various situations must be quite wonderful. But is it not better that you have gained this conviction in good time, that is, before beginning the work? Something else will be found ' (7th May 1895).

declare that the subject, as well as the treatment thereof, are not suitable for composition, and stage experts must know—and perhaps publishers as well.' Strecker was deeply wounded by Wolf's attitude towards his firm and agreed at once to all the composer's proposals. Schott's discontinued handling Wolf's work and he was allowed to buy back the copyrights in the first Italian songs and *Der Feuerreiter*.

For a time he was undecided whether to entrust his work to the Viennese publisher Eberle, to Brockhaus at Leipzig or to Heckel at Mannheim. In the end he decided for the last named, and arrangements were at once made for the publication of the vocal score of *Der Corregidor*. Heckel was to publish the opera on commission for Wolf, who paid the costs of printing and remained owner of the copyright, while Heckel received twenty per cent of the net profits. Heckel also took over all the other published works, except the *Elfenlied*, which Fürstner had purchased.

A copy of the manuscript vocal score of *Der Corregidor* had been prepared by one Bernhard Maresch at Graz, under the supervision of Potpeschnigg, who had succeeded in infecting the copyist with his own enthusiasm. Maresch took a real pleasure in the work, which he carried out, to the composer's intense satisfaction, with remarkable rapidity and accuracy, and for a ridiculously low fee. The expenses were actually borne by Potpeschnigg, who thanked Wolf profusely for the 'privilege' of being allowed to do so, and gave the copyist half as much again as he had asked. In all the long and tedious work involved in the preparation of the opera for publication—the copying, the writing out of the parts, the correction of the proofs of the piano reduction, full score and parts—Potpeschnigg placed himself entirely at Wolf's service and spared no effort to fulfil his wishes. His work, above all, at the exacting and tiresome revision and correction of the full score and parts, which occupied him throughout the whole of 1896, must count as one of the greatest services ever rendered to the composer by his friends.

Baron Lipperheide returned to Schloss Matzen in the middle of October, to find Wolf still deep in the task of orchestrating *Der Corregidor*. Soon the castle began to fill up with guests and, after having had the place to himself for so long, Wolf found the presence of these strangers irritating. 'A herd of tame beasts,' he called them, who took away all his pleasure in life. 'I have done everything humanly possible,' he told Rosa Mayreder, 'to adapt myself to this company, but it can't be done. There is no point of contact between these people and myself, and at the common midday meals my appetite often fails me, so that I touch scarcely any of the dishes and have to make shift after the meal with bread and butter in my little Jägerhaus, so as not to die of starvation.' After completing the scoring of the second act he thought of returning to Vienna. Conditions at Matzen, however, improved in November and a long period of splendid autumn weather followed during which the orchestration was taken a long way further towards completion. On 22nd November the third act was finished. In this month Wolf rejected a suggestion by his librettist that a cut should be made in the fourth act. 'Who the deuce put this monstrous flea in your ear?' he demanded. The fourth act was his declared favourite. It contained all sorts of precious things, to make the epicure's mouth water. The scoring of this beloved and beautiful act, after the writing of the other three had been only a plague and vexatious drudgery, would be for him a source of the purest pleasure. On 17th December, just before midnight, he laid down his pen after scoring the last pages of his opera. The prelude was begun on the 19th, completed on the 22nd, and scored in the next few days. The whole opera, after nine months of almost unbroken labour, was complete to the last detail.

The composer spent Christmas happily at Matzen with the Lipperheides. Presents and loving congratulations were not lacking, as this letter to Melanie shows:

Your dear letter of the 23rd has moved me to tears, although I was not at all in a mood for weeping. I received the letter and the parcel together and so I wept and laughed at the same time. Ah, what splendid things this precious treasure chest contains! Only too much, only too much! I sink beneath such burdens of obligation. The wonderful cigarette holder I inaugurated straight away—unfortunately only with a wretched Herzegovina, and of that, too, only a battered stump. The new holder is much finer even than the previous one. And then the beautiful and practical dressing-case, and the pure gold cuff-links—probably the gift of your husband, for which I heartily thank him! I almost forgot the superb Malaga grapes—Frasquita's grapes. How *can* one forget such things?

In a letter to Grohe at this time the baroness wrote:

Friend Wolf saw the Christmas tree lit up with us. He was on that evening wholly the God-gifted artist, who with his music held us bound in the loveliest spells. Unfortunately he has now left us; we hope he will return some day, to rest from the triumphs that we wish for him in richest measure. His music must surely conquer the world.

In the castle visitors' book Wolf himself wrote at the end of his stay: 'In grateful remembrance of the happiest time of my life, from 16th May to 28th December, to my dear hosts, Baron and Baroness von Lipperheide, in praise and greeting.'

Back in Vienna, he stayed with the Mayreders in the fourth Bezirk, at Plösselgasse 4. He at once began to busy himself with arrangements for the production of his opera. Grohe and other south German friends were pressing him to agree to its production at Mannheim, but for a long time he hesitated, hoping to win over one of the more important opera-houses. The idea of a first performance in Berlin had already had to be abandoned. While at Matzen he had sent a copy of the libretto and part of the manuscript vocal score to Karl Muck, but not only had the hopes aroused by his Berlin friends proved illusory, but he had had the greatest difficulty in even regaining possession of his manuscript. Letters, postcards and telegrams had all been ignored, until at length he had had to threaten legal action. Meanwhile, Frau Mayreder had learned that Kapellmeister Fuchs, of the Vienna Opera, was in favour of the production of *Der Corregidor*. 'If the text is only half reasonable,' he was reported to have said, 'it will unquestionably be performed.' Accordingly, on 30th December, Wolf called to present his score personally to the director, Wilhelm Jahn. But here he met with another rebuff. He did not succeed in securing an interview with Jahn and was told by an underling that he would have to submit his work formally in the usual way, and that even if it were accepted it could not possibly be performed in the current season. Wolf was incensed that the walls of Jericho did not at once fall down before him. 'Am I then a mere beginner, a Heuberger or a Kienzl?' he asked. 'My work is too good for that. The directors must come to me, not I to them. Out there at Mannheim they are already waiting for it.' He sought elsewhere for compensation. On 1st January he told the Baroness Lipperheide:

Happily Prague offers me better prospects, where my friend Franz Schalk . . . holds the position of first conductor at the German Theatre. The first performance of *Der Corregidor* will therefore take place at Prague, the town which had the honour of presenting Mozart's *Don Giovanni* for the first time. I have already taken the initial steps regarding a performance. Director Neumann of Prague is known as an exceptionally circumspect and experienced man; and as for friend Schalk, I can fully rely on him. The good Viennese will follow later on, but then they will have to pay dearly for their pleasure.

These confident hopes, too, were doomed to disappointment, for reasons that are not clear. It is probable, however, that it was found impossible to fit the new opera into the programmes for the current season at Prague and that Wolf, whose heart was set on an immediate performance, himself cut short the negotiations. By 20th January he was resigned to his opera being first heard in the Court and National Theatre at Mannheim. The intendant, August Basser-mann, and the Kapellmeister, Hugo Röhr, stimulated by Grohe and Heckel, approached their task with enthusiasm. The contract was made out on 11th February and signed by Wolf on the 14th. He was to receive 6 per cent of the net receipts from each performance and the Mannheim Theatre was to pay him 700 marks for the score and orchestral material, this sum being the approximate cost of the writing out of the parts and a copy of the full score. The first performance was provisionally fixed for 22nd May.

Meanwhile, in Berlin, Paul Müller had founded the Hugo Wolf Verein, a society formed for the purpose of spreading knowledge of Wolf's music. Its inaugural concert was given on 30th January. The existence of this society in Berlin was a source of great satisfaction to Wolf, particularly as Müller, apart from a brief encounter in 1892, was personally unknown to him, and thus inspired wholly by enthusiasm for his work.

All through the autumn and first part of the winter, while he had been working at Matzen on his opera, Wolf's health had been perfect. With his return to Vienna, however, there had recommenced the familiar long succession of ailments—chronic coughs and colds, inflammation of the throat and eyes, headaches and insomnia. For weeks on end he was never free from fever, aches and pains. In this condition he was plagued by the task of preparing his opera for publication and performance. The copying of the full score and writing out of the parts was carried out at Graz under the supervision of Potpeschnigg. Maresch worked at high pressure on the score, while at least two other copyists were engaged on the parts. Wolf himself was kept busy on the proof sheets of the vocal score. Against the advice of Heckel he had insisted on dealing directly with Röder's, the music printers at Leipzig, and consequently had involved himself in a great deal of unnecessary trouble. He was quite unfitted for the task of proof correcting, and it tired and worried him excessively. No sooner had he sent off one batch of corrections than he began to discover numerous fresh mistakes. Every time he looked at the score he found something further to correct and when, after going through

the whole text several times, he imagined that he had at last secured a
flawless set of proofs, Potpeschnigg was able to surprise and dismay
him with a long catalogue of additional errors.

At this same time he was further preoccupied with another, not less
difficult, task—the seeking out of a suitable dwelling in which to set
up a home of his own.   For nearly ten years now he had been living
the life of a nomad, moving from the shelter of one friend's hospitable
roof to that of another, in Vienna, at Perchtoldsdorf, at Unterach,
Rinnbach, Traunkirchen and Matzen.   The last apartment for
which he had actually paid rent had been that in the Kumpfgasse,
which he had left in 1887.   It was an amazingly long period for a
man to be 'without fixed abode.'   No wonder that he puzzled the
income tax authorities as to his way of living!   Now, however, that
he was in receipt of an annual allowance from Baron Lipperheide
and the others, and was, moreover, the composer of an opera that
was, as he thought, shortly to blaze its way throughout the theatres
of the German-speaking world, he decided that it was time to set up
an independent home.   It cost him much time and trouble to discover a vacant dwelling that conformed to his requirements, but in
February he was able to tell the Baroness Lipperheide:

After long wandering and searching I succeeded yesterday in finding a
charming flat looking out into a garden in a very distinguished-looking
house in the Piaristengasse, not far from the centre of the town.   Naturally
it is an unfurnished flat, and, when the time draws near, my first thought
will be to furnish it.   To begin with I shall only get the merest necessities:
bed, writing-desk, chairs, and a few cupboards.   But when the royalties
begin to flow in (may this time be none too distant!) luxury and comfort
will also follow.

To his mother he wrote of the 'divans and arm-chairs, carpets,
pictures, palm-trees, tapestries, and all the devil's stuff that really
makes a dwelling comfortable' that he would purchase after the
success of his opera.   He had no sooner arranged to take this flat
than he found another, at Schwindgasse 3, which he liked better and
he impetuously took that one too, so that after being so long without
a home of his own, he suddenly found himself in possession of *two*,
neither of them furnished or habitable at the time.   Fortunately he
was able to sublet the flat in the Piaristengasse without much
difficulty.   He looked forward to entering into possession of his
Schwindgasse apartments when he returned from Mannheim after
the production of his opera.

It might have been expected that this period of many preoccupations and indifferent health would have been far from propitious for the reappearance of Wolf's shy and fugitive creative gift, but on 23rd March he left the Mayreders' house and once again settled down in the Werners' summer residence at Perchtoldsdorf, and there, in little more than a month, he completed the twenty-four songs of the second part of the *Italian Song Book*. He worked with his customary rapidity and sureness of touch, though there were short periods when his ideas refused to flow. Between 25th March and 3rd April he wrote eight songs; in the next eight days only one. Then he added four more in two days, after which there was another break of five barren days before the last eleven songs were completed in as many days.[1]

. . . .

The second part of the *Italian Song Book* has all the characteristic delicacy and refinement of the earlier volume. Although more than four years had elapsed since the last of the first part of the song-book had been composed, Wolf was able to take up his pen where he had laid it down and at once revert to his uniquely beautiful Italian manner. The musical material used is of the same incomparable quality, though sometimes drawn out to unusual lengths, as in *Und steht Ihr früh am Morgen auf*, and sometimes, as in *Heut' Nacht erhob ich mich*, concentrated more than ever before. It is tempting to discover in this later collection a further sublimation of Wolf's musical style and thought, and, indeed, the two songs mentioned may well claim to represent the final consummation of his art in this form. While we are under their spell we have no choice but to declare them the crown of the whole song-book. But afterwards the recollection returns of the sheer perfection of many of the earlier Italian masterpieces—sparkling, glowing jewels of song that may be matched, as pearls are matched for a necklace, but never surpassed—and we are content to recognize the impossibility, as well as the lack of all necessity, of deciding whether the second part of the *Italian Song Book* represents in any way an advance upon the first.

Wolf himself told Edwin Mayser that the second part contained more absolute music than the first. Many things in it, he said, could be played equally well by a string quartet. We see what he meant by the latter statement when we examine a song like *Wohl kenn' ich Euren Stand*, the style of which is more contrapuntal, and less

[1] For details of the dates of composition see Appendix II, p. 490.

pianistic, than anything in the earlier volume.   But the music is here
still exquisitely expressive of the mood of the poem—it is poetic, not
'absolute' music.   The idea of Wolf as absolute musician is, indeed,
almost inconceivable, but here and there in the second part of the
Italian Song Book we do have the feeling that the music is oddly
detached from the subject-matter of the songs.   Examples of this are
seen in the accompaniments of *Ich liess mir sagen* and the discon-
certing *Nicht länger kann ich singen*.   The effect is as though the
composer had been revelling in Bach's suites, and had been unable
completely to withdraw his mind again to his own musical domain.

Here and there in the second volume Wolf's inspiration seems
momentarily to flag.   *O wüsstest du, wie viel ich deinetwegen*, for
instance, is an unsuccessful humorous piece.   *Lass sie nur gehn* and
even *Verschling' der Abgrund* seem lacking in spontaneity; the middle
section of *Benedeit die sel'ge Mutter* is music written to a Wolfian
formula but not with his customary imaginative fire.   But where
there are so many perfect things, such a rich hoard of beauty, these
occasional lapses are scarcely worth remarking.

The general characteristics of the Italian songs have been indicated
already in discussing the earlier volume.   A few brief comments upon
some features of the second part of the song-book will have to suffice
here.

The series of character-sketches of women in and out of love is
continued in the second volume.   *Mein Liebster hat zu Tische mich
geladen* and *Ich liess mir sagen* are further songs of mockery.   It is
worth while considering that each of these fantastically humorous
poems had originally some point of contact with reality.   It must
have been by the real failure of a not too wealthy or not over-generous
admirer to provide refreshment of the expected quality that the
Italian original of *Mein Liebster hat zu Tische* came into being.   The
disappointed beauty, in the *rispetto*, viciously exaggerates the defects
of the entertainment.   According to her, there was neither wine nor
glasses, the table was small, the bread as hard as a stone and the knife
blunt.   The unavailing hacking at the stale bread with a blunt knife
is cleverly suggested in Wolf's song.   *Ich liess mir sagen* pokes fun at
poor Toni's appetite, which, although he is in love, is still formidable.
Schweig' einmal still draws an unfavourable comparison between a
serenader's voice and that of a donkey.   In *Ich hab' in Penna* an
exultant beauty enumerates her twenty-one different admirers.
'Masterpiece' is perhaps rather a ponderous word to apply to these

little humorous thumb-nail sketches, but they all have great vividness, wit and sparkle. The verve and sheer exuberance of *Ich hab' in Penna*, in particular, are altogether irresistible.

More important, however, are those women's songs which express deeper feelings and more complex emotional states. *Du sagst mir, dass ich keine Fürstin sei* is made a more interesting character-study because Wolf was not content to take the words at their face value. As in *Wer rief dich denn?*, in the first part of the *Italian Song Book*, he saw behind the girl's rebuke a desperate heartache, which comes unmistakably to expression, in particular in the piano part of the song, at 'Du spottest mein um meine Niedrigkeit.' *Wie soll ich fröhlich sein* likewise has points of contact with *Wer rief dich denn?*. The situation is the same. A one-time lover has become remiss in his attentions, but the woman this time, instead of expressing her injured pride, pleads only for release from tormenting uncertainty. A last gleam of hope appears in the emphasis on 'wenn' in the phrase 'Was kommst du, wenn's die Deinen ungern sehn,' precisely resembling that on the same word in *Wer rief dich denn?*. The close of *Wie soll ich fröhlich sein*, with the crashing discords of the piano postlude, gives the lie to the suggestion in the last words of the poem that the speaker is reconciled to Heaven's decree. It is not clear whether *Was soll der Zorn* is a song for a man or a woman. 'Mein Schatz,' in the first line of the poem, would be used in addressing either sex. The Italian original makes it clear that the speaker is a woman, but that is not a reliable guide to Wolf's attitude to Heyse's translation. The song may be a man's reply to *Wie soll ich fröhlich sein*, which it follows in the order of the song-book. But probably, here as elsewhere in the volume, Wolf did not bother himself about the point and the song may with propriety be sung by either man or woman.[1] *Was soll der Zorn* is one of the most deeply felt of all the Italian songs. There are only twenty bars, but within that space is concentrated what burning intensity of feeling! The air is heavy with tragedy; some desperate deed must shortly, one feels, bring the only possible release for the agony of this character.

Towards the end of the volume there are some surpassingly beautiful 'straight' love-songs for women. *Gesegnet sei das Grün*, a

[1] Wolf's letters give some indications of his attitude towards such problems, but show that he was not always consistent. He objected to *Auf einer Wanderung* being sung by a woman. *Ganymed* he regarded as a soprano song. *Grenzen der Menschheit* was suitable for contralto or bass. But, quite inexplicably, he allowed Frieda Zerny to sing one of the *Peregrina* songs.

song in praise of all things green, the colour worn by the singer's lover, is, with the single exception of the passage about the rose at the end of *Auch kleine Dinge*, the only expression of love of nature in all the *Italian Song Book*. It comes like a breath from Maierling in springtime. It is interesting to note how the figure that pervades, in various guises, the piano part of this song echoed again in the composer's mind in 1897, when he was working on the ill-starred *Manuel Venegas*. In the Spring Chorus which was to have opened that opera there occurs a two-bar passage which, in spite of rhythmic differences, is strikingly reminiscent of *Gesegnet sei das Grün*. It appears first at the words 'Komm zu begrüssen das herrliche Kind' (vocal score, p. 6), but when, after interruptions, the Spring Chorus is concluded a little later, the words with which this passage is associated are 'Lass dir gefallen schmuckloses *Grün*' (vocal score, p. 28). There is nothing more exquisitely wrought in all Wolf's work than *O wär' dein Haus durchsichtig wie ein Glas*. The texture of the song is itself transparently beautiful. There is not a note that could possibly be altered. Every quaver, every demisemiquaver, fits into its place in the delicate pattern of the whole. The simple but striking little figure,

Ex. 18

which is reiterated throughout the whole piano part of this song perhaps requires elucidation. This little patter of notes has no connection with the raindrops mentioned in the last line of the poem, but rather derives from the *first* line. It is a sort of musical symbol for the flash and glitter of sunlight on glass-houses.

It was inevitable that a composer like Wolf should often reflect in his music ideas and images occurring in the words of the poems he set. The language of music, however, is too difficult for us always to be able to recognize the relationship between a musical phrase and the idea or verbal image from which it is derived. When we can do so we gain new insight into the workings of the composer's mind and often new understanding of the right interpretation of his works. The claim is not being made here that Wolf's music is merely illustrative. Between the crude representation of events described in the poem, such as the firing of the huntsman's gun in the Mörike song *Der Jäger*, and 'absolute' music there lies a whole world of 'poetic'

N

musical expression in which the mind of the composer, consciously or unconsciously, is influenced, to a greater or less degree, by the words and thoughts of his chosen poet. Sometimes the idea behind a musical motive is unmistakable. Thus the accompaniment of *Und steht Ihr früh am Morgen auf*, in the second part of the *Italian Song Book*, is suggestive of the chiming of bells, although not directly representational of them. There is no direct reference to such bells in the text, but the mention of the mass and the beloved at her devotions gave the composer his cue and led to the chiming figure which in this song evokes so wonderfully the atmosphere of a peaceful Sunday morning.

Benedeit die sel'ge Mutter is distinct from all the rest of the Italian songs in that it is based not on a *rispetto* or *velota* but on a Venetian folk-song. Wolf uses, exceptionally, a straightforward A-B-A form for his song. There is no repetition of the first stanza in Heyse. The song is unquestionably a beautiful one, but, for all that, not entirely successful. The opening, chaste and reticent, is flatly contradicted by the yearning and fiery passion of the middle section, at the end of which we have been led too far from the initial mood of the song to accept its return without a shock. Heyse's passionate second stanza, the source of the discrepancy of mood between the two sections of Wolf's song, is hardly justified by the original Italian poem, as comparison will show:

> Ammirando la vaghezza
> Di bellezza così rara,
> Ti confesso, mia cara,
> Mi facesti sospirar;
> E nel petto mi sentii
> Una fiamma si vivace,
> Che disturba la mia pace
> Mi fa sempre delirar.

This is a long way from Heyse's

> Wenn ich aus der Ferne schmachte
> Und betrachte deine Schöne,
> Siehe wie ich beb' und stöhne. . . .

One sees how impossible it was to end on this note after beginning in a mood so different, but the mere repetition of the opening stanza did not give unity to this unsatisfactory poem.

Wenn du mich mit den Augen streifst is one of the great love-songs of the world. It opens in this way:

Ex. 19

Langsam, doch leidenschaftlich

Wenn du mich mit den Au-gen streifst und lachst,

The rhythm set by the first bar of the voice part is taken up in the second bar in the piano part and dominates the greater part of the song. It recurs in the piano part in ten out of its twenty bars, including six consecutive bars at the climactic point of the song. It might have been thought that this simple rhythmic division of the bar of common time:

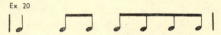

Ex. 20

would have already occurred frequently in the body of Wolf's work, but in point of fact it is extremely rare, and nowhere is it used with any particular emphasis except in this second volume of the Italian songs, where it becomes of outstanding importance. There can be little doubt that it must have had some special significance for Wolf. If an unknown song of his were discovered in which this 'fingerprint' occurred, we should be able at once to surmise the year, and almost the month, of its composition. *Wenn du mich mit den Augen streifst* was completed on 18th April 1896. Ten other songs were composed after it in the latter part of April, and in three of these this same rhythm occurs incidentally, while two more are pervaded by it from beginning to end. In *Was soll der Zorn*, in *Benedeit die sel'ge Mutter* and in *Heut' Nacht erhob ich mich* it is used in the piano parts for a few bars, in *Wenn du, mein Liebster, steigst zum Himmel auf* in thirteen out of twenty bars and in *Was für ein Lied* in twelve out of twenty bars, in all these cases in connection with melodic phrases of a type closely akin to that used for the opening of *Wenn du mich mit den Augen streifst*. The possibilities that Wolf saw in this phrase, and the inspiration that he found in the words and emotions of this poem, were not exhausted by the single song; he drew upon them again when he came upon poems similar in mood, or reflecting similar moods. *Wenn du mich mit den Augen streifst* is a song of utter devotion, rising to a great climax of passionate expression. *Wenn du, mein Liebster, steigst zum Himmel auf* is its feminine counterpart. The woman is here allowed to sing out her whole heart, as the men are generally throughout the Italian volumes. In *Was für ein Lied*, the last of the Italian songs in order of composition, though the first in the published order of the second volume, the poet seeks for a song that shall worthily hymn the praises of his beloved. It must be something the like of which no one in the world has ever before conceived or heard. Wolf found that song; it echoes with wonderful sweetness in the piano part of *Was für ein Lied*. It is, however, clearly enough a derivative of his own *Wenn du mich mit den Augen streifst*.

There are a few further songs which, however inadequate words may be to give more than an inkling of their beauty, must at least be mentioned here. Such are *Schon streckt' ich aus im Bett die müden Glieder*, perhaps the finest of all Wolf's variations on the theme of the 'Italian Serenade,' *Sterb' ich, so hüllt in Blumen*, with its almost voluptuous sense of amorous contentment,[1] and *Wie viele Zeit verlor ich*, that most delicious of lover's fancies, the playful spirit of which is founded on such intense emotion that, though we may smile, we are yet moved to tears. Finally, there is *Heut' Nacht erhob ich mich*, the most concentrated, the most intimate, of all the many beautiful love-songs in the Italian volume. It seems almost a profanation to perform such a song in a public concert-hall, for one feels that it was intended for one pair of ears alone. Its piercing sweetness, its unspeakable tenderness, cannot be indicated in words. There are only eighteen bars, but within that space a world of exquisite feeling.

> Auch kleine Dinge können uns entzücken,
> Auch kleine Dinge können teuer sein.

On that note, with hearts full of thankfulness to the composer for some of the most precious and perfect of all artistic achievements, we may conclude this brief survey of the *Italian Song Book*.

     .   .   .   .

Wolf remained at Perchtoldsdorf until 5th May, when he returned to the Mayreders' house in Vienna. Insistent requests were now

---

[1] Ernest Newman, in his notes to the Hugo Wolf Society's gramophone records, writes of this song's 'sense of resignation, of deathbed repose.' This is, I think, to take too literal a view of the poem. The Hugo Wolf Society's record of *Sterb' ich, so hüllt in Blumen* is anything but a model. For one thing, the tempo is just half that required by Wolf's metronome marking.

being made that he should go at once to Mannheim, where all manner of difficulties were being encountered in the study of his opera. He had himself never displayed any great enthusiasm for the idea of performance there, regarding it in the light of a temporary expedient forced upon him by the failure of Berlin, Vienna and Prague to meet his wishes in this season. He was not very gracious, or grateful, to the Mannheim authorities. At first he had wished his opera to be performed in April, in spite of the very brief period that would then have remained for the study of the work after the delivery of the orchestral material—the vocal score, too, would not have been available at that time. He grumbled because Weingartner's *Genesius* was to be produced before *Der Corregidor*, believing that his own work would suffer in consequence, and hinting that he was not disinclined, in such circumstances, to withdraw it, in spite of having contracted with the Mannheim Theatre for its production. He calmly suggested that *Genesius* could be deferred or turned down altogether, but when it was found necessary to put off the production of *Der Corregidor* for another week he threatened that neither he nor the librettist would in that case attend the performance.

The earliest rehearsals had shown that the hastily copied orchestral parts were chock-full of errors and the composer's presence at Mannheim was called for to clear up a thousand doubtful points. Yet he still prevaricated, obviously reluctant to embark on the sea of tribulation that he foresaw awaiting him in the preparation of his opera for public performance. It was only when Grohe, in an outspoken letter, urged upon him the necessity of his attendance if the work was to be performed at all, and suggested that it was cowardly of a father to desert his own child in time of trouble, that Wolf summoned up his courage and marshalled his will-power to face the inevitable conflict with the practical world of the theatre. After a week spent in preparations for his entry into his Schwindgasse flat after his return to Vienna, he departed on 12th May for Stuttgart. There he spent a few days at the Hotel Marquardt, renewing acquaintance with his numerous friends in the district. The vocal score of *Der Corregidor* had just been published and he took it everywhere with him, playing the whole opera through to Faisst and his mother, the Maysers, and the Klinckerfuss family. He lingered at Stuttgart until the 17th, when, at the pressing request of Kapellmeister Röhr, he made his way to Mannheim.

Straight from the railway station they led him to an orchestral rehearsal where, as he told Frau Mayreder, what he endured defied all description, so that he would have liked best to be up and away from Mannheim at once.   He showed himself so hopelessly ill-equipped to control the orchestral rehearsals that some of the players formed the opinion that he could not be the composer of the work at all, or, at least, had got someone else to orchestrate it for him.   The solo rehearsals from the piano score went somewhat better, but here again hostility was soon aroused by his intense impatience and irritability. Only Joachim Kromer (Tio Lukas) and Hans Rüdiger (Corregidor), of all the cast, were at all acquainted with the style of Wolf's music and the opera was considered extremely difficult.   The singer who took the part of Repela, and achieved with it considerable success at the actual performance, at first declared the music unsingable and wished to retire from the engagement.   The part of Frasquita was badly miscast, being entrusted to a soubrette, Frl. Hohenleitner, who had been only a very short time on the stage.   Wolf bitterly lamented that Anna Sorger, the Corregidora, had not been given the more important role of the miller's wife.   Frl. Hohenleitner's difficulties in mastering her part were largely responsible for the delays in the production of the opera, which was deferred from 24th May to 31st May and then to 7th June.

Wolf's nerves were in a pitiful state, and difficulties at the rehearsals led to frequent scenes which increased the opposition to *Der Corregidor* and its composer among the cast and in the orchestra.   His manner was also characterized by a good deal of arrogance.   He demanded that the singers should all be in their places ready for the rehearsal before he got there—irrespective of whether he came in late himself or not.   His outspoken criticism was widely resented.   More than once revolution threatened to break out and it required all the diplomacy of Grohe and Dr. Bassermann, the intendant, to avert a catastrophe.   It was only owing to the constant care and watchfulness of these two men that the opera was ever brought to public performance at Mannheim.   Hugo Röhr, the conductor, went to great trouble at the rehearsals, but with him, too, Wolf had disagreements.   Röhr expected from the composer more consideration and recognition than he received and, although rehearsals of *Der Corregidor* were unusually numerous, was blamed by Wolf for stinting his work in this respect.   The question of *tempi*, too, was a constant point of dissension between composer and conductor.

On Wagner's birthday, 22nd May, Wolf played the whole second volume of the *Italian Song Book* to Grohe, Emil Heckel, senior, and his two sons.   His joy in his latest compositions was unbounded and it seemed almost as if they had for him far more importance than the whole troublesome *première* of his opera.   One song, *Ich hab' in Penna*, he would play to any one who would listen to it, sometimes two or three times over.   Its successful completion was a source of particular satisfaction to him, as he had intended to include it in the first part of the *Italian Song Book* but had then failed to strike the right mood in his music.[1]   He took especial pleasure in rattling off the difficult piano postlude with amazing virtuosity.

The day of the performance of *Der Corregidor* arrived.   Wolf's friends had come from near and far to be present on the great occasion, and in the morning of 7th June he called his intimates together to hear the Italian songs.   As the room he had rented for the rehearsal period, directly opposite the theatre, was unsuitable for such a gathering, he led the friends to Heckel's piano showroom.   As no one was about, he had the room opened up on his own authority and there, in blissful self-forgetfulness, he sang, with Faisst's assistance, all his new songs.   *Der Corregidor*, the fate of which preoccupied the minds of all the friends, he scarcely mentioned.

As the time of the performance drew nearer the tension and excitement among Wolf's friends increased, but he himself gave no sign of any emotion.   He chose out Paul Müller and Heinrich Werner, perhaps because they were the quietest of the group, to accompany him everywhere that day.   After lunch he paid visits to several acquaintances and then returned to his room.   Kapellmeister Röhr called to see him there to clear up a few outstanding points, but Wolf gave scant attention and soon sent him away.   The afternoon passed in conversation.   Müller and Werner tried to persuade Wolf to rest a little before the excitement of the evening, but at first he would not hear of this.   Then, at about six o'clock, half an hour before the performance was due to commence, he suddenly lay down on a divan and fell asleep, or pretended to do so.   His self-control, in the circumstances, was amazing, and in *him*, scarcely credible.   All the strength of his will was being applied to the mastery of his

---

[1] See Müller's 'Erinnerungen an Hugo Wolf' (*Die Musik*, Berlin, March and April 1903).   In letters to Kauffmann on 15th October 1892, and to Grohe on 27th October and 2nd November of the same year, Wolf mentions twenty-*three* completed Italian songs then in the hands of the printer.   The published volume contained only twenty-two.   Was an early version of *Ich hab' in Penna*, perhaps, included in Part I of the *Italian Song Book* and withdrawn before publication?

own secret expectancy and inner emotion.   For a quarter of an hour he lay there, until Müller aroused him, and a little later Werner urged that it was time to leave.   Wolf replied, with perfect tranquillity: 'I believe you are excited.   How strange!   I am quite calm.   We've still got five minutes.'   Then at last he set out, sauntering slowly across the square to the theatre, in his light grey summer suit and hat, his normal daily wear.   He was not to be persuaded to don his evening clothes and had no intention of making an appearance on the stage.   'I wouldn't dream of it,' he said.   'They won't get a sight of me.'   Similarly he refused to sit, as was customary, in the intendant's box.   A place was found for him in one of the 'reserve boxes,' above the two tiers of boxes normally in use.   It would seem that this reserve accommodation was utilized as an overflow for the gallery, and there in the darkness at the back of the box, Wolf sat in one of the last rows of seats.

During the performance of the Prelude he gave various signs of vexation.   The solo oboe made a wrong entry and Röhr, as usual, and in spite of Wolf's often-repeated objections, set *tempi* that were too fast.   The first act went smoothly enough, although the festal conclusion did not have the expected effect.   There was loud applause, which, however, died away after the appearance of the singers.   After the second act enthusiasm among the audience was greater and calls for the composer were heard.   Wolf remained still, leaning back in his seat, without sound or movement.   The conductor appeared, then the intendant, to lead him down to the stage. He only said: 'I'm not going.'   He began to criticize the performers. Then there came a number of his friends who had found out his retreat and among them Rosa Mayreder and her husband.   Wolf stood up, looked at his librettist in silence for a moment, and then threw his arms round her neck and burst into tears.

The friends dispersed again, as the performance was about to continue.   Then, as the first bars of the third act were heard, Potpeschnigg, who had arrived at Mannheim very shortly before the performance began, tired and feverish, after a railway journey of twenty-three hours from Graz, and had only just learned where Wolf was to be found, appeared in the box to greet him.[1]   As he took his seat beside them a silent handshake, a brotherly kiss and the single

[1] I here follow the account of Heinrich Werner, which is totally at variance with that published under Potpeschnigg's name in the *Alpenländische Monatshafte* (Graz) for February 1924.   There is grave doubt whether this article, and others in the same periodical, were really written by Potpeschnigg.

word 'Enrico!' spoken in a tone expressive of heartfelt gratitude, were Potpeschnigg's reward for all he had done to make the performance possible. It was Potpeschnigg who finally succeeded, after the conclusion of the third act, in persuading Wolf to appear on the stage. He owed it to his *work*, he said; its success would not be manifest without the personal appearance of the composer, and at that Wolf went down to receive the homage of the crowd. Amidst laurel wreaths and garlands that fell about his feet, he stood abstracted, profoundly earnest in mien, on his pale face traces of the overpowering emotion that could no longer be concealed. His dark, burning eyes seemed to gaze away, over the heads of the cheering audience, far beyond into the unknown future. It was the fulfilment of that old, often-repeated dream, of which he had once spoken to Hellmer. He bowed briefly and took one of the laurel wreaths in his hand; the rest he did not seem to be aware of. Then he drew the singers, the conductor and the intendant before the curtain and it appeared as if in this moment of triumph all hostile feeling between him and the opera-house personnel had vanished.

Similar scenes were repeated after the last act, and all those present had the decided impression that Wolf's opera had indeed achieved an outstanding success.

After the performance Bassermann had arranged a little celebration. Wolf agreed to be present, provided there were no speeches about him. All the friends were there but, except for Hildebrandt, the stage-manager, who had taken the small part of Tonuelo, the meeting was boycotted by all the singers. The reason for this was that Wolf had, at the last moment, particularly incensed them by refusing to appear at a charity concert, because he disapproved of the rest of the programme. Their absence, however, certainly did not upset him, or in any way spoil the evening. Surrounded by his friends, he was in the best of humours and even sat through a number of speeches—Bassermann had broken the ice by pretending that he was not addressing Wolf at all, but the Corregidor. Later he stood up and expressed his thanks in a few simple words. Bassermann presented him with an honorarium of 200 marks. This sum of money, of which, owing to the expenses of the publication of his opera and his recent re-purchase of copyrights from Schott's, he stood in great need, he had the misfortune to lose. He put it in a drawer in his lodgings at Mannheim and forgot it. He refused the offer of a friend to replace the money.

* N

Der Corregidor was given a second performance at Mannheim a few days later, on 10th June. But on the day before this performance Wolf had already left for Stuttgart again. It was well that he did so, for to stay would only have brought him bitter disillusionment. Before this second performance most of his friends had departed, the theatre was half empty, and the hostility of the singers and players came to open expression. The performance was bad. The critics had been almost wholly favourably inclined after the first performance but now their judgments were in some cases reversed. A Mannheim newspaper spoke of 'wire-pulling' and of cliques and claques, and opposed the idea expressed in some quarters that Wolf had, in allowing his opera to be performed at Mannheim, granted a favour to the theatre and its public. Clearly enough, the opinions of the performers had been passed on to the journalists. Heinrich Werner, who had stayed for the second performance, afterwards had supper with the intendant and found him depressed. He had decided that Wolf's opera could not be performed again in that season and spoke of the cuts that would be necessary if it were to be revived in the autumn. It was not revived. Röhr left Mannheim for Munich, several of the singers also departed, and *Der Corregidor* was laid aside.

The same fate has pursued Wolf's opera ever since its first performance. From time to time it has been revived, has achieved a *succès d'estime*, has delighted the connoisseur and lover of Wolf's music and has then been quietly dropped. Nowhere has it succeeded in establishing itself in the repertory. The reasons are not far to seek, either for the secure place the best of its music holds in the hearts of the composer's devoted admirers, or for the comparative failure of the work as a whole on the stage. Into *Der Corregidor* Wolf put much lovely music, but unfortunately he expended his energies on a libretto that was unworthy of his genius.

How it came about that he was able to convince himself, when he read the book for the second time, that it was both dramatically effective and of high poetic value has always been, and still remains, an inexplicable mystery. Earlier he had rejected it with contempt, as he had rejected innumerable other librettos during the five or six years of his unceasing search for an operatic subject, and during that time, it might have been thought, he had had occasion enough to ponder the needs of the stage. Yet, shortly after rejecting Schaumann's reasonably effective treatment of the same story, he uncritically accepted, and clung to, in spite of the warnings of some of his friends, this amateurish, hopelessly undramatic piece of poetic carpentry. The only possible explanation seems to be that while, at his first examination, at a time when he was as yet unembittered by the failure of his years long search, he saw the book for what it was, by the time that it came into his hands for the second time his need for self-expression in operatic form had become so intensified that he judged it less from an objective view of its dramatic qualities than from the subjective response within him to the purely lyrical opportunities it offered him. Wolf was, in his mature years, essentially a miniaturist; Rosa Mayreder's *Corregidor* libretto offered him a succession of short scenes and songs well within the range of his powers and, his overwhelming, long-thwarted desire to write an opera blinding him to everything else, he clutched desperately at the opportunity to discharge the pent-up musical forces within him.

The result was less an opera than another song-book, with orchestral accompaniment. We should know, from internal evidence, without that of Wolf's letters and the dates in his manuscript, that in its composition he worked from point to point, without consideration of dramatic, or, in its larger sense, of musical form. No one will ever discover in *Der Corregidor*, as Alfred Lorenz has in the music-dramas of Wagner, an underlying tonal and formal architecture as logical and considered as that of any classical symphony. Frau Mayreder followed Alarcon's narrative all too faithfully and made no attempt to rethink the story in terms of the stage. Wolf accepted her libretto, just as it stood, with its manifold redundancies, its artificial 'curtains,' its desperate dramatic shortcomings and lack of any real sense of growth or climax, and into this flawed and misshapen mould he poured the precious metal of his genius.

One of the most baffling experiences of those who had to co-operate with Wolf in the production of his opera at Mannheim was the discovery that he was indifferent to, and even unaware of, what was happening on the stage. When he was approached for his opinion about certain scenic alterations, it was found that not only had he not noticed anything different, but that he had paid no attention at all to the picture presented by his opera on the stage. He told them that such matters were not his business and referred them to the librettist. Such an attitude was strange indeed in an earnest student of Wagner, who had, in his *Salonblatt* days, on many occasions harshly criticized the Vienna Opera for discordancies between music and stage action. The explanation, undoubtedly, is that Wolf's own music was, for him, continually evocative of mental images so convincing that the crude realities of the footlights were as nothing to the spectacle played out before his mind's eye. All Wolf's music, indeed, is extraordinarily suggestive of motion and gesture. We think of the opening of the great monologue of Prometheus, as he draws himself up to hurl his defiance in the face of Zeus, of the pictorial effect of such a phrase as 'und neiget Euch und beugt die Knie ingleichen' in the Italian song *Und steht Ihr früh am Morgen auf*. We know, also, that Wolf told Kauffmann that he imagined a scenic background to each of his songs—for example, in *Gesang Weylas*, the protective deity of Orplid sitting on a reef in the moonlight, accompanying herself on the harp. But these imaginative scenes and gestures have nothing in common with those of the theatre. In *Der Corregidor* a sense of disparity between music and action, between the characters as suggested to the imagination by the music and as actually observed on the stage, is often striking. The power and authority with which the Corregidor's office is invested is often depicted in the orchestra, but little of it can be suggested by the hapless buffoon on the stage. The dumb bishop, whose arrival brings the first act to such a dramatically lame conclusion, is unworthy of the noble processional music that he evoked in Wolf's imagination. The purely orchestral interlude which depicts, during the change of scenes in the third act, the nocturnal flight of Frasquita and Repela, is like a return to reality after the unconvincing stage actions that have preceded it.

'Without *Die Meistersinger*,' Wolf wrote to his librettist, '*Der Corregidor* would never have been composed.' There are various points of resemblance between the two works. They are alike in their genial atmosphere, their blended lyricism and drama, and their juxtaposition of grotesque comedy and deep pathos. In Wolf's opera the declamation, the use of *leit-motive*, and in particular the incessant polyphonic web of sound in the orchestra, reveal the Wagnerian impress. Except for the Fandango in the first act, and Frasquita's interrupted song, 'Auf Zamora geht der Feldzug,' in the second, there is not a lot of 'local colour' in the opera,[1] but nevertheless a certain incompatibility is felt between the Spanish setting of the story and the generally *Meistersinger*-like tone and sentiment of the music. Wolf himself seems to have recognized the difficulty of

---

[1] I find it difficult to believe, as did Prince Bojidar Karageorgevitch and Decsey, that the love duet in the second act has any connection at all with the Spanish folk-song *Se me morio mi bonita*' (see Decsey, iv, p. 22).

presenting the Spanish scene with the apparatus that Wagner bequeathed to his followers.   He once remarked to Ferdinand Löwe that Bizet had had a far easier task in his *Carmen*, since he was not bound to the polyphonic style in his use of the orchestra.   As Richard Capell has suggested, Wolf and Frau Mayreder would perhaps have been better advised to transfer the whole plot boldly to a German or Austrian setting.

The story of *The Three-cornered Hat* is fairly well known, especially since Falla employed it as the basis of his popular ballet.   The version used by Wolf is, briefly, as follows: The scene is Andalusia, the year 1804.   The amiable, hunchbacked miller, Tio Lukas, has a lovely wife, Frasquita.   Don Eugenio de Zuniga, the Corregidor (magistrate), who is elderly and also hunchbacked, visits the mill and makes love to Frasquita, who is, however, as virtuous as she is beautiful and gay.   Made to look ridiculous at his first attempt, the Corregidor renews his love-making in the evening of the same day. He arranges for Lukas to be called away to the house of the Alcalde (mayor), so that Frasquita is left alone in the mill.   After a period of uneasy solitude she hears a cry for help outside.   Thinking it is Lukas, she rushes to the door and opens it—to admit the dripping wet Corregidor, who has had the misfortune to fall into the mill-stream. When he has recovered a little he presses his attentions on her, first offering a wished-for official appointment for her nephew and then, when she indignantly rejects this bribe, threatening her with his pistol.   She nearly frightens the life out of him with Lukas's blunderbuss and the Corregidor falls down in a faint.   Frasquita departs to seek Lukas at the Alcalde's house and the Corregidor is put to bed in the mill.

Meanwhile Lukas has tricked the Alcalde and his friends into drinking heavily and escaped.   He arrives home to find the door unlocked and the Corregidor's clothes spread out before the fire. On the table he sees what he takes to be the price of his wife's honour, the document giving the official appointment to her nephew, and through the bedroom keyhole he catches sight of the Corregidor's head on his own pillow.   After thoughts of murder, he conceives a form of vengeance satisfying to his injured pride—the Corregidor, too, has a lovely wife!   He changes into the Corregidor's clothes, seizes the three-cornered hat, the emblem of authority, and leaves the house.

The Corregidor wakes up, finds his clothes gone, and puts on Tio

Lukas's, so that he is assaulted by his own followers, in mistake for the miller, when they arrive in search of the fugitive. He is given another beating by his own servants when, in the early hours of the morning, he demands admittance to his own house. His wife, Donna Mercedes, tells him her husband has long been home and in bed beside her. The plot is then rapidly disentangled. While the Corregidor is changing into his own clothes we learn from Mercedes and the servants that Lukas's presence in the house was discovered, that he told his story, and that Mercedes decided to teach her real husband a lesson by seeming to admit the success of Lukas's venture. The miller and his wife are reconciled and everything ends happily. The only person who does not get an explanation is the Corregidor, who is left wondering to his dying day what really happened that night in his wife's bedroom.

Undoubtedly the love of Tio Lukas and his Frasquita was the theme nearest to Wolf's heart; in all the tender scenes of conjugal felicity he is altogether inimitable. Outstanding are the duets, in the first two acts, between the miller and his wife, the first expressive of gentle raillery and heartfelt affection, and the second, more formal but not less beguiling, wholly blissful and content. Only a bachelor like Wolf could have imagined that married life could ever really be like that! Frasquita's theme is of truly bewitching loveliness. In its initial form it is eloquent of goodness of heart and a certain emotional simplicity; in its later manifestations it is transformed to express the heroine's agitated solicitude or passionate exaltation. Tio Lukas surely deserved a better theme. The suspicion cannot be dismissed that his brief, stolid motive, that of the Corregidor, and the theme of 'Authority' which appears in the second act were all chosen chiefly because they allowed of so many ingenious contrapuntal developments, the advantages of which will be obvious when it is considered that the composer had to portray the Corregidor in the miller's clothes and the miller in the Corregidor's. The cynical Repela, the Corregidor's snuff-taking, sneezing servant, is well characterized in Wolf's music, although this figure, as developed by Frau Mayreder from the Garduna of Alarcon's novel, is a disturbing influence that would have been better eliminated. The Corregidor's own theme excellently suggests his pompous officiality and is also capable, in some of its many transformations, of indicating that his dignity is not all that he thinks it—the three-cornered hat is sometimes worn tilted over one ear. Don Eugenio de Zuniga, however, can be eloquent, too, or, rather, Frasquita can inspire him to eloquence. 'Süsse Zauberin Frasquita' he sings to a magically beautiful phrase, 'Alles, was du willst, mein Herz,' with just the right blend of fire and devotion, and from 'Aber wenn dein Blick, Frasquita' onwards he pleads his case with a power and passion that many a younger man might envy him and that might well have prevailed against a heart less steadfast than the lovely Frasquita's. It is evident that the Corregidor must have been a formidable wooer in his youth. Frasquita's attempt at a reconciliation, with the offering of the first grapes from the miller's celebrated vines, is accompanied by an exquisite theme, one of the beauties on account of which *Der Corregidor* is treasured by all who know it, which, however, after twenty bars disappears from the score, never to return.

One of the most affecting episodes in the opera is the scene of Frasquita in solitude, in the second act. She decides to keep watch until the morning, and her tender solicitude and love for Lukas are painted in a most expressive passage, freely developed out of her own theme and that of the miller. Then she takes the bellows and blows up the fire, to the accompaniment of a miniature *Feuerzauber*, and sings to the flames and the friendly old kettle bubbling on the hob. There has never been another composer with the ability to reproduce with such fidelity the atmosphere and sentiment of such homely domestic scenes. Frasquita next takes her distaff and settles herself near the fire to spin. To exquisite music she tries to banish the thoughts of impending evil that throng about her, to open her heart to the consolations of hope. The lyricism of her music is interrupted by passages in the rhythms of ordinary speech, as practical considerations break into the poetry of her thoughts.

It is not known whether it was Wolf or his librettist who first conceived the idea of incorporating existing songs from the *Spanish Song Book* in the text of the opera. Frasquita sings *In dem Schatten meiner Locken* in the first act to lull the Corregidor into the belief that her husband is asleep, and in the second act, after being worsted by his intended victim, the Corregidor himself brings the first scene to an end with *Herz, verzage nicht geschwind*. The songs are fitted cleverly enough into their places in the text, but the procedure is a sufficiently desperate one, and indicative of Wolf's need of a succession of brief lyrical opportunities rather than a properly cumulative dramatic action.

After a brilliantly attractive orchestral intermezzo, the second main

scene of the second act represents a falling away from the general
level of the opera up to this point.　Wolf was not too happy in the
company of the drunken Alcalde and his companions.　The effect of
this scene is somewhat scrappy, although it contains some delightful
musical incidents, notably the good-night canon and Pedro's wine-
soaked melodies.

One of Wolf's major defects as a composer of opera lies in the
excessive rapidity of his stage action, leading to effects of restlessness
and the failure to establish firmly the atmosphere of the different
scenes.　One instance of this is seen in the musical picture of Frasquita in solitude described above, which is evidently intended to
cover a much greater passage of time than it actually does suggest.
The whole episode does not last longer than about five minutes, and
some four minutes after we have watched Tio Lukas walk out of the
door of the mill we are told that he must be already nearly half-way
to his destination, the house of the Alcalde.　Stage time does not
necessarily stand in close relationship to actual time, but it must at
least give the impression of doing so, and here it fails to do that.
Again, in this scene in the Alcalde's house, it only takes five or six
minutes, after the arrival of Tio Lukas, for him to accept the necessity of spending the night there, to drink the others under the table
and send them off to bed.　One minute later he is out of the window
and on his way back to the mill, and in another two and a half
minutes his absence is discovered.　If things moved with the rapidity
suggested by the stage action in this scene it is difficult to see how the
central events of the story could possibly have been spread over a
whole night—from supper-time at the mill, at the beginning of the
second act, to dawn on the following morning, at the opening of the
fourth.　As a song-writer Wolf was skilled in presenting his characters at single, isolated moments of time; the time factor in opera was
new to him and brought with it problems that he did not solve.　For
this, however, his librettist is equally to blame with him.　If she had
not been intent on reproducing so many minor incidents of Alarcon's
novel, she would have been able to give the composer room to expand
his music at points where expansion, for dramatic purposes, was
necessary.

Wholly superfluous, and ineffective on the stage, is the scene which
opens the third act, showing how the miller and his wife pass without
seeing each other and Repela attaches himself to Frasquita.　Luckily
it is quite short, and after an orchestral interlude, covering the change

of scenes, we are back in the mill for the finest scene of the whole
opera. Lukas's monologue of jealousy gave Wolf his one great
dramatic opportunity, and he rose magnificently to meet it. Here at
least the claims of music are equated with those of the theatre. Each
stage of the unhappy miller's hour of torment—his initial stupe-
faction, his despairing unwillingness to believe his own eyes, the tense
and dreadful moment when he steals towards the door of the bedroom
with murder in his heart, his self-pity and sense of helpless inferiority,
and finally his savage exultation, when he discovers a way to pay out
the seducer in his own coin—is depicted by Wolf with extraordinary
power and mastery, and the whole combines to form one of the
greatest scenes in all operatic literature. Motives from various
earlier episodes are employed in the orchestra and given new significance and eloquence. When Lukas first dares to express the idea
that he may find his wife and the Corregidor together in the bedroom,
there recurs a theme that had accompanied his confident assertion, in
the love duet of the first act, that Frasquita would always belong only
to him. When he can no longer doubt that his enemy has attained
his desires, he stands there in silence, covering his face with his hands,
while the Corregidor's theme resounds with awful power over his own
poor, impotent motive. When he reflects that even if he killed
Frasquita and her lover the world would yet resound with mocking
laughter over his misery, the orchestra reintroduces a theme that
appeared in the first pages of the score but which, up to this point,
has not been heard again. It is associated with the neighbour who
first hints to Lukas that some of those who visit his mill do so perhaps
less on account of his famous vines than because his wife is so
attractive. On its return it is enveloped in derisive trills and turns,
and presented over a broken, stumbling version of Lukas's own
motive. Such ingenious touches as these, however, are only significant details in a canvas on a grand scale, splendidly drawn, formally
satisfying, and glowing with colour—Wolf's unique masterpiece in
the domain of opera. Comparison is sometimes made with Ford's
great monologue in the second act of Verdi's *Falstaff*. Both scenes
present the jealous husband erroneously convinced of his wife's
infidelity; both, in their emotional intensity, stand out from the
generally light-hearted tone of their surroundings—though Verdi's
is not, like Wolf's, really tragic. The thoughts and memories that
haunt the mind of Lukas, like those by which Ford is tormented,
are reflected by the use in the orchestra of musical phrases

from earlier scenes. Wolf's music, however, is perfectly individual, and not derivative. There is no evidence that he knew Verdi's opera. *Falstaff* was given two performances in Vienna, by the original company from La Scala, on 21st and 22nd May 1893, but Wolf was at that time staying in the Salzkammergut. The work was not produced again in Vienna before *Der Corregidor* was written.[1] He may, of course, have seen a score. One point that does suggest that he took a hint from Verdi is the comical re-entry of the villain as the sequel to the jealousy monologue—the emergence of the Corregidor in his night-clothes, accompanied by a humorous diminution of his theme on the bassoons, makes an effect closely matching the swaggering reappearance of Falstaff, dressed up to the nines.

After the romantic poetry of the night-watchman's call, the fourth act degenerates, with Repela's burlesque serenade, to the level of farce, to be redeemed, after the Corregidor has been beaten for the second time, by the appearance of Donna Mercedes. The Corregidor's wife is seen on the stage for the first time in this act, although her splendid theme, the embodiment of *grandezza* and stately graciousness, has already been conspicuously employed in the first act and in Lukas's monologue. She is given music of exceptional loveliness and aristocratic distinction, which for subtlety of characterization is hardly surpassed anywhere in the whole of Wolf's work in lighter vein. The passage beginning 'Mein Gatte, der Corregidor' may be cited as a notable example. Wolf manages to convey the essential nobility of her character, and also her charm and serene humour, while her dignified reserve does not preclude a certain archness in hinting at the secrets of the bedchamber. But in spite of the lustre imparted by Donna Mercedes to many pages of this fourth act, its musical qualities are insufficient to counterbalance its hopeless dramatic failings. Almost the whole act is given up to the narration of events that are over before the curtain rises. First Lukas has to be given a true account of what happened to Frasquita after he left her alone in the mill—all of which is already familiar to the audience —and then what occurred, off stage, in the Corregidor's house when Lukas arrived there has to be told. The expectations aroused by the miller's great monologue in the previous act are left unsatisfied; the culmination of the story occurs in the interval between the third and fourth acts, leaving only misunderstandings to be cleared up on the stage.

[1] The first Vienna performance of *Falstaff* in German was given under Mahler on 3rd May 1904.

Various attempts have been made to reshape the opera, but none of them, not even Wolf's own, succeeded, because none of them went far enough.   The faults of *Der Corregidor* are too fundamental to be corrected by mere cuts and rearrangements; the whole second half of the libretto needed rewriting and setting to music afresh, and since Wolf himself did not undertake the latter task, it is now too late for any one to do so.

If the whole opera had only remained in the style and on the level of the scenes at the mill, it would assuredly have won all hearts by its music alone.   If the librettist had cut out the drinking scene, the scene of Frasquita's nocturnal flight, the clowning of Repela throughout the opera, and, in the last act, had boldly tackled the representation of the events *inside* the Corregidor's house, what a masterpiece we might have had!   As things are, Wolf's opera must remain for ever at once the delight and despair of all his admirers.

After he left Mannheim on 9th June, Wolf's journey back to Vienna was made in several stages.   He first stayed for a week as the Nast family's guest at Stuttgart, giving a concert there on the 15th, with the assistance of Emma Gerok, Karl Lang and Faisst.   Certain other non-musical developments during this time must now be considered.

During his visits to Stuttgart in this year, before and after the production of *Der Corregidor*, Wolf had renewed acquaintance with Margarethe Klinckerfuss, the daughter of one of the friends he had made there two years earlier, and between the thirty-six-year-old composer and this girl of nineteen there developed, during these few weeks, an intimate relationship which, according to the lady herself, amounted to a secret engagement to be married.   The story has been outlined by Frl. Klinckerfuss in a book of reminiscences, *Aufklänge aus versunkener Zeit*.[1]

The African explorer Johannes Wissemann was a distant relative of the Klinckerfuss family, and before his departure on what was to prove his last voyage a secret pledge of troth had been exchanged between him and Margarethe.   Wissemann's last letter was dated 9th April 1895, reached Stuttgart on 2nd June, and was replied to at once.   This reply was returned a few months later with the information that Wissemann had died of blackwater fever on the Zambesi.   Margarethe Klinckerfuss was still suffering from the effects of this blow when Wolf reappeared on the Stuttgart scene in 1896.   In the

[1] Port-Verlag, Urach, 1947.

course of a walk together, after he had briefly indicated to her—
without actually naming Frl. Zerny—that he had experienced disillusionment over the singer to whom he had been attached when last
at Stuttgart, she confided to him the story of her love for Wissemann
and his death in Africa.

In such a state of heart Hugo Wolf and I met each other again on his
return to Stuttgart. Then in the Hoppenlau cemetery, after he had first
confided to me his bitter experience, I told him, too, of my heart's distress.
Thereupon he drew my attention to a passage in Shakespeare's *Romeo and
Juliet* that reveals how a deeply wounded heart is doubly receptive of new
impressions. At these words he looked me quietly in the eyes, almost
beseechingly. We walked up and down between the tombstones, side by
side. Then, when we sat down on a concealed bench, Hugo Wolf, without
speaking, held both my hands fast in his own and I, with beating heart,
permitted it. I felt as if a burden had fallen from my heart, all the more
as I had experienced and suffered that girlish love wholly in secret. 'Poor
child, may I console you?' said quietly the voice of Hugo Wolf beside me—
and he employed for the first time the 'Du.'

Frl. Klinckerfuss describes how they returned, as they wished to
keep their meeting to themselves, by separate ways to her home in the
Kanzleistrasse, where Wolf's 'consolation' took the form of a suggestion that they should play a Bruckner symphony together as a
piano duet. After the *adagio* he kissed her lightly on the brow and
said: 'How unanimous we are, as though we had practised together
all our lives,' and quoted Goethe's poem to Frau von Stein:

> Sag, was will das Schicksal uns bereiten?
> Sag, wie band es uns so rein genau?
> Ach, Du warst in abgelebten Zeiten
> Meine Schwester oder meine Frau. . . .

From this beginning there grew an intimacy between them that
found expression in the course of various unofficial meetings. Wolf's
letters of this period show him planning to revisit Kauffmann at
Tübingen; they show also that he did not, in fact, do so. Nevertheless, he *was* in Tübingen once with Margarethe Klinckerfuss,
incognito, and she also made an unofficial trip to Mannheim to see
him during the *Corregidor* rehearsals. Although they believed
themselves unobserved, they were seen there by Emil Heckel, as
came out many years later. This relationship with Frl. Klinckerfuss
was, no doubt, the real reason why, at Mannheim, as his letters show,
he frequently thought of abandoning the rehearsals, which brought
him so much annoyance, and returning to Stuttgart for a few days,

and why he chose in fact to return there after the production of *Der Corregidor*.

The scene of another episode recorded in these memoirs is the Klinckerfuss family's country house 'Heidfried' on the Feuerbacher Heide.

One evening there as he took leave of my parents, he detained me at the door and whispered that he would like once more to return to me alone. After the 'Good night' of my parents I awaited him under our great walnut-tree and I heard Hugo Wolf sing Schumann's song of longing, *Der Nussbaum*, as he again advanced towards me. He wished to experience with me, on the flat roof of our house, the clear, starry night. We went inside the house, upstairs, and up the little winding staircase that led to the roof. Timelessly we both sat there, hand in hand, in silent understanding, on a rolled-up, thick carpet. When I looked up at Hugo Wolf, who had raised his pale face towards the firmament, I noticed how tear upon tear rolled down his cheeks. He pressed his folded hands before his brow, while he sang quietly to himself Beethoven's melody to the words: 'Die Himmel rühmen des Ewigen Ehre.' Not until morning was near did we descend again and Hugo Wolf 'talpte zu Tal,' as he put it, using an expression of Richard Wagner's.

Altogether, what with his experiences of 1894 and those of 1896, Stuttgart must have become for Wolf a place of poignant memories.[1]

Nevertheless, it is permissible to doubt whether this relationship had for Wolf the significance attached to it by Frl. Klinckerfuss. That he found her attractive is certain. But was he really in love with her? Did he ever seriously consider the possibility of marrying her? Frl. Klinckerfuss writes: 'When Hugo Wolf, almost bashfully, spoke to me of a common future, it was always in Vienna, where he hoped, after his *Corregidor* and his songs should have brought him success and an income, to prepare for me too a second home.' Is this credible? Or did he, 'beyond good and evil' as he considered himself, permit himself to trifle with the affections of an attractive and infatuated girl? Or was this brief idyll, perhaps, something that

[1] I should like to record here that I am convinced that this episode between Wolf and 'das kleine Klinckerfüssle,' as he called her, did actually take place at Stuttgart in 1896 and is not, as has been ungallantly suggested to me in other quarters, a product of the lady's imagination. In the form in which the Wolf reminiscences in *Aufklänge aus versunkener Zeit* were first sent to me there were, it is true, serious chronological discrepancies. The affair seemed to be actually coincident with that with Frieda Zerny! But reference to the letters of Johannes Wissemann established the fact that he died in 1895 and not, as Frl. Klinckerfuss had believed when she set down her memoirs, in 1893, and with that the chief obstacles to the acceptance of her story disappeared. Faisst seems to have known something of the affair, judging from a remark of his in a letter of 20th January 1900 to the Marchese Casanova.

could take root and develop, up to a point, in the special circumstances of his Stuttgart environment, where he was for a short time a loved and honoured guest, but which was bound to wither and die in the conditions of his normal life in Vienna? He wrote Margarethe Klinckerfuss one intimate letter, and this he insisted on her destroying—it was buried, as it were, among the ivy covering the grave of the once celebrated Mozart singer, Agnes Schebest-Strauss, in the Hoppenlau cemetery at Stuttgart. His later letters were official ones, which gave no indication of the intimacy that had existed between them. He never saw her again. Twice, in later letters to Faisst, he refers to her,[1] but it requires the eye of faith to read as much as Frl. Klinckerfuss does into these passages. The second reference is particularly unconvincing: 'That your extensive plans for the popularization of Wolf's songs are already assuming tangible form and shape is highly gratifying. The little Klinckerfüssle will, it is to be hoped, be the right person for the part. That your mouth waters for such honey I can easily imagine. Don't become *too* fond of dainties, however, you Sweet-tooth.' (10th August 1897.) The last sentence in the original language ('Werde mir nur nicht zu genäschig, Du Leckermaul') has a possessive air, certainly, as though Faisst were trespassing on Wolf's preserves in showing interest in the little Klinckerfüssle, but is it credible that he would have written thus about someone with whom he was really in love and whom he considered himself engaged to marry?

One other interesting point arises out of these reminiscences, and that concerns Wolf's religious beliefs. At Stuttgart, we are told, as they passed the Marienkirche Wolf looked earnestly at his companion and remarked what a beautiful custom it was that Catholic churches were always open.

We went inside and Hugo Wolf knelt for a long time, fervently praying. I was a witness of his submissive, reverent bearing in the church, and in this devout disposition we both felt ourselves *one* heart and *one* soul. The fact that he was a Catholic and I a Protestant could never have led to discord between us. Hugo Wolf would never have composed his *Geistliche Lieder*, and many another song, if he had not been deeply religious.

The idea expressed in the last-quoted sentence is too naïve to require refutation. But it must be stated that Wolf's attitude towards religion is not in doubt. He was neither a Catholic nor a Protestant, but a freethinker, like his father before him. He had

---

[1] In two passages omitted from the letters as published in book form.

been brought up in a Catholic environment, and his mother was a good Catholic to the end of her days. Whether Wolf himself, in earlier years, ever passed through a religious phase is unknown. It is certainly not unlikely. But long before 1896 he had made up his mind about such things and, influenced largely by Nietzsche, had rejected Christianity entirely. Eckstein has described how foreign to Wolf, 'a man of the world, through and through,' was Bruckner's pious Catholicism. Wolf described himself as an 'Unbeliever' in a letter to his mother on 29th April 1892, and in a letter to Rosa Mayreder, another Nietzschian, on 7th September 1897, wrote: 'As you know, on the subject of Christianity I share your views completely, which, however, does not hinder me at all from appreciating its artistic sides.' In Heinrich Werner's diary, where Wolf's conversation is recorded, we find the following:

Then we turned to Nietzsche. Wolf says that one allows oneself to be carried away so easily by this man because he makes everything so clear to one, explains so lucidly, speaks so winningly, but one must take everything with a pinch of salt. The last work of Nietzsche, *The Antichrist*, is something downright annihilating of Christianity, something demoniacal; all papal bulls, compared with it, are rubbish, nothingness. [3rd February 1895.]

What was this disciple of Nietzsche doing on his knees, 'fervently praying,' in that Stuttgart church? We can only conclude that, unless the lady's memory or imagination, or both, have been playing her tricks, this episode must have occurred in connection with the confession by Frl. Klinckerfuss of her childish love for Wissemann, and that Wolf, for the comfort of his young companion, offered a prayer for the repose of the soul of the dead explorer.

On 17th June Wolf left Stuttgart for Traunkirchen, via Munich and Salzburg. After another week spent with the Köcherts at Traunkirchen he finally reached Vienna on the 24th, taking up temporary residence again with the Mayreders.

On 4th July he took possession of his new flat in the Schwindgasse, high up on the fourth floor, at the back of the building, facing the courtyard and garden, and soon in letters to his friends he was describing with touching pride the amenities of the first real home of his own that he had ever possessed. It was owing to the generosity of Faisst that he was able to settle himself in this new place of refuge. He was still in debt over the printing of the vocal score of his opera, with further expenses to follow on account of the preparation of a definitive version of the full score, and he would not have been able to take the Schwindgasse flat if Faisst had not, in the previous March, made him a present of 1,000 marks. The money had been sent anonymously, but Wolf knew well from whom it came. 'Let me kiss and embrace you, you dear, good man, friend, brother, and companion,' he now wrote. 'I can only exclaim like Florestan "May you be rewarded in a better world!"' Other friends assisted in the furnishing of the new home. The first and largest room had to remain for the time completely bare. Wolf used to say: 'That will one day be my reception-room for the opera directors who will crowd here to secure my *Corregidor*.' The interior of the second room, the study, is known from photographs that have often been reproduced. Against one wall stood the old cherry-wood Bösendorfer piano, taken out of storage, now that he had, for the first time, a room big enough to keep it in. Near it was a book-case, with his editions of Schiller, Shakespeare, Goethe, and Mörike, the collected writings of Wagner, and the rest of the little library he had accumulated in the years since boyhood. Many of these volumes had been finely bound for him by his friends. His collection of scores, consisting for the most part of works by Beethoven, Berlioz, Bruckner, Liszt, Wagner and Weber, filled the lower part of the book-case. In one corner of the study, by the window, stood a large writing-desk, a present from Potpeschnigg, to whose grandfather, the poet Karl von Holtei, it had once belonged. Before the desk was a red-striped cane arm-chair with a leather cushion, and near by a little Japanese smoking-table. On the opposite side of the room to the piano was a divan, provided by Rosa Mayreder, and on the floor a Persian carpet, the gift of Melanie Köchert, who had also supplied kitchen utensils and a wash-stand. The walls were hung with two prints after Böcklin, a portrait of Beethoven, a water-colour by Rosa Mayreder, two humorous drawings, the work of Anton Katzer, an old friend and fellow student of Edmund Lang's, illustrating episodes, real and imaginary, from Wolf's life, and a theatre bill from Mannheim surmounted by a laurel wreath. A portrait of Wagner stood on the writing-desk. The bedroom contained only an iron bedstead, a commode and the indiarubber bath. In the kitchen were Wolf's trunks and boxes.

It was simple enough—a pleasant, quiet, sunny retreat, but by no means luxurious. To Wolf it was paradise. 'At last I can be quite on my own,' he told Grohe, 'and can do just what I like. The feeling of absolute freedom and independence fairly intoxicates me.

I often want to cry out aloud with delight over it. My life is now like a wonderfully beautiful morning dream.' In these rooms he lived quietly and happily for the next fifteen months, except only for two short holidays. He had occasional trials, as when he discovered bugs in his bedroom, so that the whole place had to be fumigated, or detected hollow places in the dividing wall between him and his neighbours, necessitating the invasion of bricklayer and plasterer. Later on he had some trouble with a noisy family on the floor below his flat, and did not rest until he had got them ejected and had arranged for his friend Larisch to take the rooms in their place. But on the whole he was well content with his home in the Schwindgasse.

He had plenty to occupy him at this time. At first all his attention was taken up with the revision of the full score of *Der Corregidor*. Röhr had discovered a lot of errors, but had overlooked as many more, and for some time Wolf was kept busy with alterations and improvements. Towards the end of July he sent Grohe a variant to the fourth act of the opera—a later letter to Potpeschnigg indicates that this involved two short cuts. When he was completely satisfied with the full score, there would be the parts to be collated and altered, before the material was sent off to be lithographed and reproduced. He had also the proofs of the second part of the *Italian Song Book* on his hands. He was invited to stay again at Schloss Matzen in August and left Vienna on the 4th, taking his work with him. Among the other guests were Faisst, Paul Müller and Kauffmann's son Max, while Potpeschnigg, with his family, was staying at nearby Brixlegg. It rained all day and every day, and Wolf spent most of the time in the Jägerhaus with his head buried in his scores. When cramp or eye-strain made a pause necessary, he would go down to Brixlegg to invite Potpeschnigg to come for a walk in the rain. The two of them, tempted by a rise of the barometer, once set out on a longer excursion but were caught, far from home, in a cloud-burst.

Wolf, by this time, had had enough of Brixlegg and made arrangements to go at once with Potpeschnigg to Graz. They left on 16th August, broke their journey at Toblach, visited Cortina and district on the 17th and 18th, then spent a day by the Wörthersee, in Carinthia, and arrived at Graz on the 20th. It was while they were exploring the neighbourhood of Toblach and Cortina that Wolf was introduced to Denza's *Funiculì, funiculà*. The travellers were on their way back to catch their train at Toblach and had entered an inn at Misurina. Two Italians at the next table began to sing the popular

Neapolitan song, to the accompaniment of guitar and mandoline. Wolf was enraptured, gave money to the performers, and kept on calling out 'Da capo!' until he had obtained endless repetitions, which he applauded like a man possessed. In the end Potpeschnigg had almost to drag him away.[1] *Funiculì, funiculà* became from that time on one of Wolf's passions. He made it, as he told Kauffmann, his 'Morning and Evening Prayer,' which he never tired of repeating.

It must have been at this time, also, that Potpeschnigg made a tragic discovery concerning the true state of his friend's health. During the railway journey Wolf got a cinder lodged in his eye, and on arrival at Graz Potpeschnigg took him to a Dr. Elschnigg to have it removed. Afterwards the doctor told Potpeschnigg that the pupils of Wolf's eyes showed the inability to expand or contract that is a symptom of incipient general paralysis.

Wolf stayed with Potpeschnigg at Graz until 1st September, both men sitting all day long at a table, collating the parts of *Der Corregidor* with the revised score. Then Wolf returned to Vienna, to his Schwindgasse home, and took up the same task again there, while Potpeschnigg continued his labours on Wolf's behalf at Graz. For the next three months they were both kept busy in this way.

There is little of importance to relate about Wolf's activities during this period.

In September he made new friends in Karl Mayr, the historian, and his fiancée, the singer Clementine Schönfield, from Munich, who called on him at the Schwindgasse flat. Clementine Schönfield sang many of his songs, including *Herr, was trägt der Boden hier*, which Wolf had never heard performed before. This singer afterwards, at Munich and elsewhere, did much to make his music known.

He was saddened to hear of the death of the Baroness Lipperheide on 12th September. She had been one of his best friends and he had deep respect and affection for her. After her death he did not again visit Schloss Matzen. On 11th October Bruckner died, after a protracted illness. Wolf had long been one of his greatest admirers; he had described him to Paul Müller as 'the only one among the living before whom I bow my head.' The funeral on 13th October brought the customary posthumous honours, after a lifetime of neglect, and Wolf, who wished to pay his last respects to the dead Master, was

---

[1] This was only one incident in the adventures of Wolf and Potpeschnigg in the Cortina district. A most entertaining account, too long for quotation here, of the events of 17th–18th August is to be found in the introduction to the published volume of Wolf's letters to Potpeschnigg.

incensed at being turned away from the doors of the Karlskirche, as he could not claim membership of the Singverein, the organizers of the ceremony.

The never-ending task of collating the parts of his opera with the score did not leave him much time for other musical activities, but on 23rd October he succeeded in completing the splendid song *Morgen-stimmung*, to words by Reinick. For nearly two months he had had the hastily sketched composition on his hands, before he found time to work it out thoroughly and give it permanent form. The completion of this song enabled him to fulfil a long-cherished wish; *Morgenstimmung* was published shortly afterwards with two other settings of Reinick, the *Gesellenlied* of 1888 and the *Skolie* of 1889, the volume being dedicated to Ferdinand Jäger. At the same time as these Reinick songs, Heckel also brought out the three songs from the incidental music to *Das Fest auf Solhaug*. The first of Gudmund's two songs underwent considerable revision before publication.

Correspondence between Joseph Schalk and his brother Franz shows that the latter was anxious to produce Wolf's opera at Prague in this season, and that his director, Angelo Neumann, was also agreeable, but that the project was held up by Wolf not replying to any of the letters Franz Schalk wrote to him on the subject. He could be singularly short-sighted and obstinate at times. His mind was now set on the production of the opera in either Berlin or Vienna. Potpeschnigg was trying to arrange a reconciliation with Karl Muck, preliminary to the reopening of the question of a Berlin performance, while Wolf himself made various attempts to get in touch with Jahn or Johann Fuchs. For a time there was a possibility that the opera might be given two performances at the Deutsches Volkstheater in Vienna, for the benefit of charity. The Countess Kilmannseg and Count Wilczek were interested in the proposal, but it came to nothing. In the end Wolf succeeded in cornering the elusive Fuchs (the 'metronome' of the *Salonblatt* criticisms), and on 19th December played through *Der Corregidor* to him, at the opera-house. Fuchs was non-committal, but assured Wolf that he would recommend the work to Jahn, the director. He gave his opinion, however, that further cuts, more drastic than those already undertaken, would be necessary in the fourth act. The narration was quite impossible, and it would be best if the whole second half of the act were omitted and replaced by something new, but quite short. Fuchs also recommended that a more extended introduction be written for the third act. These criticisms Wolf now accepted, though still unhappy about his precious last act. He set to work at once on the new introduction to the third act, and Rosa Mayreder undertook the revision of her libretto in accordance with Fuchs's suggestions.

Wolf was all the time itching to get on with a second opera. *Maria Schweidler, die Bernsteinhexe*, over which he had enthused at Matzen in 1895, had apparently by this time been rejected, as had, quite recently, *Eldas Untergang*, an original opera book of Rosa Mayreder's. At Wolf's pressing request, that lady was now working on a new version of *Manuel Venegas*, his old passion and source of vexation. She approached the task, however, in no spirit of enthusiasm, the subject being antipathetic to her. Wolf told Grohe: 'I fear that Frau Mayreder is still suffering too much from the depression that my necessary refusal of an opera poem of her own invention has occasioned. But what else could I have done in this difficult situation? I cannot set to music a text that in no way interests me.' He had proposed that she should attempt a *Manuel Venegas* and she had agreed. 'But now she laments continually about the fearful difficulties that stand in the way of a dramatic adaptation, for which naturally I cannot blame her, for this damned *Manuel Venegas* really has its snags.' She was shortly after this to suggest Gerhart Hauptmann's *Versunkene Glocke* as a substitute, a proposal that powerfully attracted Wolf, but which he abandoned when he learned, from friends of the dramatist, how improbable it was that Hauptmann would permit the mutilation of his work for operatic purposes.

Christmas was spent quietly and happily in the Schwindgasse. Presents arrived from far and near, among them considerable additions to the furnishings of Wolf's flat. Melanie Köchert's presents included a rocking chair, which transported him into the seventh heaven, he said, an occasional table, silver cutlery and a large white goatskin rug. He received from other friends books and scores. Paul Müller sent a fine illustrated edition of *Don Quixote* and a copy of the poems of Michelangelo, with the German translations of Walter Robert-Tornow. This last Wolf immediately recognized as a new incentive to composition. For the time, however, he had other songs in preparation, *Keine gleicht von allen Schönen* and *Sonne der Schlummerlosen*, two settings of poems by Byron, translated by Otto Gildemeister. The first, begun on 18th December, was apparently given its final form on Christmas Day, after a week's interrupted labour; the second, begun on the 29th, was finished on New Year's Eve.

It is surprising that more attention has not been paid to these late flowers of Wolf's genius. Somehow the songs have remained unexplored and unknown. One is a setting of Byron's lines to the moon, 'Sun of the sleepless, melancholy star,' which had been made use of, before Wolf's time, by Loewe, Mendelssohn and Schumann, although, curiously enough, all four composers used different translations; the other is 'There be none of Beauty's daughters.' The theme of waking misery amid a sleeping world recurs from time to time in Wolf's work, as does that other related theme of longing for rest, and the songs that he wrote on these subjects are among his least impersonal utterances. *Sonne der Schlummerlosen* is the saddest and most desolate of all these haunted nocturnes. *Keine gleicht von allen Schönen* is even more remarkable than its companion, though strangely unlike anything the original English poem could possibly have suggested. Wolf seems to have brooded upon the words until they have become charged with his own intenser imagination. The whole song is of dream-like beauty, glowing, especially in its middle section, with subdued but rich colouring, while the words are floated upon a vocal line of such artistry as even Wolf himself seldom achieved. The final cadence is of striking originality and loveliness.

The Byron songs were published, a little later, by Heckel, together with the Heine song *Wo wird einst*, from 1888, and the *Lied des transferierten Zettel*, from *A Midsummer Night's Dream*, of 1889.

By 11th January 1897 Wolf was already in possession of the revised text of the fourth act of his opera, and busy on the orchestration of the enlarged introduction to the third act, in which the original five bars were expanded to fifty-two. The alteration of the last act involved the sacrifice of about fifteen pages of the original printed vocal score, from 'Ja Sennora,' at the foot of p. 186, to 'Und ich rath' Euch, Caballero,' in the last line of p. 201. He began the composition of the variant, to fill this gap, on 26th January, and had it finished and scored by 19th February. In the new version of the opera the Corregidor arrests Lukas and is about to have him marched off to jail, when the morning bells begin to sound, giving Donna Mercedes the idea of laying the whole case before the bishop—a prospect which so terrifies the Corregidor that he is forced to climb down and let Lukas go free. The makeshift nature of this revised version is unhappily obvious; it cuts out the narration, but leaves

untouched the heart of the problem, of which the only really satisfactory solution would have been to make the narration unnecessary
by playing out on the stage the events of which it tells.   Wolf himself
believed that the time would come when the original would be preferred to the 'stage version.'   The variant runs to sixty-four bars.
When the bells begin to sound, the bishop's motive, from the conclusion of the first act, where it originally only appeared in the role of
a counterpoint,[1] is reintroduced, with the chiming accompaniment
of the Italian song *Und steht Ihr früh am Morgen auf*—an exquisite
passage:

After completing the revised fourth act, the composer made an
alteration to the conclusion of the first act, giving it a more idyllic and
less pompous character, and, in view of its subsequent employment,
allowing the bishop's motive to dominate the scene.

[1] In the vocal score it does not appear at all.

If Fuchs's assurance that he would recommend the opera to Jahn was anything more than an empty phrase it did not bring about any positive result, and for the time there was no possibility of the hoped for performance in Vienna.

On 22nd February Wolf made what was to be his last public concert appearance, in a recital at the Bösendorfersaal, with Jäger and Sofie Chotek. He had wished another singer, Hermine Bosetti, to perform, with Jäger, the complete Hatem-Suleika sequence from the Goethe volume, but at the last moment the director of the Vienna Conservatoire had refused to give permission for Frl. Bosetti to appear. Frl. Chotek, the substitute, nevertheless did well, and Jäger was in really wonderful form and voice. The hall was reasonably well filled, the applause was enthusiastic, and more than half the songs on the programme had to be repeated. Wolf himself was surprised at the warmth of his reception. He was particularly pleased at the acclamation that greeted *Morgenstimmung*, finely interpreted by Jäger, and, contrary to his usual practice, rose from the piano and bowed in response to the applause. Financially, too, the evening was a success, Wolf finding to his surprise that it had earned him a profit of 140 gulden.

After the concert he became friendly with two men who henceforward were numbered among his most active adherents—Michael Haberlandt and Walter Bokmayer. Haberlandt was curator of the Vienna Natural History Museum, teacher of Sanskrit at the university, ethnologist and author, a man of learning and wide culture, modest, but of great energy and tenacity of purpose when his enthusiasm was aroused, as it had been in the course of the concert in the Bösendorfersaal. He and Wolf at once took a liking to each other, a strong mutual attachment grew up between them, and in a surprisingly short time Haberlandt gained greater influence over Wolf than was enjoyed by almost any other of his friends. Some of those whose love for Wolf was of longer standing may not have been too well pleased with this development, but the composer's own letters show how warm and genuine was the affection and esteem he had for Haberlandt. Certainly, by his subsequent activities, this new friend fully deserved the honour of Wolf's intimacy. It was he who eventually succeeded in overcoming doubts and indifference and establishing a Hugo Wolf Verein in Vienna, where such an association had long been held to be impossible. During the rest of Wolf's lifetime his devotion was unceasing. As chairman of the Vienna

Hugo Wolf Verein he took on his own shoulders a great part of the cares and arduous responsibilities involved in the maintenance of the composer during the long years of his mental collapse, and after his death continued to work in his interests. Haberlandt's deeds speak for themselves. With Bokmayer Wolf's acquaintance was less rapid in development, and much less intimate. Bokmayer was a rich manufacturer living at Mödling, not far from Perchtoldsdorf. He was also a keen amateur singer, with a well-trained tenor voice, and instituted public and private Wolf concerts at Mödling, Wiener Neustadt, and elsewhere. He first earned the composer's approval by the discrimination with which he selected and arranged his programmes. During the later part of this year Wolf was a frequent visitor to his villa at Mödling.

March 13th brought the composer's thirty-seventh birthday; it was a day of particular happiness for him. He was, as he put it, 'bombarded with flowers from all sides.' His friends, from the most recent to dear old 'Aunt Bertha,' of blessed Maierling memory, vied with one another to do him honour. Presents and countless congratulations and good wishes arrived from near and far, including some from people who were quite unknown to him. It may be that the news had got about that it was unlikely that he had much time left him in which to be happy, and that all who loved him were moved to do what they could to bring joy into his life and demonstrate their affection while it was still possible. In the evening the Vienna friends assembled to hear him play the revised version of *Der Corregidor* from beginning to end. Those present on this occasion included the Mayreders, the Langs, Haberlandt and his wife, Joseph Schalk, Heinrich Werner and Richard Hirsch. Wolf was in what he considered 'famous voice,' and everything went splendidly. Afterwards a festal and most memorable day was concluded by the entertainment of his guests in a private room in the Brauner Hirsch, his favourite restaurant.

All in all, this was for Wolf a time of considerable present happiness and eager anticipation of the future. He was established in a comfortable home of his own and relieved from all his more pressing monetary anxieties. He could look back on great achievements in the past, knowing full well the value of the work he had done. Recent developments gave promise of increasingly wide recognition of his genius. Above all, he felt that quickening within him that betokened important new works soon to be born. He awaited with

MELANIE KÖCHERT

impatience Frau Mayreder's libretto for *Manuel Venegas*, and yet another operatic project claimed his attention for a time. He wrote to Grohe: 'The creative impulse is now stirring powerfully within me, and I can hardly wait any longer before letting fly. Do you know Kleist's *Amphitrion*? That is ideal material—the true "heavenly comedy." I have recently read this wonder-work again and was more than ever enchanted. I should like best to set to work straight away on *Amphitrion*.' Then the arrival of the complete first act of Rosa Mayreder's *Manuel Venegas* sent everything else out of his head. 'If the two following acts fulfil what the first act promises,' he told Heckel, '*there has been nothing like it since Wagner*. The mine is laid, the thunderstorm approaches. Now look out!' A little later another letter told Grohe: 'This first act is magnificent beyond all bounds and in every respect. Exposition, construction, language, except for a few trivialities that have been eliminated— everything ravishing and truly sublime!' The future did indeed seem to be rich in promise.

XIV

THE SWORD OF DAMOCLES

THE last of all the songs that Hugo Wolf was destined to create were settings of Robert-Tornow's translations of poems by Michelangelo. They were written in the Schwindgasse, in the second half of March 1897, while he was awaiting the completion of Rosa Mayreder's *Manuel Venegas* libretto. Three Michelangelo settings were afterwards published—*Wohl denk' ich oft*, composed on 18th March; *Alles endet, was entstehet*, which Wolf originally called *Vanitas Vanitatum*, composed on the 20th; and *Fühlt meine Seele*, composed between the 22nd and 28th. A fourth song, entitled *Irdische und himmlische Liebe*, and beginning 'Zur Schönheit meine Blicke suchend gleiten,' was written at about the same time, but was afterwards destroyed by its composer as not being up to standard.

'Naturally the sculptor must sing bass,' Wolf told Edmund Hellmer, and this remark should have sufficed to dispose of the suggestion, sometimes put forward, that here, after half a lifetime, the subjective note is again to be discerned in his music. He had been reading Hermann Grimm's biography of Michelangelo, and it is the sculptor himself who is depicted in these songs. 'They are truly antique,' Wolf wrote to Faisst, 'as far as can be in modern music.'

Wohl denk' ich oft contrasts present fame with past neglect. In Wolf's own description, given in a letter to Grohe, it 'begins with a melancholy introduction, and holds fast to this tone until the line before the last,' then 'takes on unexpectedly a vigorous character (developed from the previous motive) and closes festively with triumphal fanfares, like a flourish of trumpets sounded for him [Michelangelo] by his contemporaries in homage.' The music has a noble gravity and majesty, with great strength and simplicity in its harmonies and rhythms. It was Wolf's unfulfilled intention to orchestrate his Michelangelo settings, and the close of this first song, in particular, would have gained greatly thereby.

The above-quoted letter to Grohe continues:

More significant, however, seems to me the second poem, which I consider the best that I have so far knocked off. . . . If in your emotion over it you don't lose your reason, you cannot ever have possessed any.

408

It is truly enough to drive one crazy, and moreover of a staggering, truly antique, simplicity. You will open your eyes. I really stand in awe of this composition, for over it I fear to lose my senses. Such perilous things I am now producing to the public danger.

Alles endet, was entstehet takes rank among Wolf's supreme achievements. The transitoriness of all earthly things, the inevitability of death and corruption, is the theme, and it is treated with that 'rigorous, bitter, inexorable truth—truth to the point of cruelty' which the composer told Kauffmann was for him the supreme principle in art. Here is no sentimentalization of death, nor any artificial romantic horrors, but the awful facts, indicated with a chilling objectivity, and without one grain of mortal comfort thrown into the balance against them. For one moment, at

> Menschen waren wir ja auch,
> Froh und traurig, so wie ihr,

these dead voices are quickened again with human emotion, before they fade and dissolve into the timeless, impersonal lament of all creation. This is not a song that we can bear to hear often; it is too bleak, too inhuman. It is a vision of dry bones, and in giving musical form to this vision Wolf seems to have eliminated every note that is not essential, to have reduced his art, too, to its bare anatomy. We cannot like, or love, this song; it is too terrible to take to our hearts. But we must recognize its greatness, its truth and universality. It is a measure of Wolf's genius that he could so impressively treat so vast a subject within the confines of the forty-five bars of his song.

Fühlt meine Seele is less abstract in style and less remote from the emotional world of ordinary humanity. The same melancholic, brooding spirit is felt behind it, but in the course of the song emerges from the slow-pulsed reserve of the opening to the free expression of a powerful erotic emotion. The severity characteristic of the Michelangelo settings as a whole is here tempered by richer harmonic colour, a more agitated and declamatory vocal line, and the employment in the piano part, at 'ist es ein Klang, ein Traumgesicht' and subsequently, of a chromatically descending motive that at once recalls the sensual longing of the *Peregrina* songs in the Mörike volume. The natural austerity of the man melts in love's torment, and in the noble peroration he lays his heart in submission at the feet of his mistress.

It had been Wolf's intention to set at least six of the Michelangelo poems to music, but apart from *Irdische und himmlische Liebe*, which he himself rejected as unworthy of its companions, he did not succeed in completing any more songs.   On 7th April he went back once more to the Werners' house at Perchtoldsdorf, hoping that its friendly atmosphere would exercise its old stimulating effect, but after only one day there he returned to the city.   The weather was cold and unpleasant, and the rather primitive conditions of life at Perchtoldsdorf in such circumstances contrasted unfavourably with the comfort of the Schwindgasse flat.   Furthermore, a card had arrived to announce the imminent arrival of Humperdinck, who was passing through Vienna on his way to Budapest.   On 9th April Humperdinck and his wife called to see Wolf.   He took them in the morning to see the Kunsthistorisches Museum, and then accompanied them to a restaurant.   There, for the first time, something strange in his manner gave warning of the tragedy to come.   He changed his seat several times, in order, as he gave out, to avoid being seen by acquaintances, and was irritable and out of humour.   In the afternoon the Humperdincks visited other friends, meeting Richard Wallaschek, with whom they returned at five o'clock to the Schwindgasse, to hear Wolf play *Der Corregidor*.   Humperdinck was impressed by what he heard of the opera, but after the first two acts had to leave, on account of another engagement.   Wolf seemed displeased at having to break off the performance, but promised to play through the remainder when Humperdinck passed through Vienna again on his way back from Budapest.   He accompanied his guests to their carriage and after they had entered it himself closed the door for them, but then, as though he had forgotten something, suddenly turned and ran away, without saying good-bye.   That was the last time Humperdinck saw his friend, for when he returned from Budapest, five days later, Wolf had disappeared.   Decsey says, apparently on Humperdinck's authority, that Wolf 'had gone into the country.'   His letters show that he was, in fact, still living in the Schwindgasse.   It may be that he was 'not at home' to Humperdinck.

There is no doubt at all that the overwhelming success of *Hänsel und Gretel* rankled bitterly in Wolf's heart.   On 10th April he wrote to Kauffmann:

Yesterday Engelbert Humperdinck, on his way to Budapest, presented himself at my dwelling in order to hear me play *Der Corregidor*, which till then, shamefully enough, he did not know, as he—naturally!—is too poor to procure a copy for himself and my publisher refused to give him one gratis. However, we did not get further than one-third of the opera as his complete lack of interest very much vexed me. Now on the one hand I find it quite understandable that a composer who has enriched the repertoire of all the barrel-organs should have no ear for the more distinguished music of another, but on the other hand it is extremely deplorable that suchlike music-making enthusiasts should be blazoned forth as the appointed successors of Wagner. If the situation among the favourite disciples of Wagner is no better than this, then the cultivation and understanding of true art is indeed in a bad way. And Humperdinck—*horribile dictu*—was in fact a favourite disciple of the Master's, and rejoiced no less—in spite of, or perhaps just on account of, *Hänsel und Gretel*—in the special favour, too, of the Master's wife.

It is charitable to ascribe the unpleasant tone of this letter to the mental instability consequent on the progress of his disease, of which there were indications at the time when it was written. The passage quoted foreshadows the astonishing letters, compounded of exaggerated self-esteem, confused thinking and unreasoning hostility towards those to whom he was most indebted, which were written later in this same year in Dr. Svetlin's asylum. It will be noticed that Wolf attributed his breaking off in the middle of the performance of his opera to his own vexation at his visitor's 'lack of interest,' while Humperdinck himself told Decsey that the music made a deep impression upon him, but that he had to leave to fulfil another engagement. Humperdinck's diary does not contain any indication of his reactions to *Der Corregidor*, but shows that he was, in fact, due at the Burgtheater to see Hauptmann's *Die versunkene Glocke* at seven o'clock, two hours after his visit to Wolf began.

At Easter another visitor came to the Schwindgasse—Paul Müller, the founder of the Berlin Hugo Wolf Verein. In his reminiscences he has left an account of how Wolf, who was at the time without a servant, did everything with his own hands with touching solicitude for his guest's comfort. He made the beds, refusing to allow Müller to assist, and at meal-times helped him generously to cream and sugar, and piled his plate with good food in a manner that brooked no refusal. Müller has also recorded some of his conversations with Wolf on musical and other subjects. *Tristan* then represented, for Wolf, the peak of Wagner's creation. Of Schubert's six hundred songs half could be destroyed without anything being lost; of Schumann's two-thirds had enduring worth. Cornelius he admired as a poet: 'He had the right to make his own opera texts,' he said. Franz he rejected almost entirely; *Gewitternacht* was the only piece for which he had a good word. Knowing that Müller was an admirer of Brahms, he attacked him repeatedly, but without making much impression. When he learned that Wolf had no liking for such literary figures as Theodor Storm and Wilhelm Raabe, Müller believed he had found the key to Wolf's hatred of Brahms, in the natural antipathy existing between the north German and the southerner. In all these conversations Müller stoutly maintained his own points of view. 'He knew well how to value frankness and independence of mind,' he afterwards wrote. He would, perhaps, have been less complacent on this point if he had seen what Wolf, after his visit, wrote about him to Faisst: [1]

Paul Müller, who was for four days my guest, has fortunately sheered off again. I must confess that on closer acquaintance Müller sinks in my estimation. I felt the lack in him particularly of personality. He is only a commonplace person, such as run around in thousands. Lack of refinement of feeling is only too acutely perceptible. Also his mental horizon seems to me to be somewhat limited. In short, I was very much disappointed and disenchanted, and so the poorer for one more illusion. *Vanitas vanitatum!*

In April the first invitations were sent out to prospective members of Haberlandt's Vienna Hugo Wolf Verein. Wolf himself understood that it was necessary for him to stand somewhat apart from the society. Not only could he not sanction some of the artistic compromises which it would be necessary to make in order to spread the knowledge of his work, but his personal presence would have been embarrassing to his friends, liable as he was, by outspoken comment or undisguised hostility, to bring to nothing their efforts to win over this or that singer or critic. He made merry over his friends as they sat in Haberlandt's house writing out, addressing and dispatching the invitations to those who, it was hoped, would give the Hugo Wolf Verein their support. He began to raise objections when some of the names were read out. 'What!' he cried, 'are you going to invite him too? That idiot?' He was told, politely but firmly, that he had no say in the matter. Soon he went out, to return 'when the air was clearer.'

It was not long before the society had enrolled a hundred members, and the first meeting was fixed for 14th May. Haberlandt became chairman, Dr. Robert Steinhauser vice-chairman, Gustav Schur treasurer, and Heinrich Werner secretary. The other members of the committee were Hellmer, Larisch and Karl Mayreder. The

[1] Letter of 23rd April 1897, a passage omitted in the published version. Faisst had recently quarrelled with Müller.

founders contributed a minimum of 50 gulden to the funds of the society, the ordinary members 5 gulden each.   Later additions to the subsidizing members included Grohe, Hildebrandt, Anna Reiss, Johanna Steinhauser, Bokmayer, Baron Lipperheide, Heinriette Faisst and Franz Edler von Wertheim.   Frl. Anna Reiss was a well-to-do lady, about sixty years of age, who had entertained Wolf during his stay at Mannheim.   She had known Wagner and Liszt and distinguished herself, in earlier years, as an amateur singer.   She came to Vienna for the inaugural meeting of the Hugo Wolf Verein and from this time forward contributed 200 gulden a year towards Wolf's living expenses, on the lines of the fund started by Baron Lipperheide, Grohe and Hildebrandt, but without her name being disclosed to the composer.   The money was handed over each quarter by Larisch, and Wolf gave a receipt: ' Received from a source unknown to me, 50 gulden.'

The artists performing at the society's first meeting on 14th May were Sophie Chotek, Hermine Bosetti and Ferdinand Jäger the younger, son of the great singer who had battled so long on Wolf's behalf.   The elder Jäger was not asked to sing on this occasion owing to the deterioration of his voice and the necessity of cultivating the public interest and forestalling criticism.   The piano parts were performed by Ferdinand Foll, who was very active in this and other fields during the subsequent proceedings of the Vienna Hugo Wolf Verein.   The concert was a brilliant success.   Wolf himself was not present, but joined in the celebrations afterwards, when about thirty enthusiasts assembled in the Pschorrbräu to do him honour.   He laughed till the tears ran down his face when Haberlandt proposed the health of the new-born society, whose name, in view of Wolf's extreme shyness and sensitiveness, he did not dare to pronounce. All forms of ceremony were abhorrent to Wolf, but he rejoiced visibly over the successful foundation of the society and the affection and esteem of his many friends.

The Hugo Wolf Verein in Vienna gave twenty-six public concerts in the course of its existence, continuing and augmenting the work that the Wagner Verein had done for the composer since 1888. Actually no less than fifty-six of the members of the Hugo Wolf Verein were also members of the Wagner Verein.   The most onerous duties of the new society were incurred, within a few months of its foundation, as the result of Wolf's illness, when his entire support, his medical treatment and the administration of his affairs were laid in

its charge.   In view of these services it was granted, by an extraordinary piece of legislation—which did not remain undisputed by
the Wolf family—the copyrights in the letters of the composer and in
all posthumous compositions.   When, its work completed, the Hugo
Wolf Verein was dissolved in December 1905, it made over these
rights to the Wagner Verein, from whose loins it may be said to have
sprung.

Meanwhile, at the beginning of May 1897, Rosa Mayreder had
finished her *Manuel Venegas* libretto.   Wolf visited the authoress,
presented her with a bouquet and thanked her with tears in his eyes.
His initial enthusiasm, however, gradually declined.   The libretto
was sent off on the round of his friends in south Germany, to Kauffmann, Grohe, Heckel and Karl Mayr, and this time he paid
more heed to the warnings he received.   Soon he was himself
declaring that in its original form Frau Mayreder's book would not
do.   Judging from an account of it given by Wolf in a letter to Paul
Müller, it seems to have been, dramatically considered, almost
incredibly naïve.   The consequences of slavishly following the course
of events as portrayed in Alarcon's novel were even more unfortunate
than they had been in the case of *Der Corregidor*.   In the third act the
hero had only six lines of verse to sing and Soledad, the heroine, had
only *one word*.   Wolf finally gave up all idea of setting to music this
version of the story when Haberlandt, in whose judgment he had
great reliance, added his voice to those of the other friends.   The
surrender of *Manuel Venegas*, on which his heart had been set, and
which he had pursued for so long, was a severe blow.   For a time he
thought of trying to revise Frau Mayreder's text himself.   Then
Haberlandt, who had given the death-blow to Wolf's earlier hopes,
resurrected them by discovering another collaborator.   This was
Moritz Hoernes, his friend and colleague at the Vienna University.
Hoernes studied the novel and sketched out his ideas on the presentation of *Manuel Venegas* on the stage at a personal meeting with Wolf,
who was impressed.   On 1st June, evidently very shortly after this
meeting, he asked Hoernes to prepare a scenario.   On the 4th he was
able to tell his mother that the scenario was already in his hands and
was quite exquisite.   Hoernes was a poet *comme il faut*.   If the execution of the libretto was as satisfactory as its plan, he was made for life.

At this time he occupied himself with the revision of the score of
Dem Vaterland and with the preparation of a new edition of the
Goethe volume.   A number of alterations were made to the songs,

the most important in *Kennst du das Land?* and *Grenzen der Mensch-heit*. The latter was revised for bass voice, the passages 'nirgends haften dann die unsichern Sohlen' and 'und viele Geschlechter reihen sich dauernd' being partly rewritten.

The performance of *Der Corregidor* at the Vienna Opera became again a possibility with the appointment of Gustav Mahler as Kapellmeister. Mahler called on Wolf and showed interest in his opera. Nearly twenty years after they had shared a garret as impecunious students the two composers again struck up a friend-ship. There is no evidence that Wolf ever seriously considered Mahler as a creative artist, though he recognized his wonderful powers as an operatic conductor. Later remarks of Mahler's, such as that made to Oskar Fried: 'Of the thousand songs by Wolf I only know three hundred and forty-four, but those I don't like,' do not suggest that he had any understanding at all for Wolf's art. Never-theless, after making every allowance for Wolf's incurable optimism in such matters, for his tendency to regard a possibility as a certainty, passages in his letters seem to establish the fact that Mahler had promised to bring *Der Corregidor* to performance in Vienna. On 4th June Wolf told his mother:[1]

Der Corregidor will now certainly be performed in the coming season. I have to-day received the explicit assurance of the new Kapellmeister Mahler (an old friend of mine). Mahler is now the almighty in the Vienna Opera. He will himself prepare and conduct my work, which is all the more desirable as Mahler, more than any other, is qualified to fulfil my intentions.

Later Wolf told several of his friends that Mahler would put on *Der Corregidor* at the end of January, or in February.[2]

In this month of June Wolf attempted to learn to ride a bicycle. He hoped at first to be able to go with Haberlandt on a cycling tour later in the summer, but he fell off his machine so frequently that after a short time he gave up the lessons. He described himself as being 'veritably tattooed with bruises and abrasions.' It is thought that his malady may have already begun to affect his sense of balance. Additional indications that all was not well with him were the feeling of leaden tiredness that overcame him from time to time and the

---

[1] In a letter not included in the *Familienbriefe*. Printed by Decsey in 'Aus Hugo Wolfs letzten Jahren,' in *Die Musik* (second October number, 1901).

[2] See the letters of 10th August, to Faisst, and 11th August, to Potpeschnigg. On 18th August Wolf told Potpeschnigg that in a conversation Mahler had cast doubt on the possibility of performing *Der Corregidor* in Vienna in this season. On 1st September, however, he again declared, this time in a letter to Müller, that the opera would be produced in January or February.

* O

frightful dreams that pursued him at night, of which he often complained.

On 8th July he received the complete *Manuel Venegas* libretto from Hoernes. It was brought to him in Vienna by Haberlandt. At once he set out with it for the latter's house at Perchtoldsdorf, where on the terrace overlooking the garden he read it through in solitude. When Haberlandt at length quietly approached, he found tears running down Wolf's pale face. So overpowering was Wolf's emotion that Haberlandt himself could not hold back his tears, and the two friends embraced in silent joy. On the next day Wolf told Grohe that Shakespeare himself could not have handled the material more dramatically or more poetically than Moritz Hoernes had done.

After a short visit, lasting only a few days, to the Köcherts' country house at Traunkirchen, the composer returned to Vienna towards the end of July in an extremely restless and excited state. On the 29th of this month, with the Spring Chorus, he began his music for *Manuel Venegas* and for ten days or so made good progress. Then he was brought to a standstill. He sought to establish the various motives to be employed in the opera, but repeatedly found that he was not in the right mood. The necessity to collate and correct another copy of the full score of *Der Corregidor*, the definitive version of the work, further held up the progress of *Manuel Venegas*. It was not until the second week of September that the opera began to go forward with the old irresistible impetus. He hoped then to be able to complete the first act in a fortnight. In spite of the fierce heat he could not be induced to leave his home in the centre of the city; he cancelled a projected holiday trip with Haberlandt and Hellmer, shut himself up in the Schwindgasse and worked furiously at his second opera from early morning until late at night, with only a short break at midday for a hasty meal in a nearby restaurant. Friends who called to see him were either refused admittance, or more or less politely shown the door after the exchange of only a few words. It is said that for the first time in his life he made use of alcoholic stimulants to keep himself going.

On 14th September he sent Melanie Köchert a most remarkable letter:

DEAR FRIEND,

I must depict for you the eventful fourteenth of September, however little you deserve it on account of the clumsy consignment of *Lebkuchen*.[1]

[1] Cakes made with barley-flour and honey.

The day began with my preparing in myself the needful frame of mind for the great monologue of Manuel, which I burned to set to music. But in that I fared badly in the morning, or rather, I fared like Beckmesser in the third act, whose brain was haunted by all the unpleasant recollections of the past night. I wished to compose the monologue, and yet I thought all the time about what I had to say to-day to my saucy Poldi.[1] I was determined to throw at her head her choicest stupidities and delivered her whole lectures aloud to myself in wrathful tones, struck an attitude, and threw angry glances at the stove, which I pictured to myself as the offender. For you must know I had made up my mind to retain Poldi not a day longer. I looked forward with suspense to her evening visit at six o'clock.

Meanwhile midday drew near. A good, modest luncheon at the restaurant 'Zum braunen Hirschen' calmed me down to some extent. A good Havana cigar of Bokmayer's and a glass of Marsala did *their* part to improve my temper. I applied myself again to my work and plunged into the monologue and—oh wonder of wonders!—suddenly the musical fountain-head began to stream from every pore and with such vehemence that I could scarcely follow in writing it down. One strophe after the other took on tangible shape and form; it was as if I wrote down all the notes out of the air. By the evening I had the whole monologue finished, a thing I should not have thought possible, for the monologue runs to sixteen long iambic verses.

Now that really was an achievement and I began to feel something like respect for myself. At the same time there still came to mind—in the shadowy background, to be sure—*Poldi*, but forthwith disappeared once more from the scene.

But then—oh horror!—the door-bell rang. I open—Heinrich Werner pokes his swan's neck round the door, in one hand a pat of butter, in the other a milk loaf of excellent quality. To take in this precious booty and to slam the door was the work of a moment.

Shortly afterwards the bell rings again. Damnation! I skip to the door, see through the peep-hole a man of very distinguished appearance, and recognize in him the young Scheu. 'What do you want?' I ask. 'I wished only to congratulate you on the acceptance of *Der Corregidor* at the local Opera.'

I: 'Damn it, what do I care for *Der Corregidor*? Now the word is— *Manuel Venegas*.'

Showed the ass, for he knew no more about the performance than I know myself—and that is little enough—what was so far written of *Venegas*, for which, however, this moon-calf evinced not the slightest interest, whereupon I complimented him out. *He* was scarcely outside when— tinkle, tinkle—sounds the bell once more. The Devil! Is all hell then loose to-day? I open once more. Foll. Ah well! To him I played then straight away, at his request, twenty pages of the new opera, and it was moving to see how this icicle visibly warmed up. Yes, yes, the musicians will open their eyes.

---

[1] His servant.

Finally, Poldi turns up. Fourth scene, last act.

I (*friendly*): 'Now, my good Poldi, have you nothing to say to me?'

Poldi: 'I? Don't know.' (Says this rather crossly, after she had coldly saluted me.)

I: 'What, no apology?'

Poldi: 'Apology? What for?'

'Well,' I say, 'allow me then to pay you back a few compliments with reference to your behaviour yesterday.' And I flew into a frightful rage and trembled with emotion and began thus: 'Do you know what you are? You are the most impertinent, the most infamous, the most insolent, the cheekiest, the most malicious of females. Understand?' Great astonishment on her part. Withal she maintained her complete equanimity, replied calmly and without showing a sign of agitation to the flood of my reproaches and abuse. That impressed me, on the one hand, but on the other hand it threw me into a still greater rage. Finally I paid her off, demanded from her the door-key, and left the flat, which Poldi meanwhile tidied up. I went to Edmund's, there to disburden my heart, and told him the story. When I come home Poldi is still there, in tears, and completely distracted. Suddenly she knocks on the door of my study, throws herself at my feet, and begs my pardon in floods of tears. Whereupon we both *howled* and the curtain fell. Moving tableau. Reconciliation.

Now you will admit that I too can be a good child, when I relate my adventurous experiences so nicely for you. What do I get in reward? That is surely worth a whole sackful of Nuremberg *Lebkuchen*. This time, I think, I have spoken clearly, or do you still misunderstand me always? Ah, with you, my dear friend, it is sometimes so difficult to come to an understanding! Meanwhile ten o'clock is here. I have been almost an hour writing this epistle, in spite of the fact that it has simply streamed from my pen. Good night, and turn over a new leaf!

Poldi comes again from to-morrow, in the early hours of the morning. After the great scene I had to rush round again to Edmund, to cancel arrangements with his servant. She was not at home, only Fritz and Edmund were present.

Now before the door of Edmund's flat I met with yet another adventure, before witnesses (three skivvies).

I ring. Nobody answers the bell. I ring a dozen times over. Nobody opens. I bang with my stick on the door and knock louder than ever Repela knocked in *fortissimo*. Nobody stirs. I begin to belabour the door with both feet, and I must confess that kicks like those have I never dealt out to any object before. At length there shuffles to the door Edmund, whom I greeted with a whole flood of imprecations. He excused himself by saying the feeble electric bell was the cause of my troubles. But what about my knocking? He heard only my kicks. That would have taken a lot of overhearing!

Now, however, enough joking. Cordial regards from your extremely merry

HUGO WOLF.

Next day he sent an exultant postcard to Haberlandt: 'Yesterday afternoon the whole of Manuel's monologue written at one go, in spite of numerous interruptions by visitors. Call for next Sunday afternoon *all* the faithful to the colours. I will play from the new opera.' It was arranged that the friends were to assemble at Bokmayer's house at Mödling. Two days later there came a further communication in the form of a sheet of manuscript music paper, covered with hasty pencil sketches, including the motive of Manuel's love for Soledad. Between the lines was scrawled: 'Piping hot! Straight from the frying-pan! Am beside myself! Sell me up! Am blissful! Raving!' Haberlandt was disquieted, and at the risk of annoying the composer by further interrupting his work, called at the Schwindgasse to see him. Wolf, looking like a ghost, opened the door and stared at his visitor, then led him inside and spoke excitedly and confusedly of his new opera. Haberlandt begged him to take some rest, but was assured by Wolf that he had never felt so divinely well in his life and had never created anything so beautiful before. He sat down at the piano and played and sang the fragmentary *Manuel Venegas* with radiant happiness apparent in his eyes and voice. Tears of joy trickled down through his thin beard and fell on the keyboard, whence he wiped them off like a child with the sleeve of his jacket. Performance of the music seemed to have calmed him and when Haberlandt left he felt no particular anxiety about his friend.

Melanie Köchert was with her family at Traunkirchen at this time. The last two surviving written communications to her are scribbled on visiting-cards:

Won't you come here for one day and hear *Manuel Venegas*? The great monologue must be counted among the most profoundly felt things in all music so far created. Come! But alone! By that time I shall have reached the fifth scene, the entry of Don Trinidad.

In haste, your
H. W.

15th September 1897.
On Sunday I play the opera at Perchtoldsdorf to all the faithful.

Potpeschnigg abandons a dying sister and comes on Sunday to Mödling. If on the same day you don't put in an appearance I shall never again set foot in your house.

In great haste, yours
HUGO WOLF.

Have just conceived the love-motive. I am raging like a volcano. [Postmark, 17th September 1897.]

On Saturday, 19th September, Hellmer was joined by Wolf at his table in the restaurant Zum braunen Hirschen in the Alleegasse. Wolf seemed very excited and restless, grew angry with the waiter about the delay with his food and grumbled about it when it was brought him. He seemed to be quite ravenously hungry, for he picked up the chop he had ordered and simply tore the meat away from the bone and gulped it down like an animal. Hellmer was surprised and alarmed and became increasingly so when Wolf leaned forward and told him, confidentially but impressively: 'I have become director of the Court Opera.' He did not know what to think— whether it was intended as a joke, whether Wolf had been made the victim of a hoax, or whether the whole affair was to be attributed to some temporary aberration due to overwork and over-excitement about *Manuel Venegas*. Wolf was not to be led away from the subject. Again and again he asserted as a fact that he was the new director of the Vienna Opera, and when Ferdinand Foll joined them at their table Wolf continued in the same strain. Afterwards he took Hellmer and Foll back to his Schwindgasse apartments to hear the new music. After he had played it through he embraced both friends, exchanged the 'du' and drank brotherhood with them. He talked at length about matters that in normal circumstances he would have died rather than have discussed—his poverty, his family affairs and his relations with women. He compared one of his friends to 'Der Sehrmann,' an empty, self-satisfied figure, drastically depicted in Mörike's poem *An Longus*, of which Kauffmann had given him the original manuscript. He read this poem aloud and declared his intention of setting it to music. The visit then came to an end.

Early next morning, on Sunday, 20th September, the day on which the friends were bidden to assemble at Bokmayer's house, Hellmer, who lived with his parents near the Perchtoldsdorf railway station, heard, while he was still dressing, Wolf's voice in the garden below. He hurried down and found his mother deep in conversation with the composer. Wolf had already repeated to her the same crazy story that had obsessed him on the previous day—that he was the new director of the Vienna Opera. He produced from his pocket, and read through, a long address to the opera-house *personnel*, concluding with the dismissal of Mahler from his post. Over this conclusion he showed diabolical glee. His distracted mien, the maniacal glare of his eyes, set in the deathly pallor of his face, the words he spoke and the obstinacy with which he asserted and reasserted what could not be true—these things made it impossible any longer to doubt that Hugo Wolf had gone mad.

Afterwards the friends learned what had led up to this calamity. A short time before he had paid a visit to the office where Mahler had already begun work as provisional director of the opera. Upon Mahler's desk the score of Rubinstein's opera *The Demon* had been lying. Wolf had made some derogatory remarks about this work, and a dispute had ensued, in the course of which Mahler had said some uncomplimentary things about *Der Corregidor*, and in spite of the fact that he had promised to produce it, had expressed doubt as to whether, after all, the opera would be performed in Vienna. With rage and bitterness in his heart, Wolf had left Mahler's office vowing revenge for this severe disappointment, and his mental distress as a result of this interview, coming at a time when he was already in the fever of creation, had unhappily provided the spark that had kindled a conflagration in his brain and brought on the long threatened insanity. Brooding upon revenge, he had conceived the idea of himself becoming director of the opera and so getting rid of Mahler and removing the last obstacle in the way of *Der Corregidor*'s success in Vienna. This idea obsessed him until he believed it was true.

Now with violent words he insisted that Hellmer should accompany him straight away to Mauer, about an hour's walk from Perchtoldsdorf, where the opera singer Hermann Winkelmann had a villa; Winkelmann he would order to come to Bokmayer's in the afternoon to sing *Manuel Venegas*. Hellmer was scarcely allowed time to put his hat on, let alone call anybody to help him in this terrible situation. The only concession Wolf would allow was that they should go through the town and not straight across the fields. The road took them past Haberlandt's house and, as Hellmer had hoped, they encountered this friend in the market-place. Haberlandt took in the situation at a glance and acted with great presence of mind. He agreed to come with them, after he had first told his family where he was going. While Wolf stamped and fumed with impatience outside the house, Haberlandt arranged for a message to be sent to Bokmayer and for a doctor to be present when the friends assembled as arranged to hear the new opera. Then Wolf, Hellmer and Haberlandt set out for Winkelmann's villa at Mauer.

As though pursued by malignant spirits, the mad composer led them, at a furious pace, by the shortest route through rough side-roads, and all the way he was talking, talking, talking—endlessly and inexhaustibly. It was in vain that they tried to divert him from his purpose, as the slightest opposition to his wishes threw him into a fearful rage. Although none of them was personally acquainted with Winkelmann, Wolf burst into the house and introduced himself to the astonished singer as the new director of the Opera, desirous of making use of his services that afternoon at Mödling. It was only with the greatest difficulty that the real state of affairs could be conveyed to Winkelmann, who, buttonholed by Wolf, could only stare, not knowing whether to accept or dispute the claim upon him. At length, with the help of a friend who was present, he was 'called away by telephone' and did not reappear. Wolf went away extremely indignant: 'He shall suffer for that,' he said, 'refusing the first request of his director!'

They returned to Haberlandt's house. Awaiting them there at the garden gate was Heinrich Werner, who had been told of the events of the early morning and was almost dumb with shock and misery at the catastrophe that had overtaken his beloved master and friend. After a curt, ill-humoured greeting Wolf asked: 'Well, have you nothing to say to me?' and Werner knew that he was expected to offer his congratulations upon the delusory appointment, but he could not bring himself to speak. 'It is very singular,' Wolf went on, 'that one has first to remind you, in order to squeeze a few words out of you.' Werner then stammered out that what had happened had come about so suddenly that he could hardly believe it, and added that in any case he was not certain that it was any cause for rejoicing, as the duties of an opera-house director would leave no time for composition. At this Wolf burst out: 'You are a fine lot of friends to me! When one for once accomplishes something in life you are not a bit pleased.'

After a meal at Haberlandt's house, to which he did full justice, Wolf fell asleep from sheer exhaustion. It transpired that he had neither eaten nor slept for more than twenty-four hours and had been on his feet since three in the morning. His friends left him and went down into the garden, where they sat in anxious suspense. It was several hours before they saw him again in the doorway, whence a few steps led down to the garden. Silently at first he gazed at his friends, and afterwards began to speak quietly of a wonderful dream he had had. Then the hopes that had been cherished by all of them, that after this deep sleep he would awaken refreshed and in his right mind, were shattered by the reintroduction of the idea that obsessed him. He went up to Hoernes, who had joined the friends while he had been asleep, and asked, laughing to himself: 'Well, what do you say? Have you heard?' and once again madness possessed him, growing more apparent from minute to minute. He was, however, no longer domineering and quarrelsome, but blissfully, radiantly happy, as before his mind's eye there gathered ever rosier visions of the future. Tears of happiness ran down his cheeks as he spoke of his good fortune, that would enable him to support his old mother and his sisters in comfort, and bring some joy into their lives at last. All his friends, too, were to be rewarded for their faithful services by appointments at the opera-house. One of them—probably Joseph Schalk—was to be made Kapellmeister; for Heinrich Werner, as he could not talk, a position among the supernumeraries was to be held open.

He had not forgotten that he had invited his friends to assemble at Mödling to hear his new opera, which, he said, was now practically finished. He urged that it was time to set out.

It was about five o'clock when the guests waiting anxiously in Bokmayer's villa were joined by Wolf and his Perchtoldsdorf friends. The stage was set for perhaps the most fantastic scene in all the tragic farce of this thwarted and broken life. There was Wolf, animated, ecstatically happy, laughing excitedly and talking endlessly in a raised voice, and round about him the friends, scarcely able to move or speak for horror, sorrow and pity. It was like a nightmare. The more fortunate he felt himself to be, the more unfortunate he appeared to them and the more unhappy they grew.

First of all, he insisted that a lady, who, he said, had not properly shaken hands with him, should leave the room. For a time he waited impatiently for Winkelmann and when he did not arrive cried: 'So he really isn't coming! Wait! Just wait! Winkelmann is sacked!' Then he sat down at the piano in the music-room, which the Bokmayers had festively decorated for his visit, arranged the friends in a circle around him, as on former occasions when he had had new works to reveal to them, and played his *Manuel Venegas*. He repeated some passages with quite lucid explanatory remarks. The abrupt conclusion he passed over without comment. Afterwards he played the *Meistersinger* prelude, but his memory failed him half-way through and he had to break off. He announced to the whole company that he had become director of the Vienna Opera, and explained his plans for the future—the dismissal of Mahler, Winkelmann and others, and the appointment of his friends in their places.

Then he began to tell stories of his experiences with Poldi, his servant-girl, and with the housekeeper of the block of flats in which he lived.

Dr. Gorhan, of the Mödling Infirmary, a friend of Bokmayer's who had been asked to be present, had soon come to the conclusion that it was imperative that Wolf should be put in a mental home as soon as possible. The establishment of Dr. Wilhelm Svetlin, in the Land-strasse district, Leonhardgasse 3–5, was known as one of the best private asylums in the city and Larisch set out to make arrangements for Wolf to be taken there on this same evening. Some hours later the news came through over the telephone that the regulations did not permit the acceptance of patients after nine o'clock; a conveyance would be sent on the following morning.

Meanwhile Wolf had become quieter and more tractable. Prob-ably on Dr. Gorhan's advice, they took him into the dining-room and plied him liberally with food and drink until he was thoroughly comfortable and at peace with all the world. He spoke much, now that he imagined he had at length achieved success, of the early stages of his struggle. He related, with only occasional lapses into inco-herence, interesting experiences from his Conservatoire days and told of his early relations with Richter.

It was after eleven o'clock when Bokmayer and Foll took him back to Vienna by carriage. It was a wonderfully lovely autumn night. During the greater part of the journey of one and a half hours, in the course of which he exchanged the 'du' with Bokmayer, Wolf was in high good humour. But as they drew nearer to the Schwindgasse his thoughts turned continually to his housekeeper, whom he disliked and of whom he had already spoken to the friends at Mödling. As they arrived before the house he fell into a rage and when the house-keeper himself opened the door Wolf sprang at his throat. For a few moments there was a desperate struggle and it was all Bokmayer and Foll could do to separate the combatants and get Wolf away to his rooms. There he quietened down after a while, ate some fruit and, at about two o'clock, went to bed. Bokmayer and Foll then left the house.

Early next morning, before any one arrived to look after him, Wolf was out and about. He presented himself to the agent in charge of the house in the Schwindgasse as the new director of the Opera and asked that his neighbour should be given notice, as he needed the rooms for the use of his mother, whom he would bring to Vienna to live with him. Next he called at the Köcherts' house and offered one of the servants double wages if he would come and work for him. Then he returned to the Schwindgasse, where he found Haberlandt awaiting him. Haberlandt was to accompany him when, as the new director of the Court Opera, he went to be received in audience by Prince Liechtenstein, the Obersthofmeister. For this important occasion he changed into his dress clothes. The 'prince's carriage' —in reality a vehicle from the asylum, with a doctor in attendance— drew up outside the door. Wolf entered with Haberlandt and was driven away. As the carriage took its way through the narrow streets of the Landstrasse district Wolf was taken aback and inquired: 'Where then does the Obersthofmeister live?' but Haberlandt succeeded in reassuring him and when they reached Dr. Svetlin's asylum Wolf got out quietly, bade farewell to his friend, and ran quickly up the steps to the doorway, and into the care of the doctors who awaited him there.

In his home in the Schwindgasse was found the manuscript of *Manuel Venegas*—about fifty pages of the first act in vocal score. The music bears absolutely no trace of the composer's incipient insanity, or sign of any failure or weakening of his creative powers.

The version of the text of the opera that has been published is not identical with that on which the composer was working, but in essentials it is the same. It is clear that *Manuel Venegas* was founded on a much better libretto than was *Der Corregidor*. Some of Wolf's friends criticized Hoernes's rhymes, as, for instance:

> Wisst, ich komm' von Malaga,
> Und bald ist er selber da.

He told them, however, quite rightly, that such things would not be apparent in musical setting. The verses are, in general, fine, powerful stuff for the musician's purpose. The dramatic interest is cumulative from beginning to end, the acts are well contrasted, the curtains are excellent. There are many fine scenes, written with good understanding of the requirements of the operatic stage. Unhappily the composer did not reach any of the great dramatic moments of the story. There was too much that required explanation before the main action began. In that part of the opera which he did succeed in completing Wolf had introduced his hero, but he was still engaged in clarifying the situation when fate snatched the pen from his hand.

The opera fragment opens with a scene representing a street before the church of Santa Maria de la Cabeza. It is a brilliantly sunny spring morning. The town is being decorated for the procession of the image of the Christ-child. Children strew flowers about the streets and, as they do so, invite the spring itself to join with them in the adornment of the town in honour of the infant Jesus. This Spring Chorus is one of the most exquisitely beautiful of all Wolf's compositions. It is his Good Friday music, combining religious solemnity with all the tenderness and radiance of the season of nature's renewal. After this purely lyrical opening, the scenes between Vitriolo and Carlos are the means whereby the librettist, by indirect narration, conveys information about some of the events preceding the action of the opera. In these preliminary scenes the characterization is excellent and some fine themes make their appearance. Perhaps Manuel's heroic motive already threatened to recur too often. Morisco, the muleteer, is a vividly depicted minor character. With the entry of the hero the whole opera moves on to an altogether higher plane. From this point onwards to the end of the fragment, some eighteen pages of vocal score, the music is of superb quality. It is of striking strength and simplicity. The robust, effective stage declamation and the general onflowing style of the music suggest that Wolf had learned a good deal from his experiences with *Der Corregidor*. He once told Hellmer that in *Manuel Venegas* he would orchestrate like Mozart. Certainly a desire to let more light and air into his score, to liberate the vocal lines from contrapuntal entanglements like those in his first opera, is already apparent in the fragment as we know it. Manuel's moving apostrophe to his native town is perhaps the finest thing in the score. The style is markedly diatonic, the vocal phrases, even the most emotional, are plain almost to bareness. Even when, a little later, Manuel's passionate love for Soledad comes to expression, the same monumental simplicity marks his utterances. It is as if the composer had recognized that the emotional extravagance of this character would have become unbearable if too directly reflected in his music. Manuel was too consistently 'a part to tear a cat in.' He was ennobled in stage presentation by Wolf's broad, rather severe musical style. A great operatic character was here in course of development. Soledad does not appear in the *Manuel Venegas* fragment. Don Trinidad gave promise of becoming something quite out of the ordinary. On the stage a really good man who is not a bore is the greatest of rarities. The long conflict of wills between Manuel and Trinidad, the struggle in Manuel's heart between his love for the old priest and his desire for vengeance, would have been Wolf's great opportunity in the second act.　Above all, the scene of Manuel alone before the image of the Christ-child could hardly have failed to inspire him to music of overwhelming beauty and eloquence.　Then the culmination of the tragedy in the third act would surely have been unmatched in German opera for its excitement and tragic passion. These doomed, star-crossed lovers were a fit subject for the composer of the burning love-songs of the *Spanish Song Book*.

Could Wolf have carried the opera through to a successful conclusion?　It is very difficult to say.　A great popular success, such as in his heart he longed for, *Manuel Venegas* would never have brought him.　But if he could have sustained the mood in which he was working when his brain gave way something great and splendid would assuredly have emerged from his years long travail with this subject.

　・　　　・　　　・　　　・　　　・　　　・

After the doors of Dr. Svetlin's asylum closed behind him, the poor, deluded Wolf was lost entirely for two months to the sight and knowledge of his friends, the doctors having forbidden all contact with the world beyond the walls of the institution.　Rumours there were, which even found their way into some of the newspapers—for the sensation caused by the onset of his insanity had brought Wolf nearer to celebrity than any of his musical achievements had been able to do—but the authenticity of these rumours was publicly denied by Haberlandt, as chairman of the Hugo Wolf Verein.[1]　The friends were not at first allowed to visit the asylum and themselves knew little of what was going on there.　According to information collected by Decsey, probably from Dr. Svetlin, Wolf in his megalomania imagined himself the director, no longer of the Vienna Opera, but of the mental institution in which he was himself confined as a patient. He believed that he was able to cure the madness of Nietzsche: Next, in mounting delirium, he imagined himself Jupiter, and able to command the rain.　He declared his intention of instituting hunting in the Belvedere gardens.

Towards the end of November his condition improved.　Although still subject to delusions of grandeur, he was restored to his own identity, knew himself for Hugo Wolf, the composer, and was allowed

---

[1] Some of the rumours current in Vienna about Wolf's insanity were retailed by Alma Mahler in her book *Gustav Mahler: Erinnerungen und Briefe*, as late as 1940.　She told how Wolf stood in the Ringstrasse, near the museums, calling out to all passers-by that he was Mahler, director of the opera, and how, in spite of fierce opposition, he was overpowered, taken into custody and interned in the asylum.　This is contrary to all the accounts by eye-witnesses of the events leading up to Wolf's entry into Dr. Svetlin's mental home.

to undertake certain musical activities within the asylum. On 24th November he wrote a letter to Dr. Svetlin in which he asked pardon for all the 'improprieties' for which his illness had been responsible in the past weeks. He explained that he was now fully recovered and talked glibly of leaving the institution very shortly: 'If you consent, I should like to remain here until the end of the month. A longer stay seems to me no longer necessary.' He explained further that he had himself become conscious, during the composition of his second opera, of being in a highly nervous state. The cause of that had probably lain in the fact that at that time he had suddenly discovered in himself poetic talents. It had always been his dearest wish to be able to write his own librettos, but every previous attempt had failed. Hence his nervous excitement at discovering that he possessed, after all, poetic genius. Everything was now clear to him. 'Now I understand the peculiar attitude of Dr. Lang towards me,' he wrote, 'similarly my reception at Kapellmeister Mahler's, and especially the behaviour of my servant-girl Poldi. The affair with the housekeeper, too, is now comprehensible to me and not least the conduct of my former friend Frau Köchert. Haberlandt, Bokmayer, Frau Köchert and Dr. Lang had long recognized my malady and decided among themselves to cure me of it. But why this mysterious behaviour? It would surely have been possible to tell me the truth?' Now that he was fully recovered he did not wish to renew the relationship with those friends of the past: 'I blame nobody, but, as I have become a new man, I will henceforward also live in new circumstances. I have broken with my past and will from now on begin a new, fairer, above all, more fruitful life.'

A few days later he wrote a letter to Rosa Mayreder in a similar strain, compounded of would-be sweet reasonableness and evident mental disorder. The ideas he had formed about his friends' part in the events that had terminated in his confinement in Dr. Svetlin's asylum had in the meantime undergone a change. 'Dear, only friend!' he wrote,

So I may call you, for since the 24th of the month—naturally in the night from the 24th to the 25th, for all great transformations take place during sleepless nights—a regeneration has been accomplished in me. I now know that I possess true and sincere friends only in you and our dear Lino.[1] All the others, including Frau Köchert, Edmund, etc. etc., have shamefully betrayed me. They are for ever blotted out from my memory. I intend to flee to Switzerland after my discharge from the asylum and have chosen

[1] Rosa Mayreder's husband.

Lucerne for my domicile.   But now I cherish the ardent wish to see you, dearest friend, and Lino again, and to unburden my mind for once with people who understand me.   Visits from other so-called friends, male and female, I have expressly forbidden.   How much I shall have to tell you! Think how I have had to pass two whole months among the veriest madmen.   Is it to be wondered at if in such company I too came upon foolish thoughts?   But I was too sensible to become a complete fool.   So I was a fool among fools in the sense of Goethe's *Cophtisches Lied.*   But in the end I have remained he that I was, only greater, wiser, more mature—yes, I may say I am become merrier and, above all, wittier than before.   And do you know what else?   In my great need I also became a poet, and a devil of a poet too.   At last!   What I have striven for so long!   I shall write my own opera texts in future.   Only think, I have no less than four tetralogies in my head, three of comic content, and one of tragic, that makes every tragedy so far written look ridiculous.

As a sign of his special favour he informed his former collaborator that he had decided to incorporate all the first act and the beginning of the second act of her previously rejected libretto for *Manuel Venegas* in the one he was writing himself.   Hoernes's text was apparently to be abandoned.

Heinrich Potpeschnigg was another who was exempt from the general ban.   He received a number of letters from Dr. Svetlin's asylum, vehicles for the extraordinary ideas that possessed the brain of the sick composer.   In the last sentence of one of these letters, written on 2nd December, Wolf told his friend: 'I am now scoring six of the Spanish songs for *Manuel Venegas*,' and a few days later, on the 6th, he declared in another letter: 'I am working on the scoring of *ten* songs from the *Spanish Song Book, the greater part of which will appear at the beginning of the first act of Venegas.*'

It is saddening to read the grandiose ideas for the establishment of his fame with which this man of genius, in his derangement, compensated himself for a lifetime of hardship and ineffective struggle for recognition.   The letter of 6th December outlines his plans for the future:

After my liberation (supposedly on the 15th) I shall move at once to Lucerne, where I shall establish my permanent quarters.   From there I shall look around and assemble an opera company, complete with orchestra, that under my colours shall visit every state (Austria excepted) for the purpose of giving operatic performances and concerts in which, naturally, only my works—the operas *Corregidor, Venegas,* and *Penthesilea, Fest auf Solhaug, Prinz von Homburg,* etc.—shall be performed.

It is hardly necessary to point out that of the compositions mentioned, the *Prinz von Homburg* music was incomplete,

Manuel Venegas barely begun and the *Penthesilea* opera wholly imaginary.

A little later an even more fantastic scheme had taken possession of his mind. 'Yesterday a magnificent idea occurred to me,' he wrote on 9th December,

I shall *not* move to Lucerne, but to *Weimar*, for the following reasons. The intendant of the court theatre there, Herr von Vignau,[1] is an old friend and admirer of my art, whom I learned to know and value at his *salon* in Berlin. Herr von Vignau is a keen and highly intelligent lover of the arts, who at that time in Berlin sang me a number of my songs with much taste but little voice. Stavenhagen,[2] who . . . officiates at the Weimar Theatre as Kapellmeister, is said to be greatly interested in my *Corregidor* and other things. In point of fact they thought about a performance of my opera at Weimar. The matter came to nothing, as you know, owing to the lack of a score. Now I will myself rehearse and conduct my three operas, *Corregidor*, *Venegas*, and *Penthesilea*, there. But far more than that. I will, through the intervention of the intendant, seek to induce the Grand Duke to place at my disposal his entire personnel for *world tours*. Naturally the chorus and orchestra would have to be still further reinforced, and as for the soloists, if the Weimar resources should be insufficient they would have to engage them from elsewhere. Above all, I should like to make Frl. Sedlmair desert the Vienna Opera. I hope that I shall succeed. She will make a magnificent Penthesilea. I intend at first to visit only the most important towns (with the exception of the whole of Austria) and to organize two great orchestral concerts and four opera performances (*Corregidor* in both versions). Through the intervention of the Grand Duke all the court theatres in Germany . . . will be at my command. . . . I am not allowing either piano reductions or full scores of my present and future works to be printed, as *only* such performances as I myself conduct can have any value for me.

A further step towards this delusory goal was taken on 11th December, when he approached by letter the Baroness von Loën, lady-in-waiting to the Grand Duchess of Weimar. He had met this lady once in the company of his benefactress Anna Reiss. 'You must have the kindness,' he now told her,

to procure me an audience with the Grand Duke. I have an imposing programme to lay before His Royal Highness. Naturally His Serenity would have to have first acquired confidence in me, by preliminary trial of my ability, before I brought forward my proposals. My plan would consist of undertaking world tours with the resources of the Weimar theatre, like the Meiningen orchestra, that in its day caused a great, and

[1] Hippolyt von Vignau, 1843–1926, intendant of the Weimar Hoftheater from 1895 to 1908.
[2] Bernhard Stavenhagen, 1862–1914, Kapellmeister at Weimar, afterwards at Munich.

justified, sensation. But the scheme projected by me should exert an incomparably greater power of attraction on the public, since works of mine (and *exclusively* works of mine) would be performed that will *never* appear in print and so could be introduced to the public in no other way than that staged by me. The event would certainly make a prodigious sensation.

In a postscript he added:

Let the Grand Duke bear in mind that I am to-day the first and most important composer living—a delicate matter, to say that oneself—and that it would truly be no discredit to Weimar, which has glorious days behind it, to offer a modest refuge to one despised in his own fatherland.

On 15th December Potpeschnigg came to Vienna to see for himself what could be done for his friend. He could stay in the asylum only a short time, and after he had departed Wolf put into a letter some of the things he had not found time or opportunity to say. This letter was more pitiful than any that had preceded it:

Frankly, I shudder at the thought of my whole past, except the blissful hours of creation. How happy I am to be free, through my misfortune, of all my former so-called 'friends'! I have from now on no one in the world except you and the Mayreders. I shall think twice before forming new friendships. Henceforward I will regard all new acquaintances solely from the point of view of their utility. Above all I will keep the women from my neck. They shall in future be handled as *canaille*; they deserve no better. I don't recognize my friends in Germany any more. The Wolf Verein in Berlin, like that in Vienna, shall be closed down. We shall see whether I cannot have peace from my 'friends.' Ah, how I rejoice in my future hermit's life! The thought of standing alone in the world makes me giddy with happiness. To experience no more disappointments, because I hope nothing more from the world—what joy! At last, at last, alone by myself, or only with creatures who are the expression of my will, for these creatures I need for the realization of my wishes and plans. But into the inner chambers of my heart no one shall ever again gaze—you and the Mayreders, as I said before, excepted. Samson will find no second Delilah.

The Baroness von Loën, acting in conjunction with Rosa Mayreder, and on the advice of Wolf's doctors, replied so diplomatically to his letter of 11th December that he was gradually led away from his grandiose plan of employing the musical resources of the Grand Duke of Weimar, and shortly after this his brain cleared still further, giving hope that one of the periods of 'intermission,' characteristic of his disease, was at hand. A letter written by Rosa Mayreder to the Baroness von Loën on 21st December makes it clear that it was already recognized that this relief could be only temporary. Nevertheless, in favourable conditions, it could last for years; Wolf could enjoy a quiet Indian summer of happiness, and perhaps even do further creative work, before the finally inevitable renewal and intensification of his malady destroyed him.

The sick brain that, in its youth and maturity, had brought to birth so much exquisite beauty, had even in Dr. Svetlin's asylum got through an astonishing amount of work. Wolf was allowed to spend only two hours at a stretch over his manuscripts. The rapidity with which he could set down his neat and flowing musical script astounded Dr. Svetlin himself, and the good doctor was even more surprised to learn later from Potpeschnigg that some entirely *new* music had been written in his asylum, for, with a cunning not unusual in such cases, Wolf had always told him that he was merely revising and re-orchestrating his old score of *Penthesilea*. Actually, besides this work of revision—which did not go beyond the addition of extra percussion instruments and the substitution of cor anglais for one oboe—the musical products of these months included an entirely new movement for *Penthesilea*—an Interlude depicting the Amazon Queen's recollections of her childhood—forty bars in full score of a Tarantella *finale* for the *Italian Serenade* for small orchestra, extensive sketches for the first movement of an entirely new 'Third *Italian Serenade*' for orchestra, a fragment, introducing *Funiculì, Funiculà*, probably intended for the same work, the incomplete full score of the Spring Chorus for *Manuel Venegas*, an arrangement for chorus and orchestra of the Reinick song *Morgenstimmung*, retitled *Morgenhymnus*, and orchestral versions of two songs from the *Spanish Song Book*, *Wer sein holdes Lieb verloren* and *Wenn du zu den Blumen gehst*. The two last were intended for incorporation in *Manuel Venegas* and are the only survivors from the ten Spanish songs that at the beginning of December Wolf was orchestrating, or imagined he was orchestrating, for use in that opera. The scoring shows no trace of the composer's mental derangement. When Rosa Mayreder visited Wolf in the asylum she was told that the Mörike *Feuerreiter* was also going to be incorporated in *Manuel Venegas*.

Among the collection of sketches in the Vienna National Library are two pages of manuscript paper headed: 'Themes from October and November of the year 1897,' containing no less than twenty-three musical ideas, mostly of the utmost banality, which the unfortunate composer, his brain teeming, blissfully set down in Dr. Svetlin's asylum. Two of the best of these ideas he used for the first movement of the above-mentioned 'Third *Italian Serenade*.'

Nothing has survived of any music intended for the opera on the subject of *Penthesilea* referred to in the letters from the asylum; it is improbable that any such music was ever written. It is known, however, that Wolf was considering several of Kleist's dramas, including the *Prinz von Homburg* as well as *Penthesilea*, for operatic treatment, using the poet's original texts. A volume of Kleist lay always on a table by his bedside and in it he had crossed out various passages that would be omitted in his operatic versions.

After December Wolf's condition continued to improve, the delusions of grandeur left him and no more was heard of his more extravagant schemes. He still intended leaving Vienna for ever and making his home in Switzerland, but his requirements were reduced to a modest post as Kapellmeister at Basle, Zürich, Lucerne or Geneva. In January all his energies were devoted to scheming how to get out of the asylum at the earliest possible moment. His family and friends were made fellow conspirators. He had become reconciled with Melanie Köchert, who used to visit him often. Through her he was able to smuggle out letters which Dr. Svetlin had not seen, devising means whereby his liberation could be achieved. His sister Käthe was employed as companion to a Bergrat Riedl at Cilli, in southern Styria, not far from Windischgraz. Wolf had often been invited by Riedl to visit Cilli, and he now saw in this fact a possible means of effecting his escape. He knew that the doctors would not yet allow him to go to Switzerland all alone, as he wished, so in one of his smuggled letters he gave his sister complete instructions about a letter she was to write to *him*, renewing the Bergrat's invitation to stay with them at Cilli, where he would be well looked after. At the beginning of February, according to this letter dictated by Wolf to his sister, who was to send it back to Wolf for the benefit of Dr. Svetlin, they would set out, together with Riedl, for an extensive tour of Italy, including Venice, Rome, Naples and Sicily. This was calculated to break down Dr. Svetlin's last resistance to Wolf's release from the asylum. He would then be given his liberty and set out, as the doctor thought, for Cilli, but actually for Switzerland.

It is not certain that Dr. Svetlin was really taken in by this plot, or that Käthe Wolf agreed to co-operate to deceive the medical authorities. What *is* certain is that Riedl issued a hearty *genuine* invitation to Cilli, that Wolf was discharged from the asylum on 24th January and decided not to go to Switzerland after all.

Haberlandt called for him at Dr. Svetlin's institution on the day of his release and saw with what haste, taking two and three steps at a time, he fled from that place of dreadful memories. He left Vienna at once, in company with Melanie Köchert and Heinrich Werner, for the Semmering. After three days in an hotel there he left with Werner for Graz on the 27th. Next day he was at Cilli, where Riedl and his sister awaited him. But their old house in the narrow Herrngasse, with its low, vaulted roofs, together with the cold and misty weather that accompanied his arrival, depressed him and he wanted to leave Cilli at once. A friend of Heinrich Potpeschnigg's, Moritz Stallner, then placed his country house at Hochenegg, a few miles from Cilli, at Wolf's disposal, and for about a fortnight the convalescent lived there with only the old housekeeper for company, except when Käthe or Potpeschnigg visited him. He grew afraid of being left alone and often asked the housekeeper to sit and talk to him. He was comforted when he could hold her hand. Every second or third day he drove into Cilli in a carriage provided by Stallner and once he went as far as Wöllan, half-way between Cilli and Windischgraz, to meet his old mother again. He was not happy. All who knew him during this period of 'intermission' agreed that he was no longer the same man. He was gentler and more accessible than formerly, easier to get on with, but listless and melancholy. His friends longed for a little of the old pugnacity and self-assurance, but it was rarely seen. A veil seemed to lie over his spirit. 'Worn out and woebegone' was how he described himself to Faisst, and to Haberlandt he wrote: 'Don't ask me for letters. The slightest mental occupation tires me. I really believe I'm finished. I read nothing, make no music, think nothing—in short I vegetate.' He felt he would never write another note.

Once when Potpeschnigg came to see him he sat down at the piano and began to play his *Penthesilea*. All went well until he came to the new Interlude, composed in Dr. Svetlin's asylum. After a few bars of this he stopped playing, looked at the score for a few moments in silence and then cried: 'God Almighty, what have I done there?' and tore it out and destroyed it.[1] From the technical point of view the new section was perfect, but artistically it was worthless.

---

[1] Decsey (iv, p. 80), referring to this Interlude, says it was burnt by Wolf himself. On the following page he says that Wolf was going to burn it but desisted at Potpeschnigg's request. According to the earliest version of the story, in Paul Müller's 'Erinnerungen' (*Die Musik*, March and April 1903), Wolf tore the score to pieces. Müller was told of the incident by Potpeschnigg.

The confusion in Decsey and the fact that the full score of *Penthesilea*, in the

On 11th February Wolf left the wintry mist of Hochenegg for Trieste and the Istrian peninsula—at that time, of course, still within the Austrian Empire. He was accompanied and looked after by his sister Käthe and Melanie Köchert. At Trieste they took rooms in an hotel. For the first time in his life Wolf saw the sea, and he was fascinated. He loved watching the waves from the mole; he would gaze endlessly, without ever tiring of the spectacle. A trip in a sailing boat on the waters of the Adriatic was to him an incomparable experience; a gorgeous sunset over the sea held him as if in a spell. Trieste he liked, except for its noise. He took his meals for preference in an Italian restaurant and tried to enter sympathetically into the southern ways of life that had so appealed to his artistic sense and been the inspiration of so many of his compositions, but he found the reality too restless and distressing to his nerves in his enfeebled state. After various trips, which were often spoiled by cold and misty weather, to nearby places of interest on the coast—Duino on the 14th, Miramare on the 15th, Pirano and Portorosa on the 16th— the party set out on the 18th by the steamship *Danubio* for Lussin-piccolo, in search of quiet and sunshine. It turned out to be a disastrous move. As far as Rovigno all went well, but between there and Pola, the next port of call, the weather deteriorated and Wolf and his companions were prostrated by seasickness. Between Pola and Lussin, in the open sea, the sirocco blew violently and the little vessel was severely battered. Wolf thought his last hour had come, and they were all more dead than alive when at half-past ten at night they reached their destination. The *pension* Pundschuh, where they had been recommended to stay, they found already full up and were turned into a cold, bare, fireless room in a private house near by. They retired to damp beds and coughed and sneezed through the night. Wolf was suffering from one of his own particularly severe and prolonged colds, and his companions were similarly afflicted. Next day an oil stove was procured, which did little to warm the room but stank abominably. Meanwhile it rained, and they crouched

---

National Library, Vienna, gives no indication as to where the Interlude was to have been inserted, have led some to question whether the whole story is not apocryphal. But among the papers of Rosa Mayreder is a letter from Müller, dated 5th February 1898, in which he refers to 'eight pages in full score,' composed by Wolf in the asylum, about which Potpeschnigg had written to him. The description cannot apply to any of the other manuscripts of this time, and I believe that the work referred to must have been this Interlude for *Penthesilea*, which Potpeschnigg took away with him after visiting Wolf in the asylum on 15th December.

around the pestilential stove, trying to warm their hands and feet, and heartily wishing they had never left Trieste.

Later the sun appeared intermittently through the clouds and they were able to get out for a few walks. But the once tireless Wolf now found himself exhausted after very short distances on foot. When all the easily accessible places of interest had been visited there was nothing to do but sit and watch the breakers. Restless and miserable, unable to smoke owing to chronic catarrh, he would have liked to leave Lussin after the briefest of stays, but while the sirocco continued he dared not risk a repetition of the experiences of the outward journey. It was nine days before comparative calm enabled the party to take ship for Abbazia, on the mainland. From Abbazia they made a trip to Lovrana on the 28th but there too no suitable accommodation could be found and the ill-fated Adriatic holiday was then finally abandoned.

They returned to Cilli, and after another visit to Wöllan to see his mother, Wolf left for Graz. Frau Köchert travelled in the same train but went on back to Vienna, having discharged her self-imposed duties of watching over the convalescent during his tour of the south.

At Graz Wolf called to see his eldest sister, the poor, abandoned Modesta, struggling to bring up her numerous family of little Strassers. As he told Käthe in an unpublished letter on 3rd March,[1] he found Modesta at home 'with her entire young brood' and she was highly surprised and delighted to see him. In the evening he went out and purchased a few little delicacies for supper—delicacies no doubt rare enough in his sister's household. They were all about to settle down to a pleasant evening together when the malignant fate, which so consistently contrived to ruin Wolf's last few poor months of freedom, played another of its petty, spiteful tricks upon him. Just as the supper was served he was seized with violent stomach pains, had to lie down at once, and so was deprived of the pleasure of participating in the little treat he had prepared for his nephews and nieces. A room usually occupied by a lodger at Modesta's house was vacant for two days and Wolf stayed there for that time. 'At Modesta's I like it very much,' he told Käthe, 'but I could not put up with it permanently. Shall I be able to put up with *anywhere* permanently? This question disquiets me somewhat.'

'I hope Potpeschnigg hears nothing about my stay here,' says

---

[1] In the Prussian State Library, Berlin.

another sentence in this unpublished letter to Käthe Wolf of 3rd March. Now only a very short time before this Wolf had sent Potpeschnigg affectionate postcards from Duino and Lussinpiccolo. How did it come about that while at Graz he wished to avoid this devoted friend? It is a pitiful story. Potpeschnigg had written to Wolf's mother, preparing her for her son's visit, a letter in which he had revealed that the apparent recovery could only be temporary in character, that Wolf was really held fast in the grip of an incurable disease of the brain. *This letter had been shown to Wolf at Wöllan.* Whether he accepted the fact that he was bound inescapably to end his days in a madhouse we do not know; he knew, at any rate, that Potpeschnigg thought so, and on this account wished to have no more to do with this friend.

On 4th March Wolf left Graz for Salzburg, where he looked round for a suitable dwelling but found nothing. Next day he heard that the Vienna Wagner Verein was including some of his works in a festival concert in celebration of the twenty-fifth anniversary of its foundation, and on the 6th, to every one's surprise, he hurried back to the city in which so much of his life had been passed, but which, only six short weeks before, he had left 'for ever.'

The fact that he showed interest in his music again was indicative of an improvement in his condition. Although still feeling the tiring effects of his journeyings, he was gradually regaining physical and mental strength. Not wishing ever to see the house in the Schwindgasse again, he was pleased when he learned that it had been relet. He settled himself in the Hotel Tegethoff for the time, while his friends looked round for a new home.

Wolf's misfortune, and the publicity resulting from it, had increased considerably the official and public interest in his work. His friends, too, delighted to have him back amongst them, redoubled their attentions and did everything in their power to make him happy and comfortable. His thirty-eighth birthday, on 13th March, brought him countless congratulations, letters and telegrams from near and far, a whole roomful of flowers, honorary membership of the Wagner Verein and news from Faisst of the opening ceremony of a new Hugo Wolf Verein at Stuttgart. Further, an elegant new apartment was found for him in his favourite district, 'auf der Wieden,' at Mühlgasse 22, on the fourth floor of a new building, with a sunny outlook and quiet surroundings. Entirely new furniture was provided by the Köchert family.

Wolf was delighted with his new home; rather than leave it he refused an invitation to spend April with the Marchese della Valle di Casanova at Pallanza. He began to occupy himself with his music again, reconsidered Hoernes's text for *Manuel Venegas*, improved the ending of *Dem Vaterland*, and saw a new edition of the Eichendorff songs through the press, in which *Erwartung*, *Die Nacht* and *Waldmädchen* did not appear.

On 29th April *Der Corregidor* was produced, in the revised version, at Strassburg; a second performance followed on 13th May. The composer was not present on either occasion, nor did he show much interest in the efforts of Kapellmeister Lohse and Intendant Krückl of the Strassburg Stadttheater.

On 21st May Wolf accompanied the Köchert family to Traunkirchen for the summer. The 'Kreutzerhaus,' a cottage a few minutes' walk from 'Puchschacher,' was rented for him, and a servant-girl, 'Liesi,' brought from Windischgraz as housekeeper. Faisst was the Köcherts' guest at Traunkirchen during the Whitsuntide holidays and there was much music-making during his visit, as it rained nearly all the time. Altogether, the weather was not too kind during this last summer of Wolf's in the Salzkammergut, although there were some periods of sunshine when he could bathe and sail on the lake, as he so loved to do. In July he received a visit from Paul Müller. Müller relates that he was warned by Melanie Köchert not to ask about *Manuel Venegas*, as Wolf had already received numerous inquiries, which had led to long hours of brooding over the fragmentary first act, but not to any further progress with the work. However, in a letter to Potpeschnigg, with whom in July he had become reconciled, Wolf declared that he intended to set to work seriously on the task of completing his second opera in the coming winter, and would for that reason not return to Vienna but settle at Schloss Orth, near Gmunden, in solitude and quiet. In August he went so far as to terminate the lease of the fine new Mühlgasse home that his friends had provided for him. He had lived in it for only two months.

He told Müller that in the winter he also intended to write a new work for chorus and orchestra, a setting of Nietzsche's magnificent poem, *An den Mistral*. Here surely was promise of a masterpiece. At the beginning of September the Michelangelo songs were published. Before this, from copies in Faisst's possession, they had been performed several times by Moritz

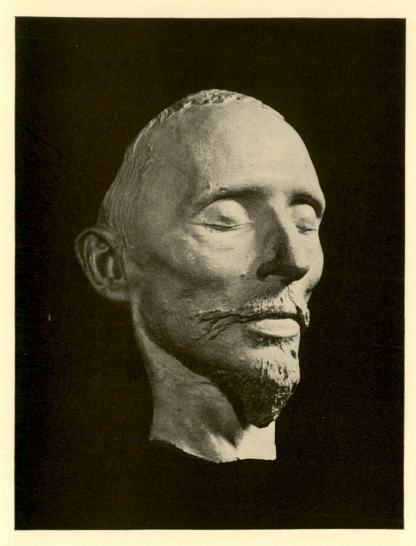

HUGO WOLF.   DEATH MASK

Frauscher, and for this singer Wolf intended to make orchestral versions.

Hopes of a quietly happy and productive future were increasing, when something went wrong again in Wolf's brain. One morning at the beginning of October the 'Kreutzerhaus' was found deserted. Search was made in the vicinity. He had been seen wandering on the railway line, which passes just behind the Köcherts' property. After some time he appeared on the edge of a nearby wood, dripping wet and shivering with cold. Sensing the onset of madness again, he had tried to drown himself in the Traunsee, but contact with the water had reawakened his instincts of self-preservation and he had swum to the shore. Then he had wandered in the woods, ashamed of what he had attempted to do. He allowed himself to be led away quietly and put to bed. There was none of the blissful exaltation of the days preceding his earlier attack. He was now tormented by ideas of persecution. He himself asked to be put in a mental home, 'only for God's sake not Svetlin's.' A telegram was sent to Haberlandt, who made the necessary arrangements with the Lower Austrian Landesirrenanstalt, in the Alsergrund district of Vienna. Two attendants were dispatched to Traunkirchen to fetch Wolf, and on 4th October, after an uneventful journey, he entered the asylum as a first-class patient.

The maintenance of Wolf in the Landesirrenanstalt became the principal responsibility of the Vienna Hugo Wolf Verein. Already, when he was in Dr. Svetlin's care, various sums had been contributed by friends in Austria and Germany. They included 2,000 kronen annually from the munificent Faisst and his mother, 2,000 marks from the Mannheim friends, and considerable sums from the Berlin Hugo Wolf Verein and the Kauffmann family. Now the Austrian Emperor Franz Joseph made a grant of 600 florins a year towards the cost of Wolf's upkeep in the asylum and the Ministry of Culture and Education one of 400 florins a year for the propagation of his works.

In the Landesirrenanstalt Wolf's condition at first deteriorated. He grew terribly depressed, was sullen and clearly in revolt against his environment. When he encountered people in the corridors he used to push them roughly out of his way. He would stand about for a long time, his body bent slightly forward, hands thrust into his trouser pockets, with bowed head, staring at the ground in front of him, biting his lips, with an expression of inner torment on his face. He suffered again from delusions and, among other things, raved a

P

good deal about Brahms.   He spoke of his fears that his body would
be dismembered, his skin stripped off.

Early in 1899 he improved greatly.   Periods of derangement alternated with others when he appeared almost normal.   He took part
in the few amusements permitted to the asylum patients, played
skittles, asked for books and music and received visits from his
friends.   It was heart-rending when, as often happened, he wanted to
leave the asylum with the visitors.   Everything was done that could
be done to make life agreeable for him in his last periods of normality.
He was allowed a piano in his own room, of which he made good use.
A few sheets of music written in 1899 are still in existence.   One page,
dated 4th May, has barely decipherable scribblings in the margins, in
which the name of Brahms, and something about regicide and the
Prinz von Homburg can be made out.   Another torn sheet of paper,
which Haberlandt took away with him after a visit, has, among other
confused scrawlings, a draft of two concert programmes, in which
compositions of Liszt and Bruckner appear with his own works.
The first item on the first programme is: 'Wolf.   Overture to the
opera *Penthesilea*, composed 1883.'   He often played duets with one
of the asylum officials, August Stiglbauer, a member of the Wagner
Verein and an admirer of Wolf's music.   He sang and played his
songs and passed many pleasant hours in Stiglbauer's company.
When he was alone he played over and over again the second movement of Beethoven's Sonata in E minor, Op. 90—that divine song of
sanity and consolation.

In the early summer he was allowed to go out for little excursions,
with his friends and two attendants, beyond the asylum walls.   Unhappily his sight was at this time becoming affected and he saw the
familiar scenes as though in a distorting mirror.   He would not
recognize that the change was in himself, but looked at the external
world with a disbelieving smile on his lips, or grew angry over the
poor imitation of the Ringstrasse, or the bad copy of the Stefansturm,
that he saw in the course of his walks.

On two occasions he was taken to Perchtoldsdorf, to the Werners'
house in the Brunnergasse where so many lovely songs had come into
existence in happier days.   The first visit was on a hot day in July.
He recognized his old friends and seemed pleased to see them, but
refused food and drink, because, he said, it was all poisoned.   As
soon as he thought himself unobserved, he slipped out of the garden
gate and climbed the Hochberg, as had been his daily custom in

earlier years.   Heinrich Werner followed close on his heels and stood beside him on the summit.   Wolf's gaze passed slowly over the beloved prospect—the town, the church, the mighty stone tower, the vineyards on the plain and the farther hills of the Wiener Wald. After a long silence he said very quietly: 'Yes! Everything there is still as it was in the old days—nothing there is bewitched.' Then pain and anger overcame the unhappy man as he caught sight at a distance of the two asylum attendants, seeking their charge.

Werner accompanied him part of the way back.   In the carriage Wolf turned suddenly to his young friend and asked to be given money.   He would get out at Liesing railway station and make his escape to the south.   It was Werner's painful duty to refuse to help him, which he did on the pretext that he had no money with him at the time.

On the second and last visit, not long afterwards, Wolf was in a surly mood.   He would not rest in the house but ran out at once into the garden and through the gate into the vineyards beyond.   His friends and attendants followed and when he saw that he could not get away he turned and came back in an exhausted condition.   For a long time he obstinately refused to return to the asylum, but at length, after long persuasion from all his friends, he jumped with a bad grace into the carriage and left Perchtoldsdorf for ever.

Thoughts of escape appear in a letter he wrote to his eldest sister on 15th July:

What are you doing then, dear Modesta?   Couldn't you send a few lines to the principal doctor, saying that you are willing to provide for me? It would be best if you could visit me.   It seems to me you have quite forgotten me.   You must call me to mind again.   Visit me as soon as possible.   Perhaps you can set me free.   Say that you will take over the care of me.   I must get out of the asylum.   We shall get on very well together, but see that I attain my freedom.   A certain F. was here, who with his sister (as he makes out)—and she is very like you—yesterday left the asylum.   Ah, have pity on me, and think of the happy days that we spent together with Strasser.   Perhaps you can induce Gilbert to accompany you here.   In short, *save* me, if I am still to be saved.

Among the unpublished letters in the Vienna City Library is the following forlorn little message to Faisst:

DEAREST FRIEND!

It would be very nice of you if after such a long pause you would once again let me have a sign of life.   As you may suppose from these lines, things are not exactly going as well with me as they might.   Perhaps we

shall meet next time somewhere in Tyrol, or in Switzerland, whither
I should most like to go.   Unfortunately I am still confined in an institution, where I am looked after, and fear very much I shall never get out
again.   However, if it should be granted to me to belong once more to
human society, I shall turn to you again.   For the present only the most
cordial greetings from your faithful

HUGO WOLF.

Do you remember the couplets that you sang to us in Puchschacher:
'But black, but black, was always my favourite colour?'   How long ago
was that?

After the summer of 1899 his condition allowed of no more outside
excursions or music-making.   His memory began to fail and the
fairly rapid progress of his malady brought on various new delusions.
He was seized with anxiety that some frightful evil and cruel torments
awaited both himself and his friends.   Sometimes he doubted even
his own identity. 'If I were only Hugo Wolf,' he would say.   His
ideas were markedly negative in character—everything was untrue,
an empty show; he himself was dead; the whole world made of card-
board.   He refused his food and was unable to sleep without artificial
aids.   Symptoms of paralysis began to increase.   His handwriting
became unrecognizable and he stuttered and stumbled a lot in
speaking, with moments of complete dumbness.

As time went on he came more and more to resemble an unruly
child, and had to be treated like one.   At about Christmas, 1899,
Potpeschnigg came from Graz to see him.   Wolf had been behaving
badly and was confined in a sort of railed bed, like a cage, that stood
in one corner of the room.   He recognized the visitor's voice at once
and as he entered pleaded from behind the bars: 'Please, Potpeschnigg, let me out, let me out!'   At Potpeschnigg's request the attendants, rather doubtfully, opened one side, and one of them said: 'If
you are going to behave, Herr Wolf, you may come out.'   Wolf, like
lightning, put his hand outside the rails and turned the screw so that
the other side of the contraption fell away, then he leaped out,
embraced and kissed his friend, broke away, ran to the table, poured
himself out a glass of wine and quickly gulped it down.   While he
was thus occupied the attendant took the opportunity to approach
from behind and then put his arms round the patient and carried him
like a little child to his bed. 'Now, Herr Wolf,' he said, 'tell us
nicely what you've had to eat.'   Wolf began to complain that all the
food was bad, but was persuaded afterwards to admit the truth, that
he liked it all very well—the soup, the *Schnitzel* with apple sauce, the

puddings.   Potpeschnigg sat down on the bed and for a while Wolf spoke to him quietly and reasonably, asking after his wife and family. Suddenly he stared at the visitor: 'No!   How queer you look!   It's terrible!   You're in a bad way.   You've only got one hand left!' Potpeschnigg was sitting against the light and part of his cloak covered one hand.

Wolf next inquired after the Baroness Lipperheide.   'But she's dead.'   'Yes, so you think!'   Then he became anxious that perhaps his friend would be prevented, as he himself was, from leaving the asylum.   He turned to the attendant: 'You, Karl, for God's sake see that the doctor gets out, that they don't keep him in here.   It's dreadful.   In Svetlin's there was at least no railed bed.'   He kissed and embraced Potpeschnigg again and urged him to depart.   For a long time he stared after him to see that he really did manage to make his escape.

Edmund Lang received one day the following pitiful letter, put together at intervals in a shaky hand, in alternating pencil and ink.

DEAREST EDMUND!

Would you do me the great favour and make me happy by visiting me here?   You could also take the opportunity of seeing your brother Karl, whom a strange fate has also led to this institution.   Perhaps if you hurry you will find me here still alive and unmutilated.   Your address, I suppose, is still the old one, assuming that you are staying in Vienna and have not yet gone into the country. . . .   As your whereabouts are not known to me, I address these lines to the Mayreders, for their further kind dispatch.   It is to be hoped that all will yet end well, although my situation takes on continually a worse and more menacing aspect.   I must be on my guard every moment against being assaulted.   So hurry to your poor

WÖLFING.

Greetings to your dear wife and to the dear children.   If only I were in better spirits!   My situation must be reckoned among the most frightful in all the world.   My brother Gilbert was here three times, the last time with a new hat, which, however, did not please me on account of the air-holes, and which I therefore gave him back to exchange.   Meanwhile Frau Melanie K. has procured me another hat.

Do come!   Here it is dreadfully lonely and the people around me adopt continually a threatening attitude towards me.   My condition is truly not an enviable one, and the less so because I cannot succeed anyhow in making myself understood.   *They simply won't understand me*, and that makes me impatient and so I aggravate my own situation.   What I have suffered! And the most dreadful torments threaten me.   Ah, if you could only take me away from here!—but that is almost out of the question.   In short, I am condemned to suffer *eternally* and without respite.   What that means you will best understand. If only I had never come here! They should never have brought me into a madhouse at all, and then everything would have turned out differently.

What of my future? It does not bear thinking about. No water, nothing to drink, perhaps no fluids at all will be given me and I shall have to languish miserably—apart from the other torments that are in store for me.

May God in Heaven forgive me, if I consciously sin against him.

Into this purgatory, three times a week, without fail, came Melanie Köchert with her eldest daughter Ilse. What could be done she did, from finding a hat without the air-holes to which his sick fancy took objection to consoling him in his blackest hours with the comfort of her presence—the one person who had understood him completely, who loved and served him unfalteringly to the end and in whom he trusted. Does not this noble woman deserve the gratitude of posterity? Where did she find the courage for this last protracted, agonizing service?

At the beginning of 1900 paralysis began increasingly to affect Wolf's powers of speech. There were still brighter intervals. As late as 10th April 1901 he was taken, supported by two attendants, into the garden, where he lay quietly in the spring sunshine. It must have been during such a temporary improvement in his condition that, in 1901, he saw his mother for the last time. A letter from the seventy-seven-year-old Katharina Wolf describes her visit to the asylum. On a previous occasion Hugo had been violent and abusive. 'Who is this woman?' he had demanded, while his mother stood weeping in a corner of the room. But now he lay quite quietly on his bed, gave no trouble, ate what he was given and only refused when he had had sufficient. He spoke very little and in an almost inaudible voice, so that it was difficult to catch his words, but showed great interest in everything that went on in the room. Katharina told the doctor about her husband's death in 1887, and how Hugo had arrived at Windischgraz scarcely an hour before the end, and how his father had still been conscious and had caressed him and cried: 'Hugo, my Hugo!' While she was recounting all this within Wolf's hearing, he wept and sobbed aloud. He smiled happily when his mother told him that his sister Käthe was married to a mining official named Salomon, a dear, honest fellow he would be sure to like. He asked: 'Has he matriculated?' and said he would go to Cilli and Römerbad in the summer. His mother told him that Salomon would certainly invite him and promised all sorts of things that she knew would never really be possible, because she saw how they pleased him.   When she told him that Max and Gilbert were at home for a month, he began to cry again.   His mother consoled him by saying that in the spring he would be able to go home himself.

One of his last utterances concerned the art to which his whole life had been dedicated.   But he wished now to hear nothing more about it.   He broke off with two words: 'Loathsome music!'

In the latter half of 1901 Wolf's malady increased its hold. Paralytic convulsions began to torture him.   Henceforth he spent day and night on his bed, sleeping most of the time, refusing nourishment, waiting for death.   In March 1902 a severe attack of bronchitis seemed likely to cut short his sufferings before the final stages of general paralysis.   The doctors gave him up and his death was expected within a few days.   But his heart was still sound and he recovered, to live in torment for another year.

A short notice about his condition appeared in the Vienna newspaper *Die Zeit* for 4th January 1903: 'His eyes stare without expression into nothingness.   Often the attendant strokes him.   But in the face of the insane Master no perceptible alteration can be detected. With rough pity the attendant asks: "How goes it, old fellow?"   But there comes no answer to this either, only sometimes an unintelligible sound.'

Not long after this, in the middle of February, he contracted a violent cold, which brought on inflammation of the lungs, and a week later the long-drawn-out tragedy came to its tardy conclusion. When it was seen that the end could not be much longer delayed, the Köcherts, Haberlandt and Heinrich Werner spent many hours watching by the bedside, but it so happened that none of his friends was present when at three o'clock in the afternoon of Sunday, 22nd February 1903, after dreadful paralytic convulsions in his last hours, Wolf died in the arms of Johann Scheibner, his faithful asylum attendant.

The body was terribly wasted and shrunken, so that, as it lay on the bier, it more resembled a white wooden doll than the mortal remains of a vital human being, but the features, for a brief period after death, appeared as if transfigured, with an expression of singular youthful radiance.

During the years of his illness, Wolf's art, largely through the tireless activities of his friends in the Hugo Wolf Verein, had won extensive recognition throughout the German-speaking countries. Now with his death, in the way of the world, fame and honours were showered upon him.　Streets were named after him, commemorative tablets, unveiled with fitting ceremony, sprang up wherever he had lived and worked and suffered.　*Der Corregidor* was produced in various cities, and great and famous singers no longer hesitated to include his works in their programmes.　How far circumstances had changed is revealed by the fact that in the year of his death his family were able to sell to the firm of Peters the copyrights of the works published in his lifetime for no less than 260,000 marks.

Wolf had once expressed a wish to be buried in the quiet church-yard at his well-beloved Perchtoldsdorf.　This wish was disregarded in favour of a 'Grave of Honour,' within a few yards of the final resting places of Beethoven and Schubert, in the Central Cemetery of Vienna.

At three o'clock in the afternoon of 24th February the funeral procession left the Landesirrenanstalt for the Votivkirche.　It was Carnival Tuesday in Vienna, and the body was borne among gaily decorated horses and carriages, through streets thronged with masked revellers—Harlequins, Columbines, clowns and jesters, with their balloons and coloured ribbons.　The public was still indifferent, but the church was crowded with artistic notabilities.　Besides official representatives of the city of Vienna, the Gesellschaft der Musik-freunde, the Conservatoire and other institutions, everybody of importance in the musical world was there—composers, conductors, singers and critics, many of them men who in Wolf's lifetime had never raised a finger to help him.　From farther afield had come deputations from the Styrian Tonkünstlerverein and the town of Windischgraz.

After the service Wolf's own early chorus *Ergebung* was sung from behind the altar by the Wiener a cappella Chorverein under Eugen Thomas, and at the heart-rendingly sad passage,

> O mit uns Sündern gehe
> Erbarmend ins Gericht,
> Ich beug im tiefsten Wehe
> Zum Staub mein Angesicht!

many eyes were wet.　Then the 'Trauermusik,' inspired by the death of Wagner, from the slow movement of Bruckner's seventh Symphony, was played in an arrangement for brass instruments by Ferdinand Löwe.

Afterwards, in the Central Cemetery, over the open grave which was to be a temporary resting place while the 'Grave of Honour' was being prepared, Haberlandt bade farewell to his friend in a noble oration, concluding with a beautifully appropriate adaptation of one of Wolf's most moving songs:

> Zur Ruh, zur Ruh, ihr müden Glieder,
> Schliesst fest euch zu, ihr Augenlider,
> Du bist allein, fort ist die Erde—
> Nacht muss es sein, dass Licht dir werde!

The tired limbs were indeed at rest at last, the eyes shut fast upon a scene of public homage such as he would undoubtedly have shrunk from, but perhaps accepted as a tribute to the demonic power of genius that expressed itself through him. 'When I can compose no more,' he had once said, 'you may throw me on a dunghill.' Instead, they buried him beside Schubert and Beethoven, where, surely, he sleeps proudly and at peace. The tragedy of what he was and what he became, of the blithe and lovely spirit brutally soiled and broken, fades before the enduring worth of the work he did succeed in committing to paper—only a fragment, maybe, of the music he had it in him to write, if circumstances had allowed, but enough to ensure him a modest place among the immortals, in the hierarchy of musicians, and the grateful love of inarticulate humanity, for whom he sang of truth and beauty.

APPENDIX I

HUGO WOLF: A BIBLIOGRAPHY—
PRINCIPALLY BIOGRAPHICAL

In this attempt at a comprehensive Hugo Wolf bibliography my aim has been to record every book and all the articles in periodicals and newspapers which contain letters, personal reminiscences or valuable biographical material of any description. Only the more important writings on the music are included, my purpose having been principally biographical. Similarly, I have not catalogued the early critical articles and concert notices which appeared during Wolf's own lifetime, although they may be considered to have a certain biographical value. Some of the best of them appear in the *Gesammelte Aufsätze über Hugo Wolf*, collected and reprinted by the Vienna Hugo Wolf Verein in the years 1898–1900.

The bibliography has been reduced to the most compact form compatible with the scope of the undertaking. The details of publication of the various articles are generally those of their first appearance, but whenever they have subsequently been reprinted in book form I have preferred to list them in this form, as being more easily accessible. The various volumes of Wolf's own letters are listed under Wolf's own name. Many letters, however, have been published in the course of personal reminiscences, or with editorial commentaries that deserve separate mention, and in these cases I have followed the title-pages or the authors' names and given a cross-reference under the name of the composer. Many valuable letters, that have never appeared in book form, lie buried in the files of periodicals and newspapers; in all such cases I have given an indication of the contents.

For every article appearing on this list, a dozen have been examined and rejected as containing nothing of any importance. *All* personal reminiscences of the composer have been included, however slight their original contribution to our knowledge of Wolf's life and personality. My sifting of this vast mass of material was interrupted by the war before it was completed. In Vienna in 1945–6 I was able to do a good deal towards filling in the gaps and bringing the work up to date. A compilation of this kind can never be exhaustive, but I believe my bibliography covers at least ninety-five per cent of the ground.

Abraham, Gerald   'Hugo Wolf,' in *Lives of the Great Composers*, edited by A. L. Bacharach (London, 1935).

'Ald.'   'Hugo Wolf. Zu seinem 50. Geburtstage,' *Tagespost* (Graz), 12th March 1910. Includes three otherwise unpublished letters to Philipp Wolf.

448

Antal, F. G. 'Hugo Wolfs erstes Jahr in Wien,' *Neue Freie Presse* (Vienna), 13th March 1910. Contains two letters from Philipp Wolf to Katharina Vinzenzberg and two letters from Hugo Wolf to Anna Vinzenzberg.

Auer, Hans 'Hugo Wolf, der Sohn der Untersteiermark,' *Marburger Zeitung*, 20th–21st February 1943.

Bahr, Hermann *Buch der Jugend* (Vienna, 1908).
Selbstbildniss (Berlin, 1923).
See also under 'Various Authors,' *Gesammelte Aufsätze über Hugo Wolf, I. Folge*, with an introduction by Bahr.

Batka, R., and Nagel, W. *Allgemeine Geschichte der Musik* (Stuttgart, 1909–15). Band III, p. 252, reproduces *Die Verlassene*, an otherwise unknown unfinished song by Wolf.

Bauer-Lechner, Natalie *Fragmente. Gelerntes und Gelebtes* (Vienna, 1907).

Besch, Otto *Engelbert Humperdinck* (Leipzig, 1914).

Bettelheim-Gabillon, Helene *Im Zeichen des alten Burgtheaters* (Vienna, 1921).

Bieri, Georg *Die Lieder von Hugo Wolf* (Berne, 1935).
'Hugo Wolfs Lieder nach verschiedenen Dichtern,' *Schweizerische Musikzeitung* (Berne), June 1935. Apparently a chapter omitted from the above.

Bistron, Julius 'Hugo Wolf, der tragische Tondichter,' *Neues Wiener Journal*, 25th December 1929. Contains two letters to Joseph Schalk.

B., J. (i.e. Julius Bistron) 'Erinnerung an Hugo Wolf,' *Neues Wiener Journal*, 22nd February 1933.

Bock, Gustav 'Erinnerungen an Hugo Wolf,' *Die Signale*, (Leipzig), 25th May 1931.

Böhmer, Curt 'Biographisches in zwei unveröffentlichten Briefen Wolfs,' *Die Musikwelt* (Hamburg), Jg. 5, Heft 5.

Bruckner, Anton *Gesammelte Briefe, Neue Folge, herausgegeben von Max Auer* (Regensburg, 1924). Contains one letter from Wolf.

Conrad, M. G. Reminiscences of Wolf, used and extensively quoted by Decsey, published in the *Münchner Neueste Nachrichten* in or before 1904. Not traced.

Davison, L. B. 'Persönliche Erinnerungen an Hugo Wolf,' *Münchner Neueste Nachrichten*, 26th April 1913.

Decsey, Ernst 'Aus Hugo Wolfs letzten Jahren,' *Die Musik* (Berlin), second October number and first

Decsey, Ernst

November number, 1901.   Contains a letter to Wolf's mother, not included in the *Familienbriefe*.

'Ein Jugendchor von Hugo Wolf.' *Festblätter zum 6. deutschen Sängerbundesfest in Graz.* Heft 3, 15th May 1902.   Wolf's early chorus *Geistesgruss* was here published for the first and only time.

'Hugo Wolf und die ersten Freunde seiner Kunst,' *Tagespost* (Graz), 8th June 1902.

'Hugo Wolf Miszellen.'   In *Ein Musikbuch aus Österreich* (Vienna, 1904).   Includes a letter from Wolf to Richard Genée.

Hugo Wolf, 4 volumes:

  I. *Hugo Wolfs Leben* (1860–87), Berlin and Leipzig, 1903.

  II. *Hugo Wolfs Schaffen* (1888–91), Berlin and Leipzig, 1904.

  III. *Der Künstler und die Welt* (1892–5), Berlin and Leipzig, 1904.

  IV. *Höhe und Ende* (1896–1903), Berlin and Leipzig, 1906.

  These volumes contain many extracts from Wolf's letters, facsimiles, etc., that have never been reprinted.

Hugo Wolf. Das Leben und das Lied (Berlin, 1919).   Republished in 1921 with slight alterations.   This is a condensation for popular consumption of the above four volumes, with a small amount of additional material taken chiefly from Antal, Kukula, Bahr and the *Familienbriefe*.   It is frequently confused with the complete reprint in a single volume of the four parts of Decsey's original work.   It lacks entirely, however, the weight and authority of the latter and contains many errors.

—de— (Decsey)

'Aus Hugo Wolfs Knabenzeiten,' *Tagespost* (Graz), 13th March 1902.

'Hugo Wolf als Kritiker,' *Tagespost* (Graz), 17th August 1901.   Includes a letter to Josef and Modesta Strasser that has never been reprinted.

Eckstein, Friedrich

Alte unnennbare Tage (Vienna, 1936).   Contains a number of previously unpublished letters.

'Die erste und die letzte Begegnung zwischen Hugo Wolf und Anton Bruckner,' in *In Memoriam Anton Bruckner, herausgegeben*

	von Karl Kobald (Vienna, 1924). Contains a small amount of information not included in the chapter of the same title in *Alte unnennbare Tage*.
Ehrmann, Alfred	*Hugo Wolf: Sein Leben in Bildern* (Leipzig,1937).
Faisst, Hugo	'Erinnerungen an Hugo Wolf' (published anonymously), *Neue Musik Zeitung* (Stuttgart), 19th December 1901 (considered as 1902, No. 1).
Fournier, August	*Erinnerungen* (Munich, 1923).
Geiringer, Karl	'Hugo Wolf and Frida von Lipperheide, some unpublished letters,' *The Musical Times*, August and September 1936. Contains nineteen letters to the Baroness von Lipperheide, which have never been published in the original German.
Göllerich, August, and Auer, Max	*Anton Bruckner*, Band IV, Teil 1–4 (Regensburg, 1936).
Grohe, Oskar	'Aus Hugo Wolfs Leben,' *Rosengartenblätter* (Mannheim), 1903. Reprinted in the *Neue Musik Zeitung* (Stuttgart), 25th February 1904. 'Hugo Wolfs Mannheimer Tage,' *Badische Kunst* (Karlsruhe), 1905.
Grunsky, Karl	'Hugo Wolf-Fest in Stuttgart,' *Festschrift*, 1906. Contains about 60 pages of annotations. *Hugo Wolf* (Leipzig, 1928). 'Offener Antwort an Hans Richter,' *Die Musik* (Berlin), second December number, 1906.
Gutmann, Albert	*Aus dem Wiener Musikleben, 1873–1908* (Vienna, 1914). Contains an unimportant letter, reproduced in facsimile. A second volume was announced, which was to have contained a chapter on Wolf, but it was never published.
Haberlandt, Michael	'Zur Erkrankung Hugo Wolfs,' *Neues Wiener Tagblatt*, 12th October 1897. *Hugo Wolf. Erinnerungen und Gedanken* (Leipzig, 1903). *Zweite erweiterte Auflag* (Darmstadt, 1911). The various letters quoted in this book have all been reprinted in full in Heinrich Werner's *Hugo Wolf in Perchtoldsdorf*.
Halm, August	'Erinnerungen an Hugo Wolf,' *Der Kunstwart* (Dresden-Munich), May 1928.
Hattingberg-Graedener, Magda	*Hugo Wolf. Vom Wesen und Werk des grössten Liedschöpfers* (Vienna-Leipzig, 1941).

Hécaen, Henri	*Manie et Inspiration Musicale. Le cas Hugo Wolf* (Bordeaux, 1934).
Heckel, Karl	*Hugo Wolf in seinem Verhältnis zu Richard Wagner* (Munich, 1905). Reprinted from the *Süddeutsche Monatshefte* (Munich) for June 1905. Contains extracts from Wolf's correspondence with Heckel.
	'Hugo Wolf,' *Münchner Neueste Nachrichten*, 13th September 1922.
Hellmer, Edmund	'Aus Hugo Wolfs Leben,' *Deutsche Zeitung* (Vienna), 23rd March, 18th August, 20th November 1900, 2nd–3rd April 1901, 21st–22nd May 1902, and 5th–6th October 1904.
	'Erinnerungen an Hugo Wolf,' *Neues Wiener Tagblatt*, 6th–7th June 1902.
	Hugo Wolf, Erlebtes und Erlauschtes (Vienna, 1921).
	'Das Vöglein. Eine Geschichte aus Hugo Wolfs jungen Tagen,' *Neue Freie Presse* (Vienna), 18th June 1924.
	'Hugo Wolfs Jugendliebe,' *Die Presse* (Vienna), 5th December 1948.
Hellmer, Hans	*Erinnerungen an Hugo Wolf*. Published in an unidentified Graz newspaper, on or about 13th March 1920.
	'Begegnung mit Hugo Wolf,' *Neue Zeit* (Graz), 10th January 1946.
Helm, Theodor	'Fünfzig Jahre Wiener Musikleben (1866–1916).' Published serially in *Der Merker* (Vienna) in the years 1915–20.
Hernried, Robert	'Hugo Wolf in Mannheim,' *Die Neue Musik Zeitung* (Stuttgart), 5th January and 2nd February 1922. English translation in *The Musical Quarterly* (New York), January 1940. Contains Wolf's correspondence with Dr. Bassermann, the intendant of the Mannheim Opera-house.
	'Hugo Wolfs "Vier Opern," mit einem ungedruckten Briefe des Tondichter,' *Der Türmer* (Stuttgart), January 1928. Contains a letter to the Baroness von Loën. English translation in *The Musical Quarterly* (New York), January 1945. The letter was reprinted by Hernried in *Anbruch* (Vienna) for February 1937.
	'Unbekanntes von Hugo Wolf,' *Wiener Zeitung*, 29th March, 5th April, 12th April 1936. Consists of a reprint of the above two items

together. The activities of this author raise a point of literary ethics. Can a letter still be described as 'unpublished' when it appears in print for the fourth or fifth time?

Huschke, Konrad	*Unsere Tonmeister Untereinander*, iv and v (Pritzwalk, 1928).
'Iron'	'Gespräch mit dem Bruder Hugo Wolfs,' *Wiener Journal*, 26th February 1928.
Kalbeck, Max	*Johannes Brahms. III, zweiter Halbband* (Berlin, 1912).
	'Ein Musikbuch aus Österreich,' *Neues Wiener Tagblatt*, 9th March 1904.
Karpath, Ludwig	*Begegnung mit dem Genius* (Vienna, 1934).
	'Die Affäre Hugo Wolf-Max Kalbeck,' *Neues Wiener Journal*, 19th February 1933.
	Lachende Musiker (Munich, 1929).
Kienzl, Wilhelm	'Die Hugo Wolf Bilder von Clementine von Wagner,' *Zeitschrift für Musik* (Regensburg), February 1933.
Kinsky, Georg	'Musikhistorisches Museum von Wilhelm Heyer in Köln. Katalog von Georg Kinsky. Vierter Band,' *Musik Autographen* (Cologne, 1916).
Kleinschmidt, W.	'Hugo Wolf in Darmstadt,' *Darmstädtes Tagblatt*, 14th March 1930. Contains two previously unpublished letters.
	'Zur Ausstellung von Hugo Wolf Andenken im Foyer des Landestheaters,' *Blätter des Hessischen Landestheaters* (Darmstadt), No. 15, 18th April 1936. Contains four previously unpublished letters.
Klinckerfuss, Margarethe	'Weitere Ergänzungen zu Hugo Wolfs Briefen, mit einem unveröffentlichten Brief Wolfs,' *Die Neue Musik Zeitung* (Stuttgart), 1st February 1925. Contains a letter to Johanna Klinckerfuss and some, but not all, of the passages omitted from the published version of the letters to Faisst.
	Aufklänge aus versunkener Zeit (Urach, 1947).
Klose, Friedrich	*Meine Lehrjahre bei Bruckner* (Regensburg, 1927).
Kostenzer, Ludwig	'Mein Nachbar Hugo Wolf,' *Neues Wiener Journal*, 10th May 1925.
Krobath, Karl	'Ein Schreiben Hugo Wolfs aus kranker Zeit,' *Tagespost* (Graz), 27th December 1908. A letter to Thomas Koschat.
Kuba, Fritz	'Hugo Wolfs Musik zu Kleists Schauspiel *Prinz Friedrich von Homburg*,' *Jahrbuch der Kleist-Gesellschaft*, Band 17 (Berlin, 1937).

Kukula, Richard	'Erinnerungen an Hugo Wolf,' *Neue Freie Presse* (Vienna), 23rd February 1903.
	'Hugo Wolf. Persönliche Erinnerungen, *Prager Tagblatt*, 25th February 1903.
	'Persönliche Erinnerungen an Hugo Wolf,' *Der Merker* (Vienna), 15th June 1918.
	Erinnerungen eines Bibliothekars (Weimar, 1925).
Lang, Marie	'Hugo Wolfs Entwicklungszeit,' *Die Zeit* (Vienna), 3rd January 1904.
	'Wie der *Corregidor* entstand,' *Die Zeit* (Vienna), 23rd February 1904.
Legge, Walter	'Hugo Wolf's Afterthoughts on his *Mörike-Lieder*,' *The Music Review*, August 1941.
Leibbrand, Werner and Balet	'Hugo Wolf und seine Geisteskrankheit,' *Die medizinische Welt*, *Sonderabdruck*, No. 17 (1930).
Litterscheid, Richard	*Hugo Wolf* (Potsdam, 1939).
Mahler, Alma	*Gustav Mahler. Erinnerungen und Briefe* (Amsterdam, 1940). English translation (abridged) by Basil Creighton, *Life and Letters of Gustav Mahler* (London, 1946).
Marilaun, Karl	'Erinnerungen der Kammersängerin Rosa Papier-Paumgartner,' *Neues Wiener Journal*, 3rd October 1918.
Mayr, Karl	'Erinnerungen an Hugo Wolf, herausgegeben von Sebastian Röckl,' *Hochland* (Munich), May 1936.
Mayreder, Rosa	'Hugo Wolfs zweite Oper,' *Deutsche Musiker-Zeitung* (Berlin), 7th, 14th and 21st July 1928. Contains four letters which were not included in the volume of Wolf's correspondence with Rosa Mayreder.
	'Über die Operndichtung *Der Corregidor*,' *Die Glocke* (Vienna), 1st June 1936.
	See also Hugo Wolf, *Briefe an Rosa Mayreder, mit einem Nachwort der Dichterin des 'Corregidors.'*
Morold, Max	*Hugo Wolf* (Leipzig, 1912).
Müller, Paul	'Erinnerungen an Hugo Wolf,' *Die Musik* (Berlin), second March number and first April number, 1903.
	'Hugo Wolf' (*Moderne Essays*, Heft 34–5), Berlin, 1904.
	Hugo Wolf. Verzeichnis seiner Werke, mit einer Einführung (Leipzig, 1908).
Navrátil, Karl	'Hugo Wolf,' *Neue Zeitschrift für Musik*

	(Leipzig), 22nd April 1903. Highly inaccurate and quite unimportant, except that it contains fragments of an unpublished letter, clearly written when Wolf was in Dr. Svetlin's asylum. The complete text of this letter would be of considerable interest.
Newman, Ernest	*Hugo Wolf* (London, 1907).
	Hugo Wolf (Leipzig, 1910). A German translation, by Hermann von Hase, of the above. The German edition contains various facsimiles and photographs that were not in the English edition.
	Notes to gramophone records published by the Hugo Wolf Society, 6 volumes (London, 1932–8).
Ochs, Siegfried	*Geschehenes, Gesehenes* (Leipzig, 1922). Contains a facsimile of a letter from Wolf.
Orel, Alfred	'Hugo Wolf,' *Das Joanneum*, Band III (Graz, 1940), *Musik im Ostalpenraum.*
	Hugo Wolf (Vienna, 1947).
Pörner, Hans	'Jugenderinnerungen an Hugo Wolf,' *Deutsch-österreichische Tages-Zeitung*, 3rd March 1933.
Potpeschnigg, Heinrich	'Ein Erlebnis mit Hugo Wolf,' published in an unidentified newspaper.
	'Hugo Wolf bei der Mannheimer Uraufführung des *Corregidors*,' *Alpenländische Monatshefte* (Graz), February 1924.
Rath, Hans Wolfgang	*In Memoriam Detlev von Liliencron* (Frankfurt, 1909). Contains two of Wolf's letters to Liliencron.
Rauschenberger, Walther	*Ahnentafeln berühmter Deutscher. Fünfte Folge, Lieferung 8. Ahnentafel des Komponisten Hugo Wolf* (Leipzig, 1940).
Refardt, Edgar	*Brahms, Bruckner, Wolf. Drei Wiener Meister des 19. Jahrhunderts* (Basle, 1949).
Reger, Max	'Hugo Wolfs künstlerischer Nachlass,' *Süddeutsche Monatshefte* (Munich), 1904, No. 2.
Richter, Hans	'Offener Brief an den Herausgeber der *Musik*,' *Die Musik* (Berlin), first November number, 1906.
	'Schlusswort,' *Die Musik* (Berlin), second December number, 1906.
Rolland, Romain	*Musiciens d'aujourdhui* (Paris, 1908). English translation by Mary Blaiklock, *Musicians of To-day* (London, 1915).
Rosen, Waldemar	'Hugo Wolfs musikalischer Nachlass,' *Allgemeine Musikzeitung* (Berlin), 30th April and 7th May 1937.

S., H. von	'Von Hugo Wolf. Erinnerungen einer Wiener Dame,' *Die Zeit* (Vienna), 18th July 1903.
Salomon-Wolf, Käthe	'Aus Hugo Wolfs Jugend. Erinnerungen an meinen Bruder,' *Neues Wiener Tagblatt*, 26th February 1928.
	'Aus Hugo Wolfs letzten Lebensjahren,' *Stadtblatt der Frankfurter Zeitung*, 24th March 1928.
	'Hugo Wolfs Jugend. Mitteilungen der Schwester des Tondichters,' *Volkszeitung* (Vienna), 15th March 1933.
Schalk, Franz	*Briefe und Betrachtungen, mit einem Lebensabriss von Victor Junk, veröffentlicht von Lili Schalk* (Vienna, 1935). Contains correspondence between Franz and Joseph Schalk, with references to Wolf.
Schmid, Wilhelm	'Ährenlese zur Biographie Hugo Wolfs,' *Die Musik* (Berlin), October 1925. Contains five letters from Wolf to Schmid, a telegram to Kauffmann, a card from Liliencron to Wolf, a letter from Clara Mörike to Wolf and a letter from Dr. J. Bubinek to Kauffmann concerning Wolf's condition in the asylum.
	'Hugo Wolf und der Tübinger Kreis. Kleine Ergänzungen aus unveröffentlichten Briefmaterial u. aus persönlicher Erinnerungen,' *Die Neue Musik Zeitung* (Stuttgart), 1st January 1925. Contains passages omitted from the published letters to Kauffmann.
Schmieder, Wolfgang	*Musikerhandschriften in drei Jahrhunderten* (Leipzig, 1939). Includes a letter of Wolf's to Breitkopf & Härtel.
Schmitz, Eugen	*Hugo Wolf* (Leipzig, 1906).
Schultz, Helmut	'Hugo Wolf,' in *Die grossen Deutschen. Neue Deutsche Biographie, herausgegeben von Willy Andreas und Wilhelm von Scholz. Fünfter Band* (Berlin, 1937).
Schur, Gustav	*Erinnerungen an Hugo Wolf, nebst Hugo Wolfs Briefen an Gustav Schur, herausgegeben von Heinrich Werner* (Regensburg, 1922).
Specht, Richard	'Ein Gespräch mit Brahms,' *Die Zeit* (Vienna), 7th May 1903.
Sternfeld, Richard	'Zum Gedächtnis eines Meisters des deutschen Liedes,' *Deutsche Revue* (Stuttgart-Leipzig), July 1903. Contains several letters from Wolf to Sternfeld.
Stolzing-Cerny, Josef	'Meine Erinnerungen an Hugo Wolf,' *Münchner Neueste Nachrichten*, 13th March 1935.

Tausche, Anton	*Hugo Wolfs Mörike-Lieder* (Vienna, 1947).
Tischler, Gerhard	'Ein bislang unbekanntes Portrait von Hugo Wolf,' *Allgemeine Musikzeitung* (Berlin), 22nd March 1940.
Ullrich, Hermann	'Hugo Wolf in Salzburg. Ein Beitrag zu seiner Biographie,' *Allgemeine Musikzeitung* (Berlin), 17th April 1925.
Umlauft, Friedrich	'Ein lustiges Jahr mit Hugo Wolf,' *Neues Wiener Journal*, 13th March 1920.
Vancsa, Max	'Hugo Wolfs letzte Lebensjahre, Tod und Begräbnis,' *Die Musik* (Berlin), second March number, 1903.
	'Hugo Wolfs *Corregidor* in Wien,' *Neue musikalische Presse* (Vienna), 19th March 1904.
Varges, Kurt	*Der Musikkritiker Hugo Wolf* (Magdeburg, 1934).
(Various authors)	*Gesammelte Aufsätze über Hugo Wolf:*
	I. Folge (Berlin, 1898).
	II. Folge (Berlin, 1899).
	'*Der Corregidor*' *von Hugo Wolf. Kritische und biographische Beiträge zu seiner Würdigung. Redigiert von Edmund Hellmer* (Berlin, 1900). Published by the Hugo Wolf Verein of Vienna.
Vorberg, Gaston	*Zusammenbruch. Pathographische Abhandlung. Teil I.* (*Lenau, Nietzsche, Maupassant, Wolf*) (Munich, 1922).
Voss, Richard	*Aus einem phantastischen Leben* (Stuttgart, 1920).
Walker, Frank	'New Light on Hugo Wolf's Youth,' *Music & Letters*, October 1939.
	'Hugo Wolf's Vienna Diary, 1875–6,' *Music & Letters*, January 1947. German translation by Willi Reich, with the original text of Wolf's diary, in *Schweizerische Musikzeitung* (Berne), December 1947.
	'The History of Wolf's *Italian Serenade*,' *The Music Review*, August 1947.
	'*Ghasel*—a song wrongly attributed to Wolf,' *The Musical Times*, September 1947.
	A letter to the editor of *The Music Review* for November 1941 contains details of an unknown version of Wolf's six *Geistliche Lieder* for chorus.
Weingartner, Felix	*Lebenserinnerungen* (vol. i), Zürich-Leipzig, 1928.
Werner, Heinrich	'Hugo Wolf und Richard Wagner,' *Österreichische Rundschau* (Vienna), 10th May 1906.

Werner, Heinrich

Hugo Wolf in Maierling: eine Idyll (Leipzig, 1913). Contains many letters.

'Die Uraufführung von Hugo Wolfs *Corregidor*,' *Der Merker* (Vienna), 1st September 1913.

'Hugo Wolfs *Corregidor* in Wien,' *Der Merker* (Vienna), 1st March 1920.

Der Hugo Wolf-Verein in Wien (Regensburg, 1921).

'Erinnerungen an Hugo Wolf,' *Die Einkehr, Unterhaltungs-Beilage der Münchner Neuesten Nachrichten*, 26th August 1922.

'Hugo Wolf. Zur zwanzigsten Wiederkehr des Todestags,' *Neues Wiener Tagblatt*, 20th February 1923.

Hugo Wolf in Perchtoldsdorf (Regensburg, 1924). Contains many letters.

'Hugo Wolf und Anton Bruckner,' *Neues Wiener Tagblatt*, 24th November 1924.

'Hugo Wolf und seine heilige drein Könige, nach ungedruckten Briefen Hugo Wolfs,' *Neue Freie Presse* (Vienna), 18th January 1925. Contains letters to Ilse and Hilde Köchert.

'Hugo Wolfs erste und letzte Wohnung in Wien,' *Neues Wiener Tagblatt*, 2nd January 1926.

'Hugo Wolfs Wohnstätten in Wien,' *Wiener Neueste Nachrichten*, 16th May 1926.

'*Corregidor*-Proben mit Hugo Wolf,' *Wiener Neueste Nachrichten*, 25th June 1926.

'Der kranke Hugo Wolf,' *Die Einkehr, Unterhaltungs-Beilage der Münchner Neuesten Nachrichten*, 26th and 29th September 1926.

Hugo Wolf und der Wiener Akademische Wagner-Verein (Regensburg, 1927). Contains many letters.

'My Childhood's Memories of Hugo Wolf,' translated by Marie Boileau, *The Monthly Musical Record*, September 1927. Does not seem to have been published in German.

'Hugo Wolf in Maierling. Zwei ungedruckte Briefe Wolfs aus dem Jahr 1881,' *Almanach der deutschen Musikbücherei auf das Jahr 1922* (Regensburg, 1921). Contains two previously unpublished letters.

Wolf, Hugo

Briefe an Emil Kauffmann, herausgegeben von Edmund Hellmer (Berlin, 1903).

'Hugo Wolfs Briefe an schwäbische Freunde,' *Süddeutsche Monatshefte* (Munich), 1st May 1904.

Wolf, Hugo

Briefe an Hugo Faisst, herausgegeben von Michael Haberlandt (Stuttgart, 1904).

'Ungedruckte Briefe von Hugo Wolf an Paul Müller,' *Jahrbuch der Musikbibliothek Peters für 1904* (Leipzig, 1905).

Briefe an Oskar Grohe, herausgegeben von Heinrich Werner (Berlin, 1905).

Musikalische Kritiken, herausgegeben von Richard Batka und Heinrich Werner (Leipzig, 1912).

Familienbriefe, herausgegeben von Edmund Hellmer (Leipzig, 1912).

'Ein ungedruckter Brief von Hugo Wolf, mitgeteilt von Paul Tausig,' *Der Merker* (Vienna), 1st April 1912. The name of the recipient of the letter is not given. The original, however, was once listed in an autograph dealer's catalogue as a letter to Heinrich Rauchberg.

Briefe an Rosa Mayreder, mit einem Nachwort der Dichterin des 'Corregidors,' herausgegeben von Heinrich Werner (Vienna, 1921).

Briefe an Henriette Lang, nebst den Briefen an deren Gatten, Prof. Joseph Freiherr von Schey, veröffentlicht von Heinrich Werner (Regensburg, 1922).

Briefe an Heinrich Potpeschnigg, herausgegeben von Heinz Nonveiller (Stuttgart, 1923).

'Unveröffentlichte Briefe Hugo Wolfs an seine Mutter und Schwester Käthe, herausgegeben von Heinrich Werner,' *Deutsche Rundschau* (Berlin), November 1925.

'Briefe Hugo Wolfs an seine Schwester Käthe,' *Neue Freie Presse* (Vienna), 25th July 1926.

'Briefe Hugo Wolfs aus dem Irrenhaus. Aus den Erinnerungen Rosa Mayreders, mitgeteilt von Käthe Braun-Prager,' *Die Musik* (Berlin), October 1929. A reprint of the letters included in Rosa Mayreder's 'Hugo Wolfs zweite Oper' (see above).

'Vier Briefe Hugo Wolfs an Dr. Heinrich Welti,' *Schweizerische Musikzeitung* (Berne), February 1947.

For further correspondence of Wolf's see:

F. G. Antal   *Hugo Wolfs erstes Jahr in Wien.*
Julius Bistron   *Hugo Wolf, der tragische Tondichter.*

Curt Böhmer — *Biographisches in zwei unveröffentlichten Briefen Wolfs.*

Anton Bruckner — *Gesammelte Briefe.*

Ernst Decsey — *Aus Hugo Wolfs letzten Jahren.*
Hugo Wolf Miszellen.
Hugo Wolf.

—de— (Decsey) — *Hugo Wolf als Kritiker.*

Friedrich Eckstein — *Alte unnennbare Tage.*

Karl Geiringer — *Hugo Wolf and Frida von Lipperheide.*

Albert Gutmann — *Aus dem Wiener Musikleben*

Karl Heckel — *Hugo Wolf in seinem Verhältnis zu Richard Wagner.*

Robert Hernried — *Hugo Wolf in Mannheim.*
Hugo Wolfs 'Vier Opern.'

W. Kleinschmidt — *Hugo Wolf in Darmstadt.*
Zur Ausstellung von Hugo Wolf Andenken im Foyer des Landestheaters.

M. Klinckerfuss — *Weitere Ergänzungen zu Hugo Wolfs Briefen.*

Karl Krobath — *Ein Schreiben Hugo Wolfs aus kranker Zeit.*

Rosa Mayreder — *Hugo Wolfs zweite Oper.*

Karl Navrátil — *Hugo Wolf.*

Siegfried Ochs — *Geschehenes, Gesehenes.*

Hans W. Rath — *In Memoriam Detlev von Liliencron.*

Wilhelm Schmid — *Ährenlese zur Biographie Hugo Wolfs.*
Hugo Wolf und der Tübinger Kreis.

Wolfgang Schmieder — *Musikerhandschriften in drei Jahrhunderten.*

Gustav Schur — *Erinnerungen an Hugo Wolf.*

Richard Sternfeld — *Zum Gedächtnis eines Meisters des deutschen Liedes.*

Heinrich Werner — *Hugo Wolf in Maierling.*
Hugo Wolf in Perchtoldsdorf.
Hugo Wolf und seine heiligen drei Könige.
Hugo Wolf und der Wiener Akademische Wagner Verein.
'Hugo Wolf in Maierling' (*Almanach der deutschen Musikbücherei auf das Jahr 1922*).

Fritz Zangger — *Das ewige Feuer im fernen Land.*

Hermann Zumpe — *Persönliche Erinnerungen.*

Anon. — *Ein Opernplan Hugo Wolfs.*
Deutsche Nachrichten.
Das Zeitbild.
Radio Woche.
Briefe von Strindberg, Weininger und Hugo Wolf.
Ein unbekannter Brief von Hugo Wolf.

Zangger, Fritz — *Das ewige Feuer im fernen Land* (Celje, 1937).
Contains two early letters of Wolf's to Franz Pecharz.

Zumpe, Hermann   *Persönliche Erinnerungen nebst Mitteilungen aus Tagebüchern und Briefen mit Geleitwort von Ernst von Possart* (Munich, 1905). Contains three letters from Wolf.

Anon.   'Ein Opernplan Hugo Wolfs,' *Der Merker* (Vienna), 1st March 1913. Contains three early letters. The name of the recipient is not given, but it was Dr. G. Winter. The originals are in the possession of the Vienna Gesellschaft der Musikfreunde. These three letters also appeared in the *Wiener Zeitschrift für Musik*, January–February 1908. This number of *Der Merker* contains also a facsimile of an otherwise unpublished letter, the content of which shows it to have been addressed to Moritz Hoernes.

Deutsche Nachrichten (Zagreb), 23rd March 1940, reproduces in facsimile an otherwise unknown letter from Wolf to his mother.

'Ein irrsinniger Componist,' *Neues Wiener Tagblatt*, 9th October 1897.

Radio Woche (Vienna) for 10th–17th March 1935 reproduces in facsimile a letter from Wolf to his sister Käthe.

'Ein unbekannter Brief von Hugo Wolf.' A letter to Emma Fulda, published in an unidentified newspaper of unknown date.

Das Zeitbild (Vienna), 22nd April 1933, contains a facsimile of a card to Wolf's sister Käthe.

'Briefe von Strindberg, Weininger und Hugo Wolf,' *Die Fackel* (Vienna), No. 568–71, May 1921, includes one letter from Wolf to Karl Kraus.

Berichte aus dem Irrenhaus. Aufzeichnungen eines durch dreissig Jahre im Wiener Irrenhaus Internierten über das Schicksal und den Aufenthalt interessanter Anstalts-Insassen. Unter Zugrundelegung von Wärter-Aussagen, ärztlichen Feststellungen, Schilderungen von Mitpatienten und persönlichen Äusserungen, sowie schriftlichen Zeugnissen der behandelten Personen. Vienna, no date (1924). Includes a chapter on Wolf in the asylum.

The Musical Courier (New York), 23rd February 1928. A Hugo Wolf number. Reproduces some unusual photographs.

APPENDIX II

WOLF'S COMPOSITIONS

THE following is as exhaustive a catalogue of Wolf's compositions, published and unpublished, lost and destroyed, as can be prepared to-day. I believe it to be practically complete.

The names of the original publishers, or, in the case of unpublished works, of the possessors of the manuscripts, are indicated by letters in the right-hand column. The date of publication is given in brackets after the letters indicating the publisher's name, so that the presence of a date in this right-hand column shows at once that the work is available in print. Where there is no date, the composition is unpublished, except in a few special cases, indicated in footnotes.

The key to the letters used is as follows:

Publishers:

F.	Fürstner, Berlin.
H.	Heckel, Mannheim.
Hof.	Hofmeister, Leipzig.
L.	Lacom, Vienna.
LK.	Lauterbach & Kuhn, Leipzig.
MWV.	Musikwissenschaftlicher Verlag, Leipzig and Vienna.
P.	Peters, Leipzig.
Sch.	Schott, Mainz.
TJ.	Tischer & Jagenberg, Cologne.
W.	Wetzler, Vienna.

Possessors of Manuscripts:

NLV.	National Library, Vienna.
CLV.	City Library, Vienna.
WWM.	Formerly in Hans Wamlek's Wolf Museum at Windischgraz (Slovenjgradec). Present whereabouts unknown.
GW.	Formerly in the possession of Gilbert Wolf, at Windischgraz; given by him to Walter Woschnagg, Sostanj (Schönstein). Present whereabouts unknown.
S.	Family of Wolf's youngest sister Adrienne.
K.	Köchert family, Vienna.
VK.	Hofrat Prof. Viktor Keldorfer, Vienna.

Most of the original manuscripts of the published works are in the National Library, Vienna. Others are in the City Library, Vienna, and the Prussian State Library, Berlin (Keller songs and orchestral version of *Der Feuerreiter*).

Such manuscripts of famous songs as come into the hands of autograph dealers from time to time are generally only copies made by Wolf for his publishers.

462

The works are here catalogued under the following headings:

I. PIANO MUSIC

Sonata, Op. 1, 1875 . . . . **CLV.**
    MS. incomplete. Adagio in E flat, leading to Allegro in D and Minuet and Trio in E flat.
    Dedicated to Philipp Wolf.
    MS. undated, but other evidence (see pp. 14–15) shows that the sonata was begun at Marburg on 11th April 1875 and continued on 12th, 13th, 15th and 29th April.

Variations, Op. 2, 1875 . . . . **CLV.**
    MS. undated.

Variations (fragment), 1875? . . . . . **CLV.**
    MS. undated. No apparent connection with Op. 2. Variation IV, Moderato, and the beginning of Variation V.

Sonata in D major, Op. 7 (or 8) (unfinished), 1875 . . . . **CLV.**
    Allegro ma non troppo, Allegretto and an unfinished Adagio.
    MS. undated. Op. 8 written in pencil on MS., Op. 7 on a separate cover.

Sonata in G major, Op. 8, 1876 . . . . . **CLV.**
    MS. incomplete. Allegro giocoso, Largo e sostenuto, Scherzo and Trio, and Rondo (allegro). The last pages of the last movement seem to have been lost. Beginning of first movement dated 9th January; beginning of last movement dated 6th February 1876.
    Mentioned by Wolf in the letter to his parents of 15th March 1876.

Fantasie, Op. 11 (unfinished), 1876 . . . . CLV.
 Begins Andante, 22 bars, followed by
 9 bars erased.
 Dated 15th February, 1876.
March for piano duet, Op. 12 (unfinished), 1876 . . . . CLV.
 The first part is complete; only the
 heading of the Trio is written out.
 Dated 16th February 1876.
 The title is illegible on the MS., but
 the work is referred to as a March
 in a note in Wolf's diary (see p.
 38).
Sonata in G minor, Op. 13 (or 14) (un-
 finished), 1876 . . . . CLV.
 Op. 13 on MS., Op. 14 on cover.
 First movement, Allegro maestoso,
 begun on 13th March and finished
 on 31st March. Second movement, Adagio, theme only, 8 bars,
 composed on 1st April.
 Mentioned by Wolf in the letter to his
 parents of 15th March 1876.
Rondo Capriccioso in B flat, Op. 15, 1876 . . . MWV. (1940) [1]
 Begun 4th April, finished 4th June.
 Dedicated, in Greek characters, to
 the Ritter Fischer von Ankern.
 The word 'Fantasie,' which appears
 at the top of the score, after the
 date, is not part of the title of
 the work, as was thought when
 the Wolf Verein catalogue of
 these MSS. was compiled, but
 probably records the place where
 the Rondo Capriccioso was begun.
 There was a favourite café-restaur-
 ant of this name near Schloss Hetzendorf. The place-name 'Hetzendorf' appears at a later point in the
 MS. The Rondo Capriccioso
 was scored by Wolf at Windischgraz in August 1876, and in this
 form was later employed as finale
 of a B flat Symphony.
Wellenspiel (unfinished), 1877 . . . . . S.
 No. 1 of a projected set of *Sechs*

[1] In an appendix to the full score of the Scherzo and Finale (see Wolf's
Symphony in B flat below, p. 471).

Charakterstücke, composed in January. About 60 bars.

Verlegenheit (fragment), 1877   .   .   .   .   CLV.
One of a projected set of *Charakterbilder für das Klavier*. Four bars only, composed in Vienna, 23rd February.

Humoreske, 1877   .   .   .   .   .   .   CLV.
Composed at Windischgraz, 9th–26th September.

Schlummerlied, 1878.   .   .   .   .   .   Sch.   (1910)
Published under the title *Wiegenlied*. No. 1 of *Aus der Kinderzeit, Kleine Stücke für das Pianoforte*. Composed in Vienna on 20th May. The *Schlummerlied* is identical with an *Albumblatt für Frl. Mizzi Werner*, dated 31st July 1880. The latter date is evidently not that of composition.

Scherz und Spiel, 1878   .   .   .   .   .   CLV.
No. 2 of *Aus der Kinderzeit*.
Composed in Vienna on 20th May, the same day as the *Schlummerlied*.
The *Humoreske* above is at present enclosed with these two pieces as part of *Aus der Kinderzeit*, with which, however, it has no real connection.

Fantasie über Lortzings 'Czar und Zimmermann'.   .   .   .   .   .   WWM.
A performance was broadcast from Graz in 1943.

Reiseblätter nach Gedichten von N. Lenau, für das Pianoforte   .   .   .   .   Lost
The title-page only has survived (CLV.). The handwriting is already formed, resembling that of 1878 or 1879.

Fantasie in C (*C minor*), 1878   .   .   .   .   .   Lost
Two title-pages have survived (CLV.), both with the date 1878.

Sonata in F sharp minor, 1879?   .   .   .   .   .   Lost
The title-page only has survived (CLV.). This is not dated. A letter from Wolf to his father of 7th April 1879 says: 'I am now writing a piano sonata, which won't be

bad.' The formed handwriting on
this title-page suggests that it may
be identified with the work referred
to in Wolf's letter.
It seems improbable that this sonata
was ever completed.

*Paraphrase über 'Die Meistersinger von
Nürnberg' von Richard Wagner,*
about 1882 . . . . VK.

*Paraphrase über 'Die Walküre' von
Richard Wagner,* about 1882 . . . . VK.
Both the above 'Paraphrases' were
given by Wolf to Dr. Joseph Reitzes.

Canon, 1882 . . . . NLV.
Composed at Maierling on 6th July.
As letters show, Wolf was at this time
giving piano lessons to Lotte
Preyss. This little canon (with
fingering) was undoubtedly written
for this youthful pupil.

II. SHORT CHORUSES, A CAPPELLA
OR WITH PIANO ACCOMPANIMENT

Wanderlied (Goethe), Op. 4, No. 1, 1875 . . . Lost
Auf dem See (Goethe), Op. 4, No. 2, 1875 . . . Lost
Op. 4 is missing among the early MSS.
Wolf's intention of arranging these
two Goethe songs from Op. 3 for
chorus is shown by remarks on the
MSS. of the songs.
The alto part of the choral version
of *Auf dem See* is all that has sur-
vived (GW.).[1]

Die Stimme des Kindes (Lenau), Op. 10, 1876 . . CLV.
For male voice chorus with piano.
Mentioned by Wolf in a letter to his
parents on 15th March 1876. Probably composed in February.

Im Sommer (Goethe), Op. 13, No. 1, 1876 . . . CLV. and S.
Geistesgruss[2] (Goethe), Op. 13, No. 2, 1876 . . . CLV. and S.
Mailied[3] (Goethe), Op. 13, No. 3, 1876 . . . CLV. and S.
For male voice chorus, unaccom-
panied. Op. 12 on some MSS.

[1] Facsimile in the Zagreb newspaper *Deutsche Nachrichten* for 23rd March 1940.
[2] Published in Heft 3 of the *Festblätter zum 6. deutschen Sängerbundesfest* (Graz, 1902).
[3] Published in Decsey's *Hugo Wolf*, vol. i.

Im Sommer is mentioned in Wolf's letter to his parents of 15th March 1876, which shows that it was begun on 28th February. A fragmentary MS. shows that Wolf began to revise it on 4th December 1876.

Geistesgruss undated, but composed in early March.

Mailied begun on 11th March, finished 3rd April.

These three choruses are dedicated to Philipp Wolf.

Wanderers Nachtlied (Goethe), 1876 .   .   .   .   Lost

Die schöne Nacht (Goethe), 1876   .   .   .   Lost

For male voice chorus, unaccompanied.

Mentioned on the cover of the Goethe choruses, Op. 13, where, however, the *Wanderers Nachtlied* is erased and replaced by *Geistesgruss*. Possibly only projects, never carried out.

Fröhliche Fahrt (Edmund Höfer), Op. 17, No. 1, 1876 .   .   .   .   .   .   CLV.

For mixed chorus, unaccompanied.

Composed 6th–7th May, in the Prater, Vienna. Revised on 6th September at Windischgraz.

Im stillen Friedhof (Ludwig Pfau), 1876   .   .   .   CLV.

For mixed chorus with piano.

Begun 10th May, finished 28th May.

Mailied (fragment), 1876 .   .   .   .   .   .   CLV.

For male voice chorus, unaccompanied.

Seven bars only, composed on 13th June, then erased and begun again as a solo song.

No connection with the *Mailied* (Goethe) above. Text begins: 'Willkommen, lieber, schöner Mai' (Hölty?).

Grablied (Lenz Lorenzi), 1876 .   .   .   .   CLV.

For mixed chorus, unaccompanied.

Undated, but composed in the Lechner Wald, near Windischgraz, in the summer months during the Conservatoire holidays.

Wahlspruch (?) . . . . ?
For male voice chorus.
Listed in Liepmannssohn's catalogue
No. 174 of *Musiker-Autographen*.
Five bars.
In a letter to his parents of 7th April
1883 Wolf writes: 'Gilbert sent me
three *Wahlsprüche* [mottoes], which
I shall set to music (all three). Per-
haps I'll get the 20 ducats.'
A letter from Philipp Wolf of 6th
January 1800 asks Hugo to write a
Wahlspruch for a Gesangverein
founded at Windischgraz: 'For
male voice chorus, and as you
think best, all three lines, or leave
out the top one.' The text of the
Wahlspruch is quoted in Liepmannssohn's catalogue as:
'Das Menschenherz wird nie
  erkalten,
So lang des Liedes Zauber walten.'
Sechs geistliche Lieder nach Gedichten
  von Eichendorff, 1881. . . . . LK. (1903)
For mixed chorus, unaccompanied.
1. *Aufblick*, undated.
2. *Einklang*, composed Vienna, 14th
   April.
3. *Resignation*, composed Vienna,
   1st April.
4. *Letzte Bitte*, composed Vienna,
   22nd April.
5. *Ergebung*, composed Vienna, 28th
   April.
6. *Erhebung*, composed Vienna, 30th
   April.
The published version was revised
by Eugen Thomas. Details of
some variants from a copy of these
choruses found among the posthumous papers of Arnold Mendelssohn were published in *The Music
Review* for November 1941. This
copy differs considerably from that
used by Thomas. The title of the
second chorus is not *Einklang* but
Einkehr, and the order of the fourth
and fifth pieces is reversed. The

conclusion of *Ergebung* is extended by eight bars and the last four bars of *Resignation* are quite different from the version used by Thomas. Mendelssohn's is almost certainly an earlier form of the score, which must have still represented Wolf's intentions up to at least 1890. Wolf's letters show that he thought of publishing the Eichendorff choruses in 1892, and again in 1894. It is very likely that it was on one of these occasions that he revised the work.

III. CHAMBER MUSIC

String Quartet in D major (fragment), 1876 . . . CLV.
32 bars of a Presto, a fugal exposition, dated 9th March.

Piano Quintet (fragment), 1876 . . . . . S.
18 bars, begun at Windischgraz on 13th September, continued in Vienna on 18th October.

Sketches for a Violin Sonata (fragment), 1877 . . . . MWV. (1940) [1]
7 bars in a sketch-book (NLV.), dated 10th November, composed 'in the post-wagon.' Mentioned by Wolf in a letter to his parents of 13th November.

String Quartet in D minor, 1878–84 . . . . LK. (1903)
For a summary of the very complicated and confused history of this work see p. 106 (footnote). Helmut Schultz and Waldemar Rosen (see Bibliography) have expressed the opinion that Josef Hellmesberger, who edited the quartet for its posthumous publication, made unjustifiable alterations in Wolf's text. These allegations are based on an examination of a copy of two movements of the Quartet and a set

---

[1] Published in the critical apparatus accompanying the full score of the Scherzo and Finale, in the mistaken belief that these sketches might have some connection with Wolf's early Symphony.

of parts with corrections in Wolf's hand (VCL.). In this copy the slow movement comes after the scherzo-like *Resolut* movement. But it would be unwise to condemn Hellmesberger's edition before Wolf's original MS. has been rediscovered. The incomplete sketches in the National Library, Vienna, show that the original order of the movements was as Hellmesberger printed them, and a facsimile reproduction of the first page of the MS., which appeared in the Christmas supplement of a Viennese newspaper in 1903,[1] is identical in every detail with the published version. A footnote shows that the MS. in 1903 remained in possession of the publishers, who have, however, long been out of business. Where it is to-day I have not been able to discover.

Intermezzo in E flat, for string quartet, 1886 . . . NLV.

Begun in Vienna, in April, and finished at Murau on 1st October. A letter from Wolf to Grohe on 16th April 1890 referred to this work as a *Humoristisches Intermezzo*. A copy of a score with this title, in the possession of the Vienna Hugo Wolf Verein in 1906, seems to have disappeared.

Serenade in G, for string quartet, 1887 . . . LK. (1903)

Composed in Vienna, 2nd–4th May. The sketches and MSS. (NLV.) all entitle the work, simply, *Serenade*. Wolf referred to it as an *Italienische Serenade* in the letter to Grohe of 16th April 1890, and gave this title also to the orchestral transcription which he made in 1892. There exist a few bars of a projected second movement for the string

---

[1] *Die Weihnachts-Zeit, Beilage zu No. 446 der Wiener Tageszeitung 'Die Zeit' vom 25. Dezember 1903.*

quartet version of the *Serenade*,
dated Perchtoldsdorf, 15th May
1889. (VCL., among some *Corregidor* fragments.)

IV. ORCHESTRAL MUSIC, WORKS FOR CHORUS AND ORCHESTRA, CONCERTOS, ETC.

Violin Concerto, Op. 6 (unfinished), 1875 . . . . CLV.
Not scored.
Maestoso, Scherzo and Trio, and
25 bars of an unfinished Adagio, in
a reduction for violin and piano.
MS. undated. Mentioned in a letter
of December 1875, which, however, refers to *three* completed
movements.

*Orchestral transcription of Beethoven's
'Moonlight' Sonata* (unfinished), 1876 . . . S.
Wolf was working on this at Hetzendorf in July. First movement
begun on 4th, finished on 6th;
second movement begun on 7th,
finished on 9th; last movement
begun on 10th and left incomplete.

Symphony in B flat (*G minor*) (fragments), 1876–7 . . . . MWV. (1940)
For the complicated history of this
work see pp. 42–3 and pp. 48–50.
A Scherzo and Finale have been published, the latter being an orchestral
version of the Rondo Capriccioso
for piano. The scoring of the
Finale was completed by the editor,
Helmut Schultz. An appendix to
the full score includes all the surviving fragments of other movements of the Symphony in its
earlier form (B flat) and later form
(G minor).

Overture on Byron's 'The Corsair,' 1877–8 . . Lost
Mentioned in Wolf's letters to his
father of 2nd January and 17th
February 1878, from the first of
which we learn that the first
sketches dated from 27th December
1877.

Q

A theme in a sketch-book (NLV.),
dated 14th January 1878, reproduced in the appendix to the full
score of the Scherzo and Finale (see
Symphony above), was undoubtedly intended for *The Corsair*, and
not for the Symphony.

Die Stunden verrauschen (Gottfried
Kinkel), for *soli*, chorus and or-
chestra (unfinished), 1878.   .   .   .   . CLV.

Mentioned by Wolf in a letter to his
parents on 10th April as 'almost
completely sketched out.' The
surviving fragment consists of
twelve and a half pages, of which
ten and a half pages are fully
scored. On the last two pages only
the voice parts are written out.
Dated at the beginning 'Vienna,
27th March 1878,' and at the top of
the seventh page 'Waidhofen a.d.
Ybbs, 11th September 1878.'

Symphony in F minor, 1879   .   .   .   . Lost

Mentioned by Wolf in a letter to his
father on 10th May 1879.

It seems improbable that this Symphony was taken very far.

Penthesilea, symphonic poem after the
tragedy of Heinrich von Kleist,
1883–5 .   .   .   . LK.   (1903)
                                                          and MWV. (1937)

For a discussion of the probable dates
of composition see the footnote on
p. 144.

The version published in 1903 was
revised and cut. That published
in 1937 represents Wolf's original
intentions, except that it includes
the revisions of the scoring made by
him in Dr. Svetlin's asylum in
1897.

An additional Interlude for inclusion
in this work was composed in the
asylum in 1897 and later destroyed
by Wolf himself.

Christnacht (Platen), for *soli*, chorus,
and orchestra, 1886–9.   .   .   .   . LK.   (1903)

Begun on 24th December 1886,
finished in May 1889.

Elfenlied (Shakespeare), for soprano
solo, women's chorus and or-
chestra, 1889–91 . . . . F.   (1894)
Composed 11th May 1889, scored
in October 1891. Probably originally intended for an opera based
on *A Midsummer Night's Dream.*
Translation by A. W. von Schlegel.

Der Feuerreiter (Mörike), Ballad for
chorus and orchestra, 1892 . . . . . Sch.   (1894)
An elaboration of the song of 1888,
completed in October and November 1892.

Dem Vaterland (Reinick), for male
voice chorus and orchestra, 1890–8 . . . Sch.   (1895)
Originally a song, composed 12th   (vocal score)
May 1890. Choral arrangement   and H. (1902)
made at about the same time and   (full score)
scoring completed, according to a
letter, on 4th June. This version
remains unpublished (NLV.). In
May and June 1894 a second version was completed and this in its
turn was revised in 1897 and again
in 1898.

Italienische Serenade, for small orchestra, 1892 . . . . LK.   (1903)
An arrangement of the *Serenade*
for string quartet of 1887. First
mentioned in a letter to Strecker of
10th February 1892. Wolf was
working on it at Döbling in April
and May of that year and it seems
likely that he completed it at that
time, although the evidence is not
decisive. It then became the first
movement of a projected suite in
several movements. Various fragments of other movements are
known:
(*a*) NLV. A sketch on two staves,
but with indication of orchestration, 30 bars composed at Döbling
on 5th January 1893, the beginning
of a 'second movement,' *Langsam,
klagend*, in G minor and 4–4 time.
(*b*) Mentioned by Decsey, vol. iii,
p. 153. 28 bars for orchestra,

scored at Traunkirchen on 2nd July
1893. Again a slow movement, but
whether identical with the above
(*a*) is uncertain, as the MS., at
one time in the possession of the
Vienna Hugo Wolf Verein, has
disappeared.

(*c*) NLV. A sketch on two and
three staves, with indications of orchestration, 43 complete bars and
2 bars with one part only sketched
in, in G major and 6–8 time, composed on 8th March 1894. There
is no heading, but a letter to Frieda
Zerny of 12th March quotes the
opening theme, with the indication
presto, and says that the movement
was 'intended to take the place of a
scherzo' in the *Italian Serenade*.
Letters to Grohe of 16th March
and 9th June 1894 show that this
movement was actually completed
by Wolf, but only this sketch of its
beginning has survived.

(*d*) CLV. Five and a half pages in
full score, not in Wolf's hand, the
beginning of a 'third movement,'
Tarantella. The string parts are
complete to the 40th bar, the others
to the 37th. Dated 2nd December
1897.

For a discussion of Reger's editing
of the *Italienische Serenade* for its
posthumous publication see pp.
309–10.

Wächterlied auf der Wartburg (Scheffel),
for male voice chorus and orchestra (unfinished), 1894 . . . . . NLV.

Sketches and fragments survive.

Referred to by Wolf in letters to
Sternfeld on 14th July and to
Kauffmann on 16th July. One page
of sketches is dated 5th July 1894.
An arrangement of the song of 1887.

Morgenhymnus (Reinick), for mixed
chorus and orchestra, 1897. . . . . P. (1910)

An arrangement of the song *Morgenstimmung* of 1896.

MS. (CLV.) dated 12th, 13th, 14th, 15th, 16th and 17th December, when Wolf was in Dr. Svetlin's asylum.
The published version was revised by Willibald Kähler.

Dritte Italienische Serenade (unfinished), 1897 . . . . NLV.

Including indicated repetitions, 170 bars of the first movement of this work exist, written out on two staves, with indications of the intended orchestration. MS. dated 18th December 1897. Material taken from two pages of MS. (also NLV.) containing 23 'Themes from October and November of the year 1897.'

In a sketch-book (NLV.), mostly devoted to *Penthesilea* (1883), is a fragment of 40 bars, dated 20th December 1897, introducing *Funiculì, Funiculà*. It seems likely that this was intended to form part of the *Third Italian Serenade*.

V. OPERAS AND INCIDENTAL MUSIC

König Alboin, Romantic Opera in 4 Acts (unfinished), 1876–7 . . . . . Lost

Mentioned by Wolf in a letter to Anna Vinzenzberg of 31st August 1876. All that survives is a half-sheet of MS. with 21 bars of music accompanying a duel in the third act, dated Windischgraz, 9th April 1877 (NLV.). The libretto was by Paul Peitl.

Incidental Music to Kleist's 'Prinz Friedrich von Homburg' (unfinished), 1884 . . . . CLV.

Two fragments survive:

I. *Trauermusik* for the end of Act II. 20 bars in full score, dated Schladming, 30th August 1884.

II. *Melodram: 'Das Leben nennt der Derwisch eine Reise,'* Act IV, Scene iii (complete). Dated Schloss Gstatt, 22nd August 1884.

In a sketch-book (NLV.) occurs a fine theme, dated Schladming, 4th September 1884, undoubtedly intended for this work.

Incidental Music to Ibsen's 'The Feast at Solhaug,' 1890–1 . . . . . . H. (1903)

I. Introduction.

II. Margit's Ballad, *Bergkönig ritt durch die Landeweit.*

III. Gudmund's first song, *Ich wandelte sinnend allein.*

IV. March and Chorus, *Bei Sang und Spiel.*

V. Introduction and Chorus, *Nun streichet die Fiedel.*

VI. Chorus, *Es locket ins Freie.*

VII. Gudmund's second song, *Ich fuhr wohl über Wasser.*

VIII. Introduction to Act III.

IX. Chorus, *Wir wünschen Fried und Glück.*

X. Chorus, *Gottes Auge wacht.*

For the dates on the (incomplete) sketches (NLV.) see footnote on p. 280.

German translation of Ibsen by Emma Klingenfeld. The three songs were published separately by the composer, with certain alterations, in 1897.

Der Corregidor, Opera in 4 Acts, 1895 . . . H. (1896)
Text by Rosa Mayreder, after Alarcon's *El Sombrero de tres Picos.* (vocal score)
and H. (1904)
(full score)

Manuel Venegas, unfinished Opera, 1897 . . . H. (1902)
Text by Moritz Hoernes, after Alarcon's *El Niño de la Bola.* (vocal score)

The vocal score of the fragmentary first act is published. The full score of the Spring Chorus, in Wolf's scoring, completed by F. Langer, was issued separately in 1904 (H.). The incomplete MS. score of this chorus (CLV.) is dated 6th January 1898.

VI. SONGS, ETC.

(a) UNPUBLISHED OR POSTHUMOUSLY PUBLISHED

Das taube Mütterlein (fragment)   .   .   . no date WWM.
Soldatenlied (fragment)   .   .   .   . no date WWM.
Der Morgen (fragment)   .   .   .   . no date WWM.
Frühlingslied .   .   .   .   .   . no date Lost
    Title-page only, in Philipp Wolf's
    handwriting, is known (WWM.).
Die Sterne (voice part only)   .   .   . no date S.
Gebet (voice part only)   .   .   .   . no date S.
    A setting of Friedrich Kind's 'Leise,
    leise, fromme Weise,' from *Der
    Freischütz.*

All the above are very early works, from 1875 or earlier.

*Fragments of a ballad-like composition
    for soprano, baritone and piano*   .   . no date CLV.
    6 pages, without beginning or end.
    About 1875.
Meine Harfe [1]   .   .   .   . ? Hof.   (1903)
    Described as a 'Lied-Entwurf von
    Hugo Wolf, in versuchsweiser
    Neuschöpfung   vollendet   von
    August Ludwig.'
Nacht und Grab (Zschokke), Op. 3,
    No. 1   .   .   .   . 1875 CLV.
Sehnsucht (Goethe), Op. 3, No. 2   .   .   . 1875 CLV.
Der Fischer (Goethe), Op. 3, No. 3   .   .   . 1875 CLV.
Wanderlied (Goethe), Op. 3, No. 4   .   .   . 1875 CLV.
Auf dem See (Goethe), Op. 3, No. 5 .   .   . 1875 CLV.
Der Raubschütz (Lenau), Op. 5 (un-
    finished) .   .   .   . 1875–6 CLV.
    The opus number suggests it was
    begun in 1875. Mentioned in
    Wolf's diary, entry of 13th Febru-
    ary 1876. Revised, according to
    one MS., on 24th June 1876.
Frühlingsgrüsse (Lenau)   .   .   .   3 Jan. 1876 CLV.
    Erroneously dated 1875 by Wolf.
    Originally Op. 6, then Op. 9, No. 1,
    but eventually excluded from Op.
    9. Two versions, of which one is
    incomplete, exist in MS.

[1] I have not seen this curiosity. August Ludwig was editor of the *Neue
Berliner Musikzeitung* at the time of Wolf's second visit to Berlin, in 1894, but
there is no record of the two men having met.   Ludwig earned rather dubious
fame by a completion of Schubert's 'Unfinished' Symphony, consisting of a
'Philosopher's Scherzo' and 'March of Fate.'

Meeresstille (Lenau), Op. 9, No. 1 . . . 1876 CLV.
    MS. undated.
Liebesfrühling (Lenau), Op. 9, No. 2 . 29 Jan. 1876 CLV.
Erster Verlust (Goethe), Op. 9, No. 3 . 30 Jan. 1876 CLV.
Abendglöcklein (Vincenz Zusner), Op. 9,
    No. 4 . . . . . . 18 Mar.–
    Although part of Op. 9 according   24 Apr. 1876 CLV.
    to Wolf's cover for this group of
    songs, this opus number is erased
    on the MS., and replaced first by
    Op. 13, and then by Op. 14.
Mai (Goethe), Op. 9, No. 5 (unfinished)   25 Apr. 1876 CLV.
    Two versions exist, neither quite
    complete. Revised on 1st May
    1876.
Der goldene Morgen, Op. 9, No. 6 . 1 May 1876 NLV.
    Mentioned on the cover of Op. 9
    (CLV.), but survives only in a
    sketch-book from 1876–8
    (NLV.).
Perlenfischer (Otto Roquette) . . 3 May 1876 NLV.
    In the same sketch-book as the
    above.
Mailied (unfinished) . . . . 13 June 1876 CLV.
    18 bars, all erased. Originally for
    chorus.
'*Horch, wie still es wird im dunklen*
    Hain' (Lenau) . . . . 1876 or 1877 CLV.
    Lenau's title is *Stille Sicherheit*.
    MS. undated. The handwriting is
    not the earliest, and the fact that
    the song is for baritone suggests
    that it is about contemporaneous
    with *Ein Grab* and the three Heine
    songs of December 1876.
'*Als ein unergründlich Wonnemeer*'
    (Lenau) . . . . 1876 or 1877 CLV.
    On the back of the above. Lenau's
    title is *Scheideblick*. MS. undated.
    A fragment of an orchestral version
    exists (S.).
Ein Grab (Paul Peitl)   Vienna 8–10 Dec. 1876 MWV. (1936)
    On one MS. the poet's name is
    given as Paul Günther—a pseudo-
    nym of Peitl's.
Mädchen mit dem roten Mündchen
    (Heine) . . . . . 17 Dec. 1876 MWV. (1936)
Du bist wie eine Blume (Heine) . . 18 Dec. 1876 MWV. (1936)

Wenn ich in deine Augen seh (Heine)   .   21 Dec. 1876 MWV. (1936)
[*Ghasel* (Platen), dated 17th August
1876, and published by MWV.
(1936), is not by Wolf.[1]]
Bescheidene Liebe   .   .   .   .   1876 or 1877 LK.   (1903)
   MS. undated.
Abendbilder (three odes by Lenau)   .   4 Jan.–
                              24 Feb. 1877 MWV. (1936)
Ständchen (Körner)   Windischgraz   25 Mar.–
   One MS. is dated 5th March, but   12 Apr. 1877 MWV. (1936)
   this seems to have been an error in
   copying.
Andenken (Matthisson)   Windischgraz 23–25 Apr. 1877 MWV. (1936)
An * (Lenau)   Windischgraz   27 Apr.–
                             8 May 1877 LK.   (1903)
Wanderlied ('aus einem alten Lieder-
   buche')   Windischgraz 14–15 June 1877 LK.   (1903)
Die Verlassene [2] (unfinished)
             Windischgraz   19 June 1877 S.
   17 bars.
Der Schwalben Heimkehr (Herlossohn)   Aug.–
   Begun at Windischgraz, completed in   29 Dec. 1877 MWV. (1936)
   Vienna.
Das Lied der Waise (Friedrich Steine-
   bach) (unfinished) Windischgraz   10 Oct. 1877 CLV.
   31 bars.
Wunsch (Lenau) (unfinished)   Vienna   26 Nov. 1877 CLV.
   52 bars.
Traurige Wege (Lenau)   Vienna 22–25 Jan. 1878 LK.   (1903)
   One MS. has the additional date 3rd
   February 1878.
So wahr die Sonne scheint (Rückert).   8 Feb. 1878 CLV.
Ich sah die blaue unendliche See (Hoff-
   mann von Fallersleben) (fragment)   15 Feb. 1878 CLV.
   6 bars only.
Nächtliche Wanderung (Lenau)   .   . 19–21 Feb. 1878 LK.   (1903)
   Dated 19th February on one MS.,
   21st February on another. The
   latter also bears a third date, 11th
   March.
Auf der Wanderschaft (Chamisso)
              Vienna 20–23 Mar. 1878 CLV.
   Two versions exist in MS., with
   rhythmic differences.

---

[1] See '*Ghasel*—a song wrongly attributed to Wolf,' *The Musical Times*, August
1947.
[2] The MS. is reproduced in Batka and Nagel's *Allgemeine Geschichte der Musik*
(Stuttgart, 1909–15), Band III, p. 252.
   * Q

Was soll ich sagen? [1] (Chamisso) (un-finished) 31 bars.	Vienna	1 Apr.–4 May	1878	CLV.
Geschiedensein . . . . . . Mentioned by Wolf in a letter to his parents of 10th April 1878.		.	1878	Lost
Das Kind am Brunnen (Hebbel)	Vienna	16–27 Apr.	1878	LK. (1903)
Knabentod (Hebbel)	Vienna	3–6 May	1878	MWV. (1936)
Sie haben heut Abend Gesellschaft (Heine)	Vienna	18–25 May	1878	TJ. (1927)
Über Nacht (Sturm)	Vienna	23–24 May	1878	LK. (1903)
Ich stand in dunkeln Träumen (Heine)	Vienna	26–29 May	1878	LK. (1903)
Das ist ein Brausen und Heulen (Heine)	Vienna	31 May	1878	LK. (1903)
Wo ich bin, mich rings umdunkelt (Heine)	Vienna	3–4 June	1878	LK. (1903)
Aus meinen grossen Schmerzen (Heine)	Vienna	5 June	1878	LK. (1903)
Mir träumte von einem Königskind (Heine)	Vienna	16 June	1878	TJ. (1927)
Mein Liebchen, wir sassen beisammen (Heine) . . . . . . Precise date of composition unas-certainable. The MS. belonged to Walter Krieg and was destroyed by fire in 1945, during the battle for Vienna. The MS. of the *Lieder-strauss* (formerly in the Heyer Museum, Cologne), which includes this and six of the other Heine songs, gives the date 'Summer 1878' for the whole collection. The six other songs were composed in the order in which they appear in the *Liederstrauss*. This makes it seem likely that *Mein Liebchen, wir sassen beisammen* was com-posed between 16th and 22nd June.		.	1878	TJ. (1927)
Es blasen die blauen Husaren (Heine)	Vienna	22 June	1878	TJ. (1927)
Manch Bild vergessener Zeiten (Heine) (unfinished) 30 bars.	Vienna	24 June	1878	CLV.

[1] Reproduced in facsimile in Heinrich Werner's *Der Hugo Wolf Verein in Wien* (Regensburg, 1921).

Frühling, Liebster (Rückert) (unfinished) Vienna 34 bars.	20 July 1878	CLV.
Liebesfrühling (Hoffmann von Fallersleben) Waidhofen	9 Aug. 1878	MWV. (1936)
Auf der Wanderung (Hoffmann von Fallersleben) Waidhofen	10 Aug. 1878	MWV. (1936)
Ja, die Schönst! Ich sagt es offen (Hoffmann von Fallersleben) Waidhofen	11 Aug. 1878	MWV. (1936)
Gretchen vor dem Andachtsbild der Mater Dolorosa (Goethe) Waidhofen	22 Aug.– 9 Sept. 1878	MWV. (1936)
Nach dem Abschiede (Hoffmann von Fallersleben) Waidhofen	31 Aug.– 1 Sept. 1878	MWV. (1936)
Die Nachtigallen schweigen (Hoffmann von Fallersleben) (fragment) Waidhofen 4 bars only.	10 Sept. 1878	CLV.
Es war ein alter König (Heine) Vienna	4 Oct. 1878	LK. (1903)
Mit schwarzen Segeln (Heine) Vienna	6 Oct. 1878	MWV. (1936)
Spätherbstnebel (Heine) Vienna	7 Oct. 1878	MWV. (1936)
Ernst ist der Frühling (Heine) Vienna	13–17 Oct. 1878	LK. (1903)
Schön Hedwig (Hebbel)	?	Lost
Mentioned on an existing title-page (K.) for *Drei Balladen von Friedrich Hebbel*, the other two being *Das Kind am Brunnen* and *Knabentod*, above.		
Der Kehraus (Eichendorff)	?	Lost
Das zerbrochene Ringlein (Eichendorff) . .	?	Lost
Der traurige Jäger (Eichendorff) . . .	?	Lost
The title-page of the above three *Romanzen von J. v. Eichendorff* has survived (K.).		
Der schwere Abend (Lenau)	?	Lost
Verschwiegene Liebe (Eichendorff) . . .	?	Lost
The above two songs are mentioned on an existing title-page (K.) for two volumes of *Lieder u. Gesänge nach Lenau u. Eichendorff*. A sketch of the voice part of *Verschwiegene Liebe* (quite distinct from the setting of 1888) survives (CLV., *Konvolut von Skizzen*, No. 29).		

Acht Lieder aus 'Des Knaben Wunder-
horn' . . . . ? Lost
Only the title-page is known (WWM.)
[*Wiegenlied* ('Su, su, su, du Wind-
chen') is an arrangement by Hum-
perdinck, to words by Adelheid
Wette, of Wolf's piano piece
Schlummerlied (see p. 465).]

Herbstentschluss (Lenau) Windischgraz		8 July 1879	MWV. (1936)
Frage nicht (Lenau) Windischgraz		21 July 1879	MWV. (1936)
Herbst (Lenau) Windischgraz		24 July 1879	MWV. (1936)
Herbstklage (Lenau) (unfinished)			
Windischgraz		11 Sept. 1879	CLV.

42 bars.

Wie des Mondes Abbild zittert (Heine)
    Vienna   13 Feb. 1880   MWV. (1936)
Der   kriegslustige   Waffenschmied
    (Lenau) (fragment)   Vienna   28 May 1880   NLV.
18 bars.
Nachruf (Eichendorff)   Vienna   7 June 1880   MWV. (1936)
Nachtgruss (Eichendorff) (unfinished)
    Vienna   2 Nov. 1880   CLV.
30 bars.
Sterne mit den goldnen Füsslein (Heine)
    Vienna   26 Nov. 1880   MWV. (1936)
Das gelbe Laub erzittert (Heine) (frag-
    ment)   Vienna   7 Dec. 1880 (?) CLV.
8 bars.
Suschens Vogel (Mörike)   Vienna   24 Dec. 1880   MWV. (1936)
An die Wolke (Lenau) (fragment)
    Vienna   7 Jan. 1881   NLV.
1 bar only.
A variant to *Mir träumte von einem*
    Königskind (Heine) . . .   20 Jan. 1881   NLV.
9 bars, replacing bars 10–18 in the
setting of 1878.
In der Fremde I ('Da fahr ich still im
    Wagen') (Eichendorff)
    Windischgraz   27 June 1881   MWV. (1936)
In der Fremde II ('Ich geh' durch die
    dunklen Gassen') (Eichendorff)
    (fragment)   Vienna   3 Feb. 1882   NLV.
Not identical with the setting of the
same poem listed below.   18 bars.
Wohin mit der Freud'? (Reinick) Vienna   31 Dec. 1882   MWV. (1936)
Rückkehr (Eichendorff)   Vienna   12 Jan. 1883   MWV. (1936)
Ständchen (Reinick)   Vienna   19 Jan. 1883   MWV. (1936)
Nachtgruss (Reinick)   Vienna   24 Jan. 1883   MWV. (1936)

In der Fremde VI ('Wolken, wälderwärts gegangen') (Eichendorff)

	Vienna	30 Jan. 1883 MWV. (1936)
Frühlingsglocken (Reinick)	Vienna	19 Feb. 1883 MWV. (1936)
Liebesbotschaft (Reinick)	Vienna	18 Mar. 1883 MWV. (1936)
Liebchen, wo bist du? (Reinick)	Vienna	12 Apr. 1883 MWV. (1936)

In der Fremde II ('Ich geh' durch die
dunklen Gassen') (Eichendorff)

	Vienna	3 May 1883 MWV. (1936)

Die Tochter der Heide (Mörike)

	Rinnbach-Ebensee	11 July 1884 MWV. (1936)
Die Kleine (Eichendorff)	Vienna	8 Mar. 1887 MWV. (1936)

Die Spröde (Goethe) (fragment)

	Döbling	13–14 Feb. 1889 NLV.

10 bars of piano introduction, distinct from the setting in the Goethe
volume. Dated 13th February on
one MS., 14th on another.

Dem Vaterland (Reinick) Perchtoldsdorf   12 May 1890 CLV.
The MS. in the City Library, Vienna,
is only a copy, not in Wolf's hand.
The first page of Wolf's MS. is
reproduced in the German translation of Ernest Newman's *Hugo
Wolf*. At the time of the publication of that book it was in the possession of Heinrich Potpeschnigg.
Present whereabouts unknown.

Frohe Botschaft (Reinick) Unterach   25 June 1890 MWV. (1936)
Irdische und himmlische Liebe (Michel-
angelo, trans. Robert-Tornow)   Mar.–Apr. 1897 Lost
Mentioned by Wolf in a letter to Paul
Müller on 6th April 1897. Des-
troyed by the composer.

(b) PUBLISHED BY THE COMPOSER

Sechs Lieder für eine Frauenstimme .   .   .   .   . W. (1888)

Morgentau ('aus einem alten Liederbuche'[1]	Windischgraz	6–19 June 1877
Die Spinnerin (Rückert)	Vienna	5–12 Apr. 1878
Das Vöglein (Hebbel)	Vienna	2 May 1878
Mausfallensprüchlein (Mörike)	Maierling	18 June 1882
Wiegenlied im Sommer (Reinick)	Vienna	17 Dec. 1882
Wiegenlied im Winter (Reinick)	Vienna	20 Dec. 1882

[1] Of five MS. copies of *Morgentau* (NLV. and CLV.), two give the name of the
poet as Albert Reinhold. On one of these this name is erased. All the
complete copies bear the date 19th June, but the melody alone, not quite in its
final form, appears already in a sketch-book (NLV.) with the date 6th June.

Sechs Gedichte von Scheffel, Mörike, Goethe und Kerner . . W. (1888)

Zur Ruh, zur Ruh! (Kerner)	Vienna	16 June 1883
Der König bei der Krönung (Mörike)	Vienna	13 Mar. 1886
Biterolf (Scheffel)	Vienna	26 Dec. 1886
Wächterlied auf der Wartburg (Scheffel)	Vienna	24 Jan. 1887
Wanderers Nachtlied (Goethe)	Vienna	30 Jan. 1887
Beherzigung ('Feiger Gedanken') (Goethe)	Vienna	1 Mar. 1887

Gedichte von Eduard Mörike . . . . . W. (1889)

Der Tambour	Perchtoldsdorf	16 Feb. 1888
Der Knabe und das Immlein	Perchtoldsdorf	22 Feb. 1888
Jägerlied	Perchtoldsdorf	22 Feb. 1888
Ein Stündlein wohl vor Tag	Perchtoldsdorf	22 Feb. 1888
Der Jäger	Perchtoldsdorf	23 Feb. 1888
Nimmersatte Liebe	Perchtoldsdorf	24 Feb. 1888
Auftrag	Perchtoldsdorf	24 Feb. 1888
Zur Warnung	Perchtoldsdorf	25 Feb. 1888
Lied vom Winde	Perchtoldsdorf	29 Feb. 1888
Bei einer Trauung	Perchtoldsdorf	1 Mar. 1888
Zitronenfalter im April	Perchtoldsdorf	6 Mar. 1888
Der Genesene an die Hoffnung	Perchtoldsdorf	6 Mar. 1888
Elfenlied	Perchtoldsdorf	7 Mar. 1888
Der Gärtner	Perchtoldsdorf	7 Mar. 1888
Abschied	Perchtoldsdorf	8 Mar. 1888
Denk' es o Seele	Perchtoldsdorf	10 Mar. 1888
Auf einer Wanderung	Perchtoldsdorf	11 Mar.[1] 1888
Gebet	Perchtoldsdorf	13 Mar. 1888
Verborgenheit	Perchtoldsdorf	13 Mar. 1888
Lied eines Verliebten	Perchtoldsdorf	14 Mar. 1888
Selbstgeständnis	Perchtoldsdorf	17 Mar. 1888
Erstes Liebeslied eines Mädchens	Perchtoldsdorf	20 Mar. 1888
Fussreise	Perchtoldsdorf	21 Mar. 1888
Rat einer Alten	Perchtoldsdorf	22 Mar. 1888
Begegnung	Perchtoldsdorf	22 Mar. 1888
Das verlassene Mägdlein	Perchtoldsdorf	24 Mar. 1888
Storchenbotschaft	Perchtoldsdorf	27 Mar. 1888
Frage und Antwort	Perchtoldsdorf	29 Mar. 1888
Lebewohl	Perchtoldsdorf	31 Mar. 1888
Heimweh	Perchtoldsdorf	1 Apr. 1888
Seufzer	Perchtoldsdorf	12 Apr. 1888
Auf ein altes Bild	Perchtoldsdorf	14 Apr. 1888
An eine Äolsharfe	Perchtoldsdorf	15 Apr. 1888
Um Mitternacht	Perchtoldsdorf	20 Apr. 1888
Auf eine Christblume I	Perchtoldsdorf	21 Apr. 1888
Peregrina I	Perchtoldsdorf	28 Apr. 1888

[1] According to Decsey, vol. ii, pp. 15–16, this song was not completed until a fortnight after this date.

Peregrina II	Perchtoldsdorf	30 Apr.	1888
Agnes	Perchtoldsdorf	3 May	1888
Er ist's	Perchtoldsdorf	5 May	1888
In der Frühe	Perchtoldsdorf	5 May	1888
Im Frühling	Perchtoldsdorf	8 May	1888
Nixe Binsefuss	Perchtoldsdorf	13 May	1888
Die Geister am Mummelsee	Perchtoldsdorf	18 May	1888
An den Schlaf	Unterach	4 Oct.	1888
Neue Liebe	Unterach	4 Oct.	1888
Zum neuen Jahre	Unterach	5 Oct.	1888
Schlafendes Jesuskind	Unterach	6 Oct.	1888
Wo find' ich Trost?	Unterach	6 Oct.	1888
Karwoche	Unterach	8 Oct.	1888
Gesang Weylas	Unterach	9 Oct.	1888
Der Feuerreiter	Unterach	10 Oct.	1888
An die Geliebte	Unterach	11 Oct.	1888
Auf eine Christblume II	Perchtoldsdorf	26 Nov.	1888
Gedichte von Eichendorff		. L. (1889)	
Erwartung	Vienna	26 Jan.	1880
Die Nacht	Vienna	3 Feb.	1880
Der Soldat II	Vienna	14 Dec.	1886
Der Soldat I	Vienna	7 Mar.	1887
Die Zigeunerin	Vienna	19 Mar.	1887
Waldmädchen	Vienna	20 Apr.	1887
Nachtzauber	Vienna	24 May	1887
Verschwiegene Liebe	Vienna	31 Aug.	1888
Der Schreckenberger	Composed in the Retten-bach-Wildniss, near Ischl	14 Sept.	1888
Der Glücksritter	Composed in the post-wagon on the road from Ischl to Weissenbach	16 Sept.	1888
Seemanns Abschied	Unterach	21 Sept.	1888
Der Scholar	Unterach	22 Sept.	1888
Der Musikant	Unterach	22 Sept.	1888
Der verzweifelte Liebhaber	Unterach	23 Sept.	1888
Unfall	Unterach	25 Sept.	1888
Der Freund	Unterach	26 Sept.	1888
Liebesglück	Unterach	27 Sept.	1888
Das Ständchen	Unterach	28 Sept.	1888
Heimweh	Unterach	29 Sept.	1888
Lieber alles	Unterach	29 Sept.	1888

Erwartung, Die Nacht and *Waldmädchen* were withdrawn by the composer from the revised edition of 1898, but reprinted posthumously (H. 1904).

Gedichte von Goethe . . . . L. (1890)		
Harfenspieler I	Vienna	27 Oct. 1888
Harfenspieler II	Vienna	29 Oct. 1888
Harfenspieler III	Vienna	30 Oct. 1888
Philine	Vienna	30 Oct. 1888
Spottlied	Vienna	2 Nov. 1888
Anakreons Grab	Vienna	4 Nov. 1888
Der Schäfer	Vienna	4 Nov. 1888
Der Rattenfänger	Vienna	6 Nov. 1888
Gleich und Gleich	Vienna	6 Nov. 1888
Dank des Paria	Vienna	9 Nov. 1888
Frech und Froh I	Vienna	14 Nov. 1888
St. Nepomuks Vorabend	Vienna	15 Nov. 1888
Gutmann und Gutweib	Vienna	28 Nov. 1888
Ritter Kurts Brautfahrt	Döbling	9 Dec. 1888
Der Sänger	Döbling	14 Dec. 1888
Mignon ('Kennst du das Land?')	Döbling	17 Dec. 1888
Mignon II	Döbling	18 Dec. 1888
Mignon I	Döbling	19 Dec. 1888
Frühling übers Jahr	Döbling	21 Dec. 1888
Mignon III	Döbling	22 Dec. 1888
Epiphanias	Döbling	27 Dec. 1888
Cophtisches Lied I	Döbling	28 Dec. 1888
Cophtisches Lied II	Döbling	28 Dec. 1888
Beherzigung	Döbling	30 Dec. 1888
Blumengruss	Döbling	31 Dec. 1888
Prometheus	Döbling	2 Jan. 1889
Königlich Gebet	Döbling	7 Jan. 1889
Grenzen der Menschheit	Döbling	9 Jan. 1889
Ganymed	Döbling	11 Jan. 1889
Was in der Schenke waren heute	Döbling	16 Jan. 1889
Solang man nüchtern ist	Döbling	16 Jan. 1889
Ob der Koran von Ewigkeit sei?	Döbling	17 Jan. 1889
Sie haben wegen der Trunkenheit	Döbling	18 Jan. 1889
Trunken müssen wir alle sein	Döbling	18 Jan. 1889
Phänomen	Döbling	19 Jan. 1889
Erschaffen und Beleben	Döbling	21 Jan. 1889
Nicht Gelegenheit macht Diebe	Döbling	21 Jan. 1889
Hochbeglückt in deiner Liebe	Döbling	23 Jan. 1889
Wie sollt' ich heiter bleiben	Döbling	23 Jan. 1889
Als ich auf dem Euphrat schiffte	Döbling	24 Jan. 1889
Dies zu deuten bin erbötig	Döbling	24 Jan. 1889
Wenn ich dein gedenke	Döbling	25 Jan. 1889
Komm, Liebchen, komm	Döbling	25 Jan. 1889
Hätt' ich irgend wohl bedenken	Döbling	26 Jan. 1889
Locken, haltet mich gefangen	Döbling	29 Jan. 1889
Nimmer will ich dich verlieren	Döbling	30 Jan. 1889
Frech und Froh II	Döbling	2 Feb. 1889

Der neue Amadis	Döbling	5 Feb. 1889
Genialisch Treiben	Döbling	10 Feb. 1889
Die Bekehrte	Döbling	12 Feb. 1889
Die Spröde	Perchtoldsdorf	21 Oct. 1889

Spanisches Liederbuch, nach Heyse und Geibel . .		Sch. (1891)
Wer sein holdes Lieb verloren (Anon., trans. Geibel)	Perchtoldsdorf	28 Oct. 1889
Ich fuhr über Meer, ich zog über Land (Anon., trans. Heyse)	Perchtoldsdorf	31 Oct. 1889
Preciosas Sprüchlein gegen Kopfweh (Cervantes, trans. Heyse)	Perchtoldsdorf	31 Oct. 1889
Wenn du zu den Blumen gehst (Anon., trans. Heyse)	Perchtoldsdorf	1 Nov. 1889
Alle gingen, Herz, zur Ruh (Anon., trans. Geibel)	Perchtoldsdorf	2 Nov. 1889
Nun wandre, Maria (Ocaña, trans. Heyse)	Perchtoldsdorf	4 Nov. 1889
Die ihr schwebet um diese Palmen (Lope de Vega, trans. Geibel)	Perchtoldsdorf	5 Nov. 1889
Die du Gott gebarst, du Reine (Nicolas Nuñez, trans. Heyse)	Perchtoldsdorf	5 Nov. 1889
Bedeckt mich mit Blumen (Anon., trans. Geibel)	Perchtoldsdorf	10 Nov. 1889
Seltsam ist Juanas Weise (Anon., trans. Geibel)	Perchtoldsdorf	14 Nov. 1889
Treibe nur mit Lieben Spott (Anon., trans. Heyse)	Perchtoldsdorf	15 Nov. 1889
Und schläfst du, mein Mädchen (Gil Vicente, trans. Geibel)	Perchtoldsdorf	17 Nov. 1889
In dem Schatten meiner Locken (Anon., trans. Heyse)	Perchtoldsdorf	17 Nov. 1889
Herz, verzage nicht geschwind (Anon., trans. Heyse)	Perchtoldsdorf	19 Nov. 1889
Sagt, seid Ihr es, feiner Herr (Anon., trans. Heyse)	Perchtoldsdorf	19 Nov. 1889
Klinge, klinge, mein Pandero (Alvaro Fernandez de Almeida, trans. Geibel)	Perchtoldsdorf	20 Nov. 1889
Herr, was trägt der Boden hier (Anon., trans. Heyse)	Perchtoldsdorf	24 Nov. 1889
Blindes Schauen, dunkle Leuchte (Rodrigo Cota, trans. Heyse)	Perchtoldsdorf	26 Nov. 1889
Bitt' ihn, o Mutter (Anon., trans. Heyse)	Perchtoldsdorf	26 Nov. 1889
Wer tat deinem Füsslein weh? (Anon., trans. Geibel)	Perchtoldsdorf	5 Dec. 1889

Auf dem grünen Balkon (Anon., trans. Heyse)	Perchtoldsdorf	12 Dec.	1889
Sie blasen zum Abmarsch (Anon., trans. Heyse)	Perchtoldsdorf	13 Dec.	1889
Führ' mich, Kind, nach Bethlehem (Anon., trans. Heyse)	Perchtoldsdorf	15 Dec.	1889
Wunden trägst du, mein Geliebter (Jose de Valdivivielso, trans. Geibel)	Perchtoldsdorf	16 Dec.	1889
Ach, wie lang die Seele schlummert (Anon., trans. Geibel)	Perchtoldsdorf	19 Dec.	1889
Ach, des Knaben Augen (Lopez de Ubeda, trans. Heyse)	Perchtoldsdorf	21 Dec.	1889
Mühvoll komm' ich und beladen (Don Manuel del Rio, trans. Geibel)	Perchtoldsdorf	10 Jan.	1890
Nun bin ich dein (Juan Ruiz, Archpriest of Hita, trans. Heyse)	Perchtoldsdorf	15 Jan.	1890
Trau' nicht der Liebe (Anon., trans. Heyse)	Perchtoldsdorf	28 Mar.	1890
Weint nicht, ihr Äuglein (Lope de Vega, trans. Heyse)	Perchtoldsdorf	29 Mar.	1890
Schmerzliche Wonnen und wonnige Schmerzen (Anon., trans. Geibel)	Perchtoldsdorf	29 Mar.	1890
Ach, im Maien war's (Anonymous Romance, trans. Heyse)	Perchtoldsdorf	30 Mar.	1890
Eide, so die Liebe schwur (Anon., trans. Heyse)	Perchtoldsdorf	31 Mar.	1890
Geh', Geliebter, geh' jetzt (Anon., trans. Geibel)	Perchtoldsdorf	1 Apr.	1890
Liebe mir im Busen (Anon., trans. Heyse)	Perchtoldsdorf	2 Apr.	1890
Deine Mutter, süsses Kind (Don Luis el Chico, trans. Heyse)	Perchtoldsdorf	2 Apr.	1890
Mögen alle bösen Zungen (Anon., trans. Geibel)	Perchtoldsdorf	3 Apr.	1890
Sagt ihm, dass er zu mir komme (Anon., trans. Heyse)	Perchtoldsdorf	4 Apr.	1890
Dereinst, dereinst, Gedanke mein (Cristobal de Castillejo, trans. Geibel)	Perchtoldsdorf	11 Apr.	1890
Tief im Herzen trag' ich Pein (Camoens, trans. Geibel)	Perchtoldsdorf	12 Apr.	1890
Komm', o Tod, von Nacht umgeben (Comendador Escriva, trans. Geibel)	Perchtoldsdorf	14 Apr.	1890
Ob auch finstre Blicke glitten (Anon., trans. Heyse)	Perchtoldsdorf	16 Apr.	1890

Da nur Leid und Leidenschaft (Anon., trans. Heyse)	Perchtoldsdorf	20 Apr. 1890
Wehe der, die mir verstrickte (Gil Vicente, trans. Heyse)	Perchtoldsdorf	27 Apr. 1890

Alte Weisen, Sechs Gedichte von Keller	. . .	Sch. (1891)
Tretet ein, hoher Krieger	Unterach	25 May 1890
Singt mein Schatz wie ein Fink	Unterach	2 June 1890
Wie glänzt der helle Mond	Unterach	5–23[1] June 1890
Das Köhlerweib ist trunken	Unterach	7–23[1] June 1890
Wandl' ich in den Morgenthau	Unterach	8–23[1] June 1890
Du milchjunger Knabe	Unterach	16 June 1890

Italienisches Liederbuch, nach Paul Heyse (Part I) .	.	Sch. (1892)
Mir ward gesagt, du reisest in die Ferne	Unterach	25 Sept. 1890
Ihr seid die Allerschönste	Unterach	2 Oct. 1890
Gesegnet sei, durch den die Welt entstund	Unterach	3 Oct. 1890
Selig ihr Blinden	Unterach	4 Oct. 1890
Wer rief dich denn?	Döbling	13 Nov. 1890
Der Mond hat eine schwere Klag' erhoben	Döbling	13 Nov. 1890
Nun lass uns Frieden schliessen	Döbling	14 Nov. 1890
Dass dochge malt all' deine Reize wären	Döbling	29 Nov. 1891
Du denkst mit einem Fädchen mich zu fangen	Döbling	2 Dec. 1891
Mein Liebster ist so klein	Döbling	3 Dec. 1891
Und willst du deinen Liebsten sterben sehen	Döbling	4 Dec. 1891
Wie lange schon war immer mein Verlangen	Döbling	4 Dec. 1891
Geselle, woll'n wir uns in Kutten hüllen	Döbling	5 Dec. 1891
Nein, junger Herr	Döbling	7 Dec. 1891
Hoffärtig seid Ihr, schönes Kind	Döbling	8 Dec. 1891
Auch kleine Dinge	Döbling	9 Dec. 1891
Ein Ständchen Euch zu bringen	Döbling	10 Dec. 1891
Ihr jungen Leute	Döbling	11 Dec. 1891
Mein Liebster singt	Döbling	12 Dec. 1891
Heb' auf dein blondes Haupt	Döbling	12 Dec. 1891
Wir haben beide lange Zeit geschwiegen	Döbling	16 Dec. 1891
Man sagt mir, deine Mutter woll' es nicht	Döbling	23 Dec. 1891

[1] A letter to Melanie Köchert of 24th June 1890 shows that these three songs were not completed on the dates indicated on the MSS. (see p. 262).

Italienisches Liederbuch, nach Paul Heyse (Part II) . • . H. (1896)

Ich esse nun mein Brot nicht trocken mehr	Perchtoldsdorf	25 Mar. 1896
Mein Liebster hat zu Tische mich geladen	Perchtoldsdorf	26 Mar. 1896
Ich liess mir sagen	Perchtoldsdorf	28 Mar. 1896
Schon streckt' ich aus im Bett	Perchtoldsdorf	29 Mar. 1896
Du sagst mir, dass ich keine Fürstin sei	Perchtoldsdorf	30 Mar. 1896
Lass sie nur gehn	Perchtoldsdorf	30–31[1] Mar. 1896
Wie viele Zeit verlor ich	Perchtoldsdorf	2 Apr. 1896
Und steht Ihr früh am Morgen auf	Perchtoldsdorf	3–4[2] Apr. 1896
Wohl kenn ich Euren Stand	Perchtoldsdorf	9 Apr. 1896
Wie soll ich fröhlich sein	Perchtoldsdorf	12 Apr. 1896
O wär' dein Haus	Perchtoldsdorf	12 Apr. 1896
Sterb' ich, so hüllt in Blumen	Perchtoldsdorf	13 Apr. 1896
Gesegnet sei das Grün	Perchtoldsdorf	13[3] Apr. 1896
Wenn du mich mit den Augen streifst	Perchtoldsdorf	19[3] Apr. 1896
Was soll der Zorn	Perchtoldsdorf	20 Apr. 1896
Benedeit die sel'ge Mutter	Perchtoldsdorf	21 Apr. 1896
Schweig' einmal still	Perchtoldsdorf	23 Apr. 1896
Nicht länger kann ich singen	Perchtoldsdorf	23 Apr. 1896
Wenn du, mein Liebster, steigst zum Himmel auf	Perchtoldsdorf	24 Apr. 1896
Ich hab' in Penna	Perchtoldsdorf	25 Apr. 1896
Heut' Nacht erhob ich mich	Perchtoldsdorf	25 Apr. 1896
O wüsstest du, wieviel ich deinetwegen	Perchtoldsdorf	26 Apr. 1896
Verschling' der Abgrund	Perchtoldsdorf	29 Apr. 1896
Was für ein Lied soll dir gesungen werden?	Perchtoldsdorf	30 Apr. 1896

Drei Gedichte von Robert Reinick . . . . . H. (1897)

Gesellenlied	Perchtoldsdorf	24 Jan. 1888
Morgenstimmung	Vienna	8 Sept.– 23 Oct. 1896
Skolie	Rinnbach-Ebensee	1 Aug. 1889

[1] MS. dated 31st, but a letter to Melanie Köchert shows that this song was sketched out on the 30th.

[2] MS. dated 3rd April. A letter to Melanie Köchert shows that it was not completed until the 4th.

[3] Letters to Heinrich Potpeschnigg and Melanie Köchert show that Wolf was not at first satisfied with *Gesegnet sei das Grün* and *Wenn du mich mit den Augen streifst*. He told Potpeschnigg that he had burnt them and afterwards that he had written them out again from memory. To Melanie Köchert he wrote that he considered them inferior to the others and put them aside in an unfinished state. But after a few days he changed his mind. *Gesegnet sei das Grün* he wrote out again on 17th April, but retained on his MS. the original date of composition. The case of *Wenn du mich mit den Augen streifst* was rather different. It was written out again on the 18th (it must originally have been composed on the 13th, 14th or 15th), but as it still dissatisfied its creator it was 'completely reshaped' on the 19th and the MS. of the song in its definitive form bears this date.

Drei Gesänge aus Ibsens 'Das Fest auf Solhaug' . . . H. (1897)
   Gesang Margits   Döbling   7 Jan. 1891
   Gudmunds I. Gesang   Döbling   30 Oct. 1891
                             Revised 12 Nov. 1896
   Gudmunds II. Gesang   Vienna   7 Mar. 1891
German translation by Emma Klingenfeld.

Vier Gedichte nach Heine, Shakespeare und Lord Byron . . H. (1897)
   Wo wird einst (Heine)   Perchtoldsdorf   24 Jan. 1888
   Lied des transferierten Zettel
     (Shakespeare, trans. A. W. von
     Schlegel)   Perchtoldsdorf   11 May 1889
   Keine gleicht von allen Schönen
     (Byron)   Vienna   18–25 [1] Dec. 1896
   Sonne der Schlummerlosen (Byron)   Vienna   29–31 [1] Dec. 1896
Both Byron poems translated by Otto Gildemeister.

Drei Gedichte von Michelangelo . . . . . . H. (1898)
   Wohl denk' ich oft   Vienna   18 Mar. 1897
   Alles endet, was entstehet   Vienna   20 Mar. 1897
   Fühlt meine Seele   Vienna   22–28 Mar. 1897
Translation by Walter Robert-Tornow.

VII. SONGS WITH ORCHESTRAL ACCOMPANIMENT

Auf ein altes Bild . . . scored		1889	P.	(1904)
Seufzer . . . . scored	28 May	1889	P.	(1904)
Karwoche . . . . scored	29 May	1889	P.	(1904)
Der Rattenfänger . . . scored	5 Feb.	1890	H.	(1902)
Er ist's . . . . scored	20 Feb.	1890	P.	(1904)
Gesang Weylas . . . scored	21 Feb.	1890	H.	(1903)
Schlafendes Jesuskind . . scored		1890	P.	(1904)
Mignon ('Kennst du das Land?') (first version, lost by Wolf but subsequently recovered by the Vienna Hugo Wolf Verein) . . scored		1890	P.	(1904)
Ganymed . . . . scored		1890	Lost	
Anakreons Grab (first version) . scored		1890	Lost	
Prometheus . . . . scored	12 Mar.[2]	1890	H.	(1902)
In der Frühe . . . scored	6 May	1890	P.	(1904)
An den Schlaf . . . scored	4 Sept.	1890	P.	(1904)
Gebet . . . . . scored	4 Sept.	1890	H.	(1903)

[1] Letters show that one of the Byron songs was completed on 25th December and the other on 31st December.

[2] This is the only date on the MS., but a letter of Wolf's to Grohe of 16th April 1890 suggests that the scoring of *Prometheus* was not at that time completed.

Neue Liebe	scored	5 Sept.	1890	P.	(1904)
Wo find ich Trost? . .	scored	6 Sept.	1890	H.	(1902)
Auf eine Christblume I . .	scored	25 Sept.	1890	CLV.	
Not quite complete.					
Harfenspieler I . . .	scored	2 Dec.	1890	P.	(1904)
Harfenspieler II . . .	scored	4 Dec.	1890	P.	(1904)
Harfenspieler III . . .	scored	4 Dec.	1890	P.	(1904)
Denk' es, o Seele . . .	scored	4 May	1891	P.	(1904)
Geh', Geliebter, geh' jetzt .	scored		1892	Lost	
Fragmentary sketches survive (NLV.).					
Mignon ('Kennst du das Land?') . . .	scored	31 Oct.	1893	P.	(1904)
Re-orchestrated after the loss of the score of 1890, above.					
Anakreons Grab . . .	scored	13 Nov.	1893	H.	(1902)
Re-orchestrated after the loss of the score of 1890, above.					
Epiphanias (fragment) . .	scored	25 Apr.	1894	NLV.	
Wer sein holdes Lieb verloren .	scored	1–4 Dec.	1897	MWV.	(1937)
Wenn du zu den Blumen gehst .	scored	5–6 Dec.	1897	MWV.	(1937)
Both the above intended for inclusion in *Manuel Venegas*.					

Orchestral versions of *In dem Schatten meiner Locken* and *Herz, verzage nicht geschwind* are incorporated in *Der Corregidor* (1895).

GENERAL INDEX

493

INDEX OF COMPOSITIONS MENTIONED IN THE TEXT